Rev/MEL Buhler
P.O. Bx A
Oakville - WA 98568
206 273-9936

Sept 4, 1994 to Aug 27, 1995

Adult Teacher

The Radiant Life Series of Adult Bible Studies
Based on Outlines From the Evangelical Curriculum Commission

3

September 1994-August 1995

RADIANT LIFE

SUNDAY SCHOOL
CURRICULUM AND LITERATURE DEPARTMENT

NATIONAL DIRECTOR	David J. Torgerson
EDITOR IN CHIEF	Gary L. Leggett
ADULT EDITOR	Paul W. Smith
ADULT ASSISTANT EDITORS	Scott Harrup
	Richard L. Schoonover
EDITORIAL ASSISTANT	Fannie Mae Hall

International Standard Book Number 0-88243-435-7
Gospel Publishing House Order Number 02-0435
Printed in the United States of America

TABLE OF CONTENTS

FALL 1994

WINTER 1994-95

TABLE OF CONTENTS, cont'd.

Index Of Study Texts
Volumes 1,2, and 3

TEACHER GROWTH SERIES

HOW TO USE
THE ADULT TEACHER

by Marvin L. Smith

The *Adult Teacher* is a Bible-centered curriculum, written by Spirit-filled authors with a goal to clearly communicate the teachings of Scripture. From Genesis to Revelation, the Bible is surveyed in a period of 7 years. All major Church doctrines are also presented, and subjects designed to help students become spiritually mature are discussed.

This "How To Use" section has been divided into four parts. Part 1 contains help-ful advice and direction to equip adult teachers for service in the classroom. It explains what the curriculum, the teacher, and class session should do. Part 2 introduces the various parts of this *Adult Teacher*. Part 3 lists the steps in study preparation. Part 4 illustrates each step in study preparation with an example. It should enable teachers to compare their own thought processes and planning sequences with the sample to discover new ways of study preparation.

PART 1: INTRODUCTORY SUGGESTIONS

What The Curriculum Should Do

Good curriculum should provide guidance, resources and training. "Curriculum," comes from a Greek word which means racetrack, or the boundaries of a race. Curriculum is like a racetrack in that it provides the boundaries (guidance) for teaching.

Curriculum provides guidance for instruction in three areas. First, curriculum ensures that information will not be omitted. Second, curriculum monitors material to avoid imbalanced teaching. Third, good curriculum weeds out false teaching and doctrinal errors.

In addition to guidance, a good curriculum should provide resources. When discussing curriculum resources, it is important to remember that
THE BIBLE IS
THE PRIMARY TEXTBOOK!
As a resource, the *Adult Teacher* is a guidebook intended to provide clear exposition of the Scriptures under consideration and make application appropriate to the age in which we live. Each study of the *Adult Teacher* contains more than enough information for one class period. Extra material helps teachers to customize objectives to meet the needs of students.

Good curriculum will also provide some type of teacher training. Teachers need a series of short, instructional topics packaged among studies for quick reference. This volume of the *Adult Teacher* contains 12 articles from the Teacher Growth Series.

What The Teacher Should Do

Before preparing the study, effective teachers study the Word (and the world), pray for guidance, and know their students.

Study preparation and personal Bible study are very similar types of activities; however, they have different functions. Study preparation without personal Bible study is like cooking a large meal but not eating what was prepared. Even though teachers may spend time in study preparation studying the Bible, they should not neglect feeding their own souls with God's Word. Teachers also need to be scholars of today's culture so that they can make bridges between the Bible and today's world.

Prayer for guidance means that teachers submit their own thoughts and direction to the Master Teacher. Sometimes it is difficult for teachers to recognize the difference between their own zeal and the voice of the Lord. Frequently, they will read a book and, because it met a need in their lives, assume the book is perfect for their class. This trap is avoided when teachers bathe each study in prayer. Only then can they trust their hunch or insight to be the Lord's direction. The less the prayer, the more a good idea could become God's "will" for the class.

Perhaps the most important responsibility of teachers is to know their students—their values, their needs, their interests, and their level of spiritual maturity. This knowledge is not available to curriculum editors and writers; they cannot anticipate the crisis needs nor the wonderful victories represented in classes. Awareness of an illness or a financial need gives teachers opportunity to build a supportive class environment. The result moves teachers beyond "teaching studies" to "teaching students."

What The Class Session Should Do

Adult teachers must ensure that each class session provides opportunity for fellowship, learning, and practice.

Fellowship is more than a coffee pot and donuts. Helping students know each other is the teacher's responsibility. Teachers set the pace by being vulnerable—sharing victories and pain with equal sensitivity. Sometimes teachers need to structure interaction so that adult students reveal parts of their lives to fellow students. In a large class, fellowship can be encouraged by dividing the class into groups of four to six and asking all to share how their faith in Christ was challenged in the past week. Fellowship results in knowing a person so well that burden sharing is not awkward.

The class session should provide opportunity for learning. Greater learning takes place when students are actively involved in the teaching/learning process. Effective teachers have a knack for gaining the attention of adult students and thrusting them into discussion or other learning activities. Lecture is carefully employed to provide significant information so that the discussion does not regress into a "pooling of ignorance." The goal for each class session is to encourage each student to participate in some way. In larger classes, some discussion should take place in small groups.

Finally, the class session should provide an opportunity to practice skills that are essential to Christian maturity. Give adults class time to practice skills that are desirable outside the classroom. For example, parents can practice talking to their children about moral issues (e.g. biblical teaching on sex) by role-playing situations during class. If teachers want adult students to study God's Word or share Christ with friends outside of class, then they should provide class time to study the Bible or practice sharing Christ with each other during class.

PART 2: INTRODUCING THE *ADULT TEACHER*

Many features have been designed into the *Adult Teacher* to facilitate study preparation. This second volume in a seven-volume set contains 1 year's worth of studies divided into four 13-week quarters. Each quarter contains 2 unit introductions, 13 studies, and 3 Teacher Growth Series articles. The following overview should provide enough orientation to effectively use this book.

Unit Introduction

Each unit in the *Adult Teacher* is introduced with a brief summary of what to expect within the studies of that unit. The unit introduction should be read to help get a clear understanding of the direction the unit will take. This will enable teachers to more effectively prepare for each individual class session.

The Studies

Each study in the *Adult Teacher* consists of the following features to help teachers present the study in a clear, logical manner:

Objective—provides direction for the study; written in general terms so that each teacher can customize them to fit each class.

Golden Text—provides focus for the class and lends itself to Bible verse memorization.

Central Truth—provides direction for the teaching and application of the Scriptures.

Study Text—a listing of passages which will be explored, analyzed, and discussed.

Scripture Setting—provides the main portion of the study text in both the King James Version and the New International Version printed in parallel column format. This can be used to compare the two versions during class or as a responsive reading. It can also help to focus the teacher's attention on the text under consideration while comparing with other texts in the Bible.

Outline—offers a general overview of the study and is expanded in the Commentary section.

Teacher Preparation—lists various methods for teaching that need advance attention and planning. Any items needed for the class session will be included here as well.

Opening Thoughts—gives a brief introduction to the study to help prepare students to receive the material which will be presented to the class.

Bible Commentary—the main body of the study; most of the teaching session will come from this section. It is divided into main points and subpoints according to the Outline.

After each header, the portion of Scripture to be studied in the main point has been printed from the King James Version. In addition, a section called Clarification has been provided immediately following the Scripture portion to clarify any words from the King James Version that may be unfamiliar.

The Notes section is a blank space in which teachers can add their personal remarks and notations.

The Bible Commentary is a valuable resource because it provides key background information about the Bible passage. Discussion questions are printed in the appropriate places to ask them. In addition, Teaching Tips recommend creative ways to involve students in the class session. Effective teachers know their students and know which questions or Teaching Tips to use to meet their needs.

Life Response—the most important part of every study. Jesus never taught for merely "head" knowledge; He sought a commitment or life response from those He met. It is important that teachers plan the study well enough to include adequate time for proper application.

Evangelism Outreach—brings out one of two aspects of evangelism for the class. First, the study is brought to bear on any unsaved students' lives. Opportunity can be given, as the Spirit leads, to invite unsaved students to accept Christ as their Savior. Or second, reaching the lost for Christ may be stressed in an evangelism emphasis that encourages adult students to reach out to those around them.

Daily Bible Readings—provided for further study. Teachers may wish to use these as devotional themes throughout the week, one reading per day, to prepare themselves spiritually for teaching the study. Adult students can be encouraged to read the same list, which is reproduced in their quarterlies.

Teacher Growth Series

Three articles from the Teacher Growth Series (TGS) are inserted at the beginning of each quarter of the *Adult Teacher*. With 36 articles in the series, the Teacher Growth Series supplies valuable information for the teacher to help in every phase of the teaching ministry. The topics and where they can be found in this bound edition of the *Adult Teacher* are listed on page v.

PART 3: STUDY SESSION PLANNING

After studying God's Word and the world in which we live and after praying for guidance and after considering your students' needs, then begin to prepare the study. The "3 to 1" rule—at least 3 minutes of study for each minute of class time—is useful to know how much time is needed for study preparation. Thus a teacher should invest a *minimum* of 2 1/4 hours to prepare for a 45-minute class.

The following steps are intended to give teachers a mental framework in which to budget time for planning studies:

1. Skim the study

(10 minutes)

The first step in study preparation is to become familiar with the contents and direction of the study. Teachers should take about 10 minutes to skim the study early in the week (usually Sunday afternoon). During the week, they are able to locate news events or other resources that pertain to the topic.

2. Pray for guidance

(20 minutes)

After skimming the material, the prepared teacher prays for guidance and direction. This is the best time to pray for class members because the Holy Spirit will steer a teacher's thoughts toward their needs. Note: The teacher should also bathe each step of preparation in prayer.

3. Study the Bible Commentary

(30 minutes)

There are several things teachers can do to study this section.
• First, read through the Study Text from the Bible, paying close attention to the relationship between the Scriptures and their interpretation in the Bible Commentary section. Avoid the temptation to memorize and recite the Bible Commentary section in class by exploring these relationships.
• Second, list those issues which are raised in the Bible Commentary that might meet needs of students.

• Third, consider the Teaching Tips as potential activities.
• Fourth, examine the questions and understand how each is answered in the Bible Commentary section.
• Last, focus on elements that seem to "leap off the page."

4. Write the Study Objective

(15 minutes)

No other part of study preparation is more misunderstood than the study objective. At the beginning of each study is the SUGGESTED objective. Teachers should customize each study objective to fit their own classes. It is a statement about the one main concept or idea that is intended for student awareness, interaction, or change. A customized objective can begin with the words, "Each student will . . ." followed by a verb such as believe, accept, change, respond with, etc. Each part of the study and each activity should be geared to accomplish the objective.

5. Plan the Life Response

(10 minutes)

Once the study objective is determined, the teacher knows how to plan for a student response to the study. The suggested Life Response in the *Adult Teacher* may need some refocusing in order to meet your objective. Use the Life Response as a means to close the class session in prayer or in a time of personal dedication. Often the Evangelism Outreach section will contain the proper response to the objective.

6. Prepare the Opening Thoughts

(10 minutes)

A good start is critical to a successful sesson. Try to begin class with a story or activity that will capture the attention of adult students. Although vital to developing a topic, avoid initiating class with definitions. Check out the Opening Thoughts or Teacher Preparation sections for useful ideas. Case studies and news items lend themselves to an interesting start.

7. Organize the Bible Commentary
(10 minutes)

Teachers may want to follow the recommended Outline in the *Adult Teacher*. However, by far the best approach is for the teacher to allow personal insight to flow from the Bible and study materials. Decide on two or three main points to emphasize during class and just highlight the other ideas brought out in the *Adult Teacher*.

8. List discussion questions
(10 minutes)

Key questions are listed in the Bible Commentary section. Each teacher must determine if these questions will provide the discussion needed for the class. Take the time to carefully select or write two to five questions that will stimulate class discussion.

9. Select the Pre-Session Activity
(5 minutes)

Effective teachers involve incoming adults before the class session actually begins. Take 5 minutes to decide how students can prepare for the class session or even interact with the objective while drinking coffee and sharing with their friends. The Teacher Preparation or Opening Thoughts sections may contain useful ideas.

10. Pray for the anointing
(10 or more minutes)

By now, study preparation is completed. It is time to again ask for help from the Holy Spirit. Request anointing for delivering the material and for students to receive the teaching.

11. Gather needed materials
(5 minutes)

The final step is to organize and collect all materials. Many teachers invest too much time collecting resources while neglecting prayer or Bible study. Following this time budget will help teachers avoid imbalance in study preparation.

PART 4: LESSON PLANNING EXAMPLE

Many instructional decisions are made by teachers during lesson preparation and during the actual class session. This "journal" illustrates how a teacher would make a series of instructional decisions in planning for just one study. It is hoped that the following will guide and challenge teachers in their lesson preparation.

This example is drawn from the study for October 9, 1994, "Salvation For All People" (pages 40-46). Please take a few minutes to skim its contents. In addition, the form "Planning The Session" (page xiv) will be used to illustrate study planning. A blank form and directions for its use appear on pages xv and xvi.

Sunday, October 2, 9:00 p.m.

After reading the October 9 study for the first time, I am disappointed in my lack of advanced planning. The Checklist (page 40, right column) recommended students invite their unsaved friends or loved ones. It is now Sunday evening and I missed a wonderful opportunity today to announce this to the class.

Sunday, October 2, 9:10 p.m.

It feels awkward to pray knowing that I lost a splendid chance to invite unsaved friends and loved ones to Christ this Sunday. Yet I decide to rest in the gift of God's great grace. My prayers shift to members of the class. These adults are growing in Christ, but I am not certain if they are intentionally sharing the gsopel. I lift each student in prayer, asking the Lord to help me minister the Word to their needs.

Monday, October 3, 7:15 p.m.

As I read the Bible Commentary section, my attention is drawn toward the first question, "What did Paul mean when he said, 'Christ is the end of the law' (Romans 10:4)?" (page 42, right column). Even though many studies this quarter have focused on the relationship between law and grace, my class will benefit from a discussion based on this question.

Other potential issues surface as I continue studying:
• There is much discussion potential in the statement, "Faith in Christ is not grounded in a philisophy, but in actual historic events" (page 43, top of left column).
• How believing and confession go together.
• Salvation is for everyone (Joel 2:32; Romans 10:13).
• How some add requirements to the gospel (Teaching Tip 3).
• Urgency for evangelism.
• Evangelism is not limited to ministers.
• The relationship between faith and hearing God's Word.
• Who is a missionary?
• "Roman Road" evangelism method (page 46, "Evangelism Emphasis").

At this point, I seem to be focused on the first discussion question, "What did Paul mean when he said, 'Christ is the end of the law' (Romans 10:4)?" I also intend to concentrate on the issues of personal evangelism.

Monday, October 3, 7:55 p.m.

Because I seem so focused on the first discussion question, I believe I have received direction from the Holy Spirit and am now ready to write my own lesson objective. My first attempt at writing an objective is: Adults will discuss how Christ is the end (or goal) of the law. Because I want to designate a significant portion of class time to issues of personal evangelism, I rewrite the objective using material from the Life Response section (page 46): Adults will discuss how to share the "three ingredients to saving faith" with others.

Monday, October 3, 8:10 p.m.

The Life Response is clearly in view now. I want to involve each student in a role-play exercise to practice sharing the gospel in class. My excitement is growing because more and more ideas are coming into my mind! I decide to call two members who are gifted in personal evangelism and ask them to role-play a situation where one shares the gospel with the other. In fact, I will ask one (or both) to start class by sharing a recent witnessing opportunity.

Monday, October 3, 8:35 p.m.

I have just called two members of the class. Both will be prepared to share a recent witnessing opportunity (as Opening Thoughts) and to share the gospel as a role play (as part of Life Response).

Thursday, October 6, 7:40 p.m.

My next step in study preparation is to organize the Bible Commentary. I decide to organize the material around the "three ingredients to saving faith" (Life Response, page 46):
1. Understand the Bible's report concerning Jesus Christ.
2. Heart belief in this report.
3. Public confession.
If there is adequate time, I will include Teaching Tip 3 with the first ingredient. Most of the discussion questions will be used as printed.

Thursday, October 6, 8:05 p.m.

The Presession Activity should deal with issues of personal evangelism. I decide to use a "graffiti poster" with the heading, "When I share the gospel with others, I feel . . ." I will need to obtain about 5 sheets of large newsprint and marking pens.

Friday, October 7, 10:30 a.m.

I called the church office to request 8 to 10 marking pens and 5 large sheets of newsprint to be placed in my classroom.

Saturday, October 8, 8:30 a.m.

As I pray for the anointing on the study plans and the class members, I recall the words, "How beautiful . . . are the feet of those who bring good news" (Isaiah 52:7, NIV). My prayer is that every member of the class will have "beautiful feet"—that they will all be eager to share the gospel with friends and loved ones.

The sample "Planning The Session" form on page xiv demonstrates how the thoughts accumulated during this study planning example could be recorded. It should contain key thoughts or transition points which are mentally checked off as the session unfolds each Sunday.

Planning The Session

Title: *SALVATION FOR ALL PEOPLE*

Scriptures: *ROMANS 10:4-17*

Objective: *ADULTS WILL DISCUSS HOW TO SHARE THE "THREE INGREDIENTS TO SAVING FAITH" WITH OTHERS.*

PRE-SESSION ACTIVITY   Time Required

"GRAFFITI POSTER" WITH HEADING: *MATERIALS NEEDED:*   **5** min.
"WHEN I SHARE THE GOSPEL WITH   *5-7 SHEETS OF NEWSPRINT*
OTHERS, I FEEL..."   *8-10 MARKING PENS*

OPENING THOUGHTS   Time Required

Teaching Methods   Materials Needed   **10** min.

2 CLASS MEMBERS SHARE CURRENT EXAMPLE   *NONE*
OF WITNESSING CHRIST TO OTHERS
Transition: *IN TODAY'S CLASS, WE WILL PRACTICE SHARING THE GOSPEL USING THE "THREE INGREDIENTS TO SAVING FAITH".*

BIBLE COMMENTARY   Time Required

Teaching Methods   Materials Needed   **20** min.

1 *NEED TO UNDERSTAND THE BIBLE'S REPORT CONCERNING JESUS CHRIST*
   READ ROMANS 10:4-8
   ASK: WHAT DID PAUL MEAN WHEN HE SAID, "CHRIST IS THE END OF THE LAW"?
   EMPHASIZE: "FAITH IN CHRIST IS NOT GROUNDED IN A PHILOSOPHY, BUT IN
   ACTUAL HISTORIC EVENTS."   USE → TEACHING TIP #3.

2 *ON THE BASIS OF THIS REPORT, THERE MUST BE A HEART BELIEF IN*
   THAT MESSAGE.   READ ROMANS 10:9-10.
   ASK: HOW DOES ONE BELIEVE WITH THE HEART?
   ASK: WHAT DOES IT MEAN TO "CONFESS WITH THY MOUTH THE
   LORD JESUS?

3 *THERE MUST BE PUBLIC CONFESSION.*

   LECTURE → ROMANS 10:11-13   *PG. 43-44*

4

LIFE RESPONSE   Time Required

Teaching Methods   Materials Needed   **20** min.

LECTURE → "URGENCY FOR EVANGELISM" (ROMANS 10:14,15) PG. 45
ROLE PLAY → 2 CLASS MEMBERS SHARE "THREE INGREDIENTS TO SAVING FAITH".
ROLE PLAY → DIVIDE CLASS INTO GROUPS OF 2-3 AND ASK THEM TO SHARE
"THREE INGREDIENTS".

Total Time: **50** min.

Planning The Session

Study:_____ Date:_____

Title:_____

Scriptures:_____

Objective:_____
_____
_____

PRE-SESSION ACTIVITY   Time Required

_____ min.

OPENING THOUGHTS   Time Required

Teaching Methods   Materials Needed   _____ min.

Transition:_____

BIBLE COMMENTARY   Time Required

Teaching Methods   Materials Needed   _____ min.

1

2

3

4

LIFE RESPONSE   Time Required

Teaching Methods   Materials Needed   _____ min.

Total Time: _____ min.

Planning The Teaching Session

Every teaching session for Sunday School should be carefully planned. By using the planning sheet on the next page (page xvi), the following instructions, and the example explained in the "How To Use" section (pages viii through xiv) when you are preparing to teach, you will be able to clearly present the material that the Holy Spirit guided you to study.

The planning sheet (page xvi) is laid out in the same order as each study in the *Adult Teacher*. This sheet should be photocopied for each study and used when preparing and teaching the study. If this planning sheet is followed carefully, you will be able to tailor the study so only those points which are important to the needs of your class will be covered. You will also ensure that there will be time to cover each point of the study adequately leaving enough time for a good conclusion.

THE FOUR-STEP APPROACH

The teaching session is divided into the same three sections as the studies in the *Adult Teacher* with space for a fellowship/prayer activity added. These four steps on the planning sheet are Pre-Session Activity, Opening Thoughts, Bible Commentary, and Life Response.

Pre-Session Activity

Although most teachers take time for prayer requests and prayer, most do not account for the time they take in class for prayer or fellowship. They end up not having enough time to finish the study properly. The Pre-Session Activity space gives a place for the teacher to plan what activity should begin the class and how long it should take.

Opening Thoughts

Opening Thoughts is used to introduce the study and capture the attention of the class. Refer to both the Teacher Preparation and Opening Thoughts sections in the *Adult Teacher* to decide the most appropriate attention-getting activity/ teaching method.

Bible Commentary

Bible Commentary contains the "meat" of the study. The majority of the teaching session is contained in this part. Write the title of each main point after the numbers. This will clearly divide the main points and help keep the teaching methods and materials needed for each main point separated.

Life Response

In Life Response the study is brought to a close and final application is brought to bear on the students' lives. Although you should know your students well, the Holy Spirit knows them better. Let Him help you plan the best way to present the material in this section of the study.

KEY ELEMENTS OF THE FOUR-STEP APPROACH

Each section on the planning sheet has three columns, key to accomplishing the goals of the teaching session. These columns are Teaching Methods, Materials Needed, and Time Required.

Teaching Methods

Under this column write a list of the teaching methods you will use to teach the session. Lecture, discussion, question and answer, and buzz groups are the most common methods. Your *Adult Teacher* contains various suggestions of other teaching methods to make the teaching session creative and interesting. Two books which may also help you to develop creative teaching methods for your classroom are:
• *40 Ways To Teach In Groups* by Martha M. Leypoldt (©1967, Judson Press, Valley Forge, PA)
• *24 Ways To Improve Your Teaching* by Kenneth Gangel (©1974, Victor Books, Wheaton, IL).

Materials Needed

Under Materials Needed, you should list everything you will need to teach the study. This will ensure that you will have such things as chalk, paper, and pencils ready for the teaching session.

Time Required

This last column is probably the hardest to fill in, but the most essential one in planning the teaching session. It is critical that you estimate the amount of time you plan to use for each of the four steps in the teaching session. By estimating and writing down the time you will take for each part of the study, you will ensure you cover the important parts of the study that you were led by the Holy Spirit to study.

After finishing your time estimates, add the time required for each of the four sections. The time you fill in as your total time should equal the time for the teaching session.

UNIT 1

INTRODUCTION

TRUTHS FROM ROMANS

The Book of Romans is probably the most important theological discussion of the believer's salvation ever written. Within its chapters, the apostle Paul explained what it means to be a Christian, how to become a Christian, and how to live as a Christian. The studies in this unit will simplify difficult theological concepts about salvation that believers need to understand.

The first two studies, "God's Plan To Save Sinners" and "Justification," discuss the Christian's relationship with Jesus Christ. The two main salvation themes of Romans, God's righteousness credited to believers and justification by faith, are clearly explained.

But just understanding salvation is not enough. Each believer must continue to grow in Christ. Paul asked, "Shall we continue in sin that grace may abound?" (Romans 6:1). The answer is obvious: "Certainly not!" (verse 2, NKJV). Yet believers continue to struggle with sin and the baser elements of their nature. The following three studies address how a Christian can live victoriously in this present world.

"Call To Holy Living," "Life In The Spirit," and "The Overcoming Life" (studies 3-5) give crucial instruction on Christian living. Although God calls all believers to be holy, He does not expect them to do it on their own. He has sent the Holy Spirit to empower each of them to overcome sin, the flesh, and the devil by faith.

The remaining studies deal with the practicality of the Christian life. "Salvation For All People" (study 6) calls for all believers to tell others of the abundant life they have in Christ. Study 7, "Practical Christian Living," explains how believers can interact with others, obeying the commandment that fulfills all others: love one another. Study 8 concludes this unit with a discussion of the Christian's obligation to serve others for Christ's sake.

How to Adapt Curriculum to Other Cultures

by Paul W. Smith

Is the curriculum in your hand written for a culture different from the one you are teaching? If so, each study in this quarterly must be modified to meet the needs of your class.

The gospel can only be communicated using words, phrases, and sentences familiar to the audience. Unless the teacher communicates in ways that the students can understand, the message of the gospel will be unclear and ineffective.

Be sensitive to the students' cultural background and values.

Although the truths of the Bible remain the same, explanations of the concepts and application of these Bible truths must be varied according to the audience. It is not just a matter of translating the study into another language.

If your cultural background is different from that of your students, there are several things you could do to make the cultural transition.

● Develop a close rapport with one or two class members in order to get feedback from the teaching of the study. These students could critique your teaching to ensure that every aspect of the teaching session is communicated to the students.

● Seek input from a person within the culture in order to develop illustrations that properly convey the Bible truths of the study to the class.

● Team teach with a person who understands the culture of the class to better convey the truths of the Bible study. Also, use interactive methods with the class—encourage them to help you apply the Bible to their lives.

Adjust illustrations to the students' environment.

Take the time to see where your students live. Visit with them. Get to know them as individuals. Discover the things in their environment that can clearly illustrate the Bible truths you want to communicate. Not everything in the study will apply to your class. Eliminate the irrelevant materials and find something that will apply. Ask your students for help. If they are coming to class, they want to learn—they will help you to teach them, if you but ask.

Adjust vocabulary to the learning level of your students.

If your class is in the inner city and consists of an ethnic group that communicates in different terms than you normally would, get to know those terms. Become intimately acquainted with their language. After all, you are in the classroom to communicate the truths of the gospel so they can be saved and mature in Christ.

The Key

The key to adapting curriculum to another culture is knowing your students and their culture intimately. Take the time to be with them, to learn about their needs. When you know them, you will have no difficulty adapting this curriculum so the truths you present will be thoroughly communicated to each person in your class.

"Teacher Growth Series" brings you information on every phase of your teaching ministry. Three articles per quarter can be read, shared with other teachers, and filed for future reference. Articles dealing with the same topics are presented at each age level from early childhood through adult. The "Teacher Growth Series" covers 36 different topics.

Characteristics of Adults

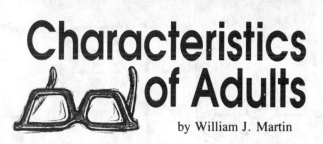

by William J. Martin

It is important that teachers have an understanding of the age-level characteristics of their students. It would be counterproductive to use preschool teaching methods with adult students. Understanding age-level needs will help ensure that teaching leads to real learning.

Not all adult students can be taught the same way. For teachers to influence learning they must be sensitive to the various needs and differences among their students. This will help them see opportunities during class time for allowing students to share problems. Usually there are others in the class who are experiencing the same circumstances. Each one will probably have something to say which will help the others. Seeing a situation from more than one viewpoint can be of great help in coping with a troublesome situation.

The wise teacher will stress fellowship and relationships. By allowing time for fellowship and involving everyone in the learning process, the teacher will help build and strengthen friendships.

The teacher should also work hard to make practical application of every study. Adults need biblical truth that will work for them as they live out their lives. The Bible is relevant to adults today as much as it was centuries ago, but the students may not always be able to see the practical side of a study. For instance, many Old Testament studies are based on historical incidents. The teacher should present the historical background, but it is important also to show how the principles that stand out in the passage are applicable to people in every time. If the study is discussed only as an incident in biblical history, many students will miss the practical application.

Since adults are different at various stages in life, they have different expectations of Sunday School and teaching. It is a challenge to the teacher to have enough variety in approaches to the Bible study to meet the needs of all students.

It is imperative that adult teachers use teaching methods suited to adults. Frequent uninterrupted lecture, one teacher making all class decisions, and little student involvement do not maintain the interest of most adults. On the other hand, allowing class input for decisions affecting the class, entrusting class members with responsibility, and teaching to meet the needs expressed by the class are ways of encouraging adults in the learning process. This will result in students who learn to express the gospel in their lives.

From time to time, new problems may crop up among class members. If students find themselves facing circumstances they have never dealt with before, the teacher should prayerfully find ways to apply biblical truth to the issues. Never forget it—the Bible has the answers.

The adult teacher should realize that students seem also to need a guide in certain transitional stages. They want an older person to be a role model, to provide encouragement, one to whom they can be accountable and from whom they can seek advice. This is especially true of young adults.

There are many stages of adult needs. Among them are: young adult, young married, mid-life, senior adult, singles, parents, divorced, and widowed. It is the teacher's responsibility to know as much as possible about the adults he teaches. That contributes much to being an effective adult teacher.

"Teacher Growth Series" brings you information on every phase of your teaching ministry. Three articles per quarter can be read, shared with other teachers, and filed for future reference. Articles dealing with the same topics are presented at each age level from early childhood through adult. The "Teacher Growth Series" covers 36 different topics.

MONDAY
TUESDAY
WEDNESDAY
THURSDAY
FRIDAY

Creative Lesson Planning

by William J. Martin

A survey in a Sunday School publication revealed some interesting facts. Of some 260 responding teachers, 131 said they seldom or never use a written study plan. This raises some interesting questions. Must teachers have a study plan? If so, what kind?

A written study plan indicates advance preparation. A good study plan provides a place to list the theme, objectives or learning goals, teaching methods, resources, time frames, and evaluation.

Thought must go into choosing teaching methods that will meet learning goals. Advance work is needed to secure necessary resources. The teacher must know the study completely in order to plan the use of time. When a study plan is utilized it provides a wholesome self-discipline which helps ensure interesting and productive teaching. Thus, adult teachers should make the effort to prepare written study plans. A Teacher Planning Form has been provided at the beginning of this quarterly that you may find helpful in planning the teaching session.

Take plenty of time for planning. The worst kind of preparation takes place on Saturday night or Sunday morning. That is much like trying to prepare a five-course formal dinner 10 minutes prior to serving. It cannot be done. It is impossible to teach adequately what has been seen for the first time only the evening before. It is better to study 30 minutes each day than 4 hours on Saturday night.

Preparation should begin at the beginning of the quarter. Previewing studies in advance allows time for special projects and assignments. An early preview also gets the teacher thinking about the subject for the quarter and ways to communicate the biblical truth.

A weekly plan might look like this:

Monday: Read the Bible text, the *Adult Teacher Guide,* the student materials, and review the Adult Teaching Helps Packet.

Tuesday: Study the learning goals. Think about how to teach so those goals are met.

Wednesday: Develop a preliminary outline of the study. Begin with the one on the first page of each study of the *Adult Teacher Guide.* Highlight the areas you want to emphasize. Fill in additional information you desire to share. Add personal touches as you familiarize yourself with the biblical content.

Thursday: Plan teaching methods and activities. Review the "Teaching Tips" provided in the quarterly. Decide which ideas are best suited to your class. You may want to develop one or two of your own.

Friday: Secure the necessary resources. If you want to order a film, Friday will be too late. In fact, there are some things that must be done at the beginning of the quarter. Other materials such as work sheets, books, pencils, maps, illustrations, and overhead transparencies can be secured as late as Friday.

Saturday: Write the final study plan and review your week's planning.

Sunday: Teach well. Evaluate later in the day.

Every step of the preparation should be accomplished with prayer. Remember: prayer and planning are a powerful combination. In addition, expect the Holy Spirit to give you thoughts as you move along.

"Teacher Growth Series" brings you information on every phase of your teaching ministry. Three articles per quarter can be read, shared with other teachers, and filed for future reference. Articles dealing with the same topics are presented at each age level from early childhood through adult. "The Teacher Growth Series" covers 36 different topics.

God's Plan To Save Sinners

CENTRAL TRUTH

The gospel of Jesus Christ is the good news of salvation for all mankind.

GOLDEN TEXT

The grace of God that brings salvation has appeared to all men. Titus 2:11 (NIV)

STUDY TEXT

Romans 1:1 through 3:26

OUTLINE

1. Revealed In The Gospel
   A. God's Power Revealed
   B. God's Righteousness Revealed

2. Revealed In God's Justice
   A. Sin Must Be Judged
   B. No Partiality With God

3. Revealed In Redemption
   A. Apart From The Law
   B. Redeeming Sacrifice

OBJECTIVE

To review God's redemptive plan and appreciate His love for humanity.

✓ CHECKLIST

☐ Study the teacher and student quarterlies carefully.
☐ Take note of any questions in the *Adult Student Guide* that would contribute to valuable classroom discussion.
☐ Display the unit poster in a prominent place in the classroom.
☐ Make sure the classroom is equipped with an overhead projector and that the projector works before the class starts.
☐ Look over the overhead transparencies "Sins Of The Pagan World" and "Sins Of The Religious World."
☐ Be prepared to discuss with the class why God responds similarly to sin even though it takes different forms in different groups of people. Be sure to note what these sins have in common.
☐ Fill out the "Planning The Session" sheet from the teaching helps packet to ensure that you cover every area of the lesson adequately.

DAILY BIBLE READINGS

Monday: Man's Sinfulness. Psalm 14:1-4
Tuesday: A Sinful City. Jonah 3:1-10
Wednesday: Forgiveness For Sin. Psalm 32:1-5
Thursday: Salvation Offered. John 4:7-15
Friday: Reconciliation Through Christ. 2 Corinthians 5:14-21
Saturday: Jesus The Savior. Hebrews 2:9-18

v.17 Therefore if any man be in Christ, he is a new creature: old things are passed away; behold, all things are become new

King James Version

Romans 1:14. I am debtor both to the Greeks, and to the Barbarians; both to the wise, and to the unwise.

15. So, as much as in me is, I am ready to preach the gospel to you that are at Rome also.

16. For I am not ashamed of the gospel of Christ: for it is the power of God unto salvation to every one that believeth; to the Jew first, and also to the Greek.

17. For therein is the righteousness of God revealed from faith to faith: as it is written, The just shall live by faith.

18. For the wrath of God is revealed from heaven against all ungodliness and unrighteousness of men, who hold the truth in unrighteousness.

2:6. Who will render to every man according to his deeds:

7. To them who by patient continuance in well doing seek for glory and honor and immortality, eternal life:

8. But unto them that are contentious, and do not obey the truth, but obey unrighteousness, indignation and wrath,

9. Tribulation and anguish, upon every soul of man that doeth evil; of the Jew first, and also of the Gentile;

10. But glory, honor, and peace, to every man that worketh good; to the Jew first, and also to the Gentile:

11. For there is no respect of persons with God.

3:21. But now the righteousness of God without the law is manifested, being witnessed by the law and the prophets;

22. Even the righteousness of God which is by faith of Jesus Christ unto all and upon all them that believe; for there is no difference:

23. For all have sinned, and come short of the glory of God;

24. Being justified freely by his grace through the redemption that is in Christ Jesus:

25. Whom God hath set forth to be a propitiation through faith in his blood, to declare his righteousness for the remission of sins that are past, through the forbearance of God;

26. To declare, I say, at this time his righteousness: that he might be just, and the justifier of him which believeth in Jesus.

New International Version

Romans 1:14. I am obligated both to Greeks and non-Greeks, both to the wise and the foolish.

15. That is why I am so eager to preach the gospel also to you who are at Rome.

16. I am not ashamed of the gospel, because it is the power of God for the salvation of everyone who believes: first for the Jew, then for the Gentile.

17. For in the gospel a righteousness from God is revealed, a righteousness that is by faith from first to last, just as it is written: "The righteous will live by faith."

18. The wrath of God is being revealed from heaven against all the godlessness and wickedness of men who suppress the truth by their wickedness.

2:6. God "will give to each person according to what he has done."

7. To those who by persistence in doing good seek glory, honor and immortality, he will give eternal life.

8. But for those who are self-seeking and who reject the truth and follow evil, there will be wrath and anger.

9. There will be trouble and distress for every human being who does evil: first for the Jew, then for the Gentile;

10. But glory, honor and peace for everyone who does good: first for the Jew, then for the Gentile.

11. For God does not show favoritism.

3:21. But now a righteousness from God, apart from law, has been made known, to which the Law and the Prophets testify.

22. This righteousness from God comes through faith in Jesus Christ to all who believe. There is no difference,

23. For all have sinned and fall short of the glory of God,

24. And are justified freely by his grace through the redemption that came by Christ Jesus.

25. God presented him as a sacrifice of atonement, through faith in his blood. He did this to demonstrate his justice, because in his forbearance he had left the sins committed beforehand unpunished—

26. He did it to demonstrate his justice at the present time, so as to be just and the one who justifies those who have faith in Jesus.

God has chosen the proclamation of the gospel to be His means to bring humanity to faith in himself. This gospel is God's message to His creation, a message that they absolutely must hear and understand. Without understanding the message, people would not be able to believe the gospel and be saved. For that reason, Paul declared that he was not ashamed of the gospel (Romans 1:16).

God longs to see His beloved children back in right relationship with himself, and He has made a way for this to happen: the sacrifice of His beloved Son. Only love beyond comprehension could motivate such a sacrifice, and it is precisely this love which is at the very heart of His gospel. The Bible declares that "God commendeth his love toward us, in that, while we were yet sinners, Christ died for us" (Romans 5:8).

BIBLE COMMENTARY

1. Revealed In The Gospel

A. God's Power Revealed
Romans 1:14-16

To Paul, the gospel was exceedingly precious. Its message declared the very thing that man most needed to hear, the way back to God. The words "not ashamed" (verse 16) actually were intended to emphasize Paul's feeling toward this gospel. He was proclaiming that, far from being ashamed of it, he gloried in the gospel message.

The reason for Paul's reverence is rooted in what the gospel can do. The gospel is God's power that operates unto salvation for all people, whether Jew or Greek. The source of this power is God, who works through the gospel to save sinners. It is His gospel and it is powerful because He works through it.

This power does not work unconditionally in an individual, however. The power of the gospel only works when accompanied by faith, for it produces salvation only in those who believe (verse 16). When a person believes the message, the gospel powerfully begins its work. Faith ignites the gospel's power.

Ask: "What examples from the Bible demonstrate how faith ignited God's saving power?"

TEACHING TIP 1: Have the students give the name of an individual from the Scriptures and how faith brought God's salvation. Be sure to have a number of good biblical examples ready to answer this question. Consult Hebrews chapter 11 as a resource. Noah, Abraham, Rahab, and Paul himself are some excellent examples that can be used.

Throughout His dealings with humanity, God has made faith a requirement before manifesting His power, though how faith originates is a wondrous mystery. One thing is clear, when people believe, God works. The gospel, when accompanied by faith, becomes "the power of God unto salvation."

NOTES

B. God's Righteousness Revealed
Romans 1:17

The theme of Paul's letter to the Romans is found in verse 17. The righteousness of God has been revealed to humanity in the person of His Son Jesus Christ.

The phrase "the righteousness of God" has a twofold meaning. It means both His personal, righteous nature and the means by which God makes sinful men right with himself. This latter meaning is most important to Paul's argument, which he developed later in Romans when he introduced the concept of justification.

The context of the word "revealed" suggests it means more than merely revealing God's righteousness to our understanding. God's righteousness has been brought to us to effect our salvation. God has acted to deliver us and make us acceptable in His sight. In light of this, Paul again underscored the importance of faith.

Faith is the instrument that brings this righteousness to us. The righteousness that we receive is by faith when we first believe and it is by faith until the day we are called to heaven ("from faith to faith," verse 17). To support this Paul quoted from Habakkuk the prophet: "The righteous will live by faith" (verse 17, NIV). It was this verse that drove the truth of justification by faith to the heart of Martin Luther and ultimately drove him back to the truth of Christianity. Faith in Christ brings God's righteousness to man. Salvation can never be earned. We are not, nor can we ever be, good enough to merit it.

Ask: "Why do some people find it difficult to accept that the gift of salvation is free?"

TEACHING TIP 2: Perhaps some in the class could share their own struggles with accepting the free gift of salvation. Or you may wish to lead a discussion of the reasons or excuses people use for not accepting Christ as their Savior. Conclude that the most common problem people have in accepting Christ is pride.

Pride will always be one of man's greatest stumbling blocks. While the world persists in dividing human beings into categories of "good" and "bad," God sees them differently. He sees them as either willing or unwilling to accept the reality of their need of a Savior. The Bible declares that "God resisteth the proud, but giveth grace to the humble" (1 Peter 5:5).

NOTES

2. Revealed In God's Justice

A. Sin Must Be Judged
Romans 1:18

The declaration that "the wrath of God is revealed from heaven against all ungodliness" (verse 18) stands in striking contrast to the revelation of the righteousness of God, which was stated in verse 17. While a way has been made for man to be made right with God, some will not choose that way. Those who refuse God's loving offer will certainly face God's wrath.

God is holy and His holiness requires that all sin be judged. While God is patient with men and endures their rebellion, He cannot allow their sin to stand in His eternal presence. His justice requires that those who hold the truth in unrighteousness—that is, stifle or suppress the truth by their wickedness—be punished.

Sin truly makes God angry, and divine anger is just as real as divine love. Because men are in rebellion against God, God's wrath is revealed against them as long as they reject the way to forgiveness.

In the Old Testament, God consistently judged both the sins of His chosen nation Israel and those of the nations which surrounded her. When Israel sinned, God lovingly called her to repent and was extremely patient toward her rebellion. There came a time, however, when the nation had to be punished. God's holiness required it. He sent the Assyrians and later the Babylonians to be agents of His judgment. Even though He preserved a remnant through captivity, those who rebelled were destroyed.

God has not changed, nor will He ever change. He will always stand against sin and rebellion. God will never be overcome with permissiveness. There will not be any last minute change of heart on His part. What God has promised, He will most certainly do. Man should never miscalculate when it comes to divine judgment.

NOTES

B. No Partiality With God
Romans 2:6-11

TEACHING TIP 3: Display the two overhead transparencies taken from Romans 1:21-32 and 2:1-11: "Sins Of The Pagan World" and "Sins Of The Religious World." As the class looks at the first transparency and then the second, ask the following two questions. Pause after the first question and allow the students to reflect on their answer. Then ask the second. You will want to get responses to both questions.

1. Which group of sins is most repulsive? Why?
2. Do you think God's response is the same as yours?

People often categorize sin according to how it offends them personally. While we separate sins into categories, God is impartial. To Him all sin is offensive and worthy of judgment.

The sins of the Gentile world were both highly visible and easily recognized. One reason for this was the fact they were mostly external in nature. Verses 29-31 of Romans 1 list no fewer than 21 sins that give evidence of total rebellion against God. This rebellion spawned behavior that brought increasing degradation to the pagan world. Those who practiced such things were clearly destined for God's judgment.

Not all sin is equally visible, however. To the Jew, the sins described in Romans 1 were abhorent. They readily agreed that such depravity was worthy of judgment. What the Jews failed to understand was that they were guilty before God as well. Paul declared that they were guilty of "the same things" (Romans 2:1, NIV). By this he meant that they were guilty of sins that, though different in kind, were the same in principle. Sin constitutes rebellion before God no matter what form it takes.

The Jews were guilty of a kind of sin that was more difficult to recognize. It was also more difficult to address because such sin frequently escaped examination. The sins of the religious world were equal in magnitude as far as God was concerned. God "will render to every man according to his deeds" (verse 6), and God will bring "tribulation and anguish, upon every soul of man that doeth evil; of the Jew first and also of the Gentile" (verse 9).

Paul's conclusion declared God's impartiality. God will judge the sin of the Jew and Gentile alike. He will give no person special consideration, "For there is no respect of persons with God" (verse 11).

The meaning is clear. God has purchased our redemption and liberated us from sin's power. This is strictly an act of His grace and entirely independent of the Law (compare verses 21 and 24). God has intervened effectively to change man's direction and provide salvation for him.

Man's redemption did not come cheaply. The price was indescribably great. It cost God the humiliating death of His Son at the hands of those who deserved punishment. God was willing to pay this price because He loves us in a way that we cannot possibly comprehend.

3. Revealed In Redemption

A. Apart From The Law
Romans 3:21-24

God has a remedy for man's problem. The words "but now," found in verse 21, indicate God's dramatic intervention to deliver man from his predicament. A new way to bring about man's acceptance with God has been established, one that has been witnessed to by the Law and the Prophets. This way is that of faith in Christ. While Romans 3:9-20 characterized humanity's enslavement to sin and subsequent judgment, in verses 21-26 we see their deliverance.

Paul further defined how we can be made righteous: by having faith in Jesus Christ (verse 22). This righteousness is made available to everyone who believes. Although there were some Jews who felt that their righteousness was through the Law, Paul explained that "there is no difference: for all have sinned," both Jews and Gentiles, "and come short of the glory of God" (verses 22,23). This indicates that there is no one who does not need the salvation offered to us. There is no one who does not need to be delivered from sin.

The agent of deliverance for those who believe is "the redemption that is in Christ Jesus" (verse 24). Redemption is the act of purchasing someone out of slavery with the purpose of making this person free. It literally means to buy back. This, of course, is exactly what God has done for us. We were once slaves of sin, but now we are set free and belong to Christ.

TEACHING TIP 4: To conclude this section, have the students close their eyes and listen while you slowly read John 3:16 to them. You may wish to lead them in a time of praise for the redemption that God purchased for us by sending Jesus to be sacrificed for our sins.

NOTES

B. Redeeming Sacrifice
Romans 3:25,26

The word "propitiation" (Romans 3:25) is key to understanding a very important concept in the mind of Paul. This word expresses the idea of an atoning sacrifice that effectively turns away God's wrath. Christ's death has brought God's mercy to bear on sinful man. In doing so God's wrath toward man has been averted. God's holiness has been satisfied by the substitutionary death of Jesus.

Ask: "Why is it necessary for God's wrath to be turned away?" As noted earlier, Paul declared that God's wrath is revealed against all man's ungodliness and unrighteousness (1:18). Man is under the sentence of God's wrath. Sin automatically faces the retribution of a holy God. Therefore, sin must not only be removed, but provision must be made to free us from His anger.

In dying for us, Jesus brought acceptance instead of wrath. Instead of the judgment that we deserve, God has given us the eternal life that we don't deserve. The result is that in redeeming us God has freed us from both the bondage of sin and the punishment for sin.

The wonderful news of the gospel is that Christ's death has reconciled us to God. We are at peace with Him because of Christ's sacrifice. There is no fearful expectation of judgment. You belong to Him. He has paid for you with His blood.

NOTES

LIFE RESPONSE

I am not ashamed of the gospel of Christ: for it is the power of God unto salvation to everyone that believeth; to the Jew first, and also to the Greek'' (Romans 1:16). These words not only sum up the heart of the apostle Paul toward Christ's gospel, but they express a truth that ought to be central to all believers. Like Paul, we ought to glory in the gospel.

The reason for this should be obvious. The gospel is God's wonderful news that reveals both His love for us, and the details of His all-encompassing plan to bring about our salvation. Apart from this gospel we would be separated from God, facing certain judgment and utterly without hope. Nothing else could have changed these circumstances.

But what about the people you know—your unsaved friends—who are outside of God's grace? The gospel is also God's power to save them as well. God uses people like you to proclaim His message to people who would not otherwise hear. What will happen if you do not? The Bible declares, "How then shall they call on him in whom they

have not believed? and how shall they believe in him of whom they have not heard? and how shall they hear without a preacher? and how shall they preach, except they be sent?'' (Romans 10:14,15). You have a wonderful treasure to share with the world and a tremendous responsibility to share it. Many people are waiting to hear, and God is depending on you to tell them.

EVANGELISM OUTREACH

This study provides many opportunities for presenting the gospel to those who don't know Christ. The importance of faith in relation to salvation should be stressed. Remind the class that the gospel is God's power for salvation only to those who believe.

Plan for a time at the end of the class to give people the opportunity to respond to the gospel. Close the meeting with a special prayer asking God to reveal himself to the class. Be prepared to pray with any individual who wants to accept Christ. ⌂

Justification

CENTRAL TRUTH

Justification means a person is made righteous in God's sight.

GOLDEN TEXT

Since we have been justified through faith, we have peace with God through our Lord Jesus Christ. Romans 5:1 (NIV)

STUDY TEXT

Romans 5:1-21

OUTLINE

1. Justified Through Faith
   A. Declared Righteous
   B. Peace, Grace, And Hope

2. Reconciled Through Christ
   A. By His Death
   B. By His Life

3. Redeemed By Grace
   A. Need For Grace
   B. Gift Of Grace

OBJECTIVE

To understand biblical justification and acknowledge our position in Christ.

CHECKLIST

☐ Read the *Adult Student Guide* and the *Adult Teacher Guide*.
☐ Note any questions that will stimulate classroom discussion.
☐ Review study 1, noting the emphasis on the righteousness of God.
☐ Familiarize yourself with the emphasis on justification in Romans 4.
☐ Duplicate enough of the work sheet "Adam And Christ: Downfall And Deliverance" so every student will have one.
☐ Look over the work sheet for Teaching Tip 5 "Adam And Christ: Downfall And Deliverance," from the teaching helps packet. The contrast between the fall of man and the redemption of man presents an opportunity to declare the triumph of grace over sin.
☐ Be sure to make the connection between grace (God's unmerited favor) and justification (God's righteousness imparted).

DAILY BIBLE READINGS

Monday: Pardon.
Isaiah 55:1-8
Tuesday: Justification.
Habakkuk 2:1-4
Wednesday: Faith.
Galatians 3:22-29
Thursday: Adoption.
Galatians 4:4-7
Friday: Peace.
Philippians 4:4-7
Saturday: Redemption.
Revelation 5:9-13

Scripture Setting

King James Version

Romans 5:1. Therefore being justified by faith, we have peace with God through our Lord Jesus Christ:

2. By whom also we have access by faith into this grace wherein we stand, and rejoice in hope of the glory of God.

3. And not only so, but we glory in tribulations also; knowing that tribulation worketh patience;

4. And patience, experience; and experience, hope:

5. And hope maketh not ashamed; because the love of God is shed abroad in our hearts by the Holy Ghost which is given unto us.

6. For when we were yet without strength, in due time Christ died for the ungodly.

7. For scarcely for a righteous man will one die: yet peradventure for a good man some would even dare to die.

8. But God commendeth his love toward us, in that, while we were yet sinners, Christ died for us.

9. Much more then, being now justified by his blood, we shall be saved from wrath through him.

10. For if, when we were enemies, we were reconciled to God by the death of his Son; much more, being reconciled, we shall be saved by his life.

11. And not only so, but we also joy in God through our Lord Jesus Christ, by whom we have now received the atonement.

12. Wherefore, as by one man sin entered into the world, and death by sin; and so death passed upon all men, for that all have sinned.

17. (For if by one man's offense death reigned by one; much more they which receive abundance of grace and of the gift of righteousness shall reign in life by one, Jesus Christ.)

18. Therefore, as by the offense of one judgment came upon all men to condemnation; even so by the righteousness of one the free gift came upon all men unto justification of life.

19. For as by one man's disobedience many were made sinners, so by the obedience of one shall many be made righteous.

20. Moreover the law entered, that the offense might abound. But where sin abounded, grace did much more abound:

21. That as sin hath reigned unto death, even so might grace reign through righteousness unto eternal life by Jesus Christ our Lord.

New International Version

Romans 5:1. Therefore, since we have been justified through faith, we have peace with God through our Lord Jesus Christ,

2. Through whom we have gained access by faith into this grace in which we now stand. And we rejoice in the hope of the glory of God.

3. Not only so, but we also rejoice in our sufferings, because we know that suffering produces perseverance;

4. Perseverance, character; and character, hope.

5. And hope does not disappoint us, because God has poured out his love into our hearts by the Holy Spirit, whom he has given us.

6. You see, at just the right time, when we were still powerless, Christ died for the ungodly.

7. Very rarely will anyone die for a righteous man, though for a good man someone might possibly dare to die.

8. But God demonstrates his own love for us in this: While we were still sinners, Christ died for us.

9. Since we have now been justified by his blood, how much more shall we be saved from God's wrath through him!

10. For if, when we were God's enemies, we were reconciled to him through the death of his Son, how much more, having been reconciled, shall we be saved through his life!

11. Not only is this so, but we also rejoice in God through our Lord Jesus Christ, through whom we have now received reconciliation.

12. Therefore, just as sin entered the world through one man, and death through sin, and in this way death came to all men, because all sinned.

17. For if, by the trespass of the one man, death reigned through that one man, how much more will those who receive God's abundant provision of grace and of the gift of righteousness reign in life through the one man, Jesus Christ.

18. Consequently, just as the result of one trespass was condemnation for all men, so also the result of one act of righteousness was justification that brings life for all men.

19. For just as through the disobedience of the one man the many were made sinners, so also through the obedience of the one man the many will be made righteous.

20. The law was added so that the trespass might increase. But where sin increased, grace increased all the more,

21. So that, just as sin reigned in death, so also grace might reign through righteousness to bring eternal life through Jesus Christ our Lord.

No matter what adverse circumstances the believer may face, he can rejoice because his greatest need has already been met. He has been made right with his Creator and can confidently expect to live eternally with Him.

How can the Christian be so assured? The Bible declares that through the death, burial, and resurrection of Jesus Christ God has accomplished this. All we have to do is believe it. This fact of our being made right with God is called justification. There is no more glorious reality than that of God imparting to us the righteousness of His Son, Jesus Christ.

Yet God wants this fact to be more than a doctrinal truth. He wants it to be a life-changing reality. He wants it to fill our minds and hearts, both enriching our fellowship with Him and bringing us peace.

BIBLE COMMENTARY

1. Justified Through Faith

NOTES

A. Declared Righteous.
Romans 5:1

Justification is an important aspect in our salvation experience. To be justified means "to be declared righteous." It is not "just-as-if-I'd-never sinned," but "I did sin, but my sin is not charged to my account. Because of my acceptance of Christ's atoning work on the cross, I have been declared righteous in the sight of God." Justification is God's way of dealing with the sins of those who have accepted His salvation.

Notice Paul's statement in Romans 5:1, "Being justified by faith." Justification only comes by faith. Paul had stated that Abraham's faith was "credited to him as righteousness" (4:3, NIV). Abraham did not "earn" his righteousness by his works. He believed God, even before his works (that is, circumcision, verses 9-12).

In the same way, our faith is credited to us as righteousness (verses 23-25). It is our faith in Christ Jesus, and only that faith, that allows us to be "declared righteous" in the sight of God.

B. Peace, Grace, And Hope
Romans 5:2-8

Having established that God has made a way to justify sinners, and having declared that faith is the means by which we are made right in His sight, Paul went on to enumerate the benefits of this justification. The first of these benefits listed by the apostle is that of peace with God.

Faith in Christ makes a relationship with God a reality by removing the enmity between God and man that was brought about by sin. Man's separation from God has many evidences in the world. These evidences include rebellion, fear, loneliness, guilt and despair. Peace with God, however, brings with it a sense of belonging, trust, and assurance. These are by-products of our having made peace with God through faith in the work of Jesus Christ His Son.

Ask: "How does understanding the meaning of justification help us experience the peace of knowing that we are saved?" When God made us right with himself, He did something much more than declare a theological, theoretical truth. By declaring that we are at peace with Him, He has made experiencial peace possible. God wants our new relationship with Him to transform our lives.

In verse 2, Paul declared that we have access into God's grace through faith in Jesus Christ. The word translated "access" symbolizes the ushering of someone into the presence of a royal or exalted person. Here it applies to the believer's introduction into the wonderful realm of God's grace.

Access to God's grace brings access to His divine presence. We are encouraged to "come boldly unto the throne of grace, that we may obtain mercy, and find grace to help in time of need" (Hebrews 4:16). Having been justified, we now have confident access into the presence of God. We can come boldly because we are righteous in Christ, and accepted before His throne.

TEACHING TIP 1: Perhaps a person in the class would be willing to share an experience of feeling unworthy to be in God's presence and how God changed this attitude. Usually this feeling accompanies a particular failure. You may wish to come prepared yourself in case no one responds. Be sure to stress the important application of grace and justification to our feelings of unworthiness. God wants us to know that our acceptance is based on Christ's work, not our works.

A third benefit of our justification is hope. Hope is the confident expectation of good. It looks to the future happily, trusting in the plan and purpose of God. That is why Paul wrote that we "rejoice in hope of the glory of God" (Romans 5:2). We confidently expect our ultimate victory and future glory.

Hope brings great joy to believers because their future is assured. The greatest and most essential need of their lives has been met. They are saved. They will forevermore live and reign with their Savior.

When we understand the true implications of God's justifying work, we can't help but rejoice. The more we meditate on the hope we have in Christ, the greater our rejoicing. We belong to Jesus for all eternity.

Ask: "How does hope in the future benefit us in the present?"

TEACHING TIP 2: To stimulate the thinking of the class, ask them to read 1 John 3:1-3. These verses teach us that the hope of eternal life helps us in our pursuit of holiness. This is one suggestion. There may be other ideas the students may wish to express.

NOTES

2. Reconciled Through Christ

A. By His Death
Romans 5:9,10

In Romans 5:10, reconciliation means to bring about a change in relationship with God. Our relationship was once simply that of sinners awaiting judgment. Now we are described as being "reconciled to God by the death of his Son" (Romans 5:10).

Our relationship with God has totally changed because of Christ. Instead of wrath, our relationship is one of acceptance. God has accepted us because of Christ. God now calls us His children. We are now treated as righteous because we have been "justified by his blood" (verse 9).

The work of reconciliation could only be initiated by God. Since we sinned against God, only God could offer forgiveness and atonement. He alone has both the ability and desire to make things right. God did this at great cost to himself. He had to become man, live on earth, and be shamefully treated to the point of being killed.

Even though the cost was enormous, God's love was far greater. Christ's death was the greatest possible demonstration of that love. Only His death could make atonement for sin and save us from the wrath of a holy God. It was a price that He freely paid because He loves us.

NOTES

B. By His Life
Romans 5:10,11

Verse 10 states that we are not only reconciled to God through the atoning death of Christ on the cross, but our salvation is dependent on the fact He lives. The phrase "we shall be saved by his life" refers to the resurrection life of Christ. Christ not only died, but was raised from the dead and now lives in an exalted state at the right hand of the Father. He not only died to save us, but He also lives to keep us. He is presently interceding before the Father as our Advocate.

The resurrection of Christ also implies that there is power available to the believers.

Because Jesus Christ is alive, He can bring aid in our struggle against sin. Our salvation is not only the result of a decision to receive Christ, it is also a continuing life which results in transformed character. Christ's power both transforms and keeps us. If He did not live, we could not live for Him.

TEACHING TIP 3: Reinforce the truth that God is faithful to us by producing character growth by having a circle response to the statement: "Christ has transformed my character by. . . ." After each student has shared, explain that God's power is necessary to transform us into Christ's likeness. Ask a student to read Philippians 1:6. Emphasize that Christ is continually working in us to achieve His desired objective: making believers to be like Him.

Ask: "How does the living Christ give the believer hope?" Our own frailties are obvious to us. We fall short in so many ways and are easily discouraged. Our hope, however, is not in ourselves but in Christ. Knowing this, we can be confident because He will never forsake us. Christ's promises can be trusted. Though we fail Him, He will never fail us. Paul spoke strongly to this when he declared, "For I know whom I have believed, and am persuaded that he is able to keep that which I have committed unto him against that day" (2 Timothy 1:12).

NOTES

3. Redeemed By Grace

A. Need For Grace
Romans 5:12-14

Man's need for grace is made clear in Scripture. Paul proclaimed that Adam's offense is the focal point of man's problem. Because of Adam's sin, all humanity has received a sinful nature.

Romans 5:12 declares that when sin came into the world through Adam it brought death. Even though through Adam mankind has received a nature bent toward sin, we cannot simply blame Adam for our problems. The clause "all have sinned" indicates that we are all active participants in sin.

The conclusion is obvious. Man's tendency toward sin has been passed on. Children don't have to be taught to sin—it comes naturally. As children grow to adulthood, they grow more sophisticated at sinning, but their selfish nature is clearly manifested.

Sin cannot be tolerated by God, but it can be forgiven. People need God's grace. Grace literally means God's unmerited favor which is bestowed upon man without regard to his merit. This grace is a person's most pressing need. Without it, he has no hope.

Ask: "How would you respond to people's aversion to the concept of sin?"

TEACHING TIP 4: Ask the class to discuss how unbelievers might respond to the idea of sin and their need for God's grace to be saved. Point out that people often compare themselves to others whose sins are more evident. Continue the discussion with the following commentary.

People sometimes have a nebulous idea of what sin is. This is becoming more and more prevalent in our culture, which for the most part has rejected moral authority. It is becoming increasingly difficult to categorize something as wrong. In the midst of this, we need the help of the Holy Spirit to bring people to an understanding of their need for grace.

NOTES

B. Gift Of Grace
Romans 5:15-21

God's grace is a free gift that is offered to sinful humanity. Just as sin came through one man, Adam, so God's free gift of grace comes by way of one agent, Jesus Christ. Paul contrasted the trespass of Adam and the obedience of Christ with their respective consequences in verses 15 and 18. Adam's offense brought death and condemnation upon all men. Christ's obedience, however, nullified the result of Adam's sin by paying its penalty. Jesus took our sin and the penalty that came with it and provided us with the free gift of eternal life in its place. What a contrast! Adam's disobedience brought sin, death, and condemnation. But the obedience of Christ resulted in grace, life, and justification.

This passage presents the human race as being in union with either Adam or Christ. People are born "in Adam," but they can only be "in Christ" through faith in His work on Calvary. In Adam they are spiritually dead and awaiting judgment. But in Christ, they have received eternal life through this gift of His grace. The old union is gone and a new solidarity takes its place.

All this is due to the sacrificial act of Jesus. He took our sins as His own and bore the penalty that belonged to us. In doing so, He took our condemnation and imparted His righteousness in place of it. Paul summed this up beautifully when he proclaimed that God "made him to be sin for us, who knew no sin; that we might be made the righteousness of God in him'' (2 Corinthians 5:21).

Ask: **"In what ways does God's grace impact you in your daily life?"** God's grace is not merely a one time expression of divine favor. We continually need His mercy and forgiveness. To be human is to be frail. God's grace exceeds our sin and failure, and will present us faultless before His throne. It is only because of God's grace that we can have assurance of eternal salvation.

NOTES

LIFE RESPONSE

Justification is more than a theological concept. It is a reality that, when understood, is totally life changing. Man, the crown of creation, has been made right with his Creator. Now each of us can have a personal relationship with God.

Yet not only can we be made right with God, we can be secure in that new relationship. This means that the greatest need of our lives has already been met by God. Our sins have been forgiven, and the shackles of guilt and fear have been broken. We now are clothed in the righteousness of Christ. What a joy to know that God does not see our sin: He sees only the righteousness of the Lord Jesus Christ.

None of this is in any way deserved. It all comes by way of grace, God's unmerited favor. The great gulf that separated us from God has been bridged. We don't have to feel alienated from Him anymore. The basis for fellowship has been established by Jesus Christ through His death on Calvary's cross. God has given the greatest gift possible to the most undeserving of creatures: the forgiveness of sin.

In Christ, we stand before God faultless and totally complete. When we received His righteousness in place of our own, we received a foundation upon which we could place our future for all eternity. What a joy to know that God did for us the one thing that we could not do. He made a way for us to be righteous in His sight. All we have to do is receive it by faith.

EVANGELISM OUTREACH

The unbeliever's only hope is to be reconciled to God through Jesus Christ. Human pride is a hindrance, but the gospel, accompanied by the conviction of the Holy Spirit, can penetrate pride.

The Bible declares that God is ''not willing that any should perish, but that all should come to repentance'' (2 Peter 3:9). Jesus died to this end, to provide a way for sinners to be reconciled to the Father. Give an opportunity for any unsaved students to accept Christ as their personal Savior.

Call To Holy Living

CENTRAL TRUTH

Every believer is called to a life of holiness.

GOLDEN TEXT

Now that you have been set free from sin and have become slaves to God, the benefit you reap leads to holiness, and the result is eternal life. Romans 6:22 (NIV)

STUDY TEXT

Romans 6:1-23

OUTLINE

1. Dead To Sin
   A. Abuse Of Grace
   B. Analogy Of Baptism

2. Alive In Christ
   A. Resurrection Power
   B. Continual Appropriation

3. Servants Of Righteousness
   A. Exclusively Christ's
   B. A Good Master

woe is me for I have seen the Lord — sin is purged whom shall I send & who will go for us .. Here am I send me.

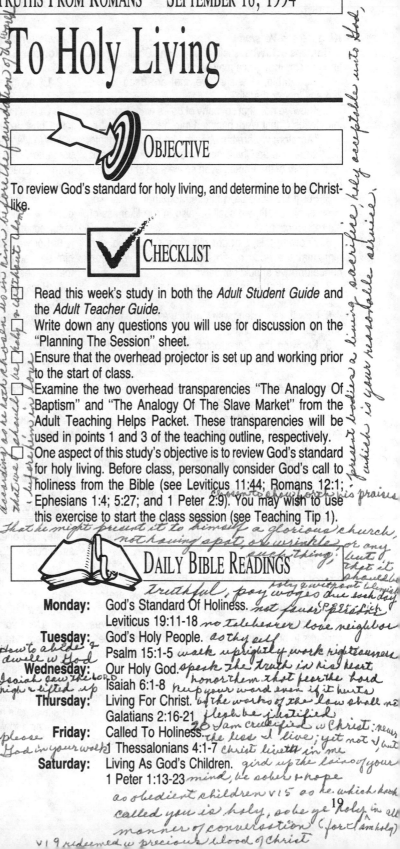

OBJECTIVE

To review God's standard for holy living, and determine to be Christ-like.

CHECKLIST

- Read this week's study in both the *Adult Student Guide* and the *Adult Teacher Guide*.
- Write down any questions you will use for discussion on the "Planning The Session" sheet.
- Ensure that the overhead projector is set up and working prior to the start of class.
- Examine the two overhead transparencies "The Analogy Of Baptism" and "The Analogy Of The Slave Market" from the Adult Teaching Helps Packet. These transparencies will be used in points 1 and 3 of the teaching outline, respectively.
- One aspect of this study's objective is to review God's standard for holy living. Before class, personally consider God's call to holiness from the Bible (see Leviticus 11:44; Romans 12:1; Ephesians 1:4; 5:27; and 1 Peter 2:9). You may wish to use this exercise to start the class session (see Teaching Tip 1).

DAILY BIBLE READINGS

Monday: God's Standard Of Holiness. *holy & without blemish* Leviticus 19:11-18 *no talebearer love neighbor*
Tuesday: God's Holy People. *as thy self* Psalm 15:1-5 *walk uprightly work righteousness*
Wednesday: Our Holy God. *speak the truth in his heart* Isaiah 6:1-8 *honor them that fear the Lord keep your word even if it hurts*
Thursday: Living For Christ. *by the works of the law shall no* Galatians 2:16-21 *flesh be justified*
Friday: Called To Holiness. *I am crucified w Christ: never the less I live; yet not I, but* 1 Thessalonians 4:1-7 *Christ liveth in me*
Saturday: Living As God's Children. *gird up the loins of your* 1 Peter 1:13-23 *mind, be sober & hope*

as obedient children v15 as he. which hath called you is holy, so be ye holy in all manner of conversation (for I am holy) v19 redeemed w precious blood of Christ

King James Version

Romans 6:1. What shall we say then? Shall we continue in sin, that grace may abound?

2. God forbid. How shall we, that are dead to sin, live any longer therein?

3. Know ye not, that so many of us as were baptized into Jesus Christ were baptized into his death?

4. Therefore we are buried with him by baptism into death: that like as Christ was raised up from the dead by the glory of the Father, even so we also should walk in newness of life.

5. For if we have been planted together in the likeness of his death, we shall be also in the likeness of his resurrection:

6. Knowing this, that our old man is crucified with him, that the body of sin might be destroyed, that henceforth we should not serve sin.

7. For he that is dead is freed from sin.

8. Now if we be dead with Christ, we believe that we shall also live with him:

9. Knowing that Christ being raised from the dead dieth no more; death hath no more dominion over him.

10. For in that he died, he died unto sin once: but in that he liveth, he liveth unto God.

11. Likewise reckon ye also yourselves to be dead indeed unto sin, but alive unto God through Jesus Christ our Lord.

12. Let not sin therefore reign in your mortal body, that ye should obey it in the lusts thereof.

13. Neither yield ye your members as instruments of unrighteousness unto sin: but yield yourselves unto God, as those that are alive from the dead, and your members as instruments of righteousness unto God.

14. For sin shall not have dominion over you: for ye are not under the law, but under grace.

15. What then? shall we sin, because we are not under the law, but under grace? God forbid.

16. Know ye not, that to whom ye yield yourselves servants to obey, his servants ye are to whom ye obey; whether of sin unto death, or of obedience unto righteousness?

17. But God be thanked, that ye were the servants of sin, but ye have obeyed from the heart that form of doctrine which was delivered you.

18. Being then made free from sin, ye became the servants of righteousness.

New International Version

Romans 6:1. What shall we say, then? Shall we go on sinning so that grace may increase?

2. By no means! We died to sin; how can we live in it any longer?

3. Or don't you know that all of us who were baptized into Christ Jesus were baptized into his death?

4. We were therefore buried with him through baptism into death in order that, just as Christ was raised from the dead through the glory of the Father, we too may live a new life.

5. If we have been united with him like this in his death, we will certainly also be united with him in his resurrection.

6. For we know that our old self was crucified with him so that the body of sin might be done away with, that we should no longer be slaves to sin—

7. Because anyone who has died has been freed from sin.

8. Now if we died with Christ, we believe that we will also live with him.

9. For we know that since Christ was raised from the dead, he cannot die again; death no longer has mastery over him.

10. The death he died, he died to sin once for all; but the life he lives, he lives to God.

11. In the same way, count yourselves dead to sin but alive to God in Christ Jesus.

12. Therefore do not let sin reign in your mortal body so that you obey its evil desires.

13. Do not offer the parts of your body to sin, as instruments of wickedness, but rather offer yourselves to God, as those who have been brought from death to life; and offer the parts of your body to him as instruments of righteousness.

14. For sin shall not be your master, because you are not under law, but under grace.

15. What then? Shall we sin because we are not under law but under grace? By no means!

16. Don't you know that when you offer yourselves to someone to obey him as slaves, you are slaves to the one whom you obey—whether you are slaves to sin, which leads to death, or to obedience, which leads to righteousness?

17. But thanks be to God that, though you used to be slaves to sin, you wholeheartedly obeyed the form of teaching to which you were entrusted.

18. You have been set free from sin and have become slaves to righteousness.

Last week's study on justification focused on the new standing we have in Christ Jesus. Today we turn our attention to the call to holy living. Now that we are in Christ, we must become like Him. This ongoing journey to Christlikeness is a process with pitfalls along the way. The old nature has to be continually treated as dead and this new life in Christ Jesus must be aggressively pursued.

We are new creatures and we have a new Master to obey. We have been set free and now, by God's grace and power, we must stay free. Paul addressed this issue in Romans 6:1: "Shall we continue in sin that grace may abound?" He not only answered this question, but gave instruction on how to bear the fruit of holiness and find perfect freedom in Christ. We shall explore these answers in this week's study.

BIBLE COMMENTARY

1. Dead To Sin

A. Abuse Of Grace
Romans 6:1-3

TEACHING TIP 1: Ask the students to define the word "holiness," writing their responses on the chalkboard or a blank transparency. Since the biblical concept of holiness is often misunderstood, ask the class to give some examples of how holiness may have been misinterpreted in times past. Stress that holiness always begins in the heart and works outward.

Romans 6 begins with Paul's having anticipated an objection on the part of those who would abuse God's wonderful gift of grace. The insinuation was that God could actually be glorified through sin because sin underscores God's mercy and compassion. In other words, the more we sin, the more God's grace is seen to be grace (verses 1,2).

Paul recoiled at such a suggestion. His response, translated "God forbid" in the King James Version, was the strongest negative that could be stated in Greek. Various translations have rendered this phrase as "By

no means" (NIV), "Certainly not!" (NKJV), and "May it never be!" (NASB). The argument represents a ridiculous contradiction. A person cannot die to sin on the one hand, and on the other hand still live in it. A Christian in no way can be so double-minded. He cannot be both dead and alive to the same thing simultaneously. Either he resolves to be dead to sin or alive to it. He cannot maintain two attitudes toward sin. Paul's presupposition here is absolutely fundamental. The Christian must maintain a steadfast attitude of being dead to sin. Grace must never be treated as though it is cheap. As a result of being justified, the Christian is accounted as right with God. He must now dedicate himself to pursue the holy life. The only way he can do this is to continually focus on his new identity in Christ. Sin has no place in this new identity.

Ask: "What are the inherent dangers for the Christian in maintaining a carefree attitude toward sin?"

TEACHING TIP 2: Have the students brainstorm for examples of how people's perception of their identity affects their actions. Point out that a person who sees himself as a child of God must live in a way that is consistent with this understanding. There is only one life-style that is acceptable for a child of God and that is a holy life-style.

NOTES

B. Analogy Of Baptism
Romans 6:4-7 *he that is dead is freed from sin*

Baptism illustrates this new identity in Christ. Paul saw it as a clear description of the believer's union with Jesus Christ. The ordinance of baptism is reserved for the person who professes both faith in Christ and a desire to follow Him. It is applicable only for one who has been regenerated by the Holy Spirit.

Ask: "Should baptism be done by immersion or sprinkling? Why?" Baptism is not only a public confession of one's faith in Christ, it is also an outward declaration of a work that has taken place within. It declares that we have died with Christ, have been buried with Him, and now have been raised with Him to walk in newness of life. This is perfectly portrayed through baptism by immersion. We are submerged into the water, indicating our death and burial. We are then raised from the water, indicating our new life in Christ.

It is imperative that the Christian see himself as dead to sin. He must view his sinful nature as something that is no more. This does not mean that his struggle against sinful passions is over. It simply means that he treats his sinful nature as dead, refusing to respond to it.

This is seen clearly in verse 6. Paul declared that our old self was crucified with Christ, in order to render our sinful natures powerless, and break sin's hold over our

lives. This crucifixion is in the past. The tense used by Paul in the Greek indicates that the work has already taken place. The result is that sin has indeed been rendered powerless and we are no longer in its deadly grasp.

TEACHING TIP 3: Display the overhead transparency "The Analogy Of Baptism." Briefly review the ordinance of baptism, pointing out the reasons for it and relating each to Paul's teaching on being dead to sin.

NOTES

Col 3:1-3 If ye then be risen w Christ, seek those things which are above, where Christ sitteth on the right hand of God. Set your affection on things above not on things on the earth. For ye are dead, & your life is hid with Christ in God.

2. Alive In Christ

A. Resurrection Power
Romans 6:8-10

The believer is not only dead to sin, but he has been quickened by the Spirit and is now alive in Christ Jesus. Just as the work of Christ was not complete without the resurrection, so our transformation is not fully accomplished until we are united with Him in this new resurrected life. Paul declared that since we died with Christ, we will also live with Him (verse 8). We are truly risen with Christ, and we must now seek after those things that please Him because we belong to Him (Colossians 3:1-3). *above*

Our death to sin cannot be realized without our being made alive by Christ's resurrection power. Then our uniting with Christ in the likeness of His death will result in our being raised in the likeness of His resurrection at the last day (Romans 6:5).

However, this cannot be a reality unless His power is manifested in us today in the form of holy lives. Holiness is not optional. Yet it can only be acquired through divine power not human strength. God seeks to manifest a new Christlike character in each of us. And this character can only become a reality when the same power that raised Christ from the dead becomes our supply.

NOTES

B. Continual Appropriation
Romans 6:11-14

Even though our bodily resurrection is something that we await, resurrection power is available to us as we pursue holy living. Our call is to live as if the bodily resurrection has become a reality. This is our new and permanent identity. As we continually cooperate with the Holy Spirit, He works to accomplish the Father's purpose in us.

Ask: "How can we be holy and live as if the bodily resurrection is a reality?" We do this as we regularly "reckon" or consider ourselves to be dead to sin and alive to God through Christ (verse 11). As we daily remind ourselves of our union with Christ in His crucifixion and resurrection, we both affirm our new identity and appropriate Christ's power. Sin is rendered powerless because it has been effectively resisted.

This "reckoning" is our choice, one that we must make continually. Verses 12 and 13 remind us that submission is necessary in our progression toward Christlike character. Our members must not be yielded as "instruments of unrighteousness"; they must be yielded as "instruments of righ-

teousness." We are to respond to God "as those that are alive from the dead."

Ask: "Why do Christians often fall into the trap of believing that they can conquer sinful habits through their own striving?" We are used to being self reliant. Our natural tendency is to think that habits can be overcome through our own will power. But it is important to remember that our pursuit of Christlikeness is a lifetime quest. We complicate things when we depend on our own strength.

> TEACHING TIP 4: Help the students understand how reckoning themselves to be dead to sin will help them overcome sin. Have them imagine themselves to be dead and placed in a coffin. Then ask: "What reaction would you have if someone were to hit you or if something were to tempt you to sin?" The answer is obvious—they would have no reaction. This is similar to Paul's statement to consider ourselves to be dead to sin. If we are dead, we will not react. If we yield ourselves to God, we will not yield to temptation.

To whom will the Christian yield? The choice is clear. He must choose either sin or Christ. Both Christ and Satan are looking for channels to use for their purposes. When someone yields to sin, Satan can use him as a channel to do his bidding. But your responsibility as a child of God is to yield your life to Christ and be an instrument of righteousness for His glory.

NOTES

3. Servants Of Righteousness

A. Exclusively Christ's
Romans 6:15-19

Just as Paul used the analogy of baptism earlier in this chapter, he continued his exhortation to holiness by using the illustration of the slave market of the first century. The institution of slavery was deeply rooted in the first century. The fact slavery was common provided the apostle with a backdrop that was clearly a picture of the Christian's condition.

Ask: "What aspects of the master-slave relationship can be compared to the Christian's battle with sin?" A master had total dominion over his slave. This ownership could only be severed under two circumstances. The first was death. Obviously a dead slave could not follow his master's orders. The Christian, as we have already seen, must consider himself to be dead to the sinful nature, and therefore unable to heed his former master's dictates (see verses 6,7).

There was a second circumstance, however, that removed a slave from his master's ownership. If he was sold in the slave market, as many slaves eventually were, he became the exclusive property of his new owner. There was no such thing as joint ownership: he was under total dominion of his master. However, Paul stated that the Christian became slave to the one he obeyed. The professing Christian, therefore, has to choose either sin or Christ as his master. One choice leads to bondage and then death, while the other leads to freedom and righteousness (verses 16-18). Becoming a slave of righteousness automatically sets the believer free from his former bondage.

Because Christ purchased you with His blood, you are now exclusively Christ's. Yet the choice is still set before you. You cannot serve two masters. You must pursue either righteousness or sin. As a Christian, you can no longer serve sin. Neither can you be double minded. When you served sin, it was your master. Now that you are under new ownership, you must become a wholehearted servant of righteousness.

TEACHING TIP 5: Display the overhead "The Analogy Of The Slave Market." Take time to contrast the masters, slaves, and the orders of both. The last item on the transparency, "wages," should not be explained until discussed in the next section.

NOTES

B. A Good Master
Romans 6:20-23

A slave's well-being was entirely dependent on what kind of master he had. In the Roman world he had no rights or legal recourse. He was mere property. If the slave was fortunate enough to have a kind master, he would be well-treated. If not, he could face a harsh existence.

This illustrates the kind of contrast evident between the reign of sin and that of Christ. Sin is a horrible taskmaster. It ravages a human being, seeking his destruction. Verse 23 states, "The wages of sin is death." Eternal death is the awful wage paid to those who serve sin.

Jesus Christ, on the other hand, is a good, benevolent Master. He does not pay us the wage due us, but rather offers us a most precious gift, one beyond comprehension. It is the free gift of eternal life, that comes only as a result of being His slave (verse 23). The slave of Christ has a whole new destiny, eternal life and freedom.

This most wonderful gift is also the reward of a lifetime of service. In the meantime, our good Master treats us with kindness, filling our lives with good things as we serve Him. Christ's character is being developed in us, as we yield ourselves to become servants of righteousness. Verse 22 summarizes the benefits of obedience to Jesus Christ. It declares that we have been set free fom sin. And this leads to holiness which results in eternal life.

We have exchanged one owner for another. God's Word declares that our bodies are temples of the Holy Spirit. Therefore, we do not belong to ourselves; we belong to God. Because of this, we must seek to glorify God with our bodies (1 Corinthians 6:19,20). When we become exclusive servants of our good Master, Jesus Christ, our lives will reap wonderful benefits. And in the end we will enjoy eternal life.

NOTES

LIFE RESPONSE

The pursuit of holiness is not an option for the believer, as some seem to think. God requires that all who profess to be citizens of His kingdom pursue His holiness. Leviticus 11:44 states, "I am the Lord your God: ye shall therefore sanctify yourselves, and ye shall be holy; for I am holy."

God's kingdom is built on His character. Believers become citizens of God's kingdom by faith, having been adopted into His family. They become heirs of His bountiful riches, which will be revealed in the life to come.

We who will receive this inheritance, must be partakers of God's holy character, being conformed into the image of God's Son. This Christlikeness is the focal point of the Holy Spirit's work in us. However, He can accomplish His work in us only as we cooperate with Him.

Every day we make choices that will either accelerate or hinder the development of Christ's character within us. The choices we make are results of the identity that we affirm for ourselves. We either choose to identify with our sinful pasts, or we understand that our lives are now hidden in Christ. When we choose to be conformed to Christ and pursue holiness faithfully, we recognize that the old identity is worthless and must be discarded. The end result is that we become dead to sin and alive to God. We become dedicated servants of righteousness. When this occurs we are well on our way to being Christlike.

EVANGELISM OUTREACH

Jesus called His followers lights of the world. By this He meant that they were the only ones able to demonstrate the difference God can make in people's lives. They reflect God's light to the world.

The light within us that must shine before the lost is Christ—He is the light of the world (John 9:5). When we allow Christ to make us holy in this sinful world, we glorify God and point the way to Him. Allow Christ to make you a light in this dark world. ⌂

Life In The Spirit

GOLDEN TEXT

Those who are led by the Spirit of God are sons of God. Romans 8:14 (NIV)

CENTRAL TRUTH

The Holy Spirit leads believers into the fulness of spiritual life.

STUDY TEXT

Romans 7:21 through 8:17

OUTLINE

1. Walk In The Spirit
   A. Dead To The Law
   B. New Law At Work

2. Reject The Sinful Nature
   A. Delivered From Sin
   B. Quickened By The Spirit

3. Live As God's Children
   A. New Obligation
   B. Spirit Of Adoption

OBJECTIVE

To consider our life in Christ and yield to the work of the Holy Spirit.

CHECKLIST

- [ ] Read this week's study from the *Adult Student Guide*.
- [ ] Write down any questions you wish to use to generate class discussion.
- [ ] Review the previous three studies in order to give a brief thematic overview of the last three sessions.
- [ ] Make copies of the work sheet "Christian Identity Crisis?" and pass them out at the beginning of the class. Refer to the Teaching Tips throughout the study for instructions on how to use the work sheet.
- [ ] Fill in a copy of the work sheet "Christian Identity Crisis?" so you will be able to offer your students help in filling in theirs.
- [ ] Use the main points of the work sheet at the end of class to serve as a review. Stress the need to assume our proper identity in Christ.
- [ ] Fill in a copy of the "Planning The Session" sheet to ensure that you cover all of the points of the study adequately.

DAILY BIBLE READINGS

Monday: Transformed By The Spirit.
Isaiah 32:15-18

Tuesday: Indwelt By The Spirit.
Ezekiel 36:24-32

Wednesday: Anointed By The Spirit.
Zechariah 12:8-10

Thursday: Guided By The Spirit.
John 16:7-15

Friday: Empowered By The Spirit.
Acts 2:1-11

Saturday: Strengthened By The Spirit.
Ephesians 3:14-21

SCRIPTURE SETTING

King James Version

Romans 8:1. There is therefore now no condemnation to them which are in Christ Jesus, who walk not after the flesh, but after the Spirit.

2. For the law of the Spirit of life in Christ Jesus hath made me free from the law of sin and death.

3. For what the law could not do, in that it was weak through the flesh, God sending his own Son in the likeness of sinful flesh, and for sin, condemned sin in the flesh:

4. That the righteousness of the law might be fulfilled in us, who walk not after the flesh, but after the Spirit.

5. For they that are after the flesh do mind the things of the flesh; but they that are after the Spirit, the things of the Spirit.

6. For to be carnally minded is death; but to be spiritually minded is life and peace.

7. Because the carnal mind is enmity against God: for it is not subject to the law of God, neither indeed can be.

8. So then they that are in the flesh cannot please God.

9. But ye are not in the flesh, but in the Spirit, if so be that the Spirit of God dwell in you. Now if any man have not the Spirit of Christ, he is none of his.

10. And if Christ be in you, the body is dead because of sin; but the Spirit is life because of righteousness.

11. But if the Spirit of him that raised up Jesus from the dead dwell in you, he that raised up Christ from the dead shall also quicken your mortal bodies by his Spirit that dwelleth in you.

12. Therefore, brethren, we are debtors, not to the flesh, to live after the flesh.

13. For if ye live after the flesh, ye shall die: but if ye through the Spirit do mortify the deeds of the body, ye shall live.

14. For as many as are led by the Spirit of God, they are the sons of God.

15. For ye have not received the spirit of bondage again to fear; but ye have received the Spirit of adoption, whereby we cry, Abba, Father.

16. The Spirit itself beareth witness with our spirit, that we are the children of God:

17. And if children, then heirs; heirs of God, and joint-heirs with Christ; if so be that we suffer with him, that we may be also glorified together.

New International Version

Romans 8:1. Therefore, there is now no condemnation for those who are in Christ Jesus,

2. Because through Christ Jesus the law of the Spirit of life set me free from the law of sin and death.

3. For what the law was powerless to do in that it was weakened by the sinful nature, God did by sending his own Son in the likeness of sinful man to be a sin offering. And so he condemned sin in sinful man,

4. In order that the righteous requirements of the law might be fully met in us, who do not live according to the sinful nature but according to the Spirit.

5. Those who live according to the sinful nature have their minds set on what that nature desires; but those who live in accordance with the Spirit have their minds set on what the Spirit desires.

6. The mind of sinful man is death, but the mind controlled by the Spirit is life and peace;

7. The sinful mind is hostile to God. It does not submit to God's law, nor can it do so.

8. Those controlled by the sinful nature cannot please God.

9. You, however, are controlled not by the sinful nature but by the Spirit, if the Spirit of God lives in you. And if anyone does not have the Spirit of Christ, he does not belong to Christ.

10. But if Christ is in you, your body is dead because of sin, yet your spirit is alive because of righteousness.

11. And if the Spirit of him who raised Jesus from the dead is living in you, he who raised Christ from the dead will also give life to your mortal bodies through his Spirit, who lives in you.

12. Therefore, brothers, we have an obligation—but it is not to the sinful nature, to live according to it.

13. For if you live according to the sinful nature, you will die; but if by the Spirit you put to death the misdeeds of the body, you will live,

14. Because those who are led by the Spirit of God are sons of God.

15. For you did not receive a spirit that makes you a slave again to fear, but you received the Spirit of sonship. And by him we cry, "Abba, Father."

16. The Spirit himself testifies with our spirit that we are God's children.

17. Now if we are children, then we are heirs—heirs of God and co-heirs with Christ, if indeed we share in his sufferings in order that we may also share in his glory.

The eighth chapter of Romans is filled with references to the Holy Spirit—at least 18. No other chapter in Paul's epistles has come close to this number. (First Corinthians 12, for instance, which focuses on the gifts of the Spirit has only 11 such references.)

The reason for this should be apparent: the theme of Romans 8 is life in the Spirit. This life is not possible without the Holy Spirit's having control over our lives. He has a great work to do in all of our lives, and He is never satisfied with a work half accomplished. Romans 8 exhorts us to yield control of our lives to the Spirit. Then we will find the freedom we desire.

In today's study, we are to consider our life in Christ. The result of our study is that we may more fully yield our lives to the work of the Holy Spirit.

BIBLE COMMENTARY

1. Walk In The Spirit

A. Dead To The Law
Romans 7:21-23

The difference between Romans 7 and Romans 8 is like the difference between night and day. Chapter 7 is filled with frustration and failure as Paul struggled hopelessly against sin. This frustration can be true of both an unbeliever trying to live a moral life or a believer trying to conquer sinful habits by human effort alone.

The main point of Romans 7 is that the Law is powerless to bring about victory over sin. The Law, in effect, is God's standard of righteousness. It is rigid and unyielding. Its demands are relentless. The Law can be satisfied by nothing less than full compliance to its statutes.

The Law is weak in that it cannot provide the power to comply with its demands. People wanting to adhere to its requirements are overcome by another law that is more powerful than their desire to keep the demands of the Law. This law is the principle of sin. Paul testified to his own personal struggle to comply with the Law's requirements in Romans 7. His heart delighted in keeping its precepts, but his sinful nature overwhelmed him and made him captive to the things that he wanted to resist (verses 22,23). There is no power in a standard. Only a greater power can bring about complete and lasting victory over sin.

The Christian must recognize the futility of seeking righteousness through the Law. That was not the Law's purpose. Its purpose was to show us that we were helpless sinners in need of deliverance. It proved to us, beyond a shadow of doubt, that we needed God's grace and mercy in Jesus Christ. Galatians 3:24 declares, "Wherefore the law was our schoolmaster to bring us unto Christ, that we might be justified by faith." For believers, the Law has fulfilled its purpose. It has brought us to Christ. Now we must no longer be subject to the Law, but alive to the power of the Holy Spirit.

NOTES

B. New Law At Work
Romans 7:24 through 8:4

Once the Law accomplished its purpose, that of bringing us to Christ, power was needed to effect our sanctification. Romans 7 ends with Paul's cry of frustration, "Oh wretched man that I am! who shall deliver me from this body of death?" (verse 24).

Having shown us the frustration of trying to be victorious over sin through the Law, Paul pointed to the way of victory. He declared that a new law is now in effect, "the law of the Spirit of life in Christ Jesus" (8:2). This law could do what the law of Moses could not. It could break the power of the law of sin and death. This new law is nothing less than the powerful working of God's Holy Spirit who resides in the life of every believer. The Holy Spirit has the power to conquer sin, and bring victory to the Christian because of Christ's victory over sin at Calvary.

This new law has another surpassing benefit, the absense of condemnation. Condemnation comes from both a sense of guilt and a fear of punishment. But we are justified, declared not guilty, because of the work of Christ. Even though we have fallen short of God's righteous standard, Christ has met that standard, and now His righteousness is our own. We are now free to appropriate both the Spirit's power and God's mercy as we yield to God's purpose for our lives. The Spirit now can lead us into the fullness of the life that is under His control.

TEACHING TIP 1: Have students refer to the work sheet entitled "Christian Identity Crisis?" Ask the class to list the respective characteristics of each law from verses 1-4. Ask if any had been guilty in the past of seeking victory over sinful habits through the wrong law (point 1 on the work sheet). Perhaps someone would be willing to share a brief testimony.

Ask: "How can pursuing victory through the wrong law bring about an identity crisis on the part of the Christian?" The Christian has no hope for the future apart from God's power. Our victory is wholly dependent on our taking possession of that power. When we determine to walk in the Spirit and not in our own strength, we will be empowered by the Spirit to meet God's standard of righteousness (verse 4).

NOTES

2. Reject The Sinful Nature

A. Delivered From Sin
Romans 8:5-8

The child of God needs to be set free from the dominion of the sinful nature. No one comes to Christ totally free from the old baggage of the life of the flesh. This baggage must be shed in favor of the new life that is Spirit controlled.

The life of the flesh is governed by only one principle, and that is the principle of its own desires. The life of the flesh is completely corrupt and totally under the control of sinful impulses. When a person is dominated by the flesh, he is absorbed in carnal thoughts and practices. He becomes morally bankrupt, both unwilling and unable to change the course of his life. In Romans 8:6-8 Paul listed characteristics of the life of the flesh. They lead to spiritual death (verse 6), lawlessness (verse 7), and the inability to please God (verse 8). Man's only hope is to be delivered from this condition.

Verses 5-11 provide a contrast between the life dominated by the sinful nature and the one dominated by the Spirit. The life of the Spirit produces a mind directed toward spiritual things, which in turn brings life and peace instead of death (verses 5,6). The spiritual mind is subject to the law of God, which in turn pleases God. The life that is "in the Spirit" is one that has been delivered from sin's power and now chooses to follow the new leadership of the Holy Spirit.

Ask: "What can we do to weaken the old nature and strengthen the spiritual man?"

TEACHING TIP 2: Have students offer practical suggestions that will accelerate the demise of the sinful nature's control and the building of the Spirit-controlled life. Emphasize the need to starve the one and feed the other.

NOTES

B. Quickened By The Spirit
Romans 8:9-11

As we have already seen, striving to do the right thing is useless, unless believers avail themselves of the power of the Spirit of God. This resource is available to those who are saved because the Spirit of God now lives in them (verses 9,10). The Holy Spirit who indwells the believer does so with a purpose. This purpose is to develop Christlikeness in the child of God by transforming his character.

The Holy Spirit quickens us with the same power that raised Jesus from the dead. This same power is available to us in our battle with our sinful natures. Power that can raise the dead is certainly able to give us the victory.

Although at one time we were dead in our sins, God has made us alive by the power of the Spirit. We are now able to make right choices because the Spirit has broken sin's control over us. But in order to make those right choices, we must place ourselves under the Holy Spirit's control. Only then will we have the power to reject the desires of our sinful nature. But we must first allow God's power to work in us.

TEACHING TIP 3: Have the class refer back to the work sheet. Review point two "The Wrong Domination." Ask the class to contrast the "Life Of The Flesh" and the "Life Of The Spirit" from verses 6-10. Stress that when the Spirit of God is in control of our lives, these characteristics will be evident. Life in the Spirit is not a vague concept that cannot be tested, but rather a way of life with specific characteristics.

Ask: "What should the Christian do when he gives in to temptation and sins?" When a Christian sins he has "an advocate with the Father, Jesus Christ the righteous" (1 John 2:1). By confessing our sins to Him, He forgives and restores (1:9). We then need to dedicate ourselves afresh to God and receive His power to live righteously.

NOTES

3. Live As God's Children

A. New Obligation
Romans 8:12-14

The believer in Christ has a new obligation that sharply contrasts with the obligation to the sinful nature. Romans 8:12 begins Paul's conclusion to all that he had previously stated concerning the Christian's new spiritual pursuit. He concluded that it is a gross contradiction for the Christian to yield obedience to that from which he has been set free. "Therefore, brothers, we have an obligation—but it is not to our sinful nature, to live according to it" (NIV). On the contrary, the believer's obligation is to put to death the deeds of the old nature (verse 13). He is further obligated as one who is called a son of God, to be led by the Spirit that indwells him (verse 14). The phrase "led by the Spirit" implies the Spirit's rule and direction. As the child of God responds to the direction of the Spirit he proves that he belongs to God's family.

Ask: "What responsibilities come with belonging to a family?" The conduct of an individual in a family affects the family's name. As sons of God we are obligated to uphold the character of God that the Church presents to the world.

TEACHING TIP 4: Again refer to the work sheet "Christian Identity Crisis?" Under number 3 "The Wrong Obligation," have the students list the obligations we have to both the flesh and the spirit after we have come to Christ. Point out that allegiance to our former identity constitutes an extremely critical identity crisis. As children of God our allegiance must be to Christ and His presence in us. Ask the class to note the differing characteristics.

B. Spirit Of Adoption
Romans 8:15-17

While on the one hand Christians have an obligation to exhibit the character consistent with their identity as sons of God, they also are the recipients of the assurance sonship brings (verses 15,16).

Verse 15 alludes to two spirits that are different in every way. The first is the spirit of bondage, which leads to fear. Sin produces fear in the lives of those who are controlled by it. There is a sense of uncertainty that comes with not knowing the outcome of life. People who are in bondage to sin are under the judgment of the Law and fear the eventual outcome of their lives.

Contrast that with the Spirit of adoption which Paul declared to be the possession of every believer. This Spirit doesn't lead to fear, but rather a sense of belonging to God. With this identification comes a closeness to God where we can say, "Abba, Father."

The phrase "Abba, Father" occurs in only two other places in the New Testament (Mark 14:36; Galatians 4:6). The first word "Abba" is an Aramaic expression for father that denotes intimacy. The second word is its translation, "Father." Another way to translate this phrase would be, "Abba (that is to say, Father)."

This expression was used by Jesus himself in Gethsemane. There He prayed to His Father asking whether it was possible for the cup of God's wrath against sin (represented by the cross) to be taken from Him. The obvious intent is that believers can use the same intimate expression that Jesus used in speaking to His Father because we have been adopted in God's family.

God has adopted us as His sons. We are not foster children, but adopted children. A foster child is insecure not knowing whether the relationship is temporary or permanent. We, however, are adopted into God's family, joining His only begotten Son as heirs to all that He possesses. And He has given us the Spirit of adoption, who reminds us of our sonship.

Ask: "Why do some Christians respond to God as if they are fearful slaves and not sons?" Although revealing sonship is the work of the Spirit, it must be received by faith. It takes faith to be saved and likewise, faith is necessary in order to receive the full assurance of sonship.

NOTES

LIFE RESPONSE

Christians face the challenge of living a spiritual life. The Holy Spirit is the Teacher, assisting us in living this new life. He also provides the power that makes this kind of living possible.

A life in the Spirit is filled with many obstacles. There is a sinful nature that resists the Holy Spirit continually. This nature must be withstood at every turn. Instead of fulfilling the desires of the flesh, we are called to assume our new identity in Christ. This involves recognizing the privilege of being called a son of God, and walking worthy of this calling.

In seeking to fulfill God's wonderful calling, we are prone to falling into the trap of trying to accomplish this in our own strength. As Paul discovered, this leads to a dead end. It is one thing to *recognize* what is good, and altogether another thing to *do* what is good. God's purposes can only be accomplished in the power of the Holy Spirit. Only He can deliver us from sin and develop the character of Christ in us.

The development of the character of Christ is the goal of every Christian's journey. We have an obligation to pursue His character. When we pursue it, we cooperate with the Holy Spirit who builds Christ's character. As we yield to the work of the Spirit, we enter the fullness of spiritual life, and in doing so fulfill our identity in Christ. "For as many as are led by the Spirit of God, they are the sons of God" (Romans 8:14).

EVANGELISM OUTREACH

Just as the Holy Spirit's power is necessary in order for us to live godly lives, so He enables us to share the gospel with those who are outside of God's family. Point out that a very important aspect of life in the Spirit is proclaiming the gospel to those that are unsaved.

The task of proclaiming the gospel is a spiritual task. It takes boldness that comes from God's Spirit. As we depend on the Holy Spirit, we will receive all that is necessary to do the job effectively. ⌒

The Overcoming Life

CENTRAL TRUTH

Faith in Christ enables believers to live the overcoming life.

GOLDEN TEXT

In all these things we are more than conquerors through him who loved us. Romans 8:37 (NIV)

STUDY TEXT

Romans 8:18-39

OUTLINE

1. Hope
   A. Right Attitude Toward Suffering
   B. Foretaste Of Heaven

2. Assurance
   A. Supernatural Assistance
   B. Steps To Glorification

3. Confidence
   A. No Condemnation
   B. No Separation

OBJECTIVE

To realize that we can be overcomers and determine to live such a life.

CHECKLIST

☐ Read the *Adult Student Guide*.
☐ Note any questions you wish to include in this week's study for further discussion.
☐ Make a copy of the work sheet "Sufferings Of This Present Time" from the teaching helps packet for each student. Use the work sheet during Teaching Tip 1.
☐ Make sure you have enough pencils and extra Bibles on hand for students to use.
☐ Assign a student to prepare a report on a biblical personality whose faith brought him through temptations and trials victoriously. Good subjects to choose from include Joseph, Esther, Job, Daniel, Paul, or any of those mentioned in Hebrews 11.
☐ Fill out a copy of the "Planning The Session" sheet from the teaching helps packet. This will help ensure that you have enough time for every part of the study you planned to use.

DAILY BIBLE READINGS

Monday: Hope Requires Trust.
Job 19:23-27
Tuesday: Hope Anchors The Soul.
Hebrews 6:11-20
Wednesday: Confidence Brings Strength.
Isaiah 30:15-18
Thursday: Confidence Is Rewarded.
1 John 5:10-15
Friday: Faith Moves Mountains.
Matthew 17:14-21
Saturday: Faith Pleases God.
Hebrews 11:1-6

King James Version

Romans 8:22. For we know that the whole creation groaneth and travaileth in pain together until now.

23. And not only they, but ourselves also, which have the firstfruits of the Spirit, even we ourselves groan within ourselves, waiting for the adoption, to wit, the redemption of our body.

24. For we are saved by hope: but hope that is seen is not hope: for what a man seeth, why doth he yet hope for?

25. But if we hope for that we see not, then do we with patience wait for it.

26. Likewise the Spirit also helpeth our infirmities: for we know not what we should pray for as we ought: but the Spirit itself maketh intercession for us with groanings which cannot be uttered.

27. And he that searcheth the hearts knoweth what is the mind of the Spirit, because he maketh intercession for the saints according to the will of God.

28. And we know that all things work together for good to them that love God, to them who are the called according to his purpose.

29. For whom he did foreknow, he also did predestinate to be conformed to the image of his Son, that he might be the firstborn among many brethren.

30. Moreover, whom he did predestinate, them he also called: and whom he called, them he also justified: and whom he justified, them he also glorified.

31. What shall we then say to these things? If God be for us, who can be against us?

32. He that spared not his own Son, but delivered him up for us all, how shall he not with him also freely give us all things?

33. Who shall lay any thing to the charge of God's elect? It is God that justifieth.

34. Who is he that condemneth? It is Christ that died, yea rather, that is risen again, who is even at the right hand of God, who also maketh intercession for us.

35. Who shall separate us from the love of Christ? shall tribulation, or distress, or persecution, or famine, or nakedness, or peril, or sword?

36. As it is written, For thy sake we are killed all the day long; we are accounted as sheep for the slaughter.

37. Nay, in all these things we are more than conquerors through him that loved us.

New International Version

Romans 8:22. We know that the whole creation has been groaning as in the pains of childbirth right up to the present time.

23. Not only so, but we ourselves, who have the firstfruits of the Spirit, groan inwardly as we wait eagerly for our adoption as sons, the redemption of our bodies.

24. For in this hope we were saved. But hope that is seen is no hope at all. Who hopes for what he already has?

25. But if we hope for what we do not yet have, we wait for it patiently.

26. In the same way, the Spirit helps us in our weakness. We do not know what we ought to pray for, but the Spirit himself intercedes for us with groans that words cannot express.

27. And he who searches our hearts knows the mind of the Spirit, because the Spirit intercedes for the saints in accordance with God's will.

28. And we know that in all things God works for the good of those who love him, who have been called according to his purpose.

29. For those God foreknew he also predestined to be conformed to the likeness of his Son, that he might be the firstborn among many brothers.

30. And those he predestined, he also called; those he called, he also justified; those he justified, he also glorified.

31. What, then, shall we say in response to this? If God is for us, who can be against us?

32. He who did not spare his own Son, but gave him up for us all—how will he not also, along with him, graciously give us all things?

33. Who will bring any charge against those whom God has chosen? It is God who justifies.

34. Who is he that condemns? Christ Jesus, who died—more than that, who was raised to life—is at the right hand of God and is also interceding for us.

35. Who shall separate us from the love of Christ? Shall trouble or hardship or persecution or famine or nakedness or danger or sword?

36. As it is written: "For your sake we face death all day long; we are considered as sheep to be slaughtered."

37. No, in all these things we are more than conquerors through him who loved us.

A thletes who participate in Olympic events start their training months and even years ahead of time. Many hours are spent conditioning both body and mind. The athletes sometimes suffer excruciating pain in the process. Nerves and muscles are constantly taxed to their limits. No sacrifice seems too great for the chance to win a medal and experience a few moments of glory as an Olympic champion.

Many Christians want to live an overcoming life but do not wish to go through the necessary training to do so. Self-discipline and self-control may not be easy, but they are essential. Just as men and women train for athletic events to win a brief moment of glory, so Christians must strengthen themselves spiritually keeping in view the goal of living an overcoming life and ultimately of being like Christ.

BIBLE COMMENTARY

1. Hope

A. Right Attitude Toward Suffering
Romans 8:18

Starting at verse 18, Paul began to contemplate the time when Christians will receive the end result of their faith, the salvation of their souls (1 Peter 1:9). Abruptly Paul brought in the idea of suffering and contrasted present troubles with future glories. Js 18

TEACHING TIP 1: Distribute copies of the work sheet "Sufferings Of This Present Time" to each student. Divide the class into pairs or small groups. (In a sanctuary class this can be done easily by simply having two people in one row interact with two people in the row behind them.) Ask each group to look up the passages on suffering and describe the benefits Christians today will have as a result of suffering according to these verses. Then have them compare their results with Romans 8:18. Regroup to discuss student responses.

Ask: "What does the term 'reckon' in Romans 8:18 mean in this context?" Although the secular use of the Greek word for "reckon" concerned entering accounts into a ledger (and is used this way in Romans 4), Paul was probably referring to a "judgment of faith." That is, a Christian's thinking is changed because of the facts established by the reality of Christ's work. Accordingly, "reckon" would mean to "think, or make a right judgment." It is used this way in 6:11, "reckon ye also yourselves to be dead indeed unto sin." In the context of 8:18, Paul compared the facts of Christ's work and promise of eternal life with the suffering Christians experience in this life.

In the early days of the Church, suffering was often the inevitable result of professing Christ. Paul was concerned that Christians not allow the adversities of this life to blind their eyes to the coming eternal glories. Fear can cause us to lose sight of God's promises.

Ask: "What should the Christian's attitude be toward suffering?" The phrase "earnest expectation" is one word in the Greek language. It means to stretch the head forward; to watch eagerly with outstretched head. It is the picture of someone looking forward with expectation. In verse 18, Paul referred to sufferings that will fade into the shadows in the light of the glory to come (see also 2 Corinthians 4:17). Christian suffering is done in hope. So, though a Christian may suffer, he has the hope of eternal life and the glories to be experienced there.

NOTES

B. Foretaste Of Heaven
Romans 8:19-25

Romans 8:19-22 should be read in light of Genesis 3:17. When man sinned, the rest of creation was "not willingly" involved. Creation is pictured in the pangs of childbirth. In the coming of the Holy Spirit on the Day of Pentecost, men and women received and continue to receive a foretaste of the glory to come. They now long for the full realization of what God has prepared for those who love Him (1 Corinthians 2:9).

During times of suffering, believers must walk by faith. But at the same time hope looks onward, hope expects, hope anticipates. Hope does not see suffering as a harsh obligation.

Ask: "How does having hope in suffering enable the Christian to wait expectantly for Christ's return?" Paul was aware of both the human and the world situations. But he was also aware of the redeeming power of God. Life for the Christian is not to wait in despair for the inevitable end to a world filled with sin, decay, and death. Life for the Christian is an eager anticipation of divine liberation. It is expectantly "looking for that blessed hope, and the glorious appearing of the great God and our Savior Jesus Christ" (Titus 2:13).

2. Assurance

A. Supernatural Assistance
Romans 8:26,27

Starting with Romans 8:26, Paul moved from the subject of hope to that of the help the Holy Spirit can bring believers, especially in prayer. This brings encouragement and comfort to even the weakest saint. Someone once wrote:

The devil trembles when he sees
The weakest saint upon his knees.

Paul spoke of three sighings or groanings in this chapter. All of creation is groaning in anticipation of the new heavens and the new earth (verse 22). Along with creation, humanity is groaning in anticipation of their glorified bodies (verse 23). These groanings are a result of the oppression and opposition brought about by sin.

The third groaning is different. Paul contrasted the weakness of the flesh with the divine assistance provided by the Holy Spirit. In His groanings, the Holy Spirit becomes our prayer Partner. When we do not understand how we should pray, He joins with us to pray for the needs on our hearts.

TEACHING TIP 2: Have someone read John 14:15-18,25,26; 16:7-15. As these verses are being read, emphasize the Holy Spirit's ministry to the believer as Comforter, Teacher, and Guide by writing these terms on the chalkboard or a blank overhead transparency in large block letters. Also point out that His ministry is to glorify the Father and the Son.

Ask: "Why did Paul write that 'we do not know what we should pray for as we ought' (or as it is necessary)?" One reason is we cannot see the future. We do not know what tomorrow may bring. Although we may be quite sure that we know God's will, things may happen that seem opposite to what we understand God's will to be. In addition, we do not always know what is best for us in any given situation. When Jesus was faced with the agony and pain of the cross, He prayed that He would not have to endure it. Yet in the agony of Gethsemane, Jesus cried out, "Nevertheless, not my will, but thine, be done."

The Holy Spirit intercedes for the saints according to the will of God. He understands our weaknesses. He knows our limitations. However, His assistance is not without some effort on our part. He "helps" us by bringing us the assistance we need to pray. When we struggle in prayer, trying to put into words the burdens of our hearts, the Holy Spirit comes alongside and helps us lift our burdens to the throne. There are some who feel that praying in tongues may be included in this expression. But whether we speak in tongues or, like Hannah, mouth words heard only by God (1 Samuel 1:9-18), prayers uttered with the help of the Holy Spirit include the longings that come from the very depths of the heart. Everyday words cannot express these yearnings. But the indwelling Holy Spirit intercedes and His mind knows the will of the Father. Thus, when we pray allowing the Holy Spirit to assist us, there is perfect communication between the Father, the Holy Spirit, and us.

NOTES

B. Steps To Glorification
Romans 8:28-30

Ask: "How do we know the Holy Spirit's intercession will be answered?" Since the Holy Spirit knows the mind of the Father, we can be assured that the Holy Spirit intercedes for us "according to the will of God" (verse 27). This is the reason Paul could write with such confidence that God makes all things work together for good to those who love Him, even in suffering (verse 28). We could be like Jacob and say, "Everything is against me" (Genesis 42:36, NIV). Or we could be like Joseph and be faithful to God regardless of our circumstances. Then in the end we would be able to say, "The devil meant to do me evil, but God worked all things out for my good and His glory."

Romans 8:29,30 presents some interesting problems, specifically because the words "predestinate" and "foreknow" are used. If predestinate means God not only knows who will be saved and all that will happen to them but determines and causes it to happen as well, then the remainder of chapter 8 does not make sense. Neither do all of the warnings against sin and the admonitions to be holy. However, if predestinate indicates that the way, rather than the individual, has been predetermined, then these two verses and the following verses fit quite well. When a person becomes a Christian and follows God's will, the way to glorification has been determined beforehand.

The word "foreknow" does not mean to determine ahead of time. Rather, it indicates God can see the future as easily as the past. This does not mean that He is personally responsible for all that happens. The *way* to glorification of those *in Christ* has been predetermined. (It is interesting to note that the Scriptures never use the word "predestinate" in conjunction with the damnation of the unsaved. Rather, the word is used exclusively of believers.) Thus, for those who are in Christ, there is a sequence of events that leads to glorification.

NOTES

3. Confidence

A. No Condemnation
Romans 8:31-36

Ask: "Will we always understand why we go through certain trials?" It is sometimes difficult to sense God's hand in some of the trying circumstances we go through. However, some who have been Christians for a long time can probably look back and confirm that God was working in their lives despite any pain, anger, or resentment they may have felt at the time.

As Christians we need to learn to trust God implicitly. Then we can accept things that come our way without fighting against them. One of the great biblical truths in relation to suffering and persecution is in verse 31: *God is for us.*

If God has justified us, what person or power can condemn us. The Christian will face no prosecutor at the Judgment Seat of Christ. Our defense Attorney will be there to intercede in our behalf. Since God has acquitted us, no one can condemn us.

Paul enlarged the "who" of verse 31 to include "what" in Romans 8:35. Natural disasters have been known to bring people closer together. This is true in the spiritual realm as well. When Paul faced persecution, it only drew him closer to Christ. His response was to say, "I consider my life worth nothing to me, if only I may finish the race and complete the task the Lord Jesus has given me—the task of testifying to the gospel of God's grace" (Acts 20:24, NIV).

NOTES

B. No Separation
Romans 8:37-39

Whatever the circumstance, Paul confidently affirmed, "We are more than conquerors." The Greek for the phrase "more than conquerors" is used only once in the New Testament. When Paul thought of the Christian warrior who is not perturbed by any affliction or defeat, the normal Greek word for conqueror was almost too weak a term. In order to describe the Christians' supreme victory, Paul used a word that indicates that we are "superconquerors."

Adult Teacher Guide

Ask: "How could Paul speak the words of Romans 8:37-39 with such conviction?" Paul's words "I am persuaded" (verse 38) indicate a fixed conviction developed from experience. Paul was firmly convinced that nothing in the experiences of death or life: nothing in the realm of invisible powers (angels, principalities, demonic powers), nothing in time (things present, things to come), or nothing in space (height, depth) could come between him and Christ.

In verses 38 and 39, Paul covered all of the things that people dread—life, death, supernatural powers, outer and inner space. Then in case he had omitted anything, Paul added "nor any other creature." The term "creature" here can refer to anything created. *Nothing* can separate us from the unchangeable, infinite, constant, all-sufficient, eternal, and triumphant love of God. What a comfort to the lonely and fearful.

NOTES

LIFE RESPONSE

Romans 8 has been called the "Chapter of Chapters" for the life of the believer. It flows out as the answer to the apostle's cry, "O wretched man that I am! who shall deliver me?" (7:24). In earlier chapters, Paul demonstrated that man is guilty because of sin. He explained the wonderful truths regarding justification by faith and salvation by grace. He set forth the challenge of sanctification when he said, "Let not sin therefore reign in your mortal body, that ye should obey it in the lusts thereof. . . . but yield yourselves unto God" (6:12,13).

In chapter 8, Paul wrote of the divine resources available to help Christians live an overcoming life. This chapter has been appropriately titled "Life In The Spirit." In the person of the Holy Spirit, we have a divine Ally who has come to be our Helper, Counselor, Teacher, and Guide.

This study emphasized several important truths. We have been set free from the power of sin and death and adopted into the family of God. Yet this freedom is not a freedom from obligation. It is the freedom we have as children of God to fulfill our responsibilities to our Heavenly Father. It is also the freedom to enjoy the blessed privileges of this relationship.

The trying experiences of life can be faced in the power of the Holy Spirit. God is for us, Christ is in us, and the Holy Spirit is with us. This chapter begins with no condemnation, it ends with no separation, and in between there is no defeat.

EVANGELISM OUTREACH

Christians do not have to fight their battles alone. Encourage those who have not been filled with the Holy Spirit to seek His fullness. Point out that in order to fight supernatural enemies we need supernatural power. Jesus has sent the Holy Spirit to help Christians live overcoming lives.

If you have any unsaved students, you could challenge them with Romans 3:23; 6:23; 10:9,10,13. Make it clear that hope, assurance, and confidence come only through a right relationship with God. ▭

Salvation For All People

CENTRAL TRUTH

All who repent of sin and confess Christ will be saved.

GOLDEN TEXT

It is with your heart that you believe and are justified, and it is with your mouth that you confess and are saved. Romans 10:10 (NIV)

STUDY TEXT

Romans 10:4-17

OUTLINE

1. Confess Christ
   A. Righteousness For Everyone
   B. Jesus As Lord

2. Call On The Lord
   A. All-Sufficient Gospel
   B. Universal Gospel

3. Believe God's Word
   A. Hearing The Message
   B. Faith And The Word

OBJECTIVE

To recognize that the plan of salvation extends to all persons and seek to share its message.

CHECKLIST

☐ This is a study on salvation. Plan ahead of time to encourage those students who are Christians to invite unsaved friends or loved ones.

☐ You may wish to schedule a special class prayer meeting during the week.

☐ At the end of class, be sure to set aside a special time of prayer for any unsaved who may come into your class.

☐ Ask your pastor for suggestions on putting together a few packets of basic materials for new Christians. Perhaps include a list of outreach opportunities to get them involved in the church. New converts will grow as they share their new-found faith.

☐ Read through this week's study in the *Adult Student Guide* and write down any discussion questions you may want to use.

☐ Familiarize yourself with the "Roman Road" transparency.

DAILY BIBLE READINGS

Monday:	Confession Of Sin. Proverbs 28:12-14
Tuesday:	Seeking God's Forgiveness. Daniel 9:4-7,17-19
Wednesday:	Believing On Christ. John 3:11-18
Thursday:	Repenting Of Sin. Acts 2:37-41
Friday:	Saved By Faith. Acts 16:25-34
Saturday:	Cleansed From Unrighteousness. 1 John 1:5-10

SCRIPTURE SETTING

King James Version

Romans 10:4. Christ is the end of the law for righteousness to every one that believeth.

5. For Moses describeth the righteousness which is of the law, That the man which doeth those things shall live by them.

6. But the righteousness which is of faith speaketh on this wise, Say not in thine heart, Who shall ascend into heaven? (that is, to bring Christ down from above:)

7. Or, Who shall descend into the deep? (that is, to bring up Christ again from the dead.)

8. But what saith it? The word is nigh thee, even in thy mouth, and in thy heart: that is, the word of faith, which we preach;

9. That if thou shalt confess with thy mouth the Lord Jesus, and shalt believe in thine heart that God hath raised him from the dead, thou shalt be saved.

10. For with the heart man believeth unto righteousness; and with the mouth confession is made unto salvation.

11. For the Scripture saith, Whosoever believeth on him shall not be ashamed.

12. For there is no difference between the Jew and the Greek: for the same Lord over all is rich unto all that call upon him.

13. For whosoever shall call upon the name of the Lord shall be saved.

14. How then shall they call on him in whom they have not believed? and how shall they believe in him of whom they have not heard? and how shall they hear without a preacher?

15. And how shall they preach, except they be sent? as it is written, How beautiful are the feet of them that preach the gospel of peace, and bring glad tidings of good things!

16. But they have not all obeyed the gospel. For Isaiah saith, Lord, who hath believed our report?

17. So then faith cometh by hearing, and hearing by the word of God.

New International Version

Romans 10:4. Christ is the end of the law so that there may be righteousness for everyone who believes.

5. Moses describes in this way the righteousness that is by the law: "The man who does these things will live by them."

6. But the righteousness that is by faith says: "Do not say in your heart, 'Who will ascend into heaven?' " (that is, to bring Christ down)

7. "Or 'Who will descend into the deep?' " (that is, to bring Christ up from the dead).

8. But what does it say? "The word is near you; it is in your mouth and in your heart," that is, the word of faith we are proclaiming:

9. That if you confess with your mouth, "Jesus is Lord," and believe in your heart that God raised him from the dead, you will be saved.

10. For it is with your heart that you believe and are justified, and it is with your mouth that you confess and are saved.

11. As the Scripture says, "Anyone who trusts in him will never be put to shame."

12. For there is no difference between Jew and Gentile—the same Lord is Lord of all and richly blesses all who call on him,

13. For, "Everyone who calls on the name of the Lord will be saved."

14. How, then, can they call on the one they have not believed in? And how can they believe in the one of whom they have not heard? And how can they hear without someone preaching to them?

15. And how can they preach unless they are sent? As it is written, "How beautiful are the feet of those who bring good news!"

16. But not all the Israelites accepted the good news. For Isaiah says, "Lord, who has believed our message?"

17. Consequently, faith comes from hearing the message, and the message is heard through the word of Christ.

Most people will do almost anything but admit "I have sinned." We try to explain human behavior by heredity, the environment, or an unhappy childhood. However, by far the greater percentage of people's problems are brought on by themselves. Every sin is related to the disobedience of Eve and the first Adam. The only hope for salvation and reconciliation to God is in the Second Adam, Jesus Christ.

The way to reconciliation with God has not changed. It is still the same biblical route it has always been: believe God's Word, call upon the Lord, repent and turn from sin, accept Christ as Savior, confess Him before others, and live for Him daily.

Today's study focuses on the plan of salvation. As we examine the Scriptures, examine your heart to see if Christ really lives in you.

BIBLE COMMENTARY

1. Confess Christ

A. Righteousness For Everyone
Romans 10:4-8

TEACHING TIP 1: Display the "Roman Road" transparency throughout the class period and refer to it periodically. Alert students ahead of time to be prepared to pray with any who may respond at the end of class.

In the first eight chapters of Romans, Paul systematically argued that righteousness did not come by the Law. He declared that all men, both Jews and Gentiles, need salvation. He indicated that the Law could not make ineffective the power of sin and could not provide power to live a holy life. Paul declared that only through the death, burial, and resurrection of Christ, and our identification with Him, can we find the salvation, justification, and righteousness we need.

Paul's heart was broken as he saw his own people, the Jews, rejecting their Messiah. In the midst of three chapters where Paul shared his burden concerning Israel's salvation, he gave a clear message of sal-

vation. But this message is not just for the Jews. This message of salvation is for everyone, including us today.

Paul did not condemn the Jews. They were zealous for God, but in the wrong way. They made the tragic mistake of trying to earn their own righteousness. Theirs was a religion of meticulous law keeping. But Paul said the righteousness of God cannot be obtained by human merit or effort (3:20).

Ask: "What did Paul mean when he said, 'Christ is the end of the law' (Romans 10:4)?" Paul was not saying Christ destroyed the Law. He wanted the Jews to understand that in reality Christ fulfilled all the Law stood for. The Greek term for "end" here could also be translated "goal" or "termination." Christ is the goal to which the Law led. Paul made this clear when he told the Galatians, "The law was our schoolmaster to bring us unto Christ" (Galatians 3:24). All that is now needed is for man to accept the grace, mercy, and love that God freely offered through the sacrifice of Christ on Calvary.

Romans 10:6,7 reinforces this idea. Paul applied the words of Moses in Deuteronomy 30:11-14 to Christ. This truth declared that no one needs to go to heaven and bring Christ down again to earth. The Incarnation is already a reality. Nor do men have to bring Christ again from the dead. He is risen! The resurrection of Christ was already an historic fact. God's mighty work of redemption has already taken place. Now all that is necessary is a personal faith in what God has provided.

When Paul spoke of "the word of faith" in verse 8, he was referring to the Christian message. This is the message which Paul preached. This preaching brings the gospel to bear upon our lives. Jesus Christ is the center of this message. Faith in Christ is not grounded in a philosophy, but in actual historic events.

NOTES

B. Jesus As Lord
Romans 10:9,10

Believing in Christ includes believing in the events that took place at Calvary. Belief in the death, burial, and resurrection of Christ and confession that He is Lord are prerequisites to salvation. Believing and confession go together.

Ask: **"How does one believe with the heart?"** The heart in verse 9 is not referring to the muscle beating in the chest of every person. Rather Paul was speaking of the seat of our emotions, intellect, and will. To believe with the heart means to make a conscious decision concerning Christ's redemptive work and act on that decision. Our justification comes when this belief takes place (verse 10).

Ask: **"What does it mean to 'confess with thy mouth the Lord Jesus'?"** In the Early Church confessing Christ involved more than just saying the words. In some instances it meant life or death when instead of saying "Lord Caesar," Christians would

say "Lord Jesus." Calling Jesus "Lord" indicates total obedience to His will.

TEACHING TIP 2: We live in a world that is constantly enticing the attention of the believer away from the Lord. Brainstorm with your class the various areas of life where they need to submit to Christ's lordship.

NOTES

2. Call On The Lord

A. All-Sufficient Gospel
Romans 10:11,13

Ask: **"What is meant by the statement 'the Bible is our all-sufficient rule for faith and practice'?"** The Bible supplies us with all we need to know in order to live the kind of lives we should, both physically and spiritually. Peter stated that God's power "hath given unto us all things that pertain unto life and godliness" (2 Peter 1:3).

Thirty years ago a medical doctor commented that if all the people in the world would accept the principles and teachings of Christ relative to peace, joy, unselfishness, and clean living, then over half of the difficulties, diseases, and sorrows of the human race would be wiped out. If simply applying the teachings of Jesus to our modern society could bring results such as this, think of the added physical, spiritual, and eternal benefits for Christians who have committed their lives to God.

Paul appealed to the Jews to abandon their way of legalism and accept God's "by grace through faith'' way. The Law said ''do and you shall live.'' The gospel says, ''It is finished.'' Now the invitation is ''Believe and you shall be saved.''

In his discussion on the subject of righteousness based on faith alone, Paul quoted Isaiah 28:16 twice (Romans 9:33; 10:11). In this messianic prophecy nothing is said regarding the Law. Faith alone is the basis. Jesus told the Jews on one occasion that they should have known this. From Moses to Malachi, prophetic fingers pointed toward the coming of the Messiah. Jesus pointed out that the very Scriptures the Jews searched testified of Him. But they stubbornly refused the witness of the prophets, the Father, and the Son of God himself (John 5:30-47).

Romans 10:11 could well read, ''Whosoever believeth on him shall not be disappointed.'' This word in the Old Testament refers to the shame and disappointment that come to one whose faith or hope is shown to be in vain. In other words, when we put our trust in God and His Word and follow His plan of salvation, we will never be disappointed or regret our decision.

Yet Paul not only wrote that salvation is by faith alone, he clearly stated that it is for everyone. To support this, he quoted Joel 2:32 in Romans 10:13. There are no limitations! Anyone and everyone can be saved! The gospel is sufficient for all, and it is all-sufficient!

NOTES

B. Universal Gospel
Romans 10:12

Paul referred to what ''the Scripture saith'' four times in the Book of Romans

(4:3; 9:17; 10:11; 11:2). Paul was emphasizing that justification by faith is not some new idea he invented. Justification by faith has *always* been God's way of salvation. This was the message Paul preached. He was not ashamed of the gospel of Christ. To Paul the gospel was ''the power of God unto salvation to everyone that believeth'' (1:16). Those who believe the gospel and are saved will not be ashamed or disappointed in the gospel's effect on their lives.

In Romans 3:22 the words ''for there is no difference'' have an ominous sound. They pass sentence on both Jew and Gentile. Yet just as both Jew and Gentile stand guilty before God (''for all have sinned,'' verse 23), they also may be lavished with God's saving mercy (''for there is no difference,'' 10:12). When it comes to salvation, Jesus is the same Lord over all who have accepted Him as Savior. The rich, forgiving grace of God is available ''unto all that call upon him'' (verse 12).

TEACHING TIP 3: This section stresses the all-inclusiveness of the gospel with such words as *all* and *whosoever*. Although repentance (including believing in the heart and confessing with the mouth) is the only condition for salvation, there are many groups that make additional requirements. Brainstorm with the class for a few minutes as to what requirements some have added to the simplicity of the gospel. Some examples are:
- the observance of specific rituals and laws in order to be saved.
- membership in a particular church is required.
- water baptism according to a specific formula is necessary in order to be saved.

Emphasize that these and other added requirements are not stated in the Scriptures. It is God who set up the condition of repentance for salvation, not man. And faith remains as the *only* basis for salvation!

the feet of them that preach the gospel of peace, and bring glad tidings of good things'' (verse 15). The feet of the gospel messengers are beautiful because they are bringing the message of God's saving grace to the sinner, the message of peace to the troubled, the message of healing to the sick, and the message of eternal hope for all.

NOTES

3. Believe God's Word

A. Hearing The Message
Romans 10:14,15

Ask: "How do Paul's comments in verses 14 and 15 put responsibility upon Christians today?" These two verses stress the urgency for evangelism. The gospel is good news for all, but it is no news for those who have never heard. In order for the gospel to truly be good news for all, someone must spread the Word.

Notice Paul's progression in these verses. In order for mankind to call out for salvation, they must believe. If they have not heard the message of the gospel, how can they believe? How are they going to hear unless someone is sent to tell them? This task is not limited only to those who are ordained ministers. All Christians have a stewardship of the gospel. When it comes to the task of evangelism no one is exempt.

In verse 15 Paul quoted from Isaiah 52:7 which refers to the good news of Zion's coming release from exile. In the New Testament, Paul treated these verses as foreshadowing the release from the bondage of sin. As the Old Testament herald had announced to Zion, "Your God reigns!" so now the New Testament preachers of the gospel proclaim, "God is still on the throne!" This is the same message we proclaim today. Jesus is Lord! He has provided release from the bondage of sin.

The beauty and glory of spreading the gospel is also seen in the prophetic word of Isaiah quoted by Paul, "How beautiful are

B. Faith And The Word
Romans 10:16,17

Twice in the Book of Proverbs the writer stated that "There is a way which seemeth right unto a man; but the end thereof are the ways of death" (14:12; 16:25). This was precisely the situation of the Jews. It is the plight of all who reject God's way of salvation and substitute their own. Man's ways bring death, but God's way brings life.

Paul finalized his message concerning faith and hearing by showing the relationship of faith to the Word of God. The word for "report" in verse 16 is the same word that is translated "hearing" twice in verse 17. Faith to believe is intimately related to the message that is proclaimed. This message is the gospel.

TEACHING TIP 4: Ask a student to read Romans 10:17. The word "hearing" is actually a noun that means message or report. Have the students think of ways other than literally hearing the Word of God preached that would cause people to understand the gospel and be saved. Write these suggestions on the chalkboard or a blank transparency (one suggestion would be gospel tracts). Challenge the students to consider using one of these to help someone have faith in Christ.

If we have been saved and are not sharing the good news of the gospel with others, then this passage is for us. Just as we are stewards of our time, talents, and finances, so we are also stewards of the gospel message. Our lives and our language should bear witness to what God has done for us. From this day on, the lives of many people will touch ours. We may be the only gospel witness that some see or hear. What a challenge to fulfill the command of Christ and let our lights shine before men so that they can see our good works and God will be glorified. Paul stated, "God was in Christ, reconciling the world unto himself . . . and hath committed unto us the word of reconciliation" (2 Corinthians 5:19). If we do not take the gospel message to those who have not heard, who will?

NOTES

LIFE RESPONSE

The term "missionary" is not found in the Bible. The dictionary defines a missionary as one who undertakes a mission, especially a religious mission. Yet this word is not used just to refer to those who go to foreign lands. Whether on the homefront or foreign fields, Christians have a responsibility to proclaim the gospel to all people. The Great Commission is God's clarion call to every Christian to accept the role of missionary or Christian witness. Wherever we go, whatever we do, we are ambassadors for Christ.

Today's study has shown that there are three ingredients to saving faith. First is the need for understanding the Bible's report concerning Jesus Christ. Next, on the basis of this report, there must be a heart belief in that message. Finally, there must be public confession. As Christians, we must spread the good news that "Jesus saves." Without this message, saving faith is not possible. Unless men and women hear the good news, they are doomed.

Throughout Israel's history God's hands were stretched out as He appealed to Israel to come to Him and serve Him with a whole heart. Christ is still holding out His hands and saying "Come unto me . . . and I will give you rest" (Matthew 11:28). The last words of the Spirit in the Book of Revelation are "Whosoever will, let him take the water of life freely." Let us do our part to ensure that the lost hear the good news that Jesus still saves.

EVANGELISM OUTREACH

Refer to the Roman Road transparency. Point out that we must believe what God's Word says about sin and salvation. No matter how good a person may be, man's righteousness is but filthy rags in God's sight.

Emphasize that in order to be saved we must "call" upon the Lord. The same Lord who heard the publican's prayer, "God be merciful to me a sinner," is more than ready to hear the cry of every repentant soul. Encourage students to share the gospel message with someone this week. ⌂

Practical Christian Living

CENTRAL TRUTH

Our life-style reveals the quality of our commitment to Christ.

GOLDEN TEXT

Make sure that nobody pays back wrong for wrong, but always try to be kind to each other and to everyone else. 1 Thessalonians 5:15 (NIV)

STUDY TEXT

Romans 13:1-14

OUTLINE

1. Be A Good Citizen
   A. Respect For Civil Authority
   B. Pay What You Owe

2. Keep God's Commandments
   A. Debt To Love Others
   B. Love Fulfills The Law

3. Be Spiritually Alert
   A. Wake Up!
   B. Put On Christ

OBJECTIVE

To know that the Christian life is applicable to daily living and determine to serve Christ each day.

CHECKLIST

☐ Review the student guide for any questions you may wish to use for discussion.

☐ Hand out copies of the work sheet "Laws Of The Land" at the beginning of the class. Allow about 5 minutes for the students to rate themselves. Let the students know these sheets are not to be handed in. This may help them to be completely honest.

☐ Ask a student to prepare a brief report on "zealots" using a Bible dictionary or encyclopedia.

☐ One of your objectives for this study should be to help students develop godly values and motivations, rather than being motivated by fear of punishment. So be sensitive to the leading of the Holy Spirit.

☐ Fill out a copy of the "Planning The Session" sheet from the teaching helps packet to ensure that you cover during the teaching session everything you studied.

DAILY BIBLE READINGS

Monday:	God Ordains Government.	
	1 Samuel 10:24-27	
Tuesday:	Honor Rulers.	
	1 Peter 2:13-17	
Wednesday:	Honesty Pleases God.	
	Proverbs 16:6-13	
Thursday:	Love Is Encouraged.	
	John 15:12-17	
Friday:	Good Works Are Expected.	
	Acts 4:32-37	
Saturday:	Faithfulness Is Rewarded.	
	Matthew 6:1-4	

King James Version

Romans 13:1. Let every soul be subject unto the higher powers. For there is no power but of God: the powers that be are ordained of God.

2. Whosoever therefore resisteth the power, resisteth the ordinance of God: and they that resist shall receive to themselves damnation.

3. For rulers are not a terror to good works, but to the evil. Wilt thou then not be afraid of the power? do that which is good, and thou shalt have praise of the same:

4. For he is the minister of God to thee for good. But if thou do that which is evil, be afraid; for he beareth not the sword in vain: for he is the minister of God, a revenger to execute wrath upon him that doeth evil.

5. Wherefore ye must needs be subject, not only for wrath, but also for conscience' sake.

6. For, for this cause pay ye tribute also: for they are God's ministers, attending continually upon this very thing.

7. Render therefore to all their dues: tribute to whom tribute is due; custom to whom custom; fear to whom fear; honor to whom honor.

8. Owe no man any thing, but to love one another: for he that loveth another hath fulfilled the law.

9. For this, Thou shalt not commit adultery, Thou shalt not kill, Thou shalt not steal, Thou shalt not bear false witness, Thou shalt not covet; and if there be any other commandment, it is briefly comprehended in this saying, namely, Thou shalt love thy neighbor as thyself.

10. Love worketh no ill to his neighbor: therefore love is the fulfilling of the law.

11. And that, knowing the time, that now it is high time to awake out of sleep: for now is our salvation nearer than when we believed.

12. The night is far spent, the day is at hand: let us therefore cast off the works of darkness, and let us put on the armor of light.

13. Let us walk honestly, as in the day; not in rioting and drunkenness, not in chambering and wantonness, not in strife and envying:

14. But put ye on the Lord Jesus Christ, and make not provision for the flesh, to fulfil the lusts thereof.

New International Version

Romans 13:1. Everyone must submit himself to the governing authorities, for there is no authority except that which God has established. The authorities that exist have been established by God.

2. Consequently, he who rebels against the authority is rebelling against what God has instituted, and those who do so will bring judgment on themselves.

3. For rulers hold no terror for those who do right, but for those who do wrong. Do you want to be free from fear of the one in authority? Then do what is right and he will commend you.

4. For he is God's servant to do you good. But if you do wrong, be afraid, for he does not bear the sword for nothing. He is God's servant, an agent of wrath to bring punishment on the wrongdoer.

5. Therefore, it is necessary to submit to the authorities, not only because of possible punishment but also because of conscience.

6. This is also why you pay taxes, for the authorities are God's servants, who give their full time to governing.

7. Give everyone what you owe him: If you owe taxes, pay taxes; if revenue, then revenue; if respect, then respect; if honor, then honor.

8. Let no debt remain outstanding, except the continuing debt to love one another, for he who loves his fellowman has fulfilled the law.

9. The commandments, "Do not commit adultery," "Do not murder," "Do not steal," "Do not covet," and whatever other commandment there may be, are summed up in this one rule: "Love your neighbor as yourself."

10. Love does no harm to its neighbor. Therefore love is the fulfillment of the law.

11. And do this, understanding the present time. The hour has come for you to wake up from your slumber, because our salvation is nearer now than when we first believed.

12. The night is nearly over; the day is almost here. So let us put aside the deeds of darkness and put on the armor of light.

13. Let us behave decently, as in the daytime, not in orgies and drunkenness, not in sexual immorality and debauchery, not in dissension and jealousy.

14. Rather, clothe yourselves with the Lord Jesus Christ, and do not think about how to gratify the desires of the sinful nature.

The apostle Paul indicated in the Book of Romans that Christians are citizens of two kingdoms, spiritual and civil. Therefore as Christians, we have a responsibility to obey both.

The world often judges Christians by the way these responsibilities are carried out. We can be good citizens without being good Christians, but we cannot be good Christians without being good citizens.

Because of our actions, people can either glorify God or speak evil of the good we do (Romans 14:16). Our conduct can cause men to bless God or blaspheme and slander the name of God (1 Timothy 6:1; Titus 2:5). Jesus gave us guidance in the Sermon on the Mount: We are to let our lights shine before the world so that people can see our *good* works. Then they will bless God and be converted.

BIBLE COMMENTARY

1. Be A Good Citizen

A. Respect For Civil Authority
Romans 13:1-5

> TEACHING TIP 1: Distribute the work sheet "Laws Of The Land" to use as an introduction to the study. Let the students have a little fun with it, but point out that often it is disobedience in little things in a society that paves the way for greater crimes.

As members of society, we are responsible to be good citizens. Good citizens respect authority, even if that authority falls short of its divine intention. The fact civil government is "ordained of God" (Romans 13:1) does not mean God approves of a government that is corrupt, officials that are ungodly, or legislation that is unjust. But in its fundamental nature, civil authority was instituted by God to be beneficial to citizens. People sometimes twist the law to their advantage, but it was initiated to protect the good and resist or punish the bad.

Ask: "How did Paul treat lawbreakers in his treatise on civil law?" Paul had no sympathy for those who broke the law. He equated resisting civil authority to resisting God (verse 2). If we break the law and suffer punishment, we cannot blame the law for the result of our own sin.

Yet Paul was not advocating blind obedience to a government that openly defies God and morality. Rather he was stating a general principle. The security of any society depends upon a stable government and obedient citizens. Lawbreaking will imperil any society. History has proven what happens when civil authority is ignored and people do that which seems right in their own eyes.

Ask: "What if a government goes beyond its limits?" Paul did not discuss this possibility but the apostles gave us an example of those who said "no" to unwarranted demands (Acts 5:29). Christians, of all people, should respect authority, obey the laws of the land, and pay their "dues" (debts, taxes). These responsibilities should be carried out, not out of fear of punishment, but because this is one way of practicing the principles for Christian living as set forth in God's Word.

The Christian has a higher principle for submission than fear. Paul believed that the believer should submit "for conscience' sake" (Romans 13:5). This means the believer has an obligation toward God to obey civil authority.

filing for bankruptcy for inability to pay is not God's way. Whatever a Christian owes, he should pay.

Paying our debts includes more than just financial obligations. We are to pay our taxes and have respect for all authority, giving honor to those whose office warrants it. As Christian citizens we have a God-given obligation to translate Christian principles into civic responsibilities.

NOTES

Early Christians were regarded by some to be a Jewish sect. Consequently they were looked upon with suspicion. This meant that it was necessary for them to be especially careful of public behavior. No Christian is exempt from good citizenship. Paul made this very plain when he wrote, "Let every soul be subject unto the higher powers" (verse 1). Abuses of civil authority do not invalidate biblical principles.

NOTES

2. Keep God's Commandments

A. Debt To Love Others
Romans 13:8

Following Paul's discussion of public debts (taxes) in Romans 13:6,7, he wrote concerning private or personal debts. "Owe no man anything" is not necessarily a prohibition against borrowing. But we should never borrow beyond our ability to pay. Solomon warned that the rich rule over the poor and the borrower becomes the servant of the lender (Proverbs 22:7).

Paul's exhortation to "let no debt remain outstanding" is followed by "except the continuing debt to love one another" (Romans 13:8, NIV). There is no way that we can repay the debt of love that Christ demonstrated for us in dying to pay for our sin. In the same way, we owe a debt of love to everyone—Christian and unbeliever—until all have heard the gospel.

The concept of love found in verse 8 is first introduced in chapter 12 where Paul urged Christians to let love be "without dissimulation" or hypocrisy (verse 9). In other words, Christian love is to be genuine, free from insincerity. In verse 10 Paul used a term that is only found here in the New Testament. The phrase "kindly

B. Pay What You Owe
Romans 13:6,7

God set up governments to be His servants. Although they are not infallible, the people who work in government service are still worthy of honor. They are also worthy to be supported. Since, as Paul stated, public servants give full-time service to governing, they need to be supported by the taxes of those whom they govern. "This is also why you pay taxes" (Romans 13:6, NIV).

The first part of verse 7 could well read "pay your debts." Failure in this area has destroyed the testimony of many Christians. Building up incredible short-term debts, then

50

affectioned'' (KJV) or ''devoted'' (NIV) is from a compound Greek word that combincs two words for ''love'' to mean ''devoted to family affection.'' This term indicates that Christians are bound by a family tie. It also defines the type of brotherly love Christians are to show to one another. It is as though Paul were saying, ''Love each other as Christians as though you were flesh and blood family members.''

As the family of God, it should go without saying that we love one another as Christ loved us. But Paul found it necessary to remind the Roman Christians that love toward one another is paramount. If we try to keep the Ten Commandments we will fail. However, if we realize that ''he that loveth another hath fulfilled the law'' (13:8), we need never live in bondage to the Law.

NOTES

B. Love Fulfills The Law
Romans 13:9,10

Five times in the Sermon on the Mount, Jesus clarified the Old Testament Law (''Ye have heard . . . but I say''). Jesus went beyond a prescribed set of rules and regulations and set forth divine principles applicable to any situation.

There are many questions regarding worship, divine guidance, and daily living that cannot be settled by rules. But there is one principle that includes everything in its all-embracing power. That is the fundamental principle of love.

For this reason Paul emphasized a debt that we can never cancel. It is not by chance that his emphasis on the debt of love comes after his discussion on public and private debts. One of the best ways to get rid of the pain involved in doing a duty we find

disagreeable is to do it in the spirit of love as unto Jesus Christ. This love is not sentimental emotion. It demands practical action that seeks the best for others. This debt of love is one Christians never pay off.

Ask: ''Why did Paul mention some of the Ten Commandments here?'' The first four commandments have to do with relationships between God and humanity (Exodus 20:2-11). The last six, including the ones Paul mentioned, have to do with human relationships (verses 12-17). Paying the debt of love will keep us from doing what is wrong to others.

TEACHING TIP 3: Taking the six commands from Exodus 20:12-17, brainstorm with the class as to what love will *not* do to others. Then take time to have the class give suggestions as to what a person *will do* because he is filled with God's love. Use the following commentary of Romans 13:9,10 to follow up this discussion.

If we love, we will respect the spouse of another person and not allow physical passions to sweep us into sinful actions. If we love, we will not deliberately harm or seek to destroy another human being. If we love, we will not take what does not belong to us. If we love, we will not lie. If we love, we will not have an unwholesome desire for the ''things'' of others.

If our lives are dominated by a love for God and a love for our neighbors (all humanity) then no other law is needed. The law of love fulfills all other laws.

NOTES

3. Be Spiritually Alert
A. Wake Up!
Romans 13:11,12

The reason for Paul's emphasis on practical principles for Christian living now becomes clear. Christians live in the light of eternity. The solemn appeal in Romans 13:11 reaches beyond Paul's day. If early Christians lived in an attitude of constant expectancy of the second coming of Christ, how much more should we. We must never make the mistake of the scoffers of the last days (2 Peter 3:4). They forgot the lessons of history. But, Peter said, one thing is certain, "The day of the Lord will come" (verse 10) and Christians must be ready.

Ask: "To what day was Paul referring in Romans 13:12?" In this context, "day" possibly refers to death, but probably refers to the Second Coming. Either way Christians should be prepared. The term "sleep" comes from the Greek word from which we get our English "hypnosis." It could refer to spiritual conformity to the world. As Christians, we must never allow Satan to lull us into the kind of sleep where we cease to work for the Lord.

When Christ described the days that would precede His second coming, He told His disciples, "When these things begin to come to pass, then look up" (Luke 21:28). Paul echoed Christ's words when he said, "It is high time to awake out of sleep" (Romans 13:11).

NOTES

B. Put On Christ
Romans 13:11-14

TEACHING TIP 4: Divide the chalkboard or a blank transparency into three columns (students in a sanctuary class could use a sheet of paper). Write the following headings at the top of each:

CAST OFF   PUT ON   WALK
(verse 12)   (verse 12)   (verse 13)

Brainstorm for a few minutes on things to "cast off," things to "put on," and ways in which Christians should "walk." Have the students also include an example from Scripture, such as walking in wisdom (Colossians 4:5).

The expressions Paul used, casting off and putting on, emphasize personal responsibility. We must throw off or get rid of anything that could prevent us from rising to be with the Lord when He appears.

Paul instructed the Romans to "behave decently, as in the daytime" (verse 13, NIV). Those things that people do under cover of darkness must never be a part of a Christian's life-style.

Paul listed a series of sins opposite to Christian holiness. Intemperance refers not only to drunkenness but also to excessiveness in feasting, carousing, and revelry (rioting). The word "chambering" can refer to those who place no value on marital fidelity. "Wantonness" refers to those so caught up in the grip of lust that they dare to do publicly things it would be unsuitable for anyone to do. Finally, there are sins of strife (discord) and envy. It is significant that Paul put these sins on the same level as the other horrible sins.

The words "cast off" and "put on" are decisive words that leave no place for compromise or indecision. We must renounce the carnal excesses and sins of the flesh and spirit. There is absolutely no substitute for purity, abstinence, and self-control.

52

Ask: "How can Christians achieve purity, abstinence, and self-control?" This kind of moral excellence is impossible apart from the strength and power that only Christ can give (Philippians 4:13). We are not to make any provision for gratifying our sinful nature (Romans 13:14). Christ is our complete Provision. We are to "put on" Christ, receiving Him as Savior and living by His teachings. We are to accept His standards and depend on His grace and strength to keep us day by day.

We are living in the critical season (verse 11). An anticipation of the Lord's soon return should be sufficient motive for Christians to take seriously the spiritual and ethical demands of Christ. In this passage Paul echoed the words of Jesus to His disciples, "Look up, and lift up your heads; for your redemption draweth nigh" (Luke 21:28).

NOTES

LIFE RESPONSE

Today's study emphasized the responsibilities Christians have. As Christians we are citizens of two kingdoms, spiritual and civil. Every Christian is responsible to both—no one is exempt.

Christians have an outward responsibility to civil authorities. Paul was living under Roman rule and had sometimes benefited by it. For Paul lawlessness was essentially resistance to God. Paul was not advocating blind obedience. He was, however, implying that the security of any society depends upon a stable government. That government requires individual responsibility on the part of its citizens.

Christians have an upward responsibility to keep God's commandments. Paul alluded to the words of Jesus in Matthew 22:34-40 when he stated that loving God and loving our neighbor is the fulfullment of all laws. Our "neighbor" is not just the folks next door or our Christian brothers and sisters. Modern travel and communications have made the world a "neighborhood." If we love, we will respect. If we love, we will not harm. If we love we will not take what isn't ours. If we love, we will not lie. If we love, we will control our desires. Love for God and for our fellow human beings fulfills all other laws.

Christians also have an inward responsibility to themselves. Each day we are one day nearer to Christ's coming. Both inwardly and outwardly, we are to be ready to be caught up with Him for eternity.

EVANGELISM OUTREACH

To be able to obey the commandment, "Thou shalt love thy neighbor as thyself" (Romans 13:9), a person must first obey the most important commandment—to love God. But this cannot be accomplished if no relationship with God has been established. To do this, a person must accept Jesus Christ as his Lord and Savior. Allow time at the end of class to give an opportunity for any unsaved students to accept Christ. Then they will be ready for Christ's return. ▭

Obligations To Others

Central Truth

All who follow Christ must give of themselves in service to others.

Golden Text

We who are strong ought to bear with the failings of the weak and not to please ourselves.
Romans 15:1 (NIV)

Study Text

Romans 15:1-13,30-33

Outline

1. Help Others
   A. Christ, Our Example
   B. Plea For Unity

2. Accept Others
   A. God's Promises Proven
   B. God's Blessings Experienced

3. Pray For Others
   A. Partners In Prayer
   B. Anticipated Results

Objective

To survey our responsibilities to others and strive to fulfill them.

Checklist

☐ Read through the *Adult Student Guide.*
☐ Write down any questions you may wish to use for discussion.
☐ Copy the work sheet "Responsibilities To Weaker Brothers And Sisters In Christ" from the teaching helps packet for each student. Fill in a copy so you will be better prepared to lead a discussion and answer student questions.
☐ Hand out strips of paper with the following Scriptures printed on them: 2 Samuel 22:50; Psalm 18:49; Deuteronomy 32:43; Psalm 117:1; Isaiah 11:10; Genesis 12:3. Ask students to be prepared to read them during the second main point. Point out that Paul's teachings regarding the Gentiles are rooted in Old Testament prophecies. They are not his own ideas.
☐ Fill out a copy of the "Planning The Session" sheet from the teaching helps packet for this week's study. Ensure that you have all teaching methodologies and questions listed that you have planned to use.

Daily Bible Readings

Monday:	Strive For Unity. Philippians 2:1-4
Tuesday:	Be Considerate Of Others. Exodus 23:1-9
Wednesday:	Be Humble. Philippians 2:3-8
Thursday:	Be Patient. Psalm 37:7-11
Friday:	Be Hospitable. 1 Peter 4:9-11
Saturday:	Support Others Through Prayer. James 5:13-20

SCRIPTURE SETTING

King James Version

Romans 15:1. We then that are strong ought to bear the infirmities of the weak, and not to please ourselves.

2. Let every one of us please his neighbor for his good to edification.

3. For even Christ pleased not himself; but, as it is written, The reproaches of them that reproached thee fell on me.

4. For whatsoever things were written aforetime were written for our learning, that we through patience and comfort of the Scriptures might have hope.

5. Now the God of patience and consolation grant you to be likeminded one toward another according to Christ Jesus:

6. That ye may with one mind and one mouth glorify God, even the Father of our Lord Jesus Christ.

7. Wherefore receive ye one another, as Christ also received us, to the glory of God.

8. Now I say that Jesus Christ was a minister of the circumcision for the truth of God, to confirm the promises made unto the fathers:

9. And that the Gentiles might glorify God for his mercy; as it is written, For this cause I will confess to thee among the Gentiles, and sing unto thy name.

10. And again he saith, Rejoice, ye Gentiles, with his people.

11. And again, Praise the Lord, all ye Gentiles; and laud him, all ye people.

12. And again, Isaiah saith, There shall be a root of Jesse, and he that shall rise to reign over the Gentiles; in him shall the Gentiles trust.

13. Now the God of hope fill you with all joy and peace in believing, that ye may abound in hope, through the power of the Holy Ghost.

30. Now I beseech you, brethren, for the Lord Jesus Christ's sake, and for the love of the Spirit, that ye strive together with me in your prayers to God for me;

31. That I may be delivered from them that do not believe in Judea; and that my service which I have for Jerusalem may be accepted of the saints;

32. That I may come unto you with joy by the will of God, and may with you be refreshed.

33. Now the God of peace be with you all. Amen.

New International Version

Romans 15:1. We who are strong ought to bear with the failings of the weak and not to please ourselves.

2. Each of us should please his neighbor for his good, to build him up.

3. For even Christ did not please himself but, as it is written: "The insults of those who insult you have fallen on me."

4. For everything that was written in the past was written to teach us, so that through endurance and the encouragement of the Scriptures we might have hope.

5. May the God who gives endurance and encouragement give you a spirit of unity among yourselves as you follow Christ Jesus,

6. So that with one heart and mouth you may glorify the God and Father of our Lord Jesus Christ.

7. Accept one another, then, just as Christ accepted you, in order to bring praise to God.

8. For I tell you that Christ has become a servant of the Jews on behalf of God's truth, to confirm the promises made to the patriarchs

9. So that the Gentiles may glorify God for his mercy, as it is written: "Therefore I will praise you among the Gentiles; I will sing hymns to your name."

10. Again, it says, "Rejoice, O Gentiles, with his people."

11. And again, "Praise the Lord, all you Gentiles, and sing praises to him, all you peoples."

12. And again, Isaiah says, "The Root of Jesse will spring up, one who will arise to rule over the nations; the Gentiles will hope in him."

13. May the God of hope fill you with all joy and peace as you trust in him, so that you may overflow with hope by the power of the Holy Spirit.

30. I urge you, brothers, by our Lord Jesus Christ and by the love of the Spirit, to join me in my struggle by praying to God for me.

31. Pray that I may be rescued from the unbelievers in Judea and that my service in Jerusalem may be acceptable to the saints there,

32. So that by God's will I may come to you with joy and together with you be refreshed.

33. The God of peace be with you all. Amen.

The Christian's attitude toward others can affect the viewpoint outsiders have of the Church. There is nothing more damaging to the witness of the Church than to have the conduct of its members condemned by unbelievers.

The apostle Paul was very jealous for the reputation of the Church. He insisted that Christians should live in such a way that they do not invite the censure of sinners.

There is much truth to the axiom, "Actions speak louder than words." Christians are to do more than just say they love others, they must show it by their actions (1 John 3:17,18). The love we show must be a tangible demonstration of the love that Christ showed to us by His death. Simply by helping others, we can share the love of Jesus that reaches out in a special way to the world through the Church.

BIBLE COMMENTARY

1. Help Others

A. Christ, Our Example
Romans 15:1-3

The first part of chapter 15 is, in a sense, a conclusion to Paul's instructions in the previous chapter regarding those weak in the faith. It is a summary of the attitudes and actions that characterize true Christianity. Paul stressed the relationship that God wants to exist between strong and weak believers. The rule of Christian love mentioned in Romans 12:9 and 14:21 is amplified here. To Paul "love" was an action word. If a person really loved God it would be demonstrated by the way he lived.

Ask: "Why is love for God tied so closely with obligations toward others?" The term "ought" in verse 1 is similar to the word translated "debt" in Romans 1:14. Paul had an overwhelming sense of obligation to all men. When we love God, then the things that concern God will be our concern. God is concerned with the unsaved. But He is just as concerned with the needs of those who are weak.

Paul set forth Christ as the Example we are to emulate (verse 3). Jesus set the pattern by not pleasing himself. He put aside His own desires and died on Calvary. In the same way, we are not to please ourselves, but please our neighbors. We are to put aside our own desires and "bear up" or "carry" those who are weak. The strong are to help the weak and promote their good to edification (verse 2).

TEACHING TIP 1: Distribute the work sheet "Responsibilities To Weaker Brothers And Sisters In Christ." Break the class up into three groups. Have each examine its assigned passage of Scripture. Each group should look for the positive and negative aspects of the responsibilities that we have toward weaker brothers and sisters in Christ. Reassemble the class and discuss student responses.

Christian growth will take place more readily in an atmosphere of love than under a barrage of criticism. Christ willingly chose to endure the reproaches of men, even though it meant His death on the cross (Philippians 2:7,8). As Christians, we also must seek to help our fellow believers, even if it means we give up our own rights in order for a weaker member of the Body to be brought into a fuller knowledge of Christ.

Jesus did not live to please himself or insist on His own rights. He put God's will first, leaving us an example to follow.

NOTES

B. Plea For Unity
Romans 15:4-6

Paul realized how difficult it might be for some to live the Christlike life. Therefore, Paul encouraged and exhorted them concerning what God could do for them in verses 4-6. It is not by accident that this plea follows so closely his remarks regarding Scripture. In the New Testament, the Word of God and prayer are often associated. The more thoroughly we become acquainted with God's Word, the more deeply it will transform our lives and affect our character.

Paul exhorted his readers to receive "patience and comfort" from the Scriptures (verse 4). Then he turned around and stated that God is the source of all "patience and consolation," the identical phrase in the original language (verse 5). God's Word brings patience and comfort because God is its Source. The patience God gives triumphantly bears up under any trial, any circumstance. This kind of patience is not only able to accept things, but it can turn stumbling blocks into stepping stones. This patience is active endurance, not passive resignation.

Paul prayed that the God who gives endurance and encouragement would give the saints at Rome a spirit of unity. This is one of the essential elements of the faith.

Ask: "Does being 'likeminded' mean everyone should think the same way?" Being "likeminded" (KJV) or having a "spirit of unity" (NIV) is based on Christ's

example, not on everyone's thinking the same things in the same way. Chapter 14 has already shown that there were differences of opinion on certain things. Despite any differences, the Christians at Rome were to seek the same goal with a united heart (likeminded), resulting in the restoration and maintenance of their harmony.

Just as an orchestra produces beautiful harmony when all of the instruments are in tune, so the Church can exhibit Christian unity before the world. The Church's problems will become insignificant when its members concentrate on the Lord, making Him the center of all they do. Then they will "with one mind and one mouth glorify God" (verse 6).

NOTES

2. Accept Others

A. God's Promises Proven
Romans 15:7-12

Paul's ministry and calling was to make known the mystery regarding the Gentiles' place in the family of God. This "mystery" had been hidden for ages and generations and was being revealed (Colossians 1:26). The Old Testament writers had foreseen the mercy to be shown to the Gentiles. Paul pointed this out in Romans 15:8-12.

TEACHING TIP 2: Point out that Paul's teachings regarding the Gentiles are rooted in Old Testament prophecies. They are not his own ideas. Have the assigned students read 2 Samuel 22:50; Psalm 18:49; Deuteronomy 32:43; Psalm 117:1; Isaiah

11:10. Note that these verses are the ones Paul quoted in Romans 15:9-12. Although much of the Old Testament is directed to Israel, God's ultimate purpose was for all of the people of the earth. Have the last student read Genesis 12:3.

Ask: "Was Paul changing the subject when he began speaking of God's acceptance of the Gentiles?" It is not by accident that Paul shifted his attention to the Gentiles. He was writing to the church in Rome which was made up of both Jews and Gentiles.

Paul had taken a great deal of space to deal with the salvation of the Jews in chapters 9 through 11. They were God's chosen people. The patriarchs of old were their fathers and Christ himself was a Jew as far as His human nature was concerned. In fact, one of the reasons Christ came was to prove that the promises of God were reliable. But among the promises given by God was the promise that the Gentiles would one day be fellow heirs with the Jews of God's "promise in Christ by the gospel" (Ephesians 3:6). And as Romans 15:12 and Isaiah 11:10 state: "In him shall the Gentiles trust."

Ask: "What is the connection between the Gentiles' acceptance by God and Paul's discussion on unity in the Church?" Just as Jesus came to save all people, so the Church is to welcome all people. Rich and poor, weak and strong, Jew and Gentile are to receive one another as Christ received all: without partiality.

NOTES

B. God's Blessings Experienced
Romans 15:13

After this last appeal for unity Paul closed with a benediction. He had challenged his readers to put their Christian faith into action. Jews and Gentiles were to be considered the same before God.

Paul's prayer for his readers was that the God of all hope would renew faith and expectancy in their hearts. Looking around at circumstances and events can cause us to despair. Looking up can restore hope.

Paul prayed that the God of hope would fill the saints at Rome with joy. **Ask: "What is the difference between pleasures the world offers and the joy that comes from God?"** The pleasures of the world are temporary and depend on circumstances. Whereas Christian joy comes from a consciousness of the presence of God. Included in real joy is an assurance that nothing can separate us from His love. Joy is the active or energetic side of our Christian experience.

To "joy" Paul added "peace." This is the restful side of our Christian experience. Philosophies of old sought for a life that was untroubled within. This cannot be found apart from Christ. Peace speaks of reconciliation between a person and God, and reconciliation between people.

Inner tensions and worry over external things keep many in a continual state of unrest. It is hard to get along with others when we are not at peace with ourselves and/or with God. The cure is to develop a steadfast conviction that God has everything under control. Although we, as Christians, experience troubles and problems, in Christ we have inward peace.

Ask: "How is Paul's prayer for joy, peace, and hope made possible for the believer?" God's joy, peace, and hope are only made possible through the power of the Holy Spirit. Union and communion with Christ and with fellow believers is possible when the power of the Holy Spirit permeates the atmosphere of our homes and churches. Only as we recognize our human weaknesses can the strength of God be made perfect. We can do nothing by ourselves. But we can do all things through Christ who gives us strength (Philippians 4:13).

NOTES

spiritual wickedness against which they have to wrestle (Ephesians 6:12).

NOTES

3. Pray For Others

A. Partners In Prayer
Romans 15:30,31

Paul was well aware of the dangers he faced in going to Jerusalem. That was one of the reasons he was asking the Roman Christians to be prayer partners with him. Unbelieving Jews dogged his steps everywhere he traveled. More than once they tried to kill him. Paul's prayer was that he might be delivered or rescued from their efforts.

Paul's second concern was whether or not the contribution he was taking to Jerusalem would be accepted (see verse 26). Some of the Jewish Christians were still struggling with prejudice. The Jerusalem Council had settled this question, but it seems that Paul may have been concerned that some animosity still existed.

Knowing the circumstances he possibly would face, Paul asked the saints at Rome to "strive" together with him in prayer. One Bible version translates Paul's words "Be my allies in the fight" (New English Bible). The Greek word translated "strive" is also used of contending in athletic competition and implies strenuous exercise. This is a striking description of earnest prayer. Prayer has been called the Christian's vital breath. Instead of being easy, it is often the hardest work of Christians because of the

B. Anticipated Results
Romans 15:32,33

When Paul asked the Roman Christians to pray, he had in mind that God would answer the prayer. As a result, he would be able to fulfill his mission in Jerusalem. Then, as he stated, "I may come to you with joy and together with you be refreshed" (Romans 15:32, NIV).

However, it must be pointed out that Paul always submitted himself to God's will, even if it conflicted with his plans. When speaking of helping others at the beginning of chapter 15, Paul said that the Christian's objective was not to please himself (verse 1). He intentionally expressed the condition for his return to Rome as "by God's will" (verse 32, NIV). God's will always has first place. Paul knew that!

In the months following this letter, Paul went to Jerusalem (Acts 21:15-19). There he was falsely accused by the unbelieving Jews and imprisoned (21:20 through 26:32). Although Paul did not fulfill the mission he set out to do in the manner he had planned, he still accomplished God's will. Paul did go to Rome, although it was under Roman guard (27:1 through 28:31).

Ask: "Why would God have Paul sent to Rome as a prisoner, rather than as a free man?"

TEACHING TIP 3: Ask the class to brainstorm for a few moments as to why Paul went to Rome as a prisoner.

> If Paul had intended to go to Rome anyway, why would God's plan include imprisonment? Acts 20:17-24 and 21:7-14 may help your class understand the background. Also have the students examine what happened while Paul was imprisoned—how he fulfilled his ministry as an apostle to the Gentiles—to help answer this question.

Paul added a benediction to his prayer request in Romans 15:33. It was the God of peace who would stand by Paul on his trip to Jerusalem. It would not matter if it was as a free man or prisoner. It was also the blessing of the God of peace that Paul sent to the saints at Rome. We may not experience the kinds of persecution and imprisonment that Paul experienced. But regardless of the trials we experience, it is the God of peace who alone can give the peace of God to us in our times of need.

NOTES

LIFE RESPONSE

It is interesting to note in this study that God is referred to as the God of patience and consolation. He is also called the God of hope and the God of peace.

The body of Christ is made up of many members. No two are alike. Only the God of patience and consolation can bring unity in diversity. Christ is to be the Christian's supreme Example. When Paul told the Corinthians, "Be imitators of me," it was with the stipulation "just as I also am of Christ" (1 Corinthians 11:1, New American Standard Bible). If God is put first and each Christian seeks to follow in the footsteps of the Master, the result will be a church giving harmonious glory to God.

If we look at the world only through the eyes of the news media it is difficult to be hopeful. Only the God of hope can help us to understand that there is no such thing as a "hopeless" situation. One of the responsibilities of the Church today is to accept people where they are and show them that the gospel of Christ offers hope to the hopeless. One of the things that will help bring an end to needless worry is the conviction that the God of hope has everything under control.

Finally, only the God of peace can restore the peace of God to our hearts and help us live at peace with one another. With God's peace reigning in our hearts we can pray with confidence. As we pray according to His will we can be sure He hears us and will grant our petitions (1 John 5:14,15).

EVANGELISM OUTREACH

Challenge students in several areas. Encourage them to be patient with and considerate of new Christians or those who may fall in the category of the "weaker brother." Remind students of the all-inclusiveness of the gospel. All have sinned, therefore all need to be saved. Emphasize that God is the only Source of real joy and peace. In the light of today's study on the obligations of Christians to others, encourage class members to allow Christ to reach out to others through them this week.

UNIT 2

I N T R O D U C T I O N

SPIRITUAL WARFARE

Many popular doctrines are not based on what the Scriptures state. Rather, they are based on experience or analogy and go beyond the clear teaching of the Bible. The subject of spiritual warfare seems to be very popular in Christian circles today. But are the popular views of spiritual warfare biblically sound? Do they explain what spiritual warfare really is? Although not an exhaustive study, this unit will discuss various aspects of what constitutes this warfare and how it is conducted from a biblical perspective.

The first study, study 9, will introduce your students to the nature of spiritual warfare and who really gains the victory in spiritual battles. Included in this study is a discussion of spiritual armor from Ephesians 6 and what it means to "put on the whole armor of God" (verse 10). Study 10 introduces your class to the enemy against whom Christians fight, "Satan, The Defeated Foe." Your class will understand what kind of power Satan has and what Christians can do with the authority Christ has given them.

Studies 11 and 12 focus on the spiritual warrior. The greatest help in defeating the enemy is to be thoroughly prepared and disciplined in the Christian faith. Since the attacks of the enemy are mostly against a believer's or church's spiritual weaknesses, study 11 covers the subject of "Conquering Sinful Desires." "Spiritual Disciplines" (study 12) gives insight on what self-control really involves. It will also help you encourage your students to stand firm for Christ.

The final study in the unit discusses our place in the present world. Although we live in the world, Christians are not a part of the world. Study 13 will help your students understand how they can live victoriously in this evil world and faithfully represent Christ to those who need Him.

The Christian's Warfare

CENTRAL TRUTH

Victory in spiritual warfare comes through relying on the strength of Christ.

GOLDEN TEXT

Put on the full armor of God, so that when the day of evil comes, you may be able to stand your ground, and after you have done everything, to stand. Ephesians 6:13 (NIV)

STUDY TEXT

Genesis 3:15; John 12:31-33; 2 Corinthians 2:14-16; 10:3-5; Ephesians 6:10-18

OUTLINE

1. Nature Of The Warfare
   A. Spiritual Struggles, Spiritual Power
   B. Not A Human Struggle

2. Weapons Of The Warfare
   A. Protection For The Battle
   B. Mighty Through God

3. Victory Through Christ
   A. Promise Of Victory
   B. Christ's Victory Is Our Victory

OBJECTIVE

To understand the spiritual nature of the Christian's warfare and be equipped for battle.

CHECKLIST

- [ ] Read through the teacher and student guides, noting any questions you may wish to discuss.
- [ ] To make this study personal, think of one or two examples from your own life when you have had spiritual battles. Be prepared to talk about how you confronted these situations. Also explain either how you were victorious or what you wish you had done differently.
- [ ] Display the poster "The Armor Of God—Protection For Spiritual Warfare" in a prominent place.
- [ ] From the teaching helps packet, prepare one copy of the information sheet "The Whole Armor Of God" for each student in your class. This sheet provides a description of the armor featured on the poster.
- [ ] Prepare a copy of the work sheet "Your Spiritual Warfare" for each student.

DAILY BIBLE READINGS

Monday:	Victory Through Obedience. Exodus 19:3-8
Tuesday:	Victory Through Worship. Job 1:12-22
Wednesday:	Victory Through Trust. Psalm 118:5-14
Thursday:	Victory Through Divine Strength. Isaiah 41:10-16
Friday:	Victory Through Prayer. 2 Corinthians 1:8-11
Saturday:	Victory Through Faith. Hebrews 11:32-40

SCRIPTURE SETTING

King James Version

Ephesians 6:10. Finally, my brethren, be strong in the Lord, and in the power of his might.

11. Put on the whole armor of God, that ye may be able to stand against the wiles of the devil.

12. For we wrestle not against flesh and blood, but against principalities, against powers, against the rulers of the darkness of this world, against spiritual wickedness in high places.

13. Wherefore take unto you the whole armor of God, that ye may be able to withstand in the evil day, and having done all, to stand.

14. Stand therefore, having your loins girt about with truth, and having on the breastplate of righteousness;

15. And your feet shod with the preparation of the gospel of peace;

16. Above all, taking the shield of faith, wherewith ye shall be able to quench all the fiery darts of the wicked.

17. And take the helmet of salvation, and the sword of the Spirit, which is the word of God:

18. Praying always with all prayer and supplication in the Spirit, and watching thereunto with all perseverance and supplication for all saints.

2 Corinthians 10:3. For though we walk in the flesh, we do not war after the flesh:

4. (For the weapons of our warfare are not carnal, but mighty through God to the pulling down of strongholds;)

5. Casting down imaginations, and every high thing that exalteth itself against the knowledge of God, and bringing into captivity every thought to the obedience of Christ.

Genesis 3:15. And I will put enmity between thee and the woman, and between thy seed and her seed; it shall bruise thy head, and thou shalt bruise his heel.

John 12:31. Now is the judgment of this world: now shall the prince of this world be cast out.

32. And I, if I be lifted up from the earth, will draw all men unto me.

33. This he said, signifying what death he should die.

2 Corinthians 2:14. Now thanks be unto God, which always causeth us to triumph in Christ, and maketh manifest the savor of his knowledge by us in every place.

New International Version

Ephesians 6:10. Finally, be strong in the Lord and in his mighty power.

11. Put on the full armor of God so that you can take your stand against the devil's schemes.

12. For our struggle is not against flesh and blood, but against the rulers, against the authorities, against the powers of this dark world and against the spiritual forces of evil in the heavenly realms.

13. Therefore put on the full armor of God, so that when the day of evil comes, you may be able to stand your ground, and after you have done everything, to stand.

14. Stand firm then, with the belt of truth buckled around your waist, with the breastplate of righteousness in place,

15. And with your feet fitted with the readiness that comes from the gospel of peace.

16. In addition to all this, take up the shield of faith, with which you can extinguish all the flaming arrows of the evil one.

17. Take the helmet of salvation and the sword of the Spirit, which is the word of God.

18. And pray in the Spirit on all occasions with all kinds of prayers and requests. With this in mind, be alert and always keep on praying for all the saints.

2 Corinthians 10:3. For though we live in the world, we do not wage war as the world does.

4. The weapons we fight with are not the weapons of the world. On the contrary, they have divine power to demolish strongholds.

5. We demolish arguments and every pretension that sets itself up against the knowledge of God, and we take captive every thought to make it obedient to Christ.

Genesis 3:15. And I will put enmity between you and the woman, and between your offspring and hers; he will crush your head, and you will strike his heel.

John 12:31. Now is the time for judgment on this world; now the prince of this world will be driven out.

32. But I, when I am lifted up from the earth, will draw all men to myself.

33. He said this to show the kind of death he was going to die.

2 Corinthians 2:14. But thanks be to God, who always leads us in triumphal procession in Christ and through us spreads everywhere the fragrance of the knowledge of him.

When the serpent tempted Eve in the Garden of Eden and she and Adam violated God's law, the struggle with evil began. All humanity became involved in this struggle. Christ won the ultimate victory in that struggle through His death and resurrection, but the individual battles of the war are still being fought.

As Christians, we have been redeemed by God and now, as His allies, wage war against sin, the sinful nature, and the devil. Sometimes the enemy is clearly seen. Other times, the battle is against a foe that cannot be identified.

In the middle of desperate struggles, how can we be victorious? How can we actually be prepared to fight spiritual wars? These are questions faced by God's people through the ages, and for answers we turn to God's Word.

BIBLE COMMENTARY

1. Nature Of The Warfare

A. Spiritual Struggles, Spiritual Power
Ephesians 6:10

TEACHING TIP 1: To assess the students' current knowledge and attitudes, ask them to identify the first thought, feeling, or memory that comes to mind when they hear the words "spiritual warfare." In a very large class, you may prefer to break into groups of four to six, then take a sampling of responses.

Ephesians 6:10-18 reminds us that our struggles are not merely human; they are spiritual in nature. Human struggles might be fought with purely human strength and weapons, but spiritual struggles require spiritual weapons and spiritual strength. So Paul told his readers to "be strong in the Lord, and in the power of his might," and not to depend on their own strength.

At the conclusion of his section on right living (5:22-6:9), Paul wrote, "Finally, my brethren, be strong in the Lord" (6:10). In using the word "finally," Paul was not summarizing what he had already written. Rather he was making some final application for the readers of this letter. Paul was giving them an ethical charge to take a new posture in their responsibility to God. Apparently, the Ephesians were caving in to the evil forces around them. Paul wanted them to be fully protected and fully aware!

Verse 10 uses three words that have similar meanings in English: "strong," "power," and "might."

• "Be strong" is a translation of a word that carries the idea of having some ability or capability. An alternate translation might be "be able in the Lord."

• The word translated "power" carries the idea of authority, rule, or power over someone or something. This word is the root of English words like democracy and autocratic.

• "Might" is strength in the sense of force, such as military force or pure physical strength.

So verse 10 might be translated, "As you confront evil, be capable in the Lord and in the authority that comes from His ability to make things happen." Being strong in the power of God's might means that we can confidently invoke God's name and rely on God's power to destroy evil. He has the force to overcome evil and grants His authority to us in our spiritual battles.

Ask: "What New Testament examples demonstrate being 'strong in the Lord and in the power of his might'?"

TEACHING TIP 2: Have your students brainstorm for people from the New Testament who clearly showed that they confronted evil in the power of the Holy Spirit. The Book of Acts is a good place to find this kind of example, although there are some illustrations in the Epistles. Have the students explain how these biblical characters depended on God and were strengthened by Him in their battles. Write student responses on the chalkboard or a blank transparency to show the number of examples there are for us to follow.

NOTES

B. Not A Human Struggle
Ephesians 6:11,12

Paul defined the nature of spiritual warfare in verse 12. He stated first that it is "wrestling." This is an unusual word that implies personal, hand-to-hand combat. We can't declare ourselves above any problems or think that turning our problems over to God means we will not struggle. We will each struggle, personally.

Second, Paul said that, as Christians, we don't wrestle "against flesh and blood," meaning human beings. This may include our own human nature, as well as other people. When we encounter evil, something more than a human force is at work.

Third, the forces we do wrestle are identified as principalities, powers, the rulers of

the darkness of this world, and spiritual wickedness in high places. These are all terms referring to powerful evil beings. They are forces of Satan that are at war with God for control of creation.

Ask: "How does knowing that our struggles are not just against human forces, but against spiritual forces, change what we do?" In remembering that we are not in a merely human struggle, we realize that our own efforts are not sufficient in the fight against evil. Paul stated that two things will allow us to withstand the devil's schemes: being "strong in the Lord, and in the power of his might" (verse 10) and wearing the "armor of God" (verse 11).

The purpose of putting on God's armor is to "stand against the wiles of the devil" (verse 11). The devil does not necessarily openly attack the believer. He has crafty schemes ("wiles") that he uses to deceive and slander the believer (the word for devil in verse 11 means "slanderer"). By putting on God's armor, we, as Christians, take a stand against his attacks.

NOTES

2. Weapons Of The Warfare

A. Protection For The Battle
Ephesians 6:13-17

Having informed his readers of the nature of spiritual warfare and having told them to go into spiritual warfare "strong in the Lord," Paul used the metaphor of armor to give us a specific way to do this. First, note that we are to put on the whole armor of God; no item is to be left off. Each of us as Christians will surely face spiritual warfare. Preparation for this warfare is incomplete unless we attend to all of the armor.

Ask: "What items of armor and weaponry mentioned in Ephesians 6:13-17 are for the believer's protection?" Five parts of the armor are defensive: the belt, breastplate, footgear, shield, and helmet. Together, these five items serve to protect all of a soldier's vulnerable areas. Paul used this imagery to portray the protection that is available to believers.

TEACHING TIP 3: Using the poster "The Armor Of God—Protection For Spiritual Warfare" and the information sheet "The Whole Armor Of God," point out the different pieces of armor the Christian soldier must put on in order to engage in spiritual warfare. As you discuss the pieces of a Roman soldier's armor, apply them spiritually to the Christian's warfare. After your discussion, distribute copies of the information sheet to reinforce this part of the study.

These five pieces of spiritual armor *will* protect the believer when engaged in spiritual warfare. But it is not enough to be protected. We must also engage the enemy. Peter wrote that believers must resist the devil in our afflictions (1 Peter 5:8,9). Likewise, James exhorted, "Submit yourselves therefore to God. Resist the devil, and he will flee from you" (James 4:7). This will be accomplished when we take up the "weapons of our warfare" (2 Corinthians 10:4) and use them in battle.

NOTES

B. Mighty Through God
Ephesians 6:17,18; 2 Corinthians 10:3-5

Huddling in a bunker or standing untouched in one's armor is not warfare. But Ephesians 6:17,18 lists two weapons that actually get the believer involved in warfare—the sword of the Spirit and prayer. These weapons enable the Christian to go on the offensive in spiritual warfare.

Ask: "How would the sword of the Spirit—God's Word—be helpful in spiritual warfare?" The Bible is useful in spiritual warfare because it reveals God's will and answers the accusations of the devil. When we see the world from God's perspective and understand God's will for it, we can work with Him to implement His will (see Luke 4:1-14).

Ephesians 6:18 tells us how to take the armor, how to stand, and how to wield the sword of the Spirit. Only with constant prayer and unceasing alertness can we expect to succeed in the warfare Christ has placed before us.

In 2 Corinthians 10:3-5, Paul wrote that spiritual warfare is effective where purely human argument is not. The weapons God has supplied are not fleshly or merely human ("carnal," verse 4). Rather, these weapons are spiritual.

The Corinthian church had a problem with factions, caused partly by the invasion of heretical "apostles." Therefore, Paul's focus was on the effectiveness of spiritual weapons against intellectual arguments or philosophical attacks on the gospel ("imaginations," verse 5, could also be translated as "speculations" or "arguments"). When he said that our spiritual weapons "have divine power to destroy strongholds" (2 Corinthians 10:4, RSV), this applied to any kind of evil we encounter.

God wants us to be prepared when the devil attacks. To succeed in spiritual warfare, we must first be fully protected in spiritual armor. Second, we must learn to use the Word of God effectively. And third, we must keep on praying. We cannot afford to let ourselves become complacent in any of these areas.

3. Victory Through Christ

A. Promise Of Victory
Genesis 3:15; John 12:31-33

The story of the war against evil began in the Garden of Eden, when Satan seduced Adam and Eve into disobeying God's commands. Because they had willingly rebelled against God, Satan had a right to claim them as his own. Thus, Satan won the first skirmish in the war. This battle is the subject of Genesis 3.

As a result of this battle, Adam and Eve (and through them, all humanity) were cut off from the Garden and from the eternal life for which they were created. However, God would not allow Satan to win the war. His intent to redeem creation is established from the very beginning. The need for Jesus Christ's life and death is already clear.

When God acknowledged to Satan in Genesis 3:15 that "you will strike his heel" (NIV), God also promised that "he will crush your head." This means that while Satan will do damage to humanity and its highest representative, Christ, in the end Christ will destroy Satan.

Ask: "How was the prophecy in Genesis 3:15 fulfilled?" Christ's victory over Satan came at a terrible cost. His crucifixion was necessary to defeat Satan. A few days before His death, Jesus showed that He knew in what way He would die (John 12:31-33). He also knew that this death was critical to the war against Satan, for He said that now, on the occasion of His death, "the prince of this world will be driven out" (verse 31,

NIV). As humanity's representative, yet untainted by Adam's sin, Christ died the criminal's death and overcame death once and for all. In this way, He redeemed mankind and defeated Satan.

Because Christ acted as humanity's representative when He conquered Satan, all who believe in Him can participate in His victory. We are all eligible, by faith, to put on the spiritual armor provided by Christ as a defense against Satan. Because we are now clothed with salvation, Satan has no more right to claim us. We have victory through Christ.

NOTES

B. Christ's Victory Is Our Victory
2 Corinthians 2:14

Ask: "If Christ has already won victory, what need does God have for our efforts? Why do we have to struggle?" Knowing that Christ has won victory over Satan on our behalf is a reason for confidence in spiritual warfare. It is not, however, a reason for complacency. God still has a purpose for us; we are not simply along for the ride. Our struggles are one of the ways that God causes us to mature. Our spiritual warfare is also the means by which Christ's victory is made known to the world.

As we fight our battles against temptation and evil, Christ's final victory becomes apparent. Paul used a particularly beautiful metaphor for this when he said, "Thanks be to God, who always leads us in triumphal procession in Christ and through us spreads everywhere the fragrance of the knowledge of him" (2 Corinthians 2:14, NIV). As we participate in victory after victory, we carry the "aroma" of Christ wherever we go.

Christ's victory becomes our victory, and that victory is part of the process by which God is redeeming humanity.

> TEACHING TIP 4: Distribute copies of the work sheet ''Your Spiritual Warfare'' to each student. Allow several minutes for quiet reflection and completion of the work sheet. Then, you may wish to have students pair off and share personal struggles or fears brought up during the study. Be sure to allow time for them to pray for one another.

LIFE RESPONSE

In the battle against evil, it is important to remember that we are *not* wrestling against flesh and blood. If we try to fight with human strength, we will end up exhausted, defeated, and despairing. How, then, do we fight?

First, we make sure we are clothed with salvation. If we are uncertain of God's grace-filled love for us, we may lose heart in the thick of battle and conclude that God has left us. We need to be certain that God has claimed us for His own through Christ. Christ alone is the basis of our salvation—past, present, and future!

Second, we need to immerse ourselves in the Bible. The knowledge of God's will as revealed in His Word is our weapon against evil. Would you go to war with an unfamiliar weapon? Of course not! We have to be familar with the sword of the Spirit in order to be prepared for spiritual warfare.

Third, we must develop a habit of prayer, constantly communicating with God about the battle in which we are engaged. We cannot accomplish spiritual warfare in our own strength, with our own battle plans. As we grow in our knowledge of God, drawing closer to Him, He will show us His victory. Then, truly, we will *experience* victory through Christ.

Spiritual warfare must not be entered into lightly. With proper preparation, putting on the whole armor of God, and knowing how to use spiritual weapons, God will bring us victory over all the powers of the enemy.

EVANGELISM OUTREACH

This study is ideal for an appeal to any unsaved in the class. The first step toward successful spiritual warfare is becoming a Christian. Therefore, much of this study is a review of the gospel.

To help unsaved students understand their need for salvation, focus first on the ways they experience despair in their lives. These are opportunities for spiritual warfare. Then, as you teach about how to conduct spiritual warfare, be prepared to give a clear presentation of the gospel.

Satan, The Defeated Foe

CENTRAL TRUTH

Christians can live victoriously because Christ has defeated Satan.

GOLDEN TEXT

Submit yourselves, then, to God. Resist the devil, and he will flee from you. James 4:7 (NIV)

STUDY TEXT

Matthew 4:1-11; Luke 10:17-20; Colossians 2:15; Hebrews 2:14,15; James 4:7; 1 Peter 5:8,9

OUTLINE

1. Defeated By Christ
   A. Christ's Defeat Of Satan On Earth
   B. Christ's Final Triumph Over Sin

2. Power Over Satan
   A. Christ's Power Given To Us
   B. Power Over Death

3. Resist The Devil
   A. Be Confident In Christ
   B. Resist Victoriously

OBJECTIVE

To see that Christ has defeated Satan and resist the devil by the authority of Christ.

CHECKLIST

☐ Review the material in the student guide. You may wish to do more study on what the Bible teaches about Satan, using a concordance and Bible dictionary.

☐ Duplicate the work sheet "James 4:7; 1 Peter 5:8,9—An Inductive Study" for use in Teaching Tip 3. You might use a chalkboard or overhead projector to write down student responses and questions. You will need to be very familiar with the texts and the material from the quarterly.

☐ Also duplicate copies of the sheet "Living Victoriously—My Commitment." Note that each page has enough copies for three students; cut these apart before class.

☐ Fill out a copy of the "Planning The Session" sheet from the teaching helps packet during your study preparation. This will ensure that you allow enough time for each area of the study while teaching this week's material.

DAILY BIBLE READINGS

Monday:	Satan's Defeat Foretold. Genesis 3:13-15	
Tuesday:	Satan's Fall. Isaiah 14:12-15	
Wednesday:	Satan Rebuked. Zechariah 3:1-7	
Thursday:	Satan Resisted. Luke 4:1-12	
Friday:	Try The Spirits. 1 John 4:1-4	
Saturday:	Satan Cast Down. Revelation 12:7-12	

King James Version

Matthew 4:1. Then was Jesus led up of the Spirit into the wilderness to be tempted of the devil.

2. And when he had fasted forty days and forty nights, he was afterward ahungered.

3. And when the tempter came to him, he said, If thou be the Son of God, command that these stones be made bread.

4. But he answered and said, It is written, Man shall not live by bread alone, but by every word that proceedeth out of the mouth of God.

11. Then the devil leaveth him, and, behold, angels came and ministered unto him.

Colossians 2:15. And having spoiled principalities and powers, he made a show of them openly, triumphing over them in it.

Luke 10:17. And the seventy returned again with joy, saying, Lord, even the devils are subject unto us through thy name.

18. And he said unto them, I beheld Satan as lightning fall from heaven.

19. Behold, I give unto you power to tread on serpents and scorpions, and over all the power of the enemy; and nothing shall by any means hurt you.

20. Notwithstanding, in this rejoice not, that the spirits are subject unto you; but rather rejoice, because your names are written in heaven.

Hebrews 2:14. Forasmuch then as the children are partakers of flesh and blood, he also himself likewise took part of the same; that through death he might destroy him that had the power of death, that is, the devil;

15. And deliver them, who through fear of death were all their lifetime subject to bondage.

James 4:7. Submit yourselves therefore to God. Resist the devil, and he will flee from you.

1 Peter 5:8. Be sober, be vigilant; because your adversary the devil, as a roaring lion, walketh about, seeking whom he may devour:

9. Whom resist steadfast in the faith, knowing that the same afflictions are accomplished in your brethren that are in the world.

New International Version

Matthew 4:1. Then Jesus was led by the Spirit into the desert to be tempted by the devil.

2. After fasting forty days and forty nights, he was hungry.

3. The tempter came to him and said, "If you are the Son of God, tell these stones to become bread."

4. Jesus answered, "It is written: 'Man does not live on bread alone, but on every word that comes from the mouth of God.' "

11. Then the devil left him, and angels came and attended him.

Colossians 2:15. And having disarmed the powers and authorities, he made a public spectacle of them, triumphing over them by the cross.

Luke 10:17. The seventy-two returned with joy and said, "Lord, even the demons submit to us in your name."

18. He replied, "I saw Satan fall like lightning from heaven.

19. I have given you authority to trample on snakes and scorpions and to overcome all the power of the enemy; nothing will harm you.

20. However, do not rejoice that the spirits submit to you, but rejoice that your names are written in heaven."

Hebrews 2:14. Since the children have flesh and blood, he too shared in their humanity so that by his death he might destroy him who holds the power of death—that is, the devil—

15. And free those who all their lives were held in slavery by their fear of death.

James 4:7. Submit yourselves, then, to God. Resist the devil, and he will flee from you.

1 Peter 5:8. Be self-controlled and alert. Your enemy the devil prowls around like a roaring lion looking for someone to devour.

9. Resist him, standing firm in the faith, because you know that your brothers throughout the world are undergoing the same kind of sufferings.

Current attitudes about Satan tend toward two extremes. On one end of the spectrum are those who ignore Satan, considering evil to be an impersonal force or merely the absence of good. On the other end of the spectrum are those who are obsessed with Satan's power, attributing every problem to attacks of Satan and living in fear of him. Neither of these views can be supported from Scripture.

The Bible depicts Satan as a powerful being—yet he is not all-powerful nor present everywhere. And he has already been defeated by Christ. If we do not rely on Christ's victory over Satan and try to confront him in our own power, he is indeed dangerous to us. But Satan has no more power over us than we choose to give him. When we resist the devil by the authority Christ has given us, we will be victorious.

BIBLE COMMENTARY

1. Defeated By Christ

A. Christ's Defeat Of Satan On Earth
Matthew 4:1-11

TEACHING TIP 1: Read or list on the board this background information about Satan.
• Created by God as a powerful angel, but challenged God for equality (Isaiah 14:12-15).
• Specifically credited with tempting:
  Adam and Eve (Genesis 3)
  Job (Job 1:7 through 2:7)
  Joshua (Zechariah 3)
  David (1 Chronicles 21:1)
  Paul (1 Thessalonians 2:18)
  Christians (2 Corinthians 2:11).
• Names and titles by which he is known include Satan, the devil, the deceiver, the tempter, the enemy, the evil one, the prince or the god of this world, the prince of demons, the prince of the power of the air, the adversary. His aim is to take control of God's creation.
• Satan's defeat has already been assured, but will culminate in the final events depicted in Revelation.

Jesus Christ is both human and divine. In order for Him to redeem us from sin, it was necessary that He become human. Although He was a perfect and sinless human, He suffered death on behalf of sinful mankind who deserved it. The story in Matthew 4 of the temptation of Jesus in the desert underscores His humanity.

After He was baptized by John and before He began His active ministry, Jesus was "led up of the Spirit into the wilderness to be tempted of the devil" (Matthew 4:1). During His 40-day fast, Luke 4:2 notes, Jesus was "tempted of the devil." At the end of the 40 days, Jesus was given a final challenge by Satan in the form of three temptations.

Ask: "Why did Satan tempt Jesus?" Satan made three attempts to turn Jesus aside from doing the will of God. The only way that Jesus Christ could redeem us was by taking the difficult way of the cross. Satan was trying to get Jesus to leave that difficult path by somehow taking a shortcut to rulership, bypassing His death on the cross. In his temptation, Satan thought he could also achieve Christ's downfall into sin.

In his three challenges, Satan admitted that Jesus is the Son of God. He even quoted Scripture to try to persuade Jesus to prove His deity before the appointed time. Satan tempted Christ to perform a miracle for His own comfort (turning stones into bread), to jump off the temple—a rash act that would demand God's special protection—and to worship Satan as a quick route to control of the world. Each time, Jesus stayed true to the will of God, and defeated Satan by using God's Word.

TEACHING TIP 2: On the chalkboard or a blank transparency, write the three temptations of Christ as outlined in Matthew 4:1-11. Have your students suggest how these three temptations represent the temptations that are thrown at Christians today. Ask them to specify other temptations Christians face and suggest Scripture passages that could be used to defeat Satan as Christ did.

NOTES

B. Christ's Final Triumph Over Sin
Colossians 2:15

Ask: "What is the connection between Christ's defeat of Satan in the desert and His final defeat of Satan at the cross?" Satan was unable to get Jesus Christ to bypass the way to the cross. By not yielding to Satan in the wilderness temptation, Jesus went sinless to the cross carrying our sin, and so Satan's defeat was sealed.

Paul wrote his letter to the Colossians largely to combat a form of pre-Gnostic heresy that attacked the true nature and power of Christ. Consequently, when he reviewed the gospel in chapter 2, he stressed both the divinity of Christ and the redemptive work He did for us on the cross. He reminded

the Colossians that in Christ "dwelleth all the fulness of the Godhead bodily" (2:9), then focused his attention on the defeat of sin at the cross (verse 14).

It was through this redemptive act that Jesus Christ triumphed over evil principalities and powers (verse 15). These evil cohorts are Satan and the forces he commands. Christ defeated them forever, and through Christ, we also are victorious.

NOTES

2. Power Over Satan
A. Christ's Power Given To Us
Luke 10:17-19

We are given a dramatic example of victory through the power of Christ in Luke's account of the commissioning of "the seventy" in Luke 10. (Many ancient manuscripts read "the seventy-two." While the NIV follows this variant, the KJV, RSV and NASB follow the traditional "seventy." There is probably no symbolic significance to either number.) These followers of Jesus were sent two by two into the towns Jesus himself planned to visit. Their mission was to proclaim peace, heal the sick, and announce the near coming of the kingdom of God.

These 70 disciples had an exciting experience of spiritual warfare. They discovered that when they relied on the power of Christ, demonic powers had to flee. They returned full of joy, exclaiming, "Lord, even the devils are subject unto us through thy name" (verse 17). Note, however, that it was not sufficient to have the name of Jesus as a sort of magic incantation. Acts 19:13-16 records the story of some who tried to use Jesus' name in this way and failed.

Rather, it was His authority Jesus gave the Seventy when He sent them out, which allowed them to have victory over demons.

In Luke 10:18,19, Jesus explained further about the authority He had given His disciples. Although Satan's downfall is assured through Christ's own victory, the actual working out of that defeat happens through our actions. Jesus saw "Satan as lightning fall from heaven" (verse 18) because of the victories of the Seventy. He made it clear that the authority He delegated to His followers is absolute power over the enemy, Satan.

Ask: "Can you think of any other places where the Bible refers to spiritual warfare in terms of treading on or crushing a serpent?" Jesus' reference in verse 19 to treading on serpents and scorpions should remind us of God's promise to Satan in Genesis 3. While Satan might strike at the heel of "Eve's seed," ultimately that Seed, Jesus Christ, would crush Satan's head. Christ has delegated to us the power He has over Satan.

NOTES

B. Power Over Death
Luke 10:20; Hebrews 2:14,15

Jesus celebrated with the Seventy when they came back to Him full of excitement about their successes. When He said, "Do not rejoice that the spirits submit to you" (Luke 10:20, NIV), He did not mean that we should not feel good when God uses us to triumph over the power of Satan. Rather, Jesus wants believers to rejoice so much more in their salvation that the power over demons seems nothing by comparison. "Do not rejoice . . . but rather rejoice" is a typical Hebrew form of comparison, used to strengthen the second part. He is saying, in effect, "You should *really* rejoice!"

Ask: "What is the most important result of the power Christ has given us?" When Jesus pointed the Seventy away from their joy in spiritual victory, He pointed them toward the greatest power He had delegated to them: power over the fear of death—"your names are written in heaven" (verse 20). The author of the letter to the Hebrews explained that it is the fear of death that keeps us enslaved to Satan (Hebrews 2:14,15). Because of Christ's sacrifice, we now have eternal life if we will receive it from Him. We can be free of the fear of death. Satan can no longer use his main weapon—the fear of death—against us.

TEACHING TIP 3: Sometimes Christians become more concerned about the "goodies" of salvation—spiritual power, healing, miraculous gifts, prosperity, and so on—than salvation itself. Lead a discussion on the priority of these things, many of which are wonderful benefits of salvation. You might start the discussion by rereading Luke 10:17-20 and then asking, "If Jesus were addressing this to our church, what would He say?" You may want them to complete the sentence, "Rejoice not that . . ." as Jesus might complete it today. Make sure that the discussion comes back to Jesus' positive point, that we should rejoice most because our names are written in heaven.

NOTES

3. Resist The Devil

A. Be Confident In Christ
James 4:7; 1 Peter 5:8,9

Both James and 1 Peter are "general" epistles; that is, they are addressed to large numbers of Christians, not one specific church. Both letters are addressed to the "Diaspora," or believers widely dispersed through the known world. James' style reflects the tradition of wisdom literature in its pithy, practical advice. Peter's letter has in mind believers who have already endured some persecution and expect to endure more. In each letter, the message about spiritual warfare is the same: be confident in the power Christ has given you against Satan.

TEACHING TIP 4: Distribute copies of the work sheet "James 4:7; 1 Peter 5:8,9—An Inductive Study." Teaching inductively challenges your students to develop their own Bible study skills, allows them to raise the issues that are most important to them, and stimulates them out of passivity. Do not jump in with your own ideas too readily; silence can encourage students to produce more responses. When they have found as many actions and attitudes as possible, raise the questions from the third column one at a time. Students should be asked to justify their responses from the text or other appropriate Scripture.

Ask: "What do James 4:7 and 1 Peter 5:8,9 have in common?" James wrote directly and with great certainty: "Resist the devil, and he will flee from you" (James 4:7). There was absolutely no question in James' mind. If we access the power Christ has given us, Satan does not stand a chance. Peter, too, called on believers to be firm in their resistance. We can be confident that we will be victorious because Christ has already defeated Satan.

B. Resist Victoriously
James 4:7; 1 Peter 5:8,9

Ask: "In addition to confidence, what attitudes do we need to develop in order to resist Satan successfully?" First, we need an attitude of submission, accepting and following the will of God. James 4:6 gives a clue about what James meant by "submit . . . to God" in verse 7. "God resisteth the proud, but giveth grace unto the humble." Submission is the opposite of proudly insisting on our own way.

Second, we need an attitude of determination. We need to decide that we really want to resist temptation, that we will not back down. With God's help, we will not give ourselves over to despair, self-pity, complacency, or impulsive self-indulgence.

Third, we need to be alert and aware. We are completely protected from Satan's attacks because of Christ. It might be tempting, however, to pretend that those attacks will never come. Peter warned in 1 Peter 5:8 that the attacks will come, and that believers should not be caught unaware.

Fourth, we need to avoid a self-centered point of view. "You know," Peter emphasized, "that your brothers throughout the world are undergoing the same kind of sufferings" (verse 9, NIV). We do not need to dwell on the difficulty of our own struggles. We just need to get on with doing what God expects us to do.

TEACHING TIP 5: Ask the students to consider which of these attitudes they need to work on the most. What difficulties are they experiencing in resisting Satan? If your students know each other well enough to share answers to this question, permit whole-class or small-group discussion. Otherwise, distribute the work sheet "Living Victoriously—My Commitment" and allow time for reflection and commitment.

Satan is real. He hates God and everything to do with God. He hates Jesus. He tried his best to defeat Jesus, but our Lord triumphed over him. Now Satan hates us because we have Jesus in our hearts and lives. However, we are joint heirs with Christ if we have asked Him into our lives as Savior. He longs for us to triumph with Him over Satan and to lead as many others as possible to spiritual victory.

NOTES

LIFE RESPONSE

Satan is a real, powerful, and malicious being who would like to get us to exchange our eternal life for eternal death with him and his minions. He is not merely a force, a human drive, or a non-entity. On the other hand, neither is he a fearsome, omnipotent being with the power to wrest control of our lives or force us to do his bidding against our will. Though powerful, he has been defeated once and for all by Jesus Christ.

Jesus defeated Satan's attempt on His own sinlessness in personal combat in the wilderness. Jesus also defeated Satan once and for all when He took our sin, the cause of our death, to the cross. Satan will certainly attack us, but the only weapon he could have used to destroy us, the power of death, has been ripped out of his grasp.

Because of Christ's crushing defeat of Satan, we need no longer live in fear. Christ delegated His power over Satan to us when He sent us the Holy Spirit. We can go into spiritual warfare confident of victory because of the authority and power given to us by Jesus Christ.

What will you do this week with the power over Satan that Christ has given you? Will you let it slip from your mind and just go on, day to day, as though there were no warfare? Will you let yourself be a victim the next time evil knocks at your door? Or will you determine to cultivate the mind and actions that lead to victory and live victoriously in Christ?

EVANGELISM OUTREACH

The reality of evil should be obvious to everyone, including unbelievers. Help unsaved class members understand the evil they see by explaining who Satan is and why he causes evil.

As believers, we have the opportunity to witness in the power of Christ. We can testify to the victory over Satan that Christ won, historically and in our lives. Encourage students to share with others what they have learned about the nature of evil and the Christian's victory over it.

Conquering Sinful Desires

CENTRAL TRUTH

Christians have new life in Christ and need not be bound by sinful desires.

GOLDEN TEXT

Those who belong to Christ Jesus have crucified the sinful nature with its passions and desires. Galatians 5:24 (NIV)

STUDY TEXT

Romans 7:4-6; Galatians 5:16,17,24,25; Colossians 3:1-5; 1 Peter 2:11,12

OUTLINE

1. Obey The Spirit
   A. Dead To The Flesh, Alive To The Spirit
   B. Walking In The Spirit

2. Get Rid Of Sin
   A. Liberated From Sin
   B. If You're Free, Act Like It!

3. Abstain From Sinful Desires
   A. Sinful Desires Are Harmful
   B. Abstain For Our Good And God's Glory

OBJECTIVE

To recognize the need to overcome sinful desires and determine to live a Christlike life.

✓ CHECKLIST

☐ Read the corresponding study in the *Adult Student Guide* and write down discussion questions you may use in class.

☐ You might want to start this week's study with a skit based on the conversation about grace and works in "Opening Thoughts" in the student guide. Recruit two to four class members and ask them to write or ad lib a conversation similar to the one in their quarterly. Use the skit as an attention getter at the beginning of class; you might even want to make it look like a spontaneous argument in the back or middle of the classroom.

☐ To help the class focus on the material in the second and third main points of the study, build a cross from wood or Styrofoam or draw a cross on poster board. Nail, pin or tape to it the cards provided on the work sheet "Crucify The Flesh."

☐ For Teaching Tip 4, you will need blank 3 X 5 cards for each student, pencils, and extra pins or tape for the cross.

DAILY BIBLE READINGS

Monday:	Resist Temptation. Genesis 39:7-12
Tuesday:	Stand For God. Daniel 1:8-16
Wednesday:	Watch And Pray. Luke 22:39-46
Thursday:	Walk In The Light. Ephesians 5:8-14
Friday:	Keep The Faith. Colossians 1:19-23
Saturday:	Be Complete In Christ. Colossians 2:6-10

SCRIPTURE SETTING

King James Version

Romans 7:4. Wherefore, my brethren, ye also are become dead to the law by the body of Christ; that ye should be married to another, even to him who is raised from the dead, that we should bring forth fruit unto God.

5. For when we were in the flesh, the motions of sins, which were by the law, did work in our members to bring forth fruit unto death.

6. But now we are delivered from the law, that being dead wherein we were held; that we should serve in newness of spirit, and not in the oldness of the letter.

Galatians 5:16. This I say then, Walk in the Spirit, and ye shall not fulfil the lust of the flesh.

17. For the flesh lusteth against the Spirit, and the Spirit against the flesh: and these are contrary the one to the other; so that ye cannot do the things that ye would.

24. And they that are Christ's have crucified the flesh with the affections and lusts.

25. If we live in the Spirit, let us also walk in the Spirit.

Colossians 3:1. If ye then be risen with Christ, seek those things which are above, where Christ sitteth on the right hand of God.

2. Set your affection on things above, not on things on the earth.

3. For ye are dead, and your life is hid with Christ in God.

4. When Christ, who is our life, shall appear, then shall ye also appear with him in glory.

5. Mortify therefore your members which are upon the earth; fornication, uncleanness, inordinate affection, evil concupiscence, and covetousness, which is idolatry.

1 Peter 2:11. Dearly beloved, I beseech you as strangers and pilgrims, abstain from fleshly lusts, which war against the soul;

12. Having your conversation honest among the Gentiles: that, whereas they speak against you as evildoers, they may by your good works, which they shall behold, glorify God in the day of visitation.

New International Version

Romans 7:4. So, my brothers, you also died to the law through the body of Christ, that you might belong to another, to him who was raised from the dead, in order that we might bear fruit to God.

5. For when we were controlled by the sinful nature, the sinful passions aroused by the law were at work in our bodies, so that we bore fruit for death.

6. But now, by dying to what once bound us, we have been released from the law so that we serve in the new way of the Spirit, and not in the old way of the written code.

Galatians 5:16. So I say, live by the Spirit, and you will not gratify the desires of the sinful nature.

17. For the sinful nature desires what is contrary to the Spirit, and the Spirit what is contrary to the sinful nature. They are in conflict with each other, so that you do not do what you want.

24. Those who belong to Christ Jesus have crucified the sinful nature with its passions and desires.

25. Since we live by the Spirit, let us keep in step with the Spirit.

Colossians 3:1. Since, then, you have been raised with Christ, set your hearts on things above, where Christ is seated at the right hand of God.

2. Set your minds on things above, not on earthly things.

3. For you died, and your life is now hidden with Christ in God.

4. When Christ, who is your life, appears, then you also will appear with him in glory.

5. Put to death, therefore, whatever belongs to your earthly nature: sexual immorality, impurity, lust, evil desires and greed, which is idolatry.

1 Peter 2:11. Dear friends, I urge you, as aliens and strangers in the world, to abstain from sinful desires, which war against your soul.

12. Live such good lives among the pagans that, though they accuse you of doing wrong, they may see your good deeds and glorify God on the day he visits us.

What is a spiritual warrior like? He isn't a perfect person—only Jesus was sinless. On the other hand, the warrior's life should not be indistinguishable from that of an unbeliever.

As believers, God expects us to prepare for spiritual warfare, aligning our minds with His mind. This includes becoming Christlike in every area of life, overcoming the sinful desires that continue to assault us.

How can we do this? We know that merely human effort is not enough. We know that just understanding what we do is wrong is not enough. To become more Christlike, we need to give up the way of the flesh, with its sinful failures and fleshly striving, and begin following after the Spirit. The way of the Spirit is not legalism nor lawlessness. It is a way to be completely free from the bondage of sin.

BIBLE COMMENTARY

1. Obey The Spirit

A. Dead To The Flesh, Alive To The Spirit
Romans 7:4-6

In Romans 7:1-3, Paul drew an analogy between the Law's teaching concerning marriage and the Christian's relationship to Christ. According to the law, when a spouse died, the widow was no longer bound by law to her husband. She was free to belong to another. As for us, we have died to the Law and now belong to Jesus Christ. We are no longer bound by the Law as the source of our salvation. Like the widow, we are free from duty to the Law.

TEACHING TIP 1: Note that Paul's purpose in Romans 7:1-3 was not to teach about marriage or divorce. He used these features of the Law regarding marriage which serve to support his point about the Law. The comments about marriage are incidental and may be incomplete. Do not allow students to get on a tangent here about divorce and remarriage. If they are interested, after class refer them to passages which teach about marriage more directly.

Because of Christ's death, we are saved by grace and are not bound to the Law which we are unable to fulfill. This is what Paul meant when he said we are "dead to the law by the body of Christ" (Romans 7:4).

Ask: "What is wrong with the Law? Does the Law cause sin? Will being free of the Law cause us to sin more, or less? Why?" The Law does not cause sin. Rather, it is an accurate description of what it means to be a godly person. However, when we try to use the Law as a way to earn our salvation, all it does is make us conscious of how sinful we are. In this way, the Law causes us to know sin.

Freedom from the Law is not meant to be the opposite of what the Law said. Rather, it means that we are not condemned every time we fail. We are free to seek the will of God in love. In the end, we will become more godly, rather than less godly. At the same time as we die to the flesh, we are made alive to the Spirit. God's purpose in liberating us from the law is "that we should bring forth fruit unto God" (Romans 7:4) and serve God "in the new way of the Spirit" (verse 6, NIV).

determine what God really wants us to do, and put that ahead of what feels good. It truly is liberating to be able to choose God's way and not be controlled by our impulses.

NOTES

B. Walking In The Spirit
Galatians 5:16,17

Ask: "What do Romans 7:4-6 and Galatians 5:16,17 tell us about how to obey the Spirit?" From a close reading of these two passages we can glean several principles that will help us walk in the Spirit, leading to a more Christlike life.

First, there is a contrast between living in the newness of the Spirit instead of the oldness of the Law (Romans 7:4-6). Because of our new nature, our lives should produce good, godly fruit. As we walk in the Spirit, we should see the fruit of a godly character and good works. If we find ourselves trying to produce good works by a human effort, keeping a set of rules in order to prove we are Christians, we should suspect that this is the "oldness of the law." Nonetheless, if there is no change in character or works, we should ask ourselves whether we have really determined to walk in the Spirit.

Second, obeying the Spirit requires action—we are to "walk in the Spirit" (Galatians 5:16). Walking in the Spirit means having victory over sinful desires because we obey God's Word by the power of the Spirit. This will result in the fruit of the Spirit being cultivated in us.

Third, we must be wary of our emotional impulses, the self-indulgent desires that characterize our old nature. Paul wrote, "For the sinful nature desires what is contrary to the Spirit, and the Spirit what is contrary to the sinful nature. They are in conflict with each other, so that you do not do what you want" (Galatians 5:17, NIV). We need to exercise the spiritual self-discipline to

2. Get Rid Of Sin

> TEACHING TIP 2: Set up the model of the cross you prepared from the description in the Checklist. As you discuss the passages for this main point, gradually tape, pin, or nail the cards cut from the work sheet "Crucify The Flesh" to the cross. Leave the cross displayed until the end of the study, when it will be used again.

A. Liberated From Sin
Galatians 5:24,25

Since the time of Adam and Eve, no human being (except Jesus Christ) has been able to resist sinful desires. If we could, we would be able to claim salvation as a right, something earned by adherence to the Law. But because we have given in to sinful desires, Christ, in infinite love and grace, died on the cross on our behalf. He took our sin upon himself.

But to benefit from Christ's sacrifice, we have to accept His grace, and that means allowing Him to take our sin. We have to release it, let go of it, allow it to be crucified with Christ. We must give up our old nature for dead if we wish to live in the new way of the Spirit. Then it will be true, as Paul wrote, that "those who belong to Christ

Jesus have crucified the sinful nature with its passions and desires'' (Galatians 5:24, NIV). Christ has already done the work; He is willing and able to liberate us from sin.

Ask: "According to Galatians 5:24,25, what must we do to be liberated from sin? How?"

TEACHING TIP 3: Have a student read Galatians 5:24,25 to the class. Lead a brief discussion on what it means to crucify the flesh or sinful desires. Ensure that the students include the how of crucifixion in their discussion, supporting their suggestions with Scripture.

NOTES

B. If You're Free, Act Like It!
Colossians 3:1-5

Ask: "What similarities do you see between Paul's language and teaching in Galatians 5:24,25 and in Colossians 3:1-4?" Both of these passages deal with the idea that our old life or sinful nature has been crucified with Christ, and now we are resurrected with Christ into a new kind of life. The stress in Galatians 5:24,25 is on crucifying the old nature, while Colossians 3:1-4 focuses on the results of our resurrection to new life. Galatians 5:25 simply says, "If we live in the Spirit, let us also walk in the Spirit," encouraging us to take action that is consistent with what we know about our new life. Colossians 3:1-4 goes further, describing the kind of change of mind that should accompany our new life.

Paul said that since our new life is with Christ (and will reach its fulfillment when Christ returns in glory), we should set our minds on the things of God. Rather than using our minds to dwell on the things that formerly attracted us, we should use them to seek out the will of God. By so doing, we are cooperating with God in the creation of the new life He has given to us.

In Colossians 3:5, Paul turned his attention back to the old nature which is to be crucified. He listed several examples of the behaviors and attitudes that characterize the old nature. Several times in his epistles, Paul gave such lists. None of these lists are meant to be exhaustive. The phrase "such as" could easily be inserted before the list to make the passage clear.

Ask: "What do the examples Paul gave in Colossians 3:5 have in common?" Four of the five examples refer to or at least have connotations of sexual sin (however, "uncleanness," "inordinate affection," and "evil concupiscence" are not limited to sexual sin). Nothing causes us to feel more separated from God than sexual sin. Few other acts attract so much negative attention from the world as sexual sin. The last three examples all deal with attitudes that put something else ahead of God in our hearts. Putting something else ahead of God amounts to idolatry. This is exactly the opposite of what we should do with our old nature: nail it to the cross.

TEACHING TIP 4: Your class may appreciate discussion of the meanings of the words used in Colossians 3:5.
• *Fornication*—from the same Greek root as the word "pornography"; connotes any form of sexual sin.
• *Impurity*—comes from the same root as "catharsis"; refers to something that needs not just surface cleaning, but a complete purging.
• *Affection*—has to do with emotions or passions.
• *Concupiscence*— means "desire to have more"; is always used in a bad sense.

If we do not abstain from sinful desires, even if ultimately we don't carry out the sins we have thought about, the desires will still wage war against our souls. Sinful desires replace the pursuit of the will of God with thoughts that make us feel guilty and separated from God. We feel ashamed and embarrassed in the presence of God, and it is more difficult for us to accept the grace He offers us. Although our salvation is not based on what we do, or think, it is for our own spiritual good that we strive to abstain from sinful desires.

NOTES

3. Abstain From Sinful Desires

A. Sinful Desires Are Harmful
1 Peter 2:11,12

Peter reminded his readers that they are "strangers and pilgrims" in this world. In other words, this life in our fleshly bodies is only temporary. Our permanent, eternal life is elsewhere, and ultimately the things that concern us now will not matter to us then. The things that *might* take a high priority for us in this life—material comfort, the esteem of others, competition, and achievement—take a lower priority for us when we realize that they are part of a life that is passing away. As strangers and pilgrims, we should not get too attached to anything around us, or count the temporal things of this world as having any lasting importance.

Ask: "According to Peter, why should we abstain from fleshly lusts? How do fleshly lusts 'war against the soul'? " When we have an impulse or a craving to do something that is not glorifying to God, that is a "fleshly lust." It is a desire to sin. Now, we cannot stop a fleeting thought from passing through our minds. As someone said, while we cannot stop the birds from flying overhead, we can stop them from nesting in our hair. If we indulge the thought, play with it, allow it a lasting place in our minds, then we are engaging in the kind of sinful desire that will war against our souls. It is from this kind of thinking that Peter begged us to abstain.

B. Abstain For Our Good And God's Glory
1 Peter 2:11,12

When we abstain from sinful desires, we are benefiting our own souls. We are working to keep our relationship with God strong and growing. When we go farther and replace those sinful desires with an active effort to seek the will of God, we are benefiting more than our own souls. The good works that we do benefit those around us. When they realize that we are doing good because of our love for God, they will glorify God. So we have a double reason to live a Christlike life: to strengthen our relationship with God, and to give other people a reason to glorify God.

Ask: "According to 1 Peter 2:12, how should Christians relate to unbelievers?" When unbelievers make fun of Christians, or pressure us to participate in activities that are wrong, we can be tempted to keep a low profile, so that people will not speak badly of us. We say to ourselves, "Who'll know?" But Peter wrote that no matter what people say about us, if we behave as God wants us to, ultimately God will be glorified. The New American Standard Bible translates verse 12, "Keep your behavior excellent among the Gentiles." In the short term, the things people say may be unflattering, but as they consistently see us perform good works, they may be won over.

that they need to crucify, and write these down. Students can then add folded slips to the cards already fixed to the cross.

NOTES

TEACHING TIP 5: At the close of the study, return the students' attention to the cross used in the second main point. Pass out blank slips of paper to each student. As you talk about Life Response, ask them to think silently about attitudes or behaviors of the old life

---

LIFE RESPONSE

Our spiritual war is real. Satan, though already defeated by Christ, is a formidable enemy if we are not prepared for him. Satan would love to use our attachment to this world or guilt over sin to drive a wedge between us and God. To stop Satan, we must continually remember what Christ did for us: He broke the hold sin had on us, took the guilt of sin to the cross with Him, and gave us new, everlasting life. Satan has no power over us, but we need to be careful not to give him a handle he can use to enslave us again.

Spiritual warriors need to overcome sinful desires and determine to live a Christian life. The process of getting rid of sin may never be quite finished this side of heaven, but we can start right this minute. How do we start?

First, let go of sin. God has freed us from Satan's control, so we can choose not to sin. Ask God to help, and keep picturing your sinful desires as dead, crucified.

Second, abstain not only from sinful acts, but from feeding your sinful desires as well. Stop secretly playing with thoughts of sin.

Even if you do not "do" the sin, even if no one else ever knows what you are thinking, you still harm your own soul when you indulge in such thoughts.

Finally, replace sin with good works. Seek the will of God; make a wholehearted attempt to obey the Spirit, and you will live the new, Christlike life that Christ purchased for you on the cross.

EVANGELISM OUTREACH

If you regularly have a prayer time at the end of class, this would be a good week to make an appeal to the unsaved. When you discussed the Christian's freedom from the bondage of sin, unsaved students may have acutely felt their continuing bondage. They may have struggled to "be good" and failed. Remind them that Christ has already paid the price for their sin; anyone who will trust Him can be free from the bondage of sin. Make personal contact this week with any student who commits to Christ.

Spiritual Discipline

CENTRAL TRUTH

God provides the encouragement and strength Christians need for spiritual discipline.

GOLDEN TEXT

Stand firm. Let nothing move you. Always give yourselves fully to the work of the Lord, because you know that your labor in the Lord is not in vain. 1 Corinthians 15:58 (NIV)

STUDY TEXT

1 Corinthians 9:24-27; 15:57,58; 16:13; 1 Timothy 1:18,19; 6:12; 2 Timothy 2:3-5; Jude 3,20,21

OUTLINE

1. Hold On To The Faith
   A. The Fight Of Faith
   B. Built Up In The Faith

2. Exercise Self-Control
   A. Spiritual And Physical Discipline
   B. Single-Minded Self-Control

3. Stand Firm For Christ
   A. Our Discipline, God's Strength
   B. Courage To Stand Firm

OBJECTIVE

To see that a disciplined life is required for successful spiritual warfare and practice the spiritual disciplines commanded by Scripture.

✔ CHECKLIST

☐ For the study introduction (Teaching Tip 1), find a member of your church who is either a member of the military or a long-time athlete. This person should live a good example of a disciplined Christian life and be articulate enough to express the comparisons between the discipline of the military or athletics and Christianity.

☐ The tension between grace and good works may still be an issue for some of your class members this week. Review the material in study 11 so that you are prepared to deal with this. Emphasize that the spiritual discipline discussed in this week's study is not the grounds of our salvation, but a necessity for spiritual warfare.

☐ Duplicate enough copies of the work sheet "Goals for Spiritual Discipline" for each member of your class. Have enough pens on hand for students who need them.

DAILY BIBLE READINGS

Monday:	Rooted In The Word. Psalm 119:33-40
Tuesday:	Prayer And Fasting. Daniel 10:1-6,12-14
Wednesday:	Abiding In Christ. John 15:1-9
Thursday:	Sufficient Grace. 2 Corinthians 12:6-10
Friday:	Running The Race. Hebrews 12:1-6
Saturday:	Overcomer's Reward. Revelation 2:1-7

King James Version

1 Timothy 1:18. This charge I commit unto thee, son Timothy, according to the prophecies which went before on thee, that thou by them mightest war a good warfare;

19. Holding faith, and a good conscience; which some having put away, concerning faith have made shipwreck.

6:12. Fight the good fight of faith, lay hold on eternal life, whereunto thou art also called, and hast professed a good profession before many witnesses.

Jude 3. Beloved, when I gave all diligence to write unto you of the common salvation, it was needful for me to write unto you, and exhort you that ye should earnestly contend for the faith which was once delivered unto the saints.

20. But ye, beloved, building up yourselves on your most holy faith, praying in the Holy Ghost,

21. Keep yourselves in the love of God, looking for the mercy of our Lord Jesus Christ unto eternal life.

1 Corinthians 9:24. Know ye not that they which run in a race run all, but one receiveth the prize? So run, that ye may obtain.

25. And every man that striveth for the mastery is temperate in all things. Now they do it to obtain a corruptible crown; but we an incorruptible.

26. I therefore so run, not as uncertainly; so fight I, not as one that beateth the air:

27. But I keep under my body, and bring it into subjection: lest that by any means, when I have preached to others, I myself should be a castaway.

2 Timothy 2:3. Thou therefore endure hardness, as a good soldier of Jesus Christ.

4. No man that warreth entangleth himself with the affairs of this life; that he may please him who hath chosen him to be a soldier.

5. And if a man also strive for masteries, yet is he not crowned, except he strive lawfully.

1 Corinthians 15:57. But thanks be to God, which giveth us the victory through our Lord Jesus Christ.

58. Therefore, my beloved brethren, be ye steadfast, unmovable, always abounding in the work of the Lord, forasmuch as ye know that your labor is not in vain in the Lord.

16:13. Watch ye, stand fast in the faith, quit you like men, be strong.

New International Version

1 Timothy 1:18. Timothy, my son, I give you this instruction in keeping with the prophecies once made about you, so that by following them you may fight the good fight,

19. Holding on to faith and a good conscience. Some have rejected these and so have shipwrecked their faith.

6:12. Fight the good fight of the faith. Take hold of the eternal life to which you were called when you made your good confession in the presence of many witnesses.

Jude 3. Dear friends, although I was very eager to write to you about the salvation we share, I felt I had to write and urge you to contend for the faith that was once for all entrusted to the saints.

20. But you, dear friends, build yourselves up in your most holy faith and pray in the Holy Spirit.

21. Keep yourselves in God's love as you wait for the mercy of our Lord Jesus Christ to bring you to eternal life.

1 Corinthians 9:24. Do you not know that in a race all the runners run, but only one gets the prize? Run in such a way as to get the prize.

25. Everyone who competes in the games goes into strict training. They do it to get a crown that will not last; but we do it to get a crown that will last forever.

26. Therefore I do not run like a man running aimlessly; I do not fight like a man beating the air.

27. No, I beat my body and make it my slave so that after I have preached to others, I myself will not be disqualified for the prize.

2 Timothy 2:3. Endure hardship with us like a good soldier of Christ Jesus.

4. No one serving as a soldier gets involved in civilian affairs—he wants to please his commanding officer.

5. Similarly, if anyone competes as an athlete, he does not receive the victor's crown unless he competes according to the rules.

1 Corinthians 15:57. But thanks be to God! He gives us the victory through our Lord Jesus Christ.

58. Therefore, my dear brothers, stand firm. Let nothing move you. Always give yourselves fully to the work of the Lord, because you know that your labor in the Lord is not in vain.

16:13. Be on your guard; stand firm in the faith; be men of courage; be strong.

Occasionally we read articles in Christian magazines that make it sound like the Christian life is akin to floating on pink clouds of love and comfort. Surrounded by God's unconditional grace and unconditional love, we pass our lives in a bubble of bliss.

Pop! Paul and Jude are going to burst that bubble in today's study. We are saved by God's unconditional grace, but we still have to face a world of fierce and deadly spiritual warfare.

Any soldier who would try to go into war with no discipline and no training would quickly find himself bruised and bloodied, if not broken. Spiritual warfare is no different. Training and discipline are indispensable for the Christian! The time has come to prepare for spiritual warfare with spiritual discipline.

BIBLE COMMENTARY

1. Hold On To The Faith

A. The Fight Of Faith
1 Timothy 1:18,19; 6:12; Jude 3

TEACHING TIP 1: Start today's session by interviewing an experienced member of the military or an athlete from your congregation. Ask your guest questions about the training necessary for his work or sport, hardships he endured, and the rewards. Ask: "What would happen if you allowed your daily discipline to lapse for a while?" Then ask him about his relationship with Christ and the development of spiritual discipline. If time permits, you may allow class members to ask questions also.

First Timothy 1:18,19 is part of the introduction to this Pauline letter. This letter was written around A.D. 63 from Macedonia, to Timothy, who was in Ephesus.

Ask: "What was Paul's purpose in writing to Timothy?" First, this letter was written to guide and encourage Timothy in the management of a church under attack by heretical teachers. Secondly, prophecies had been given to Timothy, possibly at the time of his ordination (4:14). But in order to fulfill these prophecies, Timothy needed encouragement. Paul's letter gave Timothy the encouragement he needed to carry on spiritual warfare in fulfillment of these prophecies. In 1:18, Paul was literally saying that "by means of" or "in the strength of" these prophecies Timothy was to fight the good fight. This fight was probably to be waged against false teachers threatening the church at Ephesus.

Paul also encouraged Timothy to hold on to his faith and a "good conscience" (verse 19). Some had not done so, and instead of fighting the good fight, had actually "shipwrecked" (made ruin of) their faith.

Fighting the "good fight of faith" has two aspects (6:12). There is the life here and now, which we were living when we made our "good confession," that is, our initial confession of faith. It is in this life that we wage this warfare.

Secondly, our spiritual warfare will result in eternal life. As we are victorious in this fight, we too will take hold of this eternal life to which we have been called.

Ask: "What does Jude 3 tell us about contending for the faith?" In verse 3, Jude used the word "faith" as synonymous with the gospel. In this context, the faith is what God has revealed about how His love and grace have been extended to us. Jude was concerned with keeping the faith pure because the churches to which he wrote were being invaded by heresy. Jude said, "I felt I had to write and urge you to contend for the faith that was once for all entrusted to the saints" (verse 3, NIV). The faith is something to be contended or fought for.

It is important to contend for the truth of God's Word. The truths of the gospel cannot be negotiated. Doctrinal error begins when God's truth is discarded for the philosophy of man.

Ask: "How can we contend for the Word of God?"

TEACHING TIP 2: Brainstorm with the students for ways in which they can contend for the faith as revealed in God's Word. Their discussion should include the various situations in which they would commonly find themselves, such as work, home, shopping, and vacations. Although such issues as abortion and euthanasia are areas in which Christians need to make themselves heard, the idea behind this discussion is to get the students to recognize how every area of their lives will be involved in contending for the faith in some way.

NOTES

B. Built Up In The Faith
Jude 20,21

In Jude's letter he addressed his attention to the behaviors and attitudes we must cultivate in order to hold on to the true gospel.

Ask: "What behaviors and attitudes are we urged to cultivate in Jude 20 and 21?" First Jude said, "Build yourselves up in your most holy faith" (Jude 20, NIV). Remember that Jude previously used *faith* as synonymous with *gospel*. This suggests that the means to building ourselves up in faith involves mental effort. Verse 20 encourages us to study that we may be stronger in our understanding of the gospel.

Then Jude advised his readers to pray in the Holy Spirit. Ask: "How can Christians pray in the Holy Spirit?"

TEACHING TIP 3: You may wish to take a few moments and explore the different ways to pray in the Spirit. Use the following verses to guide the discussion: Jude 20,21; 1 Corinthians 14:4,12-15; 1 John 5:14,15.

When we pray in the Spirit, we are built up. As we pray, we are to seek the Spirit's will and pray in agreement with the Spirit. We will be prepared for spiritual warfare when we are filled with the Spirit and fighting in the way the Spirit directs.

Finally in Jude 21, we are told to keep ourselves in God's love. This is a lifelong process. Jude's exhortation is that we continue until God's love and grace culminate in our eternal life.

NOTES

2. Exercise Self-Control

A. Spiritual And Physical Discipline
1 Corinthians 9:24-27

Chapters 7 through 14 of 1 Corinthians are apparently Paul's answer to a letter the Corinthians had sent him in which they had asked him several questions about Christian practices. First Corinthians 8:1 indicates that they had asked him whether it was permissible to eat meat that had been offered to idols. Rather than give a simple answer, Paul spent chapters 8 through 10 discussing the basis for placing self-imposed limits on the believer's liberty in Christ.

While we are no longer under the Law and thus free, it is sometimes better for us and for the advancement of the gospel if we choose to limit our liberty. In 1 Corinthians 9:24-27, Paul used the analogy of an athlete to show why believers need to be self-disciplined. An athlete can refrain from training or run lackadaisically if he wants, but what would be the point? An athlete with the goal of winning will be self-disciplined, and so too should the Christian with the goal of spiritual victory.

Ask: "What physical activities would have an impact on one's spiritual condition? How could physical self-discipline help with spiritual warfare?"

TEACHING TIP 4: Divide the class into buzz groups to discuss these questions for a few minutes. Then have the groups share the results of their discussion. Encourage the class to think beyond the traditional forms of intemperance (such as smoking and drinking) to include other forms of excessive or impulsive behavior that distract believers from their true goals.

What we do with our bodies does make a difference in our spiritual lives. If an activity makes us feel guilty, that guilt causes us to feel separated from God. If an activity dulls our minds and senses or damages our bodies, we will not have the capacity to do the work God gives us. If an activity takes all our time and attention, it will squeeze God out of our lives. Controlling ourselves physically is part of spiritual discipline.

NOTES

B. Single-Minded Self-Control
2 Timothy 2:3-5

The first half of chapter 2 of Paul's second letter to Timothy is a charge to Timothy to be strong, to continue in the work of Christ no matter what hardship he must endure. Like a soldier or an athlete, Timothy had to keep his eyes on the goal and not be deterred by any difficulties along the way.

The word translated "endure hardness" in 2 Timothy 2:3 is a unique one in the New Testament, occurring only in this book. Paul specifically chose a word that means suffering hardship with others, not suffering alone. He is emphasizing that the discipline required of Timothy (and of us) is not a solitary endeavor; we are not alone in hardship. All Christians have in common this experience of suffering. We can take courage from our unity with the rest of the body of Christ in the midst of hardship.

Ask: "Paul used two analogies in 2 Timothy 2:4,5 to explain the discipline required of Christians. What characteristics do they have in common?"

TEACHING TIP 5: Allow time for students to identify the two analogies. Then, have the students make suggestions as to common characteristics. Allow the list to grow until it includes self-discipline, desire to win, and single-minded focus (or similar ideas).

Neither a soldier nor an athlete in training can afford to let his life be filled with distractions. Just so, we need to be focused, single-minded in the pursuit of our goal. We must single-mindedly exercise the discipline to keep God first in our lives in order to be effective spiritual warriors.

NOTES

3. Stand Firm for Christ

A. Our Discipline, God's Strength
1 Corinthians 15:57,58

As Paul neared the end of his first letter to the Corinthians, he turned from answering the Corinthians' questions about practical matters to reminding and reassuring them of the ultimate truths of the faith: Christ's sacrificial death and resurrection and our eventual resurrection to eternal life. Knowing that our eternal life is assured through Christ's death liberates us from guilt over our inadequacies. It is God's strength and grace that will give us victory.

God expects us to live a disciplined life. Living in a self-controlled way prepares us for spiritual conflict. An unprepared warrior is likely to be taken off guard and defeated. But, as Paul said, "Thanks be to God, which giveth us the victory through our Lord Jesus Christ" (1 Corinthians 15:57). We need to build our spiritual strength like an athlete who exercises every day. We need to use our strength when our self-control is challenged. But it is God's strength that will give us victory. We can rely on Him.

Ask: "How can Paul command weak, fallible human beings to be 'steadfast, unmovable' (verse 58)? Does God really expect us to be that strong?" Notice that verses 57 and 58 are connected by the word "therefore." That means the victory God gives us through Jesus Christ is the cause or source of our ability to do the things commanded in verse 58. Because God gives us strength, we are able to be "steadfast, unmovable, always abounding in the work of the Lord" (verse 58). Because our victory does not rest on our own strength, we can be productive in the Lord's work.

NOTES

B. Courage To Stand Firm
1 Corinthians 16:13

Paul's closing exhortations to the Corinthians (16:13) echo what he told them at the end of chapter 15, with a slight difference. In both passages Paul reminded the Corinthians to "stand firm" or to "be steadfast." But verse 58 emphasizes that standing firm in the faith implies productivity for God. The stress is on the work we will be able to do for God if we are steadfast. On the other hand, 16:13 puts the stress on the courage and strength we need in order to be steadfast.

Ask: "According to 1 Corinthians 16:13, how should we live a disciplined Christian life?" Paul's admonition in this verse is fourfold:
1. "watch ye" or be alert;
2. "stand fast [or firm] in the faith;"
3. "quit you like men," or be courageous;
4. "be strong."

First, like a soldier on watch, we must be alert to be effective. This is one aim of the discipline we impose on ourselves: the elimination of distractions that could draw us away from the work of God. The other three admonitions—stand firm in the faith, be courageous, be strong—all show us that effort is required. We must have the courage to hold on, to be disciplined, to be single-minded in our pursuit of God's will. It takes both God's strength and our will and self-control to stand firm for Christ.

TEACHING TIP 6: For the closing activity, distribute the work sheet "Goals For Spiritual Discipline" to each class member. Explain that goals and action steps should be practical and concrete. For example, a goal for active faith might be "Five hours of service weekly for a Christian agency." The action plan might be "Make five phone calls this week to locate agency." Circulate through the class, helping students complete their plans.

NOTES

LIFE RESPONSE

A popular slogan among exercise buffs is "Just Do It." It is a phrase that cuts through all our excuses, defenses, and insecurities. It is what Paul and Jude would say to us today: "You're afraid to try? You think you'll fail? You have habits you think you can't overcome? You have too many other things to do? Stop procrastinating; just do it. Be strong; be self-controlled; hold on to the faith."

"But," we say, "I really can't. I've tried to overcome this habit and I've tried to be self-controlled, but I am not strong enough." This excuse is deceptive, for it is actually true. We do not have the willpower to live a completely consistent, godly life. But the excuse is deceptive because it is irrelevant. The strength and encouragement we need to live a disciplined life come from God. What we have to do is have the courage to begin. We must set out on the road to that godly, disciplined life in the confidence that God will sustain us and give us success.

Do you want to live a disciplined life? Then stop theorizing, intellectualizing, procrastinating, and debating. You probably know what area of your life needs more discipline; if not, ask God, and listen to His answer. Begin by making a plan; write it down. List the area that needs discipline, and next to it write a step-by-step plan on what to do. Then follow it. Have the courage to be "steadfast, unmovable, always abounding in the work of the Lord" (1 Corinthians 15:58).

EVANGELISM OUTREACH

One of the greatest criticisms of the Church today is that Christ's followers are often inconsistent and hypocritical. Too many of us preach about a life we do not live. A Christian who admits his inadequacies but puts an all-out effort into living a disciplined life will not be criticized as hypocritical. A disciplined Christian life makes others want to know more about the Lord. Show your students that such a life is not only for their own benefit, but for the benefit of those who need Christ. ▱

Victory Over The World

CENTRAL TRUTH

Victory over the world comes through faith in Christ.

GOLDEN TEXT

The world and its desires pass away, but the man who does the will of God lives forever. 1 John 2:17 (NIV)

STUDY TEXT

John 15:18-21; 16:33; 17:14,18; James 4:4; 1 John 2:15-17; 5:3-5

OUTLINE

1. Opposed By The World
   A. Not Of The World
   B. Sent Into The World

2. Love Not The World
   A. God Or The World—
      Not Both
   B. The World Will Pass Away

3. Overcome The World
   A. Victory Through Christ
   B. Faith Overcomes The
      World

OBJECTIVE

To understand that Christians can live victoriously in this evil world and strive faithfully to represent Christ.

CHECKLIST

☐ Read the *Adult Student Guide* and write down any questions that you may want to discuss during class.

☐ For the first teaching tip it will help to have a concordance and at least two study Bibles for each group of three to five students in your class. Ask class members the week before to bring any they own, in addition to what you can supply.

☐ For Teaching Tip 3, duplicate copies of the work sheet "Outline Of 1 John 5:3-5" for each student. If you wish to use this outline for a whole class discussion, copy the work sheet onto a transparency instead.

☐ Fill out the "Planning The Session" sheet from the teaching helps packet to help ensure that you cover all of the material that you studied in preparation for the teaching session. Remember to remain flexible if the class seems to flow in a slightly different direction than planned. Let the Holy Spirit guide you.

DAILY BIBLE READINGS

Monday:	Be Confident. Psalm 27:1-6
Tuesday:	Be Strengthened. Isaiah 40:28-31
Wednesday:	Be Transformed. 2 Corinthians 3:12-18
Thursday:	Be Prayerful. 1 Thessalonians 5:17-25
Friday:	Be Godly. Titus 2:11-15
Saturday:	Be Faithful. Hebrews 10:35-39

SCRIPTURE SETTING

King James Version

John 15:18. If the world hate you, ye know that it hated me before it hated you.

19. If ye were of the world, the world would love his own; but because ye are not of the world, but I have chosen you out of the world, therefore the world hateth you.

20. Remember the word that I said unto you, The servant is not greater than his lord. If they have persecuted me, they will also persecute you; if they have kept my saying, they will keep yours also.

21. But all these things will they do unto you for my name's sake, because they know not him that sent me.

17:14. I have given them thy word; and the world hath hated them, because they are not of the world, even as I am not of the world.

18. As thou hast sent me into the world, even so have I also sent them into the world.

James 4:4. Ye adulterers and adulteresses, know ye not that the friendship of the world is enmity with God? whosoever therefore will be a friend of the world is the enemy of God.

1 John 2:15. Love not the world, neither the things that are in the world. If any man love the world, the love of the Father is not in him.

16. For all that is in the world, the lust of the flesh, and the lust of the eyes, and the pride of life, is not of the Father, but is of the world.

17. And the world passeth away, and the lust thereof: but he that doeth the will of God abideth for ever.

John 16:33. These things I have spoken unto you, that in me ye might have peace. In the world ye shall have tribulation: but be of good cheer; I have overcome the world.

1 John 5:3. For this is the love of God, that we keep his commandments: and his commandments are not grievous.

4. For whatsoever is born of God overcometh the world: and this is the victory that overcometh the world, even our faith.

5. Who is he that overcometh the world, but he that believeth that Jesus is the Son of God?

New International Version

John 15:18. If the world hates you, keep in mind that it hated me first.

19. If you belonged to the world, it would love you as its own. As it is, you do not belong to the world, but I have chosen you out of the world. That is why the world hates you.

20. Remember the words I spoke to you: 'No servant is greater than his master.' If they persecuted me, they will persecute you also. If they obeyed my teaching, they will obey yours also.

21. They will treat you this way because of my name, for they do not know the One who sent me.

17:14. I have given them your word and the world has hated them, for they are not of the world any more than I am of the world.

18. As you sent me into the world, I have sent them into the world.

James 4:4. You adulterous people, don't you know that friendship with the world is hatred toward God? Anyone who chooses to be a friend of the world becomes an enemy of God.

1 John 2:15. Do not love the world or anything in the world. If anyone loves the world, the love of the Father is not in him.

16. For everything in the world—the cravings of sinful man, the lust of his eyes and the boasting of what he has and does—comes not from the Father but from the world.

17. The world and its desires pass away, but the man who does the will of God lives forever.

John 16:33. I have told you these things, so that in me you may have peace. In this world you will have trouble. But take heart! I have overcome the world.

1 John 5:3. This is love for God: to obey his commands. And his commands are not burdensome,

4. For everyone born of God overcomes the world. This is the victory that has overcome the world, even our faith.

5. Who is it that overcomes the world? Only he who believes that Jesus is the Son of God.

In this unit, we have considered several aspects of preparation for spiritual warfare. We have seen that Satan, our foe, has been defeated. We have learned what armor the Lord has provided for warfare and how to put it on. We have discussed the mental, physical, and spiritual basic training we need before we go to battle. In today's study, we will see the point of all this preparation: victory over the world.

As Christians, we are engaged in a real war. And like any war, it has its moments of darkness, times when we will feel utterly surrounded by evil, cut off from our home base. It is a long war, one in which we spend our entire lives fighting behind enemy lines. We need to know that however dark the nights, however hard the trials, we can live victoriously over the world, the flesh, and the devil. Today's study tells us how.

BIBLE COMMENTARY

1. Opposed By The World

A. Not Of The World
John 15:18-21

Ask: "While Jesus was on earth, how did the people who heard Him respond to Him? Was rejection a frequent experience for Him or a rare one?"

TEACHING TIP 1: To answer the question above, divide the class into groups of three to five. Make sure each group has several Bibles and a concordance. Assign each group one gospel and ask them to skim it, making note of people's responses to Jesus, both positive and negative. In each group, one member should serve as recorder while the other members divide up responsibility for skimming the book. After about 5 minutes, ask each recorder to summarize his or her group's findings. Don't worry if the groups do not have time to finish skimming the Gospels. Five minutes will be enough to get a sample of the ways people responded to Christ.

In John 14 through 17, John reported some of the most moving and personal words of Christ we find anywhere in the New Testament. The setting is the Last Supper, and it is Jesus' last chance to talk heart-to-heart with His disciples before He (and they) must endure the trial of His death. He spoke eloquently to them of His love for them, the love the Father has for them, and the love they should share with one another (15:9-17). Then, in sharp contrast, He spoke of the hatred the world has for Him and for His followers.

The world hated and rejected Jesus because He was so different from it. Jesus was the very embodiment of the love of God the Father. The world, under the dominion of Satan, is godless by choice.

Jesus told the disciples about the world's hatred for Him in order to warn them about what they would experience (verse 18). Any follower of Christ is certain to experience the hatred of the world, because the world hates Christ himself.

Ask: "Some unbelievers are people with good moral values, people we respect. How should we expect such people to respond to Christians?" When Christ chose us, He chose us "out of the world" (verse 19). We are not just followers of one

*different from Word used
hate father + mother
(willing to forsake)

of the world's many religions and philosophies. We are not of the world. This means we do not share the world's nature, its values, or its goals. We are in opposition to the world. So it is inevitable that the world, meaning all who have rejected God's grace, will oppose us. Of course, just as some formerly worldly people heard Christ and responded to His message, some will hear and respond to us also (verse 20).

Ask: "How did Jesus expect His followers to respond when the world persecuted them?" In verse 21, Jesus reminded His disciples that those who persecute them are really not reacting to them personally but to Him. We should not be surprised, even when good, upright people of the world reject us, because Jesus has told us to expect it. Furthermore, we should not "take it personally," feeling singled out or picked on when we encounter rejection, because we are not being rejected. By rejecting us, the world simply proves that it does not know God. We cannot expect the world to treat us any better than it treats our Lord.

NOTES

B. Sent Into The World
John 17:14,18

Just before Jesus went out to the Garden where He would be betrayed and arrested, He prayed for His disciples. This is the prayer known as Jesus' high priestly prayer. Jesus committed himself and His followers into the hands of the Father. This is, in a sense, the moment at which Jesus "passed the torch" to His disciples, leaving them to complete the ministry which He began.

Jesus said again that the world would hate the disciples because they no longer belonged to the world. But here He showed another reason why the world would hate

the disciples. Jesus was sending the disciples into the world for the purpose of bringing God's Word to it. Just as He confronted the world with its failings, so too would the disciples confront the world with the evidence of its sin. Consequently, the world would not ignore the disciples; it would either accept or reject them and their message.

So the world hates us for two reasons. First, it hates us because we have been chosen out of the world, made separate and distinct from it. But second, it hates us because we have been sent back into the world to illuminate the distinction between the people of God and people without God.

NOTES

2. Love Not The World

A. God Or The World—Not Both
James 4:4

The first half of James 4 is addressed to people who, though Christians, are still trying to keep their worldly values and way of life. You might think of them as people who have enlisted in an army but not undergone basic training—they belong to God, but they are not looking or acting like His soldiers yet. James used a strong, ugly word for these people: adulteresses. This term indicates spiritual unfaithfulness. New Testament believers are considered the bride of Christ (Ephesians 5:32,33). Such people have committed themselves to God, but are still trying to maintain alliances (or affairs) with the world.

This helps us understand what James meant when he wrote, "You adulterous people, don't you know that friendship with the world is hatred toward God?" (James 4:4, NIV). James was not referring to friendships between Christians and unbelievers. Nor was he saying we should not

Christ Does Not have a Hard Bride

have compassion for the lost or try to bring the love of God to the world. Rather, he was talking about adopting worldly values which amounts to being adulterous toward God. If you make yourself one with the world, if you strive to be like it, or develop your character with worldly values, then you are opposed to God. One is either opposed to the world or to God. We choose— one or the other, not both.

This is also the point in 1 John 2:15. John frequently thought and wrote in terms of contrasts and opposites. His contrast of love of the world against love of the Father is one of eight such passages in this short letter. Just a few verses back, he contrasted light and darkness; the contrast between love of the world and love of the Father is meant to be just as dramatic.

John wrote, "Love not the world, neither the things that are in the world" (verse 15). But this is the same John who quoted Jesus saying that "God so loved the world" (John 3:16). Like James, John did not mean we should not have compassion for the world. Rather, we are not to love it in the sense of being attached to it, wrapped up in it. The world is opposed to God; if we love the world and want to be part of it, then we do not love God.

NOTES

phrasing in order to find the answer to this question. Ask the students to paraphrase 1 John 2:15-17 on paper. Tell them to rewrite it as though they were explaining it to a child. Have volunteers read their paraphrases and answer the question based on their reading of the text.

John listed three characteristics of the love of the world: "All that is in the world, the lust of the flesh, and the lust of the eyes, and the pride of life, is not of the Father, but is of the world" (1 John 2:16). Lust of the flesh ("the cravings of sinful man," NIV) refers to the impulses to sin which we allow to take residence inside us. Lust of the eyes is essentially greed. It is gazing at material things or the attractions of a worldly life-style and longing for them. Even if we do not start working to acquire those attractions, we indulge lust of the eyes if we let that longing become an important part of our thought-life. Pride of life is putting a high value on the things we have been able to do or acquire, a self-centered way of viewing the world. Loving the Father requires that we have His values and priorities, which are opposed to the lustful, prideful values of the world.

Do you feel a sting of regret when you contemplate giving up your longing for the things of the world? John has an answer: all this stuff is dust and not worthy of our love. "The world and its desires pass away, but the man who does the will of God lives forever" (1 John 2:17, NIV).

NOTES

B. The World Will Pass Away
1 John 2:15-17

Ask: "What are the characteristics of someone who loves the world?"

TEACHING TIP 2: Have students practice the Bible study skill of para-

3. Overcome The World

A. Victory Through Christ
John 16:33

Christ's conversation with His disciples at the Last Supper contained warnings of difficulties to come. Jesus' last words to them before His high priestly prayer acknowledged this: "These things I have spoken unto you, that in me ye might have peace. In the world ye shall have tribulation: but be of good cheer; I have overcome the world" (John 16:33). Although they would definitely suffer from the opposition of the world, the disciples did not need to be sorrowful, fearful, or full of self-pity. They could be at peace, because Jesus had assured them that the ultimate victory in the conflict with the world would be theirs.

Ask: "According to Jesus, why is it possible for the disciples to have peace and good cheer despite tribulation?" Note that the source of the disciples' peace is Christ. They can be at peace in tribulation because He has overcome the world. Our victory comes directly from Christ's victory, not from our own ability or effort. Therefore, there is no chance that we will fail to overcome the world if we trust Christ. Our victory is assured; Christ has overcome the world already.

NOTES

B. Faith Overcomes The World
1 John 5:3-5

TEACHING TIP 3: The work sheet "Outline Of 1 John 5:3-5" is a study of the structure of these three verses. Using it will encourage your students to do closely detailed Bible study. Distribute copies to the students to complete before you continue the study.

In 1 John 2 we learned that the opposite of the love of the world was the love of God. When we choose to enter Christ's army, we are to transfer our love and concern from the ways of the world to the ways of God.

Ask: "How do we know we are loving God in the way that John intended?" John defined love for God: "This is love for God: to obey his commands" (1 John 5:3, NIV). Loving God means we search for what He wants us to do, through reading His Word and through prayer. Then when we know what He wants, we do it. As John said, this is not a burden. We obey God because we love Him. And, since He loves us too, obedience leads to good for us. Loving God allows us to participate in Christ's victory over the world.

Three times in 1 John 5:4,5 John answered the question, "Who will overcome the world?" Ask: "What are John's three answers to the question 'Who will overcome the world'?" First, John said that "everyone born of God overcomes the world" (verse 4, NIV). Here he used the language reminiscent of the words of Jesus in John 3, when He spoke about being born again and being born of the Spirit. The one who will overcome the world is the one who, in a sense, has turned his back on his earthly life to begin a whole new life.

John's second answer to the question, "Who will overcome the world?" is: we will, by our faith. By faith and trust, we identify ourselves with Jesus Christ and His victory. Faith is relying on Jesus instead of our own efforts to reconcile us with God; faith is doing what God wants us to do in the certainty that Jesus has reconciled us. We are saved by faith in Jesus Christ, and this faith gives us victory over the world.

Finally, John put his answer in the clearest possible terms: "Who is it that overcomes the world? Only he who believes that Jesus is the Son of God" (1 John 5:5, NIV). If you believe that Jesus is the Son of God, sent by God to die for our sins and reconcile us; if you know that you need Jesus to reconcile you to God; if you have accepted His offer of redemption; and if you are now living the life of one in love with God instead of the world; then you are the one that overcomes the world. Victory in spiritual warfare is yours through faith in Christ.

TEACHING TIP 4: Tie together the five studies in this unit by giving the "Unit Review" test from the teaching helps packet.

NOTES

LIFE RESPONSE

We can live behind enemy lines and not be defeated. We can live victoriously in an evil, opposing world. By withstanding the world's opposition and achieving victory over it, Jesus Christ has given us the ability to be victorious, too. It is in our hands to take hold of the victory Christ has already given to us.

We are in a war. Would you expect your enemy to treat you well? The world is the enemy in our spiritual war, and it will certainly oppose us, just as it opposed Christ before us. Accept the fact; do not be surprised or disheartened when you encounter opposition. See it as evidence that you are on the right side. As Jesus said, "If you belonged to the world, it would love you as its own. As it is . . . the world hates you" (John 15:19, NIV).

Do not fall into the trap of getting too attached to the world, like a prisoner who joins forces with his captors. You are not a prisoner of the world; Jesus has given you victory over it. Do not surrender that victory by getting attached to the things the world has to offer you. All the material posses-sions and fleshly pleasures are like dust. Even now, they are meaningless, decaying away. The victory that Christ has given you lasts forever.

Do not love the world; love God. And how can you love God? The answer is simple: obey His commands. Find His will for you and do it. Then you will find that victory through Christ really is yours.

EVANGELISM OUTREACH

To call unsaved class members to a relationship with Jesus, return to 1 John 5:4,5. Those who believe Jesus Christ is the Son of God and put faith in Him will have victory over the world. Ask students to consider their struggles with sin, failed attempts to overcome habits that imprison them, a perpetual sense of guilt or inadequacy, or the feeling of being alone in the world. Tell them that Jesus is on their side, and explain the way of salvation, offering to pray with any who are interested.   ⌐⌐

UNIT 1

INTRODUCTION

MOSAIC LAW AND NEW TESTAMENT COUNTERPART

When we compare the biblical records of God's law and His grace, we may think they have little or nothing in common. The Old Testament system of seasonal religious ceremonies and daily personal observance was minute in detail and, as Paul repeatedly explained in his epistles, impossible to keep perfectly. The full expression of God's grace through Christ, however, offered an open invitation to full communion through faith between those once bound by sin and a holy Heavenly Father.

In reality, Mosaic law was never divorced from God's grace. God gave His laws to His people to teach them His requirements for holy living. Even though they were unable to perfectly keep those laws, they could put their faith in God and count on His mercy. When Christ came, He personally fulfilled the requirements of the Law in His perfect life, and satisfied the Law on behalf of all sinners everywhere through His sacrificial death and resurrection.

The studies in this unit examine different facets of God's plan for salvation, illustrating its expression under Mosaic law and through Christ's ministry. "Saved By The Blood" (study 1) will show how Old Testament blood sacrifices pointed ahead to Christ's perfect sacrifice. "Living By God's Commandments" (study 2) connects the specific commands of the Law with the overarching call of Christ to love God and others. The third study, "Called To A Priestly Ministry," highlights the common priesthood of all believers under Christ. After the Christmas study, study 5 looks more closely at "Jesus Christ, Our Mediator," again showing the strong connection between the Israelites' sacrifices and Christ's death. "Living A Pure Life" (study 6) sheds light on the foundational principles of righteousness behind the requirements of the Law. Finally, "Christ And The Law" and "Contrasting Law And Grace" each give attention to the full manifestation of God's grace in the New Testament era.

TEACHER GROWTH SERIES

REAL PEOPLE NEEDS

By Terry L. Terrell

So you have a class of adults! Possibly your church does not have sufficient teachers, facilities, or number of adults to place them in separate classes. What do you do?

Don't do what is done too often: "Good morning, class. Today our study text is Joshua 6,7. What did Israel do as they advanced in Canaan?"

If a teacher presents a study this way, class members' thoughts will probably range far afield. A middle-aged couple may be worrying about their son who didn't come home until 3 a.m. A widow can't get over the loss of her husband. A young single girl is leaving for college and wonders how she'll make it financially away from home. An older man wonders why God hasn't healed him so he won't need cancer surgery.

The teacher must meet the real needs of real people. He is not to be just a lecturer who stands before his class and spouts biblical facts like a fountain. Like Christ, the teacher must reach out to people, help them when he can, and direct them to God and the Word for help when he doesn't have the answers.

So what do you do in class to meet the needs of those lost in their own thoughts? First, make your studies relevant. Even though you are teaching, for example, from the Book of Joshua, remember that Joshua was human and had times of success and failure as we all do. How did he respond to the unpredictable changes of life? Make him relevant to your class members.

Then, encourage classroom sharing. Incidents that occurred in one person's life and were successfully (or sometimes unsuccessfully) dealt with can be of help to others when shared with them. This kind of interacting doesn't happen by accident. You must be sensitive to the needs and hurts of your class and encourage discussion in specific areas as the Holy Spirit directs you.

Next, urge the people to pray for one another—in the classroom and outside the class in private or group settings. It is appropriate in the classroom for members to share problems relating to the study and then to "bear one another's burdens" in prayer.

People experiencing problems need help and fellowship, so you should provide opportunities for both. Studies from books with such widely varied messages as Joshua, Ezra, Acts, and others often show people helping one another. As they did, they grew spiritually, emotionally, and even socially. Part of the teacher's responsibility is to encourage the same kind of growth by providing opportunities for class members to help one another.

Naturally related to this is the teacher's responsibility to provide fellowship opportunities for class members. If you have a class with a wide age range, don't always combine all age groups—and don't always segregate all age groups when planning socials. Young marrieds need to be with other young marrieds, but at times they will benefit by being with more mature couples. The latter may even serve as exemplary role models for young marrieds.

Recognize the special needs of your class members. Ask the introverted young single male who loves to fish to share his thoughts on being a "fisher of men." This may help him feel he is a real part of the class. And others will get to know him better.

A couple whose children have all left home may enjoy sharing some thoughts on committing our children to the Lord. This will be appreciated not only by other older parents, but also those with young children.

The man entering the hospital for cancer surgery may be helped by hearing others share their experiences during sickness: how they were strengthened through the trial and the opportunities it gave them to witness for Christ.

Most of all, teacher, your class will learn from you. If you read the Word, it is more likely they will. If you pray, their desire to pray will be strengthened. You are the key.

"Teacher Growth Series" brings you information on every phase of your teaching ministry. Three articles per quarter can be read, shared with other teachers, and filed for future reference. Articles dealing with the same topics are presented at each age level from early childhood through adult. The "Teacher Growth Series" covers 36 different topics.

INVOLVEMENT IS THE KEY

By David Reddout

Radiant Life adult curriculum provides a variety of tools and resources designed to involve students in the learning experience.

Among these resources is the *Adult Student Guide*. This 64-page study guide is closely correlated with the content of the *Adult Teacher Guide*. It is recommended that both teacher and students be completely familiar with the content of the student quarterly.

The *Adult Student Guide* format contains important features such as the Central Truth, Golden Text, and Scripture Setting as printed in the *Adult Teacher Guide*. A brief introduction provides a lead-in to the Bible study.

Commentary & Application comprises the greater portion of the *Adult Student Guide* format. It is written to correspond with the major outline headings in the *Adult Teacher Guide*.

When teaching the Bible study, you may want to refer to statements made in the *Adult Student Guide*. It may be beneficial to have students read portions of the commentary aloud from time to time. This should help promote discussion.

Student interaction can also be encouraged through reference to statements and questions under each main heading. Be prepared for students to raise questions during the study discussion. You may wish to incorporate some of the questions and statements in your own presentation. Or you may plan beforehand for students to present reports concerning issues raised with the questions in the study.

An important resource for young adult students is *Pathways For Young Adults Student Guide* (often simply referred to as "Pathways." This 48-page quarterly features two pages of Bible study commentary for each week, written in a contemporary, conversational style. Each study is closely correlated with the *Pathways For Young Adults Teacher Guide*. Articles are included in the student quarterly which are reprinted from Christian publications and relate to subjects in a number of the studies in the quarter.

These features in *Pathways* lend themselves to student involvement and interaction. Students can be invited to discuss or share thoughts from the commentary as well as related issues presented in the reprinted articles.

Consider having students present synopsis reports on the various articles in *Pathways*. Reports may be followed by class discussion. Or you may wish to highlight contents of the articles during your study presentation.

When presenting the Bible study, be careful to avoid continual use of the lecture approach. Undoubtedly, various questions and concerns will arise as study topics are presented. Give the students opportunity to interact as much as possible.

As you plan your weekly study presentation, keep the following points in mind regarding student materials:

1. Become thoroughly familiar with the content of the *Adult Student Guide* and/or *Pathways For Young Adults Student Guide*.

2. Anticipate questions or points of discussion that may arise. Or plan to discuss purposely various points of emphasis in the commentary and life application sections of the student quarterly.

3. Plan ways to involve the students directly through reports or guided discussion of student quarterly materials.

4. Encourage the students to share thoughts, opinions, or questions that arise from their personal study.

As with the *Adult Teacher Guide* and *Pathways For Young Adults Teacher Guide*, the *Adult Student Guide* and the *Pathways For Young Adults Student Guide* are tools and resources that, if used effectively, can help make study presentations come alive. The key is involvement. When the students in your class move from passive to active participation, Sunday School becomes a life-changing experience.

"Teacher Growth Series" brings you information on every phase of your teaching ministry. Three articles per quarter can be read, shared with other teachers, and filed for future reference. Articles dealing with the same topics are presented at each age level from early childhood through adult. The "Teacher Growth Series" covers 36 different topics.

TEACHER GROWTH SERIES

TEACHING AND WINNING

By John T. Maempa

"Go . . . make disciples" is Jesus' command. This involves first, reaching individuals with the gospel and training them to reach others. "Until all have heard" must be our goal.

But how? Teachers may view the classroom as the place to teach God's Word to God's people. This is true, but we need to be sensitive to those who attend our classes but have not made a commitment to Christ. What are some ways we can be responsive to their needs?

First of all, a teacher's life must be bathed in prayer. Not just "Lord bless my class," but prayer where each member is called by name and their needs lifted to God. This helps us to be more aware of those who have not made a commitment to the Lord.

Secondly, be sensitive to the Holy Spirit. Sometimes in the classroom a remark by the teacher or a member will start a chain reaction which will result in a person's being ready to accept Christ. If we feel we must first finish the study, we may miss the opportunity to lead this person to the Savior. When someone indicates a desire to know Him, that is the best time to introduce them to Him. Delay could be dangerous.

Thirdly, the Sunday School class is not a miniature church service. As an effective teacher, you should know your class members and their level of commitment. Salvation appeals need not be made to a class of committed Christians. However, the opportunity for interested persons to respond to Christ's love should be given. It might be an invitation to remain after class for further discussion or an opportunity for people to pray quietly. Perhaps instructions for the prayer can be given so that no one will feel intimidated. A simple lifting of a hand, nodding of the head, or other kind of response might help the individual take the first step toward Christ.

Whatever method you use, keep it as clear as possible what you are asking. Beware of using vocabulary which is understood only by Christians. Perhaps speaking in relationship terms—of knowing Christ, of becoming part of God's family—will make the concept of salvation clearer.

We need to remove as many barriers as possible between the unsaved and Christ. The end of the study may not be the best time for an invitation. Asking people to come to the front may create a barrier for some. Jesus talked to people by wells, in trees, beside pools, along the road, as well as in the synagogue. He approached each one individually, simply, and made it easy for them to accept Him.

Classroom evangelism should focus on the individual without intimidating him or her. It should involve language clear and simple enough for all to understand and an invitation that makes it easy enough for all to respond.

As we focus on the individual, we will find the classroom to be a rich harvest field for the Kingdom, but we can't stop there. Many people have made a commitment to Christ but haven't continued to follow Him. Christ contacted Zaccheus when he was "up a tree," then He went home with him.

Evangelism is more than having people "repeat after me." Follow-up is very important. Sometimes we need to explain to converts what has happened, give guidance about Bible reading, and support them with our presence. All of us need to know that someone cares about us. When people are saved, we want to be sure they know we are interested in their becoming growing members of God's family.

The Evangelism Outreach section at the end of each study in the *Adult Teacher Guide* is a brief reminder to reach out to the unsaved members of the class. The instructions are not detailed, but they are intended to emphasize the importance of soul winning in the Sunday School setting. Some studies lead more easily to an altar call than others, but the teacher should always have the challenge of evangelism in focus.

"Teacher Growth Series" brings you information on every phase of your teaching ministry. Three articles per quarter can be read, shared with other teachers, and filed for future reference. Articles dealing with the same topics are presented at each age level from early childhood through adult. The "Teacher Growth Series" covers 36 different topics.

Saved By The Blood

CENTRAL TRUTH

Jesus shed His blood on the cross to save from sin all who will believe in Him.

GOLDEN TEXT

The blood of Jesus, his Son, purifies us from all sin. 1 John 1:7 (NIV)

STUDY TEXT

Leviticus 16:1-34; 17:11; John 19:17-37; Ephesians 1:3-7; Hebrews 9:23-28

OUTLINE

1. Blood Atonement
   A. High Priest's Responsibility
   B. Blood Of The Sacrifice

2. The Lamb Of God
   A. Behold The Lamb
   B. The Lamb Crucified

3. Redeemed By Christ's Blood
   A. Bought Back And Released
   B. The Final Sacrifice

OBJECTIVE

To show the significance of Christ's blood in God's plan of redemption and grow in appreciation for the Atonement.

CHECKLIST

☐ Display the unit theme poster "Two Mountains."
☐ Make copies of the work sheet "The Lamb Honored Forever" from the Adult Teaching Helps Packet. Work through a copy yourself prior to class.
☐ When introducing the material, explain that you will be studying how the Law pointed to Christ's coming and the contrasts between the Law and the gospel. Stress the significance of having an opening study about the blood of Jesus, since blood atonement is the very foundation of the gospel.
☐ Using a concordance, scan the biblical passages that mention the blood—both of sacrificial animals and of Christ. This will give you an understanding of the amount of Scripture dedicated to the teaching of blood atonement.

DAILY BIBLE READINGS

Monday: Blood Of The Lamb.
Exodus 12:1-13
Tuesday: Saved By The Blood.
Exodus 12:21-27
Wednesday: Blood Of The Covenant.
Exodus 24:1-8
Thursday: Blood Of The Cross.
Colossians 1:19-23
Friday: Cleansed By The Blood.
1 John 1:1-7
Saturday: Redeemed By Christ's Blood.
Revelation 5:1-10

King James Version

Leviticus 16:15. Then shall he kill the goat of the sin offering, that is for the people, and bring his blood within the veil, and do with that blood as he did with the blood of the bullock, and sprinkle it upon the mercy seat, and before the mercy seat:

16. And he shall make an atonement for the holy place, because of the uncleanness of the children of Israel, and because of their transgressions in all their sins: and so shall he do for the tabernacle of the congregation, that remaineth among them in the midst of their uncleanness.

17. And there shall be no man in the tabernacle of the congregation when he goeth in to make an atonement in the holy place, until he come out, and have made an atonement for himself, and for his household, and for all the congregation of Israel.

18. And he shall go out unto the altar that is before the Lord, and make an atonement for it; and shall take of the blood of the bullock, and of the blood of the goat, and put it upon the horns of the altar round about.

19. And he shall sprinkle of the blood upon it with his finger seven times, and cleanse it, and hallow it from the uncleanness of the children of Israel.

17:11. For the life of the flesh is in the blood; and I have given it to you upon the altar to make an atonement for your souls: for it is the blood that maketh an atonement for the soul.

John 1:29. The next day John seeth Jesus coming unto him, and saith, Behold the Lamb of God, which taketh away the sin of the world!

19:17. And he bearing his cross went forth into a place called the place of a skull, which is called in the Hebrew Golgotha:

18. Where they crucified him, and two others with him, on either side one, and Jesus in the midst.

Ephesians 1:3. Blessed be the God and Father of our Lord Jesus Christ, who hath blessed us with all spiritual blessings in heavenly places in Christ.

7. In whom we have redemption through his blood, the forgiveness of sins, according to the riches of his grace.

New International Version

Leviticus 16:15. He shall then slaughter the goat for the sin offering for the people and take its blood behind the curtain and do with it as he did with the bull's blood: He shall sprinkle it on the atonement cover and in front of it.

16. In this way he will make atonement for the Most Holy Place because of the uncleanness and rebellion of the Israelites, whatever their sins have been. He is to do the same for the Tent of Meeting, which is among them in the midst of their uncleanness.

17. No one is to be in the Tent of Meeting from the time Aaron goes in to make atonement in the Most Holy Place until he comes out, having made atonement for himself, his household and the whole community of Israel.

18. Then he shall come out to the altar that is before the Lord and make atonement for it. He shall take some of the bull's blood and some of the goat's blood and put it on all the horns of the altar.

19. He shall sprinkle some of the blood on it with his finger seven times to cleanse it and to consecrate it from the uncleanness of the Israelites.

17:11. For the life of a creature is in the blood, and I have given it to you to make atonement for yourselves on the altar; it is the blood that makes atonement for one's life.

John 1:29. The next day John saw Jesus coming toward him and said, "Look, the Lamb of God, who takes away the sin of the world!"

19:17. Carrying his own cross, he went out to the place of the Skull (which in Aramaic is called Golgotha).

18. Here they crucified him, and with him two others—one on each side and Jesus in the middle.

Ephesians 1:3. Praise be to the God and Father of our Lord Jesus Christ, who has blessed us in the heavenly realms with every spiritual blessing in Christ.

7. In him we have redemption through his blood, the forgiveness of sins, in accordance with the riches of God's grace.

Atonement through blood sacrifice was not something introduced in the New Testament. In fact, God gave the first lesson on the subject in the Garden of Eden when He provided coats for Adam and Eve by killing innocent animals.

Physically, the very life of everyone is in the blood. The outpouring of blood is the outpouring of life. This is what happened when Old Testament sacrifices were carried out. Animals that were sacrifices for sin poured out their life so the lives of the sinners could be spared. On the cross, Jesus poured out His life so the deserved judgment for our sin does not fall on us.

No title given to Jesus evokes more feelings of tenderness than "the Lamb of God." Our thoughts go immediately to One who is innocent, unresisting, and submissive to the work of atonement He accomplished.

BIBLE COMMENTARY

1. Blood Atonement

A. High Priest's Responsibility
Leviticus 16:15-22

TEACHING TIP 1: Read the passage with the students. On the chalkboard write "Two Pictures Of Atonement." Under this heading, write "Sin Atoned For" on one side and "Sin Carried Away" on the other side. Under the first heading write, "The Substitute Dies." This describes the first goat that was killed. Under the second heading write, "The Substitute Carries Away Sin." This describes the second goat, commonly called the scapegoat. This will help keep the students' attention on your discussion of both aspects of atonement.

Ask: "Why was no other person allowed behind the veil with the high priest while he was making atonement for the people?" On the shoulders of one man rested the entire responsibility for making atonement for the nation's sins. If he failed, the people would not be reconciled to God. This reminds us of the lone responsibility our High Priest, the Lord Jesus, had when He bore the sins of the whole world. No one else among the Israelites but the high priest had been designated for this work on the Day of Atonement and no one else but Jesus has been designated our High Priest.

Atonement includes not just deliverance from punishment but the removal of guilt from the sinner's record. The first goat represented Jesus' taking our punishment so we will not have to be punished. The second goat represented His work of putting our sins out of God's sight to be remembered against us no more.

When the priest confessed the nation's sins over the live goat, those sins were symbolically transferred to the animal. When he disappeared from the people's view as he was led into the desert, it assured everyone their sins would not be brought back to confront them.

NOTES

B. Blood Of The Sacrifice
Leviticus 17:11

Leviticus 16 describes the Day of Atonement, the most solemn day of the year for the Israelites. Jews today call it Yom Kippur and still approach it with great reverence. Leviticus 17:11 focuses specifically on the issue of blood sacrifice. "It is the blood that maketh an atonement for the soul" is a truth that does not change. There is no other way for sin to be dealt with.

Ask: "Since under the requirements of the Law sacrifices were made constantly, why did God require this special Day of Atonement?" The offerings of the Law were temporary in nature. None could make a perfect atonement for sin. Even with the daily, weekly, and monthly sacrifices, sin was never fully atoned for. The other sacrifices throughout the year involved the sins of individuals. The sacrifices on the Day of Atonement were for the nation as a whole. Atonement even had to be made for the tabernacle where worship was constantly carried out.

The Day of Atonement reminded the people just how widespread and entrenched sin is. It would break their fellowship with God unless atonement was constantly made. Even the high priest was required to make atonement for himself before he could carry out the rest of the sacrifices.

If these solemn ceremonies emphasize one great truth, it is that God does not take sin lightly. People today have difficulty comprehending this because our society has become so permissive. In those days God required a constant outpouring of the life of innocent substitutes to maintain fellowship with His people. Even though the Mosaic system was temporary, it taught a truth that has never changed—sin separates humanity from God and only sacrificial blood can bring reconciliation. God brought forgiveness through faith to the Israelites through the blood sacrifices He allowed in place of judgment for their sin. That blood pointed ahead to the ultimate salvation bought through Christ's blood shed on behalf of sinners everywhere and throughout time.

2. The Lamb Of God

A. Behold The Lamb
John 1:29

To a nation longing for deliverance from the tyranny of Rome, John the Baptist introduced Jesus as the Lamb of God, not the conquering king they may have been expecting. In announcing that the Lamb of God would take away the sin of the world, John made it clear that sin, not political freedom, is every person's primary problem. Satanic bondage is far worse than the rule of an earthly tyrant. Spiritual freedom is to be prized even above deliverance from a dictator's rule.

When the people on the banks of the Jordan heard John talking about a lamb, their minds would have gone back to the time when God gave instructions for the first Passover (Exodus 12:1-20). It was the death of a lamb substituting for the firstborn of every household that made the Passover a night always to be remembered.

The Greek word translated "takes away" in John 1:29 means to lift up and carry away. It pictures a heavy load being removed from someone and taken out of their sight. Nothing could describe better what Jesus' death on Calvary did for us. Despite all human efforts to evade the subject, sin is a burden that becomes heavier and more galling with every passing day. It cannot be removed by reformation or good works. It cannot be rationalized or reasoned away. Sin can only be removed from one's record and its stain cleansed from one's soul when that person accepts the sacrifice of God's Lamb, His only begotten Son, and believes in Him as Savior.

Ask: "Why did John not say merely 'your sins' instead of 'the sins of the world'?" Whether he was conscious of it or not, John's inspiration came from the Holy Spirit who, even then, was declaring to Israel that God loved the whole world, not just one nation. His Son came to redeem all people, not one race.

TEACHING TIP 2: Although the term "Lamb of God" does not occur again in the Gospels, it is emphasized elsewhere. Have a student read Acts 8:32, where the Ethiopian eunuch was reading about the lamb from Isaiah 53. Have another student read 1 Peter 1:18,19, where the apostle recalled the Passover lamb as a type of Jesus. Distribute the work sheet "The Lamb Honored Forever" from the Adult Teaching Helps Packet. The sheet contains a list of references showing how often Jesus is called the Lamb in Revelation. Allow a few minutes for students to read some of the references. Urge them to examine the remainder at home during the week.

NOTES

B. The Lamb Crucified
John 19:17,18,32-34

When a criminal was to be crucified he was forced to carry his own cross. This added to his public humiliation. Anyone seeing such an individual would know that here was someone finally being punished

for his crimes, getting what he deserved. What condescension we see in Jesus as He carried His cross through the city streets! Like a common criminal, He was made a public spectacle, the object of the crowd's hatred and scorn. He was not a sinner himself, but like the innocent Passover lamb, He was to die in the place of the condemned.

It seems that putting Jesus between the two thieves instead of on one side or the other was deliberate. It made Him appear to be the worst of all. Christ reached out in compassion even to these thieves. One of them responded to Him, calling Him "Lord." Before this thief died he was assured a place in heaven with Christ.

Ask: "What evidence is there that God was in control of the whole situation even though Jesus' enemies appeared to have triumphed at the moment?" The Roman government tried to keep peace with the Jews by tolerating many of their religious customs. Since the Jews did not want the bodies of Jesus and the thieves remaining on their crosses on the Sabbath, they asked Pilate to have their legs broken to hasten their death.

After the Roman soldiers broke the thieves' legs they saw that Jesus was already dead. Breaking His legs was unnecessary. Little did they realize that in not breaking any of Jesus' bones they were fulfilling Scripture and keeping the biblical type intact. God's strict rule for the Passover lamb was that none of its bones were to be broken (Exodus 12:46; Numbers 9:12). When a soldier pierced Jesus' side with his spear, he was fulfilling the prophecy of Zechariah 12:10, which John quoted.

NOTES

3. Redeemed By Christ's Blood

A. Bought Back And Released
Ephesians 1:3,7

"Redemption through his blood" (Ephesians 1:7)—this is the unshakable foundation of the gospel. Reject the truth of Christ's atoning blood, and you have nothing left in the gospel but a shell of a story about a good man who was martyred.

People must be redeemed because they are separated from their Creator by a deliberate choice to disobey Him. When Adam and Eve first sinned they fell into slavery to sin. They brought on themselves God's just decree of death.

To redeem is to buy back, or pay a price on behalf of someone else. The redeeming blood of Christ paid the cost of humanity's sin. That cost was so high that the human mind cannot grasp it. The price was the life of One who was totally sinless.

The Old Testament sacrifices were only types and shadows of the final sacrifice that was to come. The blood of animals could not actually take away sin. It was God's temporary arrangement to teach people about the coming Savior. Christ is the totally sinless One whose blood cleanses us once and for all.

Ask: "What is the connection between redemption and forgiveness?" Christ redeemed us by paying the price for our sin. When that redemption is put into effect in our lives through faith, our sins are forgiven. We are morally clean in God's sight. God's forgiveness means a release from the punishment due us for our transgressions.

Human attempts at righteousness can never earn our redemption and forgiveness. Those blessings flow from one source—the grace of God. That grace is so boundless that Paul spoke of its riches in Ephesians 1:7. God has not bestowed these riches on us in a small measure; He has lavished them upon us. He has literally plunged us into a river of grace.

B. The Final Sacrifice
Hebrews 9:24-28

The Book of Hebrews is the New Testament's counterpart to the Book of Leviticus. It was written to people who had accepted Jesus but were now tempted to return to the bondage of the Law. Consequently, much of the theme of this book is Christ's superiority to everything in the Law.

TEACHING TIP 3: As a background for this Hebrews passage, ask the students to turn to Leviticus 16:29-34. Ask several students to take turns reading it to the class.

Old Testament priests ministered in a man-made sanctuary. The fact God was so precise about how it was constructed and furnished shows He had a pattern to follow. Hebrews 9:24 tells us the pattern was the heavenly sanctuary ("the figures of the true"). It is in the heavenly sanctuary that Christ ministers for us. Note the word "now" in verse 24. His intercession as our High Priest is an ever-present blessing. He is there for us at this moment.

If Christ's sacrifice were imperfect like the Old Testament offerings, He would have had to suffer constantly from the moment sin entered the world. Thank God, this is not true. The word "once" in verse 26 is a triumphant one. The high priest under the Law went into the Holy of Holies every year on the Day of Atonement. Jesus made His offering once. Since it was a perfect sacrifice, no repetition is needed.

Ask: "What is the significance of the expression 'in the end of the world'?" This means literally "the consummation of the ages." Jesus' death and resurrection inaugurated the final stage of God's plan of grace. When these great events occurred, God's plan for human history began moving toward its climax. That climax is heralded in verse 28.

Just as there is a finality about our own death, there is a finality about Christ's death (verses 27 and 28). It will never happen again; the transaction has been completed.

When He returns it will be to rule as King, not to deal with sin and die on a cross.

NOTES

LIFE RESPONSE

A Christian once testified, "I am not what I should be. I am not what I want to be. But one thing is certain: I am not what I used to be." We should not dwell on our past sinful condition to the point of bringing back guilt feelings. However, we should never lose sight of what we were apart from God's grace and what we have become through the gospel. Nor should we forget the price paid to bring us into this wonderful relationship with the Lord.

Not many people are willing to shed their blood for another—especially if that one is an enemy. Yet that is exactly what Jesus did. Sin made us His enemies, but He poured out His life to redeem us. Salvation is free, but it is not cheap. We can never repay our Savior for what He did, but we can show by our consistent living that we appreciate how much He loves us.

The Law's work has been completed, but the Law was necessary during the time of its observance. Understanding how the Law relates to the work of Christ helps us read the Old Testament through different eyes. It is not a mass of ritual that has no signif-icance for us. It prepared the world for Jesus' coming and such preparation was an important part of God's plan. As we read the account of the Passover we can see the blood of God's perfect Lamb on the "doorposts" of our heart. When we see the high priest at the mercy seat—the atonement cover— we rejoice that our High Priest intercedes for us in heaven.

EVANGELISM OUTREACH

Some of the discussion in this study may seem too theological for unsaved students. Make an effort to keep your teaching clear. This study presents an excellent opportunity to emphasize the lost condition of the human heart and Christ's atoning death as the only means of salvation. Allow time at the end of class for an altar call or invite students to remain after dismissal if they wish to discuss their questions. Keep your teaching evangelistic throughout the study in preparation for this invitation.

Living By God's Commandments

CENTRAL TRUTH

Obedience to God's commandments brings His blessings.

GOLDEN TEXT

" 'Love the Lord your God with all your heart and with all your soul and with all your strength and with all your mind'; and, 'Love your neighbor as yourself.' " Luke 10:27 (NIV)

STUDY TEXT

Exodus 20:1-17; Luke 3:14; 4:8; 10:25-28; 16:18; Ephesians 4:28; Colossians 3:20; 1 Timothy 5:3,4; Hebrews 13:5; James 2:10-12

OUTLINE

1. Honor God
   A. The Basis Of All Commandments
   B. Serve God Only

2. Treat Others Right
   A. Honor Parents
   B. Don't Commit Murder
   C. Don't Commit Adultery
   D. Don't Steal
   E. Don't Bear False Witness
   F. Don't Covet

3. Obey The Greatest Commandment
   A. Summarizing The Law
   B. Obey From The Heart

OBJECTIVE

To examine the relationship between the Ten Commandments and New Testament teaching and determine to be obedient.

CHECKLIST

☐ Ask a student ahead of time to read aloud to the class the Ten Commandments from Exodus 20:1-17.

☐ Familiarize yourself with the three overhead transparencies from the teaching helps packet. Read the student guide and review the questions in both the teacher and student material.

☐ Because the study deals with the commandments individually, decide during your preparation how much time you can allot for each. Do not allow any student to sidetrack the discussion onto one issue. Use the "Planning The Session" sheet from the Adult Teaching Helps Packet to help you.

☐ Be sure to give the proper emphasis to the New Testament Scriptures which show how the Ten Commandments relate to believers today.

DAILY BIBLE READINGS

Monday: Command To Obey. Deuteronomy 6:17-25

Tuesday: Command To Be Strong. Joshua 1:1-9

Wednesday: Command To Praise God. Psalm 150:1-6

Thursday: Command To Repent. Acts 17:22-31

Friday: Command To Love Others. John 15:12-17

Saturday: Command To Live Right. 1 Thessalonians 5:12-22

SCRIPTURE SETTING

King James Version

Exodus 20:3. Thou shalt have no other gods before me.

7. Thou shalt not take the name of the Lord thy God in vain: for the Lord will not hold him guiltless that taketh his name in vain.

8. Remember the sabbath day, to keep it holy.

Luke 4:8. And Jesus answered and said unto him, Get thee behind me, Satan: for it is written, Thou shalt worship the Lord thy God, and him only shalt thou serve.

Exodus 20:12. Honor thy father and thy mother: that thy days may be long upon the land which the Lord thy God giveth thee.

Colossians 3:20. Children, obey your parents in all things: for this is well-pleasing unto the Lord.

Exodus 20:13. Thou shalt not kill.

James 2:10. For whosoever shall keep the whole law, and yet offend in one point, he is guilty of all.

11. For he that said, Do not commit adultery, said also, Do not kill. Now if thou commit no adultery, yet if thou kill, thou art become a transgressor of the law.

Exodus 20:14. Thou shalt not commit adultery.

Luke 16:18. Whosoever putteth away his wife, and marrieth another, committeth adultery: and whosoever marrieth her that is put away from her husband committeth adultery.

Exodus 20:15. Thou shalt not steal.

Ephesians 4:28. Let him that stole steal no more: but rather let him labor, working with his hands the thing which is good, that he may have to give to him that needeth.

Exodus 20:16. Thou shalt not bear false witness against thy neighbor.

Luke 3:14. And the soldiers likewise demanded of him, saying, And what shall we do? And he said unto them, Do violence to no man, neither accuse any falsely; and be content with your wages.

Exodus 20:17. Thou shalt not covet thy neighbor's house, thou shalt not covet thy neighbor's wife, nor his manservant, nor his maidservant, nor his ox, nor his ass, nor any thing that is thy neighbor's.

Hebrews 13:5. Let your conversation be without covetousness; and be content with such things as ye have: for he hath said, I will never leave thee, nor forsake thee.

Luke 10:27. And he answering said, Thou shalt love the Lord thy God with all thy heart, and with all thy soul, and with all thy strength, and with all thy mind; and thy neighbor as thyself.

New International Version

Exodus 20:3. You shall have no other gods before me.

7. You shall not misuse the name of the Lord your God, for the Lord will not hold anyone guiltless who misuses his name.

8. Remember the Sabbath day by keeping it holy.

Luke 4:8. Jesus answered, "It is written: 'Worship the Lord your God and serve him only.' "

Exodus 20:12. Honor your father and your mother, so that you may live long in the land the Lord your God is giving you.

Colossians 3:20. Children, obey your parents in everything, for this pleases the Lord.

Exodus 20:13. You shall not murder.

James 2:10. For whoever keeps the whole law and yet stumbles at just one point is guilty of breaking all of it.

11. For he who said, "Do not commit adultery," also said, "Do not murder." If you do not commit adultery but do commit murder, you have become a lawbreaker.

Exodus 20:14. You shall not commit adultery.

Luke 16:18. Anyone who divorces his wife and marries another woman commits adultery, and the man who marries a divorced woman commits adultery.

Exodus 20:15. You shall not steal.

Ephesians 4:28. He who has been stealing must steal no longer, but must work, doing something useful with his own hands, that he may have something to share with those in need.

Exodus 20:16. You shall not give false testimony against your neighbor.

Luke 3:14. Then some soldiers asked him, "And what should we do?" He replied, "Don't extort money and don't accuse people falsely—be content with your pay."

Exodus 20:17. You shall not covet your neighbor's house. You shall not covet your neighbor's wife, or his manservant or maidservant, his ox or donkey, or anything that belongs to your neighbor.

Hebrews 13:5. Keep your lives free from the love of money and be content with what you have, because God has said, "Never will I leave you; never will I forsake you."

Luke 10:27. He answered: " 'Love the Lord your God with all your heart and with all your soul and with all your strength and with all your mind'; and, 'Love your neighbor as yourself.' "

Christians are not under the ceremonial laws and ritual of the Old Testament. As we studied last week, Christ's death fulfilled the symbolism of the sacrificial system. This has led some to conclude that nothing in the Old Testament is of any concern or relevance to us.

However, being under grace does not mean we are free to choose our own standards of right and wrong. The Ten Commandments set forth briefly and concisely how God wants His people to live. Has He changed His mind about honoring parents, murder, adultery, or stealing? Sin is sin whether it was committed in the days of Moses or in the 20th century.

Jesus lived in obedience to the Ten Commandments and taught us to do likewise. He also gave us a clearer perspective of these commandments.

BIBLE COMMENTARY

1. Honor God

A. The Basis Of All Commandments
Exodus 20:3,7,8;

Ask: "How many of the problems in social relationships today can we trace to the fact the majority of society does not have a relationship with God?" We are not just "higher animals" with superior social skills. God created us with the capacity to worship and commune with Him. Only when this worship and communion are a reality can relationships with others be fully established.

With this in mind, we see that the first commandment is the basis of all the others. We are not to have any other gods before God (Exodus 20:3). Think about it. When we honor God, how can we murder, steal, commit adultery, or slander? If we truly honor God, these characteristics cannot co-exist in our lives!

TEACHING TIP 1: Read Exodus 20:4 to the class. Display the overhead transparency "No Other Gods" from the Adult Teaching Helps Packet. Use it to emphasize that other gods besides idols can cause people to break this commandment.

In studying the history of Israel, we see that falling into idolatry was always a major problem. The second commandment was a crucial addendum to the first. God created people with the need to worship. If they do not worship God they will reach out for other things to which they can give their devotion. We cannot evade our relationship to the second commandment just because we might not worship a piece of wood or metal. There are many other things people in so-called civilized countries are worshiping today.

Looking back at verse 3, there is a difference of opinion about the meaning of the Hebrew word translated "before." Whether it means "in place of" or "in addition to," the principle is the same. We must not have other gods in place of the true God, nor have others in addition to Him. He must claim the only place in our worship and the supreme place in our love.

The third commandment's prohibition against taking God's name "in vain" (verse 7) condemns more than just cursing. Cursing is the most flagrant misuse of God's name and has become widespread. Even Christians use expressions that involve God's name. The Hebrew word translated "in vain" refers to anything that is unreal or worthless. In the Old Testament it is used of idols. To take God's name in vain is to treat it as something that has no real value.

God's name reminds us of His character. It involves His very nature, His person. The NIV translates this commandment, "You shall not misuse the name of the Lord your God." This certainly covers a wide area.

The fourth commandment concerns our use of time. God gives people 6 full days out of every week to do their own work. Every seventh day is to be especially honored as "the Lord's Day." This reminds us especially that God created everything and that we owe Him respect and honor as Creator.

In the Old Testament, God made the Sabbath a sign of the covenant between himself and Israel (Exodus 31:14-17). The vast majority of Christians worship on Sunday instead of Saturday in celebration of our Lord's resurrection on the first day of the week. This still retains the principle of setting apart one day out of seven in recognition of God's claims on our time and our responsibility to worship Him. Acts 20:7 and 1 Corinthians 16:2 indicate believers gathered on the first day of the week for worship.

NOTES

B. Serve God Only
Luke 4:8

Among the temptations Satan used against Jesus was a direct attack on this foundational commandment. He insisted that Jesus break the very first one and worship, not just idols, but Satan himself. Jesus' response was not to argue or try to reason with the tempter, but to hurl the Word at him. "It is written!" is one weapon before which Satan cannot stand. What God has written is written forever. It will never be repealed or changed. It cannot be diluted. The words "him only" exclude any person or object to which we might give our worship and service instead of God.

Had Satan been able to get Jesus to yield in His commitment to the first commandment, breaking the others would have been easy. The same is true of us. As we keep God first in our lives He will help us obey the commandments He has established.

2. Treat Others Right

A. Honor Parents
Exodus 20:12; 1 Timothy 5:3,4; Colossians 3:20

It is fitting that the fourth commandment, the first guiding our relationships with others, concerns the family (Exodus 20:12). From the cradle, the family is the environment in which our personalities and relationship skills are molded. A godly family, in which children submit to the wise guidance of Christian parents, is the best environment possible. But even within a secular society, peace and stability rest on the foundational family unit and the need for children to honor their parents.

A blessing is attached to the fourth commandment. When children honor their parents, it contributes to their well-being and length of life. God's undergirding of the home and family by this commandment shows us the sanctity of these relationships.

The lifelong context of honoring one's parents is seen in the care of widows in the Early Church. The Church assumed responsibility for widows who had no family to care for them. However, Paul insisted that if there were children or grandchildren, they were to repay the service to them as children by caring for their parents when they could no longer care for themselves (1 Timothy 5:3,4). Paul also gave the strongest possible reason for children obeying parents and thus honoring them: it is pleasing to the Lord (Colossians 3:20).

B. Don't Commit Murder
Exodus 20:13; James 2:10-12

In the fifth commandment, God declared for all time the sanctity of human life: "You shall not murder'' (Exodus 20:13, NIV). This is a point which sorely needs emphasis in our day when murder of unborn children in the womb is rampant, when "doctor-assisted suicides" are in the headlines, and there is increasing pressure to consider euthanasia favorably.

James used the prohibition against murder to make a significant point. In James 2:10-12 he emphasized the unity of God's law. **Ask: "Why does breaking one commandment make one guilty of breaking them all?"** We begin to understand God's law when we study and apply it as one great unit, not breaking it up into separate commandments. All of the Ten Commandments are an expression of the will of God and of His character. To violate one of them is to show unconcern for the directions God has given for living.

C. Don't Commit Adultery
Exodus 20:14; Luke 16:18

As the sixth commandment protected the sanctity of human life, the seventh commandment protected the sanctity of marriage and family ties (Exodus 20:14). Adultery violates the principle God established when He created the first man and woman. He declared then that husband and wife are one flesh (Genesis 2:24). The integrity of marriage depends on the faithfulness of spouses to one another. Nothing threatens our society today more than the flagrant breaking of this law by so many.

Luke 16:18 is a brief excerpt from Jesus' teaching on divorce and remarriage. There is not space here to consider also His statements recorded by Matthew and Mark. In this day of easy divorce and remarriage, it is important to remember that Jesus extended the scope of the commandment against adultery to include divorcing one's spouse and marrying another.

D. Don't Steal
Exodus 20:15; Ephesians 4:28

This commandment declares an individual's right to own property and the sanctity of that property. To deprive someone of

property by outright stealing, cheating, or any other form of theft breaks God's law.

It may seem strange that in Paul's day he had to remind Christians of this commandment. This shows that the temptation to take something from others is always present. With his admonition, Paul also emphasized the honorable character of work. Among other things, it enables the worker to help others who are in need.

E. Don't Bear False Witness
Exodus 20:16; Luke 3:14

There are two kinds of false witness connected with Exodus 20:16, and both may cause a person to suffer damage or loss. The Hebrew word translated "witness" applied especially to testimony in a court of law. If such testimony was false it could injure an individual's reputation or threaten him with financial disaster. God made careful provisions to assure the integrity of witnesses in legal proceedings (Deuteronomy 19:15-21).

We can be sure God also condemns the kind of false witness that is done more privately. It may be more subtle but can prove just as destructive as false testimony in court. Lying about someone may not result in the loss of tangible possessions, but can very well ruin a reputation. The ninth commandment was God's protection against a person's life being damaged by either public or private lies.

Although the soldiers John the Baptist addressed in Luke 3:14 were probably Jewish, they could have been Roman. In either case, it was not unusual for these individuals to use false accusations to extort money from the people. As we know from our observations today, human nature has not changed in 20 centuries.

F. Don't Covet
Exodus 20:17; Hebrews 13:5

The tenth and final commandment focuses on inward desires and thoughts rather than outright acts (Exodus 20:17). The danger of covetousness lies in what it can lead to. People have been driven to violent acts because they were eaten up with covetousness. They have taken by force what was not theirs because they had wanted it so intensely. Thus we see the safeguard God was providing for His people in this commandment. Covetousness disrupts our relationships with others because we focus on their possessions rather than who they are. Most certainly covetousness can destroy our relationship with God, because those desires become more important to us.

Hebrews 13:5 is God's antidote to a covetous spirit. He has promised never to leave or forsake us, which means He will always provide for our needs. Recognizing this produces peace and contentment in our hearts instead of a jealous, covetous spirit.

TEACHING TIP 2: Having considered these individual commandments, display the transparency "Keep The Wall Intact" from the Adult Teaching Helps Packet to summarize the discussion. It illustrates the truth of James 2:10—breaking one law makes one guilty of breaking them all.

3. Obey The Greatest Commandment

A. Summarizing The Law
Luke 10:25-27

TEACHING TIP 3: Ask a student to read Luke 10:25-27 to the class. Display the overhead transparency "The Greatest Commandment" from the Adult Teaching Helps Packet during the concluding discussion of the study. You will strengthen your discussion by referring to the parallel account in Matthew 22:34-40.

Ask: "How are the commandments in this passage of Scripture a summary of the Law?" Whether the lawyer's question in verse 25 was sincere or hostile, it brings an important truth into sharp focus. All the teaching of the Law, including the Ten Commandments, centers on one's relationship to God and, by extension, to others. When the greatest commandment is obeyed, obedience to the other commandments will follow.

Being a Jewish lawyer meant this man was an authority on the countless ways in which the Law impacted everyday life. He would also have been familiar with the extensive traditions connected with the Law in his day by such groups as the Pharisees and Sadducees. But this man recognized the heart of the Law—loving God and loving others.

As we apply the Bible to our lives, we can sometimes lose sight of this truth. We can begin to categorize our life-style in detail, searching for any area that might be sinful. How much simpler to focus on what it means to love God and others completely. Whenever we have a question about something we are about to do, we can ask if that action would demonstrate our love for God or affirm our godly love for someone else.

NOTES

B. Obey From The Heart
Luke 10:28

Ask: "Did Jesus' answer in Luke 10:28 mean that a person can be saved by good works?" No, Jesus was emphasizing that when people obey the greatest commandment, their lives will be in right relationship with God. We could never keep this commandment in our own strength. Only through the new birth and the nature the

Holy Spirit gives us at salvation can we love God with our whole being and our neighbor as ourselves.

This passage emphasizes that the real keeping of God's commandments is not a mechanical exercise. It comes from the heart—a heart that has become right with God through the experience of salvation. Living under God's grace, we do not have to focus on the legality of the Bible's requirements for living. Rather, throughout our Christian experience we can obey those guidelines out of love for God and with the confidence that He is helping us.

LIFE RESPONSE

It is important to note that the New Testament emphasizes the Ten Commandments. They are still God's guidelines for living for His people. Jesus lifted these commandments from the narrow perspective of the religious leaders in order to teach that obedience must come from the heart. He also made it clear that there can be outward observance of the commandments while the heart rebels against them. One of the clearest examples of this is when He said adultery in the heart makes one as guilty in God's sight as the outward act.

We cannot pick which commandments we want to obey and disregard the others. Though they are 10, they really comprise one law. Breaking one makes us guilty of breaking them all.

The Ten Commandments are not "the ten suggestions," as some want to think. God does not give us the option to decide what we can choose for our own life-style. His commandments are absolute—a concept our permissive age detests. As believers we cannot compromise in obeying God's laws.

Some will say, "We live in a different day. It isn't possible to live this way now." This is, of course, one of Satan's lies. When we obey God out of love for Him and others, keeping His commandments is not a burden. It is a delight. Such obedience is the natural outflow of a heart made clean by the blood of Jesus. When we accept what Jesus has done for us, we are empowered to live for God.

EVANGELISM OUTREACH

You may notice negative reactions to this study from unsaved students. Some might even try to argue, but do not allow them to. Be loving and kind in presenting the study, but be very firm. Your students are bombarded every day with the devil's propaganda, and some probably are convinced the Bible's teachings are out-of-date. Pray that the Holy Spirit will bring conviction during your presentation. Allow time for an altar call at the end of class, and be quick to respond to students' questions.

Called To A Priestly Ministry

CENTRAL TRUTH

Every believer is called by God to a priestly ministry.

GOLDEN TEXT

You are a chosen people, a royal priesthood, a holy nation, a people belonging to God, that you may declare the praises of him who called you out of darkness into his wonderful light. 1 Peter 2:9 (NIV)

STUDY TEXT

Leviticus 8:10-12; 21:10-12; Hebrews 4:14 through 5:10; 1 Peter 2:9; Revelation 1:4-6; 20:6

OUTLINE

1. Levitical Priesthood
   A. Chosen And Anointed
   B. Separated Unto God

2. Christ's Priesthood
   A. Above All Others
   B. Eternal Priesthood

3. Believers' Priesthood
   A. Royal Priesthood
   B. Reigning With Christ

OBJECTIVE

To understand the biblical concept of priestly ministry and accept the role God planned for us.

CHECKLIST

☐ At least a week ahead of time, select a student to give a report to the class about the holy anointing oil used for anointing priests and the tabernacle furniture and vessels. Have the student use Exodus 30:22-33 and a Bible encyclopedia.

☐ During your own study, read additional commentaries that consider how the holy anointing oil is a type of the Holy Spirit. Use this teaching to impress students with the continuing role of the Holy Spirit's ministry in our relationship to God.

☐ Note the suggestion in Teaching Tip 2 that you familiarize yourself with the Bible's teaching about Melchizedek. You could also ask another student to prepare a report on this priest.

☐ Develop discussion questions around the information sheet mentioned in Teaching Tip 3. Make copies for the students.

DAILY BIBLE READINGS

Monday: A Caring Priesthood.
Genesis 14:17-20
Tuesday: An Anointed Priesthood.
Exodus 40:9-15
Wednesday: A Pure Priesthood.
Leviticus 10:1-11
Thursday: An Unchangeable Priesthood.
Hebrews 7:15-25
Friday: A Holy Priesthood.
1 Peter 2:1-6
Saturday: A Royal Priesthood.
1 Peter 2:7-10

SCRIPTURE SETTING

King James Version

Leviticus 8:10. Moses took the anointing oil, and anointed the tabernacle and all that was therein, and sanctified them.

11. And he sprinkled thereof upon the altar seven times, and anointed the altar and all his vessels, both the laver and his foot, to sanctify them.

12. And he poured of the anointing oil upon Aaron's head, and anointed him, to sanctify him.

21:10. And he that is the high priest among his brethren, upon whose head the anointing oil was poured, and that is consecrated to put on the garments, shall not uncover his head, nor rend his clothes;

11. Neither shall he go in to any dead body, nor defile himself for his father, or for his mother;

12. Neither shall he go out of the sanctuary, nor profane the sanctuary of his God; for the crown of the anointing oil of his God is upon him: I am the Lord.

Hebrews 4:14. Seeing then that we have a great high priest, that is passed into the heavens, Jesus the Son of God, let us hold fast our profession.

5:1. For every high priest taken from among men is ordained for men in things pertaining to God, that he may offer both gifts and sacrifices for sins:

2. Who can have compassion on the ignorant, and on them that are out of the way; for that he himself also is compassed with infirmity.

3. And by reason hereof he ought, as for the people, so also for himself, to offer for sins.

4. And no man taketh this honor unto himself, but he that is called of God, as was Aaron.

5. So also Christ glorified not himself to be made a high priest; but he that said unto him, Thou art my Son, today have I begotten thee.

6. As he saith also in another place, Thou art a priest for ever after the order of Melchizedek.

1 Peter 2:9. But ye are a chosen generation, a royal priesthood, a holy nation, a peculiar people; that ye should show forth the praises of him who hath called you out of darkness into his marvelous light.

Revelation 1:6. [Christ] hath made us kings and priests unto God and his Father; to him be glory and dominion for ever and ever. Amen.

20:6. Blessed and holy is he that hath part in the first resurrection: on such the second death hath no power, but they shall be priests of God and of Christ, and shall reign with him a thousand years.

New International Version

Leviticus 8:10. Moses took the anointing oil and anointed the tabernacle and everything in it, and so consecrated them.

11. He sprinkled some of the oil on the altar seven times, anointing the altar and all its utensils and the basin with its stand, to consecrate them.

12. He poured some of the anointing oil on Aaron's head and anointed him to consecrate him.

21:10. The high priest, the one among his brothers who has had the anointing oil poured on his head and who has been ordained to wear the priestly garments, must not let his hair become unkempt or tear his clothes.

11. He must not enter a place where there is a dead body. He must not make himself unclean, even for his father or mother,

12. Nor leave the sanctuary of his God or desecrate it, because he has been dedicated by the anointing oil of his God. I am the Lord.

Hebrews 4:14. Therefore, since we have a great high priest who has gone through the heavens, Jesus the Son of God, let us hold firmly to the faith we profess.

5:1. Every high priest is selected from among men and is appointed to represent them in matters related to God, to offer gifts and sacrifices for sins.

2. He is able to deal gently with those who are ignorant and are going astray, since he himself is subject to weakness.

3. This is why he has to offer sacrifices for his own sins, as well as for the sins of the people.

4. No one takes this honor upon himself; he must be called by God, just as Aaron was.

5. So Christ also did not take upon himself the glory of becoming a high priest. But God said to him, "You are my Son; today I have become your Father."

6. And he says in another place, "You are a priest forever, in the order of Melchizedek."

1 Peter 2:9. But you are a chosen people, a royal priesthood, a holy nation, a people belonging to God, that you may declare the praises of him who called you out of darkness into his wonderful light.

Revelation 1:6. [Christ] has made us to be a kingdom and priests to serve his God and Father—to him be glory and power for ever and ever! Amen.

20:6. Blessed and holy are those who have part in the first resurrection. The second death has no power over them, but they will be priests of God and of Christ and will reign with him for a thousand years.

The subject of priesthood may seem strange to Christians because they have been exposed to the wrong concepts. The office of priest was introduced in the Old Testament because people lost direct access to God through the Fall. This role of intermediary between worshiper and deity was continued as long as the ceremonial regulations of the Law were in force.

However, the New Testament also mentions the ministry of priests, declaring that it belongs to every believer. Jesus Christ fulfilled the requirements of the Law perfectly in His life and became the perfect sacrifice for our sins in His death and resurrection. Through Him, all believers have direct access to God. Many of the Old Testament regulations concerning priests are beautiful illustrations of the Christian's privileged position.

BIBLE COMMENTARY

1. Levitical Priesthood

A. Chosen And Anointed
Leviticus 8:10-12

TEACHING TIP 1: Ask a student to read Leviticus 8:10-12 to the class. Have the student you had prepare the report about the anointing oil relate the regulations concerning its ingredients and use. It may be helpful for the student to read Exodus 30:22-33 to the class, making any appropriate comments in conjunction with the text.

Looking back at Leviticus 8:10-12, note the items which were to be anointed. Pouring the oil on them meant that they were permanently dedicated for sacred purposes. There seems to be little if any disagreement among evangelical scholars that this oil was a type of the Holy Spirit. God forbade anyone to try to make a compound that sought to imitate it. The oil was never to be used for common purposes. God's Spirit was to anoint every facet of the priestly ministry. As Spirit-filled believers, we recognize the Spirit as empowering our lives for the Lord's service. His anointing is to be just as pervasive in all we do and think.

Not just anyone could become a priest. From the 12 tribes of Israel, God set aside the tribe of Levi to serve in the tabernacle—and later the temple. From this tribe, one family was chosen to be priests. Aaron was the first high priest, and only his descendants were to be priests serving under the high priest. When the high priest died, his successor was his oldest son. The Scriptures give special attention to the high priest's qualifications and activities because he was a picture of Jesus, our High Priest.

The priests were the mediators between God and the people. When the people made sacrifices, they had to bring them to the priests, who followed God's prescribed rules for all the offerings. No Israelite approached God directly, for sin had broken the relationship between God and humanity. Yet God has always desired to restore this relationship, so He ordained these mediators to intercede on the people's behalf because of their sin. They had access to God because He ordained them and qualified them for such ministry. The priests stood between the people and God, representing the people to God and God to them.

Testament?'' We see the fulfillment of Old Testament priestly anointings when Jesus was baptized by John the Baptist in the Jordan (Matthew 3:13-17). When He came up out of the water, the Holy Spirit descended on Him in bodily form like a dove. At the same time the Father spoke from heaven, declaring that this was His beloved Son in whom He was well pleased. Jesus was officially anointed for His ministry of redemption, including His continuing ministry in heaven as our High Priest.

NOTES

B. Separated Unto God
Leviticus 21:10-12

There were more regulations concerning the high priest than the other priests because there could be no violation of the way he pictured the coming ministry of Jesus. The high priest was responsible for the national atonement of the people on the Day of Atonement. His ministry within the holiest portion of the sanctuary required special attention to ceremonial cleanliness as listed in Leviticus 21:10-12.

The prohibition against the high priest's uncovering his head or rending his clothes pertained to signs of mourning for the dead. God was so strict about the high priest's behavior that He forbade him to show any signs of grief even for the death of close relatives. He was not to touch a dead body, for under the Law that brought defilement. God was using such means to illustrate the importance of spiritual cleanness.

The prohibition concerning the high priest's leaving the sanctuary apparently pertained also to times of mourning. His chief mission was to be in the sanctuary to intercede for the people. This is a clear picture of the truth that our High Priest never leaves the heavenly sanctuary to engage in any other business but intercession for us.

Verse 12 further emphasizes the sacredness of the anointing oil, calling it "the anointing oil of his God." This reminds us that we must always approach our relationship with the Holy Spirit (of whom the oil is a type) with great reverence.

Ask: "What counterpart to the anointing of the high priest is there in the New

2. Christ's Priesthood

A. Above All Others
Hebrews 4:14-16

When the Holy Spirit inspired the writer of Hebrews, He led him to call Jesus not just a "high priest" but a "great high priest" (verse 14). This indicates that Christ is above every earthly high priest who ever served. Jesus is also superior to the Levitical priests because He continues to perform His ministry in heaven. Above all, He is the Son of God. No one can even approach His greatness.

Nothing could be more encouraging to us than to know that although Jesus is no longer on earth, He sympathizes with every weakness we face. When we remember He has been on earth and felt the full force of temptations and tests as we do, we see we are not dealing with One who is aloof and far removed from our situation. He understands each of us as no one else can—not even those who are closest to us.

Ask: "Why does the writer follow this description of Jesus by encouraging us to

come to Him for help?" It is one thing for people to understand our problems, and sometimes quite another for them to do something about them. They may be powerless to help. Not so with Jesus. We can come to Him in confidence that from His throne of grace there will flow just the grace we need. "In time of need" (verse 16) means that the help Jesus gives us will be appropriate to the time. Needs vary. What is a problem one time may not be at another. In each case, our High Priest will give us the appropriate help.

NOTES

B. Eternal Priesthood
Hebrews 5:1-10

Ask: "Why did the writer of Hebrews quickly change from speaking of Jesus to describing earthly high priests?" The theme of the Book of Hebrews is the absolute supremacy and sufficiency of Jesus in revealing and mediating God's grace. In describing the high priests, the writer was offering a comparison that would help his readers understand Christ's ministry to them.

The Law, or old covenant, was incapable of truly enacting God's grace in people's lives as Jesus did through God's new covenant. This was a crucial truth for those to whom the epistle was directed, because they were in danger of turning from Christ back to the Mosaic ritual.

It was true that the Old Testament high priest was also sympathetic, but this was because of his own weaknesses and failures. In fact, he even had to offer sacrifices for the sins he committed before he could intercede for the people. What a contrast this is to our sinless High Priest!

The writer then spoke of a similarity between Christ's priesthood and the Levitical order. No one could be a high priest by his own choice. He served only by divine appointment. Likewise, Jesus is our High Priest because His Father appointed Him. In verse 5 the writer quoted Psalm 2:7 and in verse 6 he quoted Psalm 110:4.

The reference to the order of Melchizedek is connected to the statement that Jesus is High Priest forever. This is in contrast to every Old Testament high priest, whose terms were limited by their inevitable deaths. Each one was succeeded by another. Melchizedek, however, was the only priest in his order. He was neither preceded nor followed by a priest. So it is with Jesus—He did not succeed another high priest and there will never be one to follow Him. He is our all-sufficient High Priest forever.

TEACHING TIP 2: The subject of the Melchizedek priesthood may not be familiar to your students. Prepare yourself for any questions the students may have by studying Genesis 14:18-20 and Hebrews 7:1-21 ahead of time. You may wish to ask a student to prepare a brief report on Melchizedek using other resources.

Hebrews 5:7,8 emphasizes that Jesus is one with us not only because of His temptations but also because of His sufferings. Through these sufferings He learned submission to His Father and obedience to God's will. Thus He has set an example for us when we suffer.

The expression "being made perfect" in verse 9 does not mean that Jesus was imperfect and had to suffer to achieve perfection. This expression is connected to the statement that Jesus became the author of eternal salvation. His work of redemption was perfected, or brought to completion, through His sufferings.

present age. Physically they are still in this world, but spiritually no longer a part of it.

"Peculiar" as used in this passage does not mean what it suggests today. Christians may indeed seem peculiar to sinners, but the original word describes a people who belong to God in a special way.

All of these wonderful descriptions of believers point to one goal we must always keep in focus: our mission is to bear testimony to the One who called us out of darkness into the glorious light of the gospel.

NOTES

3. Believers' Priesthood

A. Royal Priesthood
1 Peter 2:9

First Peter 2:9 introduces a turning point in Peter's exhortation to the exiled Christians who received his letter. He had just mentioned those who are disobedient, who stumble because they rebel against the Word. Then he wrote, "But you." What a contrast between the rebels and these saints who were suffering for their faith. Although they had been scattered and forced from their homes, they had a high standing in heaven—their real home.

Peter employed several expressions to describe the relationship believers have with the Lord. First, they are a chosen people. Everyone has to make a personal decision to accept Christ, but it is God who has taken the initiative to reach lost souls. Before He created the world, God foresaw the entrance of sin and planned for His Son to redeem us. He has sent the Holy Spirit to draw sinners to himself. There is a double choosing—we make a choice to accept Christ, but He has already chosen to save us when we repent and believe.

Ask: "Why did Peter speak of a royal priesthood?" Royalty reminds us of dignity and majesty, of those whose manner befits their high station. Since Jesus is King as well as High Priest, we are part of His royal family.

These royal priests are also a holy nation. They are the true Church, the body of Christ. They are set apart, or sanctified, for His use. They have been called out from the

B. Reigning With Christ
Revelation 1:4-6; 20:6

The Holy Spirit inspired John to continue the picture of our royal priesthood. As John began writing the Book of Revelation he broke into a doxology, declaring that in cleansing us with His blood, our Lord Jesus has made us kings and priests (1:5,6). John was a prisoner, but that was only from the human viewpoint. In God's eyes he belonged to a royal priesthood. Some of the churches to whom he wrote were experiencing persecution, but they were God's priests and kings regardless of what people did to them.

Ask: "To whom was John referring in Revelation 20:6?" John was not just referring to the martyrs he had mentioned in verse 4. Rather, verse 6 refers to everyone who has part in the first resurrection, which means all believers. As God's priests, they will share in Christ's reign during the Millennium. It is as though the Holy Spirit chose to end this book with a reminder to Christians of their high and holy calling.

TEACHING TIP 3: To summarize this study, distribute the information sheet ''God's Priests—Old Testament And New'' from the teaching helps packet. This will help the students understand the believer's priesthood and how the Levitical priesthood pointed to New Testament believers.

Give the students time to read the points with the accompanying passages. Then discuss how our identity as God's priests should shape our life-style. Explain that belonging to God's holy priesthood makes the need for holy living more imperative.

LIFE RESPONSE

Christians today live in an age that is shallow and carnal. Unbelievers trample on everything sacred. The world in general has a totally distorted concept of what it means to be a Christian. To many it means simply that they are not openly heathen. Others associate Christianity with church membership and certain religious activities.

We need to remind ourselves that we live by the Bible, not public opinion. We must not be pressured into adopting the world's light and frivolous view of Christianity. Believers have been called out from the present age to keep themselves separated from the attitudes, philosophies, and life-style of the ungodly. Old Testament priests were a distinct body that everyone recognized. New Testament priests must be just as distinct by the way they live each day.

It is no light thing for God to call us His royal priesthood. We must always be careful to measure up to the standards of royalty and priestly conduct. But can we actually live such a life in the midst of an age like ours? If we were depending on our own strength, the answer would be a resounding no. But the inner strength of the Holy Spirit makes us victors over the strongest spiritual opposition.

As a royal priesthood we look forward to a wonderful future. Jesus has prepared an eternal home for us in heaven. And we will share in His reign. The things that Jesus is preparing for us are beyond human description.

EVANGELISM OUTREACH

It may seem difficult to conclude this kind of study with an altar call to the unsaved. However, you should never miss an opportunity to call them to Christ no matter what the week's study is. This week you may wish to make the altar call for Christians, challenging them to a greater ministry of intercessory prayer. As they respond and are in prayer, the Holy Spirit may use their prayers to touch the hearts of unsaved students. Be sensitive and alert to such an opportunity.

The Joy Christ Brings

CENTRAL TRUTH

Christ's birth is a special reason for the world to rejoice.

GOLDEN TEXT

Today in the town of David a Savior has been born to you; he is Christ the Lord. Luke 2:11 (NIV)

STUDY TEXT

Luke 1:26-38; 2:1-20

OUTLINE

1. Miraculous Birth
   A. Born Of A Virgin
   B. Born In Bethlehem

2. Angelic Announcement
   A. Unlikely Audience
   B. Good News Proclaimed

3. Joyful Response
   A. Shepherds' Proclamation
   B. Mary's Contemplation

OBJECTIVE

To review the events surrounding Christ's birth and rejoice because of His coming.

✓ CHECKLIST

☐ Read the following material thoroughly, as well as study 4 of the *Adult Student Guide*.

☐ Familiarize yourself with the work sheet "If God's Ways Were Our Ways . . ." found in the Adult Teaching Helps Packet. Make copies of the work sheet for the students and be prepared to use it with Teaching Tip 2. Be sure to set aside enough time in your presentation to allow adequate discussion of the work sheet.

☐ Read Luke's entire account of the birth of Jesus (1:1 through 2:40). Contrast Luke's account with Matthew's, which is much shorter (1:18 through 2:12). Note Matthew's inclusion of the Wise Men and Luke's reference to the shepherds. It is widely accepted that Matthew wrote to a Jewish audience, while Luke wrote to a Greek audience. This may help you answer any questions from your students regarding these differing details.

DAILY BIBLE READINGS

Monday:	Sure Prophecy. Isaiah 9:2-7
Tuesday:	Source Of Peace. Isaiah 53:1-5
Wednesday:	God's Anointed Son. Psalm 2:1-12
Thursday:	Miraculous Conception. Luke 1:26-35
Friday:	Virgin Birth. Matthew 1:18-25
Saturday:	Cause For Rejoicing. Matthew 2:1-11

SCRIPTURE SETTING

King James Version

Luke 2:1. It came to pass in those days, that there went out a decree from Caesar Augustus, that all the world should be taxed.

2. (And this taxing was first made when Cyrenius was governor of Syria.)

3. And all went to be taxed, every one into his own city.

4. And Joseph also went up from Galilee, out of the city of Nazareth, into Judea, unto the city of David, which is called Bethlehem, (because he was of the house and lineage of David,)

5. To be taxed with Mary his espoused wife, being great with child.

6. And so it was, that, while they were there, the days were accomplished that she should be delivered.

7. And she brought forth her firstborn son, and wrapped him in swaddling clothes, and laid him in a manger; because there was no room for them in the inn.

8. And there were in the same country shepherds abiding in the field, keeping watch over their flock by night.

9. And, lo, the angel of the Lord came upon them, and the glory of the Lord shone round about them; and they were sore afraid.

10. And the angel said unto them, Fear not: for, behold, I bring you good tidings of great joy, which shall be to all people.

11. For unto you is born this day in the city of David a Savior, which is Christ the Lord.

12. And this shall be a sign unto you; Ye shall find the babe wrapped in swaddling clothes, lying in a manger.

13. And suddenly there was with the angel a multitude of the heavenly host praising God, and saying,

14. Glory to God in the highest, and on earth peace, good will toward men.

20. And the shepherds returned, glorifying and praising God for all the things that they had heard and seen, as it was told unto them.

New International Version

Luke 2:1. In those days Caesar Augustus issued a decree that a census should be taken of the entire Roman world.

2. (This was the first census that took place while Quirinius was governor of Syria.)

3. And everyone went to his own town to register.

4. So Joseph also went up from the town of Nazareth in Galilee to Judea, to Bethlehem the town of David, because he belonged to the house and line of David.

5. He went there to register with Mary, who was pledged to be married to him and was expecting a child.

6. While they were there, the time came for the baby to be born,

7. And she gave birth to her firstborn, a son. She wrapped him in cloths and placed him in a manger, because there was no room for them in the inn.

8. And there were shepherds living out in the fields nearby, keeping watch over their flocks at night.

9. An angel of the Lord appeared to them, and the glory of the Lord shone around them, and they were terrified.

10. But the angel said to them, "Do not be afraid. I bring you good news of great joy that will be for all the people.

11. Today in the town of David a Savior has been born to you; he is Christ the Lord.

12. This will be a sign to you: You will find a baby wrapped in cloths and lying in a manger."

13. Suddenly a great company of the heavenly host appeared with the angel, praising God and saying,

14. "Glory to God in the highest, and on earth peace to men on whom his favor rests."

20. The shepherds returned, glorifying and praising God for all the things they had heard and seen, which were just as they had been told.

For some, Christmas brings out goodwill that is not evident the rest of the year. It is a time to be reminded of the best in people, and at least for a time to put aside hard feelings. Many see it as an appropriate occasion to give help to the less fortunate in our society. But while they have their place, these attempts at goodwill and public displays of charity do not really exemplify the meaning of Christmas. They only represent flawed, human love.

God meant the birth of His Son to be an occasion of eternal hope for the world. The believer, having received the forgiveness of sins and the gift of eternal life, is able to experience the blessing that this wonderful season provides. Christ made a way for us to become children of His Father. Christmas reminds us that in heaven's family true love and joy can be found.

BIBLE COMMENTARY

1. Miraculous Birth

A. Born Of A Virgin
Luke 1:26-38

The Old Testament proclaimed that the Messiah was to be born of a virgin. "Therefore the Lord himself shall give you a sign; Behold, a virgin shall conceive, and bear a son, and shall call his name Immanuel" (Isaiah 7:14). The Hebrew word translated "virgin," while often referring to a young girl of marriageable age, was understood by the Jewish scholars of the Greek Septuagint (a translation of the Old Testament from Hebrew to Greek in the third and second centuries B.C.) and the New Testament writers to specifically refer to virginity.

The New Testament fulfillment of this prophecy is found in Luke 1:26-38. The appearance of Gabriel declaring the nature of this miraculous conception was greeted by faith on Mary's part: "Behold the handmaid of the Lord; be it unto me according to thy word" (verse 38).

Ask: "Why is belief in the Virgin Birth vital to the Christian faith?" There is a strong relationship between the virgin birth of Christ and His nature. Jesus Christ is both fully God and fully man. Because the Virgin Birth circumvents natural law, accepting its truth is a matter of faith. Christians believe that God is a God of miracles. The words of the angel Gabriel are especially instructive: "For with God nothing shall be impossible" (Luke 1:37).

NOTES

B. Born In Bethlehem
Luke 2:1-7

The Old Testament also proclaimed where the Messiah was to be born—in Bethlehem (Micah 5:2). Bethlehem, which literally means "house of bread," was the birthplace of David and perhaps Joseph also. As the Bread of Life, Jesus would be born in this humble town.

The events that brought about His birth in Bethlehem were truly miraculous. Joseph and Mary lived in Nazareth. Joseph, however, was required to go to his ancestral home of Bethlehem in order to register for the new tax decreed by Caesar Augustus (Luke 2:1).

The miraculous fulfillment of the prophecy of Christ's birthplace was aided by an emperor who ruled from faraway Rome. In accordance with God's sovereign plan, Caesar Augustus decided that a new tax was necessary and desirable for the empire. Little did he know that he was being used for a higher purpose, to provide the occasion for the fulfillment of prophecy, declared long before his time. God can and does use many things to accomplish His eternal purposes. Men and women are continually being used to bring about God's sovereign objectives, often without their slightest knowledge.

Mary accompanied Joseph on this tedious journey (Luke 2:5). They lived in Palestine, a part of the Roman province of Syria which required women 12 years of age and older to pay a poll tax. So Mary was probably required to register in person. The circumstances were harsh, but God's purposes were accomplished. The Messiah would be born in Bethlehem.

The journey from Nazareth to Bethlehem was approximately 70 miles. Without question, it was a difficult one for a woman so close to giving birth. God, however, was their strength and protection as He brought them to the appointed place of this tremendous event.

Luke's description of Jesus' birth is a very simple one. He merely stated that when the pregnancy came to term, Mary gave birth to her firstborn son (Luke 2:6,7). Little is made of the humble circumstances, only that there was no room at the inn. It is not expressly stated that Jesus was born in a stable. Many infer this from the laying of the Baby in a manger, which was a feeding trough for animals.

The simple account of the birth of Jesus stands in contrast to the miraculous account of His conception. Others would soon come to witness this great event by paying homage to the Baby, but His birth was accomplished in great humility.

NOTES

2. Angelic Announcement

A. Unlikely Audience
Luke 2:8,9

Shepherds were not a highly regarded group of people at the time of Christ's birth. They were not considered to be exceptionally honest or trustworthy by the religious leadership of the day. That does not mean, however, that the shepherds who witnessed Jesus' birth were of that sort. They were very likely devout, humble men. The fact they were chosen by God to witness this great event reveals God's concern for those who are powerless in a world that reveres people of power and preeminence.

Some have speculated that these shepherds were tending sheep that were to be used in the temple sacrifices. In support of this is the location of the shepherds near Bethlehem. The rabbinic authorities had declared that animals found between Jerusalem and a spot close to Betheleliem could be taken for temple use.

Whatever their specific duties were, these shepherds were in the open country in the dark of night. Against this darkness, the angels' appearance would have been especially startling. Luke 2:9 indicates that the shepherds were initially greatly frightened by the appearance.

NOTES

B. Good News Proclaimed
Luke 2:10-14

Ask: "What was the purpose of the angel's announcement as given in Luke 2:10,11?" The purpose of the announcement was to proclaim good news of great joy to all people. The basis of this great news was the birth of One whose greatness is declared by the titles given Him.

"Savior" means deliverer. The Jewish nation had long been looking for deliverance. The leaders of the nation, however, interpreted deliverance solely in the political sense. They expected to be delivered from their Roman oppressors.

The Greek word "Christ" and its Hebrew counterpart "Messiah" mean "Anointed One." **Ask: "What were the Jews expecting in this 'Anointed One'?"** The expectation of the Jewish people was not for deliverance in a general sense, but for the emergence of a specially anointed Deliverer, the Messiah. This expectation had become one of a coming King, as the prophets began referring to the Messiah with increasing specificity (Isaiah 9:6,7; Jeremiah 23:5,6; Ezekiel 21:26,27; Zechariah 9:9).

While the Jews had focused their attention on the description of their Messiah as a king, the angel's message to the shepherds focused on His title, "Lord." While the term when applied generally means ruler, in this context it refers to someone much greater. The title "Lord" was also the translation of the personal name for God, "Yahweh." The angel's use of the full title "Christ the Lord" speaks of the Baby in the greatest sense possible. This child was not only the Anointed One that was long expected, but deity as well. He is God, just as Isaiah and Jeremiah had prophesied.

Ask: "When taken together, how do the titles _Savior, Messiah,_ and _Lord_ proclaim good news?" One had come who was to meet the needs of all people, not just those of the nation of Israel. He was to be not only Israel's Messiah, but Savior of the world. God's love is not confined to one nation, but is extended to all people everywhere.

Today, the nations of the world continue to hear this good news. Some people are hearing the story of Jesus' birth and its meaning for the first time. After nearly 2,000 years great numbers are still being added to God's kingdom. The good news believed by the shepherds on that night is transforming the hearts of multitudes today.

3. Joyful Response

A. Shepherds' Proclamation
Luke 2:15-18,20

The shepherds' initial response indicated the wonder they felt over the angelic pronouncement. They wanted to see this tremendous event for themselves (verse 15). Verse 16 suggests an urgency on their part. They undoubtedly marveled at the fact they were chosen to witness the Messiah's birth. Even though they were considered among the lowest of their society, God counted them as people of value and worth.

Ask: "How might the shepherds' station in life have affected their response to the angels' announcement?" The shepherd of that day endured a life of hardship and danger. His responsibility included protecting his sheep from wild animals such as wolves, bears, and even lions. He seldom had enough food to eat and often suffered exposure to the elements, living in caves or makeshift shelters. His life was an extremely difficult one and his expectations in this life were limited. The words of the angel without question prompted great joy.

The shepherds' joy is evident in verses 17, 18, and 20. Luke stated that after hearing the angel's announcement and seeing the Son of God for themselves, the shepherds spread the word of His birth. Their testimony was sufficiently convincing to amaze all who heard. The shepherds glorified God and praised Him for what they had seen. Even though He was only a Baby, the Son of God had begun the work of bringing hope to the world.

TEACHING TIP 3: Allow a brief time for some in the class to share testimonies of their joyful response to the good news of Jesus Christ. Ask specifically how this new hope changed their outlook toward difficult circumstances they face.

In all likelihood, the shepherds remained shepherds. They still faced danger and hardship. But the joy Christ gives is far more important than a change in our present circumstances. It is the by-product of an eternal hope that changes our response to life's trials and hardships. Jesus does not necessarily remove hardship, but He will always give us joy in the midst of trials.

NOTES

B. Mary's Contemplation
Luke 2:19

Mary's response to the angel's proclamation as told by the shepherds was essentially an internal one. Luke's record of her reaction consisted of only one brief statement (verse 19). He attributed no comments by Mary, giving the impression that she said nothing.

While the shepherds declared their joyful response, Mary kept and pondered the things said about her Son in the depths of her heart. Even though the shepherds undoubtedly spoke of things that she already believed, they were a welcome confirmation. Mary could only sit and wonder how it would all be fulfilled.

TEACHING TIP 4: Have someone read Luke 1:30-35 and 2:10-14. Ask the class to compare Gabriel's words to Mary concerning Jesus with the words of the angel spoken to the shepherds which were repeated to her.

Ask: "What are the similarities between the pronouncements to Mary and to the shepherds?" Both declare Christ's kingly reign and at least hint of His deity. These things, however, are more easily proclaimed than understood. The more they are pondered the more awesome they become.

Mary treasured and pondered the words of the shepherds. She treasured them for what she understood, and pondered them to more fully comprehend their meaning. One can only imagine what Mary was feeling as she contemplated all the words spoken to her about the Child. No woman had ever been given such honor. None had ever been so highly favored.

Jesus, King of kings and Lord of lords, came to earth to establish His great Kingdom. We can only partially understand the significance of this wondrous event. God has invited all people to become His children and live eternally as joint heirs of this kingdom with Jesus Christ, His Son.

Mary and the shepherds responded with faith to the words of the angelic messengers. As they believed they were filled with joy. This same joy can be ours as we receive Christ as Lord and King.

NOTES

LIFE RESPONSE

The meaning of Christmas is Jesus Christ, His birth and mission. All the other trappings, as warm and inviting as they may be, must not overshadow Him in our celebration of this event. God became Man in order to reconcile us to himself. The angelic proclamation was "good tidings of great joy" (Luke 2:10).

The joy of salvation is the only basis for the true celebration of Christmas. Sadly, many Christians get caught up in the materialistic pursuits that accompany the holiday season and allow these pursuits to crowd out the wonderful birth of their Lord and Savior. The giving and receiving of gifts is not wrong in itself. It is only wrong when the story of Christ's birth is overshadowed. Too many believers are so busy shopping that they scarcely have the time to consider the great eternal significance of this time.

Have the pressures of the season robbed us of the greater joy of Christmas' true meaning? If so, it is not too late to change the way we celebrate. Today, we can turn our hearts toward Jesus, acknowledge His love for us, and rejoice at His coming. If we do, we will experience a greater and more lasting joy.

Just as importantly, we can share with others the true meaning of Christmas. The Holy Spirit can guide us in using the opportunities that come our way during this time of year to openly talk of the birth of Jesus Christ.

EVANGELISM OUTREACH

Jesus' titles in Luke 2:11 provide an excellent basis for a salvation appeal to the unbeliever. The good news is that the Baby born in Bethlehem is Savior, Messiah, and Lord. Point out that Christmas is a time when people's hearts may be more apt to listen to the message of God's love.

The lost need to hear the good news of the Incarnation. Some of those who need to hear this message are in our own families. Encourage the class to be mindful of any additional opportunities to share Christ. ▭

Jesus Christ, Our Mediator

CENTRAL TRUTH

Christians have the assurance that Christ is interceding for them.

GOLDEN TEXT

He is able to save completely those who come to God through him, because he always lives to intercede for them. Hebrews 7:25 (NIV)

STUDY TEXT

Exodus 32:1-35; Luke 22:31,32; Romans 8:31-34; Hebrews 7:25; 1 John 2:1,2

OUTLINE

1. Our Sacrifice
   A. Need For Atonement
   B. God's Love Demonstrated

2. Our Advocate
   A. Judgment Averted
   B. Help In Time Of Need

3. Our Intercessor
   A. Picture From The Past
   B. Jesus Prays For Us

OBJECTIVE

To show the all-sufficiency of Christ's mediatorial work and trust Him completely.

CHECKLIST

☐ Read the *Adult Student Guide* and write down the questions you wish to include in your teaching.

☐ Review the questions and teaching tips in the *Adult Teacher Guide.* You may want to write some questions of your own to encourage discussion of the material in the commentary.

☐ Review the context of the individual verses under study to get a total picture of what each passage teaches.

☐ Make a copy of the work sheet "Our Confidence" from the Adult Teaching Helps Packet for each student. Write your own paraphrases to compare with those of the students.

☐ Give careful thought to the Evangelism Outreach at the end of your presentation. This study is particularly suited to an invitation for accepting Christ as Savior.

DAILY BIBLE READINGS

Monday: Willing Sacrifice. Isaiah 53:6-12

Tuesday: Humble Submission. Psalm 22:14-18

Wednesday: Prayer For Believers. John 17:6-15

Thursday: Prayer For Unity. John 17:16-25

Friday: Complete Sacrifice. Hebrews 9:23-28

Saturday: Effective Advocate. 1 John 2:1-6

King James Version

Exodus 32:30. It came to pass on the morrow, that Moses said unto the people, Ye have sinned a great sin: and now I will go up unto the Lord; peradventure I shall make an atonement for your sin.

Romans 8:31. What shall we then say to these things? If God be for us, who can be against us?

32. He that spared not his own Son, but delivered him up for us all, how shall he not with him also freely give us all things?

1 John 2:2. [Jesus Christ] is the propitiation for our sins: and not for ours only, but also for the sins of the whole world.

Exodus 32:11. And Moses besought the Lord his God, and said, Lord, why doth thy wrath wax hot against thy people, which thou hast brought forth out of the land of Egypt with great power, and with a mighty hand?

12. Wherefore should the Egyptians speak, and say, For mischief did he bring them out, to slay them in the mountains, and to consume them from the face of the earth? Turn from thy fierce wrath, and repent of this evil against thy people.

13. Remember Abraham, Isaac, and Israel, thy servants, to whom thou swarest by thine own self, and saidst unto them, I will multiply your seed as the stars of heaven, and all this land that I have spoken of will I give unto your seed, and they shall inherit it for ever.

14. And the Lord repented of the evil which he thought to do unto his people.

Romans 8:33. Who shall lay any thing to the charge of God's elect? It is God that justifieth.

34. Who is he that condemneth? It is Christ that died, yea rather, that is risen again, who is even at the right hand of God, who also maketh intercession for us.

1 John 2:1. My little children, these things write I unto you, that ye sin not. And if any man sin, we have an advocate with the Father, Jesus Christ the righteous.

Exodus 32:31. And Moses returned unto the Lord, and said, Oh, this people have sinned a great sin, and have made them gods of gold.

32. Yet now, if thou wilt forgive their sin—; and if not, blot me, I pray thee, out of thy book which thou hast written.

Luke 22:31. And the Lord said, Simon, Simon, behold, Satan hath desired to have you, that he may sift you as wheat:

32. But I have prayed for thee, that thy faith fail not: and when thou art converted, strengthen thy brethren.

Hebrews 7:25. Wherefore he is able also to save them to the uttermost that come unto God by him, seeing he ever liveth to make intercession for them.

New International Version

Exodus 32:30. The next day Moses said to the people, "You have committed a great sin. But now I will go up to the Lord; perhaps I can make atonement for your sin."

Romans 8:31. What, then, shall we say in response to this? If God is for us, who can be against us?

32. He who did not spare his own Son, but gave him up for us all—how will he not also, along with him, graciously give us all things?

1 John 2:2. [Jesus Christ] is the atoning sacrifice for our sins, and not only for ours but also for the sins of the whole world.

Exodus 32:11. But Moses sought the favor of the Lord his God. "O Lord," he said, "why should your anger burn against your people, whom you brought out of Egypt with great power and a mighty hand?

12. Why should the Egyptians say, 'It was with evil intent that he brought them out, to kill them in the mountains and to wipe them off the face of the earth'? Turn from your fierce anger; relent and do not bring disaster on your people.

13. Remember your servants Abraham, Isaac and Israel, to whom you swore by your own self: 'I will make your descendants as numerous as the stars in the sky and I will give your descendants all this land I promised them, and it will be their inheritance forever.'"

14. Then the Lord relented and did not bring on his people the disaster he had threatened.

Romans 8:33. Who will bring any charge against those whom God has chosen? It is God who justifies.

34. Who is he that condemns? Christ Jesus, who died—more than that, who was raised to life—is at the right hand of God and is also interceding for us.

1 John 2:1. My dear children, I write this to you so that you will not sin. But if anybody does sin, we have one who speaks to the Father in our defense—Jesus Christ, the Righteous One.

Exodus 32:31. So Moses went back to the Lord and said, "Oh, what a great sin these people have committed! They have made themselves gods of gold.

32. But now, please forgive their sin—but if not, then blot me out of the book you have written."

Luke 22:31. "Simon, Simon, Satan has asked to sift you as wheat.

32. But I have prayed for you, Simon, that your faith may not fail. And when you have turned back, strengthen your brothers."

Hebrews 7:25. Therefore he is able to save completely those who come to God through him, because he always lives to intercede for them.

A mediator is one who interposes between two parties with the goal of bringing about reconciliation. He must have the confidence and trust of both sides. Frequently we hear of a mediator being called to settle a labor dispute when negotiations have come to an impasse.

Sin broke humanity's relationship with God. God wanted the relationship restored; however, sin has no place in His holy presence. Under the Law, the high priest stood between God and the people as a mediator, but this was only a temporary arrangement.

In God's time the perfect and eternal Mediator came. He is God the Son, so He could approach the Father. He became Man so He could reach out to lost people everywhere. Jesus Christ made it possible for sinful humanity to be forgiven and to establish communion with a holy God.

BIBLE COMMENTARY

1. Our Sacrifice

A. Need For Atonement
Exodus 32:30

The Israelites had committed a terrible sin while Moses was on Mount Sinai receiving God's laws. The people had persuaded Aaron to make a golden calf which they proclaimed as their god and proceeded to worship. We can imagine Moses' horror at the scene as he returned from the presence of a holy God!

The Israelites realized they had sinned and had already felt God's judgment. However, they could not be forgiven until an atonement was made. Moses was so dedicated to the people he led out of Egypt that he was willing to offer himself as their substitute.

Ask: "Could Moses have made atonement for the people as he desired?" He erred in thinking he could do such a thing, for no sinful human can atone for another. However, Moses understood the divine principle in dealing with sin. There must be the sacrifice of an innocent substitute before sin can be erased from the record.

Moses' attitude shows he realized the serious consequences of sin. He was keenly aware that this terrible outbreak of idolatry had to be dealt with. This meant that some kind of atonement had to be made.

NOTES

B. God's Love Demonstrated
Romans 8:31,32; 1 John 2:2

In Romans 8:31,32, Paul was building up to the mighty climax of the chapter in verses 38 and 39 where he listed everything that we might mistakenly think could separate us from God's love. **Ask: "What did Paul mean when he asked in verse 31, 'If God be for us, who can be against us?' "** Paul wanted believers to know that all the opposition they will ever encounter cannot outweigh the truth that God is for them. Neither can that opposition overcome the victory God can help them win.

TEACHING TIP 1: Take a few moments and have members of the class mention some of the things that can be against us. List suggestions on the

In verse 32 Paul gave the greatest proof for knowing God loves us—the sacrifice of His Son. That ultimate proof has cost God dearly. Yet He paid the price willingly, not even sparing His own Son. Never forget that the Son was not an unwilling sacrifice, for He laid down His life freely for the salvation of sinners. He did so knowing He would be victorious.

Since God has shown He is for us by such a sacrifice, we can be certain that through His Son all our needs shall be met. What He gives He gives "freely," in other words, graciously out of His favor.

"All things" does not mean God will cater to our every whim. It does mean that we shall lack nothing that pertains to our spiritual well-being and the legitimate needs of life. Since God has been so gracious in giving us His very best—His only begotten Son—we can be certain of His continuing provision throughout life.

John also described Christ's sacrifice in 1 John 2:2. John referred to Jesus himself as the "propitiation" (KJV) or "atoning sacrifice" (NIV). "Propitiation" is a theological word with which we may not be familiar. It is a sacrifice that atones for sin and satisfies the requirements of God's law. This sacrifice propitiates or satisfies the judgment of a holy God. It makes it possible for Him to show mercy and forgiveness to the sinner.

The Greek word for "propitiation" in the New Testament does not mean the same as the Greeks used it. To them it simply meant appeasement, which is not the complete sense in which Christ's sacrifice was made. The heathen believed that the more sacrifices they made to their false gods the less those gods would be inclined to be angry with them.

The Scriptures put Christ's redemptive work on a much higher plane than this. Christ's sacrifice does not only appease God, but satisfies His holy demand for sin's judgment and offers the redeemed sinner perfect fellowship with himself. The Law kept pointing to this perfect sacrifice. Now it has been made and we have good news to give the whole world. We can tell every sinner, "God loves you. If you don't believe it, just look at what happened on the cross."

NOTES

2. Our Advocate

A. Judgment Averted
Exodus 32:11-14

Moses recognized that in their sinful condition the Israelites needed someone to plead their case. Their terrible idolatry made it impossible for them to approach a holy God in their own name. Moses himself stood in the gap as their advocate. His plea was not on the basis of the people's deserving mercy, for they did not. God would have been justified in wiping them out. Moses based his appeal on the honor of God's own name.

Ask: "In what sense did God 'repent' in this situation?" It is unfortunate that the way "repent" is now used makes it difficult for people to understand biblical statements about God's repenting. God does not change His mind whimsically. If He changes His actions it is because people have given Him reason to do so. God cannot be untrue to His own character, which means He cannot overlook sin. In this case, Moses' plea for God's covenant people resulted in God's showing mercy and not destroying the nation. It should be noted, however, that God only limited the extent and delayed the time of His judgment.

Moses' role on behalf of Israel was used by God to roughly illustrate that of Christ as the perfect Advocate on behalf of the world. God was merciful to Israel, but their sin was still present. He knew He would have to deal with it later (verses 33,34). Christ's role as our Advocate is founded on the shedding of His blood for our sins. When we accept the Atonement by faith, God will never again remember our sins against us.

NOTES

B. Help In Time Of Need
Romans 8:33,34; 1 John 2:1

In Romans 8:33,34 Paul dealt with the matter of condemnation for believers' sins. Who can press charges against them for past sins if those sins have been washed away by the blood of Jesus? There are those who would try. Satan is the great accuser who tries to bring charges against the redeemed (Revelation 12:10).

However, as Paul emphasized, it is only God who has the right to make such charges. He has justified everyone who has accepted His Son; He has declared them righteous. If there are any charges to be pressed, only He can bring them.

In verse 34 the apostle pointed out that if Christ condemned us after forgiving us, He would be denying the effectiveness of His own work on the cross. His resurrection proves that God accepted that redemptive work. When Satan would bring thoughts of condemnation to our minds, we can point to Calvary and the open tomb and say: "There is the evidence that my sins have been dealt with. You can no longer condemn me for them."

TEACHING TIP 2: Lead a brief discussion concerning the use of the word "advocate" today. Usually it is employed in legal proceedings. It may also apply to a spokesman for a group interested in some cause. Often this is an issue before a branch of government and threatens to damage the interests of the people involved, for example, building a freeway through a residential area. Then use the following to expand the students' understanding of the biblical emphasis.

The term *advocate* as applied to Jesus Christ goes much farther than its present-day usage. The Greek word occurs five times in the New Testament. First John 2:1 is the only verse where it is translated "advocate." It is rendered "Comforter" in John 14:16,26; 15:26; and 16:7, and refers to the Holy Spirit. He came to be our Advocate when Jesus returned to heaven. The Greek word means literally "called to one's side to give aid."

In 1 John 2:1, John spoke of our Advocate in connection with the commission of sin. First of all, he urged believers not to sin. He was not giving them any license to feel they could sin because they could count on God's forgiveness. However, John recognized that believers do sin. They are not perfect. When they fail the Lord, it is likely they will have to deal with feelings of condemnation, aggravated by Satan. For the encouragement of such believers, John reminded us that we have an Advocate who pleads our case before God.

NOTES

3. Our Intercessor

A. Picture From The Past
Exodus 32:31,32

The idolatry of the Israelites while Moses was on Mount Sinai was the greatest tragedy that had happened since they left Egypt. Moses feared God would destroy the whole nation for this sin. In his plea he did not minimize what they had done and named the sin without hesitation: "This people have sinned a great sin, and have made them gods of gold" (verse 31).

Moses then put himself in the place of the whole nation, asking God to let the blow of judgment fall on him instead of them. If God could not forgive the people, Moses wanted his own name to be blotted out of God's book (verse 32). In this act, Moses demonstrated the true nature of intercession, putting himself in the place of those for whom he was interceding.

Sometimes we use the term *intercede* in a rather light or even frivolous way. We need someone's help but do not feel we can approach him. So we ask a mutual friend to "intercede" for us.

Of course we cannot think of Christ's intercession on such a human plane, but the principle is the same. Not only has Christ offered himself as our substitutionary sacrifice and continued to plead our cause before God in heaven's court, but He faithfully brings our needs to God. **Ask: "In what way did Moses' intercession point to the intercessory ministry of Jesus?"** Sin had doomed the human race to everlasting death. Jesus put himself between a holy God and sinful man when He died on the cross; the blow of judgment fell on Him. If we will believe on Him and accept His sacrifice, we will be saved.

NOTES

B. Jesus Prays For Us
Luke 22:31,32; Hebrews 7:25

The Cross represents Christ's all-sufficient sacrifice on behalf of all sinners. But beyond the point of salvation, there are many trials that believers face. It is comforting to know that Christ's intercessory ministry before the Father is aimed at meeting our specific needs.

Peter was a man with many faults, but Jesus knew what Peter could become through spiritual discipline and the power of the Holy Spirit. He knew Peter would fail Him, but Jesus would not respond by abandoning him. Jesus warned Peter he would experience Satan's attack, but Jesus tenderly assured Peter He had already prayed for him. Jesus had pleaded his case even before Peter's denial of his Lord took place. Despite Satan's efforts, Peter's faith would remain intact even though his actions were a picture of failure. Afterward, Peter would repent and recover. He would turn back to the path of faithfulness and become a leader in the Early Church. This would not be attributable to Peter's own strength, but to the intercession of the Lord who loved him.

Peter was not a "special case" when it comes to Jesus' prayers for His followers. The writer of Hebrews makes this clear: "He is able also to save them to the uttermost that come unto God by him, seeing he ever liveth to make intercession for them" (verse 25). **Ask: "What is the meaning of the expression, 'to the uttermost'?"** This salvation is total and complete. The deliverance Christ petitions when interceding for us will be lacking in nothing. We must note the qualification, of course. Such a salvation is for them "that come unto God by Him." There is no other way but Jesus.

This complete salvation is based on the fact Jesus is alive forevermore and engaged continually in intercession for those who come to Him. In our Christian walk, there will never be a time when this intercession will cease. It will continue whether we are walking a path of joyous victory or whether we falter and come short of what we should be. This is the kind of High Priest we have!

TEACHING TIP 3: To summarize the study, distribute the work sheet ''Our Confidence.'' Give the students time to paraphrase the three key verses. Ask several of them to read their paraphrases. They should be reminded not to change the meaning of any passage, but simply to express them in what we might call ''everyday'' language.

LIFE RESPONSE

If Jesus were only a good man, an outstanding teacher, or a worthy example, we would not have the great assurance this study gives us. Teachers and examples serve their purpose, but in a world of tests and trials, we need someone who can help us, guide us, and sustain us.

Dying on the cross and rising again from the dead proves that Jesus is the Son of God and the Savior of sinners. His resurrection and the outpouring of the Holy Spirit are evidences that He is at God's right hand. And we know that in this position of authority, He is our Mediator and Intercessor.

We should do our best with God's help not to fail and, above all, not to sin. However, we are human and we are all too aware of our weaknesses. If we fail, we can be certain Satan will be on the scene quickly to attack us with condemnation and discouragement. At such times we can rely on the truth that our Advocate is pleading our case before His Father's throne. He is not there to condemn us. He represents our cause in the highest Court of all. He will restore us when we fail (as He did Peter). He will forgive us when we repent and confess.

We cannot simply sit back and enjoy the benefits we receive through Christ's ministry. We must have a heart of compassion for the lost, just as Moses felt compassion for the idolatrous Israelites. Unlike Moses, we can approach the throne of God confidently in Jesus' name on behalf of those who are bound by sin.

EVANGELISM OUTREACH

Remind unsaved students that only Jesus Christ can forgive sin—any sin, no matter how bad or unforgivable it may seem. Only Jesus is able to cleanse sin completely and make those who believe in Him righteous. In addition, emphasize that as Christians they would then have an Advocate, Jesus Christ, who would be available to assist them with any problem, at any time.

Plan your class time to allow for an altar call. Be prepared to stay after class to pray with any who wish to be saved.

Living A Pure Life

Central Truth

God wants purity of life to be characteristic of His people.

Golden Text

I am the Lord your God; consecrate yourselves and be holy, because I am holy. Leviticus 11:44 (NIV)

Study Text

Leviticus 10:8-10; 11:44,45; Numbers 19:14-20; Deuteronomy 7:6-11; Titus 2:11,12; 1 Peter 1:15,16; 1 John 3:1-3

Outline

1. Call To Pure Living
   A. Set Apart From Evil
   B. God Is The Standard

2. Instructions For Pure Living
   A. Abstain From Alcohol
   B. Shun All Defilement

3. Motivation For Pure Living
   A. Set Free From Bondage
   B. Anticipate Christ's Return

Objective

To know God wants His people to be holy and determine to live pure lives.

Checklist

☐ Familiarize yourself with the two overhead transparencies from the Adult Teaching Helps Packet. These transparencies supplement the third main point.

☐ Read the *Adult Student Guide* in order to tie it closely to your teaching. You will want to be familiar with the questions in the *Adult Student Guide*.

☐ You may need to consult a commentary or Bible dictionary for additional insights into the Mosaic ceremonies described in this study. Make sure you have a clear concept of how these laws of cleanliness illustrate the spiritual truth of holy living.

☐ Emphasize practices that must be shunned as well as positive biblical behavior that should be followed daily. Be ready to answer questions while discouraging arguments.

Daily Bible Readings

Monday:	Purified For Service. Numbers 8:18-26
Tuesday:	Personal Purity. Numbers 19:11-13,17-22
Wednesday:	Prayer For Purity. Psalm 51:1-10
Thursday:	Purity Of Heart. James 4:1-8
Friday:	Call To Purity. Titus 2:11-15
Saturday:	Means Of Purification. 1 John 1:8 through 2:2

King James Version

Leviticus 11:45. I am the Lord that bringeth you up out of the land of Egypt, to be your God: ye shall therefore be holy, for I am holy.

1 Peter 1:15. But as he which hath called you is holy, so be ye holy in all manner of conversation;

16. Because it is written, Be ye holy; for I am holy.

Leviticus 10:9. Do not drink wine nor strong drink, thou, nor thy sons with thee, when ye go into the tabernacle of the congregation, lest ye die: it shall be a statute for ever throughout your generations:

10. And that ye may put difference between holy and unholy, and between unclean and clean.

Numbers 19:17. And for an unclean person they shall take of the ashes of the burnt heifer of purification for sin, and running water shall be put thereto in a vessel:

18. And a clean person shall take hyssop, and dip it in the water, and sprinkle it upon the tent, and upon all the vessels, and upon the persons that were there, and upon him that touched a bone, or one slain, or one dead, or a grave.

Titus 2:11. For the grace of God that bringeth salvation hath appeared to all men,

12. Teaching us that, denying ungodliness and worldly lusts, we should live soberly, righteously, and godly, in this present world.

Deuteronomy 7:6. For thou art a holy people unto the Lord thy God: the Lord thy God hath chosen thee to be a special people unto himself, above all people that are upon the face of the earth.

8. But because the Lord loved you, and because he would keep the oath which he had sworn unto your fathers, hath the Lord brought you out with a mighty hand, and redeemed you out of the house of bondmen, from the hand of Pharaoh king of Egypt.

1 John 3:2. Beloved, now are we the sons of God, and it doth not yet appear what we shall be: but we know that, when he shall appear, we shall be like him; for we shall see him as he is.

3. And every man that hath this hope in him purifieth himself, even as he is pure.

New International Version

Leviticus 11:45. I am the Lord who brought you up out of Egypt to be your God; therefore be holy, because I am holy.

1 Peter 1:15. But just as he who called you is holy, so be holy in all you do;

16. For it is written: "Be holy, because I am holy."

Leviticus 10:9. You and your sons are not to drink wine or other fermented drink whenever you go into the Tent of Meeting, or you will die. This is a lasting ordinance for the generations to come.

10. You must distinguish between the holy and the common, between the unclean and the clean.

Numbers 19:17. For the unclean person, put some ashes from the burned purification offering into a jar and pour fresh water over them.

18. Then a man who is ceremonially clean is to take some hyssop, dip it in the water and sprinkle the tent and all the furnishings and the people who were there. He must also sprinkle anyone who has touched a human bone or a grave or someone who has been killed or someone who has died a natural death.

Titus 2:11. For the grace of God that brings salvation has appeared to all men.

12. It teaches us to say "No" to ungodliness and worldly passions, and to live self-controlled, upright and godly lives in this present age.

Deuteronomy 7:6. For you are a people holy to the Lord your God. The Lord your God has chosen you out of all the peoples on the face of the earth to be his people, his treasured possession.

8. But it was because the Lord loved you and kept the oath he swore to your forefathers that he brought you out with a mighty hand and redeemed you from the land of slavery, from the power of Pharaoh king of Egypt.

1 John 3:2. Dear friends, now we are children of God, and what we will be has not yet been made known. But we know that when he appears, we shall be like him, for we shall see him as he is.

3. Everyone who has this hope in him purifies himself, just as he is pure.

The Lord called Israel to have a separate and distinct life-style from the heathen. Israel was to serve as a beacon to the rest of the world. The surrounding nations that observed them in the centuries before Christ saw a people who were commanded by their God to shun idolatry and immorality—a people who were blessed by God when they obeyed and punished when they rebelled. In the days following Christ's first coming, the world was impacted by the teaching and example of Christians whose lives were transformed by their Savior.

God's regulations about outward cleanness in the Old Testament illustrate the necessity of moral cleanness. This truth is constantly repeated and emphasized in the New Testament. Today's believers are the Body God has called out to be separate and distinct from the world system.

BIBLE COMMENTARY

1. Call To Pure Living

A. Set Apart From Evil
Leviticus 11:44,45

Leviticus 11:44,45 summarizes God's purpose for the many laws He gave the Israelites. To maintain a covenant relationship with Him, they had to be like Him.

Ask: "Why were God's commandments about pure living repeated so often?" The Israelites were not in a sterile moral environment. They were surrounded by heathen who worshiped idols and indulged in all manner of degraded living. The temptation to yield to pressure from the heathen was constant. Furthermore, the wicked were not passive about their desire to impose their standards on the godly. They flaunted their vileness openly. They sought intermarriage between the Israelites and themselves. When such marriage alliances occurred, it always resulted in God's people being dragged down instead of their lifting up the heathen.

TEACHING TIP 1: Lead a brief discussion concerning parallels between Israel's position and moral influence among the heathen and the Christian's situation in this present age. You may want to put a summary of students' comments on the chalkboard.

The statement, "I am the Lord your God," is not a cliche. God introduced His commandments about holy living with a reminder of who He is. God himself is always the standard of holiness. Furthermore, He is the One to whom His people are accountable for their behavior. This is a truth we must keep in focus at all times in this day of moral permissiveness.

Ask: "What attribute of God is emphasized most in the Old Testament?" God's holiness is mentioned more often than any other characteristic of His nature. The word *holy* occurs again and again in the Book of Leviticus because it was the "handbook" for the priesthood. As God's New Testament priests, we can learn much from this book.

Since the Israelites were under the authority of a holy God, they had to sanctify themselves. It is unfortunate that the word *sanctify* has sometimes been associated with extreme legalism and man-made rules. The Hebrew word most frequently used in the Old Testament for *sanctify* referred to what was separated as sacred and holy. It was distinct from the common or profane. Only if God's people maintain this separation from the world system can they enjoy an unbroken, unimpeded relationship with Him.

The Hebrew words translated "sanctify" and "holy" in Leviticus 11:44 are the verbal and adjectival forms of the same word. This reinforces God's call to His people to be distinct and separate from the heathen, just as He is.

Under the Law, God illustrated defilement by forbidding contact with certain things, including animals which He designated as unclean. This only pointed to the larger danger of spiritual defilement. For Christians, this happens not from touching dead bodies or unclean animals, but from yielding to the unclean moral atmosphere around us. We cannot afford to become desensitized to the sinful world in which we live. Our victory lies in keeping the holiness of God himself before our spiritual eyes.

Over and over God reminded His people that they now enjoyed the blessings of their relationship with Him because He had delivered them from the terrible bondage of Egypt. While they were slaves, they could hardly have been called a people. Now they were free. They were a people God called His own. He bound himself to them by a covenant sealed with His own Word. As long as they recognized Him as their God, worshiping and serving Him, that covenant relationship would be maintained.

NOTES

B. God Is The Standard
1 Peter 1:15,16

We must recognize that there are two sides to our relationship with the Lord. He has delivered us from the slavery of sin and keeps us by His power daily. However, we have our own personal responsibility to obey His Word and vigorously resist all of the temptations of Satan and the world system he controls. We must not try to place on God the responsibility which is our own.

Peter wrote his letters to believers who had been scattered to various locations. They, too, were living among idolaters whose lives were vile and lawless. They faced temptations daily. The apostle felt it necessary to repeat God's commandment to Israel: "Be ye holy; for I am holy" (1 Peter 1:16). Turning an eye backward to their former life of spiritual ignorance, Peter warned his readers not to pattern their behavior after the standards they formerly held. God was now their standard. He is holy, and He will be satisfied with nothing less from those who profess to serve Him.

NOTES

2. Instructions For Pure Living

A. Abstain From Alcohol
Leviticus 10:9,10

God's commandment against the priests' drinking wine or any other strong drink while performing their duties could not have been stronger. They would die if they disobeyed. The law was not temporary; it was intended for every generation of priests.

God's reasons were clear. Consuming alcohol would cloud the priests' minds and affect their ability to reason. People will do things under the influence of alcohol that they would never do otherwise. Their inhibitions disappear; their convictions are weakened and sometimes destroyed.

As the spiritual leaders of the people, the priests needed to have at all times a clear conception of the difference between right and wrong. They had to be able to distinguish between what was holy and what was common, between what God had designated as clean and as unclean. The congregation looked to these men for guidance, and their judgment in providing that guidance could never be clouded by strong drink.

> TEACHING TIP 2: Discuss with the students the different approaches Christians have taken toward alcoholic beverages. But do not allow the discussion to sidetrack the study. Also avoid emotional interaction between students with varying points of view. Use the following commentary to guide class discussion.

Ask: "What does this Scripture tell us about total abstinence versus moderation or 'social' drinking?" Believers today are God's priesthood. They must be as separate and distinct from the present age as the Old Testament priests were separated for their duties. Christians cannot afford to indulge in a practice which would influence them to compromise scriptural truth and engage in questionable behavior.

NOTES

B. Shun All Defilement
Numbers 19:17,18; Titus 2:11,12

Numbers 19:17,18 refers to the means of gaining ceremonial cleansing after becoming unclean. The strict guidelines in this chapter are primarily for those who came in contact with a dead body. **Ask: "Why would God use dead bodies as a picture of spiritual defilement?"** Death was not in the human picture until sin entered. Death represents the ultimate consequences of sin. It destroys what is beautiful and useful. When death comes, a once healthy looking body soon begins to deteriorate and decay. What physical death does to the human body, sin does to the human spirit.

Titus 2:11,12 summarizes what these Old Testament Scriptures teach in type and symbol. Paul reminded us that being under grace instead of the Law does not free us from obeying God's command to be pure.

Ask: "What did Paul mean when he stated, 'God's grace that brings salvation has appeared to all people'?" Grace did not appear as an abstract principle, but as a Person. When God's Son appeared on earth, the grace of God offered salvation from sin to everyone, not just a favored few.

Through grace we are not only saved; we are taught. Once converted we still have much to learn about living to please God. God's grace as manifested in Christ teaches us what we could not otherwise know. Grace "teaches us to say 'No' to ungodliness and worldly passions" (Titus 2:12, NIV).

> TEACHING TIP 3: Looking at Titus 2:12 in the King James Version, lead a discussion about the three words, "soberly, righteously, and godly." Draw out from the students what they see in these characteristics as they apply to their own lives.

The believer must live soberly, which means in a self-controlled manner. Christians must be disciplined, keeping their own nature under a tight reign. Living righteously refers to one's relationship with others. It means to be upright and just. Living godly refers to our relationship with God. We are to be reverent and devout.

The miracle of it all is that God's grace enables us to live "soberly, righteously, and godly, in this present world" (verse 12), surrounded by every force and influence that would pull us away from Him. Let no one claim that such a life is impossible. God's grace makes victorious living a reality.

NOTES

3. Motivation For Pure Living

A. Set Free From Bondage
Deuteronomy 7:6-11

TEACHING TIP 4: Display Overhead Transparency 1 "Motivation For Pure Living: Old Testament" from the Adult Teaching Helps Packet while discussing Deuteronomy 7:6-11. Give the students opportunity to connect each of the points with their own experience.

Because Israel was God's people, anything but holy living would be inconsistent with such a relationship. The word "special" in Deuteronomy 7:6 refers to a possession that belongs to no one else. Of all the other nations on earth, God had called Israel for His own. Who would want to violate the laws of the God who had bestowed such matchless privileges on them? **Ask: "How did God's choice of a small nation demonstrate the way He often works?"** The natural mind expects God to look upon the mighty, the powerful, and the great. But God delights in confounding such carnal thinking. He operates according to His divine will. His actions are also based on a divine love that refuses to be limited by human standards of greatness (verse 7).

Israel had the assurance of God's own covenant, His Word, to secure this relationship. Nothing could have demonstrated His love for them more than delivering them from slavery in Egypt. That deliverance from human bondage serves to illustrate the freedom from sin's bondage offered to all who will come to Christ. We are saved from sin and set apart as God's chosen people today. We are called to live holy lives in response.

Israel was warned that their relationship with God depended on their continued obedience. If they became disobedient and lawless they would face His judgment. Those who rejected God's laws would be visited with judgment that even affected future generations. We see this truth lived out in our own day. As people and nations have embraced the truth of the gospel, they have enjoyed God's favor. When society rejects God, it begins on a road to destruction that can ruin the lives of their children as well.

NOTES

B. Anticipate Christ's Return
1 John 3:1-3

TEACHING TIP 5: Display Overhead Transparency 2 "Motivation For Pure Living: New Testament" from the Adult Teaching Helps Packet while discussing 1 John 3:1-3. Solicit input from the students for each point.

John reminded believers of the privilege of being in God's family. Children of God must be careful not to bring reproach on the family name or reputation.

Ask: **"In what sense does the world not recognize those who are God's children?"** Their identification with Jesus Christ makes certain that the world's attitude toward them will be the same as it was toward Him. The world did not give Jesus the recognition He deserved. In the same way, the world seeks to ignore Christians and what they stand for.

But while being unrecognized by the world, God's children have a future the world will never have. They are looking for the coming of Jesus, knowing that when He appears they will be like Him. Such a hope is the most powerful incentive to purity that could be named.

NOTES

LIFE RESPONSE

The world's ridicule of Christianity must never be allowed to sway us. We have done more than join a church or participate in religious ceremonies. We have heard the call of God through His Spirit and have left the old life of sin to become part of His family. This is a miraculous experience, a new birth. God has now put His new nature within us by His indwelling Spirit.

This raises the Christian life to the highest plane. Our call has come from God himself and it is to Him we must always be accountable. Whatever the standards of the world around us, our guidelines for living must be from the Bible. Because it is God's Word, its standards do not change no matter what century we live in. Principles of holiness are declared in both Testaments, and God's principles remain constant.

God's people in Old Testament days were like beginning students in the school of holy living, for they did not have the light we have today. Patiently God taught them His ways, often using the things of earth to illustrate spiritual truth. We must be just as careful about spiritual defilement as they had to be of physical contamination.

When we see Jesus face-to-face, that will be the goal toward which pure living has been propelling us. We want to be ready each moment for that great event when we are forever ushered into His glorious presence. The lessons in holiness in this life will be the foundation for the perfect union we enjoy with Him then.

EVANGELISM OUTREACH

While this study is aimed primarily at Christians, it affords an opportunity to emphasize to unsaved students what it means to be a Christian. We are not doing unbelievers a favor by playing down God's demand for separation from the world. Unsaved students must be reminded that the Lord will give them the strength to live an overcoming life. Do not hesitate to conclude this study with an altar call, allowing time for response and prayer at the end of the class period.

142

Christ And The Law

CENTRAL TRUTH

Through faith in Christ's atoning work we are freed from the condemnation of the Law.

GOLDEN TEXT

Christ redeemed us from the curse of the law by becoming a curse for us. Galatians 3:13 (NIV)

STUDY TEXT

Matthew 5:17-20; Luke 2:21-24; 24:25-27,44; Galatians 3:11-14; 4:4,5

OUTLINE

1. Christ, Born Under The Law
   A. Obedience To The Law
   B. In The Fullness Of Time

2. Christ Fulfilled The Law
   A. The Law Must Be Fulfilled
   B. The Law Testifies Of Christ

3. Christ, Redeemer Of Sinners
   A. Justified By Faith
   B. Redeemed From The Curse

OBJECTIVE

To understand how Christ fulfilled the Law and appropriate His redemptive work.

CHECKLIST

☐ Be sure to read the student guide and accompanying questions as you prepare your presentation.

☐ Become familiar with the work sheet "Works Or Faith?" Make enough copies for the students and yourself. Fill in your work sheet in order to offer the students suggestions as they fill in their own responses. Question 4 will be discussed in class.

☐ Next week's study (study 8) discusses the Law in contrast to grace. It would be helpful to read through that study before you begin preparations for this week so you can avoid any overlapping.

☐ Matthew 5:17-20 is part of the Sermon on the Mount. Scan chapters 5 through 7 to see how these verses tie in with Jesus' explanation of the principles of His kingdom.

DAILY BIBLE READINGS

Monday:	Power To Deliver.	
	Exodus 13:1-5	
Tuesday:	Assurance Of God's Presence.	
	Ezra 9:5-9	
Wednesday:	Promise Of Deliverance.	
	Isaiah 14:1-7	
Thursday:	Do Not Return To Bondage.	
	Galatians 4:1-9	
Friday:	Liberty In Christ.	
	Galatians 5:1-6	
Saturday:	Rejoice In Freedom.	
	Hebrews 2:10-18	

SCRIPTURE SETTING

King James Version

Luke 2:21. When eight days were accomplished for the circumcising of the child, his name was called Jesus, which was so named of the angel before he was conceived in the womb.

22. And when the days of her purification according to the law of Moses were accomplished, they brought him to Jerusalem, to present him to the Lord;

23. (As it is written in the law of the Lord, Every male that openeth the womb shall be called holy to the Lord;)

24. And to offer a sacrifice according to that which is said in the law of the Lord, A pair of turtledoves, or two young pigeons.

Galatians 4:4. When the fulness of the time was come, God sent forth his Son, made of a woman, made under the law,

5. To redeem them that were under the law, that we might receive the adoption of sons.

Matthew 5:17. Think not that I am come to destroy the law, or the prophets: I am not come to destroy, but to fulfil.

18. For verily I say unto you, Till heaven and earth pass, one jot or one tittle shall in no wise pass from the law, till all be fulfilled.

Luke 24:25. Then he said unto them, O fools, and slow of heart to believe all that the prophets have spoken:

26. Ought not Christ to have suffered these things, and to enter into his glory?

27. And beginning at Moses and all the prophets, he expounded unto them in all the Scriptures the things concerning himself.

44. And he said unto them, These are the words which I spake unto you, while I was yet with you, that all things must be fulfilled, which were written in the law of Moses, and in the prophets, and in the psalms, concerning me.

Galatians 3:11. That no man is justified by the law in the sight of God, it is evident: for, The just shall live by faith.

12. And the law is not of faith: but, The man that doeth them shall live in them.

13. Christ hath redeemed us from the curse of the law, being made a curse for us: for it is written, Cursed is every one that hangeth on a tree:

14. That the blessing of Abraham might come on the Gentiles through Jesus Christ; that we might receive the promise of the Spirit through faith.

New International Version

Luke 2:21. On the eighth day, when it was time to circumcise him, he was named Jesus, the name the angel had given him before he had been conceived.

22. When the time of their purification according to the Law of Moses had been completed, Joseph and Mary took him to Jerusalem to present him to the Lord

23. (As it is written in the Law of the Lord, "Every firstborn male is to be consecrated to the Lord"),

24. And to offer a sacrifice in keeping with what is said in the Law of the Lord: "a pair of doves or two young pigeons."

Galatians 4:4. When the time had fully come, God sent his Son, born of a woman, born under law,

5. To redeem those under law, that we might receive the full rights of sons.

Matthew 5:17. Do not think that I have come to abolish the Law or the Prophets; I have not come to abolish them but to fulfill them.

18. I tell you the truth, until heaven and earth disappear, not the smallest letter, not the least stroke of a pen, will by any means disappear from the Law until everything is accomplished.

Luke 24:25. He said to them, "How foolish you are, and how slow of heart to believe all that the prophets have spoken!

26. Did not the Christ have to suffer these things and then enter his glory?"

27. And beginning with Moses and all the Prophets, he explained to them what was said in all the Scriptures concerning himself.

44. He said to them, "This is what I told you while I was still with you: Everything must be fulfilled that is written about me in the Law of Moses, the Prophets and the Psalms."

Galatians 3:11. Clearly no one is justified before God by the law, because, "The righteous will live by faith."

12. The law is not based on faith; on the contrary, "The man who does these things will live by them."

13. Christ redeemed us from the curse of the law by becoming a curse for us, for it is written: "Cursed is everyone who is hung on a tree."

14. He redeemed us in order that the blessing given to Abraham might come to the Gentiles through Christ Jesus, so that by faith we might receive the promise of the Spirit.

When Adam and Eve fell into sin, God's plan of redemption was quickly announced—a plan in His mind even before creation. As early as Genesis 3:15, God spoke of a descendant of Eve who would conquer evil. In the centuries before Christ, God repeatedly showed people they were sinners in need of saving. Through the Law, He identified sin so no one could claim not to know what behavior was wrong in His sight. The Law also taught people they were incapable of keeping God's commands. God's people had to depend on Him for the means of atonement and forgiveness.

All of these centuries of the Law led up to the coming of Jesus. He did not come to destroy the Law, but to fulfill it. In His teaching He showed people the Law from God's perspective. True fulfillment of the Law comes through faith in Christ.

BIBLE COMMENTARY

1. Christ, Born Under The Law

A. Obedience To The Law
Luke 2:21-24

> TEACHING TIP 1: Before beginning a discussion of Luke 2:21-24, ask a student to read Leviticus 12:1-8 to the class. Then ask another student to read Luke 2:21-24.

When we compare Luke 2:21-24 and Leviticus 12:1-8, we see that Joseph and Mary were a devout Jewish family who conformed strictly to the Law. Under the Law a Jewish woman was considered ceremonially unclean when a child was born to her. **Ask: "What was the significance of this statute of the Law?"** The birth of a child, accompanied by the discharge of blood, was a reminder of sin and the mortality of the body. The ceremonial cleansing of a woman after childbirth kept before the people the truth that sin is ever present. Although Jesus was born sinless, Mary would have still been required to observe the requirements of the Law for her own benefit. The ceremony was also carried out because all of Christ's life was subject to the Law He came to fulfill.

The period of ceremonial uncleanness began a week before the circumcision of a male child and continued until 40 days of purification were complete. The mother then offered a sacrifice. The first preference was a lamb, but God made provision for the poor. In this case He accepted the sacrifice of two doves or two pigeons. This sacrifice was made when the child was presented to the Lord at the temple.

That birds were offered by Joseph and Mary instead of a lamb suggests that Jesus was born into a poor family. Thus even in His infancy, Jesus was identified not only with those who lived under the Law, but also with those considered of no great importance, those lacking social status because they were poor.

Throughout Jesus' earthly life, no one could point to a time when He had not been fully obedient to the Law. He is the Son of God, yet He did not exempt himself from the Mosaic regulations under which the rest of the Jewish people lived.

NOTES

B. In The Fullness Of Time
Galatians 4:4,5

Paul's Galatian letter was written to people who were drifting back into bondage to the Law. To attempt to please God through the legalistic standards of the Law would mean substituting those standards for faith in Christ. God had established faith in His Son as the foundation for any relationship with himself. When we accept Christ as Savior, His righteousness is credited to us. We are considered righteous in God's eyes because Jesus is righteous.

God does everything according to His divine schedule: "When the fulness of the time was come, God sent forth his Son" (Galatians 4:4). Jesus' coming to earth was not an afterthought. It was planned before the Creation. God knew Adam and Eve would fall even before He created them. However, God did not send the Redeemer immediately after the Fall. He included centuries of preparation in His plan for our redemption. During that time He used the Law as a constant reminder of humanity's total inability to obey Him perfectly.

Ask: "Why did Paul refer to Jesus as 'made of a woman' (verse 4)?" Undoubtedly this is a reference to the Virgin Birth. Born of a woman, Jesus was fully human; conceived by the Holy Spirit, He was also fully God.

Notice the connecting statements in verses 4 and 5: "made under the law, to redeem them that were under the law." To save lost humanity, Jesus had to identify himself completely with them. For approximately 33 years He lived on the same earth as everyone else. As a man He became weary, hungry, and thirsty. He resisted Satan's temptations. By subjecting himself to the Law, He was able to redeem those who were under the Law but could not keep it.

Having been redeemed from the Law's condemnation, we have been adopted into God's family (verse 5). God does not look at us as His slaves, but as His children. None of this could have happened if Jesus had not been willing to humble himself and live under the Law. Because He kept the Law instead of breaking it, He can reach out to lawbreakers and lift them out of their state of condemnation.

NOTES

2. Christ Fulfilled The Law

A. The Law Must Be Fulfilled
Matthew 5:17-20

During Christ's ministry on earth, He was often accused by His enemies of breaking the Law. Underlying this accusation was a fundamental misunderstanding of the Law. The religious leaders of Jesus' day were focused entirely on the physical details of the Law. They did not realize that the Law pointed toward the very One they were attacking, and that His life was the fulfillment of the Law. Jesus proclaimed His relationship to the Law in Matthew 5:17-20.

The term "the Law or the Prophets" (verse 17, NIV) refers to the entire body of Old Testament Scripture. God has always desired to redeem humanity from sin. Instituting the Law was a necessary step. It emphasized people's inability to please God in their own strength and their need of atoning blood for the forgiveness of sins. Whatever the specific message of the prophets or any of the other Old Testament Scriptures was, the underlying theme was redemption.

The full plan of redemption awaited the coming of Jesus to earth. Throughout the Old Testament all the types, shadows, and symbols of the Law's ceremonies pointed to the coming One. The Savior who fulfilled them all arrived and accomplished His work of redemption. Jesus emphasized His relationship to the Law by declaring that it would be fulfilled in the smallest detail (verse 18). He demonstrated His commitment to the commandments of Scripture by warning against breaking any part of this moral code (verse 19). As scrupulous as the scribes and Pharisees were, they had never fully obeyed the Law (verse 20).

TEACHING TIP 2: Jesus' statements in Matthew 5:17-20 belong to detailed teachings popularly called the Sermon on the Mount. Ask the students to scan Matthew 5-7 and note how these teachings enunciate the principles on which Christ's kingdom is based.

NOTES

B. The Law Testifies Of Christ
Luke 24:25-27,44

While on earth, Jesus lived in obedience to the Law's requirements. His death was the perfect Sacrifice to which all other sacrifices had pointed. But at the time of His crucifixion His disciples were so overwhelmed by sorrow they were unable to anticipate the true victory Christ had won. After His resurrection Jesus visited His disciples and opened their eyes to the scriptural promises that had guaranteed that victory all along. In reality, not only do the requirements of the Mosaic law point to Christ, but all of God's written Word heralds the mission of the living Word, Jesus Christ.

In Luke 24:25-27, Jesus was speaking to two disciples who were returning to their home in Emmaus. He emphasized that the death of the Messiah was not a tragic defeat, but something foretold in the Scriptures.

Verse 26 adds the words "and to enter into his glory" to stress that Jesus' death was in no way a defeat. Rather, it was the means of returning to His glory after accomplishing His work of redemption.

Ask: "What is the significance of the expression, 'beginning at Moses'?" Moses was God's spokesman in giving the Law. Referring to "Moses" was the same as referring to the Law contained in the first five books of the Scriptures. No Jew could think of the Law without thinking of Moses. Jesus' teaching on this occasion began with Moses' teaching concerning himself. "All the prophets" and "all the Scriptures" make it clear that Jesus is the theme of the whole body of the Scriptures.

In His appearance later to the whole group of disciples, Jesus repeated what He had said to the Emmaus disciples. Along with the law of Moses and the prophets He mentioned the Psalms, many of which contain messianic prophecies.

TEACHING TIP 3: Divide the class into groups of three or four students. Ask the groups to brainstorm for Scripture passages Jesus might have used when teaching His disciples about His death and resurrection. After 2 or 3 minutes, regroup the class and ask the students to share their ideas and read some of the verses they selected. The following references may help the class: Genesis 3:15; Deuteronomy 18:15; Psalm 16:10; 22:1-31; Isaiah 7:14; Micah 5:2; Zechariah 9:9.

NOTES

3. Christ, Redeemer Of Sinners

A. Justified By Faith
Galatians 3:11,12

Looking again at Paul's teaching to the Galatians concerning the purpose of the Law, we see that no one was ever able to successfully use the Law as a means of salvation. The champions of Judaism may have considered themselves "justified by the law," but this was not true "in the sight of God" (3:11). There are no exceptions; "no man is justified." "Justify" has many meanings today. As Paul used the word in this passage, it means to be declared righteous before God.

The Law was a schoolmaster, as Paul explained in Galatians 3:23-25. It kept people conscious of their guilt. The sacrifices they brought to the priests continually reminded them they were sinners. In response to the people's obedience in offering the blood sacrifices, God forgave their specific sins. But people had to continue offering these sacrifices as long as they lived.

Paul contrasted the Law with faith. Even in the Old Testament, obedience to the Law was only effective through faith. Paul quoted Habakkuk 2:4 to bolster his argument: "The just shall live by faith" (Galatians 3:11). **Ask: "Why did Paul emphasize the subject of faith?"** Christ had already fulfilled the Law. Faith remains as the means to obtain the salvation He offers. Those who depend on faith for their justification cannot depend on the Law. If their hope is in the Law, faith is excluded.

Verse 12 teaches that those who live by the Law will spend all their days trying to keep its works without ever having the assurance of being right with God. Only faith can produce that kind of peace in one's heart.

NOTES

B. Redeemed From The Curse
Galatians 3:13,14

Paul showed in Galatians 3:10 that those who would try to place their trust in the Law are under the curse of the Law. Verse 10 looks back to Deuteronomy 27:26 that pronounced a curse on anyone unable to keep *all* of the Law. The Law was not a series of unrelated commandments. Each commandment was part of the whole law of God. To break one commandment was to be guilty of breaking them all. The Law demanded perfection, which is impossible for any human. Redemption from the curse had to come in some other way than the works of the Law.

Galatians 3:13 clearly presents Christ as the One who has forever redeemed us from bondage to the Law. He took the curse of the Law on himself when He hung on the cross. Again, Paul quoted an Old Testament passage to clarify Christ's mission, Deuteronomy 21:23.

Verses 22,23 deal with the public display of a lawbreaker's corpse after execution. As a warning to everyone that such justice would be visited on others who broke the law, the corpse was hung on a tree only during daylight hours. The spectacle of the dead body reminded everyone that God's curse had fallen on that individual.

The tree on which Jesus hung was, of course, the cross. In exposing himself to public view as a criminal, Jesus was bearing the curse. This was the only way a sinful world could be redeemed. The innocent One took the place of the guilty, the cursed.

Ask: "What connection does the blessing of Abraham (Galatians 3:14) have with observing the Law or relying on faith for salvation (verses 11-13)?" The blessing of Abraham was justification by faith (verses 6-9). Abraham was the father of the Hebrew nation, but the whole world could share in this blessing of faith through Jesus Christ. The evidence of being justified by faith is receiving the promise of the Spirit. With the new birth, the Holy Spirit makes His home in believers, witnessing to their new relationship with God (Romans 8:16).

TEACHING TIP 3: Distribute the work sheet "Works Or Faith?" to the students. Ask them to look over the questions carefully. Have them consider questions 1, 2, and 3 during the week. Ask them to write out an answer to question 4 in class. Discuss their answers before continuing.

LIFE RESPONSE

If we were still under the Law we could only have a temporary sense of sins forgiven by the offering of sacrifices. Thank God, this is not the case. Jesus made himself subject to the Law during His earthly life. By His perfect obedience to the Law He fulfilled it in every respect. He then became the one perfect Sacrifice on Calvary. Because our Savior was righteous before God, we become righteous in God's eyes when we believe in Jesus. This happens through faith, not good works.

The whole world is under God's curse because of sin. Judgment hangs over the head of every unrepentant sinner. As believers, we look back to the day our Lord was hanged on a tree at Calvary and exposed to public humiliation as One who had become a curse. The price He paid that day liberates us from the slavery of works, of law-keeping. By His sacrifice Jesus made it possible for us to be right in God's eyes and receive the Holy Spirit as evidence of that justification. We are redeemed—bought back from slavery to sin!

Although we have been freed from sin's mastery, we will surely be tempted to sin again. But Christ has paid the price for our salvation, so we do not have to rely on our own efforts at righteousness when temptation comes. Instead, as we listen to the guiding voice of the Holy Spirit, we can be continually reminded that Christ's righteousness in us will give us the power to live faithfully for God.

EVANGELISM OUTREACH

Throughout this study, steer clear as much as possible from technical theological points. Concentrate on the main theme of Christ's work of redemption and His offer of salvation to all who believe. Plan the study to culminate in an altar call to the unsaved. If there is no response, you may want to invite students to stay after class to discuss their questions with you. This will give you an opportunity to pray with them and lead them to a decision for Christ. This is, of course, the evangelistic goal of the class.

Contrasting Law And Grace

CENTRAL TRUTH

By grace we are delivered from the bondage of the Law.

GOLDEN TEXT

We maintain that a man is justified by faith apart from observing the law. Romans 3:28 (NIV)

STUDY TEXT

Acts 15:1,5,10,24,28,29; Romans 3:19-23; 7:7; Galatians 3:21-26; Ephesians 2:8-10; Titus 3:4-7; 1 Peter 4:10,11

OUTLINE

1. The Law
   A. Gives Knowledge Of Sin
   B. Brings Bondage
   C. Leads To Christ

2. Grace
   A. Saves From Sin
   B. Brings Justification
   C. Enables Believers

OBJECTIVE

To discover the difference between law and grace and express thanks for God's favor given in Christ.

CHECKLIST

☐ Since this week's study has some overlap with study 7, take a few minutes to review the main points from last week's study. Emphasize that God's grace allowed Christ to die for us.

☐ Read the context of the verses in the Study Text. This will give you a clearer picture of the intent of each sub-point.

☐ Preview the *Adult Student Guide* for additional insights.

☐ Write down the questions from the *Adult Student Guide* you wish to use for discussion.

☐ The overhead transparencies "The Schoolmaster" and "The Gift Of God" in the Adult Teaching Helps Packet should help illustrate visually some of the truths in this week's study.

☐ In preparation for your teaching, seek the Holy Spirit for His direction in meeting the needs of students who are present.

DAILY BIBLE READINGS

Monday: Moral Law Given.
Deuteronomy 5:7-21

Tuesday: Obedience Required.
Deuteronomy 6:12-19

Wednesday: Blessings Of Obedience.
Deuteronomy 28:1-10

Thursday: Purpose Of The Law.
Galatians 3:21-29

Friday: Justified By Grace.
Romans 3:21-31

Saturday: New Life.
Romans 6:1-10

SCRIPTURE SETTING

King James Version

Romans 3:20. By the deeds of the law there shall no flesh be justified in his sight: for by the law is the knowledge of sin.

21. But now the righteousness of God without the law is manifested, being witnessed by the law and the prophets;

22. Even the righteousness of God which is by faith of Jesus Christ unto all and upon all them that believe; for there is no difference:

23. For all have sinned, and come short of the glory of God.

Acts 15:10. Now therefore why tempt ye God, to put a yoke upon the neck of the disciples, which neither our fathers nor we were able to bear?

24. Forasmuch as we have heard, that certain which went out from us have troubled you with words, subverting your souls, saying, Ye must be circumcised, and keep the law; to whom we gave no such commandment.

28. For it seemed good to the Holy Ghost, and to us, to lay upon you no greater burden than these necessary things;

29. That ye abstain from meats offered to idols, and from blood, and from things strangled, and from fornication: from which if ye keep yourselves, ye shall do well. Fare ye well.

Galatians 3:22. But the Scripture hath concluded all under sin, that the promise by faith of Jesus Christ might be given to them that believe.

23. But before faith came, we were kept under the law, shut up unto the faith which should afterward be revealed.

24. Wherefore the law was our schoolmaster to bring us unto Christ, that we might be justified by faith.

Ephesians 2:8. For by grace are ye saved through faith; and that not of yourselves: it is the gift of God:

9. Not of works, lest any man should boast.

Titus 3:7. That being justified by his grace, we should be made heirs according to the hope of eternal life.

1 Peter 4:10. As every man hath received the gift, even so minister the same one to another, as good stewards of the manifold grace of God.

11. If any man speak, let him speak as the oracles of God; if any man minister, let him do it as of the ability which God giveth; that God in all things may be glorified through Jesus Christ: to whom be praise and dominion for ever and ever. Amen.

New International Version

Romans 3:20. No one will be declared righteous in his sight by observing the law; rather, through the law we become conscious of sin.

21. But now a righteousness from God, apart from law, has been made known, to which the Law and the Prophets testify.

22. This righteousness from God comes through faith in Jesus Christ to all who believe. There is no difference,

23. For all have sinned and fall short of the glory of God.

Acts 15:10. Now then, why do you try to test God by putting on the necks of the disciples a yoke that neither we nor our fathers have been able to bear?

24. We have heard that some went out from us without our authorization and disturbed you, troubling your minds by what they said.

28. It seemed good to the Holy Spirit and to us not to burden you with anything beyond the following requirements:

29. You are to abstain from food sacrificed to idols, from blood, from the meat of strangled animals and from sexual immorality. You will do well to avoid these things. Farewell.

Galatians 3:22. But the Scripture declares that the whole world is a prisoner of sin, so that what was promised, being given through faith in Jesus Christ, might be given to those who believe.

23. Before this faith came, we were held prisoners by the law, locked up until faith should be revealed.

24. So the law was put in charge to lead us to Christ that we might be justified by faith.

Ephesians 2:8. For it is by grace you have been saved, through faith—and this not from yourselves, it is the gift of God—

9. Not by works, so that no one can boast.

Titus 3:7. So that, having been justified by his grace, we might become heirs having the hope of eternal life.

1 Peter 4:10. Each one should use whatever gift he has received to serve others, faithfully administering God's grace in its various forms.

11. If anyone speaks, he should do it as one speaking the very words of God. If anyone serves, he should do it with the strength God provides, so that in all things God may be praised through Jesus Christ. To him be the glory and the power for ever and ever. Amen.

We need to have a clear understanding of the Law's purpose and how it prepared the way for Jesus' coming. The Law was never intended to bring salvation. Salvation has always been by grace. The Old Testament people of God were chosen because of God's grace, not because of obedience to the Law.

Because we are under grace, we do not discard our study of the Old Testament. The Old Testament gives us valuable insights into our privileges under grace. It provides a foundation for a study and appreciation of the New Testament.

New Testament writers quoted from the Old Testament often to show how it relates to Christians. By focusing on the contrast between law and grace, They continually reminded us that salvation comes by faith in Christ.

BIBLE COMMENTARY

1. The Law

A. Gives Knowledge Of Sin
Romans 3:19-23; 7:7

Paul, in writing to these Roman Christians, emphasized that salvation was through faith, not through the Law. Several times in this book, Paul stressed the real purpose of the Law—to show that all are sinners. Those who relied on the Law for salvation needed to be reminded that instead of saving them, the Law indicted them.

No one can escape from this indictment (Romans 3:9-18). It is as though the whole world is one great courtroom with God as the judge and the human race as the accused. Each time an individual tries to plead "Innocent," the Law cries, "Guilty!" Eventually those trying to be saved by keeping the Law are stripped of their pleas and have to become silent. This includes Jews and Gentiles alike: "all the world" (verse 19).

Ask: "What did Paul mean by 'the knowledge of sin' (verse 20)?" The Law identified actions, behavior, and attitudes that God condemned as sin. Those relying on the Law to save themselves are constantly reminded that they are guilty of the things God condemns. They cannot plead ignorance, for the Law has spoken clearly.

TEACHING TIP 1: Ask the students to give examples from their experiences where God's Word spoke to them about practices they had once considered "gray areas" but now consider to be sin. Discuss how we continue to grow and learn of God's standards through careful study of His Word.

As opposed to human sinfulness, Paul introduced the subject of the righteousness of God (verse 21). This is the standard by which all will be judged. God instituted the Law as a reflection of His standard of righteousness. But the Law itself could not provide the power for achieving that righteousness. In a similar way, we become more aware of our sin as we study the requirements of God's Word. But it is not that knowledge that saves us.

We can now become righteous, but not by keeping the Law. Salvation does not depend on our doing our best to please God, for such efforts always fall short. Testimony to this righteousness apart from the Law was anticipated by the writings of the prophets and even by the Law itself.

Paul lost no time declaring how man can become righteous: "through faith in Jesus

Christ'' (verse 22, NIV). The promise is limited only by whether one believes. Those who believe in Christ acknowledge that He is God's sacrifice for sin.

God puts no difference between Jew and Gentile because all are equally guilty (verse 23). As hard as we may try to reach up to God's standards, we always fall short. On our own we can never satisfy God's demand for righteousness.

Some might want to point out that if the Law revealed God's standards, but never made righteousness possible, it must be sinful. Paul was quick to point out that the Law is not sinful (7:7). The Law brought a knowledge of sin. Without the Law we would not know that we are sinners.

NOTES

B. Brings Bondage
Acts 15:1,5,10,24,28,29

The Early Church was made up largely of Jews who had lived all their lives under the Law. It is not surprising that controversy arose concerning whether the Gentiles needed to keep the law of Moses. This was especially true in relation to the Old Testament rite of circumcision (Acts 15:1,5). We can see that old ideas, customs, and cultural practices do not always disappear the moment one becomes a Christian.

Ask: "Why did Paul condemn this adherence to the Law?" These sincere but misguided Jewish believers were bringing Gentiles who were saved by grace under the bondage of the Law. The Law was like a heavy yoke on the neck of those who tried to keep it (verse 10). Paul even admitted that all Jews of all times, not just those who

proposed this, were not able to adhere to the requirements of the Law. Thus, instead of a freedom in Christ, legalism can destroy salvation. This is totally contrary to God's will.

The council at Jerusalem was marked by both sides presenting their case vigorously. Eventually, however, it was the Holy Spirit who took charge of the meeting and brought all minds together. A letter was dispatched to the Gentile churches. This letter revealed that those who taught Gentile believers to obey the law of Moses had no authorization from the leaders in Jerusalem (verse 24). This letter also assured Gentile believers that they were not to be brought under the Law's bondage. However, the members of the council asked that Gentile believers maintain godly standards of morality and not use their liberty to offend Jewish disciples by practices which were specifically named (verses 28,29).

NOTES

C. Leads To Christ
Galatians 3:21-26

TEACHING TIP 2: During the following discussion, display the overhead transparency "The Schoolmaster" from the Adult Teaching Helps Packet.

Just as Paul had countered the false belief that the Law was sinful, he also showed that the Law did not oppose God's promises (Galatians 3:21). God had promised Abraham that salvation would come through his Seed, that is, Christ (verses 15-18). The

Law, which came 430 years later, did not contradict His promises to Abraham. The promise was intended to give life, which the Law could not do. If the Law could give life, then righteousness would come through the Law, and God's promise would have been unnecessary (verse 21).

Ask: "How does the promise given to Abraham impact our lives today?" This promise of salvation is given to all "through faith in Jesus Christ" (verse 22, NIV). We have the privilege of trusting Christ to accomplish in us the righteousness to which the Law pointed. Now that this faith has been revealed, we are free from bondage to the Law (verses 23,25).

Ask: "Why did Paul call the Law a schoolmaster (verse 24)?" The word translated "schoolmaster" is one from which we get our word "pedagogue." A pedagogue was a slave who took charge of a male child in the family, supervised all his activities, made sure he received his education, and administered discipline. However, this ended when the child became an adult. At that time this schoolmaster's work was done.

Like the schoolmaster, the Law had completed its task when Jesus died, rose again, and ascended back to heaven. We are no longer under its supervision (verse 25). We are not saved by works, but by faith in Jesus Christ. The Law has led us to Christ, and now we are God's children (verse 26).

NOTES

2. Grace

A. Saves From Sin
Ephesians 2:8-10

Grace is God's undeserved favor. Grace has always been offered to sinners. Even when we were dead in sin, God by His grace reached down to save us (Ephesians 2:1-5). This is what Paul emphasized in verse 8: "For by grace are ye saved through faith."

Ask: "Why did Paul qualify this statement by adding the phrase, 'not of yourselves'?" One of the tendencies of human nature is to try to earn favor with God by doing good works. Paul made it clear that the whole process of salvation involves nothing we could have done ourselves. Salvation is a free gift. God is the initiator of everything. He reached out to us before we ever thought of reaching out to Him. He planned redemption even before creation itself.

The works of which Paul spoke in verse 9 are not confined to keeping the law of Moses. They include any kind of self-effort or human achievement. This principle applies to our own day as much as to Paul's. Whatever activity is listed under the term works, it cannot bring forgiveness and deliverance from sin.

Verse 10 summarizes the results of the gospel. Under grace a brand new creation has come into being. Each redeemed sinner becomes a testimony to God's skilled workmanship. Former slaves to sin become devoted servants of God. Those who lived only to fulfill the lusts of the flesh are now empowered to live for God. Our lives reflect the transforming power of the gospel.

The good works to which Paul referred in verse 10 are not connected with earning salvation. They are the fruit of being saved by grace through faith in Christ. Such works are a testimony to the inward work of grace. They represent a life-style already transformed by God.

The result of this miraculous work of new birth is justification. This means to be made right—declared righteous—in God's sight. God defines the conditions by which we receive this justification. It was never possible under the Law, but grace has made the difference. We are "justified by his grace" (verse 7). We become heirs of eternal life.

Much of the blessing that awaits us as heirs is future, but salvation has also made it a present reality. Ultimately we shall live forever in heaven, but we do not have to wait until then to have eternal life. Eternal life is both a future hope and a present reality. And that gift is ours now through God's grace in Christ.

NOTES

B. Brings Justification
Titus 3:4-7

God's kindness and love toward sinful humanity are not something He suddenly displayed when Jesus came to earth. Those attributes appear repeatedly on the pages of the Old Testament even during the days of the Law. The full expression of that kindness and love, however, awaited the time when God's Son would come into the world (Titus 3:4). This love was extended toward the human race that had rebelled against Him and trampled on His laws.

Verse 5 sums up the contrast between law and grace. Our works of righteousness could not save us. Salvation is totally dependent upon God's mercy. As Paul emphasized, we are saved "by the washing of regeneration and renewing of the Holy Ghost."

Ask: "What is the significance of the term 'washing'?" Paul was using the Old Testament practice of washing to remove ceremonial defilement as a picture of the cleansing that occurs at salvation. The washing that takes place is inward. We are not only forgiven, we are cleansed from all spiritual defilement.

The Greek word translated "regeneration" actually means new birth. This supernatural renewal in the life of a repentant sinner is the work of the Holy Spirit.

In pouring out His Spirit on us so abundantly, God has made provision, not only for our rebirth, but for our continuing spiritual life (verse 6). Only by the Spirit can we grow in grace and become more Christlike.

C. Enables Believers
1 Peter 4:10,11

TEACHING TIP 3: At this point display the overhead transparency "The Gift Of God" from the Adult Teaching Helps Packet.

There is more to God's grace than the blessing of salvation. God's grace is given to every believer as a means to minister to others (1 Peter 4:10).

God's children should use their natural talents and abilities to help one another. However, the Greek word translated "gift" in verse 10 is the same one Paul used in his discussion of spiritual gifts when he wrote to the Corinthians (1 Corinthians 12:4). Peter did not give extensive teaching on this subject, but here he admonished believers to use their spiritual gifts to minister to one another. He made it clear that these gifts are part of the manifestation of God's grace. They are not of human origin and are given to individuals for the upbuilding of the Body.

Ask: "In what ways does Peter's statement in verse 11 regarding speaking apply to us?" The speaking referred to in verse 11 can apply to the wide range of utterances prompted by the Spirit including preaching and teaching. When we are speaking in these situations, we should do so as those conveying God's message. Everything that is said should be in harmony with God's Word. God desires that we edify His Church. We should have that same desire. Criticism and backbiting do not fulfill God's design for edification.

The term "minister" means "to serve" and covers many areas. It refers to serving others in whatever way God enables. Different believers have different abilities. But whatever service we render, we must do it in the strength and ability that God provides through His grace. In addition, Peter reminded believers that all of this ministry has one purpose: to glorify God through Jesus Christ.

NOTES

LIFE RESPONSE

It is hard for us to comprehend what it would be like to strive to live up to the Law's commands. Even with our best efforts, we would constantly be falling short.

Only through the miracle of the new birth is it possible to fulfill the Law. God has graciously provided the salvation we needed through His Son. By His grace He reached down to us in our sinful condition, when we had no thought of Him. When we accept His Son, we are declared righteous in His sight. We can rejoice in the One who fulfilled the Law and provided power to keep the requirements of the Law. Each of us must determine how we will respond to God's grace.

Once we have experienced God's grace, we have the responsibility to extend that grace to others. God has provided us with grace to minister. How are we using this grace to touch the lives of others?

Certainly there are those we know of who are under the bondage of sin. They need the same salvation we have freely been offered by God's grace. They need to experience the justification found through Christ in order to be free from guilt and able to worship God.

God has called every believer to minister. As we use each opportunity He provides to meet others' needs, we may be able to lead them to Christ. Ask the Holy Spirit to help you to be sensitive to the needs of those around you. The same grace that saved you will enable you to minister to others.

EVANGELISM OUTREACH

You may know students in your class who are not saved. Keep this in mind in preparing and presenting this study. They may not be concerned about problems under the law of Moses, but they know their own need of forgiveness and cleansing. Your emphasis on grace should provide a background to invite unsaved students to accept Christ. Plan for time to pray with any who respond at the close of the class period. Ask the Holy Spirit to make such an invitation the natural outcome of this study. ⌷

INTRODUCTION

WORSHIP IN THE OLD AND NEW TESTAMENTS

The Psalmist declared, ''O worship the Lord in the beauty of holiness'' (Psalm 96:9). But in the church world today we find varieties of worship styles. Some Christians sincerely worship according to rules and ritual while others have more freedom of expression. So what is true worship? In this unit you will examine biblical models of worship to help you and your students enhance your worship of God.

''Worship In Heaven'' (study 9) points to God's majesty. God is worthy of worship because of His holiness and His provision of salvation.

In study 10 you will examine attitudes concerning worship. Jesus emphasized that worship of God must be ''in spirit and in truth'' (John 4:24). Some of these elements of worship are reviewed in study 11. By examining them your worship experience can take on added dimensions.

Congregational worship was important in the nation of Israel and remains crucial in the Church today. Various ways to honor God and encourage believers through corporate worship are the focus of study 12.

This unit concludes with a study on Pentecostal worship. Study 13 highlights the joyousness of celebration found in fervent prayer in the Spirit. The gifts of the Spirit bring a new dimension of worship to the Church.

These studies can help you and your students grow in your worship experience. As you teach this unit, allow the Lord to expand your expression of worship. As you know Him better and are able to express your worship to Him more freely, you will more effectively teach your students the value and importance of worship.

Worship In Heaven

CENTRAL TRUTH

Believers anticipate the joy of worshiping God in heaven.

GOLDEN TEXT

A great multitude . . . cried out in a loud voice: "Salvation belongs to our God, who sits on the throne, and to the Lamb." Revelation 7:9,10 (NIV)

STUDY TEXT

Isaiah 6:1-4; Ezekiel 3:12,13; Revelation 4:1 through 5:14; 7:9-12

OUTLINE

1. Holy Is The Lord
   A. Revealed In The Temple
   B. Proclaimed In The Heavens

2. Worthy Is The Lamb
   A. The Lamb That Was Slain
   B. Worshiped By The Redeemed

3. Glory, Honor, And Power!
   A. Worship Ascribed To God
   B. Worshiped By A Great Multitude

OBJECTIVE

To examine the worship offered by heavenly beings and determine to join the white-robed multitude in worshiping God forever.

CHECKLIST

☐ Read the student guide and become familiar with the questions. You may want to use some of these questions for discussion.

☐ In preparation for Teaching Tip 1, you will need to work through the work sheet "Visions Of God" prior to class. This will allow you to plan where in your teaching session you will want the students to respond.

☐ You will need a chalkboard or blank overhead transparency for Teaching Tip 2. If using an overhead projector, make sure it is set up and in working order before class.

☐ Contact two students early in the week. Assign one of them to present a short report on Ezekiel and the other a short report on John. These reports should focus on the circumstances surrounding each man's exile.

DAILY BIBLE READINGS

Monday: Creator Of Heaven And Earth.
Genesis 1:1-10
Tuesday: God's Dwelling Place.
1 Kings 8:27-30
Wednesday: God Hears In Heaven.
2 Chronicles 7:1-3,12-14
Thursday: Cleansing From Heaven.
Isaiah 6:5-7
Friday: A Voice From Heaven.
Matthew 3:13-17
Saturday: New Heaven And Earth.
Revelation 21:1-7

SCRIPTURE SETTING

King James Version

Isaiah 6:1. In the year that king Uzziah died I saw also the Lord sitting upon a throne, high and lifted up, and his train filled the temple.

2. Above it stood the seraphim: each one had six wings; with twain he covered his face, and with twain he covered his feet, and with twain he did fly.

3. And one cried unto another, and said, Holy, holy, holy, is the Lord of hosts: the whole earth is full of his glory.

Revelation 4:2. And immediately I was in the Spirit: and, behold, a throne was set in heaven, and one sat on the throne.

6. And before the throne there was a sea of glass like unto crystal. And in the midst of the throne, and round about the throne, were four beasts full of eyes before and behind.

8. And the four beasts had each of them six wings about him; and they were full of eyes within: and they rest not day and night, saying, Holy, holy, holy, Lord God Almighty, which was, and is, and is to come.

5:8. And when he had taken the book, the four beasts and four and twenty elders fell down before the Lamb, having every one of them harps, and golden vials full of odors, which are the prayers of saints.

9. And they sung a new song, saying, Thou art worthy to take the book, and to open the seals thereof: for thou wast slain, and hast redeemed us to God by thy blood out of every kindred, and tongue, and people, and nation;

10. And hast made us unto our God kings and priests: and we shall reign on the earth.

7:9. After this I beheld, and, lo, a great multitude, which no man could number, of all nations, and kindreds, and people, and tongues, stood before the throne, and before the Lamb, clothed with white robes, and palms in their hands;

10. And cried with a loud voice, saying, Salvation to our God which sitteth upon the throne, and unto the Lamb.

11. And all the angels stood round about the throne, and about the elders and the four beasts, and fell before the throne on their faces, and worshipped God,

12. Saying, Amen: Blessing, and glory, and wisdom, and thanksgiving, and honor, and power, and might, be unto our God for ever and ever. Amen.

New International Version

Isaiah 6:1. In the year that King Uzziah died, I saw the Lord seated on a throne, high and exalted, and the train of his robe filled the temple.

2. Above him were seraphs, each with six wings: With two wings they covered their faces, with two they covered their feet, and with two they were flying.

3. And they were calling to one another: "Holy, holy, holy is the Lord Almighty; the whole earth is full of his glory."

Revelation 4:2. At once I was in the Spirit, and there before me was a throne in heaven with someone sitting on it.

6. Also before the throne there was what looked like a sea of glass, clear as crystal. In the center, around the throne, were four living creatures, and they were covered with eyes, in front and in back.

8. Each of the four living creatures had six wings and was covered with eyes all around, even under his wings. Day and night they never stop saying: "Holy, holy, holy is the Lord God Almighty, who was, and is, and is to come."

5:8. And when he had taken [the scroll], the four living creatures and the twenty-four elders fell down before the Lamb. Each one had a harp and they were holding golden bowls full of incense, which are the prayers of the saints.

9. And they sang a new song: "You are worthy to take the scroll and to open its seals, because you were slain, and with your blood you purchased men for God from every tribe and language and people and nation.

10. You have made them to be a kingdom and priests to serve our God, and they will reign on the earth."

7:9. After this I looked and there before me was a great multitude that no one could count, from every nation, tribe, people and language, standing before the throne and in front of the Lamb. They were wearing white robes and were holding palm branches in their hands.

10. And they cried out in a loud voice: "Salvation belongs to our God, who sits on the throne, and to the Lamb."

11. All the angels were standing around the throne and around the elders and the four living creatures. They fell down on their faces before the throne and worshiped God,

12. Saying: "Amen! Praise and glory and wisdom and thanks and honor and power and strength be to our God for ever and ever. Amen!"

God alone is worthy of our worship. Though He is worthy of much more than we are capable of giving Him, in today's world, many things try to draw our attention away from God. Activities of life demand so much of our attention we fail to spend time in His presence.

Sometimes our false concept of worship robs us of the enjoyment that God desires in our fellowship with Him. We fail to realize that worship benefits all of life. Only when we get a picture of God's holiness can we really respond in worship.

Worship also involves responding to God's Son, pictured as the "Lamb." It is through His work on the cross that we enjoy the privilege of worship. This week's study focuses on the worship that takes place around the throne of God, offering a valuable model for our own worship.

BIBLE COMMENTARY

1. Holy Is The Lord

TEACHING TIP 1: Divide your class into six groups and assign each group one of the questions on the work sheet "Visions Of God." Give them 3 to 5 minutes to examine the passages and write down their answers. As you present the first main point, ask for student response at the appropriate place in the commentary.

A. Revealed In The Temple
Isaiah 6:1-4

In Isaiah's vision recorded in chapter 6, the prophet was given a glimpse into heaven, the real Holy of Holies. **Ask: "In his vision, what were Isaiah's impressions of God (verses 1-4)?"** While Isaiah did not physically describe God, the imagery he used is powerful. He reported God's throne as "high and lifted up" (verse 1) giving the impression of God's strength, power, and authority. Isaiah's reference to the train of God's robe filling the temple calls attention to God's supreme authority.

The titles which Isaiah used to refer to God are significant because they reveal His character. In verse 1, "Lord" is translated from the Hebrew word *Adonai*, meaning "the sovereign One." This denotes that God is the supreme authority over all. The Greek equivalent to this title is given to Jesus in the New Testament. The Hebrew word *Yahweh* in verse 3 is also translated Lord. Many English versions print this name in capital letters to distinguish it from *Adonai*. The chief meaning of *Yahweh* is "One who keeps His covenants."

Isaiah also mentioned the seraphim, a specific class of angels. Although he described them as having three pairs of wings, only one pair was used for flying. The other two pairs were used to cover their faces and feet (verse 2) probably in response to God's holiness.

In verse 3 the seraphim proclaimed God's holiness: "Holy, holy, holy, is the Lord of hosts: the whole earth is full of his glory." This triple "holy" seems to indicate that the holiness of God is the summation of all that He is.

When the seraphim declared God's holiness, the doorposts of the temple reeled under their voices (verse 4). A cloud of smoke, the symbol of God's glory, then filled the temple.

While this vision is actually Isaiah's call to ministry, it reveals to us that in God's presence the angels declare God's holiness. When angels, beings created to do God's bidding, come into God's presence, they hide themselves and proclaim that God is holy. What happens when a New Testament believer has a vision of God's holy presence is described in the next section.

NOTES

B. Proclaimed In The Heavens
Revelation 4:1-8

In Revelation 4:1,2, John was caught up into heaven and, like Isaiah, was ushered into the throne room of God and into God's very presence. Around the throne John saw 24 elders clothed in white. Although commentators differ as to what these elders represent, it is likely they represent the body of Christ. Their crowns are the victors' crowns and they are clothed in white garments. Both items would indicate believers (see 1 Corinthians 9:25; Revelation 5:8-10; 7:13,14; 22:14). These 24 elders "cast their crowns before the throne" attesting to their worship of God (4:10).

Proceeding from the throne were "lightnings and thunderings and voices" (verse 5). This is reminiscent of God's speaking at Mount Sinai, further describing God's majesty and power. Stretching out before God's throne was the sea of glass, bringing to mind a picture of God's purity and holiness around the throne of God (verse 6). This concept of holiness is also seen in the four "living creatures" (NIV) who worshiped God in a manner similar to those described in Isaiah 6:3. Their repetition of

the word "holy" gives additional emphasis to that characteristic of God.

Ask: "What is the significance of the title 'Lord God Almighty' (Revelation 4:8)?" The title "Lord God Almighty" clearly proclaims God's lordship over all. He is omnipotent. He has the power to fulfill His plan for His creation. In addition, the phrase "which was, and is, and is to come" reminds us that God is eternal and unchangeable. He has existed throughout eternity past, He exists now, and He will exist for all eternity future.

These glimpses of God and His holiness inspire us to worship Him and to commit our lives to Him completely. As we become more aware of His holiness, we will respond by seeking to live lives worthy of our relationship with Him.

NOTES

2. Worthy Is The Lamb
A. The Lamb That Was Slain
Revelation 5:1-6

TEACHING TIP 2: During the following discussion, list the main components of John's vision of the scroll and the Lamb in Revelation 5:1-6 on a chalkboard or blank transparency. As you list each point, ask the students to suggest its significance. Write down their responses and supplement them with material from the commentary.

When we read Revelation 5 and are considering who God is, we might wonder why so much attention is given to a scroll sealed with seven seals. The opening of the seals heralds the death and destruction that will be poured out in judgment upon unrepentant humanity (Revelation 6:1 through 8:1). Throughout Scripture we are reminded that all humanity would fall under God's judgment were it not for the work of a Savior.

In 5:5, John's attention was then directed to the One who was worthy to open the seals. He is called "the Lion of the tribe of Judah," referring to the tribe to which Jesus belonged (Genesis 49:9,10; Matthew 1:1-17), and "the Root of David," from a prophecy that the Messiah would come from David's lineage (Isaiah 11:1). The lion is symbolic of both kingship and strength. This would be a picture of the conquering Messiah.

John looked, probably expecting to see the Lion, but instead saw the Lamb. The elder's statement is the only reference to the Lion in the Book of Revelation. The continuing references to the Lamb of God, however, identify the glorified Christ of Revelation with the crucified Savior (see John 1:29). It is probably intended to emphasize the grace of God available to everyone who reads the book. The phrase "had been slain" (Revelation 5:6) refers to Christ's sacrificial death, connecting the opening of the seals with His redemptive work.

John's continuing description is not what we would expect; he saw seven horns and seven eyes which represent the seven Spirits of God sent into all the earth. This does not mean there is more than one Holy Spirit. This could also be translated as the "sevenfold Spirit of God" (see Isaiah 11:2). This probably refers to the activity of the Holy Spirit taking the power of the Lamb into all the world.

The opening of the book was to be accompanied by a judgment against sin. As the One who had defeated sin by the Cross and the Resurrection, Christ alone could open the seals of the book.

B. Worshiped By The Redeemed
Revelation 5:7-12

Because Christ was worthy, He took the book from God's hand (verse 7). This indicated the authority given to Christ to execute God's plan for the world. When He received the book, the 4 living creatures and the 24 elders did the only thing appropriate for the occasion. They fell on their faces in worship (verse 8). To worship they employed three things: harps, representing divine worship; golden bowls filled with incense, the prayers of believers; and a new song, focusing on the redemptive work of Christ (verse 9).

Ask: "How does this song encourage us?" This is the song of the redeemed, those who have personally experienced the redemption brought about by Christ's death on the cross. Because of Calvary, salvation is available to all who will call upon the Lord. Whosoever will, regardless of race, color, or language, may come to Him.

As the scene progressed, myriads of angels joined the 4 living creatures and the 24 elders in song, worshiping the Son for who He is and what He has done (verse 11). And as part of the redeemed, we can worship Christ because of what He has done for us. He is worthy of our worship and praise.

NOTES

3. Glory, Honor, And Power!

A. Worship Ascribed To God
Ezekiel 3:12,13; Revelation 4:9-11; 5:13,14

TEACHING TIP 3: Ask for the student reports on Ezekiel and John. These reports should emphasize their experiences as exiles. Discuss with the class how each man's vision may have impacted his circumstances. Explain how we can be encouraged in the midst of our difficulties by a renewed awareness of God and His holiness.

Ezekiel 3:12,13 is at the conclusion of a vision of God's glory that began in Ezekiel 1:1. Ezekiel had been forced into exile with the other captives and was now living in Babylon (verse 1). His being lifted by the Spirit (3:12) was probably not in a physical sense, but still a part of this vision.

The phrase, "Blessed be the glory of the Lord from his place," may have been used to encourage Ezekiel. God's presence was not just in the temple in Jerusalem. Even in exile God's people could praise Him and enjoy fellowship with Him. We may not always like the situation in which we find ourselves, but we can always respond by giving glory, honor, and thanks to God knowing that He has everything under control.

Such worship is also seen in Revelation 4:9,10. The four living creatures are continually involved in giving glory, honor, and thanks to God. The 24 elders join in this praise (verse 10). In honor to Him as God, they lay their crowns before Him. As those around the throne bow before Him, they ascribe to Him power, glory, and honor. Only God is worthy of this kind of worship.

Ask: "Why is it important that we ascribe worship to God?" When we grasp who God is, it helps us to put the problems of this life into proper perspective. Worship enlarges our vision of God and increases our faith in Him.

All creation, because it was made by God, should praise Him. As John's vision continued, this was what he saw (5:13,14). Not only was this praise directed to God, it was also directed to the Lamb, Jesus Christ. One day, all creation will praise God.

NOTES

B. Worshiped By A Great Multitude
Revelation 7:9-12

John's attention was now turned to a great multitude from every nation on earth (Revelation 7:9). These people stand before the throne of God clothed in white robes with palm branches in their hands. They are the innumerable redeemed whom Christ purchased with His blood.

The white robes are symbolic of God's righteousness. This multitude is righteous because Christ's righteousness has been imparted to them. Some believe the multitude were martyred in the Great Tribulation, while others believe they are saints who suffered persecution throughout the ages. Regardless, they have been redeemed by the blood of the Lamb. The palm branches represent their triumph in overcoming great tribulation (verse 14).

This multitude was worshiping by specifically acknowledging what God had done. Notice that clear distinction was made between the Father and the Son. Both had been involved in the act of salvation. God is the Source of salvation and the Son (the Lamb) purchased salvation by His blood.

All the angels and other beings already mentioned joined the multitude in worship (verses 11,12). The "Amen" simply affirms the truth of what had been sung. Notice that the angels are around the elders and the four living creatures. Even though they have never been redeemed, they join in worship.

Ask: "How should the picture of the multitude in Revelation 7:9-12 challenge us to fulfill the Great Commission?" When we read of believers from every part of the world, we should realize our responsibility to carry the gospel everywhere. The Lord has entrusted us to tell others about what Jesus Christ has done.

Our salvation will be complete when we stand before God's throne, delivered from the presence of sin. Then we will stand with the white robed multitude and worship God forever. In preparation for that day, we can and should use every opportunity to prepare ourselves and others. Every aspect of worship in this study can be used to enrich our relationship with the Lord each day. Will we offer up to Him the worship He deserves in everything we do and say?

NOTES

LIFE RESPONSE

God is worthy of worship. As those around His throne have proclaimed throughout the ages, God is worthy because of who He is and what He has done.

Worship is an important aspect of the Christian life. Throughout Scripture there are many instances of groups as well as individuals who worshiped God. We even see examples of how those in heaven worship around God's throne. One thing is certain. All worship centers around God and His Son.

Yet worship involves more than just vocal praise. Worship is also a life-style. We worship God by the way we conduct ourselves in the everyday affairs of life. Our very lives can bring honor and glory to the One who sits on the throne.

Check your life-style today. Can those who know you sense your worship of God by the way you live? Is church the only place where you worship God? Or is even your work involved in your worship? As we realize that we are God's creation, designed to worship Him, then even the mundane, everyday tasks of life can be used as worship to our Father.

We have seen examples of pure worship in heaven. We can anticipate the day when we, too, will stand with the multitude clothed in white. The worship which we are engaged in now will continue when we are around that throne. Until then our worship can serve to enrich our walk with the Lord and bring Him the glory due His name.

EVANGELISM OUTREACH

Any unsaved students in your class may find it difficult to relate to the worship described in this week's study. Only through a personal relationship with Christ are we able to participate in worship. Just as the heavenly hosts sang of their own redemption, your students can have the opportunity to praise God for saving them. Give an invitation to accept Christ as Savior today and begin enjoying the benefits of worship. Then their entire lives can be dedicated to acts of worship that God desires.

Attitudes For Worship

CENTRAL TRUTH

To be acceptable to God, worship must be offered in the right attitude.

GOLDEN TEXT

True worshipers will worship the Father in spirit and truth, for they are the kind of worshipers the Father seeks. John 4:23 (NIV)

STUDY TEXT

Genesis 28:16-22; Deuteronomy 6:13-15; Psalms 122:1; 123:1,2; John 4:23; 16:23,24; Revelation 19:10

OUTLINE

1. Worship God Only
   A. Reverence The Lord
   B. Worship Refused

2. Acknowledge God's Presence
   A. In Difficult Situations
   B. In Spirit And In Truth

3. Worship Expectantly
   A. In God's House
   B. In Prayer

OBJECTIVE

To identify and adopt right attitudes for worship.

CHECKLIST

☐ Read the corresponding study in the *Adult Student Guide*, noting any questions you may wish to use for class discussion.

☐ Duplicate enough copies of the work sheet "Building A Memorial" so each student will have one. Use this as a time of encouragement for students who may be going through a difficult situation.

☐ Make sure to have enough copies of the work sheet "Benefits Of Church Attendance" so each student will have one. Work through this prior to class. This can also be used to generate discussion on the value of the local church.

☐ Prepare your own heart by spending time in worship this week. Allow the Holy Spirit to refresh you so you can minister effectively to your students. Be sensitive to those the Lord may be dealing with during this study.

DAILY BIBLE READINGS

Monday: Obey God's Commands.
Exodus 34:10-14
Tuesday: Reverence God.
Deuteronomy 10:12-21
Wednesday: Seek The Lord.
1 Chronicles 16:8-12
Thursday: Show Humility.
Psalm 95:1-6
Friday: Focus On Jesus.
Matthew 17:1-8
Saturday: Rejoice In The Lord.
Philippians 4:4-9

Scripture Setting

King James Version

Deuteronomy 6:13. Thou shalt fear the Lord thy God, and serve him, and shalt swear by his name.

14. Ye shall not go after other gods, of the gods of the people which are round about you;

15. (For the Lord thy God is a jealous God among you;) lest the anger of the Lord thy God be kindled against thee, and destroy thee from off the face of the earth.

Revelation 19:10. And I fell at his feet to worship him. And he said unto me, See thou do it not: I am thy fellow servant, and of thy brethren that have the testimony of Jesus: worship God: for the testimony of Jesus is the spirit of prophecy.

Genesis 28:16. And Jacob awaked out of his sleep, and he said, Surely the Lord is in this place; and I knew it not.

17. And he was afraid, and said, How dreadful is this place! this is none other but the house of God, and this is the gate of heaven.

John 4:23. But the hour cometh, and now is, when the true worshippers shall worship the Father in spirit and in truth: for the Father seeketh such to worship him.

Psalm 122:1. I was glad when they said unto me, Let us go into the house of the Lord.

123:1. Unto thee lift I up mine eyes, O thou that dwellest in the heavens.

2. Behold, as the eyes of servants look unto the hand of their masters, and as the eyes of a maiden unto the hand of her mistress; so our eyes wait upon the Lord our God, until that he have mercy upon us.

John 16:23. And in that day ye shall ask me nothing. Verily, verily, I say unto you, Whatsoever ye shall ask the Father in my name, he will give it you.

24. Hitherto have ye asked nothing in my name: ask, and ye shall receive, that your joy may be full.

New International Version

Deuteronomy 6:13. Fear the Lord your God, serve him only and take your oaths in his name.

14. Do not follow other gods, the gods of the peoples around you;

15. For the Lord your God, who is among you, is a jealous God and his anger will burn against you, and he will destroy you from the face of the land.

Revelation 19:10. At this I fell at his feet to worship him. But he said to me, "Do not do it! I am a fellow servant with you and with your brothers who hold to the testimony of Jesus. Worship God! For the testimony of Jesus is the spirit of prophecy."

Genesis 28:16. When Jacob awoke from his sleep, he thought, "Surely the Lord is in this place, and I was not aware of it."

17. He was afraid and said, "How awesome is this place! This is none other than the house of God; this is the gate of heaven."

John 4:23. Yet a time is coming and has now come when the true worshipers will worship the Father in spirit and truth, for they are the kind of worshipers the Father seeks.

Psalm 122:1. I rejoiced with those who said to me, "Let us go to the house of the Lord."

123:1. I lift up my eyes to you, to you whose throne is in heaven.

2. As the eyes of slaves look to the hand of their master, as the eyes of a maid look to the hand of her mistress, so our eyes look to the Lord our God, till he shows us his mercy.

John 16:23. In that day you will no longer ask me anything. I tell you the truth, my Father will give you whatever you ask in my name.

24. Until now you have not asked for anything in my name. Ask and you will receive, and your joy will be complete.

W hat occupies your thoughts when you worship? An honest appraisal of your priorities might give an indication of who or what you feel is important in your life.

Attitudes play an important part in worship. When in the midst of difficult circumstances, your attitude toward God will determine whether you worship Him or not. Even your attitude about where you will worship the Lord has an effect on your church attendance.

Moses challenged a new generation of Israelites to worship the Lord only. Each new generation of believers needs to accept that same challenge to worship only God.

This study will examine some attitudes that will help you focus on God. As we look at God's Word, allow the Holy Spirit to challenge you in your worship of God.

BIBLE COMMENTARY

1. Worship God Only

A. Reverence The Lord
Deuteronomy 6:13-15

The Children of Israel were again at the border of Canaan. Except for Joshua and Caleb, the generation that had left Egypt and had refused to enter for fear of the inhabitants lay buried beneath the desert sand. Moses was now preparing a new generation of Israelites to enter the Promised Land.

In his address to those Israelites, Moses reviewed some of the events of the last 40 years. This included reading the Ten Commandments (Deuteronomy 5:6-21). The Israelites were once again commanded to obey these statutes. Because they would be inhabiting a land where worshiping false gods (idols) was the norm, Moses commanded them to worship God only (6:13). One thing that would keep them true to God was the command to "fear the Lord."

TEACHING TIP 1: Write the following phrases on the chalkboard or overhead transparency: "fear the Lord," "swear by His name," and "a jealous God." Ask: "In reference to the first commandment, how do these phrases relate to our lives as Christians?" Write the students' responses on the chalkboard or overhead transparency. Use the following commentary to bring clarification.

The foundation for our understanding the fear of the Lord is in the knowledge that God can and will judge unrighteousness. The purpose of this understanding is to produce holiness and a cessation of willful sin (see Exodus 20:20; Proverbs 16:6). Moses was again emphasizing the importance of this fear at the entrance to Canaan (Deuteronomy 6:13).

To "fear the Lord," then, is to stand in awe of Him and reverence Him. We are not to take Him for granted nor treat Him flippantly. Reverence means to honor and respect. This includes having a devout relationship with Him. You cannot honor and respect One whom you do not know. Knowing God personally must be life's highest priority for the believer. As we come to know God, we know His ways and commands. Therefore, we can honor His Word by obeying it. We demonstrate respect the same way. To fear or reverence the Lord is not some intellectual exercise, but is lived out in our daily lives.

"Swear by his name" should be taken in the sense of making a commitment. Some translations use the phrase "take your oaths in his name" (NIV, NKJV). The Scriptures are emphatic that we are not to profane God's name. In this context, it was used in relation to the covenant that God established with Israel. It involved affirming their allegiance to Him. They pledged to serve Him alone and not to follow other gods (verse 14).

God is also a "jealous God" (verse 15). This is the biggest reason of all for not following other gods. He is jealous for truth. He is intolerant of any idol which draws people's worship away from Him.

The judgment God exacts against those who do worship idols is terrible. He will destroy them "off the face of the earth." He is slow to anger, but He will judge the rebellious and unrepentant. We are to worship Him alone, because He alone is God.

NOTES

B. Worship Refused
Revelation 19:10

The command to worship God only will still be valid in heaven. In his vision, John witnessed a multitude in heaven worshiping God (Revelation 19:1-8). Overwhelmed by this scene, John fell down in worship to the angel who had been showing him this event. This angel refused John's worship because the angel was only a "fellow servant" (verse 10); he was not God. The angel then commanded John, "worship God."

Jesus is also to be exalted. The phrase "the testimony of Jesus is the spirit of prophecy" indicates that the purpose of prophecy is to reveal the redemptive work of Christ.

Ask: "What things in modern society can draw our worship away from God?" Some religions acknowledge many gods. To them, the Christian God is only one

means of attaining heaven. We must affirm that God is the only God. We can also allow family, jobs, and possessions to occupy the place of prominence in our lives that only belongs to God. To worship anyone or anything else is idolatry. We are called to worship God; He alone is worthy.

NOTES

2. Acknowledge God's Presence

A. In Difficult Situations
Genesis 28:16-22

It is easy to acknowledge God's presence when everything is going well in your life. It is another thing, though, to acknowledge that God is with you when you are in the midst of a difficult situation. Jacob had stolen the blessing of the firstborn from his older brother, Esau. Now he was on his way to the home of his uncle Laban until Esau's anger subsided. Even though Jacob was probably over 70 at this time, there still may have been some apprehension about his future. While on this journey, he had an unforgettable experience with God.

In a vision, God reaffirmed the covenant He had made with Abraham and Isaac. For someone who was running away from home, the promise that God would return him safely must have been very encouraging. It was also God's way of confirming Jacob's place of promise in the lineage of Abraham.

Ask: "How did Jacob react as a result of his meeting with God?" Jacob recognized that he had been in the presence of God (Genesis 28:16). In response, Jacob built a pillar in honor of God (verse 18). This was to be a memorial commemorating the revelation of God which He had given to Jacob. His use of oil to anoint the pillar was an act of consecration.

To the Jewish people of his time, names carried significant meanings. Jacob renamed the place where the vision took place, including the neighboring city, Bethel, which means "the house of God."

Jacob also made a vow. If God would keep His word, then Jacob would serve Him (verse 21). This vow revealed a desire for God to be at work in his life, watching over him as he was away from home.

Jacob's commitment to tithing also seemed to indicate that even he understood that the tithe is an acknowledgment that all we have belongs to God. He is the Owner and we are the stewards. This is a practical way of realizing His presence in our lives.

TEACHING TIP 2: Distribute copies of the work sheet "Building A Memorial." Give the students a few minutes to answer the questions. Ask for volunteers to give their responses to question 4. (Some may wish to explain the circumstance they were in and how God met with them.) Have the students explain how they honored God when He met with them in their difficult situation.

NOTES

B. In Spirit And In Truth
John 4:23

Jacob recognized God's presence at a specific place—Bethel. If God brought him back safely, he would worship Him there. Today many people have sacred places of worship. But putting emphasis on a place can lead to controversy as to which place is right.

In His conversation with the Samaritan woman, Jesus indicated that true worship did not depend on a specific place (John 4:23). The woman's focus on the place of worship may have been a tactic to change the conversation concerning her sinful condition (verse 18). But Jesus used this diversion to teach what true worship is.

Ask: "What did Jesus mean when He told the woman that 'true worshippers shall worship the Father in spirit and in truth'?" Worshiping in spirit and truth involves an attitude that desires to know and honor God for who He truly is. "In spirit" refers to the inner consciousness that connects us to the heavenly realm. It is the human spirit within us that cries out for the reality of God. We commune with Him in spirit when we open our hearts before Him.

However, worshiping only "in spirit" can be deceptive. Real worship also calls for a passion for knowing truth as revealed by God in His Word. True worshipers will settle for nothing less. Like lovers pursuing the desire of their heart, so those who worship in spirit and truth pursue loving God according to the truth of His Word.

NOTES

3. Worship Expectantly

A. In God's House
Psalms 122:1; 123:1,2

Psalms 122 and 123 are part of a collection of psalms known as the "songs of ascents." Three times a year every Jewish male was required to come to Jerusalem to worship in various festivals (Exodus 23:14-17). It is thought that these songs were sung by the Levites in these annual processions.

Notice the words of the Psalmist in Psalm 122:1: "I was glad." There was an attitude of expectation as he came to the temple.

Ask: "What was David expecting that would have brought joy just at the thought of going to the temple?" First and foremost, David would have been expecting the presence of God. As attested to by many psalms, David longed to be in God's presence. But David also expected to be with God's people. When the time of the feasts came near, thousands of pilgrims made the journey to Jerusalem to worship God together.

Ask: "As believers, what should be our attitude toward coming to God's house?" The place of worship for the Psalmist was "the house of the Lord." Our place for worship is our church. The Psalmist realized the importance of corporate worship. The pronouns "they" and "us" dominate this verse, making it clear that worship with others is both to be desired and sought.

Some believers come to church out of duty. Some do so for prestige. But the real purpose of gathering together with fellow believers is to worship God and to fellowship with one another. While we have seen that God cannot be contained in a building, it is important that we join with other Christians in worship (Hebrews 10:25).

TEACHING TIP 3: Distribute a copy of the work sheet "Benefits Of Church Attendance" to each student. Divide the class into groups of four to five students. Assign each group one or two Scripture references. Ask the groups to evaluate the passage and list the benefits that could be applied to church attendance. After a few minutes, ask each group to share their benefit. Allow time for discussion if any students want to respond.

While Israel may have worshiped in the temple, they were well aware that God did not physically dwell there. They recognized that He lives in the heavens, which exist beyond the natural realm (Psalm 123:1).

The Psalmist used the analogy of servants and masters (verse 2) in order to explain part of our relationship with God. Just as a servant or maid would look to a master or mistress for direction, so we expectantly look to the Lord for His mercy.

NOTES

B. In Prayer
John 16:23,24

TEACHING TIP 4: Briefly relate to the students the context of John 16:23,24 (verses 16-22). Explain that Jesus was speaking of His death, with its sorrow, and His resurrection, with its accompanying joy. The phrase "in that day" (verse 23) refers to the time after His resurrection including the present.

In speaking of the time following His resurrection, Jesus told His disciples that they would no longer ask Him for anything (verse 23). They had been confused about all that Jesus had been telling them. After the Resurrection, they would no longer need to question Him about things they did not understand ("ask me nothing"). At that time they would bring their petitions to the Father in His name, not only for understanding but for provision.

Ask: "Why can we pray in Jesus' name?" Jesus opened the way for us to speak directly to the Father using the authority of His name. This authority is based on what Jesus did at Calvary. He became our atonement for sin, our substitute before the Father. This does not forbid praying directly to the Son. However, He has given us access directly to the Father simply by our praying in the authority He has given to us through His name.

Now we can ask for anything in His name. Our Father desires that we depend on Him for His provision. Yet we must balance asking for "anything" by praying according to His will (1 John 5:14,15). Otherwise, our prayers could degenerate into sinful and selfish indulgence.

Just as the Psalmist had anticipated joy when coming to God's house, we can ask God for our needs, knowing that our joy will be complete. We have confidence that God hears our petitions. We no longer need to worry or be overly concerned: God has everything under control (Philippians 4:6,7).

NOTES

LIFE RESPONSE

There are many things that clamor for our attention in today's society—our family, our jobs, our hobbies, and other leisure activities are but a few. As good as all these activities may be, we cannot allow them to crowd out our worship of God.

As believers we are called to worship God only. A look at our calendar, checkbook, or list of priorities may indicate where our devotion lies. We must not allow anyone or anything to take the place of God.

Making God first in our lives will provide stability. Even in the midst of difficult situations we will feel the presence of God. We, like Jacob, will be able to truly open our hearts to Him in worship—whatever the circumstance.

Yet our worship of God is not confined to a place. We can worship God wherever we are. In our daily tasks we can have an attitude of worship. But just because we can worship God anywhere does not mean we can forsake worship with others. When God is first in our lives there is a desire to gather with other believers to worship Him and fellowship with each other.

Worship helps us recognize the greatness of God and our dependence upon Him. When we learn to depend on Him, we can come to God with confidence knowing that He hears and answers our prayers.

Allow the Holy Spirit to examine your attitudes in worship. As your heart is open to Him, He in turn will minister to you "that your joy may be full."

EVANGELISM OUTREACH

There may be some in your class who cannot worship God because they do not know Him as Savior. They may have allowed other things to take the place of God. But God's command for first place is valid for them as well and can be used to lead them to salvation.

As you end this week's study, draw any unsaved student's attention to God's desire to answer prayer, especially a prayer of forgiveness. Give opportunity for any unsaved in your class to accept the Savior.

Dynamics Of Worship

CENTRAL TRUTH

True worship can be expressed in many ways but is always focused on God.

GOLDEN TEXT

Enter his gates with thanksgiving and his courts with praise; give thanks to him and praise his name. Psalm 100:4 (NIV)

STUDY TEXT

Psalms 28:1-9; 98:1-9; 100:4; Luke 4:16-21; 1 Timothy 4:13; 2 Timothy 4:2; Hebrews 2:12

OUTLINE

1. Rejoicing And Singing
   A. From His People
   B. From His Creation

2. Prayer And Praise
   A. God Answers Prayer
   B. Proclaim God's Majesty

3. Centrality Of The Word
   A. In Christ's Ministry
   B. In The Church

OBJECTIVE

To examine the elements of biblical worship and appreciate the variety God has provided.

CHECKLIST

☐ Read the *Adult Student Guide*. Write down any questions you wish to use for discussion.
☐ For Teaching Tip 1, early in the week contact a person who has an interest in music. Ask him to give a brief report on the importance of music in the religious life of Israel. Application should be made to present-day worship services. A Bible dictionary or encyclopedia will have the information needed for this report.
☐ The overhead transparency "Dynamics Of Worship" will be used in Teaching Tips 2,3, and 4. Make sure the overhead projector is set up and working prior to class.
☐ Luke 4:16-21 in the third main point is an excellent passage for evangelism. Be sensitive to the Holy Spirit for an opportunity to present Christ to the unsaved students in your class.

DAILY BIBLE READINGS

Monday: Musical Instruments.
1 Chronicles 25:1-6
Tuesday: Organized Choir.
2 Chronicles 5:11-14
Wednesday: Creation's Praise.
Psalm 148:1-14
Thursday: Times Of Prayer.
Daniel 6:10-13
Friday: Fellowship.
Acts 2:41-47
Saturday: Focus On The Word.
Acts 18:24-28

Scripture Setting

King James Version

Psalm 98:4. Make a joyful noise unto the Lord, all the earth: make a loud noise, and rejoice, and sing praise.

5. Sing unto the Lord with the harp; with the harp, and the voice of a psalm.

6. With trumpets and sound of cornet make a joyful noise before the Lord, the King.

28:1. Unto thee will I cry, O Lord my rock; be not silent to me: lest, if thou be silent to me, I become like them that go down into the pit.

2. Hear the voice of my supplications, when I cry unto thee, when I lift up my hands toward thy holy oracle.

6. Blessed be the Lord, because he hath heard the voice of my supplications.

7. The Lord is my strength and my shield; my heart trusted in him, and I am helped: therefore my heart greatly rejoiceth; and with my song will I praise him.

100:4. Enter into his gates with thanksgiving, and into his courts with praise: be thankful unto him, and bless his name.

Hebrews 2:12. Saying, I will declare thy name unto my brethren, in the midst of the church will I sing praise unto thee.

Luke 4:16. And he came to Nazareth, where he had been brought up: and, as his custom was, he went into the synagogue on the sabbath day, and stood up for to read.

17. And there was delivered unto him the book of the prophet Isaiah. And when he had opened the book, he found the place where it was written,

18. The Spirit of the Lord is upon me, because he hath anointed me to preach the gospel to the poor; he hath sent me to heal the brokenhearted, to preach deliverance to the captives, and recovering of sight to the blind, to set at liberty them that are bruised,

19. To preach the acceptable year of the Lord.

20. And he closed the book, and he gave it again to the minister, and sat down. And the eyes of all them that were in the synagogue were fastened on him.

21. And he began to say unto them, This day is this Scripture fulfilled in your ears.

1 Timothy 4:13. Till I come, give attendance to reading, to exhortation, to doctrine.

New International Version

Psalm 98:4. Shout for joy to the Lord, all the earth, burst into jubilant song with music;

5. Make music to the Lord with the harp, with the harp and the sound of singing,

6. With trumpets and the blast of the ram's horn— shout for joy before the Lord, the King.

28:1. To you I call, O Lord my Rock; do not turn a deaf ear to me. For if you remain silent, I will be like those who have gone down to the pit.

2. Hear my cry for mercy as I call to you for help, as I lift up my hands toward your Most Holy Place.

6. Praise be to the Lord, for he has heard my cry for mercy.

7. The Lord is my strength and my shield; my heart trusts in him, and I am helped. My heart leaps for joy and I will give thanks to him in song.

100:4. Enter his gates with thanksgiving and his courts with praise; give thanks to him and praise his name.

Hebrews 2:12. He says, "I will declare your name to my brothers; in the presence of the congregation I will sing your praises."

Luke 4:16. He went to Nazareth, where he had been brought up, and on the Sabbath day he went into the synagogue, as was his custom. And he stood up to read.

17. The scroll of the prophet Isaiah was handed to him. Unrolling it, he found the place where it is written:

18. "The Spirit of the Lord is on me, because he has anointed me to preach good news to the poor. He has sent me to proclaim freedom for the prisoners and recovery of sight for the blind, to release the oppressed,

19. To proclaim the year of the Lord's favor."

20. Then he rolled up the scroll, gave it back to the attendant and sat down. The eyes of everyone in the synagogue were fastened on him,

21. And he began by saying to them, "Today this scripture is fulfilled in your hearing."

1 Timothy 4:13. Until I come, devote yourself to the public reading of Scripture, to preaching and to teaching.

God's Word mentions a variety of ways in which to worship Him. Many Christians may have one or more "favorite" ways they use to worship the Lord. For those with a good voice who like to sing, this may be their way of expressing worship to God. Others may not be able to sing as well, but use their voices to praise Him. Some Christians may spend hours in prayer. Others may praise God spontaneously when He answers their prayers. Whatever methods are used, we must remember that worship must be grounded in the truth of God's Word.

This week's study focuses on the variety of ways to worship God. Yet He is not so much interested in the method used as He is in having His people worship Him. Allow this week's study to challenge you to worship God "in spirit and in truth" (John 4:23).

BIBLE COMMENTARY

1. Rejoicing And Singing

A. From His People
Psalm 98:1-6

> TEACHING TIP 1: Have a person who is interested in music give a brief report on the importance of music in the religious life of Israel. You should also ask for comment on the importance of music in our worship services today. The entire report should be no more than 4 minutes.

Musical worship was an important part of the religious life of Israel. Many of the psalms mention singing and playing musical instruments. Music was one way the Israelites expressed their devotion to God.

The first stanza of Psalm 98:1 calls for a new song unto the Lord. This song tells of the marvelous things that God has done. The Psalmist used metaphors to explain God's mighty acts. To the ancient Hebrews, the right hand and right arm signified power. The Psalmist explained that by God's own power He accomplished tremendous acts on behalf of His people.

Ask: "According to verse 2, what specific 'marvelous thing' had the Lord done?" The primary focus of worship in this psalm is "The Lord hath made known his salvation" (verse 2). While many theological writers argue that in the Old Testament salvation was for Israel only, this and many other Old Testament passages strongly teach otherwise. This is a clear call for all the peoples of the earth to worship the Lord. Israel was called to be His witness to these nations. They would come to know the Lord through having contact with Israel. As verse 3 reveals, the nations (various countries and ethnic groups) would see His salvation through His faithfulness to Israel (see Deuteronomy 4:5-8). They would be drawn to Him and worship Him.

This psalm gives examples of the kinds of musical instruments that were used in worship. Lyre (Psalm 98:5, NASB) is another term for harp. The horn was a ram's horn, called a shofar (verse 6). It was used throughout the Old Testament, primarily to give military signals, not melodies (Joshua 6:4). The trumpet was used by the priests, usually in pairs (Numbers 10:1-10).

This psalm is one of many Scriptures that endorsed and encouraged skillful playing of instruments unto the Lord. God deserves our very best. This is a challenge to all those who minister in music today. We need to be the very best that we can be. This means spending adequate time in preparation. God has never desired haphazard service.

The use of music in the worship service can be one of the most powerful ways in which to acknowledge God's greatness and power. Worship today should be God-centered. By singing either choruses or hymns, we can focus our attention on God.

NOTES

ist to write glorious praises to God. By putting his thoughts in writing, the Psalmist gave us further reason to rejoice in God.

TEACHING TIP 2: Display the transparency ''Dynamics Of Worship'' and answer the question under point 1 *Rejoicing And Singing*. List all student responses on the transparency.

NOTES

B. From His Creation
Psalm 98:7-9

Ask: ''What part does creation have in the worship of God?'' People are not the only part of creation that can praise the Lord. Creation will also bring praise to Him (Psalm 98:7-9). Creation reflects the glory of God. It testifies to His existence, power, and knowledge.

All creation awaits the coming of its King. On that day creation itself will be ''liberated from its bondage to decay and brought into the glorious freedom of the children of God'' (Romans 8:21, NIV).

The imagery in Psalm 98:8 is powerful. Close your eyes and imagine floods of water clapping its hands. The Psalmist used figurative language to show the joyfulness of God's creation at its redemption.

Yet there is coming a day when God will hold judgment against the peoples of the earth (verse 9). He will judge rightly because it is His nature to do so. Total and equal judgment will finally be administered.

The knowledge of God's judgment, coupled with His salvation, inspired the Psalm-

2. Prayer And Praise

A. God Answers Prayer
Psalm 28:1-9

Prayer can be an expression of worship. Through prayer we acknowledge our dependence upon God. We recognize the frailty of our human lives. We also acknowledge God's sovereignty and majesty. David wrote Psalm 28 as a plea for help and a praise for answering his prayer.

Ask: ''What characteristics of God cause us to turn to Him?'' David referred to the Lord as his Rock (verse 1), a symbol of unconquerable strength. The Lord is our Rock, the foundation of our trust.

Knowing the Lord to be trustworthy, David cried out to Him for help. He pleaded for the Lord to hear his voice (verses 1,2). Lifting hands is seen as an act of worship. ''Thy holy oracle'' is probably a reference to the Holy of Holies, symbolizing God's presence among His people.

In verses 3-5 David pleaded not to be judged with the wicked—those who by nature practice evil and speak deceptively. He had no desire to be among those who are deceitful to their neighbors. Knowing their end result, he prayed for God's justice.

Verses 6-9 are an expression of worship because God has answered David's prayer. Indeed, the Lord is "my strength and my shield" (verse 7). We also can rejoice in the fact God takes care of us. He is our strength and shield as well.

The phrase "his anointed" (verse 8) in this case is not a reference to the coming Messiah, but to the nation of Israel. The Psalmist pleaded with God to continue saving Israel, who is His inheritance (verse 9).

Through his prayer in Psalm 28, David demonstrated that God seeks to care for His own. Part of worship is to exalt God for who He is by prayer. In extolling His character through prayer, we acknowledge our dependence on God. As a result, our relationship with Him grows.

NOTES

B. Proclaim God's Majesty
Psalm 100:4; Hebrews 2:12

Just as prayer is an important act of worship, so is praise. The Psalmist declared, "Enter into his gates with thanksgiving" (Psalm 100:4). This is our call to worship.

Psalm 100 might have been sung during one of the festivals. The worshipers entered into the courts of the temple through the "gates." They would come with thanksgiving and praise. We do not come into the temple with our praise, but we enter into God's presence when we begin to offer praise and thanksgiving.

Thanksgiving is foundational to worship. **Ask: "How does an attitude of thank-**fulness cause one to respond in worship?"** A thankful attitude generally is not selfish. When we examine our lives, we discover that there are many things we have that have been graciously given us by God.

TEACHING TIP 3: Take a few moments and brainstorm with your students on the many blessings God has provided in answer to prayer. List responses under the question in point 2 *Prayer And Praise* on the transparency "Dynamics Of Worship." Then have a few students offer short prayers of thanksgiving for the items you listed.

Corporate worship is not only given to God, but also is shared with others. An important part of worship is telling others of God's greatness: "I will declare thy name unto my brethren" (Hebrews 2:12). The writer of Hebrews quoted Psalm 22:22. This psalm was viewed by the Early Church as a Messianic psalm. In it, Christ is seen proclaiming the Father to His "brethren." These brethren are all believers—the Church. By proclaiming God's name, Christ gives honor to the Father.

Ask: "How does a Christian proclaim God's name to others?" Proclaiming God's name can take many forms. Worship is one primary way. Whether in congregational singing or in special musical numbers, we can tell others of God's greatness. Testimonies of God's greatness can also be considered proclaiming God's name. In corporate worship, as we proclaim His name, not only does it honor God, but it also encourages others in their walk with the Lord.

NOTES

3. Centrality Of The Word

A. In Christ's Ministry
Luke 4:16-21

The Word of God was central to Christ's ministry. He constantly affirmed the Old Testament as God's Word. Throughout His ministry, His teaching was based on the Old Testament (see Matthew 5-7). In Luke 4:16-21, Jesus read Isaiah 61:1,2 as the foundation for His ministry.

One reason Christ emphasized the Word is it is the power of the gospel that sets people free. This is exactly what Isaiah proclaimed. And Christ has commissioned the Church to do the same things He did:

• "Preach the gospel to the poor" (verse 18)—The poor may not be the financially poor as much as the poor in spirit. To those who acknowledge their dependence upon God, the gospel is "good news" (Luke 4:18, NIV).

• "Preach deliverance to the captive" (verse 18)—The captives are those enslaved to sin. The good news is that Jesus sets people free from sin (John 8:36). Only the gospel has power to change people's lives.

• "Preach recovering of sight to the blind" (verse 18)—Jesus healed the blind several times. God's Word declares that both the physically and spiritually blind can be healed.

• "Set at liberty them that are bruised" (verse 18)—The broken, crushed, and oppressed, those injured by the events of life, can find healing and encouragement through Jesus and the Word.

• "Preach the acceptable year of the Lord" (verse 19).

Jesus made the Word of God central to all that He did. When He told that congregation in Nazareth that He was the Messiah, He used God's Word. In the next section, we will learn how the Early Church made God's Word central to their worship.

B. In The Church
1 Timothy 4:13; 2 Timothy 4:2

Scripture had an important place in the Early Church. Almost every New Testament book has references to the Old Testament. When the apostles proclaimed the "good news," the Old Testament was the basis for their teachings.

Timothy, a disciple of Paul, was pastoring the church at Ephesus. Paul wrote to his "son in the faith" to encourage him and give him practical suggestions concerning the ministry. Part of that instruction had to do with the importance of God's Word.

In 1 Timothy 4:13 Paul told Timothy to "give attendance to reading." The NIV translates this phrase "devote yourself to the public reading of Scripture." This is probably the sense of what Paul meant. Public reading of the Scriptures was necessary because there were no printing presses to mass-produce Bibles. Public reading gave everyone the opportunity to hear God's Word, understand, and believe.

Not only was the reading of Scripture important, Paul also instructed Timothy to give attendance to "exhortation" and "doctrine." After reading the Scriptures in a worship service, there would be a time of teaching (instruction in sound doctrine and Christian living) and exhortation (urging to obey the Word). The preaching and teaching of the Word increases understanding and helps to apply the Word to everyday life. Paul obviously placed a high premium on studying the Word of God. Since copies were not usually privately owned, a great deal of studying took place when believers were gathered together.

In Paul's second letter to Timothy we again find an emphasis on Scripture. As a preacher, Timothy was commanded to "preach the word" (2 Timothy 4:2). Proclaiming God's Word must be the focus in our worship services. Through preaching, God's Word can be used to "correct, rebuke, and encourage" (NIV), bringing practical application to the people who hear the message. When God's Word is proclaimed people are saved and Christians are brought to maturity in Christ. It is the Word of God that changes people's lives, bringing new life through Jesus, the Living Word.

TEACHING TIP 4: Have the students answer the questions under point 3 *Centrality Of The Word* on the transparency "Dynamics Of Worship."

Note that the first question is for general observations on how God's Word affects the worship service. The second deals with how it affects the individual. Write student answers on the transparency.

NOTES

LIFE RESPONSE

Scripture lists a variety of ways in which we can worship God. While some may appeal more to you than others, all are important.

Enthusiastic singing was one thing that attracted many to Pentecostal churches. The worship services were times of rejoicing in a newfound faith as well as the Pentecostal experience. Singing hymns and choruses, both at home and at church can be an encouragement. There is something about exalting God in song that lifts the heart.

Some might not list prayer and praise as a part of worship. Yet, when we seek God in prayer, we acknowledge His sovereignty and power. We honor God, giving Him the lordship over our lives. And praise goes hand-in-hand with prayer, as the natural response to God when He answers.

In addition, we must, like Timothy, "give attendance" to the reading of God's Word. God has called us to study the Word, practice it, and patiently teach it to others.

If you are going through a time of trial or discouragement try worshiping through

song! Or perhaps a time of prayer is what you need in order to understand how much God loves and cares for you. Then read God's Word and allow God to speak life to you in your situation. Both public and private times of worship need to be an integral part of every Christian's life. This is the way you will increase in the knowledge of God and continue in His peace.

EVANGELISM OUTREACH

There may be some in your class today who have never truly worshiped God because they are not saved. Luke 4:16-21 could be used to lead into an altar call. Emphasize the power of Christ to set people free from the bondage of sin through His Word.

Instruct the unsaved students that through repentance Christ releases the oppressed. Invite them to accept Christ today and take time to pray with those who respond. ⌷

Congregational Worship

CENTRAL TRUTH

Congregational worship honors God and edifies believers.

GOLDEN TEXT

I will extol the Lord with all my heart in the council of the upright and in the assembly. Psalm 111:1

STUDY TEXT

1 Chronicles 29:6-13,20-22; 1 Corinthians 14:4-12; Hebrews 10:23-25; 13:15,16

OUTLINE

1. Thanksgiving
   A. Gifts Of Gratitude
   B. Proclaiming God's Authority

2. Sacrifice
   A. Sacrifice Of Thanksgiving
   B. Sacrifice Of Praise

3. Edification
   A. Through Spiritual Gifts
   B. Through Faithful Worship

OBJECTIVE

To understand the importance of corporate worship and resolve to participate regularly in church services.

CHECKLIST

☐ Two of the teaching tips in this study call for student reports. Assign these early in the week so these students will have adequate time to prepare. Be sure to give them the information contained in the teacher guide that will help them in research for their reports.

☐ Read the student guide and write down any questions you want to use for discussion.

☐ Duplicate enough copies of the work sheet "Edifying One Another" from the teaching helps packet so each student will have one. Being concerned about fellow believers is an important aspect of being a member of the body of Christ. Encourage your students to be concerned about others in your church.

☐ Consider opening your class with singing and worship.

DAILY BIBLE READINGS

Monday: Sing Unto The Lord.
1 Chronicles 16:23-27

Tuesday: Give Unto The Lord.
1 Chronicles 16:28-34

Wednesday: Bless The Lord.
Psalm 103:1-5

Thursday: Living Sacrifices.
Romans 12:1-3

Friday: Spiritual Blessings.
Ephesians 1:3-14

Saturday: Unity Of The Spirit.
Ephesians 4:1-6

King James Version

1 Chronicles 29:10. David blessed the Lord before all the congregation: and David said, Blessed be thou, Lord God of Israel our father, for ever and ever.

11. Thine, O Lord, is the greatness, and the power, and the glory, and the victory, and the majesty: for all that is in the heaven and in the earth is thine; thine is the kingdom, O Lord, and thou art exalted as head above all.

12. Both riches and honor come of thee, and thou reignest over all; and in thine hand is power and might; and in thine hand it is to make great, and to give strength unto all.

13. Now therefore, our God, we thank thee, and praise thy glorious name.

20. And David said to all the congregation, Now bless the Lord your God. And all the congregation blessed the Lord God of their fathers, and bowed down their heads, and worshipped the Lord, and the king.

21. And they sacrificed sacrifices unto the Lord, and offered burnt offerings unto the Lord, on the morrow after that day, even a thousand bullocks, a thousand rams, and a thousand lambs, with their drink offerings, and sacrifices in abundance for all Israel:

22. And did eat and drink before the Lord on that day with great gladness. And they made Solomon the son of David king the second time, and anointed him unto the Lord to be the chief governor, and Zadok to be priest.

Hebrews 13:15. By him therefore let us offer the sacrifice of praise to God continually, that is, the fruit of our lips, giving thanks to his name.

16. But to do good and to communicate forget not: for with such sacrifices God is well pleased.

1 Corinthians 14:4. He that speaketh in an unknown tongue edifieth himself; but he that prophesieth edifieth the church.

12. Even so ye, forasmuch as ye are zealous of spiritual gifts, seek that ye may excel to the edifying of the church.

Hebrews 10:23. Let us hold fast the profession of our faith without wavering; for he is faithful that promised;

24. And let us consider one another to provoke unto love and to good works:

25. Not forsaking the assembling of ourselves together, as the manner of some is; but exhorting one another: and so much the more, as ye see the day approaching.

New International Version

1 Chronicles 29:10. David praised the Lord in the presence of the whole assembly, saying, "Praise be to you, O Lord, God of our father Israel, from everlasting to everlasting.

11. Yours, O Lord, is the greatness and the power and the glory and the majesty and the splendor, for everything in heaven and earth is yours. Yours, O Lord, is the kingdom; you are exalted as head over all.

12. Wealth and honor come from you; you are the ruler of all things. In your hands are strength and power to exalt and give strength to all.

13. Now, our God, we give you thanks, and praise your glorious name."

20. Then David said to the whole assembly, "Praise the Lord your God." So they all praised the Lord, the God of their fathers; they bowed low and fell prostrate before the Lord and the king.

21. The next day they made sacrifices to the Lord and presented burnt offerings to him: a thousand bulls, a thousand rams and a thousand male lambs, together with their drink offerings, and other sacrifices in abundance for all Israel.

22. They ate and drank with great joy in the presence of the Lord that day. Then they acknowledged Solomon son of David as king a second time, anointing him before the Lord to be ruler and Zadok to be priest.

Hebrews 13:15. Through Jesus, therefore, let us continually offer to God a sacrifice of praise—the fruit of lips that confess his name.

16. And do not forget to do good and to share with others, for with such sacrifices God is pleased.

1 Corinthians 14:4. He who speaks in a tongue edifies himself, but he who prophesies edifies the church.

12. So it is with you. Since you are eager to have spiritual gifts, try to excel in gifts that build up the church.

Hebrews 10:23. Let us hold unswervingly to the hope we profess, for he who promised is faithful.

24. And let us consider how we may spur one another on toward love and good deeds.

25. Let us not give up meeting together, as some are in the habit of doing, but let us encourage one another—and all the more as you see the Day approaching.

The Early Church realized the importance of community (Acts 2:42-47). As new believers, they depended upon each other in their newfound faith. As a result, these Christians grew in their spiritual life and in close relationship with each other. Worship and ministry were their goals.

Believers today also depend on one another for encouragement in their faith. Gathering together with fellow believers is intended to enhance spiritual growth and Christian fellowship. The focus of our worship is God and the emphasis of our Christian walk is ministry to others.

This week's study presents some elements that are important in corporate worship—a thankful attitude, the sacrifice of praise, and the edification of fellow believers. Allow the Holy Spirit to teach you in these areas this week.

BIBLE COMMENTARY

1. Thanksgiving

A. Gifts Of Gratitude
1 Chronicles 29:6-9

David had called the leaders of the nation of Israel together (1 Chronicles 28:1). In their presence he presented his plans for the building of the temple to his son Solomon (verses 11-19). Though God did not choose David to build the temple, David had faithfully gathered necessary supplies. After David gave of his offerings for the building of the temple (1 Chronicles 29:2-5), the leaders responded with their gifts (verses 6-8).

TEACHING TIP 1: Early in the week assign a student to calculate the current value of the gifts of both David and the leaders. Usually in the financial section of a newspaper there will be a listing of the current price of gold and silver. Use the weight measurements given in the teacher guide as the basis for figuring these costs.

The aggregate amount of their gift was enormous. Based on one modern estimate of the weights of David's day, he alone gave 110 tons of gold and 260 tons of silver. The leaders gave approximately 190 tons of gold, 375 tons of silver, 675 tons of bronze, and 3,750 tons of iron. To this amount some of the people added "precious stones" (verse 8). By today's standards, the temple was an extremely expensive building.

Because of the generosity of the giving by these leaders, there was great rejoicing among the people (verse 9). Not only did they give generously but also from a "perfect heart." In other words, they gave "freely and wholeheartedly" (NIV).

Ask: "What should be our attitude in giving?" While we may not be able to give to every appeal for finances, as believers we can prayerfully evaluate organizations and give in obedience to the Lord's leading. Giving starts with our tithe to our church. Our church's missions and building programs should also be part of our priority of giving. In all of these, our attitude should be one of generosity. While God may not ask us to empty our bank accounts, we need to evalute our giving in light of God's Word.

David also rejoiced at the generosity of the leaders. His people shared his vision of erecting a temple for God. This attitude of generosity would make Solomon's task easier. It is the same today. An attitude of generosity among the people in a local church will greatly enhance the work of the kingdom of God and bring Him glory.

Giving together is a powerful expression of worshiping together.

B. Proclaiming God's Authority
1 Chronicles 29:10-13

David voiced his and the people's gratitude to God. His prayer in verses 10-13 beautifully described God's sovereignty over Israel. Though David was Israel's king, he publicly blessed the Lord before all the people and directed their praise toward their true Ruler.

Ask: "What was the focus of David's thanksgiving to God?" He specifically addressed the Lord as the God of "Israel our father" (verse 10). This reference to Jacob reminded the people that God had faithfully kept His promises of blessing on the nation of Israel through the ages. The statement also implied that God was the ultimate king over Israel. In this, Israel was unique among the nations. Other ancient rulers claimed absolute authority over their land, often taking on divine status in the eyes of their people. Israel's king acknowledged his reliance on and accountability to God.

In verse 11, the king ascribed to the Lord characteristics of power and might. These characteristics refer to God's supreme rule over all. David was also acknowledging God's rulership of his own life.

When David stated that "riches and honor" came from God (verse 12), he was voicing the foundational truth of biblical stewardship. Everything we have belongs to God. We are just stewards. We are to give willingly and joyfully from that which the Lord has given us. By giving, we are thanking Him for who He is and what He has done for us.

David realized that the success of this "building fund" was not a result of his own efforts. It was God's power that gives "strength unto all" (verse 12). God had given the people the strength to give and He would give Solomon the strength to build. Verse 13 draws the people together in grateful praise to the Lord through the representative voice of their king.

2. Sacrifice

A. Sacrifice Of Thanksgiving
1 Chronicles 29:20-22

TEACHING TIP 2: Early in the week assign a student to study Leviticus 3:1-17; 7:11-36 and prepare a report on the requirements for the peace offerings. This would include the qualifications for the animals and the worshipers. Ask this student to give this report at this time.

David's prayer and praise recorded in 1 Chronicles 29:10-19 express his personal praise to God. He also encouraged the people to praise God (verse 20). The reaction of the people was to bow down their heads and worship the Lord and acknowledge David as God's chosen ruler.

Ask: "Why did David command the people to praise the Lord?" It is not enough for just the leader to worship. God was not just David's God. He was "the Lord your God," the "God of their fathers" (verse 20). He was the Israelites' God as well. The people needed to worship Him and recognize His authority.

The following day, the people expressed their worship through a series of sacrifices. The offerings presented in this passage was classified as a peace offering, sometimes called a thank offering (Leviticus 7:11-36). The purpose of this sacrifice was to celebrate the joy of fellowship in the presence of God (1 Chronicles 29:22). It was a grateful offering back to God of part of what was given by Him.

Not all the meat of the animal was offered to the Lord. Part of it was to be eaten by the priest and the priest's family and part was for the worshiper and his family. This occasion was a national feast, and was celebrated with great joy.

NOTES

B. Sacrifice Of Praise
Hebrews 13:15,16

Animal sacrifice was important in the Old Testament worship system. Many of the offerings included the sacrificing of a bull or goat. Even in fellowship offerings, the spilling of blood was a reminder of the separation sin has brought between humanity and God. But when Jesus went to the cross, He became our true Sacrifice. Because of this, animal sacrifices are no longer necessary. Christ's supremacy and sufficiency as revealer and mediator of God's grace is the major theme of the Book of Hebrews.

While animal sacrifices are no longer offered in worship to God, there are other sacrifices that we as believers can offer to Him. One of these is the sacrifice of praise (Hebrews 13:15). We offer this sacrifice "through Jesus" (NIV). Because He has borne our sin, we become His followers. It is through Him that we can offer acceptable sacrifices to God

Ask: "How often are we to offer this sacrifice?" The sacrifices in the Old Testament were offered at specified times. The sacrifice of praise is to be offered "continually." As believers we will use every opportunity possible to give praise to God.

Ask: "What is meant by the phrase 'the fruit of our lips'?" This may be a reference to Hosea 14:2. Instead of offering a bullock for forgiveness, God was asking for words of repentence. An important fruit of our lips is our confession of Jesus as the Source of our salvation. The fruit of our lips can also include how we converse with others. The speech of the believer should be wholesome (Ephesians 4:29). It should uplift and not tear down.

Believers are also "to do good and to share with others" (verse 16, NIV). Christians may not have animal sacrifices to offer, but it does not mean that they have nothing to offer. They can share what they have with others. This would include material possessions as well as fellowship that would encourage one another.

The last few words of this verse captures our attention—"for with such sacrifices God is well pleased." Our sacrificial sharing with others pleases God just as much as our sacrifice of praise and worship offered directly unto Him. In fact, what we do for others is to be done as unto Him.

NOTES

3. Edification

A. Through Spiritual Gifts
1 Corinthians 14:4,12

Believers are an invaluable resource to each other for personal support in the walk of faith. The members of the body of Christ are to edify, or build up, one another. When temptations seem overwhelming, when personal tragedy strikes, or when an individual's faith wavers, the Body is available to uphold the struggling member.

One of the ways believers can edify each other is through the proper use of spiritual gifts. In light of the gifts' importance, Paul wrote to the Corinthians to correct their misuse of these gifts. Continual misuse of spiritual gifts destroys their effectiveness.

After listing nine gifts of the Spirit and a treatise on the Body (1 Corinthians 12), Paul showed the importance of love in the ministry of these gifts (chapter 13). In chapter 14 he turned to their purpose and proper use. Verse 4 is part of a discussion started in verse 1 concerning the use of tongues and prophecy. By comparing prophecy to tongues Paul was not elevating one over the other, but putting each in its proper place.

The context emphasizes the edification or building up of the local, corporate body. Tongues, spoken unto God, edifies the individual. The body is not edified because they cannot understand what is spoken. Prophecy, on the other hand, edifies the church because the members can understand what is being said.

Ask: "What should be the believer's motivation for pursuing the gifts?" The gifts are not to be used for power, prestige, or ego. The only proper motivation is the desire to build up the church (verse 12). Paul urged the Corinthian believers to keep this goal in mind. Paul was not negating any gift—all gifts are important. He was encouraging the proper use of each gift.

NOTES

B. Through Faithful Worship
Hebrews 10:23-25

TEACHING TIP 3: Distribute copies of the work sheet "Edifying One Another." Divide the class into groups, each group being assigned one verse from Hebrews 10:23-25. Ask the groups to brainstorm for ways to apply their verse. After about 5 minutes, have them share their answers. Encourage your students to seek the Lord for ways to be used in edifying your local body of believers.

The writer of Hebrews was concerned that some believers were leaving Christianity and returning to Judaism. The Book of Hebrews emphasizes the complete superiority of Christ over the Law and His fulfillment of it. The writer challenged these believers to "hold fast the profession of our faith" (10:23) in spite of any persecution they might be facing. The phrase "the hope we profess" (NIV) indicates that God will fulfill His promises.

Each believer is not just to be concerned with himself. He is also to be concerned with his fellow believers (verse 24). We are to be concerned about the salvation and Christian life of others and look for ways to "provoke" or "spur one another on" (NIV) to live for God more faithfully. We are not to sit idly by and let our fellow believers waver in their faith.

Ask: "What can we do to help other believers stay true to the faith?" First, we can pray for each other. Jesus himself prayed for Peter when He knew Satan's attack was imminent (Luke 22:31,32). With God's power we can be victorious. On a more practical level, we can be available to talk with other believers. We need to listen and encourage others who are going through difficult struggles. Using the Word, we can build one another's faith to extinguish Satan's fiery darts (Ephesians 6:16). Faithfully ministering to others can help us overcome our own times of discouragement.

The writer of Hebrews elaborated on an important means of supporting one another—"not forsaking the assembling of ourselves together" (verse 25). Evidently some were intentionally avoiding corporate worship. Faithful church attendance is important. When we gather with other believers, we receive encouragement from being around those of like faith. Hearing and applying the Word brings growth and maturity to meet the demands of today's world.

The day to which the writer referred is no doubt the Day of the Lord. This phrase not only includes the Rapture, but all end-time events, including God's judgment. In light of the believer's future home and God's judgment on those outside of Christ, we need to carefully consider our spiritual life.

NOTES

LIFE RESPONSE

Thanksgiving and generosity go hand in hand. And what better place to exercise both than within the church! We have the privilege of showing our gratitude to God and building up the different ministries of the local body.

As individuals and as a body of believers we need to express our thanks to God. Sometimes we accept the blessings of God and fail to thank Him for His goodness to us. Thankfulness recognizes God as Owner of all that we have. We will then want to honor Him with our lives and possessions. Perhaps this study has reminded you to become more thankful toward God. Begin to practice this thanksgiving today both at church and at home.

True thanksgiving leads to sacrifice. We can joyfully present ourselves as living sacrifices to God. As we continually offer the sacrifice of praise, we find ourselves strengthened in the Lord. Look for ways to proclaim the Lord's name to fellow believers and to the unsaved. As you do, you will share His mercy and grace. Offering ourselves to God means offering ourselves in service to others.

When we gather with fellow Christians, the goal of our corporate worship is to build up and edify the body. Since spiritual gifts are an important part of this ministry, why not ask God to show you how you can be used in these gifts? Your life and the lives of fellow believers will be enhanced as you allow God to use you in this way.

EVANGELISM OUTREACH

The elements of congregational worship, especially the idea of sacrifice, may be foreign to any unsaved in your class. To them, sacrifice may be a negative term. Emphasize that the only way to have a sacrificial spirit comes through the sacrifice of Christ upon the cross. Explain how Christ, the sinless Son of God, became the Sacrificial Lamb and gave himself for the sins of all humanity. Allow time to pray for those who might want to accept Christ's sacrifice for them. ⌐

Pentecostal Worship

Central Truth

Pentecostal worship is characterized by freedom of expression in praise to God.

Golden Text

Be filled with the Spirit. Speak to one another with psalms, hymns and spiritual songs. Sing and make music in your heart to the Lord. Ephesians 5:18,19 (NIV)

Study Text

Exodus 15:20,21; 2 Samuel 6:5,14,15; Nehemiah 9:1-3; Acts 2:42-47; 4:23-31; 1 Corinthians 14:1-5; Ephesians 5:19,20

Outline

1. Joyous Celebration
   A. Exalting God
   B. Songs Of Encouragement

2. Earnest Prayer
   A. Prayer Of Confession
   B. Praying With Power

3. Fellowship And Ministry
   A. Strengthened Through Fellowship
   B. Ministry Through Spiritual Gifts

Objective

To review the components of Pentecostal worship and desire the Spirit's leading in every worship service.

Checklist

☐ Read this week's study in the student guide. Write down any questions you might want to use for discussion.

☐ Distribute copies of the work sheet "Ministry Through Fellowship." Use this to start the students thinking about the importance of ministry to new believers. Have them list practical ways they can minister to new converts as well as other believers.

☐ Pentecostal worship was an important expression of the Early Church. It should be for our church today also. Pray for the anointing of the Holy Spirit as you teach this week's study. There may be some in your class who have not received the baptism in the Holy Spirit. This would be a good time to encourage them to seek this special gift from God.

Daily Bible Readings

Monday: Kneeling.
2 Chronicles 6:12-15
Tuesday: Standing.
Nehemiah 9:4-6
Wednesday: Shouting.
Psalm 47:1-5
Thursday: Singing.
Psalm 47:6-9
Friday: Rejoicing.
Psalm 149:1-5
Saturday: Raising Hands.
1 Timothy 2:1-8

King James Version

Exodus 15:20. Miriam the prophetess, the sister of Aaron, took a timbrel in her hand; and all the women went out after her with timbrels and with dances.

21. And Miriam answered them, Sing ye to the Lord, for he hath triumphed gloriously: the horse and his rider hath he thrown into the sea.

Ephesians 5:19. Speaking to yourselves in psalms and hymns and spiritual songs, singing and making melody in your heart to the Lord.

Nehemiah 9:2. The seed of Israel separated themselves from all strangers, and stood and confessed their sins, and the iniquities of their fathers.

3. And they stood up in their place, and read in the book of the law of the Lord their God one fourth part of the day; and another fourth part they confessed, and worshipped the Lord their God.

Acts 4:23. Being let go, they went to their own company, and reported all that the chief priests and elders had said unto them.

24. And when they heard that, they lifted up their voice to God with one accord, and said, Lord, thou art God, which hast made heaven, and earth, and the sea, and all that in them is.

31. And when they had prayed, the place was shaken where they were assembled together; and they were all filled with the Holy Ghost, and they spake the word of God with boldness.

2:42. They continued steadfastly in the apostles' doctrine and fellowship, and in breaking of bread, and in prayers.

1 Corinthians 14:1. Follow after charity, and desire spiritual gifts, but rather that ye may prophesy.

2. For he that speaketh in an unknown tongue speaketh not unto men, but unto God: for no man understandeth him; howbeit in the spirit he speaketh mysteries.

3. But he that prophesieth speaketh unto men to edification, and exhortation, and comfort.

4. He that speaketh in an unknown tongue edifieth himself; but he that prophesieth edifieth the church.

5. I would that ye all spake with tongues, but rather that ye prophesied: for greater is he that prophesieth than he that speaketh with tongues, except he interpret, that the church may receive edifying.

New International Version

Exodus 15:20. Miriam the prophetess, Aaron's sister, took a tambourine in her hand, and all the women followed her, with tambourines and dancing.

21. Miriam sang to them: "Sing to the Lord, for he is highly exalted. The horse and its rider he has hurled into the sea."

Ephesians 5:19. Speak to one another with psalms, hymns and spiritual songs. Sing and make music in your heart to the Lord.

Nehemiah 9:2. Those of Israelite descent had separated themselves from all foreigners. They stood in their places and confessed their sins and the wickedness of their fathers.

3. They stood where they were and read from the Book of the Law of the Lord their God for a quarter of the day, and spent another quarter in confession and in worshiping the Lord their God.

Acts 4:23. On their release, Peter and John went back to their own people and reported all that the chief priests and elders had said to them.

24. When they heard this, they raised their voices together in prayer to God. "Sovereign Lord," they said, "you made the heaven and the earth and the sea, and everything in them."

31. After they prayed, the place where they were meeting was shaken. And they were all filled with the Holy Spirit and spoke the word of God boldly.

2:42. They devoted themselves to the apostles' teaching and to the fellowship, to the breaking of bread and to prayer.

1 Corinthians 14:1. Follow the way of love and eagerly desire spiritual gifts, especially the gift of prophecy.

2. For anyone who speaks in a tongue does not speak to men but to God. Indeed, no one understands him; he utters mysteries with his spirit.

3. But everyone who prophesies speaks to men for their strengthening, encouragement and comfort.

4. He who speaks in a tongue edifies himself, but he who prophesies edifies the church.

5. I would like every one of you to speak in tongues, but I would rather have you prophesy. He who prophesies is greater than one who speaks in tongues, unless he interprets, so that the church may be edified.

In the Old Testament, there were times of joyous worship. These special occasions allowed those involved to express their worship to God in an exuberant manner. It was at those times that the "joy of the Lord" was truly their strength (Nehemiah 8:10).

Pentecostal worship provides Spirit-filled believers with opportunities of joyous worship as well as ministry to others. The baptism in the Holy Spirit opens a whole new area of spiritual life for Christians. This experience is not an end of a search, but a beginning of Spirit-empowered ministry. When we allow the Holy Spirit to direct each element in our worship services God is glorified and the body of Christ will be edified.

This week, allow the Holy Spirit to refresh you and increase your desire to worship and touch other lives for Christ.

BIBLE COMMENTARY

1. Joyous Celebration

A. Exalting God
Exodus 15:20,21; 2 Samuel 6:5,14,15

TEACHING TIP 1: Begin class with a time of worship. Have a student lead in the singing of several lively choruses to set the stage for the presentation of this first main point.

Worship was never intended to be lifeless. God designed us to have emotions, and worship is one way we use our emotions to express our love of God. The Children of Israel had been oppressed for more than 400 years in Egypt. They were now free from this bondage. This called for a great celebration.

Moses led the Israelites in worship (Exodus 15:1-19). In song Moses exalted God and His power over Israel's enemy. Verses 20 and 21 record a song led by Miriam, Moses' sister. Actually, it may have been an antiphonal response, with the women led by Miriam responding with the refrain after each verse of Moses' song.

Note the joyousness of Miriam's actions. With a tambourine-like instrument she led the women in singing and dancing. Their dance was probably something of a leaping motion that was not sensual or immoral. Their celebration was filled with emotion and excitement.

David also found occasion to worship the Lord joyfully. The ark of the covenant, which symbolized God's presence among His people, had remained in the house of Abinadab for 70 years. David decided that the ark belonged in Jerusalem (1 Chronicles 13:1-6). When David and those chosen by him began to move the ark, there was great celebration. With various musical instruments they began to rejoice "before the Lord" (2 Samuel 6:5). But tragedy struck, and the ark was placed in the house of Obed-edom (verses 6-11). Three months later David again began to bring the ark back to Jerusalem (verse 12). As before, there was great rejoicing with musical instruments and singing.

To show the joyousness of this occasion, the Scripture records that David "danced before the Lord with all his might" (verse 14). The phrase "with all his might" indicates that it was wholeheartedly unto the Lord. With trumpet blasts and shouts of joy, David brought the ark to Jerusalem (verse 15).

worship in one's own language. Whatever the case, these songs were part of Pentecostal worship.

TEACHING TIP 2: Ask your students to share testimonies of times when Christian music ministered to them, helping them deal with a personal need. Ask for examples from each of the three categories in Ephesians 5:20.

NOTES

B. Songs Of Encouragement
Ephesians 5:19,20

Music must have had an important place in the New Testament church. In Paul's letter to the Ephesians he encouraged them in the use of music in their worship services. One of the results of being filled with the Spirit is being able to express worship in various forms.

Ask: "Why did Paul say that the Ephesians were to 'speak to one another' with songs?" To "speak to one another" (verse 19, NIV) should be understood in the sense of edifying one another. Not only were these songs sung in worship to the Lord, but the words of these songs were to be uplifting to those present. The goal of the worship service was to have each believer encouraged in the Lord. Spiritual music was going to be one of the ways this would be accomplished.

Paul listed various kinds of songs that were to be sung. Psalms probably referred to the Old Testament psalter. Since a majority in the Early Church were Jewish, adapting the singing of psalms would have been natural. Hymns in the pagan world were used to exalt the various gods that were worshiped. Paul may have been referring to Christian hymns which were composed to exalt Jesus as Lord. Spiritual songs may refer to songs which were sung in the Spirit, that is, songs that were sung in tongues (1 Corinthians 14:15). Some, though, think these could also have been songs of testimony based upon spiritual experiences. Others have said that spiritual songs might also have included spontaneous

2. Earnest Prayer

A. Prayer Of Confession
Nehemiah 9:1-3

Prayer is an invaluable line of communication between the believer and God. Voiced in many different ways and for many different reasons, prayer ushers the believer into a greater personal knowledge of God's presence and power. While God knows all that we think, He calls us to prayer for our own benefit. He wants us to depend upon Him, opening our hearts to Him in prayer. Because God is holy and we are prone to sin, our prayers will often include personal confession. Acknowledging our sins leads to God's forgiveness and to free and intimate communion with Him.

After the Babylonian captivity, Nehemiah came to Jerusalem to supervise the rebuilding of the city wall. After its completion, the people gathered into the city and Ezra the priest read the Law to them (Nehemiah 7:73 through 8:8). Following a celebration of the Feast of Booths, or

Tabernacles (8:13-18), the Children of Israel gathered again for a special time of prayer, confession, and hearing God's Word (9:1). This time they gathered to fast, wearing "sackclothes, and earth upon them." Throughout Scripture, there is a direct link between fasting and confession of sin. Sackcloth and ashes were also connected, demonstrating contrition.

The Israelites separated themselves from the foreigners (verse 2). This probably does not refer to the intermarriage that had taken place, but to a renunciation of any association with the heathen and their practices.

After hearing the Law read for 3 hours, they stood and confessed their sins for 3 more hours. Not only did they confess their sins, they confessed those of their fathers (see verses 4-37). These people had seen the destruction that sin brings, and had no desire to walk in the sins of their fathers.

Part of confession is repentance, which means to change direction. It involves turning from the patterns of sin. The deep conviction brought about by the Word resulted in confession and repentance.

NOTES

B. Praying With Power
Acts 4:23-31

Peter and John had been arrested for preaching the gospel. After they were threatened with punishment, they were released. When they rejoined their companions, they told them the whole story (Acts 4:23). Sensing the seriousness of the situation, all went to prayer, seeking answers from the One who has all authority.

As they prayed, they acknowledged God's creative power (verse 24). Their quote from Psalm 2:1,2 in verses 25 and 26 is significant. This was a Messianic prophecy which they correctly applied to Christ. They knew their arrest was not an attack upon them, but upon Christ (verses 27,28).

Acts 4:29 is the turning point of the prayer. They had noted the threats and now asked the Lord to do the same. Rather than backing off from preaching the gospel, however, they asked the Lord for boldness to keep on preaching. They understood that persecution and trial came with being followers of Christ.

They also understood that signs and wonders are part of the gospel (verse 30). They knew that as they preached, miracles would occur. Signs and wonders would validate the message of the gospel which they preached. When the power of God is at work, people will realize that Jesus is real and the gospel, true.

Ask: "What was the result of these believers' prayer?" An interesting event happened after they prayed—"the place was shaken where they were assembled together" (verse 31). This was not an earthquake, but a mighty move of the Holy Spirit. These believers were also "filled with the Holy Spirit" (NIV). This fresh, new filling empowered them to speak "the word of God with boldness." God's miraculous power was again manifested in their lives because they prayed. Part of Pentecostal worship is praying for the power of God to be released through our lives. As a local body of believers unite together in fervent prayer asking God for His power in their lives, God will once again give a refreshing and an empowering for ministry.

TEACHING TIP 3: After reflecting on this account from Acts, ask your students to suggest things that should happen after Pentecostal believers earnestly pray. List their responses on the chalkboard. Encourage your students to believe God for the miracles they might need in their lives or in the lives of others.

---

3. Fellowship And Ministry

A. Strengthened Through Fellowship
Acts 2:42,46,47

The Day of Pentecost brought about the glorious outpouring of the Holy Spirit. Accompanying the Baptism of the 120, multitudes heard the gospel proclaimed and the Church grew dramatically within one day. The disciples were now faced with the task of ministering to 3,000 new believers. These new converts were Jews from all over the Roman Empire. They had come to Jerusalem for the Feasts of Passover and Pentecost. Now they had also found the Messiah to which these feasts had pointed.

The new converts needed to be taught. The apostles' teaching (Acts 2:42) was designed to instruct these believers in their new faith. This teaching was based on the Old Testament and also included the teachings of Jesus, which the disciples would have heard. These new believers "devoted themselves" (NIV) to this teaching.

Ask: "Why is it important to devote ourselves to the study of God's Word?" As believers, we are clearly presented with the benefits of God's Word (2 Timothy 3:16,17). The Word will encourage, strengthen, admonish, and correct us in our Christian walk. We also need God's Word to teach us proper doctrine, so we will not be caught up with teachings that are contrary to the Word (Ephesians 4:14). The disciples knew the importance of sound teaching and provided it.

These times of gathering together were used for fellowship as well as teaching. True fellowship goes beyond casual visiting. It allows for deep friendships to form and a real opportunity for personal needs to be shared and met. The breaking of bread in verse 42 probably referred to Communion, whereas in verse 46 it referred to more general fellowship around food. Both were important. Communion would have emphasized the basis for their fellowship—the death and resurrection of Christ. The other times of fellowship would allow them to encourage one another in their newfound faith. Prayer, especially intercessory prayer for one another's needs, would flow naturally from committed fellowship.

Not only did they take their meals together for fellowship, they also did it out of necessity. Many of these new believers lived in other parts of the Empire and had no place to live in Jerusalem. Fellowship and practical assistance went hand in hand.

TEACHING TIP 4: Distribute copies of the work sheet "Ministry Through Fellowship." Give the students about 5 minutes to think of ways they can become involved in ministry to other believers, especially new Christians. Ask the students to share their suggestions and allow them to discuss their responses. Make these suggestions as practical as possible.

NOTES

B. Ministry Through Spiritual Gifts
1 Corinthians 14:1-5

Not only was fellowship and teaching an important part of the Early Church, ministry to all believers was also emphasized. These Christians realized their need for one another and their responsibility to assist fellow believers in their spiritual growth. Spiritual gifts played a major role in this ministry in the local church.

As we studied last week, the gifts of the Spirit were in operation in the Corinthian church, but some of the Corinthians were abusing these gifts. Therefore, Paul wrote to give guidance and correction in this area.

Spiritual gifts belong in the church. Paul said to "desire spiritual gifts" (1 Corinthians 14:1). But the gifts are to be operated in love (13:1-13). They belong to every believer, not just to pastors, evangelists, and others in leadership positions. The Holy Spirit intends that all members of a church can be used in the ministry of spiritual gifts to glorify God, thereby building up the body.

There are times when speaking in tongues is used to edify the believer (1 Corinthians 14:2,4). But God also intends spiritual gifts to be used to minister and edify the members of the local church (verses 3,5). Both have their place. This is the basis for Paul's teaching in chapter 14. If we fail to minister to others, the body is weakened rather than strengthened. Therefore, we are called, not just to do those things which please us, but to make sure others in the body of Christ are ministered to.

NOTES

LIFE RESPONSE

Worship can be expressed in a variety of ways. Some people worship God in a quiet manner while some worship God joyously. One of the marks of Pentecostal worship is its exuberance. People have been attracted to the Spirit-filled life through the joyful worship services found in many Pentecostal churches.

There is one element in Pentecost that enhances worship—the baptism in the Holy Spirit. While the main purpose for the Baptism is an enduement of power for witness, there is also the aspect of joy that is associated with this experience (Romans 14:17). Paul recognized this when he wrote to the church at Ephesus. He wanted their worship in song to be an expression of joy to each other and to God.

Maybe you have sensed that there is something missing in your worship experience. Maybe you are desiring more from your times of worship. Perhaps you have been baptized in the Holy Spirit, yet feel that you have allowed that experience to become a distant memory. Ask the Holy Spirit to come upon you in a fresh and new

way. Allow the refreshing of the Spirit of God to engulf and meet your desire (Isaiah 44:3). If you have never received the baptism in the Holy Spirit, seek for His filling today. God wants to fill you with His Holy Spirit (Luke 11:13). This experience not only opens an avenue of worship, but also leads to a dynamic prayer life and to spiritual ministry to others.

EVANGELISM OUTREACH

There may be some in your class who do not understand worship of any kind, let alone Pentecostal worship, because they have never accepted Christ as their Savior. One of the results of the Spirit-filled life was the evangelism that took place after the Day of Pentecost. Pray for the Holy Spirit to help you as you use the passage from Nehemiah to stress the importance of confession and repentance. Briefly explain the plan of salvation, then make an appeal for any unsaved in your class to come to Christ. ▭

I N T R O D U C T I O N

1 & 2 CORINTHIANS

Jesus said, "I will build my church; and the gates of hell shall not prevail against it" (Matthew 16:18). Believers everywhere are encouraged by these words. In the midst of difficult situations church members know that Christ is with them. By these words we also realize that the Church is not built by human efforts. But that does not mean that God does not use people. In the process of building His Church, Jesus uses imperfect humans. Sometimes personalities and personal opinions hinder what God wants to accomplish. This was part of the problem in the church at Corinth.

Paul, under the inspiration of the Holy Spirit, wrote to these believers and urged them to work together for the good of their church and each believer. His instructions are just as important for believers today.

In study 1, "Trusting God's Wisdom," you will discover the contrast between God's wisdom and worldly wisdom and how God's wisdom is important for our lives. Studies 2 "Let Unity Prevail" and 3 "Responsible Christian Living" will help you understand the importance of unity and the need for living responsible Christian lives.

Guidelines for the believer's participation in "Observing Holy Communion" are covered in study 4. "Gifts, Unity, and Love" (study 5) presents teaching on the ministry of spiritual gifts. Paul's ministry, including his suffering for the gospel, forms the backdrop of studies 6 and 8 "Facing Trials Courageously" and "Effective Christian Service." It is through his example that we are challenged for Christian service.

Sandwiched between these two studies is Easter. On Resurrection morning you will examine the significance of Christ's resurrection for each believer as you study "Authority Of The Risen Christ."

Make the Old New

By Donald Piper

Who says you can't teach an old dog new tricks? The problem is that most of us accept that saying too readily. One of the most challenging tasks for a teacher of adults is developing teaching methods that are fresh but still involve the student in the learning process. After students have progressed through our educational structure, both secular and Christian, they have been exposed to almost every method. Instead of spending hours developing "new" methods, let's use the "old" ones in "new" ways.

One effective activity for involving students is the role-play. It is more effective if it is not announced as a role-play. You will contact a student or students before class and give them specific instructions about their part. Do not introduce the role-play. At a previously determined cue, the students will act out the situation. Stop it when you see the others are aware it has been staged. Take time to ask the class questions like: "How did you feel during the role-play?" "What did you want to do?" "Why?" "What causes situations like the one portrayed to develop?"

The advantage of using this activity is that students usually develop "real" feelings, not artificial ones, toward the situation. As the teacher you must constantly monitor the tone of the role-play. Do not allow a positive setting to turn negative.

A second method not often used in the classroom is student expression. For many teachers the learning process is a simple dialogue (sometimes a monologue) between teacher (the transmitter) and student (the receiver). How do you know if the students are really receiving? You can't by simply asking. (Students quickly learn the right responses.) Challenge them by interjecting statements of non-truth in your lecture or discussion. Do it in such a way that students have the impression you are serious. When they respond to your statments, encourage them to verbalize their responses as fully as possible. Do not accept simple yes and no answers. The process of verbalization will help students firm up those inward convictions. If you use this method and they do not respond to your statments, be sure to let them know what you were doing before you go on.

Most of us have used the case study at some point in our teaching. Why not reverse the process and have the students write the case studies? Students in a group could analyze a Bible character. It does not take professional training to use the case study effectively. Most of us are already analyzing people we know and meet. After students have prepared their analysis, discuss each case as a class.

An interview can serve well in getting students involved. Instead of you acting as the interviewer, send the class out in groups to conduct their own interviews. To add interest, instruct students to record the interviews. If you have access to a video camera and a video cassette machine, have them conduct TV interviews. They are sure to come back to class with information that is both educational and entertaining.

A "Scripture search" for adults? Why not? With some modifications, the popular Scripture search game of our youth can be an effective tool for involving the adult student. Rather than simply telling students to find a particular passage, give them the Scripture and have them only read the parallel reference, but indicate its relationship to the original Scriptui

These are just a few suggestions for involving the students by using old methods in new ways. It is possible to alter the use of any teaching method to make it not only different but, more importantly, the most appropriate method for your class.

"Teacher Growth Series" brings you information on every phase of your teaching ministry. Three articles per quarter can be read, shared with other teachers, and filed for future reference. Articles dealing with the same topics are presented at each age level from early childhood through adult. The "Teacher Growth Series" will cover 36 different topics.

A Winning Combination

By Terry L. Terrell

What parts of the Bible do you remember best? Which portions of the Word are among your earliest memories?

Probably Bible stories. Right? Stories of Noah, David, Samson, Jonah, Paul, Peter, Ruth, Esther, Daniel, Adam and Eve, and of course, our Lord Jesus Christ.

Why do you remember these stories so much more easily than doctrinal discourses, historical studies, or passages of instruction? Because it is the nature of stories to stick in the mind.

Storytelling is one of the most effective ways to teach. Jesus used it constantly. Students of all ages enjoy good storytelling and remember what was said long after they have forgotten a discourse, even though the latter may be on the same subject.

This is not to suggest that only biblical stories should be presented in a class session. Adults need the instruction, encouragement, history, and doctrine taught in Scripture. These must not be neglected.

However, all of these subjects will be understood more readily when the truths are illustrated with a story from Scripture or personal experience.

How do you tell a good story? Read again the story of Jonah. At times as he stepped down into the ship heading for Tarshish, can you almost feel yourself slipping on the wet deck? Do you smell the fish and hardtack? As Jonah sails out on the Mediterranean, do you almost hear the slap of giant waves against the rolling ship? Can you sense the fear of the storm that is drying every throat? Do you nearly panic as your stomach wrenches with the nausea of seasickness?

Storytelling is filled with descriptive words that appeal to every sense of the listener. As the hearer, your student, is completely wrapped up in the story, you drop in the truth it illustrates.

With Jonah, you may want to emphasize God's protection, His mercy, the great lengths to which He goes to reach the Ninevites, or any of several other truths.

Of course, a personal illustration may be shared with the class for the same purpose. The more "bookish" the study seems, the more you need to use storytelling to bring home its truths to your class.

Sometimes when teaching that type of study, teachers are inclined to give an uninterrupted lecture.

A lecture is a form of teaching that is necessary at times. But a good lecture allows for a variety of embellishments that bring home the truths of the Bible effectively to the students.

Suppose your study is about Communion. You may choose to lecture on the subject, sharing the background of Communion, its purpose, how it is observed in the local church, and its benefits. Sounds a little dry in outline form, doesn't it?

But let's begin the lecture by talking about Communion's predecessor—Passover. Describe the first Passover as vividly as possible, then involve your students. Ask them what Passover meant. Ask them if they see parallels between Passover and Communion. In other words, break up your lecture by the use of storytelling and class discussion.

Then when students have touched on some point that is coming up in your lecture, talk about it. In dealing with the purpose of Communion, you may list a variety of purposes on a blackboard or an overhead transparency.

The most effective lecture is one that is broken up by a variety of attention getters, each one reinforcing the lecture itself. Throughout the study, however, the teacher must maintain complete control of discussion. In a lecture you cannot afford to miss the point of the study by becoming bogged down in something totally off the subject. You may have some students who persist in sidetracking the study with experiences of their own. Ask the Holy Spirit to give you wisdom to deal with this tactfully.

"Teacher Growth Series" brings you information on every phase of your teaching ministry. Three articles per quarter can be read, shared with other teachers, and filed for future reference. Aricles dealing with the same topics are presented at each age level from early childhood through adults. The "Teacher Growth Series" will cover 36 different topics.

TEACHER GROWTH SERIES

Aim at the Bull's-Eye!

By Kenneth D. Barney

It would be just an accident if a marksman hit the bulls-eye without aiming at anything in particular.

In sports, coaches talk about their "game plan." They decide on it well ahead of time—helped by viewing films of their opponents' playing. The coach aims at one objective—victory. All of his plans and his decisions about the plays he will use are geared to finishing on top.

The goal of the majority of Sunday School teachers is excellence. However, this involves more than just the desire to present a good study. All week long, study preparation should be guided by considering the question, "What do I really want to accomplish by this point?" The teacher should keep in mind whether the teaching plan being used will lead the class in the direction that will bring them the greatest spiritual benefits.

The *Adult Teacher Guide* is designed to help the teacher reach vital objectives. The first one is simple: increase the students' Bible knowledge. This is the purpose of the Bible Commentary, the largest segment. The study also contains several questions designed to help the teacher lead the students in a thorough investigation of the Scripture text.

Biblical knowledge must be applied to life situations if it is to accomplish its purpose. This is the purpose of the "Life Response." It is to help the teacher apply the biblical truth to daily living at the point in the study where such application would logically be made. This section is to help the teacher wrap up at the conclusion of the class period the relation of the Scripture text to the students' personal lives.

The final section of the study is "Evangelism Outreach." This is to help remind teachers that another important objective of Sunday School is winning souls to Christ. There may not always be unsaved people present in the class. But if there is only one, the teacher should not miss the opportunity to make it easier for that person to realize his need of Christ and accept Him as Savior.

The "Teaching Tips" are tools to assist the teacher in the presentation of the Bible study so there will not be uninterrupted lecture. Helping students discover the truth for themselves is an objective with high priority. Each teacher should, of course, adapt these teaching tips to the needs of his or her particular class.

The Adult curriculum is designed to present a balanced study of both Old and New Testaments as well as current topics viewed from a biblical perspective. This includes emphasis on vital Bible doctrines, including our Pentecostal distinctives, particularly the baptism in the Holy Spirit with the evidence of speaking in tongues. From such a systematic study will come excellent opportunities for the teacher to encourage students to be saved and filled with the Spirit, live a holy life committed to Christ's service, and pursue individual study of the Word.

During busy weeks it is easy for a teacher to plan merely to "teach a lesson." That teaching will be aflame with fire if the teacher, at the beginning of each week, sets his or her eyes on the objectives to be reached in class. Write out these objectives. Make them your "bulls-eye," and keep them in your sights all week.

"Teacher Growth Series" brings you information on every phase of your teaching ministry. Three articles per quarter can be read, shared with other teachers, and filed for future reference. Articles dealing with the same topics are presented at each age level from early childhood through adult. The "Teacher Growth Series" will cover 36 different topics.

Adult Teacher Guide

Trusting God's Wisdom

CENTRAL TRUTH

True wisdom comes only from God.

GOLDEN TEXT

For the message of the cross is foolishness to those who are perishing, but to us who are being saved it is the power of God. 1 Corinthians 1:18 (NIV)

STUDY TEXT

1 Corinthians 1:18-31; 2:1-16

OUTLINE

1. Failure Of Worldly Wisdom
   A. To Understand The Cross
   B. To Recognize God's Wisdom

2. Triumph Of God's Wisdom
   A. Through Believers
   B. Through Christ

3. Superiority Of Spiritual Wisdom
   A. Unknown By The World
   B. Revealed To Believers

OBJECTIVE

To contrast worldly and spiritual wisdom and depend on God's wisdom.

CHECKLIST

☐ Read the student guide, noting any questions that you wish to use for discussion.

☐ Duplicate copies of the work sheet "Wise Or Foolish?" for each student. This is to be used as a tool to get the students interested in this study. Do not get sidetracked in discussing each Scripture.

☐ Make sure to have enough copies of the work sheet "Unlikely Candidates For Ministry" for each student. Some of your students may not think they have any abilities with which to serve God successfully. Use this work sheet to encourage them to find a place of ministry.

☐ Become familiar with the culture of ancient Corinth. Background material can be found in commentaries or a study Bible. An understanding of the cultural situation will help you to interpret Paul's message to your students.

DAILY BIBLE READINGS

Monday: Priority Of Wisdom.
1 Kings 3:5-10
Tuesday: Wisdom Displayed.
1 Kings 3:16-28
Wednesday: Importance Of Wisdom.
Proverbs 3:13-19
Thursday: Desire Wisdom.
Proverbs 4:5-9
Friday: God's Wisdom Demonstrated.
Mark 12:14-17
Saturday: Heavenly Wisdom Defined.
James 3:13-18

King James Version

1 Corinthians 1:18. The preaching of the cross is to them that perish, foolishness; but unto us which are saved, it is the power of God.

19. For it is written, I will destroy the wisdom of the wise, and will bring to nothing the understanding of the prudent.

20. Where is the wise? where is the scribe? where is the disputer of this world? hath not God made foolish the wisdom of this world?

21. For after that in the wisdom of God the world by wisdom knew not God, it pleased God by the foolishness of preaching to save them that believe.

22. For the Jews require a sign, and the Greeks seek after wisdom:

23. But we preach Christ crucified, unto the Jews a stumblingblock, and unto the Greeks foolishness;

24. But unto them which are called, both Jews and Greeks, Christ the power of God, and the wisdom of God.

25. Because the foolishness of God is wiser than men; and the weakness of God is stronger than men.

26. For ye see your calling, brethren, how that not many wise men after the flesh, not many mighty, not many noble, are called:

27. But God hath chosen the foolish things of the world to confound the wise; and God hath chosen the weak things of the world to confound the things which are mighty;

28. And base things of the world, and things which are despised, hath God chosen, yea, and things which are not, to bring to nought things that are:

29. That no flesh should glory in his presence.

2:6. Howbeit we speak wisdom among them that are perfect: yet not the wisdom of this world, nor of the princes of this world, that come to nought:

7. But we speak the wisdom of God in a mystery, even the hidden wisdom, which God ordained before the world unto our glory;

8. Which none of the princes of this world knew: for had they known it, they would not have crucified the Lord of glory.

9. But as it is written, Eye hath not seen, nor ear heard, neither have entered into the heart of man, the things which God hath prepared for them that love him.

10. But God hath revealed them unto us by his Spirit: for the Spirit searcheth all things, yea, the deep things of God.

New International Version

1 Corinthians 1:18. The message of the cross is foolishness to those who are perishing, but to us who are being saved it is the power of God.

19. For it is written: "I will destroy the wisdom of the wise; the intelligence of the intelligent I will frustrate."

20. Where is the wise man? Where is the scholar? Where is the philosopher of this age? Has not God made foolish the wisdom of the world?

21. For since in the wisdom of God the world through its wisdom did not know him, God was pleased through the foolishness of what was preached to save those who believe.

22. Jews demand miraculous signs and Greeks look for wisdom,

23. But we preach Christ crucified: a stumbling block to Jews and foolishness to Gentiles,

24. But to those whom God has called, both Jews and Greeks, Christ the power of God and the wisdom of God.

25. For the foolishness of God is wiser than man's wisdom, and the weakness of God is stronger than man's strength.

26. Brothers, think of what you were when you were called. Not many of you were wise by human standards; not many were influential; not many were of noble birth.

27. But God chose the foolish things of the world to shame the wise; God chose the weak things of the world to shame the strong.

28. He chose the lowly things of this world and the despised things—and the things that are not—to nullify the things that are,

29. So that no one may boast before him.

2:6. We do, however, speak a message of wisdom among the mature, but not the wisdom of this age or of the rulers of this age, who are coming to nothing.

7. No, we speak of God's secret wisdom, a wisdom that has been hidden and that God destined for our glory before time began.

8. None of the rulers of this age understood it, for if they had, they would not have crucified the Lord of glory.

9. However, as it is written: "No eye has seen, no ear has heard, no mind has conceived what God has prepared for those who love him"—

10. But God has revealed it to us by his Spirit. The Spirit searches all things, even the deep things of God.

In Paul's day, only a small percentage of the population was literate. Few people ever traveled more than a short distance from their hometowns. Most people spent the majority of their time making a living with little time left over for entertainment or study. In contrast to this, Corinth was a wealthy city, therefore its people had time for the pursuit of learning and "wisdom."

In today's society, most individuals spend at least a dozen years in formal education. Many pursue graduate studies beyond college, seeking to gain knowledge as well as wisdom. We also have more leisure time than people have ever had. Paul's words to the Corinthians concerning human wisdom and spiritual wisdom apply as much to us as they did to the first readers. In the midst of a world that admires wisdom, we need to consider God's wisdom.

BIBLE COMMENTARY

1. Failure Of Worldly Wisdom

TEACHING TIP 1: Distribute copies of the work sheet "Wisdom Or Foolishness?" Divide the class into small groups and allow a few minutes for them to answer each question (or divide the questions among the small groups). Do not go over the questions at this time. After the study is complete, the students will examine each situation in the light of what they have learned to determine if they would change any answers and why.

A. To Understand The Cross
1 Corinthians 1:18-20

Many people want to have the reputation of being wise. The world we live in contains many issues that need solving, such as poverty, wars between nations, and drug abuse, to name a few. Our society admires those individuals who have the wisdom to provide answers to these problems.

Many times, though, this wisdom is based on human abilities to achieve the desired goals. This type of wisdom comes from human self-sufficiency. This is the wisdom Paul was addressing in 1 Corinthians.

The citizens of Corinth were influenced by Greek philosphy. Corinthian believers, caught up in this philosophy, were trying to call the gospel a "new wisdom." But Paul argued that the gospel was not a "new wisdom" but something that transcended the wisdom of the world. To preach the gospel with man's wisdom would actually empty this message of its power (verse 17). Therefore Paul needed to address the wisdom of God manifested through the Cross.

God's wisdom is totally different from worldly wisdom. In fact, spiritual wisdom, the message of the Cross, is so different the world calls it "foolishness" (verse 18).

Ask: "What is the 'message of the Cross?' " The message of the Cross is the promise of salvation by grace alone on the strength of Christ's sacrificial death and resurrection. Humanity cannot save itself. There is nothing in human wisdom that can achieve salvation. There is no work that mankind can perform that can merit salvation (Ephesians 2:8,9).

This message of salvation by grace is foolishness by the world's standards because people in the world believe in earning their own way. The possibility of things like the Virgin Birth and Resurrection are beyond their comprehension. That God would die to provide salvation for humanity is beyond human understanding. And yet this message is true wisdom. By it we gain eternal life, while those who reject it are doomed to perish.

To prove his argument, Paul quoted Isaiah 29:14 in 1 Corinthians 1:19. God's plan of salvation destroys the wisdom of the world. Humanity cannot outwit God. God is the final authority.

In verse 20, Paul asked, "In light of what God has done through the Cross, where are the wise of this world?" Although this is a rhetorical question, his answer is clearly understood. By the act of the Cross, God has brought judgment on the wisdom of the world.

NOTES

seem like foolishness to the Greeks. In worldly terms, God's choice to save those who accept the preaching of the Cross is foolishness.

Ask: "How is Christ the power and wisdom of God to those who believe? (verse 24)" The power of the Cross is revealed in the changed lives of those who accept Christ. These individuals have found the power that breaks the bondage of sin. Because of this, Christ is the "wisdom of God" in bringing about salvation. Those in the world discount this power and wisdom. God opens willing hearts to recognize the wisdom of the gospel.

NOTES

2. Triumph Of God's Wisdom

B. To Recognize God's Wisdom
1 Corinthians 1:21-25

With the world's wisdom, humanity cannot even know God (verse 21). God's wisdom was manifested through the preaching of salvation. Even upon hearing God's wisdom, they refuse to accept it. Those who hear and believe, God will save.

The gospel is alien to the interests of the world. The Jews were still waiting for a powerful revolutionary leader marked by magnificent miraculous signs. They were not ready for the "suffering servant" that Isaiah prophesied about.

Greek intellectuals had reduced religion to a moral or philosophical system to help them through life. A message centered on a man crucified like a criminal and belief in a miraculous resurrection would certainly

A. Through Believers
1 Corinthians 1:26-28

Part of the problem in the Corinthian church was boasting concerning various preachers and teachers (verse 12). This boasting carried over into spiritual matters. The very wisdom they were boasting about was nullified in the Cross. They also had no sufficiency in themselves for salvation. It was totally provided for in the gospel. If any of the Corinthian believers had the idea that they were truly wise, Paul let them know differently.

If there is anything more foolish to the world than the gospel, it must be the people who believe it. Paul asked the Corinthian believers to take inventory of themselves in relationship to who they were. They were not the world's prized possessions. Quite the opposite, they were the ones the world would likely pass over (verses 26). But God had chosen them (verse 27). We may not have the possessions and charisma that others in the world may display. But when God looked at us, He saw someone who was useful for His kingdom.

Ask: "What persons in the Bible had a successful ministry even though they did not feel qualified or were rejected?"

TEACHING TIP 2: Have the students suggest the names and circumstances of any individuals in the Bible who did not feel qualified to minister for God or who were rejected for some reason. Some suggestions to get the students started could be Moses, Gideon, and Peter. Stress the unlikeliness of God's choice in each case.

Some in your class may feel inadequate to minister to others. Because God has called them, they are valuable to Him. Encourage your students to seek God and let Him show them ways they can minister to others.

When God chooses His spokesmen, He doesn't pay attention to the world's standards of wisdom. He doesn't look at a community, identify the natural leaders, and call them to ministry. If He did, we could reasonably argue that we had earned God's attention. We could boast about it rather than humbly admitting that His choice of us was a matter of pure grace. God chooses the foolish, the weak, the lowly, and despised to put that attitude and those who hold it to shame (verse 28).

NOTES

B. Through Christ
1 Corinthians 1:29-31

In verse 30, Paul mentioned three things that explain God's wise plan of salvation. In this plan Christ Jesus "is made unto us wisdom" from God.

First, as part of this wisdom, Paul stated that Christ has become our righteousness. We have no righteousness in ourselves (Romans 3:9,10). Jesus Christ took our sin upon himself at the cross making us righteous (2 Corinthians 5:21).

Secondly, Jesus has become our "sanctification." Not only are we sanctified by His blood shed on the cross (Hebrews 10:10-15), He has also made possible our growth in our Christian walk.

Lastly, Paul declared that Christ is our "redemption." It is only through His death that we have been delivered from sin (Romans 3:24). By transforming us from sinful creatures into righteous servants, God's wisdom triumphs over the world. Therefore, it is not who we are but who Christ is and what He has done in us.

Ask: "How should we respond to God's provision through Christ?" Since we cannot claim any praise for ourselves for salvation, all glory for our redemption and transformation goes to God. Paul paraphrased Jeremiah 9:24 to conclude his argument: "He that glorieth, let him glory in the Lord" (1 Corinthians 1:31). God's "foolishness," the gospel Paul preached, is proven wiser than all the wisdom of men, and in this God is glorified. His plan of salvation, so difficult for the world to understand, results in all glory going to Him. Through our transformation, God's wisdom is vindicated and He is glorified.

NOTES

3. Superiority Of Spiritual Wisdom

A. Unknown By The World
1 Corinthians 2:6-9

To those who may have thought that the world's wisdom was "for the mature" Paul declared to the contrary—the gospel is wisdom for the mature (verse 6). His preaching to the Corinthians may not have been eloquent or sophisticated (worldly wise, verses 1-5), but it was spiritually wise.

Ask: **"What proves that God's wisdom is superior to the wisdom of the world?"** God's wisdom is beyond the understanding of the worldly wise. Paul said that it is "a mystery, even the hidden wisdom" (verse 7). Spiritual wisdom is superior because it is a mystery beyond human comprehension. This wisdom was destined to bring us to glory; therefore, it was hidden until the proper time to be revealed.

Moreover, the leaders of the world proved that God's wisdom was superior to theirs when they crucified Christ. Based on their worldly judgment, Jewish and Roman leaders agreed that the wisest thing to do was to crucify Him. This proved that they could not grasp the scope of God's wisdom— God's plan of redemption through Christ. Those who crucified Jesus, hoping to do away with Him, actually fulfilled God's plan. If they had realized what the results of killing Christ would be, "they would not have crucified the Lord of glory" (verse 8).

NOTES

B. Revealed To Believers
1 Corinthians 2:10-16

Ask: **"If God's wisdom is beyond human understanding, how can we expect to become spiritually wise?"** The "ma-ture" that Paul mentions in verse 6 are not spiritually elete. Paul was contrasting believers with nonbelievers. Despite the fact God's wisdom is "hidden" (KJV) or "secret" (NIV), Christians can have spiritual wisdom. To express this great truth poetically, Paul quoted Isaiah 64:4 in verses 9 and 10: "Eye hath not seen, nor ear heard, neither have entered into the heart of man, the things which God hath prepared for them that love him. But God hath revealed them unto us by his Spirit." The Spirit knows the deepest thoughts of God (verse 11). What is hidden from the wisest human interpreter is open to every Christian, because in salvation, God gave us His Spirit, not the "spirit of the world" (verse 12). As we allow the Spirit to teach us, we learn the wisdom of God, as well as words with which to express spiritual truth.

Ask: **"What are the "spiritual truths" (verse 13, NIV) which we are to teach?"** Like Paul, we who are given spiritual wisdom have been given a twofold commission. First, we have the privilege and obligation to share the message of salvation with others. And second, once the lost have been saved, they need to be discipled in the ways of God, "teaching them to observe all things whatsoever [Christ has] commanded" (Matthew 28:20).

With Paul, we know that there will be those who are not open to God's message. They consider God's wisdom foolishness because they cannot understand it (1 Corinthians 2:14). The understanding of spiritual truths requires spiritual insight. But that does not relieve us from the responsibility of sharing the gospel. There will always be those who will respond to God's truth. The Holy Spirit can open their minds to spiritual truth as He did for us.

In verse 15 Paul noted that the spiritual person makes judgments based upon spiritual perception, but is not subject to the judgment of the world. Having been given "the mind of Christ" (verse 16), we can understand God's plan, especially in the realm of salvation. Having the "mind of Christ" does not mean that we are spiritually superior, but means that we now have an obligation to cooperate with the Spirit's teaching in our lives so we can reveal God's wisdom to those who need it.

world calls wisdom. Draw a distinction between worldly wisdom and spiritual wisdom.

NOTES

LIFE RESPONSE

True wisdom comes only from God. It cannot be found in any library or laboratory, in conversation with friends, or in advice columns. In all of those places we can find human "wisdom," tips that will help us get along on earth. But God's wisdom can only be found in God's Word. The person who chooses common sense over the wisdom of God is the person who is truly foolhardy.

The events of Christ's crucifixion and resurrection are examples of the difference between human and divine wisdom. When we see Christ as an example of God's wisdom, we understand why that wisdom is so hard for the world to accept. It seems unlikely that God would have a Son, improbable that that Son would become a human and be crucified, and impossible that He would subsequently rise again. Yet, in the wisdom of God, this is the most profound and meaningful truth in the universe.

But this wisdom demands a response from us. If we desire wisdom, it is Christ himself that we must receive. We cannot rely on our own wisdom to provide us with eternal salvation. The very first step toward wisdom, then, is to accept Christ as Savior.

The Holy Spirit is faithful to open our hearts and minds to God's plan for our lives. He will help us in our understanding of God's truth. Then, day by day we can listen to the Spirit, choosing His wisdom over the world's. By doing so, we can grow in our knowledge of God.

EVANGELISM OUTREACH

The focus of Paul's teaching in this study is that the wisdom of the world can never provide salvation. God's plan of salvation centers around the Cross. There may be some in your class who have sought salvation through some other way besides the Cross. They have placed their wisdom above God's. Remind them of the temporary nature of our present existence and human "wisdom." Encourage them to accept God's true wisdom and the salvation He offers through Christ. ⌒

Let Unity Prevail

CENTRAL TRUTH

Unity gives beauty and strength to the Church.

GOLDEN TEXT

For we are God's fellow workers. 1 Corinthians 3:9 (NIV)

STUDY TEXT

1 Corinthians 1:10-13; 3:1-17

OUTLINE

1. Seek Unity
   A. Perfectly United
   B. Unity In Christ

2. Avoid Divisions
   A. By Being Spiritual
   B. True Servants Of Christ

3. Build On Christ
   A. Careful Builders
   B. Tested Works

OBJECTIVE

To understand that division in the Church is destructive and determine to contribute to unity in the Church.

CHECKLIST

☐ Use a copy of the Planning The Session sheet from the teaching helps packet to help in your preparation to teach this study.

☐ This study deals with an important topic—church unity. Become familiar with the commentary and application portions of this study. Look for ways to make practical application to your church.

☐ Teaching Tips 2 and 3 ask for student involvement in promoting unity. Have some suggestions ready for discussion if needed.

☐ Duplicate enough copies of the work sheet "Seeking Unity" so each student will have one. Work through it prior to class so you will be prepared to lead the discussion concerning seeking unity.

☐ Pray for the anointing of the Holy Spirit as you teach this study. If your church is going through a time of disunity, ask God to use this study as a tool in bringing about unity among the members of your congregation.

DAILY BIBLE READINGS

Monday:	Beauty Of Unity.	Psalm 133:1-3
Tuesday:	God Despises Discord.	Proverbs 6:12-19
Wednesday:	Sharing And Caring.	Acts 2:41-47
Thursday:	Live Unselfishly.	Romans 12:9-13
Friday:	Maturing In Unity.	Ephesians 4:11-16
Saturday:	Unified In Worship.	Hebrews 10:19-25

King James Version

1 Corinthians 1:10. I beseech you, brethren, by the name of our Lord Jesus Christ, that ye all speak the same thing, and that there be no divisions among you; but that ye be perfectly joined together in the same mind and in the same judgment.

11. For it hath been declared unto me of you, my brethren, by them which are of the house of Chloe, that there are contentions among you.

12. Now this I say, that every one of you saith, I am of Paul; and I of Apollos; and I of Cephas; and I of Christ.

13. Is Christ divided? was Paul crucified for you? or were ye baptized in the name of Paul?

3:1. I, brethren, could not speak unto you as unto spiritual, but as unto carnal, even as unto babes in Christ.

2. I have fed you with milk, and not with meat: for hitherto ye were not able to bear it, neither yet now are ye able.

3. For ye are yet carnal: for whereas there is among you envying, and strife, and divisions, are ye not carnal, and walk as men?

4. For while one saith, I am of Paul; and another, I am of Apollos; are ye not carnal?

5. Who then is Paul, and who is Apollos, but ministers by whom ye believed, even as the Lord gave to every man?

6. I have planted, Apollos watered; but God gave the increase.

7. So then neither is he that planteth any thing, neither he that watereth; but God that giveth the increase.

8. Now he that planteth and he that watereth are one: and every man shall receive his own reward according to his own labor.

9. For we are laborers together with God: ye are God's husbandry, ye are God's building.

10. According to the grace of God which is given unto me, as a wise masterbuilder, I have laid the foundation, and another buildeth thereon. But let every man take heed how he buildeth thereupon.

11. For other foundation can no man lay than that is laid, which is Jesus Christ.

12. Now if any man build upon this foundation gold, silver, precious stones, wood, hay, stubble;

13. Every man's work shall be made manifest: for the day shall declare it, because it shall be revealed by fire; and the fire shall try every man's work of what sort it is.

New International Version

1 Corinthians 1:10. I appeal to you, brothers, in the name of our Lord Jesus Christ, that all of you agree with one another so that there may be no divisions among you and that you may be perfectly united in mind and thought.

11. My brothers, some from Chloe's household have informed me that there are quarrels among you.

12. What I mean is this: One of you says, "I follow Paul"; another, "I follow Apollos"; another, "I follow Cephas"; still another, "I follow Christ."

13. Is Christ divided? Was Paul crucified for you? Were you baptized into the name of Paul?

3:1. Brothers, I could not address you as spiritual but as worldly—mere infants in Christ.

2. I gave you milk, not solid food, for you were not yet ready for it. Indeed, you are still not ready.

3. You are still worldly. For since there is jealousy and quarreling among you, are you not worldly? Are you not acting like mere men?

4. For when one says, "I follow Paul," and another, "I follow Apollos," are you not mere men?

5. What, after all, is Apollos? And what is Paul? Only servants, through whom you came to believe—as the Lord has assigned to each his task.

6. I planted the seed, Apollos watered it, but God made it grow.

7. So neither he who plants nor he who waters is anything, but only God, who makes things grow.

8. The man who plants and the man who waters have one purpose, and each will be rewarded according to his own labor.

9. For we are God's fellow workers; you are God's field, God's building.

10. By the grace God has given me, I laid a foundation as an expert builder, and someone else is building on it. But each one should be careful how he builds.

11. For no one can lay any foundation other than the one already laid, which is Jesus Christ.

12. If any man builds on this foundation using gold, silver, costly stones, wood, hay or straw,

13. His work will be shown for what it is, because the Day will bring it to light. It will be revealed with fire, and the fire will test the quality of each man's work.

O ver the years many kinds of issues have caused divisions in churches. While we cannot allow basic biblical teachings to be corrupted just to keep peace, we must work toward maintaining unity in our church in other areas.

Many disagreements seem ridiculous in retrospect—what color to paint the church or where to place the organ. In light of eternity and God's purpose for the Church,

we need to evaluate the importance of some of these issues we argue about with other Christians.

This week's study examines the lack of unity in the Corinthian church. Paul used biblical principles to show how far from the truth they were.

Use this study to find ways to promote unity among your fellow believers. Allow the Holy Spirit to use you in this area.

BIBLE COMMENTARY

1. Seek Unity

A. Perfectly United
1 Corinthians 1:10

A church that is united in its efforts to proclaim the gospel is a testimony to our Risen Lord. But a church filled with strife and division presents a negative testimony in the community. God intended the church to be a place where believers come for fellowship and encouragment. When there is division, this purpose cannot be met. To restore this purpose, Paul first had to deal with the problems of disunity.

Ask: "With all the other problems in the Corinthian church why would Paul be concerned about lack of unity?" Paul knew that in order to correct the other problems, the church would need to be united. This became his first priority.

In order to restore unity, Paul appealed to the Corinthians in the strongest possible way—"by the name of our Lord Jesus Christ" (verse 10). It was His church, not theirs. Instead of divisions over issues and personalities, they needed to be united to fulfill God's purpose. The other problems were certainly serious, but they were issues a united church could resolve. Their con-

tinued divisiveness would cause the church to self-destruct.

Therefore Paul urged them to "agree with one another" (verse 10, NIV). He was not asking for uniformity, because there is diversity in the body of Christ. But he was asking for agreement concerning the fundamental nature and truth of the gospel.

TEACHING TIP 1: Distribute copies of the work sheet "Seeking Unity" to each student. Divide the class into three groups and assign one question to each group. After 2 or 3 minutes, ask each group to report on their answers. Allow others in the class to add their own comments to each answer.

Paul appealed to the Corinthians to be "perfectly joined together in the same mind and in the same judgment" (verse 10) for two reasons. The first reason was to eliminate divisions. Paul wanted the damage divisions caused to the body of Christ to end. The second reason for agreement among the Corinthians believers was for a true unity to exist among them. True unity of hearts and minds comes when believers realize what the purpose of the Church is and unite in fulfilling that purpose. Paul wanted his friends to come to agreement and restore the unity that they once had.

NOTES

B. Unity In Christ
1 Corinthians 1:11-13

In order to promote unity in the church, Paul had to confront the issue surrounding the division. Some from the Corinthian church had told Paul the basis for these factions (verse 11). **Ask: "What issues were dividing the Corinthian Christians?"** These believers seemed to be expressing pride in themselves by attributing their wisdom to different leaders. Some were saying, "I follow Paul"; others, "I follow Apollos." Still others claimed, "I follow Cephas," one of the original Twelve. Beside these, there were those who expressed their pride above all others by affirming that they "followed Christ" (verse 12, NIV).

In their pride, they were basing their spirituality on which personality they followed rather than their relationship with Christ. These divisions showed how limited and immature their vision of the Church was.

Paul had to expose the foolishness of their pride (verse 13). By their divisions, they were treating Christ as only one of many teachers and making Paul and the others equal with Him. Using rhetorical questions, Paul focused their attention back on the center of their faith—Christ's crucifixion. They belonged to Christ, not the apostles and teachers in the church. This was cause for unity, not divison.

As believers, we are unified because we depend on Christ's sacrifice for the for-giveness of sin. We are not disciples of anyone but Christ. Divisions cause us to focus on ourselves and our "rights" as opposed to focusing on Christ and His plan for His church.

NOTES

2. Avoid Divisions

A. By Being Spiritual
1 Corinthians 3:1-4

In seeking unity, we must avoid divisions. As we grow in Christ we realize some issues are not as important as others. Maturity will cause us to seek ways to promote unity, rather than division. In urging these believers to unity, Paul pointed out that their carnality was the basis for their factions (verse 3). Their divisions were clear evidence of their carnality. He told them that he could not even speak to them as mature Christians, just as "babes in Christ" (verse 1).

The key to this passage is the use of the words "spiritual" (verse 1) and "carnal" (verses 1,3,4). Paul had already defined who the spiritual ones were. They were those who had the Spirit and understood the things of God (2:6-16).

But Paul said that he "could not speak unto [the Corinthian believers] as unto spiritual" (3:1). Even though they were saved and filled with the Holy Spirit, they were acting like those who do not have the Spirit—carnal. They were behaving like the unsaved when they quarreled over leaders.

Ask: "What place does spiritual maturity play in Christian unity?" While we cannot compromise the truth of God's Word, there are some things that we can compromise for the sake of unity. Spiritual maturity helps us realize the difference. The color of the carpet and the placement of the piano are minor issues that should not cause divisions. Rallying around one individual over another is also a minor issue. Mature Christians will not argue over these issues. They realize the importance of proclaiming the gospel and will not allow petty issues to sidetrack them from that purpose.

NOTES

B. By Being Servants
1 Corinthians 3:5-9

Ask: "How can disunity be overcome or avoided in the local church?" The cure for disunity in a local church is realizing that "we are laborers together with God" (verse 9). As Paul explained in verse 4, the Corinthians held some workers in esteem above others. This became a cause for division. This attitude was wrong in two ways.

First, although we are to give "honor to whom honor" is due (Romans 13:7), all leaders are still servants. The word translated "minister" in 1 Corinthians 3:5 would be better translated as "servant" in this context. Each believer has been called to do a task for the Lord. Whether a person is a pastor or a janitor, each has an important function in the body of Christ. To exalt one above the other is to be a respecter of persons and can cause damage to the Body.

Secondly, the Corinthians failed to recognize God as the True Source of the church's growth. It was not what Paul or Apollos or Peter or any other leader did that brought growth to the Church. Rather God causes all growth (verse 7).

To illustrate the childishness of attaching loyalties to the various leaders, Paul used the picture of a farm (verses 6-8). Paul, the founder of the Corinthian church, and Apollos, one of the pastors who helped it grow, were like farmers working in a field. One planted the seeds and the other watered and tended them. Both roles are necessary and equally important to the growth of the plants and of the Church.

But even the combined work of the one who plants and the one who waters is insufficient if the seed is not viable. Just as God causes seeds to germinate in the ground, He is also the ultimate source of growth for all churches. There is no reason for any person to be elevated above another. Rather, we must all work together with God for the good of the church.

Without God's action, neither Paul nor Apollos would have had any effect. No one worker is more important than another. But all must work together as servants to do God's will.

TEACHING TIP 2: Have your students suggest ways they can use the principles concerning Christian workers in 1 Corinthians 3:5-9 to promote unity in your church. Write their suggestions on the chalkboard or a blank transparency.

NOTES

3. Build On Christ

A. A Solid Foundation
1 Corinthians 3:10-11

Just as there are some basic principles for building a physical structure, there are also

208

basic principles for building the kingdom of God. Paul compared the Church with a building to illustrate these principles.

The first step in constructing a building is laying the foundation. To stand, a building must have a good foundation.

Paul said that he was a "wise master-builder" (verse 10) because he had laid a good foundation. As the founder of the church at Corinth, he had wanted to make sure that it got off to a good strong start. So while he had been with them, he labored to construct a good foundation. Others would build upon his work, but laying the foundation was the most important part.

But Paul knew that he was not the foundation, nor were any of the local leaders or pastors. Jesus Christ is the only real foundation any church can have (verse 11). As the foundation, Jesus is more than just the Teacher. The entire Church is built upon Him. Any work done to build up the Church must begin with this foundation.

Ask: "How can we make sure that Jesus is the foundation of our church?" If the people of the church focus on Jesus Christ as the only source of salvation as revealed in God's Word (Acts 4:12), then you can be assured that the proper foundation has been laid in the church. Everything that the church does and teaches will subsequently relate to that foundation. No church can ever be built on philosophy, worldly wisdom, or any human system or individual. By keeping Christ and His Word central, the church will start on the right foundation and continue to enjoy the blessings of a good, solid foundation.

NOTES

B. Tested Works
1 Corinthians 3:12-17

After laying the foundation, a builder would turn his attention to the rest of the building. It is useless to lay a good foundation, and then use shoddy materials for the remainder of the building. This is the point Paul is making in verses 12-17.

Each member of the church contributes uniquely to building the Church. But if Christ is our foundation, then we need to use appropriate materials to build on that foundation. Paul challenged the Corinthian believers by discussing their role as fellow laborers who are responsible for the quality of the building.

In verse 10 Paul wrote, "Let every man take heed how he buildeth thereupon." **Ask: "Why is it important that we exercise care when we work with people in the local church?"** In building, certain materials withstand fire, while others are easily consumed. Some are imperishable, others are not. Since Paul was not talking about a real building in his example, but people, the quality of the materials is important.

The material each builder puts into the building will be tested by fire (verse 13). This fire will show what kind of material was used. Each person's work will be shown to be what it is. And with this fire will come either the reward or the judgment of God. Those who have built solidly on the foundation of Christ will receive a reward (verse 14). For those who caused division—tearing down instead of building up—they will suffer loss; they will not receive a reward. They have the right foundation, Jesus Christ. But they did not build to withstand the fire. They did not do the works that God ordained for them to do (Ephesians 2:10). They will make heaven "only as one escaping through the flames" (1 Corinthians 3:15, NIV).

Paul gave the Corinthian believers a solemn warning that still applies today. "If anyone defile the temple of God, him shall God destroy" (verse 17). The temple to which Paul was referring was the Church, the body of Christ. As a body of believers, the Corinthian Church was the place where the Holy Spirit dwelt. The divisions that the believers were causing in the church were defiling (or destroying) the temple of the Holy Spirit. Instead of building a temple for God, they were destroying their church by their quarreling. To continue with their divisions would invite God's judgment.

> TEACHING TIP 3: Ask the students to read Ephesians 2:19-22. Discuss the role that unity plays concerning the presence of the Holy Spirit in the midst of a church body. Ask students to suggest things they can do to promote

unity. Explain that these things are some of the good works that build upon Christ, the foundation of the Church.

NOTES

LIFE RESPONSE

It is easy to fall into seemingly innocent habits that can in fact harm the unity of the church. After all, the world around us thrives on competition, encouraging us to "look out for Number One" and to take sides with apparently winning teams. We can begin to see the committees within the church, or the churches within our denomination, or the denominations represented in our town, as competitive teams, winning converts and contributions at one another's expense.

In working toward unity, God has commissioned us to be laborers together with Him. But this also means that we labor together with every other member of our church. We must do those things that promote unity rather than division.

As members of the body of Christ we must realize that we are not in competition with each other. Every member, no matter how lowly, is important. Each person's ministry may be different, but we can still be supportive and work together for the kingdom of God.

The Church is not a softball league, composed of competitive local churches fighting

to be the most successful soul winners. By seeking God's direction for our local church and learning to work together for unity, we will see the benefits of promoting unity and experience God's blessings upon us. Rather than fighting and causing divisions, we will then be the true Christian witness to our community that God desires.

EVANGELISM OUTREACH

When nonbelievers see Christians fighting with each other, they quite logically conclude that there is no difference between Christians and themselves. Some have never accepted Christ because they believe their behavior is as good as many Christians' behavior. Emphasize that salvation is not based on behavior and entrance into heaven is not based on how good a person is. Faith in Christ's sacrifice on the cross is the only basis for salvation. Encourage the unsaved to accept Him as their Savior.

Responsible Christian Living

CENTRAL TRUTH

Authentic Christianity demonstrates responsibility toward God and others.

GOLDEN TEXT

Religion that God our Father accepts as pure and faultless is this: to look after orphans and widows in their distress and to keep oneself from being polluted from the world. James 1:27 (NIV)

STUDY TEXT

1 Corinthians 4:1-5; 6:12-20; 8:9-13

OUTLINE

1. Be Faithful
   A. Faithful Servants
   B. True Judgment
2. Be Disciplined
   A. Sanctified Bodies
   B. Flee Immorality
3. Be Considerate
   A. Toward Other Believers
   B. Limiting Legitimate Freedom

OBJECTIVE

To realize that Christian living brings unique responsibilities and accept them.

CHECKLIST

☐ Using a copy of the "Planning The Session" sheet from the teaching helps packet, plan the time you feel you should spend on each point of the study.

☐ Read through the *Adult Student Guide.* Write down any questions you would like to discuss in class.

☐ Early in the week assign a student to present a research report on Corinth. This information can be obtained from a Bible commentary or a Bible encyclopedia. One of the items that should be covered is the immorality that prevailed in this city. This will help understand the background of Paul's teaching in this study.

☐ Make a copy of the work sheets "Guiding Principles For A Disciplined Life" and "Faithfulness" for each student. Familiarize yourself with how they are to be used in this study. You may wish to complete one of each prior to class to be able to help students should they have any difficulty.

DAILY BIBLE READINGS

Monday: Commitment To Faithfulness.
Genesis 28:16-22
Tuesday: Importance Of Faithfulness.
Luke 16:1-12
Wednesday: Disciplined Behavior.
Daniel 1:8-15
Thursday: Necessity Of Discipline.
1 Corinthians 9:24-27
Friday: Consideration Shown.
2 Samuel 9:3-7
Saturday: Consideration Encouraged.
Colossians 3:12-17

SCRIPTURE SETTING

King James Version

1 Corinthians 4:1. Let a man so account of us, as of the ministers of Christ, and stewards of the mysteries of God.

2. Moreover it is required in stewards, that a man be found faithful.

3. But with me it is a very small thing that I should be judged of you, or of man's judgment: yea, I judge not mine own self.

4. For I know nothing by myself; yet am I not hereby justified: but he that judgeth me is the Lord.

6:12. All things are lawful unto me, but all things are not expedient: all things are lawful for me, but I will not be brought under the power of any.

13. Meats for the belly, and the belly for meats: but God shall destroy both it and them. Now the body is not for fornication, but for the Lord; and the Lord for the body.

14. And God hath both raised up the Lord, and will also raise up us by his own power.

15. Know ye not that your bodies are the members of Christ? shall I then take the members of Christ, and make them the members of a harlot? God forbid.

16. What! know ye not that he which is joined to a harlot is one body? for two, saith he, shall be one flesh.

17. But he that is joined unto the Lord is one spirit.

18. Flee fornication. Every sin that a man doeth is without the body; but he that committeth fornication sinneth against his own body.

19. What! know ye not that your body is the temple of the Holy Ghost which is in you, which ye have of God, and ye are not your own?

20. For ye are bought with a price: therefore glorify God in your body, and in your spirit, which are God's.

8:9. But take heed lest by any means this liberty of yours become a stumblingblock to them that are weak.

10. For if any man see thee which hast knowledge sit at meat in the idol's temple, shall not the conscience of him which is weak be emboldened to eat those things which are offered to idols;

11. And through thy knowledge shall the weak brother perish, for whom Christ died?

12. But when ye sin so against the brethren, and wound their weak conscience, ye sin against Christ.

13. Wherefore, if meat make my brother to offend, I will eat no flesh while the world standeth, lest I make my brother to offend.

New International Version

1 Corinthians 4:1. So then, men ought to regard us as servants of Christ and as those entrusted with the secret things of God.

2. Now it is required that those who have been given a trust must prove faithful.

3. I care very little if I am judged by you or by any human court; indeed, I do not even judge myself.

4. My conscience is clear, but that does not make me innocent. It is the Lord who judges me.

6:12. "Everything is permissible for me"—but not everything is beneficial. "Everything is permissible for me"—but I will not be mastered by anything.

13. "Food for the stomach and the stomach for food"—but God will destroy them both. The body is not meant for sexual immorality, but for the Lord, and the Lord for the body.

14. By his power God raised the Lord from the dead, and he will raise us also.

15. Do you not know that your bodies are members of Christ himself? Shall I then take the members of Christ and unite them with a prostitute? Never!

16. Do you not know that he who unites himself with a prostitute is one with her in body? For it is said, "The two will become one flesh."

17. But he who unites himself with the Lord is one with him in spirit.

18. Flee from sexual immorality. All other sins a man commits are outside his body, but he who sins sexually sins against his own body.

19. Do you not know that your body is a temple of the Holy Spirit, who is in you, whom you have received from God? You are not your own;

20. You were bought at a price. Therefore honor God with your body.

8:9. Be careful, however, that the exercise of your freedom does not become a stumbling block to the weak.

10. For if anyone with a weak conscience sees you who have this knowledge eating in an idol's temple, won't he be emboldened to eat what has been sacrificed to idols?

11. So this weak brother, for whom Christ died, is destroyed by your knowledge.

12. When you sin against your brothers in this way and wound their weak conscience, you sin against Christ.

13. Therefore, if what I eat causes my brother to fall into sin, I will never eat meat again, so that I will not cause him to fall.

Have you seen the T-shirts and bumper stickers that read "Refuse To Grow Up?" Some people think that childhood is a perfect time; they don't understand why anyone would want to grow up. But if you ask children if they want to stay children forever, you will probably get a different picture. It is in our nature to grow, develop, and become mature. As we grow, we accept responsibility, first for ourselves, then for others—our children, our parents, those who need us.

Spiritual maturity is similar to physical maturity in that it, too, requires accepting responsibility. The mature Christian demonstrates responsibility toward God and others. Genuine Christian living means being faithful in service, disciplined in behavior, and considerate of others. These actions bring glory to God.

BIBLE COMMENTARY

1. Be Faithful

A. Faithful Servants
1 Corinthians 4:1,2

Faithfulness is a quality that every believer needs. Christians need to be known as those who are faithful to their word. Faithfulness also needs to be shown by our actions. When given a task to perform, whether at work, church, or home, we need to be faithful to accomplish it.

In chapter four Paul continued his teaching concerning servants. He and Apollos were first and foremost servants of Christ. The word translated "ministers" (4:1) is a general word for servants who have the oversight of the affairs of others. This is how they were to be viewed by the Corinthians—as servants of Christ.

The word translated "steward" (verses 1,2) is a different word from the one translated "minister" in verse 1. It refers to the position of manager in a large household. The master of the house entrusted to the steward the economy of the house and the well-being of all who lived there. Paul used this word to describe his relationship to Christ. As a servant, he was entrusted with the "mysteries of God."

Ask: "What are the 'mysteries of God'?" The term "mysteries of God" probably refers to the wisdom of God hidden from the world (2:6,7). This would include the message of salvation through Christ by His death on the cross. Since this wisdom had been revealed, Paul said that he had been entrusted with this message and the responsibility to share it with others. This is why he felt such an obligation to preach the gospel (Romans 1:14-17).

The primary requirement for a household steward was faithfulness (1 Corinthians 4:2). If he proved unfaithful, his failure could damage his master's estate. We have been given a sacred trust as well—the mysteries of the divine plan of salvation. We are expected to be faithful stewards of those mysteries, carefully handling and teaching them.

TEACHING TIP 1: Distribute copies of work sheet 1 "Faithfulness." Divide your students into four groups. Assign one Scripture passage to each group. Give the students about 5 minutes to examine the verses and write their responses. Ask each group to summarize their answers. Allow the class to add comments.

we see now, can determine how God will eventually judge one's service, whether our own or someone else's. When the Lord's final judgment comes, He will "make manifest the counsels of the hearts" (verse 5). Everyone will receive the reward that their faithful service has earned. We must leave that judgment to God. Our only responsibility is to ensure that we are faithful to the ministry God called us to fulfill.

NOTES

B. True Judgment
1 Corinthians 4:3-5

Responsibility and accountability go hand in hand. We are accountable to the one who assigned us our task. It is this one who will judge our faithfulness and success. Paul now began to talk about that judgment.

The Corinthian believers had evidently been judging Paul and his work (verse 3). They probably felt that his work was inferior to others'. Paul's response was not arrogant. He was not putting himself above judgment, but he realized what judgment was important—God's judgment.

In fact, Paul said that not even his own conscience was a true judge of his service (verse 4). Some of us forgive ourselves readily or make excuses for ourselves when we should not. Others are burdened by guilt that they need not carry. For all of us, the standard is the same. God judges us not by how much we achieve in human terms, but whether we are faithful.

Ask: "Why should we be careful about our judging of others?" There are times when we as believers are called upon to make judgments (see 5:12; 6:5). But, the kind of judging Paul mentioned has more to do with finding fault. Sometimes church members examine their pastor using the wrong criteria. They compare him with other ministers, assessing whether he fits into their idea of what a good preacher is. A similiar type of judgment is used on church members as well.

Paul knew the danger in this type of judgment. In summing up this teaching, he indicated that none of us, by looking at what

2. Be Disciplined

A. Sanctified Bodies
1 Corinthians 6:12-17

TEACHING TIP 2: Have the student who researched the background of the city of Corinth report at this time. This will help the class understand Paul's teaching in 1 Corinthians 6:12-17.

When you were a small child, the rules you lived by were probably very explicit. With these rules and their enforcement, our parents helped us learn to live disciplined lives. As we matured, however, the rules our parents made (and that we made for ourselves) become more like guidelines. We live by these principles because we have learned to discipline ourselves.

Some of the Corinthian believers were evidently not living according to God's Word. Paul countered some of their philosophy concerning holy living.

"All things are lawful for me" (verse 12) seems to be one of the Corinthians'

statements which indicated license to do what they wanted. Paul quickly qualified this statement, showing their error.

Not everything, even if it was lawful or permissible, would be beneficial. In fact, some things may become a controlling influence. Also, since some felt the body was temporary—for this world only—they may have felt that anything they did with their body had no eternal consequence. Paul responded to this error by teaching how the body relates to godly living, especially in the area of sexual immortality.

The body is not for "fornication, but for the Lord" (verse 13). The word translated "fornication," also translated "sexual immorality" (NIV), is a general word that can encompass any type of sexual sin. But adultery and fornication seem to be the intended meaning in this context.

To prove his point concerning the body, Paul stated that the Lord was raised from the dead and God would raise us up also (verse 14). The body is not destroyed, but resurrected. Therefore sinful actions do have an effect on our bodies.

Ask: "Why does something done with our bodies, such as immoral sexual encounters, harm our spiritual lives?" Some people like to think that there is a radical split between our physical beings and our mental-spiritual-emotional beings. Actually, the human being is an integrated whole. The believer involved in sexual sins might deny that his mind and spirit are involved. This is far from the truth. The truth is that he damages his holy union with Christ when he is involved in an unholy union.

We are members of Christ (verse 15). To take our bodies and unite them with someone else in sexual sin is wrong (verse 16). How can we take a member of Christ's body and unite it with a prostitute?

TEACHING TIP 3: Distribute copies of the work sheet "Guiding Principles For A Disciplined Life." Some in your class may be engaged in habits or activities that are harmful either physically or spiritually or both. Have your students evaluate their lives by the principles listed on this sheet. Give them about 3 minutes to answer the questions. Encourage them to take this work sheet home and keep it where it will be seen frequently as a reminder for making godly choices.

NOTES

B. Flee Immorality
1 Corinthians 6:18-20

Sexual sin cannot be tolerated. In fact, Paul told these believers to flee fornication (verse 18). There is a reason for this. First, sexual sins are against one's own body. In the strongest possible terms, Paul stated that we, as members of Christ's body, must never commit acts of fornication or adultery. Would Christ himself commit acts of sexual impurity? Never! As believers, we are united with Christ. What do you suppose happens when a member of Christ's body commits an act of sexual sin? According to verse 17, if we are Christians we are one in spirit with Christ. Only He should have mastery of our lives.

Secondly, our minds *and* our bodies are the temple of the Holy Spirit (verse 19). We are not our own. We do not have the right to do what we want with our bodies. We were bought "with a price" (verse 20). Therefore, we are obligated to direct our efforts to glorifying God with our whole person, mind, *and* body. Fornication and any other kind of immorality must not be a part of the Christian's life. Only by the Holy Spirit's help in living disciplined lives are we able to do this.

3. Be Considerate

A. Toward Other Believers
1 Corinthians 8:9-12

The body of Christ is a community of believers. As individuals within this community, we have a responsibility to one another. This means restraining ourselves from actions—sometimes not wrong in themselves—that might be offense to others. This is Paul's focus in chapter 8.

Some of the believers were probably arguing for the right to continue eating meals in the cultic temples. Their argument stemmed from the knowledge that an idol is nothing (verses 4-8). But Paul recognized that not all Christians understood this.

People without this knowledge were probably those who grew up believing in idols. Despite their newfound faith in Christ, they still had a feeling that the acts of idol worship were meaningful and may even have had some mystical effect on the meat. When they saw other believers eat meat offered to idols, they would be "emboldened" to eat meat that was offered to idols (verse 10). When they ate, they were sinning because they felt they were participating in sinful idol worship.

Paul had to address the result of this act of eating in these temples. Contrary to what the "knowledgeable" Corinthians believed, this eating was destroying the weaker believers. Notice that Paul said that this was sinning against a "brother"—someone for whom Christ died. This was a fellow Christian. The end result of this action was the destruction of this brother (verse 11). Instead of being built up, these believers were coming back under the grip of idolatry.

Ask: "How could these weak believers come back under the bondage of idolatry?" Because many of these new converts were idol worshipers before conversion, the pull of the old life was strong. By being exposed to idol worship when they did not have the strength to resist, they came back under its bondage. Sometimes today those who have been saved from drugs, prostitution, and spirit worship cannot return to their old friends, even for evangelization purposes, because of the grip that their former life had on them. We must recognize this, and provide opportunities for fellowship and Christian growth to those saved from these types of life-styles.

TEACHING TIP 4: There may be some in your class who were saved from a life-style of degradation. They may wish to share some of the temptations that they have faced after being saved and the need to reject old associations. Remind the class that there are some things that may not tempt one person, but are a great temptation to another. This is why it is so important that we are careful to live righteous lives, and even sacrifice things that we have freedom to do, in order to help weaker Christians.

NOTES

B. Limiting Legitimate Freedom
1 Corinthians 8:13

We live in a day where people demand their rights. For believers, there is a principle that overrides personal rights—love for our brothers and sisters in Christ.

Our responsibility goes beyond just avoiding what Scripture states is sin. Even things that do not interfere with our relationship with God can be problematic if we live and worship with other Christians who, for some reason, find these activities sinful. Paul said that he would not eat meat rather than influence a brother who felt eating meat offered to idols was sinful (verse 13).

Ask: "What is our responsibility toward other believers whose convictions are different from ours?" When we encourage other believers to do things that are contrary to their convictions, we are in reality urging them to sin. We sometimes do not know how God is working in the lives of individuals. Some believers' past lives were filled with all kinds of sins and temptations. They may have developed convictions concerning things, not sinful in themselves, but having the possibility of leading them to sin. As fellow believers, we need to recognize these convictions and honor them. We must not ask them to compromise their convictions. If we prefer them above ourselves, then we are truly walking in love.

NOTES

LIFE RESPONSE

Mature Christian living involves responsibilities. Christianity requires us to be faithful in our service for God. It is important to evaluate our lives in relationship to our faithfulness to God. We have the responsibility to take God's Word to the world. So, we need to ask ourselves some searching questions. Are we known as people who are faithful in service to the Lord? When given a task to do in the church, do we faithfully carry out that task until it is finished? If the answer to these questions is "no," then we need to ask the Lord to help us grow in this area.

Our bodies are the temples of the Holy Spirit who lives in us. We have the responsibility to live disciplined lives according to God's Word. To fail to do so damages our relationship with the Lord and brings reproach upon the gospel. We need to examine our lives daily, asking the Lord to help us lay aside those things that are displeasing to Him.

God has also given us responsibility for caring for our brothers and sisters in Christ. This may sometimes mean laying aside activities that are not wrong in themselves to prevent our injuring other believers in their walk with the Lord. God expects us to joyfully accept these responsibilities, willingly holding ourselves to a higher standard. This standard is not one of rights, but one of love for fellow believers. This is pleasing to the Lord and our love for others brings glory to Him.

EVANGELISM OUTREACH

This week's study outlines some of the responsibilities required for Christian living. These are high standards that the world is basically ignoring. There may be some in your class who want these standards in their lives, but don't know where to start. These standards can only be lived in the power of the Holy Spirit. Emphasize that none of us can live up to these standards without first knowing the Lord. Invite the unsaved in your class to accept Christ as their Savior and begin living according to God's Word.

Observing Holy Communion

CENTRAL TRUTH

Holy Communion is an important part of Christian worship.

GOLDEN TEXT

Whenever you eat this bread and drink this cup, you proclaim the Lord's death until he comes. 1 Corinthians 11:26 (NIV)

STUDY TEXT

1 Corinthians 11:17-32

OUTLINE

1. Carnality Rebuked
   A. Divisions At His Table
   B. Selfish Actions

2. Significance Of The Lord's Supper
   A. Broken Body
   B. Shed Blood

3. Preparing For Holy Communion
   A. Unworthy Manner
   B. Judge Yourself

OBJECTIVE

To remember the purpose of the Lord's Supper and partake of Communion worthily.

CHECKLIST

☐ At least one week ahead of time, ask five students to prepare the drama "The Potluck" from the teaching helps packet for use in Teaching Tip 1. For a change of pace, you may wish to put the skit on videotape prior to class.

☐ Duplicate copies of the work sheet "The Lord's Supper In The Gospels And Paul" and the information sheet "Questions And Answers About Communion" for each student in your class. The information sheet may be taken home for personal Bible study if you do not have time to do it in class. If you plan to use it in class, provide pencils for the students.

☐ Your class might want to finish this study by sharing Communion together. Discuss with your pastor whether this is appropriate, and whether he or she would be willing to share with you. Remember to provide enough of the elements of Communion for your class.

DAILY BIBLE READINGS

Monday: Covenant Of The Passover.
Exodus 12:13-17
Tuesday: New Covenant Promised.
Jeremiah 31:31-34
Wednesday: New Covenant Instituted.
Matthew 26:26-29
Thursday: New Covenant Explained.
Hebrews 8:6-13
Friday: Price Of The Covenant.
Hebrews 13:9-13
Saturday: Communion With Christ.
Revelation 19:5-9

King James Version

1 Corinthians 11:17. Now in this that I declare unto you I praise you not, that ye come together not for the better, but for the worse.

18. For first of all, when ye come together in the church, I hear that there be divisions among you; and I partly believe it.

19. For there must be also heresies among you, that they which are approved may be made manifest among you.

20. When ye come together therefore into one place, this is not to eat the Lord's supper.

21. For in eating every one taketh before other his own supper: and one is hungry, and another is drunken.

22. What! have ye not houses to eat and to drink in? or despise ye the church of God, and shame them that have not? What shall I say to you? shall I praise you in this? I praise you not.

23. For I have received of the Lord that which also I delivered unto you, That the Lord Jesus, the same night in which he was betrayed, took bread:

24. And when he had given thanks, he brake it, and said, Take, eat; this is my body, which is broken for you: this do in remembrance of me.

25. After the same manner also he took the cup, when he had supped, saying, This cup is the new testament in my blood: this do ye, as oft as ye drink it, in remembrance of me.

26. For as often as ye eat this bread, and drink this cup, ye do shew the Lord's death till he come.

27. Wherefore whosoever shall eat this bread, and drink this cup of the Lord, unworthily, shall be guilty of the body and blood of the Lord.

28. But let a man examine himself, and so let him eat of that bread, and drink of that cup.

29. For he that eateth and drinketh unworthily, eateth and drinketh damnation to himself, not discerning the Lord's body.

30. For this cause many are weak and sickly among you, and many sleep.

31. For if we would judge ourselves, we should not be judged.

32. But when we are judged, we are chastened of the Lord, that we should not be condemned with the world.

New International Version

1 Corinthians 11:17. In the following directives I have no praise for you, for your meetings do more harm than good.

18. In the first place, I hear that when you come together as a church, there are divisions among you, and to some extent I believe it.

19. No doubt there have to be differences among you to show which of you have God's approval.

20. When you come together, it is not the Lord's Supper you eat,

21. For as you eat, each of you goes ahead without waiting for anybody else. One remains hungry, another gets drunk.

22. Don't you have homes to eat and drink in? Or do you despise the church of God and humiliate those who have nothing? What shall I say to you? Shall I praise you for this? Certainly not!

23. For I received from the Lord what I also passed on to you: The Lord Jesus, on the night he was betrayed, took bread,

24. And when he had given thanks, he broke it and said, "This is my body, which is for you; do this in remembrance of me."

25. In the same way, after supper he took the cup, saying, "This cup is the new covenant in my blood; do this, whenever you drink it, in remembrance of me."

26. For whenever you eat this bread and drink this cup, you proclaim the Lord's death until he comes.

27. Therefore, whoever eats the bread or drinks the cup of the Lord in an unworthy manner will be guilty of sinning against the body and blood of the Lord.

28. A man ought to examine himself before he eats of the bread and drinks of the cup.

29. For anyone who eats and drinks without recognizing the body of the Lord eats and drinks judgment on himself.

30. That is why many among you are weak and sick, and a number of you have fallen asleep.

31. But if we judged ourselves, we would not come under judgment.

32. When we are judged by the Lord, we are being disciplined so that we will not be condemned with the world.

Communion is an important act of worship. Unfortunately, it is sometimes tacked on the end of a Sunday morning worship service without giving much thought to its importance. But Communion is a vital part of the Christian experience.

Communion is a time for personal reflection. We reflect upon the death of Christ and what it means to us. We can use this act of worship as a time to examine our relationship with Him.

More importantly, Communion gives opportunity for us to review our relationships with others in the body of Christ. If there is discord in any relationship, this is the time to bring restoration.

As we examine Communion together, allow the Holy Spirit to examine your life. If there are any broken relationships, commit yourself to restore each one today.

BIBLE COMMENTARY

1. Carnality Rebuked

A. Division At His Table
1 Corinthians 11:17-19

TEACHING TIP 1: Have the five students present the drama from the script found in the teaching helps packet. If the presentation is live, make sure they are ready to start at the beginning of class. If you use video, check before class to make sure the equipment is functioning and the tape, ready.

Communion is a time to focus our attention upon Christ's death upon the cross. It is also a time to realize the unity in the body of Christ. Christ died for all believers, not just a select few. But many times, we fail to think about this unity during a Communion service.

In 1 Corinthians 11, Paul gave instructions concerning proper conduct in worship, including Communion. The Corinthian believers' lack of unity was even apparent when they would partake of Communion.

They seemed to have had little regard for each other.

The situation was so bad that Paul said that their meetings were actually doing "more harm than good" (verse 17, NIV). Their problem was more than just following leaders. It extended even into their worship services (verse 18).

It is hard for us to imagine that type of setting, and yet this same situation could happen in our churches today. There are many people who come to church and take Communion who are at odds with others within the congregation. The divisions may not be as obvious as they were at Corinth, but they are still there. It is this type of situation that Paul was trying to correct.

Paul indicated that the believers' differences revealed "which of [them had] God's approval" (verse 19, NIV). The word translated "heresies" in the King James Version is more accurately translated "sect" or "division." Division in itself is never good. Yet in this case, Paul apparently meant that by contrast, the divisions pointed out those whose faith was genuine or mature.

Paul's rebuke is stinging. If they had to act like gluttons, they were to eat at home. He detested the humiliation of those who had nothing (verse 22). The Corinthians' selfish concern for themselves was destroying the sacredness of their worship and the unity of the body.

Concern for others' welfare must be a priority in the church today. If we are a body of believers united through Christ Jesus, we must minister to those in our churches who are less fortunate than we are.

NOTES

B. Selfish Actions
1 Corinthians 11:20-22

Selfishness is characteristic of the people of the world. They are looking out for themselves. They do not consider the needs of others. This type of attitude is to be expected outside of the church, but not among its members.

The Corinthians' behavior in the shared meals before worship had become so outrageous that Paul said, "When ye come together . . . this is not to eat the Lord's supper" (verse 20). In other words, whatever they were celebrating, it was not the Lord's Supper. Their selfishness was making a mockery of the celebration.

Ask: "For what specific behaviors did Paul criticize the believers in 1 Corinthians 11:21,22?" It is thought that, before worship, a shared meal—known as a love feast—was a common practice in the Early Church. Paul seemed to be referring to this love feast in these verses. But rather than sharing what they had and enjoying fellowship, the Corinthians were making these common meals an opportunity for the display of wealth and humiliation of the poor.

Some may have been bringing elegant and expensive dishes to this meal and not sharing with anyone else. There is also the possibility that the rich would come early and eat their food (verse 21). Those that worked came later. Some of this latter group may have been poor. They either had to eat what little they could afford to bring or went hungry. The result was those who could afford it became gluttonous and drunk, while the poor did without.

2. Significance Of The Lord's Supper

The Lord's Supper is an important part of our worship because it was commanded by Jesus himself. He emphasized its importance by instructing His disciples to participate in it regularly, until He comes again. Each of the first three Gospels records Jesus' words when He instituted the Lord's Supper. In His letter to the Corinthians, Paul provided another witness to Jesus' command.

A. Broken Body
1 Corinthians 11:23,24

The occasion for the first Communion was the Feast of Passover. The disciples had gathered with the Lord on the eve of His betrayal and crucifixion to partake of this very significant supper together.

Ask: "What was the Passover? How is it related to the Lord's Supper?" The Passover was an annual commemoration of God's liberation of Israel from Egypt. The covenant God made with His people at that time was demonstrated by the blood of lambs the Israelites applied to their doors, marking them as God's people (Exodus 12:13). As believers, we view the Passover lamb as a type of Jesus, who was slain for our salvation (see John 1:29). When Jesus celebrated the Passover with His disciples, He instituted a new commemoration for a new covenant.

Ask: "Why is it important for us to celebrate the Lord's Supper?" Communion is one of the most significant things Jesus commanded us to do because of what it symbolizes. The Lord's Supper symbolizes Jesus' suffering and death in our place.

TEACHING TIP 2: Distribute the work sheet "The Lord's Supper From The Gospels And Paul." Have students examine these texts noting the differences and similarities that show all four accounts came from the same event. Note the similarities and differences concerning the bread.

On the night prior to His death, Jesus celebrated the Feast of Passover with His disciples. When it came time to serve the unleavened bread, He took it in His hands and broke it. Then He said, "This is my body, which is broken for you: this do in remembrance of me" (1 Corinthians 11:24).

Breaking the bread symbolized dramatically what was going to happen to Jesus' body in a few hours. Just as eating bread was the foundation of physical life for those who ate it, so too, Jesus' broken body is necessary for our spiritual life. All that happened to Jesus happened for us—He was sacrificed for us. Each time we participate in this dramatic visual representation of breaking the bread, we remember the crucified Christ it symbolizes.

NOTES

B. Shed Blood
1 Corinthians 11:25,26

TEACHING TIP 3: Using the work sheet, "The Lord's Supper From The Gospels And Paul," point out the differences and similarities concerning the fruit of the vine in the four passages.

Ask: "What significance did Jesus give to the cup in the Passover meal?" Jesus said that the cup represented His shed blood. With the shedding of Christ's blood comes the "remission of sins" (Matthew 26:28). There is no other way for sins to be forgiven. No one can be saved except through Christ's atoning work on the cross. All of the good works and false religions of humanity cannot produce salvation.

Note in 1 Corinthians 11:26 that Paul did not indicate the frequency for partaking of this ordinance. Paul simply stated, "For as often as ye eat" (verse 26). The frequency is not the important thing. It is the fact we celebrate this ordinance that is important. Every time we partake, we remind ourselves of what Christ did on our behalf. And we proclaim this truth as well.

Communion also looks forward to Christ's return. When we take Communion, we need to remember that Jesus is coming again. This motivates us to live holy lives.

TEACHING TIP 4: If you wish to discuss questions about the way your church celebrates Communion, distribute the information sheet "Questions And Answers About Communion" at this time. Otherwise, distribute it at the end of class.

NOTES

3. Preparing For Holy Communion

A. A Reverent Attitude
1 Corinthians 11:27-29

The Lord's Supper is such a significant part of our worship that we are required to approach it with an especially reverent attitude. To destroy this reverent attitude with unchristlike attitudes was dangerous. So Paul included a warning against taking the Lord's Supper "unworthily."

Ask: "What does it mean to partake of the Lord's Supper 'unworthily' (verse 27)?" This is a very strong, almost frightening word. How awful it would be to deliberately scorn the crucified body of Christ and reject His blood that saves us from sin! Some people even avoid receiving Communion so that they will not inadvertently take it "unworthily." But the word "unworthily" is used to describe the *manner* in which Communion is received, not the *person* receiving Communion.

In the context of this chapter, the unworthy manner of the Corinthians had to do with their treatment of each other at the fellowship meal. By their mistreatment of their fellow believers, they were "guilty of the body and blood of the Lord" (verse 27).

The key to partaking in the Lord's Supper in a worthy manner is self-examination (verse 28). Paul had addressed this issue in telling the Corinthians to examine themselves in relationship to others in their local assembly. Believers today also need to take a close look at their relationships before partaking of Communion. **Ask: "What practical suggestions can you give that will help us obey Paul's command to examine ourselves prior to taking Communion?"**

TEACHING TIP 5: List the students' responses on the chalkboard or overhead transparency. Suggest that your students copy these responses and keep them in their Bibles for use as a self-examination guide before Communion. Remind them to ask for the Holy Spirit's help in this examination.

It is easy to rush from other church activities into the worship service with a to-do list still scrolling through our minds. But instead, we must take some time before receiving Communion to allow the Holy Spirit to examine our lives. We need to understand the importance of this observance.

It seems clear that this examination includes evaluating our relationship with others in the church. Have you harbored bitter feelings toward fellow believers over something they have done or said? Are you avoiding some because they are "less fortunate" than you? These are the kind of issues that need to be resolved prior to taking Communion.

Paul stated that those who continue to "eat and drink unworthily" are "not discerning the Lord's body" (verse 29). In light of the context, he probably is referring to the Corinthians' attitude toward each other. After their love feast—where not much love could be seen—they were coming together to take Communion. Each member was a part of Christ's body, but they were not "discerning" this. They were only concerned about themselves. The very observance that was to bring unity—celebrating the death of Christ—was marred by their divisions. To continue to live like this is to court God's judgment.

NOTES

B. Judge Yourself
1 Corinthians 11:30-32

The reality of God's judgment was already being seen in the Corinthian church (verse 30). Paul viewed this as a "chastening" or a discipline from the Lord. The church was indeed suffering because of the offenses that were taking place.

Paul now turned his attention upon the importance of the examination mentioned in verse 28. "If we would judge ourselves, we should not be judged" (verse 31). The judgment he referred to is the sometimes uncomfortable correction that God uses to get us back on the right path. This is not eternal judgment. It is the discipline that will help us avoid eternal judgment (verse 32). But unless we yield to God's discipline, there is the possibility of eternal judgment. That is why our judging ourselves and yielding to God is important. Our eternal destiny is at stake.

NOTES

LIFE RESPONSE

The opportunity to partake of Communion is an important part of Christian worship. It is a time to once again reflect upon the saving, forgiving grace of Jesus Christ. Therefore our attitude as we come to the Lord's table is important.

The danger inherent in the observance of any ordinance is that it may become commonplace. We can soon loose the importance of the celebration. During the observance, our minds can wander in several different directions and never focus upon what Christ has done for us.

Another danger is that we can take Communion without examining ourselves in relationship to others in the church. We may be bitter toward someone in the church who we feel has wronged us. Yet Communion is also a recognition of the body of Christ.

Right now is a good time to examine your heart. Where do you stand in relationship to others in the church? Is there someone that you need to go to and ask forgiveness for your wrong attitude? Remember, we are the body of Christ. Every believer is a member. To treat them otherwise is "not discerning the body." Do not delay in restoring that relationship.

TEACHING TIP 6: If you and your pastor feel it is appropriate, close class by sharing Communion. Allow time for self-examination. Serve in such a way that no one will feel pressured or embarrassed.

EVANGELISM OUTREACH

There may be some unsaved students in your class who have never considered the significance of Communion. Even if they have been raised in church, Communion might have been just another ritual. Use this study on Communion as an opportunity to challenge them to acknowledge their need of the sacrifice of Christ that Communion represents. Give an opportunity prior to sharing Communion for any unsaved students to accept Christ. Then, they too can share joyfully in Communion.

Gifts, Unity, And Love

CENTRAL TRUTH

Ministry among believers should be characterized by love.

GOLDEN TEXT

These three remain: faith, hope and love. But the greatest of these is love. 1 Corinthians 13:13 (NIV)

STUDY TEXT

1 Corinthians 12:1 through 13:13

OUTLINE

1. Gifts Of The Holy Spirit
   A. Many Gifts, One Source
   B. Manifesting The Gifts
2. Unity In Diversity
   A. One Body, Many Parts
   B. God's Design
3. Preeminence Of Love
   A. Gifts Without Love Equals Nothing
   B. Love Lasts

OBJECTIVE

To survey the work of the Spirit among believers and seek to serve in love.

CHECKLIST

☐ Using the "Planning The Session" sheet from the teaching helps packet, plan the areas you want to emphasize.

☐ Read the *Adult Student Guide*. Note any questions you may wish to use for discussion.

☐ Familiarize yourself with the 3 overhead transparencies from the teaching helps packet. These transparencies are designed to present biblical material as well as promote discussion. When using them, make sure to allow time for student response.

☐ Make sure an overhead projector is available. Have it set up ready to use prior to class.

☐ There may be some in your class who have never received the baptism in the Holy Spirit. Encourage them to do so. There may also be some who are Spirit-filled but have never been used in spiritual gifts. Encourage these students to be used by God in this spiritual gift ministry.

DAILY BIBLE READINGS

Monday:	Anointed By The Spirit. 1 Samuel 10:1-6
Tuesday:	Holy Spirit Promised. Joel 2:21-29
Wednesday:	Error Confronted. Acts 19:11-17
Thursday:	Priority Of Love. Romans 13:8-10
Friday:	Unity Encouraged. 1 Peter 3:8-12
Saturday:	Made Perfect In Love. 1 John 4:16-21

King James Version

1 Corinthians 12:4. Now there are diversities of gifts, but the same Spirit.

5. And there are differences of administrations, but the same Lord.

6. And there are diversities of operations, but it is the same God which worketh all in all.

7. But the manifestation of the Spirit is given to every man to profit withal.

8. For to one is given by the Spirit the word of wisdom; to another the word of knowledge by the same Spirit;

9. To another faith by the same Spirit; to another the gifts of healing by the same Spirit;

10. To another the working of miracles; to another prophecy; to another discerning of spirits; to another divers kinds of tongues; to another the interpretation of tongues:

11. But all these worketh that one and the selfsame Spirit, dividing to every man severally as he will.

14. For the body is not one member, but many.

15. If the foot shall say, Because I am not the hand, I am not of the body; is it therefore not of the body?

16. And if the ear shall say, Because I am not the eye, I am not of the body; is it therefore not of the body?

17. If the whole body were an eye, where were the hearing? If the whole were hearing, where were the smelling?

18. But now hath God set the members every one of them in the body, as it hath pleased him.

19. And if they were all one member, where were the body?

20. But now are they many members, yet but one body.

13:8. Charity never faileth: but whether there be prophecies, they shall fail; whether there be tongues, they shall cease; whether there be knowledge, it shall vanish away.

9. For we know in part, and we prophesy in part.

10. But when that which is perfect is come, then that which is in part shall be done away.

11. When I was a child, I spake as a child, I understood as a child, I thought as a child: but when I became a man, I put away childish things.

12. For now we see through a glass, darkly, but then face to face: now I know in part; but then shall I know even as also I am known.

13. And now abideth faith, hope, charity, these three; but the greatest of these is charity.

New International Version

1 Corinthians 12:4. There are different kinds of gifts, but the same Spirit.

5. There are different kinds of service, but the same Lord.

6. There are different kinds of working, but the same God works all of them in all men.

7. Now to each one the manifestation of the Spirit is given for the common good.

8. To one there is given through the Spirit the message of wisdom, to another the message of knowledge by means of the same Spirit,

9. To another faith by the same Spirit, to another gifts of healing by that one Spirit,

10. To another miraculous powers, to another prophecy, to another distinguishing between spirits, to another speaking in different kinds of tongues, and to still another the interpretation of tongues.

11. All these are the work of one and the same Spirit, and he gives them to each one, just as he determines.

14. Now the body is not made up of one part but of many.

15. If the foot should say, "Because I am not a hand, I do not belong to the body," it would not for that reason cease to be part of the body.

16. And if the ear should say, "Because I am not an eye, I do not belong to the body," it would not for that reason cease to be a part of the body.

17. If the whole body were an eye, where would the sense of hearing be? If the whole body were an ear, where would the sense of smell be?

18. But in fact God has arranged the parts in the body, every one of them, just as he wanted them to be.

19. If they were all one part, where would the body be?

20. As it is, there are many parts, but one body.

13:8. Love never fails. But where there are prophecies, they will cease; where there are tongues, they will be stilled; where there is knowledge, it will pass away.

9. For we know in part and we prophesy in part,

10. But when perfection comes, the imperfect disappears.

11. When I was a child, I talked like a child, I thought like a child, I reasoned like a child. When I became a man, I put childish ways behind me.

12. Now we see but a poor reflection as in a mirror; then we shall see face to face. Now I know in part; then I shall know fully, even as I am fully known.

13. And now these three remain: faith, hope and love. But the greatest of these is love.

Can you picture the worship services at the church at Corinth? These believers seemed to have been excited about their faith, about coming together to worship God, and about the great things God was doing among them. Paul remarked that they were greatly enriched by God and were not lacking in any of the spiritual gifts (1 Corinthians 1:4,7). But all of this zeal was sometimes misdirected because of the immaturity and self-centeredness of many of the believers at Corinth.

In this week's study, we will examine Paul's teaching concerning the use of spiritual gifts. These gifts are important for the spiritual growth and maturity of the Church. Allow this study to challenge you to be used by the Holy Spirit in the gifts. As you do, your church will benefit from God's supernatural ministry in its midst.

BIBLE COMMENTARY

1. Gifts Of The Holy Spirit

A. Many Gifts, One Source
1 Corinthians 12:4-6

When God established the Church, He provided spiritual gifts to promote growth. These gifts have not been removed simply because the Church has been around for close to 2,000 years. Every church in every age needs the power of the Holy Spirit as manifested through these supernatural gifts. When the gifts are evident in a church, there can be great growth and evangelism. But the misuse of these gifts hinders what the Spirit wants to accomplish. This is one of the reasons Paul wrote to the church at Corinth.

The Corinthian church's problem with unity also affected their use of spiritual gifts. Instead of their elevating one gift above the others, Paul wanted these believers to understand that all of these gifts came from one Source—the Holy Spirit (1 Corinthians 12:4). Each gift is an important part of God's plan for the Church. By fragmenting the church into factions, the Corinthians were fighting against the Spirit's plan for the use of spiritual gifts He had given the church.

Ask: "Why did Paul give a threefold source of the gifts in verses 4-6?" In these verses Paul stressed the diversity of these gifts in their operation, but noted that it is the "same Spirit," the "same Lord," and the "same God" that is working through these gifts. Even in diversity, all the members of the Trinity are at work in these gifts. Because of this, no one gift is more important than the others. Each one has a unique purpose to fulfill in the church. The emphasis then is on the effectual working by the power of God through these gifts.

We need to recognize the diversity of these gifts. The God who created the colors of the rainbow and all the myriad forms of life on our planet also created the diversity of spiritual gifts. But we also need to recognize the ultimate results of having God's gifts in a church. God has designed them to demonstrate His power and bring growth to the church. They all work together to accomplish God's plan.

NOTES

B. Manifesting The Gifts
1 Corinthians 12:7-11

Paul wanted these believers to understand the purpose of these gifts. In verse 7 he said they were for "every man to profit withal" (KJV) or for the "common good" (NIV). These gifts do not necessarily benefit the individuals who are used in a public manifestation of these gifts. Neither are they to be used for personal gain. These gifts are intended for the benefit of the whole church (see 14:4,5,12). This needs to be the motivation behind every use of these gifts.

In 1 Corinthians 12:8-10, Paul listed nine gifts of the Spirit.

TEACHING TIP 1: Display overhead transparency 1 "Nine Spiritual Gifts" from the teaching helps packet. As you work through this list, discuss the brief definition of these gifts. Ask your students to suggest various ways these gifts are used to build up the Church.

These nine gifts are all "manifestations of the Spirit," and they exceed normal human abilities. When these manifestations of the Spirit are in operation, there can be no doubt that God is at work.

Ask: "According to 1 Corinthians 12:11, how are these manifestations given to the church?" All of these varied manifestations of the Spirit are given as the Spirit "wills." It is according to God's will, as He determines what is best for the Body. As individuals we do not own or possess a gift or gifts of the Spirit. Neither can the gifts be said to reside within a believer. Rather, the Holy Spirit is the gift that was given to each believer when baptized in the Holy Spirit. Now He resides in each believer. As the need arises, each of these gifts is bestowed upon individuals by the Holy Spirit (verse 11).

Ask: "Which gift is the best one to have? Which ones do you think most people would want? Why?"

TEACHING TIP 2: Divide the class into groups of four or five to discuss these questions. After about 5 minutes, ask for each group to share their answers.

Every spirit-filled believer can be used in the operation of the gifts. They are not just for those in full-time ministry. Paul said that these gifts are divided "to every man" (verse 7). This means that we, as Pentecostal believers, must be open to being used by the Holy Spirit and also seeking to be used by God. Without these gifts, God's plan for the Church is incomplete.

NOTES

2. Unity In Diversity

A. One Body, Many Parts
1 Corinthians 12:18-20

God has designed His Church in such a way that it is to become a unified whole. Yet within this unity, there is also diversity. Not every member has the same abilities. As each individual member does his or her part, this brings a unified dimension to the Church. To explain this diversity, Paul compared the body of Christ to a human body.

Human bodies are made up of many parts. Each part, though different, is important. So it is with the body of Christ. It too is made up of many parts (verse 12). And each part, though different, is important to its function (verses 14-17). Without this diversity, neither a physical body nor the Church could function. Yet God, in His wisdom, designed both with a diversity that makes them unique (verse 18). Without the individual parts, there would not be a body (verse 20). But with each part working together with all of the other parts, the body becomes a unified, functioning whole.

We, the Church, are a whole, like the human body. The gifts of the Spirit are given to us so that each part will function better for the good of the whole. No matter how well a part of the Body functions, if it tries to function on its own without considering or interacting with the other parts of the Body, it is no good to the Body. The gifts are only valuable when we work in unity with the whole body of Christ.

NOTES

B. God's Design
1 Corinthians 12:21-27

Because of the way in which God designed the body, all parts are necessary. One part cannot say to the others that they are not needed (verse 21). This is the same in the church. No one can say of other members that they are not needed.

Ask: "How did God bring balance to the body?" In verses 22 through 24 of this chapter, Paul gave special attention to those parts which seem to be less spectacular or less "desirable." There are some members who need no special treatment, but there are some "uncomely parts" whom God has given greater honor because they lacked it. He reminded us that the people of the Body we consider unlovely are just as critical to the Body's function, and perhaps more critical than some of the more attractive parts.

God has designed the body so "there should be no schism [division] in the body" (verse 25). Because of this, each member should have the same concern for every member, not holding some members in esteem over others. This means that we will suffer if one member suffers (verse 26), no matter who it might be. On the other hand, we will also rejoice with a member who rejoices—and not be jealous because of the blessing that they received.

God's design for the Church today is the same as for the Corinthians. The diversity that each member brings to the church actually adds to its unity. This is true whether we are talking about being used in spiritual gifts and other areas of ministry or just being ourselves. God has designed us so we fit together with all members contributing to the proper functioning of the Body. All members are important.

TEACHING TIP 3: Display overhead transparency 2 "The Unified Church" from the teaching helps packet. Using the questions on this transparency, lead the class in a discussion on attaining and maintaining unity in your church. You will need a transparency pen to write student responses on the transparency.

NOTES

3. Preeminence Of Love

A. Gifts Without Love Equal Nothing
1 Corinthians 13:1-7

Many times we, as Pentecostals, place emphasis on spiritual gifts, and rightly so. These gifts are important for the ongoing ministry of the Church. But as important as these gifts are, they must be used properly.

Some of the Corinthian believers were evidently using these gifts to prove their own spirituality. Since spiritual gifts are part of God's design for the Church, then they must be used appropriately if they are used to build up the Church. The most well-known chapter of all of Paul's writings, 1 Corinthians 13, was written in support of this point. In the middle of Paul's discussion concerning the use of spiritual gifts, he turned his attention to the motivation for the use of these gifts.

In this chapter, Paul was not contrasting love and the gifts. Some have mistakenly used this chapter to prove that the gifts are no longer valuable. But Paul was focusing on the importance of love in the operation of these gifts.

Paul began his chapter on love by choosing three gifts that may have been prominent in the Corinthian assembly. No matter how wonderful these gifts may be, they are nothing without love (1 Corinthians 13:1-3). We must not neglect the exercise of these gifts, but we must remember their purpose—the building up of the body of Christ—and manifest them in love.

In order for believers to know the qualities of love, Paul described what godly love was like (verses 4-7).

TEACHING TIP 4: Display overhead transparency 3 "Qualities Of Love" from the teaching helps packet. Ask your students to suggest practical ways that love can be demonstrated using 1 Corinthians 13:4-7. Give the students opportunity to reflect on how they demonstrate love to others and commit

---

themselves to demonstrate love as shown in this chapter.

Whether being used in the manifestation of the gifts of the Spirit or just living our everyday lives, we must realize the preeminence of love and show love to all those whose lives we touch.

NOTES

B. Love Endures
1 Corinthians 13:8-13

In describing love, Paul explained why love needed to be manifested in the Corinthian assembly. The gifts will one day cease to be needed, but love will always be (verse 8). **Ask: "When and why will the gifts no longer be necessary?"** Gifts are temporary. Their purpose is to build the Church while we wait for Christ's coming. Once the Church is in heaven, these gifts will no longer be necessary. On the other hand, love lasts. It is the core of our relationship with God and will still be manifested in heaven.

Ask: "How will we know when the gifts of the Spirit will no longer be needed?" Paul said that everything we do now is done only with a partial understanding (verse 9). "But when that which is perfect is come, then that which is in part will be done away" (verse 10). This phrase simply means that this side of eternity, we cannot completely understand God's plan. But the "perfect" Paul mentioned in verse 10 will exist when the final goal of God for His Church has been reached. This will happen at Christ's second coming. Until then we only know in part.

Paul used the analogy of growing up to illustrate this truth (verse 11). He is not saying that spiritual gifts are immature and when we "mature" we will not need them. Right now the gifts are appropriate. They are how the Spirit is working in the Church. Rather, when Christ returns, these gifts will no longer be needed.

Even our exercise of spiritual gifts is distorted by the limited vision of eternity we have now (verse 12). But when that time comes, we will then have a complete view of God's plan for His Church.

We know that the ministry of spiritual gifts will eventually cease. This is part of our preparation for eternity. But there are three things that last: the faith or trust that brought us to God and that binds us to Him for eternity; the hope in Christ that gives us the certainty of spending eternity with Him; and love. And what surpasses all else? Love (verse 13)!

NOTES

LIFE RESPONSE

God desires to work in the Church through spiritual gifts. His plan is for a vibrant, living Church where believers are used in the manifestation of these gifts. While God has given these gifts to build up His Church as we wait for the second coming of Christ, they are not just for our personal spiritual enrichment. They are to be used to unify and strengthen others in the Body of Christ.

Although a major part of this study concentrated on the gifts of the Spirit, the motivation behind the gifts and their ultimate results are just as important. In every manifestation of a gift, love must be the motivating factor. Without love, all of our efforts are nothing. Consider ways that you can demonstrate love to those in your church.

Unity in the local church is a natural result of the gifts of the Spirit when they are manifested with the proper motivation of love. When love is in action, selfishness is laid aside. Believers seek to build others up and strive to ensure that their needs are being met. People in the church cannot help but be drawn to one another in love. This is the unity Paul encouraged in his first letter to the Corinthians.

God designed spiritual gifts to be beneficial to all the members of the local church. Allow God to use you in this way. Through them each of us can contribute to unity, growth, and the very life of the Church, Christ's Body.

EVANGELISM OUTREACH

One of the purposes of being filled with the Holy Spirit is to be empowered to witness. God can use the gifts of the Spirit as a means of drawing the unsaved into a relationship with Him.

Encourage your students to seek to be continually filled with the Holy Spirit. Then He will be able to use them not only in supernatural gifts for the building up of the body, but in witnessing to the lost. In this way, they will be a part of God's work in the world, redeeming lost humanity. ▭

Facing Trials Courageously

He doesn't take the Trial away He goes with us thru it

CENTRAL TRUTH

Christians can depend on God's help in facing trials.

GOLDEN TEXT

Our light and momentary troubles are achieving for us an eternal glory that far outweighs them all. 2 Corinthians 4:17 (NIV)

STUDY TEXT

2 Corinthians 4:6-18; 5:1-10

OUTLINE

1. Do Not Be Discouraged
   A. God's Light In Us
   B. Victorious Suffering

2. Face Trials With Confidence
   A. Death For Jesus' Sake
   B. Suffering Brings Eternal Glory

3. Seek To Please The Lord
   A. Our Eternal Dwelling
   B. An Eternal Perspective

OBJECTIVE

To consider that God has a purpose in every trial and determine to persevere.

CHECKLIST

☐ Read the student guide, noting any questions you might want to use for discussion.

☐ Duplicate enough copies of the information sheet "The Life Of Paul" from the teaching helps packet for each student. Used during Teaching Tip 4, this work sheet gives an idea of some of the hardships that Paul faced during his missionary journeys.

☐ Have the overhead projector set up and ready prior to class for the transparency "Between 1 And 2 Corinthians" (Teaching Tip 1).

☐ Copy the information sheet "Between 1 And 2 Corinthians" for each student. It is to be used in conjunction with the transparency with the same title.

☐ You may have some in your class who are currently experiencing struggles in their lives. Ask God to help you to be sensitive to their needs as you teach this study.

DAILY BIBLE READINGS

Monday: Challenge To Be Courageous.
Deuteronomy 31:1-8

Tuesday: A Courageous Woman.
Esther 4:10-17

Wednesday: Courage From God.
Psalm 46:1-11

Thursday: Unfailing Confidence.
Acts 20:17-24

Friday: Triumph Of Faith.
2 Timothy 4:5-8

Saturday: Patience Rewarded.
James 1:2-12

King James Version

God's light in us

2 Corinthians 4:6. God, who commanded the light to shine out of darkness, hath shined in our hearts, to give the light of the knowledge of the glory of God in the face of Jesus Christ.

7. But we have this treasure in earthen vessels, that the excellency of the power may be of God, and not of us.

8. We are troubled on every side, yet not distressed; we are perplexed, but not in despair;

9. Persecuted, but not forsaken; cast down, but not destroyed;

10. Always bearing about in the body the dying of the Lord Jesus, that the life also of Jesus might be made manifest in our body.

11. For we which live are alway delivered unto death for Jesus' sake, that the life also of Jesus might be made manifest in our mortal flesh.

12. So then death worketh in us, but life in you.

13. We having the same spirit of faith, according as it is written, I believed, and therefore have I spoken; we also believe, and therefore speak;

14. Knowing that he which raised up the Lord Jesus shall raise up us also by Jesus, and shall present us with you.

15. For all things are for your sakes, that the abundant grace might through the thanksgiving of many redound to the glory of God.

16. For which cause we faint not; but though our outward man perish, yet the inward man is renewed day by day.

17. For our light affliction, which is but for a moment, worketh for us a far more exceeding and eternal weight of glory;

18. While we look not at the things which are seen, but at the things which are not seen: for the things which are seen are temporal; but the things which are not seen are eternal.

5:6. Therefore we are always confident, knowing that, whilst we are at home in the body, we are absent from the Lord:

7. (For we walk by faith, not by sight:)

8. We are confident, I say, and willing rather to be absent from the body, and to be present with the Lord.

9. Wherefore we labor, that, whether present or absent, we may be accepted of him.

10. For we must all appear before the judgment seat of Christ; that every one may receive the things done in his body, according to that he hath done, whether it be good or bad.

New International Version

2 Corinthians 4:6. God, who said, "Let light shine out of darkness," made his light shine in our hearts to give us the light of the knowledge of the glory of God in the face of Christ.

7. But we have this treasure in jars of clay to show that this all-surpassing power is from God and not from us.

8. We are hard pressed on every side, but not crushed; perplexed, but not in despair;

9. Persecuted, but not abandoned; struck down, but not destroyed.

10. We always carry around in our body the death of Jesus, so that the life of Jesus may also be revealed in our body.

11. For we who are alive are always being given over to death for Jesus' sake, so that his life may be revealed in our mortal body.

12. So then, death is at work in us, but life is at work in you.

13. It is written: "I believed; therefore I have spoken." With that same spirit of faith we also believe and therefore speak,

14. Because we know that the one who raised the Lord Jesus from the dead will also raise us with Jesus and present us with you in his presence.

15. All this is for your benefit, so that the grace that is reaching more and more people may cause thanksgiving to overflow to the glory of God.

16. Therefore we do not lose heart. Though outwardly we are wasting away, yet inwardly we are being renewed day by day.

17. For our light and momentary troubles are achieving for us an eternal glory that far outweighs them all.

18. So we fix our eyes not on what is seen, but on what is unseen. For what is seen is temporary, but what is unseen is eternal.

5:6. Therefore we are always confident and know that as long as we are at home in the body we are away from the Lord.

7. We live by faith, not by sight.

8. We are confident, I say, and would prefer to be away from the body and at home with the Lord.

9. So we make it our goal to please him, whether we are at home in the body or away from it.

10. For we must all appear before the judgment seat of Christ, that each one may receive what is due him for the things done while in the body, whether good or bad.

How do you handle suffering? When the doctor gives you a discouraging diagnosis, what do you do? When you are ridiculed on your job because you are a Christian, what is your response? When you or members of your family suffer from terminal illness, how do you handle the stress?

Christianity does not immunize us from tragedy. May of us suffer heartbreaks and disasters we thought we could never handle.

We pray for healing and deliverance. Sometimes God says "yes" and our illnesses are miraculously healed, our obstacles instantly cleared away. But sometimes God has other plans.

This week's study focuses on Paul's teaching concerning suffering in the believer's life. Allow God's Word to encourage you in your difficult time. Allow His power to be at work in your life.

ILL. Anderson creek — Sebron at the end. Light of the tunnel

Darrel Beebe Solomon Islands

LU 12:50 Jesus straightened — Discouraged — not knowing the will of God

Disappointment leads to Discouragement

BIBLE COMMENTARY

Discouragement because we do not know the will of God

1. Do Not Be Discouraged

A. God's Light In Us
2 Corinthians 4:6

Discouragement is something that even believers face. At times not everything goes as planned. Sometimes tragedy, such as the death of a loved one or a serious illness, comes our way. But these times of discouragement do not have to overwhelm us.

Paul faced difficult times in his ministry. In this passage Paul gave us insight into how to come through our suffering victoriouly. For Paul, part of victorious living came from his knowledge of the purpose of his life. This knowledge came from the light of God that had shined into his heart (2 Corinthians 4:6). God, who began creation with the words "Let there be light" (Genesis 1:3) began His creative work of redemption in Paul by letting the light of His glory shine from the face of Christ into him.

The word translated "light" in the phrase "the light of the knowledge of the glory of God" (2 Corinthians 4:4) carries the idea of "illumination." God illumined the gospel to Paul's heart. And not only to Paul's heart, but to the heart of every believer.

Paul's ministry was to proclaim the gospel (Acts 9:15). But he knew that he would

Gen 1:3
Jn 1:17
Jn 8:12

suffer persecution in the process of fulfilling that ministry (verse 16). When difficulties and suffering came, he realized they were only part of serving Christ.

Ask: "Why do believers suffer?"

TEACHING TIP 1: Although there are many trite answers that people give, this question is almost impossible to answer. Poll your students to find those who feel they have at least a partial answer to why believers suffer. List their suggestions on the chalkboard or a blank transparency. Their responses should include sin and the curse evidenced in our society, persecution for a godly witness, and wrongdoing and personal sin. Use this question as a lead in to the next point.

NOTES *Positive Confession —*
If you are sick you don't have faith —

9 4
4 5
4 9

234

B. Victorious Suffering
2 Corinthians 4:7-10

We are not instantly transformed at the moment of salvation into perfect, powerful beings who never face any difficulty. We are still human beings living in a sinful world and suffering from the results of the Fall—disease, poverty, and broken relationships.

To illustrate this, Paul contrasted God's glory with our physical bodies. God's glory is like a brilliant light placed in an ordinary clay pot—an "earthen vessels" (verse 7). This reveals our temporary status. We must remember that this glory is far greater than the container. The contrast between the treasure and the vessel also proves that the power at work in us is God's, not ours.

Ask: "What are some personal situations that distress you?"

TEACHING TIP 2: Divide the class into groups of four or five students. Ask each to discuss this question. Then have them write down the problems they think about when they read 2 Corinthians 4:7-10. Ask the groups to discuss how this passage can give them encouragment to face their problems.

---

see ch. 1:8

Verses 8-10 are a study in contrasts. In our fallible humanity, we are "troubled . . . perplexed . . . persecuted . . . cast down." Yet because of the life of Jesus within us, we are not "distressed . . . in despair . . . forsaken . . . destroyed." When our troubled lives show the death of Christ, our perseverance through trouble shows His life (verse 10). With God's help we endure, and others will see the glorious light of God, the life of the resurrected Christ, through us.

Ask: "How can you explain the death of a believer in light of 2 Corinthians 4:8,9?" Paul wrote that though we are hard pressed, we are never completely crushed. We are ultimately delivered from trials. We should not, however, understand that we

will not suffer what appears from an earthly point of view to be an ultimate defeat. Though we may die physically, our faith is in the resurrected Jesus. Our final deliverance from trials will be when we are resurrected to live in God's presence forever.

NOTES *Not forsaken - Heb 13: 5+6*

the excitement of traveling long distance and you arrive at relative or friend we are excited (?) - my father dr. report -

2. Face Trials With Confidence
A. Death For Jesus' Sake   *what I know I know I know*
2 Corinthians 4:11-15

Our deliverance from death begins, in one sense, from the moment we accept God's grace. From that moment, we are no longer prisoners to the fear of death. However, in another sense, we still carry death with us at all times.

Paul continually risked danger, facing the possibility of death because of his service to Christ (verse 11). He later recorded the many forms of danger that he had experienced (11:23-29). *Perils* He faced those dangers, knowing that, through them, the life of Jesus would be revealed in him. *see Phil. 12-14*

Paul quoted from Psalm 116:10 in 2 Corinthians 4:13 to show why he continued to minister even if it meant suffering. This psalm is a hymn of thanksgiving for deliverance from danger. The Psalmist wrote of being encompassed by death, suffering distress and anguish, and then being delivered by the Lord. But in verse 10, the Psalmist indicated that even in the Old Testament, immediate deliverance in the flesh was not the only or ultimate deliverance.

With this psalm in mind, Paul wrote about facing trials with confidence, acting and speaking in faith rather than fear. Because of his confidence in the gospel he could not keep silent. The basis of his confidence also came from the fact of the Resurrection (2 Corinthians 4:14). Jesus' resurrection brought confidence that Paul himself would be resurrected. Because he understood the future glories of eternal life, he could face suffering that was temporary by comparison. Rom 8:18

Ask: "What benefit results from our suffering?" Our trials and sufferings are not pointless. When weighed against eternal life, our sufferings now are comparatively slight. As we endure trials, we grow spiritually. But others also benefit, for as they see the strength God gives us to persevere, and as they see God deliver us from trials, they are drawn to Him. Paul said that his trials were for their benefit. His continuing to minister in spite of persecution meant that more people would still hear the gospel. This in turn would cause them to give thanks "to the glory of God" (verse 15) because they too had heard the gospel.

NOTES The joy of the Lord is my strength

B. Suffering Brings Eternal Glory
2 Corinthians 4:16-18

Intense suffering can cause us to give up. Difficulties and pain can be almost overwhelming. But Paul found a strength that enabled him to continue in the midst of suffering. While it is true that our physical bodies are perishing, there is another part of us that can be renewed—the "inward man" (verse 16).

When we set our sights on the eternal rather than the temporary, we see our afflictions for what truly are "light and momentary troubles" (verse 17, NIV). Then we can see the value of these struggles because of what they produce in us. They are achieving for us an "exceeding and eternal weight of glory." In other words, our struggles help to strengthen us so we will obtain a lasting glory. It will be worth it all when we see Jesus - Life's trials will seem so small

TEACHING TIP 3: Distribute copies of the information sheet on "The Life Of Paul" to each student. Ask volunteers to relate some of Paul's "light and momentary troubles" to things which Christians experience today. Draw attention to the dangers Paul experienced as a backdrop for his teaching in this letter.

Paul could face life, including difficulties, with confidence. The most important things in this life are eternal. So instead of fixing his attention on his difficulties and complaining, Paul fixed his attention on "the things which are not seen" (verse 18).

TEACHING TIP 4: Have the students suggest some "unseen things" to which Paul may have been referring. After writing them down on the chalkboard or a blank transparency, emphasize that focusing our attention on these things will help us endure the temporary suffering we experience in this life.

NOTES Bro Judge allergy
God sure has my attention

3. Seek To Please The Lord

A. Our Eternal Dwelling
2 Corinthians 5:1-5

As believers, we need to realize that our physical bodies are only dwelling places for our spiritual being. This is not to negate the importance of the physical body, but to recognize its temporary aspect.

Paul compared our earthly life to our eternal life with God by using the analogy of dwelling places. Our life here is like a tent where we camp, waiting until God allows us to move into our real home with Him (verse 1). While we are in this "tent," we anticipate that day in which we will be released from this dwelling and shall put on that heavenly dwelling. Paul said that we "groan" (verse 2), waiting for that day.

Some in Corinth may have believed that when they died, they would be nothing but disembodied spirits. To this Paul replied that we would not be "unclothed" but "clothed" with a new body (1 Corinthians 15:50-54).

Ask: "Why did Paul return to the idea of 'groaning' while we are in our present bodies in 2 Corinthians 5:4?" Paul wanted us to understand a desire that must be a part of every believer's life. Even though we have new life in Christ, as long as we are in our physical bodies, we will have struggles because of sickness and sin. It is during these times that we desire to be "clothed with our heavenly dwelling" (NIV). Then we will no longer have mortal bodies, but fully enjoy our eternal life in immortal bodies.

God has an overarching purpose for everything that happens in our lives. Through all the ups and downs, He is preparing us for eternal life with Him. When we know that there is a purpose in our suffering, when we know that God cares for us, when we know we can depend on Him to support and encourage us, then we can face our trials with courage.

To show the reality of this eternal dwelling, God has given us "the earnest of the Spirit" (verse 5) or a down payment or deposit of what He has in store for us in heaven. The Holy Spirit's life-giving work in our present bodies is the guarantee that what God has promised will come to pass.

NOTES

B. An Eternal Perspective
2 Corinthians 5:6-10

In the midst of our struggles, we can still have confidence. We know that while we are in our bodies, we are not present with the Lord (verse 6). But, as believers our lives are not built upon sight, but faith (verse 7). Our preference, though, is to be with the Lord (verse 8).

Ask: "How can the idea that 'to be absent from the body is to be present with the Lord' change the way we look at this life?" If we understand that this world is not home, it will change the way we look at trials and the choices we make in our behavior. We will long to be with Him, and we will put less value on what happens now. Our suffering seems intense while we are in the midst of it. But if we put things in eternal perspective, suffering will become more endurable.

If we put things in eternal perspective, we will understand that the most important thing we can do is please God (verse 9). Since we will live with God for eternity, we must choose to do what will enhance our relationship with Him. We must consider first what God would have us do.

In verse 10, Paul reminded us that the choices we make now will earn us eternal rewards. "The judgment seat of Christ" to which Paul referred is not the Great White

Throne Judgment of Revelation 20:11. Rather, at Christ's judgment, believers will have to give an account for what they have done on earth. Although we have been unconditionally received into God's presence having been saved by grace, we are still accountable for making choices that please God.

TEACHING TIP 5: Memorized Scripture can help us make choices that are pleasing to God. It will also help us keep an eternal perspective through trials. Select 2 Corinthians 4:8-10; 4:16-18; or 5:8,9. Divide the class into small groups. Assign the three passages to different groups and see which group can memorize their passage error free in the shortest period of time.

NOTES

LIFE RESPONSE

No one wants to suffer. No one would choose illness, bereavement, deprivation, persecution, or humiliation. But these things do happen. When they do, it helps to know that our suffering is not without meaning.

God has a purpose in allowing us to experience times of trial. When He does not say "yes" to our prayers for immediate relief, it does not mean He has abandoned us. Rather, it means He is watching over us, using our suffering for a higher purpose, ready to deliver us when the time comes.

As difficult as it seems right now, in the middle of our pain and grief, the key to persevering courageously through trials is taking God's point of view. If we can set our minds on that which is eternal, if we can see our troubles from an eternal perspective, we can begin to realize that they truly are "light" and "momentary." The work that is accomplished for the kingdom of God through our suffering, namely our spiritual growth and the salvation of others, is worth every minute of our temporary pain.

Do not be discouraged. Though you may be under a lot of pressure from many sources, you will not be destroyed. Pray for deliverance, but pray also for courage and confidence to face trials. Ask God to help you to be pleasing to Him during this time. Remember, God is using those trials to prepare you for that "far more exceeding and eternal weight of glory" (2 Corinthians 4:17). Allow Him to do His work.

EVANGELISM OUTREACH

There may be unsaved students in class who are confused concerning suffering. They may be upset at God because of suffering in their lives or the lives of loved ones. They may be rejecting God's offer of salvation because of this. Use this week's study to show that even though Christians are not immune to suffering, they can be victorious through Christ. Christ can help us see purpose in suffering. Invite the unsaved to accept Christ and discover His purpose for their lives.

Authority Of The Risen Christ

CENTRAL TRUTH

Jesus Christ rose from the dead and lives forever.

GOLDEN TEXT

He is not here; he has risen. Matthew 28:6 (NIV)

STUDY TEXT

Matthew 27:57-66; 28:1-20

OUTLINE

1. The Burial Of Christ
   A. Care Of A Friend
   B. Fearful Precautions

2. The Resurrection Of Christ
   A. The Empty Tomb
   B. The Risen Lord

3. The Command Of Christ
   A. Waiting In Galilee
   B. Commission Given

OBJECTIVE

To understand the significance of Christ's resurrection and tell others that He is alive.

CHECKLIST

☐ Read the student guide, noting any questions you wish to use for discussion.

☐ Duplicate the work sheet "Reactions To The Empty Tomb" for each student. Fill out the work sheet prior to class so you are able to give suggestions if needed.

☐ Read the parallel accounts of the resurrection of Jesus in Mark, Luke, and John. Note the similarities and differences regarding the details in each account. Each Gospel writer gave a brief account of these events for a specific audience. Identify the audience and the reason the Gospel was written.

☐ Take note of the many contacts Jesus had with His disciples. Jesus used these appearances to absolutely convince them of the reality of the Resurrection. It is equally important to understand that Christ's resurrection was demonstrated by such infallible proofs.

DAILY BIBLE READINGS

Monday:	Resurrection Song.	Psalm 16:1-11
Tuesday:	Resurrection Promise.	Daniel 12:1-3
Wednesday:	Resurrection Message.	Romans 1:1-6
Thursday:	Resurrection Life.	Romans 6:1-11
Friday:	Resurrection Hope.	1 Corinthians 15:1-11
Saturday:	Resurrection Power.	Ephesians 2:1-10

King James Version

Matthew 27:57. When the even was come, there came a rich man of Arimathea, named Joseph, who also himself was Jesus' disciple:

58. He went to Pilate, and begged the body of Jesus. Then Pilate commanded the body to be delivered.

59. And when Joseph had taken the body, he wrapped it in a clean linen cloth,

60. And laid it in his own new tomb, which he had hewn out in the rock: and he rolled a great stone to the door of the sepulchre, and departed.

28:1. In the end of the sabbath, as it began to dawn toward the first day of the week, came Mary Magdalene and the other Mary to see the sepulchre.

2. And, behold, there was a great earthquake: for the angel of the Lord descended from heaven, and came and rolled back the stone from the door, and sat upon it.

3. His countenance was like lightning, and his raiment white as snow:

4. And for fear of him the keepers did shake, and became as dead men.

5. And the angel answered and said unto the women, Fear not ye: for I know that ye seek Jesus, which was crucified.

6. He is not here: for he is risen, as he said. Come, see the place where the Lord lay.

7. And go quickly, and tell his disciples that he is risen from the dead; and, behold, he goeth before you into Galilee; there shall ye see him: lo, I have told you.

8. And they departed quickly from the sepulchre with fear and great joy; and did run to bring his disciples word.

9. And as they went to tell his disciples, behold, Jesus met them, saying, All hail. And they came and held him by the feet, and worshipped him.

10. Then said Jesus unto them, Be not afraid: go tell my brethren that they go into Galilee, and there shall they see me.

18. And Jesus came and spake unto them, saying, All power is given unto me in heaven and in earth.

19. Go ye therefore, and teach all nations, baptizing them in the name of the Father, and of the Son, and of the Holy Ghost:

20. Teaching them to observe all things whatsoever I have commanded you: and, lo, I am with you alway, even unto the end of the world. Amen.

New International Version

Matthew 27:57. As evening approached, there came a rich man from Arimathea, named Joseph, who had himself become a disciple of Jesus.

58. Going to Pilate, he asked for Jesus' body, and Pilate ordered that it be given to him.

59. Joseph took the body, wrapped it in a clean linen cloth,

60. And placed it in his own new tomb that he had cut out of the rock. He rolled a big stone in front of the entrance to the tomb and went away.

28:1. After the Sabbath, at dawn on the first day of the week, Mary Magdalene and the other Mary went to look at the tomb.

2. There was a violent earthquake, for an angel of the Lord came down from heaven and, going to the tomb, rolled back the stone and sat on it.

3. His appearance was like lightning, and his clothes were white as snow.

4. The guards were so afraid of him that they shook and became like dead men.

5. The angel said to the women, "Do not be afraid, for I know that you are looking for Jesus, who was crucified.

6. He is not here; he has risen, just as he said. Come and see the place where he lay.

7. Then go quickly and tell his disciples: 'He has risen from the dead and is going ahead of you into Galilee. There you will see him.' Now I have told you."

8. So the women hurried away from the tomb, afraid yet filled with joy, and ran to tell his disciples.

9. Suddenly Jesus met them. "Greetings," he said. They came to him, clasped his feet and worshiped him.

10. Then Jesus said to them, "Do not be afraid. Go and tell my brothers to go to Galilee; there they will see me."

18. Then Jesus came to them and said, "All authority in heaven and on earth has been given to me.

19. Therefore go and make disciples of all nations, baptizing them in the name of the Father and of the Son and of the Holy Spirit,

20. And teaching them to obey everything I have commanded you. And surely I am with you always, to the very end of the age."

For the disciples, the morning of the Resurrection began as a time of sorrow and disorientation. They were doubtlessly questioning what direction their lives would take after the turmoil they had just experienced.

The meaning of what had taken place was beyond the disciples' comprehension. They could only hope that time would help them sort it all out. Little did the disciples know that as quickly as joy turned to sorrow, grief would again give way to a new blessedness.

The death and resurrection of Jesus represents the greatest and most meaningful event in human history. More than a mere religious commemoration, Christ's resurrection reveals the very identity of Christ and completely substantiates His teachings. This week's study focuses on the importance of Christ's resurrection in our lives.

BIBLE COMMENTARY

1. The Burial Of Christ

A. Care Of A Friend
Matthew 27:57-61

Friends are an important part of our lives. Sometimes, when we are in a difficult situation, it is a friend who helps us or gives us the encouragment we need. In this passage we find that Joseph was a friend that provided a valuable service for Jesus.

All four Gospels make mention of Joseph of Arimathea's care for the body of Jesus. Matthew referred to Joseph as a rich man and a disciple, while Mark called him an "honorable counselor." Luke indicated he was a "good man and just." These descriptions may mean that he was a member of the Jewish Sanhedrin. This faithful act on Joseph's part may have been prompted by the terrible crucifixion he had witnessed. He summoned the courage to seek Jesus' body from Pilate who commanded that it be delivered (Matthew 27:58).

Verses 59 and 60 give the details of the extent of Joseph's care for Christ's lifeless body. He wrapped it in a clean linen cloth and laid it in a new tomb cut out of a huge rock. The motivation on Joseph's part was not stated, but it is clear that this was the act of one who loved and believed in Jesus.

Ask: "In what ways could Joseph's act be described as courageous?" Joseph's request to Pilate for Christ's body came at a time when nearly all of Jesus' own disciples had fled. Peter denied knowing Jesus. Pilate had condemned Jesus as a criminal. Merely approaching Pilate for permission to take the body could have been seen as suspicious. It took great courage for Joseph to risk being identified as one of Christ's disciples by asking for the body.

TEACHING TIP 1: Have the class look up Isaiah 53:9. Ask: "What particular aspects of this Old Testament prophecy were fulfilled by Joseph?" Emphasize that God leaves no details unattended but fulfills His Word at every point. Both Christ's crucifixion with the thieves and His burial by Joseph in his grave are a direct fulfillment of prophecy.

In the end, Joseph of Arimathea had nothing to gain from his gift to this Crucified Man. He braved the risks of personal danger at the hands of Pilate and the Jewish leaders. We too are offered similar opportunities. Many times it is difficult to express our allegiance to our Lord in the face of antagonism. It is, however, our opportunity to show Christ our love and devotion.

NOTES

B. Fearful Precautions
Matthew 27:62-66

In contrast to Joseph, the chief priests and Pharisees expressed a different kind of concern. They were troubled about the burial of Christ's body. There should have been a sense of triumph on their part. But there was not.

Their concern caused these religious leaders to come to Pilate and express their nervousness (verse 62). Jesus had prophesied that He would rise again on the third day after His death. The chief priests and Pharisees told Pilate that His disciples might try to steal His body and claim that He had been raised from the dead. This would keep alive what the Pharisees saw as deception (verse 63). They urged Pilate to post a guard at the sepulchure (verse 64).

Pilate's answer to these priests, "Ye have a watch" (verse 65), has caused some controversy as to who the guard was. The phrase can be translated "Ye have a watch" (KJV) or "Take a guard" (NIV). Both are excellent translations. Some believe the phrase indicates that the chief priests were to post the temple guard at the tomb for 3 days. This could explain why the guard reported to the chief priests instead of to Pilate (28:11). However, this explanation leaves some problems unexplained.

First, the word translated "guard" is a Latin loanword and most likely indicates that the soldiers were Roman. Also why would the chief priests have to persuade the governor on behalf of the soldiers (verse 14). If they were the temple guard, there would be no consequences for their actions from the governor. However, if they were Roman soldiers, they would be executed for sleeping on watch (verse 13). This would definitely be sufficient cause for the soldiers to appeal to the chief priests to intercede on their behalf before the governor.

Regardless of which is correct, the important thing is Pilate did charge them to post a watch. This ensured that the disciples would not steal the body of Christ. It also provides further proof in the Scriptures that the Resurrection is real. The disciples could not possibly overcome an armed guard, even in the best of conditions.

As per Pilate's orders, the tomb was sealed. The guard was set. Only the Resurrection could free Jesus from the grave.

NOTES

2. The Resurrection Of Christ

A. The Empty Tomb
Matthew 28:1-8

Matthew's account of Christ's resurrection is briefer than the other gospel records. It represents a concise summary of the events of that day. Many of the details found in the other Gospels are omitted.

The women waited until the Sabbath had passed before going to the tomb (Matthew 28:1). Matthew did not give their reason for going to the sepulchure, but Mark stated that they went to anoint the body of Jesus. Prior to their arrival, there had been a supernatural tremor, and an angel rolled the stone from the entrance of the sepulchure (verse 2). This angel was brilliant with both his countenance and garment radiating. The soldiers were gripped by paralyzing fear at the sight of him. Matthew said they became like "dead men" (verses 3,4).

The women must have been startled by the angel's appearance because the angel told them not to be afraid. Jesus whom they had sought was not there for He had been raised from the dead (verses 5,6). His words may have been almost beyond belief. "He is risen" may not have made much sense to the women. But eventually they understood the meaning of what had taken place.

The angel's message also included a reference to Christ's teaching concerning His resurrection. This was no accident or unexplained mystery. Jesus's own words had proclaimed this event. As proof they were commanded to view the empty tomb as evidence of Christ's resurrection.

In verse 7 the angel commanded the women to go and give Jesus' disciples the message of His resurrection. He also told them that they would see Jesus again in Galilee. Verse 8 states that they went immediately with "fear and great joy."

Ask: "Given the circumstances of the passion week, how do you think you would have responded to this angelic pronouncement?" The women had probably witnessed many miracles but nothing like this. They were probably having conflicting emotions. Many times we want to believe but are afraid to. These women went to the tomb that morning fully expecting to find Christ's body. The events which followed so staggered them that they struggled to believe them. Soon these events were to be confirmed beyond any doubt.

NOTES

B. The Risen Lord
Matthew 28:9-15

The empty tomb together with the appearance of the angel were powerful evidences that Christ had indeed been raised from the dead. The New Testament, however, gives evidence that is far more conclusive. The four Gospels record numerous physical encounters with the risen Christ. Matthew described the first of these encounters in verses 9 and 10. As the women were on their way to deliver the news to the disciples, Jesus met them.

Verse 9 details this meeting in very physical terms. It was no mere vision on the part of these women. Matthew wrote that they "held him by the feet, and worshipped him." All of the Gospel writers enumerate a variety of occasions where Christ interacted with His followers in a physical way. Acts 1:3 sums up these occasions by stating that Jesus "showed himself alive after his passion by many infallible proofs."

While the women were rejoicing in their knowledge that their Lord was risen from the dead, the soldiers who were assigned to guard the sepulcher brought news of what they had seen to the religious leaders. These very guards that were placed around the sepulcher to prevent the disciples from stealing the body of Jesus now became witnesses of the fact the Resurrection did actually take place (verses 11). The chief priests and elders responded by bribing the soldiers to lie about what had taken place, giving them a large sum of money (verse 12). Their story was preposterous. They were to claim that the disciples stole Jesus' body while they slept (verse 13). The absurdity of this story is obvious. How could they know what took place if they were sleeping at the time? And besides, if they had been asleep on watch the penalty was death.

TEACHING TIP 2: Distribute the work sheet "Contrasting Reactions To The Empty Tomb." Divide the class into small groups and have them contrast the response of the women with those of the soldiers and the chief priests. After completing the work sheets, ask a spokesperson for each group to share their observations.

NOTES

pated by Christ's followers. They were also not gullible followers. Their immediate hesitancy only strengthens their later belief in Christ's resurrection that His followers proclaimed with such power.

NOTES

3. The Command Of Christ

A. Waiting In Galilee
Matthew 28:16,17

Jesus had risen and shown himself alive to His disciples. In fact over 500 people were witness to the resurrected Christ. Yet He was not to remain among them. In preparation for His ascension, Christ instructed them to meet Him in Galilee (verse 10). Verse 16 found the disciples already at Galilee awaiting Jesus' promised appearance.

But some disciples still were in conflict over Christ's resurrection. Matthew stated that when they saw Jesus "they worshipped Him: but some doubted" (verse 17).

The exact meaning of the expression "some doubted" is open to question. Some commentators believe that more than the 11 were present at this time. The "some" would then refer to these. It may mean that some initially doubted because He was unable to be easily identified at a distance and this caused them to doubt at first. But it may also mean that many were hesitant to believe so great an event after the letdown of the Crucifixion.

Matthew may have included this point to show that the Resurrection was not antici-

B. Command Given
Matthew 28:18-20

Ask: "What is the Great Commission?" Jesus would not be with His disciples for very long after His resurrection. It was important that they understood what He had planned for them after He ascended to the Father. He commanded them to evangelize and disciple all people everywhere. This is the Great Commission.

It would strike many as odd that God would leave the task of the Great Commission to believers who are beset with human weaknesses. The disciples who were closest to Jesus during His ministry did not prove to be either steadfast or courageous when their Lord was crucified.

Fortunately, the job of evangelizing was not left to human ability. Jesus' disciples could proclaim this message without fear because they were acting under His authority (verse 18). God has promised us His power to proclaim His message. This promise is found in some form in each of the Gospels and in Acts.

TEACHING TIP 3: Ask four students to read the following passages that include God's promise of His power to the disciples and to us: Mark 16:15-18; Luke 24:46-49; John 14:12-17;

This wonderful message of hope is for all the nations. God's love cannot be limited to one nation or people. There are populations that still await the message of the Creator's love. We are given the responsibility to declare this Word. We who have been given the right to be called an heir of His kingdom, must also accept the responsibility of proclaiming it.

Verse 20 declares that Jesus not only promised His divine power, but also His presence. Without both His presence and power we could not possibly hope to accomplish this tremendous task. Let us seek God to be filled with the Holy Spirit, and do all we can to fulfill the task Christ has given us to do.

NOTES

LIFE RESPONSE

The words "He is not here: for he is risen as he said" (Matthew 28:6), are both life changing and world changing. Since Christ has indeed risen from the dead, then all that He said pertaining to His deity are true. Since He has risen from the dead, then His teachings about God, man, salvation, and the proper way to live come from God.

The resurrection of Jesus Christ is not only the most important event in the history of mankind, it is also one of the most attested to. Lord Darling, former chief justice of England, considered the evidence for the Resurrection so overwhelming that if these facts were presented in a court of law, no intelligent jury could bring back any other verdict than "the Resurrection story is absolutely true." Even though faith is still required, reason can lead to no other conclusion if the facts are honestly considered.

The implications of the reality of the Resurrection on the believer are immense. In a world filled with confusion, the Christian has a certainty that is built on a sure foundation. The absolutes of the teachings of Christ give forth a sense of assurance and peace in a world that has lost its bearing. The Resurrection means that we too can have a new life in Christ.

This gives us a tremendous opportunity to shine as lights in the world around us. What a contrast this presents to those who are truly searching for answers. We have certainty that they can only experience in Christ.

EVANGELISM OUTREACH

The Resurrection is the culmination of all the events of Passion Week. The crucifixion of Christ was the sacrifice for the sins of every person. When Jesus rose from the dead, the redemptive work was complete. Christ's resurrection proved His death on the cross was effective.

There may be some students in your class who have never accepted this provision of salvation. Give an invitation to those in your class who do not yet have a saving knowledge of Jesus Christ. ⌂

Effective Christian Service

CENTRAL TRUTH

Every Christian is called to the ministry of reconciliation.

GOLDEN TEXT

All this is from God, who reconciled us to himself through Christ and gave us the ministry of reconciliation. 2 Corinthians 5:18 (NIV)

STUDY TEXT

2 Corinthians 5:11-21; 6:1-10

OUTLINE

1. Motivated By Christ's Love
   A. Persuading Humanity
   B. Compelling Love

2. Ministers Of Reconciliation
   A. New Creatures In Christ
   B. Christ's Ambassadors

3. Faithful In Service
   A. Day Of Salvation
   B. Faithful Through Trials

OBJECTIVE

To understand the high calling of the Christian life and dedicate ourselves to serve Christ.

CHECKLIST

☐ Read the Adult Student Guide, noting any questions that you might want to use for discussion.

☐ Assign a student to research and give a report on "The Fear of God" for Teaching Tip 1.

☐ Familiarize yourself with the overhead transparencies "God Through Christ," a portrayal of God's plan of reconciliation and our part in the plan, and "Faithful Through Trials," a phrase-by-phrase breakdown of 2 Corinthians 6:4-7.

☐ This study provides an opportunity to challenge your students in the area of evangelism. There may be some who are reluctant to share their faith with others. Emphasize the importance of the baptism in the Holy Spirit to provide the power to become effective witnesses.

☐ Consider concluding the class in prayer for unsaved family and friends and for opportunities to witness to them.

DAILY BIBLE READINGS

Monday: Responsibility.
Exodus 32:30-34

Tuesday: Accountability.
Ezekiel 3:17-21

Wednesday: Reward.
Psalm 126:1-6

Thursday: Witnessing.
John 1:6-12

Friday: Challenge.
Acts 9:10-18

Saturday: Preparation.
2 Timothy 2:10-15

SCRIPTURE SETTING

King James Version

2 Corinthians 5:14. For the love of Christ constraineth us; because we thus judge, that if one died for all, then were all dead:

15. And that he died for all, that they which live should not henceforth live unto themselves, but unto him which died for them, and rose again.

16. Wherefore henceforth know we no man after the flesh: yea, though we have known Christ after the flesh, yet now henceforth know we him no more.

17. Therefore if any man be in Christ, he is a new creature: old things are passed away; behold, all things are become new.

18. And all things are of God, who hath reconciled us to himself by Jesus Christ, and hath given to us the ministry of reconciliation;

19. To wit, that God was in Christ, reconciling the world unto himself, not imputing their trespasses unto them; and hath committed unto us the word of reconciliation.

20. Now then we are ambassadors for Christ, as though God did beseech you by us: we pray you in Christ's stead, be ye reconciled to God.

6:1. We then, as workers together with him, beseech you also that ye receive not the grace of God in vain.

2. (For he saith, I have heard thee in a time accepted, and in the day of salvation have I succored thee: Behold, now is the accepted time; behold, now is the day of salvation.)

3. Giving no offence in any thing, that the ministry be not blamed:

4. But in all things approving ourselves as the ministers of God, in much patience, in afflictions, in necessities, in distresses,

5. In stripes, in imprisonments, in tumults, in labors, in watchings, in fastings;

6. By pureness, by knowledge, by longsuffering, by kindness, by the Holy Ghost, by love unfeigned,

7. By the word of truth, by the power of God, by the armor of righteousness on the right hand and on the left,

8. By honor and dishonor, by evil report and good report: as deceivers, and yet true;

9. As unknown, and yet well known; as dying, and, behold, we live; as chastened, and not killed;

10. As sorrowful, yet alway rejoicing; as poor, yet making many rich; as having nothing, and yet possessing all things.

New International Version

2 Corinthians 5:14. For Christ's love compels us, because we are convinced that one died for all, and therefore all died.

15. And he died for all, that those who live should no longer live for themselves but for him who died for them and was raised again.

16. So from now on we regard no one from a worldly point of view. Though we once regarded Christ in this way, we do so no longer.

17. Therefore, if anyone is in Christ, he is a new creation; the old has gone, the new has come!

18. All this is from God, who reconciled us to himself through Christ and gave us the ministry of reconciliation:

19. That God was reconciling the world to himself in Christ, not counting men's sins against them. And he has committed to us the message of reconciliation.

20. We are therefore Christ's ambassadors, as though God were making his appeal through us. We implore you on Christ's behalf: Be reconciled to God.

6:1. As God's fellow workers we urge you not to receive God's grace in vain.

2. For he says, "In the time of my favor I heard you, and in the day of salvation I helped you." I tell you, now is the time of God's favor, now is the day of salvation.

3. We put no stumbling block in anyone's path, so that our ministry will not be discredited.

4. Rather, as servants of God we commend ourselves in every way: in great endurance; in troubles, hardships and distresses;

5. In beatings, imprisonments and riots; in hard work, sleepless nights and hunger;

6. In purity, understanding, patience and kindness; in the Holy Spirit and in sincere love;

7. In truthful speech and in the power of God; with weapons of righteousness in the right hand and in the left;

8. Through glory and dishonor, bad report and good report; genuine, yet regarded as impostors;

9. Known, yet regarded as unknown; dying, and yet we live on; beaten, and yet not killed;

10. Sorrowful, yet always rejoicing; poor, yet making many rich; having nothing, and yet possessing everything.

We live in a society that is characterized by broken relationships. About half of all marriages end in divorce. Of those marriages that remain intact, some of them contain strained relationships.

There is another relationship that has been broken by everyone—an individual's relationship with God. Adam and Eve broke that relationship with their act of sin. As a result, all humanity has sinned. But God has provided a way to mend that relationship. God is reconciling individuals in the world to himself through Christ.

The focus of this week's study is our part in this reconciliation. As believers, we all have the responsibility of sharing the message of God's love toward sinners. As you consider this study, think of someone you know who is not saved. Determine to share God's message with that individual.

BIBLE COMMENTARY

1. Motivated By Christ's Love

A. Persuading Humanity
2 Corinthians 5:11-13

TEACHING TIP 1: Have the assigned student give the report on the fear of God. Ensure the report presents a balanced view of both the terror of and reverence for God. This subpoint will show the part "fear" played in Paul's efforts to win the lost.

Paul knew that all humanity is going to be judged; he wanted each person to know Christ. Paul feared God, so he did his best to "persuade men" (verse 11). This fear is not a "terror" caused by disobeying God. Neither is it a fear of suffering fiery punishment in hell because of not accepting Christ. This fear is based on the knowledge that Christians will give an account for their actions at the judgment seat of Christ (verse 10). Paul knew that he was going to give an account of his life and wanted to do all he could to fulfill the ministry God gave him—winning the lost.

Ask: "How should we view Paul's motivation in relation to our ministry of reconciliation?" We as believers need to have that same motivation. All of our friends, family, and neighbors are going to stand before God to give an account of their lives. In light of eternity, they need to know Christ, and we need to tell them.

In verses 11-13, Paul gives a defense of his apostleship. Yet his defense provides more of a motivation for what he was doing rather than a specific defense for what God called Paul to be. Paul entreated the Corinthians not to think that he was boasting about himself. Rather, he explained what he was doing and why the Corinthians could take pride in what God was doing.

There were obviously those who thought Paul was out of his mind ("whether we be beside ourselves," verse 13), probably due to the visions and revelations he was experiencing or his great zeal in doing the work of God. To this Paul said, "It is to God." No one had the right to criticize the work God was doing in and through Paul. However, if what Paul was doing and teaching made him appear sober in their sight, that was for their benefit. Paul had been faithful in his apostolic ministry, and they were the result of that ministry.

B. Compelling Love
2 Corinthians 5:14,15

Behind all of Paul's ministry and defense for that ministry was his true motivation: "The love of Christ constrains us" (verse 14). **Ask: "What does the love of Christ constrain or compel us to do?"** The love of which Paul wrote is not our love for Christ, but Christ's love for humanity. This love sent Him to the cross on our behalf. His love redeemed us from certain eternal death. Because we understand this, we are convinced that Christ's death is for all (verse 14). Without Christ all humanity is "dead in tresspasses and sins" (Ephesians 2:1). Christ's love for those without Him compels us to share the gospel.

Many people, both Christians and non-Christians, have pointed to Jesus as the Supreme Example of sacrificial love. His total sacrifice of himself for others can inspire others to do great acts of unselfish compassion also. But it is clear in 2 Corinthians 5:14,15 that Paul is not principally concerned with Jesus as the Great Example, but with Jesus as the Savior. We are not merely "inspired" to service by His example, but are "compelled" to service because His love bought and paid for us.

Since Christ died on our behalf, the life we have belongs to Christ (verse 15). We have no more right to live our own lives, but only the life He chooses for each of us. We love and serve others because of the love Christ has shown us. A life of pleasing and entertaining ourselves is not just a poor choice for a Christian; as Paul saw it, it is an impossible choice. But the love of God compels us to give ourselves for others as ministers of reconciliation.

2. Ministers Of Reconciliation
A. New Creatures In Christ
2 Corinthians 5:16-19

The gospel not only changes the outward actions and habits of those individuals impacted by it, but it also changes the attitudes behind those actions. Because of the gospel, believers have a different outlook on life.

After Paul's experience with Christ, he viewed all humanity differently (2 Corinthians 5:16). He no longer judged people by superficial external appearances. Race and gender were not important. What was now important was a relationship with Jesus Christ. Paul judged people on the basis of whether they were saved or not.

Instead of the worldly perspective he held prior to salvation, Paul viewed Christ from a spiritual perspective. He saw Christ as the sacrificial Lamb by whom God reconciled the world to himself. Paul's new perspective was based on being "a new creature" in Christ (verse 17). As believers we have been re-created into something brand new, given an entirely new kind of life, established in a new relationship with God, and given a new purpose in life.

Since we are "dead to the world," we no longer see things from the world's perspective. Rather, since we are in Christ, we see things from Christ's point of view.

Ask: "How are we personally affected by seeing things from God's point of view?" Not only do we become motivated by Christ's love, but we are also given a new vision of the world because of Christ's love. Our vision now is of a world that needs to be restored to relationship with God through Jesus Christ.

When we are born again, we become new creatures in Christ and "all things are of God" (verse 18). All of the work of reconciliation and new creation was God's design. He purposed to send Jesus Christ in order to reconcile the world to himself. Even when we were separated from Him, God was not an enemy at war with us. We were the ones who rejected Him. He sought to bring back to himself the ones He loves. His means of bringing us back was the sacrifice of His only Son.

God spoke to us His words of love and forgiveness through Christ. Now that we have been reconciled to Him, He wants to continue speaking those words of love and forgiveness to the rest of the world, with us as His messengers. The reconciliation that we have received can now be passed on to others.

Ask: "What is the message God wants to give to the world?" Paul summarized the message God wants us to tell others quite well in verse 19. God wants to forgive sins, and this forgiveness comes through Jesus Christ. When God forgives an individual's sins, the trangression is no longer counted against that individual.

It is amazing that God has entrusted imperfect humans with this message. It will not be given if Christians do not give it. Like Paul, we need to sense our responsibility to be God's spokespersons to the lost.

NOTES

B. Christ's Ambassadors
2 Corinthians 5:20,21

TEACHING TIP 2: As you discuss 2 Corinthians 5:20, use the transparency "Ambassadors For Christ." Point out

that God still reconciles the world to himself through Christ, but Christians are the only representatives of Christ that the world sees.

The fact God has entrusted us with this message of reconciliation makes our calling not only a high one but a very serious one. We are His ambassadors, the only representatives the world sees.

God does not speak the message of reconciliation in a supernatural voice from the heavens. As His ambassadors (verse 20), God now makes His appeal to the world through us. It is based on God's provision for humanity's reconciliation. Christ, the One who knew no sin, became sin for us, so that we might become "the righeousness of God" (verse 21). Through Christ, God has provided a way for sinful humanity to become righteous in His sight. We must handle the message faithfully and well, so it will be heard and understood by the people to whom we are sent.

NOTES

3. Faithful In Service

A. Day Of Salvation
2 Corinthians 6:1,2

Because of the importance of this message, Paul did not want it made ineffective because of internal church problems. He reminded the Corinthian believers that as ambassadors, they were "workers together" (verse 1). They were all representatives of the same God with the same message. Paul was fearful that by their rejection of him they might also reject the message.

This is why he warned them to "receive not the grace of God in vain."

To show the urgency of his message, Paul quoted from Isaiah 49:8 in 2 Corintians 6:2. Isaiah wrote of God's "day of salvation." God had "heard" the Corinthians' prayer for forgiveness. Paul then took this idea and applied it to the Corinthians and, by extension, to all people. God had "succored" (literally, helped) them in their salvation.

"Now is the accepted time," Paul quoted, "behold, now is the day of salvation." This "now" is the day of grace in which we now live. There is still an urgency to share the message of God's grace. We must first accept God's grace while it is still being offered. Then, we must proclaim that message to lost people in a dying world.

NOTES

B. Faithful Through Trials
2 Corinthians 6:3-10

TEACHING TIP 3: As you work through 2 Corinthians 6:4-7, use the transparency titled "Faithful Through Trials" as an organizer. Cover the transparency and reveal one line at a time as you discuss each line.

As a laborer for the gospel, Paul did not want to offend in any way. This is not to say that he watered down the gospel so its truth had no effect on people's lives. But he realized that if he offended someone in a personal way, his ministry and the gospel might be discredited (verse 3). The message of reconciliation was too important to hinder its reception because of irresponsible actions on his part. In order to show his integrity, Paul mentioned that he could "commend" himself in all his actions.

It is critical that we are faithful to the message of reconciliation. Our lives must truly reflect the nature of the gospel. If we contradict with our lives what we say with our mouth or offend those to whom we are sent to minister, we are unfaithful representatives of Christ.

In verses 4 and 5, Paul continued to defend his own ministry. Few of us experience the kinds of hardships Paul endured for the sake of the gospel. No matter what difficulties confront us, we must represent the gospel faithfully as Paul did.

Paul gave three general categories of difficulties he endured: "afflictions," those times when there seems to be no escape from trouble; "necessities," pain, anguish, torture, or violent suffering at the hands of others; and "distresses," difficult times which are not the result of another's action, such as times of fasting or poverty by choice (verse 4).

Paul then listed punishments he received on behalf of the gospel as well as those chaotic events such as riots, "hard work, sleepless nights and hunger" (verse 5, NIV), that he endured in his passion to see people come to know Jesus.

In verses 6 and 7, Paul listed characteristics of Christ that a faithful representative will display, even in trials: "by pureness, by knowledge, by longsuffering, by kindness, by the Holy Ghost, by love unfeigned, by the power of God; by the armor of righteousness."

To conclude his description of faithful service in hardship, Paul used a series of contrasts between the way his life appeared to the world and the way it really was from an eternal perspective (verses 8-10).

TEACHING TIP 4: In the same manner as the transparency "Faithful Through Trials," list the contrasts in 2 Corinthians 6:8-10 on a blank transparency. Point out that Paul's emphasis is that Christianity can work in all circumstances. And as Christ's representatives on earth, we will suffer many of the hardships that Paul and other disciples experienced.

Ask: "What can we learn from Paul's list of sufferings recorded in this chapter?" Paul was willing to endure hardship for the cause of Christ. He did not shrink back from any difficult situation that came his way because of his proclaiming of the gospel. We too need to not shrink back from the verbal abuse or ridicule we receive as a result of our stand for Christ. Even in the midst of difficult times the life of Christ flows through us. We can live victoriously as faithful servants of Jesus Christ.

NOTES

LIFE RESPONSE

As believers, we have all been given the responsibility to proclaim God's message of reconciliation. We have experienced His saving grace and are new creatures in Christ. As such, we have a different outlook on life. We no longer look at life from a worldly perspective. We now judge things in relationship to eternity.

Many times we realize our responsibility, but for one reason or another, fail to fulfill it. We may not share God's message of reconciliation with others because we are afraid of ridicule or of being ostracized by family, friends, or coworkers. But we need to remember that Paul experienced far more persecution and hardship than most of us will face. Yet he continued to faithfully proclaim the message that God was reconciling the world to himself through Jesus.

Paul's motivation for ministry was both the love of God for humanity as well as the realization that all will give an account of their lives before the Lord. We need to have that same motivation at work in us. Today is still the "day of salvation." Until Christ returns, God's salvation is available to all.

Perhaps you know of someone who is not saved. Ask God to help you to take His message of reconciliation to that person. Allow His love to "compel" you to pray for the right opportunity to present this message. The same God who ministered through Paul will now minister through you. You can be the minister of reconciliation that God wants you to be.

EVANGELISM OUTREACH

This week's study presents an excellent opportunity for evangelism. God's call for reconciliation among lost humanity is at the forefront of this study. God is the One who took the initiative in reconciling humanity to himself. Emphasize God's love in sending His Son to take the sins of the world upon Him. He who was sinless became our sin offering. Appeal to the unsaved that today is the "day of salvation." Urge them not to put this decision off any longer. Offer to pray with any who respond.

INTRODUCTION

STRENGTHENING MARRIAGE AND FAMILY TIES

God designed the family as the place where biblical values are to be taught. This is why Christian families are so important. Within the Christian family the Word of God can be taught and godly values modeled.

In a world where families are disintegrating, it is important for the Church to provide biblical teaching concerning the family. The Church is only as strong as its individual families. This unit, then, is designed to teach biblical principles that will strengthen family relationships. As the Church helps strengthen its families, they can reach out to families outside of the Church and help them.

In order to build solid Christian families, we need to build our marriages upon biblical guidelines. Both "Biblical View Of Marriage" (study 9) and "Husband-Wife Relationship" (study 10) will help us learn more about how a husband and wife can work together to form a stable platform on which to build a family.

The last three studies revolve around the interpersonal relationships that are a part of a growing family. Parenting can be a challenge. Study 11 "Parental Responsibilities" looks at some biblical responsibilities of parents. The next study "Improving Intergenerational Relationships" gives the opposite side of the issue. This study examines the way parents, children, and grandparents can interact with one another from a biblical perspective.

Finally, the stresses of peer pressure and harmful addictions that are a part of many families are analyzed in "Dealing With Family Stress" (study 13). This study will help bring an understanding of the causes of these family problems and the answers God has given in His Word.

Biblical View Of Marriage

CENTRAL TRUTH

The Bible reveals God's plan for marriage.

GOLDEN TEXT

For this reason a man will leave his father and his mother and be united to his wife, and they will become one flesh. Genesis 2:24 (NIV)

STUDY TEXT

Genesis 2:18-24; Matthew 19:1-9; 1 Corinthians 7:10-16

OUTLINE

1. Purpose Of Marriage
   A. Something Is Missing
   B. Here Comes The Bride

2. God's Plan For Marriage
   A. The Perpetual Question
   B. Back To The Beginning

3. Sanctity Of Marriage
   A. Hard Hearts Miss The Truth
   B. A Practical Approach

OBJECTIVE

To know that God wants marriages to be strong and work to preserve the integrity of our marital commitments.

CHECKLIST

☐ Read the student guide. The questions at the end of each main point are designed to get the students thinking about what each passage of Scripture teaches concerning marriage. You may wish to use these questions for discussion.

☐ Bring two lumps of clay in contrasting colors to class. They will be used to demonstrate one of the principles of marriage discussed in this study.

☐ Copy the work sheet "Principles For A Godly Marriage" from the *Adult Teaching Helps Packet* for each student.

☐ There may be students present who have had unsuccessful marriages. Exercise caution so these studies will not cause those individuals to accept unnecessary blame or guilt. Pray for the Holy Spirit to give you direction and insight for this study.

DAILY BIBLE READINGS

Monday: Finding A Godly Mate.
Genesis 24:61-67

Tuesday: Avoid Immoral Behavior.
2 Samuel 11:2-5

Wednesday: The Folly Of Infidelity.
Proverbs 5:20-23

Thursday: The Virtuous Wife.
Proverbs 31:10-18

Friday: God's View Of Divorce.
Malachi 2:11-16

Saturday: Integrity Encouraged.
Mark 10:2-9

King James Version

Genesis 2:18. The Lord God said, It is not good that the man should be alone; I will make him an help meet for him.

20. And Adam gave names to all cattle, and to the fowl of the air, and to every beast of the field; but for Adam there was not found an help meet for him.

21. And the Lord God caused a deep sleep to fall upon Adam, and he slept; and he took one of his ribs, and closed up the flesh instead thereof.

22. And the rib, which the Lord God had taken from man, made he a woman, and brought her unto the man.

23. And Adam said, This is now bone of my bones, and flesh of my flesh: she shall be called Woman, because she was taken out of Man.

24. Therefore shall a man leave his father and his mother, and shall cleave unto his wife: and they shall be one flesh.

Matthew 19:1. It came to pass, that when Jesus had finished these sayings, he departed from Galilee, and came into the coasts of Judea beyond Jordan;

2. And great multitudes followed him; and he healed them there.

3. The Pharisees also came unto him, tempting him, and saying unto him, Is it lawful for a man to put away his wife for every cause?

4. And he answered and said unto them, Have ye not read, that he which made them at the beginning made them male and female,

5. And said, For this cause shall a man leave father and mother, and shall cleave to his wife: and they twain shall be one flesh?

6. Wherefore they are no more twain, but one flesh. What therefore God hath joined together, let not man put asunder.

7. They say unto him, Why did Moses then command to give a writing of divorcement, and to put her away?

8. He saith unto them, Moses because of the hardness of your hearts suffered you to put away your wives: but from the beginning it was not so.

9. And I say unto you, Whosoever shall put away his wife, except it be for fornication, and shall marry another, committeth adultery: and whoso marrieth her which is put away doth commit adultery.

New International Version

Genesis 2:18. The Lord God said, "It is not good for the man to be alone. I will make a helper suitable for him."

20. So the man gave names to all the livestock, the birds of the air and all the beasts of the field. But for Adam no suitable helper was found.

21. So the Lord God caused the man to fall into a deep sleep; and while he was sleeping, he took one of the man's ribs and closed up the place with flesh.

22. Then the Lord God made a woman from the rib he had taken out of the man, and he brought her to the man.

23. The man said, "This is now bone of my bones and flesh of my flesh; she shall be called 'woman,' for she was taken out of man."

24. For this reason a man will leave his father and mother and be united to his wife, and they will become one flesh.

Matthew 19:1. When Jesus had finished saying these things, he left Galilee and went into the region of Judea to the other side of the Jordan.

2. Large crowds followed him, and he healed them there.

3. Some Pharisees came to him to test him. They asked, "Is it lawful for a man to divorce his wife for any and every reason?"

4. "Haven't you read," he replied, "that at the beginning the Creator 'made them male and female,'

5. And said, 'For this reason a man will leave his father and mother and be united to his wife, and the two will become one flesh'?

6. So they are no longer two, but one. Therefore what God has joined together, let man not separate."

7. "Why then," they asked, "did Moses command that a man give his wife a certificate of divorce and send her away?"

8. Jesus replied, "Moses permitted you to divorce your wives because your hearts were hard. But it was not this way from the beginning.

9. I tell you that anyone who divorces his wife, except for marital unfaithfulness, and marries another woman commits adultery."

Like most everything else in society, views and ideas concerning the marriage relationship are varied. These views run the spectrum from totally conservative to wide-open liberalism. Yet a quick glance at statistics show that sinful humanity's approach to marriage is not working. Society has moved the wonderful institution of marriage away from what God the Creator meant it to be in the beginning.

God intended marriage to be fulfilling. And it can be when we bring ourselves into line with God's design. But in order to be fulfilling, marriage must operate according to the instruction manual, the Bible.

We have an opportunity to strengthen our own marriages, and to help others to strengthen their marriage relationships. This week's study gives us a biblical basis on which to build our marriage.

BIBLE COMMENTARY

1. Purpose Of Marriage

A. Something Is Missing
Genesis 2:18-20

The creation week had almost ended. Everything God created had been declared by Him as "good." But God the Creator observed that the man He had created was alone and declared it as "not good" (Genesis 2:18).

Ask: "Why was it not good for the man to be alone?"

TEACHING TIP 1: Along with their responses, be sure to include: mutual companionship and satisfaction, procreation of the human race, and an avenue for the future Redeemer of humanity to come.

Verse 18 gives God's response to Adam's plight. "I will make him a help meet for him." The key word in God's plan was "meet" meaning "suitable." Adam's counterpart had to be someone who would complete him in every way.

Every living creature had been created in pairs. As Adam named the animals, he must

have become aware of this. He had been created as a single unit. Though distinct from the rest of creation, this uniqueness must have made him realize his aloneness (verses 19,20). Something important was missing from his life. In all of creation, Adam could not find the help he longed for (verse 20). He was still painfully alone.

NOTES

B. Here Comes The Bride
Genesis 2:21-24

It became obvious that the only solution to Adam's loneliness was to create a "help meet." The answer was not in what God had already "formed" out of the ground but in what He was about to "make."

Ask: "Why did God take a portion of Adam by which to create Eve?" To accomplish this special creative act, Adam was placed in a deep sleep and a rib was removed from his side. The word "rib" can be interpreted to be both the bone itself with the flesh attached to it. To the Jews, this was significant because the rib came from near the heart, which they considered to be the seat of affection. The woman was not made from inferior substance, rather she was a special creation.

In verse 22, you can almost see a beautiful wedding as God, the Heavenly Father of the bride, "brought her unto the man" and presented her to him. Adam found what he had been missing—a completeness nothing else could provide. Adam immediately recognized that his counterpart was an intimate part of himself (verse 23). She had been made from him and would become the helper that was suitable for him.

Through this passage, we see a clear picture of God's purpose for the marriage union. God intended man and woman to complement each other and to work together as a single unit. It's here that God stated His purpose for marriage.

From the beginning, God desired marriage to be an intimate relationship. Verse 24 makes a clear statement to this effect. Man's responsibility was that he was to "cleave unto his wife" in mutual and total commitment and trust. This union was to be inseparable as they became "one flesh." They were to find their identity and completeness in one another.

TEACHING TIP 2: To illustrate what cleaving involves, take the two different colored lumps of clay you brought to class. Let one lump represent the man, the other the woman. Knead them together. Show how they are still two lumps of clay but have now become one. Point out that it is impossible to separate them.

NOTES

2. God's Plan For Marriage

A. The Perpetual Question
Matthew 19:1-3

Although God's purpose for marriage was made clear from the beginning, humanity's sinful nature perverted it. God's original design for marriage was no longer revered by many. By the time of Christ, the dissolution of marriages had become a common occurence.

The issue of divorce was further complicated by the controversy over remarriage. These issues were causing so much divisiveness among the Jewish people, that the Pharisees following Jesus selected this topic in an attempt to entrap Him.

The question posed in Matthew 19:3 was cleverly conceived. The Pharisees wanted Jesus to say something that would make Him take either too lax or too strict a view on the matter. They wanted to trap Him into perhaps saying something that would appear to contradict the law of Moses. And maybe the Pharisees thought they could get Jesus entangled in the Herod and Herodias scandal to the extent that He might end up like John the Baptist.

Among the Jews, opinions on divorce and remarriage were almost evenly divided between the teachings of two well-respected Jewish rabbis, Hillel and Shammai. Their interpretation of Deuteronomy 24:1 formed the basis of the controversy which Matthew brings up by using the phrase "for every cause" (verse 3). This phrase is significant since it is not found in parallel passages. Gentile readers would not understand the Jewish interest in this question. This phrase was the basis for a wide diversity of opinions represented by Hillel and Shammai. Both teachers permitted the divorce of a woman by a man, but disagreed sharply as to what constituted a justifiable reason.

Shammai and his followers interpreted the "uncleanness" of Deuteronomy 24:1 to refer to a gross act of indecency. This would include adultery, although not limited to it. Hillel and his followers interpreted uncleanness to mean any acceptable reason to any number of real or perceived offenses, including burning a meal.

Jesus refused to allow himself to be trapped. Instead, He directed them to the Word of God for an answer. In the process, He was able to turn their attempts to discredit Him into an opportunity to teach everyone about the divine plan that God has for the marriage relationship.

NOTES

B. Back To The Beginning
Matthew 19:4-6

Jesus immediately took His questioners back to the beginning by referring to Genesis 1:27 and 2:24. A principle of Jewish exegesis stated that the further back one could go to gather facts, the weightier that argument would be. So Jesus went back to the very beginning to present His arguments. One couldn't go further back than the creation to learn the responsibilities God had assigned to mankind.

Jesus called on the Pharisees to remember what they had read and had been taught from the Pentateuch (Matthew 19:4). It was God who had created male and female. By quoting from Genesis, Jesus clearly reminded them of God's plan for marriage.

The words recorded in verse 5, "for this cause" are God's statement concerning what is to take place in the marriage relationship. A man is to break his emotional and physical ties with his father and mother and join himself to his wife and become one flesh with her. Each time this union is formed, it is a testimony of the foundation of marriage as God intended it to be.

Ask: "What does it mean for a man to 'cleave unto his wife'?" The overriding plan and design for all marriages is permanence. The word "cleave" describes a

strong bonding that is to take place between the husband and wife. Jesus again emphasized this when He restated the "one flesh" concept in verse 6.

Jesus further indicated God's plan for permanence. If God joins man and woman together as one flesh, no man has the right to divide them.

TEACHING TIP 3: Distribute copies of the work sheet "Principles For A Godly Marriage." Allow 3-5 minutes to complete the work sheet. Ask volunteers to share their answers. (Some answers may be too personal to share. Do not force participation.) Allow time for discussion.

Believers today need to heed the importance of this command. When the Church begins to take the marriage vows seriously, then it will be able to influence the marriages of those outside of the Church. We can be an example of what God had intended marriage to be.

NOTES

3. Sanctity Of Marriage

A. Hard Hearts Miss The Truth
Matthew 19:7-9

Not to be outdone, the Pharisees came back with a question suggesting that if Jesus was correct, Moses was infringing upon God's purpose by allowing for divorce.

Jesus pointed out a flaw in the Pharisees' understanding of Moses. They said Moses *commanded* divorce (verse 7). Jesus emphasized that Moses only *permitted* it (verse 8). Jesus' response demonstrated that, in fact, Moses was trying to restore sanctity

258

to the marriage relationship. But Jesus unmasked the real problem. It was not a concern for the Law, or for the of sanctity of marriage. The real reason for divorce was the hardness of their hearts.

Ask: "What reasons do people today give for divorce?"

TEACHING TIP 4: Lead the class in a discussion concerning the state of marriage in our society. Then have the students mention ways your church could help stabilize the family. Include marriage preparation classes, marriage enrichment weekends, and pastoral teaching concerning the importance of marriage.

Christ took the side of the stricter interpretation and took a bold stand for the sanctity of marriage. He allowed only one legitimate reason for the dissolution of marriage—"fornication" (verse 9, KJV) or "marital unfaithfulness" (NIV).

In addition, the man who divorces his wife "and shall marry another, committeth adultery" (verse 9). The word translated "adultery" is a general word for sexual immorality, the same word translated "fornication." The word translated "commit adultery" at the end of the verse is the specific word for "commit adultery."

Jesus recognized that any type of sexual immorality has already broken the marriage relationship. But He was not commanding divorce, only permitting it. We must realize that God can forgive and heal a marriage broken by infidelity.

NOTES

B. A Practical Approach
1 Corinthians 7:10-16

The sanctity of marriage is an important issue for believers. In his first letter to the Corinthians, Paul instructed them concerning marriage relationships. In his teaching, we can find solid information to assist us as we face questions concerning the importance of marriage in today's society.

In 1 Corinthians 7:10,11, Paul addressed the union in which both parties are Christian. Christians are expected to stay true to their marriage vows, remaining together as man and wife as was originally intended. Paul made it clear that this is a command from the Lord. He was simply repeating what Christ had taught.

It is interesting to note that Paul also directed his statement to the women. In Jewish culture only men were allowed to initiate divorce. But the Corinthians were under Roman rule which allowed for either party to dissolve the marriage. However, if problems in the marriage arose, Paul taught that Christians should seek reconciliation, not dissolusion (verse 11).

Verses 12-16 are directed toward marriages in which a Christian is married to a non-Christian. More than likely, one marriage partner had been converted after their marriage.

In marriages where both parties are content with their relationship, marriage to an unbeliever is not a reason to initiate divorce. If dissolution occurs, it should be at the initiative of the unbeliever (verses 12-14). There was no spiritual stigma on a Christian who lived with an unbeliever if they were happy together. In fact, keeping the marriage together provided a sanctifying influence on the family.

In verse 15 Paul addressed the issue of the unbeliever refusing to remain in the marriage relationship. Again, the departure was to be initiated and completed by the unbeliever. The Christian partner was not to encourage or promote this.

Ask: "When one marriage partner becomes a believer, what could be the result

of that decision?'' Paul reminded the Corinthians, and us as well, that while a couple is together, there is always the possibility the unbelieving spouse can be won to the Lord. While God has made provision for divorce, that decision must be made according to the principles of God's Word and direction of the Holy Spirit.

LIFE RESPONSE

Have you ever noticed the photographs in the newspaper of couples who are celebrating their 50th wedding anniversary? Some of these couples have the unhappiest looks on their faces. Could it be that over the years their marriage relationship has become a burden more than a joy? God designed the marriage relationship to grow better and more satisfying with time. And it will, if we follow God's Word.

The marriage relationship is somewhat like an orchestra that blends all of its instruments together to present a beautiful rendition of a musical score. One person cannot make it reach that desirable place of beauty and satisfaction alone. It is a joint effort.

Each couple owes it to themselves to periodically evaluate their relationship and see if each one is fulfilling his or her individual responsibilities. Should problems be found, then actions should be taken to correct them. To ignore them will slowly drain the life out of the relationship. This relationship is far too valuable to allow anything like this to happen to it.

God desires for you to have the best marriage possible. Ask Him to heal any aspect of a broken relationship within your marriage. Allow the Holy Spirit to help you to express the love toward your marriage partner that God intended. As you allow God to have first place in your marriage, you will begin to experience the marriage relationship that God intended you to have.

EVANGELISM OUTREACH

The relationship between a husband and wife is to typify the relationship between Christ and His Church. There may be some in your class this week who do not understand this important aspect of their marriage relationship because they are unsaved. Explain how Christ loved each one of us and gave himself for us. His desire is that we be pure and holy. Yet this can only be accomplished through the cleansing offered through His blood. Give opportunity for any unsaved to accept Christ today. ▭

Husband-Wife Relationship

CENTRAL TRUTH

Mutual love and respect are essential for fulfillment in marriage.

GOLDEN TEXT

Each one of you also must love his wife as he loves himself, and the wife must respect her husband. Ephesians 5:33 (NIV)

STUDY TEXT

1 Corinthians 7:1-5; Ephesians 5:21-33; 1 Peter 3:1-7

OUTLINE

1. Show Loving Consideration
   A. Safeguard Against Immorality
   B. Practical Love
2. Submit One To Another
   A. God's Principle
   B. Source Of Inner Beauty
3. Follow Christ's Pattern
   A. Love Makes It Easier
   B. Advantage Of Mutual Consideration

OBJECTIVE

To learn the importance of love and respect in marriage and let these govern our marital relationships.

CHECKLIST

☐ Read the student guide noting any questions you wish to use for discussion.

☐ There are two overhead transparencies, "Paul's Guide For Demonstrating Loving Concern" and "Submission Includes," in the teaching helps packet. Make sure you have the overhead projector ready to use prior to class.

☐ Some of the material in this week's study is contrary to the philosophy of modern society. You may have students who are struggling with biblical principles in their marriages. Ask the Holy Spirit to guide your comments during the presentation of this material. Often, couples may be struggling secretly over some problem. The Holy Spirit can use your presentation to help them resolve any problems they may have.

DAILY BIBLE READINGS

Monday: A Husband's Love.
Genesis 29:15-20
Tuesday: Marital Fidelity.
Proverbs 5:15-19
Wednesday: Strength Of Love.
Song of Solomon 8:5-7
Thursday: A Married Couple Serves.
Acts 18:24-26
Friday: Love And Marriage.
Colossians 3:13-19
Saturday: Christian Role Models.
Titus 2:1-8

King James Version

1 Corinthians 7:3. Let the husband render unto the wife due benevolence: and likewise also the wife unto the husband.

4. The wife hath not power of her own body, but the husband: and likewise also the husband hath not power of his own body, but the wife.

Ephesians 5:21. Submitting yourselves one to another in the fear of God.

22. Wives, submit yourselves unto your own husbands, as unto the Lord.

23. For the husband is the head of the wife, even as Christ is the head of the church: and he is the saviour of the body.

24. Therefore as the church is subject unto Christ, so let the wives be to their own husbands in every thing.

1 Peter 3:1. Likewise, ye wives, be in subjection to your own husbands; that, if any obey not the word, they also may without the word be won by the conversation of the wives;

2. While they behold your chaste conversation coupled with fear.

3. Whose adorning, let it not be that outward adorning of plaiting the hair, and of wearing of gold, or of putting on of apparel;

4. But let it be the hidden man of the heart, in that which is not corruptible, even the ornament of a meek and quiet spirit, which is in the sight of God of great price.

5. For after this manner in the old time the holy women also, who trusted in God, adorned themselves, being in subjection unto their own husbands:

6. Even as Sara obeyed Abraham, calling him lord: whose daughters ye are, as long as ye do well, and are not afraid with any amazement.

Ephesians 5:25. Husbands, love your wives, even as Christ also loved the church, and gave himself for it;

26. That he might sanctify and cleanse it with the washing of water by the word,

27. That he might present it to himself a glorious church, not having spot, or wrinkle, or any such thing; but that it should be holy and without blemish.

28. So ought men to love their wives as their own bodies. He that loveth his wife loveth himself.

1 Peter 3:7. Likewise, ye husbands, dwell with them according to knowledge, giving honor unto the wife, as unto the weaker vessel, and as being heirs together of the grace of life; that your prayers be not hindered.

New International Version

1 Corinthians 7:3. The husband should fulfill his marital duty to his wife, and likewise the wife to her husband.

4. The wife's body does not belong to her alone but also to her husband. In the same way, the husband's body does not belong to him alone but also to his wife.

Ephesians 5:21. Submit to one another out of reverence for Christ.

22. Wives, submit to your husbands as to the Lord.

23. For the husband is the head of the wife as Christ is the head of the church, his body, of which he is the Savior.

24. Now as the church submits to Christ, so also wives should submit to their husbands in everything.

1 Peter 3:1. Wives, in the same way be submissive to your husbands so that, if any of them do not believe the word, they may be won over without words by the behavior of their wives,

2. When they see the purity and reverence of your lives.

3. Your beauty should not come from outward adornment, such as braided hair and the wearing of gold jewelry and fine clothes.

4. Instead, it should be that of your inner self, the unfading beauty of a gentle and quiet spirit, which is of great worth in God's sight.

5. For this is the way the holy women of the past who put their hope in God used to make themselves beautiful. They were submissive to their own husbands,

6. Like Sarah, who obeyed Abraham and called him her master. You are her daughters if you do what is right and do not give way to fear.

Ephesians 5:25. Husbands, love your wives, just as Christ loved the church and gave himself up for her

26. To make her holy, cleansing her by the washing with water through the word,

27. And to present her to himself as a radiant church, without stain or wrinkle or any other blemish, but holy and blameless.

28. In this same way, husbands ought to love their wives as their own bodies. He who loves his wife loves himself.

1 Peter 3:7. Husbands, in the same way be considerate as you live with your wives, and treat them with respect as the weaker partner and as heirs with you of the gracious gift of life, so that nothing will hinder your prayers.

Marriages may be made in heaven but they are maintained on earth. Anyone married for a while knows this to be true. But in order to maintain our marriages, we need to understand and apply principles on which to build them.

A marriage counselor once said, "There are no perfect marriages because there are no perfect people." While this may be true, we all can work toward having better marriages. But it requires the cooperation of both partners.

In this week's study we will look at some scriptural principles that can help make marriage better. We must recognize these principles as part of God's inspired Word. As such, we need to diligently apply them. To circumvent any of these principles greatly decreases the chance of having a strong marriage relationship.

BIBLE COMMENTARY

1. Show Loving Consideration

A. Safeguard Against Immorality
1 Corinthians 7:1,2

TEACHING TIP 1: Distribute pencils and paper to each student. Write the following sentence on the chalkboard or an overhead transparency: "I feel that the marriage relationship should. . . ." Have students complete this sentence, sharing their answers with the class.

God's plan in marriage is for each partner to mature and become closer to the other with each passing year. Sadly, far too many marriages fall short of this goal. If a marriage relationship is to reach its full potential, it is because both partners have faithfully fulfilled their God-given roles.

Some of the Corinthian believers did not realize the importance of the marriage relationship. Instead of promoting loving consideration in marital relations, they were condoning celibacy within the marriage (1 Corinthians 7:1). Paul wanted these believers to understand that God had designed a safeguard in the marriage relationship against immorality (verse 2). But in order for this safeguard to work, there must be mutual consideration between each partner in the marriage.

NOTES

B. Practical Love
1 Corinthians 7:3-5

Consideration is to be displayed not only in physical intimacy, but also in other areas of the marriage relationship. In 1 Corinthians 7:3-5 Paul dealt with three key elements that are necessary to achieve a mutual level of satisfaction and fulfillment in marriage. Paul did not intend these three components to be seen as mere duty. Rather both partners are to fulfill their roles out of love for each other. In doing this, they will be sensitive to each others feelings and needs.

According to Paul, loving consideration for one's mate is demonstrated in three key areas:

• The first area is providing for the physical and emotional needs of one's spouse (verse 3). Each spouse has needs that can only be met by the other marriage partner. It is the height of selfishness for one person to only be concerned with his or her own needs.

• The second area is relinquishing control over one's own body (verse 4). This refers to the exercise of authority. When this principle is practiced, it eliminates a self-ownership which causes individuals to seek personal satisfaction only. It also prevents one partner from being unduly under subjection to the other.

• The third manifestation of loving consideration is not depriving one another of physical intimacy (verse 5). For one partner to be celibate is defrauding the other mate of what rightfully belongs to him or her. However, Paul did make an allowance for temporary abstinence. This was to only be by mutual agreement, for a specific purpose, and only for a limited time.

It should be noted that Paul did not even remotely suggest that the duty of either partner should be carried out at the expense of the other. Paul was placing both partners on an equal level. This equality was unusual in a male-dominated society. More importantly, he was stressing giving instead of getting. In a happy marriage each partner gives to the other. When one partner strives to fulfill these three duties, that person will also find the highest degree of satisfaction and fulfillment.

Every couple can benefit by observing these principles set forth by Paul. Showing loving consideration for one's mate is not limited only to the sexual side of marriage. It needs to be demonstrated in every part of the marriage relationship.

Ask: "In what other areas can a couple show their consideration for one other?" In many families today both husband and wife work outside the home. This means that the duties that the wife would normally do can be shared by both spouses. Both spouses also need to be actively involved in child rearing, which includes spiritual training.

The motivation behind our efforts is important. If we do any of the things out of mere obligation and duty, we will not see the positive effects we might otherwise expect. Rather, we must seek to please our mates and meet their needs out of love.

NOTES

2. Submit One To Another

A. God's Principle
Ephesians 5:21-24

The word submission causes many to bristle. They do not want to submit to anyone. But our whole society is build on the principle of submission. The same is especially true in the Church.

Sometimes Paul's teaching in this passage of Scripture has been incorrectly applied to justify one person in a marriage relationship dominating the other person. But as we take a close look, we discover a far different and more positive meaning.

In Ephesians 5:21 Paul instructed the Ephesian believers to submit themselves to one another. To submit means that we are willing to serve rather than exalting ourselves over others. Paul applied this concept to marriage.

The wife is directed to submit herself to her husband "as unto the Lord" (verse 22). This phrase does not mean that she views her husband in the same light as she does the Lord. It means that bringing herself under submission is to be viewed as service to the Lord.

The submission is based on the structure that God has given for the marriage relationship. God has made the husband the head of his wife just as Christ has been made the head over the Church (verse 23).

It is important to note in the comparison that the Church, of which Christ is the head, is also called His body. This analogy gives the husband the responsibility of being the protector and the provider for his wife who has been made one flesh with him.

The wife's responsibility is to be submissive to her husband as the Church is to Christ. Submission does not mean inferiority in any way. It simply means that she recognizes him as the head and responds accordingly.

Ask: "Because a man is the head of his home, does this mean that he is in charge of all business affairs and decisions?"

The husband, as head of the house, is ultimately responsible for the home. However, this does not mean he must be the one to actually do everything. For example, take the area of finances. Some men are not good bookkeepers and money managers. As head of his home, a husband is to see that the best-qualified person handles the finances. One young husband said, "The best act of stewardship I have ever committed was when I gave my wife the checkbook."

The "in every thing" of verse 24 does not include sinful activity as some have taught. When an unsaved husband asks his wife to participate in activities that are contrary to God's Word, a higher law comes into effect. That law is obedience to Christ and His Word.

NOTES

B. Source Of Inner Beauty
1 Peter 3:1-6

TEACHING TIP 3: Display overhead transparency 2 "Submission Includes" from the teaching helps packet. Reveal each point as you discuss it in the commentary below.

There are other benefits to the wife's being in submission. God can use the inner beauty of a submissive wife as a method by which an unbelieving husband can be won to the Lord (1 Peter 3:1,2).

Peter did not suggest that a woman should not fix her hair, or wear jewelry or nice clothes. Rather she should not think of her physical beauty as the source of true beauty (verse 3). The real beauty of a Christian woman comes from the "meek and quiet spirit" which is valuable to God (verse 4).

In verses 5 and 6, Peter drew on Jewish history to demonstrate that purity of life and a submissive spirit have always been the godly women's beauty secret. It's this inner beauty that is a force in winning the unsaved mate.

NOTES

3. Follow Christ's Pattern

A. Love Makes It Easier
Ephesians 5:25-33

When we look at God's directives for marriage, we realize that they will require constant work in order to accomplish them. Just as Paul wrote some requirements for the wife, he also issued some for the husband.

In Ephesians 5:25, Paul wrote that the husband is to love his wife with the same type of love that Christ had for His Church. This love was so selfless that Christ died for the Church. Thus the true measure of a husband's love for his wife is based on how concerned he is for her needs, well-being, and safety.

The manifestations of Christ's love for His Church result in its sanctification and holiness (verses 26,27). The Church in its glory is going to bring glory to Christ. In the same way, when a husband loves his wife, she in turn brings honor to him as a husband.

When God asked the woman to submit to her husband, He wasn't even hinting that a husband may dominate his wife or treat her as a slave. Rather the couple is to develop a relationship that exhibits submission on her part and love on his. This arrangement will cause them to experience a glorious partnership with each other.

In verses 28-30 Paul once again drew upon the analogy of Christ and His Church. He stressed that the husband should love his wife just as he loves his own body. This love of one's body is not an egotistical, conceited love, but a love that stems from the inner desire for health and survival. A husband cares for his body even though it is not perfect. By the same token, he is to care for his wife and genuinely seek to meet her needs—physically, emotionally, and spiritually.

In order to again show the importance of this love, Paul referred to God's original intent in marriage (verse 31). We may not understand everything concerning this analogy, but this is God's plan (verse 32).

In Verse 33, Paul concluded his directives for good husband-wife relationships. He simply restated his basic premise. Husbands are to love their wives. Wives are to respond with honor for their husbands.

NOTES

B. Advantage Of Mutual Consideration
1 Peter 3:7

Peter, like Paul, did not focus just on wives in his letter; he included husbands as well. Peter began his instruction to husbands, by writing, "Likewise, ye husbands." This phrase does not refer to the husband's being under subjection to his wife. Rather, just as the wife is responsible to do everything in her power to promote a spiritual atmosphere in the home, so is the husband. A husband who fails to carry out his God-given responsibilities as the head of the house can do a lot of damage to the spiritual life of a home.

Peter further instructed the husband to live with his wife "according to knowledge." This phrase not only refers to the physical act of marriage, but indicates that the husband is to be "considerate" (NIV) in every area of their lives together.

This consideration will show up in a variety of ways, depending on the couple and their unique needs. These acts of consideration could be called "loving acts"—something one partner does for the other out of love for him or her. It may be something as simple as a husband being sure that there is always fuel in the car when his wife gets ready to use it. To the husband it may mean having 30 minutes of quiet relaxation after he arrives home from work.

The husband is to remember that the woman is the "weaker vessel." This is in no way derogatory. God has created man to be physically stronger. As such, he is to respect his wife in every way.

The husband must remember that his wife is equal with him spiritually in this life and in the life to come. Even now, men and women experience equally the grace of God.

Ask: "Why is it important for the husband to be considerate of and honor his wife?" A failure on the part of the husband to fulfill his responsibility can have a negative effect on his prayer life. Husbands must remember that being selfish and egotistical in their relationships with their wives can result in hindering their own relationship with God.

NOTES

LIFE RESPONSE

The relationship between husband and wife is intended to get better with every passing year. However, little things can slip into the relationship. And when they are not handled properly, they can cause a separation between the marriage partners that may widen as years pass by.

Over the years a lot of jokes have been made about marriage. But the marriage relationship is no joking matter. God takes marriage seriously. This is why He has given us principles by which to strengthen our marriages.

These principles we have studied today go against the trends of modern society. It is easy to say that the Scripture passages were written for another time and audience. But as believers, we have an obligation to obey God's Word. Do not look for ways to circumvent these principles, but find ways to apply them to your marriage in order to renew the life and joy that God desires you to have in your marriages.

Right now would be a good time for each of us to examine the relationship we have with our spouse. Are we allowing the principles of God's Word to be the guiding principles in our marriage? If there needs to be a change in behavior, God will help us make this change.

As we conclude this study let each of us determine to make our marriage what God desires it to be. God has designed us with individual roles that complement each other. Ask God to help you fulfill your role.

EVANGELISM OUTREACH

As we conclude this study, we are all made more aware of how each one of us has to work together with his or her spouse to make the marriage relationships work. There may be some unsaved people in your class who have never realized their scriptural role in marriage. Emphasize Christ's love for the Church that is typified in the marriage relationship. Christ gave himself for us. That same love is shown toward sinners. Give opportunity for any unsaved to accept Christ today. ⌷

Parental Responsibilities

CENTRAL TRUTH

God directs parents to rear their children according to scriptural principles.

GOLDEN TEXT

Fathers, do not exasperate your children; instead, bring them up in the training and instruction of the Lord. Ephesians 6:4 (NIV)

STUDY TEXT

Deuteronomy 6:1-9; 1 Samuel 3:11-14; Proverbs 13:24; 19:18; 22:6; Luke 15:20-24; Ephesians 6:4

OUTLINE

1. Teach God's Word
   A. Obey God's Commands
   B. Teach Your Children Daily

2. Employ Godly Discipline
   A. An Ounce Of Prevention
   B. Effective Discipline

3. Demonstrate Love
   A. Love Rejected
   B. Love Forgives And
      Restores

OBJECTIVE

To assess the proper role of parents and grandparents toward children and resolve to fulfill this role.

CHECKLIST

☐ Read the student guide. Write down any questions from it that you wish to use for discussion.

☐ Come prepared with some suggested opportunities to teach children in everyday life for Teaching Tip 1 if your students are hesitant to make their own suggestions.

☐ Make enough copies of the "Biblical Commands For Christian Parenting" work sheet found in the teaching helps packet. Be sure to have extra pencils or pens.

☐ You may have some parents in your class who are struggling with the task of rearing their children. Ask the Holy Spirit to lead you in your presentation. Be sensitive to parents who may be hurting because of their children's life-style.

☐ Be sure to finish the study on an encouraging note.

DAILY BIBLE READINGS

Monday: A Father's Example.
1 Kings 9:1-5

Tuesday: Maternal Influence.
2 Timothy 1:3-10

Wednesday: Lack Of Discipline.
1 Samuel 2:27-31

Thursday: Discipline Commended.
Proverbs 29:15-17

Friday: A Father's Love.
Luke 8:41,42,49-56

Saturday: A Mother's Faith.
Matthew 15:22-28

SCRIPTURE SETTING

King James Version

Deuteronomy 6:4. Hear, O Israel: The Lord our God is one Lord:

5. And thou shalt love the Lord thy God with all thine heart, and with all thy soul, and with all thy might.

6. And these words, which I command thee this day, shall be in thine heart:

7. And thou shalt teach them diligently unto thy children, and shalt talk of them when thou sittest in thine house, and when thou walkest by the way, and when thou liest down, and when thou risest up.

8. And thou shalt bind them for a sign upon thine hand, and they shall be as frontlets between thine eyes.

9. And thou shalt write them upon the posts of thy house, and on thy gates.

1 Samuel 3:11. The Lord said to Samuel, Behold, I will do a thing in Israel, at which both the ears of every one that heareth it shall tingle.

12. In that day I will perform against Eli all things which I have spoken concerning his house: when I begin, I will also make an end.

13. For I have told him that I will judge his house for ever for the iniquity which he knoweth; because his sons made themselves vile, and he restrained them not.

Proverbs 13:24. He that spareth his rod hateth his son: but he that loveth him chasteneth him betimes.

19:18. Chasten thy son while there is hope, and let not thy soul spare for his crying.

22:6. Train up a child in the way he should go: and when he is old, he will not depart from it.

Ephesians 6:4. Ye fathers, provoke not your children to wrath: but bring them up in the nurture and admonition of the Lord.

Luke 15:20. He arose, and came to his father. But when he was yet a great way off, his father saw him, and had compassion, and ran, and fell on his neck, and kissed him.

21. And the son said unto him, Father, I have sinned against heaven, and in thy sight, and am no more worthy to be called thy son.

22. But the father said to his servants, Bring forth the best robe, and put it on him; and put a ring on his hand, and shoes on his feet:

23. And bring hither the fatted calf, and kill it; and let us eat, and be merry:

24. For this my son was dead, and is alive again; he was lost, and is found. And they began to be merry.

New International Version

Deuteronomy 6:4. Hear, O Israel: The Lord our God, the Lord is one.

5. Love the Lord your God with all your heart and with all your soul and with all your strength.

6. These commandments that I give you today are to be upon your hearts.

7. Impress them on your children. Talk about them when you sit at home and when you walk along the road, when you lie down and when you get up.

8. Tie them as symbols on your hands and bind them on your foreheads.

9. Write them on the doorframes of your houses and on your gates.

1 Samuel 3:11. The Lord said to Samuel: "See, I am about to do something in Israel that will make the ears of everyone who hears of it tingle.

12. At that time I will carry out against Eli everything I spoke against his family—from beginning to end.

13. For I told him that I would judge his family forever because of the sin he knew about; his sons made themselves contemptible, and he failed to restrain them."

Proverbs 13:24. He who spares the rod hates his son, but he who loves him is careful to discipline him.

19:18. Discipline your son, for in that there is hope; do not be a willing party to his death.

22:6. Train a child in the way he should go, and when he is old he will not turn from it.

Ephesians 6:4. Fathers, do not exasperate your children; instead, bring them up in the training and instruction of the Lord.

Luke 15:20. "So he got up and went to his father. But while he was still a long way off, his father saw him and was filled with compassion for him; he ran to his son, threw his arms around him and kissed him.

21. "The son said to him, 'Father, I have sinned against heaven and against you. I am no longer worthy to be called your son.'

22. "But the father said to his servants, 'Quick! Bring the best robe and put it on him. Put a ring on his finger and sandals on his feet.

23. Bring the fattened calf and kill it. Let's have a feast and celebrate.

24. For this son of mine was dead and is alive again; he was lost and is found.' So they began to celebrate."

ce said, ''The toughest job in
s to be a parent and to do it
gnt.'' Christian parenting is sometimes
difficult because we live in an ungodly society. But parenting is a responsibility that
God has given to us.

It is sometimes tempting to delegate this
task to others. But others may not teach our
children the spiritual values we want to see
instilled in them. If we fail to teach our

children properly, we may lose a generation
who will faithfully serve God.

Many parents do not have a clear understanding of what their role as parents really
is. This week's study is designed to help
make these roles clearer and to give some
practical suggestions in performing them.

As we look at three principles of parenting, ask the Lord to help you be the parent
He desires you to be.

BIBLE COMMENTARY

1. Teach God's Word

A. Obey God's Commands
Deuteronomy 6:1-6

The Children of Israel were at the border
of the Promised Land. Soon they would be
scattered all across the hills and valleys of
their new homeland. How could this people
keep focused on God and avoid being dis-
tracted by the life-style of those around
them? God's solution was quite simple—a
consistent plan of teaching God's Word.
This would help ensure that they continue
on the path God had chosen.

Moses had just reviewed the Ten Commandments with them (Deuteronomy 5:1-
21). He made it clear that God's purpose
was for him to teach them ''the commandments, the statutes, and the judgments'' of
God (6:1). The purpose of this teaching was
twofold. First, it was to ensure that each
generation would fear (reverence and honor)
the Lord and His decrees (verse 2). Second,
teaching them to obey God's commands
would ensure that things would go well for
them and give them a long life (verse 3).

A priority for Christian parents is to establish a solid biblical foundation in their
own lives (verses 4-6). If we expect our

children to serve the Lord, then we must
set the example for them. This not only
includes faithfully attending worship services at church, but having private devotional times at home as well. We must also
model for them the Christian values that we
desire them to have. As we have established
our relationship with the Lord, then we can
properly teach our children.

NOTES

B. Teach Your Children Daily
Deuteronomy 6:7-9

Our responsibility is to teach God's Word
to our children. According to this passage
this would include truths concerning the nature of God and their love for Him and His
Word. In verses 7-9, Moses indicated that
this teaching is not a onetime occurrence,

but an ongoing process. Every day there would be opportunities for parents to use common experiences to teach their children the truths concerning God and His commandents. As these truths are addressed, they become a part of the children's lives.

Ask: "What situations in life can be used as opportunities to teach God's Word to our children?"

TEACHING TIP 1: Allow class members to discuss real-life situations that can be used as opportunities to teach scriptural principles to their children. Then use the following commentary to reinforce their understanding.

The biblical mandate in verse 7 is to "teach [God's commandments, statutes, and judgments] diligently unto thy children." Moses gave three methods of accomplishing this task. First, the parents were to talk about God's law regularly. They were to look for opportunities to teach and reinforce the principles of God's Word. Things that happen every day, both positive and negative, are tremendous opportunities to teach and reinforce God's Word.

Next, they were to bind God's law to themselves. They were to carry with them a constant reminder of the truths they had learned. Last, they were to write them on the door frames of their homes and on their gates as well. This would serve to remind their children as they entered or left their home of the God they served and of their responsibilities to Him.

Ask: "How can we apply these visual and life-style teaching methods to our Christian homes today?" One casualty of our busy society has been the family devotional time. Few families eat meals together anymore, much less have family devotions. While family devotions are necessary, the concepts presented by Moses are a natural way to instruct our families in Christian values. In this life-style teaching method, every event, opportunity, victory,

or defeat can become a practical opportunity to teach our children God's Word. Our children will be able to observe biblical truths and principles in action.

In our daily teaching, we must teach our children several important precepts—the baptism in the Holy Spirit, the soon return of our Lord, the importance of holy living, and appreciation for and obedience to the Word of God. These precepts must be written on the hearts of our children by taking the opportunities of life and teaching them how God is an everyday part of their lives. We must not just teach religious duties, but a practical and holy life-style.

TEACHING TIP 2: Hand each student a copy of the work sheet "Biblical Commands For Christian Parenting." Divide the class into small groups and have them answer the questions. After a few minutes, ask for volunteers to share practical suggestions for Christian parenting.

NOTES

2. Employ Godly Discipline

A. An Ounce Of Prevention
1 Samuel 3:11-14

God has placed the responsibility for disciplining children on parents. The end result of discipline should produce orderly conduct and a respectful submission to rules and authorities. As we discipline our children, we desire to make a difference in their behavior both now and in the future—for their good.

In 1 Samuel 3:11-14, we observe the results of failing to properly discipline one's children. Young Samuel heard God's voice for the first time (verse 4). God gave him a message that would rock the nation of Israel. Eli's sons had lived in gross sin and had shown disrespect for sacred things. Eli was aware of this and had failed to restrain them (verse 13). As a result, Eli was removed from office and his entire family was judged by God (verse 14). They were judged not only because of their sin, but because Eli had failed to discipline his sons.

Ask: "Why does God hold parents accountable for the disciplining of their children?" While God does not hold parents accountable for their children's actions, He does hold them accountable for failing to discipline their children. Parents are disobedient to God's commands if they do not properly discipline their children and take the chance that their children may not serve God. Even though disciplining children is not always easy, Christian parents are required to do it.

NOTES

B. Effective Discipline
Proverbs 13:24; 19:18; 22:6;
Ephesians 6:4

The subject of discipline generates much discussion. Views concerning the proper methods of discipline are quite diverse.

Proverbs 13:24 speaks to the issue of corporal punishment, where a child is given physical discomfort because of a willful and defiant act of rebellion. While many in to-day's society speak out against this type of discipline, we must remember that this is God's inspired Word.

Spanking has often been used for the wrong purposes. The inclusion of the word "rod" does indicate that there is a proper time and use for physically spanking a child. But it never gives anyone the right to physically harm or abuse anyone.

Spanking, as discipline, must be administered in love. It should never be administered in anger, out of frustration, or to make the parent feel better. Spanking, as discipline, should be followed by an expression of love and acceptance.

The end result of any disciplinary action is to teach children that wrong behavior always carries unpleasant consequences. Proverbs states that parents who do not discipline their children actually hate them.

Parents are also warned against being passive in regard to discipline (19:18). Discipline must be administered during the formative years of children's lives, while there is still hope for them. Failure to follow this advice can make the parent a "willing party" (NIV) to a person's death. This could refer to capital punishment under the law or by natural consequences that accompany a person's foolish behavior. Discipline is designed to prevent children from destroying their lives by sinful activities.

One of the best forms of discipline is proper training (22:6). Part of the concept of training is to cultivate a taste for the things of God. This means that parents must model godly attitudes and actions. We can never discipline our children for the things we do ourselves. Double standards will derail all disciplinary actions.

The last part of this verse should not be considered an ironclad guarantee. Many parents have had their hearts broken when they did their very best, only to have their child stray from their godly training. However, children reared in Christian homes under the influence of godly parents, are more apt to follow the training they received.

Parents can also be too strict in their discipline. In Ephesians 6:4, Paul instructed parents to not anger their children by wrong or too strict disipline. Paul wanted Christian parents to realize that part of parenting is training children in righteous living.

NOTES

3. Demonstrate Love

A. Love Rejected
Luke 15:20

Being a good parent is not always easy. Providing children with a sound biblical foundation and a well-disciplined life-style in a society with questionable values often presents a challenge.

Parents must remember that all training and discipline must be in love. Love is something we can talk about. But for love to be fully realized, it must be demonstrated. Whether children fully accept teaching and discipline or totally rebel, they must be able to see their parents' love for them and concern for their well-being.

TEACHING TIP 3: Have someone give a brief summary of the Parable of the Prodigal Son up to verse 19.

Jesus told the Parable of the Prodigal Son to demonstrate a father's love in action for a wayward child. According to Jewish law, this son had no right to return to the family as a son. He had squandered his inheritance by living a sinful life-style. But the father still loved his son. When he saw his son in the distance, he ran to him and embraced him. This suggests that perhaps the father often looked down the road for some sign of his son's return.

"How does this parable speak to parents concerning loving their children?" The father in this parable gives us a pattern for demonstrating our love today. Notice that he did not downplay the young man's mistakes, nor did he say "I told you so," rather he sought to support him and accept him. Even when our children do not live according to our standards, we still need to express our love toward them.

NOTES

B. Love Forgives And Restores
Luke 15:21-24

The son did not complete the speech that he had so carefully rehearsed. The father interrupted him and quickly sent the servant scurrying to begin the big celebration.

In Luke 15:21-24, the father made several significant and symbolic gestures toward his son that referred to more than sonship. The robe he placed on his back was a ceremonial robe for a guest of honor. The ring he placed on his hand symbolized authority. Lastly, the sandals were those only worn by a free man. And the "fatted calf" was a special animal that was kept for only the most special of occasions.

The young man was totally restored to the place he had once held. This father's love reached beyond his son's failures and saw him in need of restoration, forgiveness, and acceptance.

As Christian parents, we need to closely observe the actions of this father. We need to understand that children will make mistakes ranging from spilling milk on the new carpet to going into the depths of sin. But one of our roles as parents is to help our children get back up when they fall. Whatever their offenses, they need our love, encouragement, and support.

Some parents are too quick to criticize their children with careless and harsh statements. Verbal abuse can be as devastating as physical abuse. Certainly at times corrective measures must be taken, but they must be handled in such a way as to build up and not tear down.

Ask: "What are some ways we can show our children that we love them and are concerned with their well-being?" We can demonstrate love by going to their special events at church and school and by spending time with them. We can also show we love them by proper discipline and forgetting past mistakes once they are settled.

Parents' love for their children is a remarkable thing to observe. No matter how often this love is stepped on, it rebounds to give the child another chance. Interestingly, when Jesus wanted to teach about the characterstics of God's love, He chose as a model a father's love for his runaway son.

NOTES

LIFE RESPONSE

Parenting is both a privilege and a responsibility. Many times our children bring joy and refreshment to our lives. The times that parents spend with their children can be some of their best experiences.

It is exciting to see our children grow. We notice daily changes when our children are newborn babies. Even most teenagers have noticeable growth spurts. But with the physical growth of our children comes the responsibility for training and disciplining them.

Our children are gifts God has entrusted to us. As stewards of God's gifts, we need to train them to honor Him. We can do that by teaching our children God's Word and by using the activities that we are involved in every day to teach them godly principles.

It would be wonderful if you never had to discipline your children. Unfortunately, this is not the case. As you have examined the Scriptures concerning the disciplining of children presented in this study, perhaps you have seen areas where you need to change the way you discipline your children. Maybe

you are too strict and need to nurture and train. Perhaps you have not disciplined as you should. Allow the Lord to help you seek to discipline according to His Word.

Maybe you have children who are like the Prodigal Son. Ask God to help you to love them as you would a faithful child. Pray for them that God will work in their lives for salvation.

EVANGELISM OUTREACH

One of the greatest demonstrations of love is seen in the Parable of the Prodigal Son. The father's response toward his son indicates that he had been waiting expectantly for his son to return home. This parable also presents an example of God's love for the sinner. There may be some unsaved in your class that need to come "home" to God. Emphasize God's love for them. Let them know that God is waiting for them to come to Him. Give them opportunity to pray for salvation today. ⌐

Improving Intergenerational Relationships

CENTRAL TRUTH

Respect and care for one another are vital in family relationships.

GOLDEN TEXT

Be devoted to one another in brotherly love. Honor one another above yourselves. Romans 12:10 (NIV)

STUDY TEXT

Exodus 20:12; Luke 2:40-52; Ephesians 6:1-3; Colossians 3:20,21; 1 Timothy 5:3-8

OUTLINE

1. Strengthen Family Ties
   A. Lasting Relationships Begin Early
   B. Letting Children Grow Up

2. Teach Mutual Respect
   A. Responsible Children
   B. Understanding Parents

3. Care For Senior Adults
   A. Do Not Forget Older Family Members
   B. Provide For The Elderly

OBJECTIVE

To recognize the importance of mutual respect across generational lines and practice it.

CHECKLIST

☐ Read the *Adult Student Guide.* Write down any questions you want to use for class discussion. Especially note the description of senior adults found in the third main point.

☐ Make sufficient copies of the work sheet "Am I A Good Listener?" found in the teaching helps packet. Study this work sheet and be prepared to apply these questions to listening within the family. Be sure to have extra pencils available.

☐ Pray for wisdom and help from the Holy Spirit in presenting this study. You may have adults in your class that are having trouble in their families. Remember that you may be helping families learn to live in harmony.

☐ Suggest to your class that they plan a group activity to minister to senior adults this week.

DAILY BIBLE READINGS

Monday: Responsible To Others.
Genesis 4:1-10
Tuesday: Forgive One Another.
Genesis 33:1-11
Wednesday: Care For Family Members.
Genesis 47:7-12
Thursday: Sacrificial Love.
Ruth 1:12-17
Friday: Care For Parents.
Mark 7:9-13
Saturday: Concern For Parents.
John 19:25-27

King James Version

Luke 2:42. When [Jesus] was twelve years old, they went up to Jerusalem after the custom of the feast.

43. And when they had fulfilled the days, as they returned, the child Jesus tarried behind in Jerusalem; and Joseph and his mother knew not of it.

44. But they, supposing him to have been in the company, went a day's journey; and they sought him among their kinsfolk and acquaintance.

45. And when they found him not, they turned back again to Jerusalem, seeking him.

46. And it came to pass, that after three days they found him in the temple, sitting in the midst of the doctors, both hearing them, and asking them questions.

47. And all that heard him were astonished at his understanding and answers.

48. And when they saw him, they were amazed: and his mother said unto him, Son, why hast thou thus dealt with us? behold, thy father and I have sought thee sorrowing.

49. And he said unto them, How is it that ye sought me? wist ye not that I must be about my Father's business?

50. And they understood not the saying which he spake unto them.

51. And he went down with them, and came to Nazareth, and was subject unto them: but his mother kept all these sayings in her heart.

Exodus 20:12. Honor thy father and thy mother: that thy days may be long upon the land which the Lord thy God giveth thee.

Ephesians 6:1. Children, obey your parents in the Lord: for this is right.

2. Honor thy father and mother; which is the first commandment with promise;

3. That it may be well with thee, and thou mayest live long on the earth.

Colossians 3:20. Children, obey your parents in all things: for this is well-pleasing unto the Lord.

21. Fathers, provoke not your children to anger, lest they be discouraged.

1 Timothy 5:3. Honor widows that are widows indeed.

4. But if any widow have children or nephews, let them learn first to shew piety at home, and to requite their parents: for that is good and acceptable before God.

New International Version

Luke 2:42. When [Jesus] was twelve years old, they went up to the Feast, according to the custom.

43. After the Feast was over, while his parents were returning home, the boy Jesus stayed behind in Jerusalem, but they were unaware of it.

44. Thinking he was in their company, they traveled on for a day. Then they began looking for him among their relatives and friends.

45. When they did not find him, they went back to Jerusalem to look for him.

46. After three days they found him in the temple courts, sitting among the teachers, listening to them and asking them questions.

47. Everyone who heard him was amazed at his understanding and his answers.

48. When his parents saw him, they were astonished. His mother said to him, "Son, why have you treated us like this? Your father and I have been anxiously searching for you."

49. "Why were you searching for me?" he asked. "Didn't you know I had to be in my Father's house?"

50. But they did not understand what he was saying to them.

51. Then he went down to Nazareth with them and was obedient to them. But his mother treasured all these things in her heart.

Exodus 20:12. "Honor your father and your mother, so that you may live long in the land the Lord your God is giving you."

Ephesians 6:1. Children, obey your parents in the Lord, for this is right.

2. "Honor your father and mother"—which is the first commandment with a promise—

3. "That it may go well with you and that you may enjoy long life on the earth."

Colossians 3:20. Children, obey your parents in everything, for this pleases the Lord.

21. Fathers, do not embitter your children, or they will become discouraged.

1 Timothy 5:3. Give proper recognition to those widows who are really in need.

4. But if a widow has children or grandchildren, these should learn first of all to put their religion into practice by caring for their own family and so repaying their parents and grandparents, for this is pleasing to God.

Perhaps you know of families where parents and children are constantly bickering. Instead of solving their problems, they are allowing these problems to destroy their relationship with each other. They may no longer even speak to each other. How tragic that these families spend their lives with resentments, grudges, bitterness, and other feelings that rob them of some of life's greatest pleasures.

Often the problems begin with small, perhaps insignificant, incidents. Rather than working through problems, family members allow them to escalate and grow out of proportion.

This week's study is designed to help keep families from experiencing such tragic incidents. The scriptural guidelines presented will help produce intergenerational harmony in the home.

1. Strengthen Family Ties

A. Lasting Relationships Begin Early
Luke 2:40-48

A good relationship between parent and child is one of the most important relationships that we have. If this relationship is not properly developed, it can have a long-lasting, negative effect on the entire family. While the Scriptures do not give us a lot of detail concerning Jesus' childhood and His relationship with Mary and Joseph, what we do have is significant. Luke 2:40-51 relates an incident from the boyhood of Jesus.

Joseph and Mary were accustomed to making the annual pilgrimage to Jerusalem to observe the Passover. Jesus was 12 years of age when this event took place (verses 41,42). Jesus' attendance at this particular celebration was probably to prepare Him for a particular ceremony in the coming year. In this ceremony, He would observe the Jewish right-of-passage that would permit Him to become a responsible member of the religious community.

At the end of the Passover, the families began their journey home. Families generally traveled with the women and smaller children in one group and the men and older boys in another. Jesus could have been with either Mary or Joseph. At nightfall, as the families rejoined for their evening meal and sleep, things became quite unsettled. Mary and Joseph, supposing that Jesus had been with the other parent, discovered that Jesus was not with the group (verses 43,44).

TEACHING TIP 1: Ask if anyone in the class has ever left their children somewhere and later discovered what they had done. Have them share their feelings about the incident.

Joseph and Mary returned to Jerusalem to look for Jesus. On the third day they found Jesus in the temple area asking questions of the doctors of the Law (verses 45,46). They were astonished when they saw Jesus' understanding of the Law (verse 47).

When Joseph and Mary found Jesus, Mary began to scold Him. Notice her reaction as recorded in verse 48, ''Son, why hast thou thus dealt with us?'' She was venting her frustrations and fears.

While Mary's reaction is typical, it is a response that can hinder the development of a good relationship. Mary, without hearing the whole story, blamed her Son for the discomfort they experienced.

Ask: **"Why is it important for parents to listen to their children?"** How often do we as parents react the same way as Mary? An important key to developing good intergenerational relationships is establishing and keeping the lines of communication open. As parents we must be open to hear and understand both sides of problems.

One of the best things we can do for our children is to learn to really listen to them before we blindly pass judgment on their actions. As we listen, we can understand their feelings. Listening to their reasoning may mean that we will have to readjust our evaluation also. While we might not always agree with our children or they with us, we must keep the door of communication open.

NOTES

B. Letting Children Grow Up
Luke 2:49-51

Most parents enjoy seeing their children mature. This maturing process brings about more than physical changes, though. Maturing also brings with it a move toward independence on the part of the child. This happened in Jesus Christ's life.

Note how gently and respectfully Jesus pointed out that He was moving toward manhood (Luke 2:49). Parents sometimes have difficulty in coping with their children growing up. A failure to recognize this transition period and accept it can also damage our relationship with our children. As children leave the adolescent stage and move toward adulthood, they move further away from our control and influence. This time in life can be a time of tension and conflict for both parent and child.

As we see this transition happening, we often wonder what our role as parents is during this time. It is found in balance. We must learn to accept our children's uniqueness and give them the opportunity to develop. At the same time, we must be close at hand to help to encourage them when they need it. Fostering good relationships with our children will make these transitions easier to deal with.

Notice how Jesus submitted himself to His earthly parents and continued to live under their control and authority (verse 51). They had a disagreement with Jesus, yet He yielded to their authority during His childhood. Our children are more likely to follow the same pattern when they feel they are accepted for themselves and are allowed the opportunity to be heard.

NOTES

2. Teach Mutual Respect

A. Responsible Children
Exodus 20:12; Ephesians 6:1-3; Colossians 3:20

Several years ago the phrase "generation gap" became a common expression used to describe the differences in ideologies between younger and older generations. Unfortunately, this gap still exists today.

The Bible gives guidelines to bridging this gap that stands between many parents and their children. This relationship, like all others, is one in which both parties must work together to make it work.

Children's attitude and behavior toward their parents are important to God. In fact, one of the Ten Commandments addresses the children's relationship with their parents. Children are directed to treat their parents with honor and respect. This is not optional, it is a command from God.

Ask: "Why do you think God places such a high importance on children's respecting parents?" Children must realize that parents have been instructed to help them grow and develop into responsible adults. Christian children, like their parents, are under the authority of Christ. By respecting and honoring their parents, children respect and honor God.

Paul, in writing to the Ephesians, addressed the conduct each family member has toward others as they live Spirit-filled lives (6:1-3). A good parent-child relationship is an outgrowth of the Spirit-filled life.

Ask: "To what extent is a child with unsaved parents to obey them?" Obedience to God is of the utmost importance in one's life. Children are to obey their parents "in the Lord" (verse 1). Some have incorrectly taken this phrase to mean only if the parents are believers. A child is not bound to obey a parent in doing anything immoral, hurtful, or illegal. The directives given here are primarily addressed to homes where parents are striving to bring their children up in the fear and admonition of the Lord. Yet in every family situation, respect for the parental role is a child's responsibility.

Paul not only gave the command for obedience but the reasons as well—it is "right" (Ephesians 6:1) and "well-pleasing unto the Lord" (Colossians 3:20). This denotes a proper behavior for Christian children.

In Ephesians 6:2,3, Paul substantiated his statement by quoting the fifth commandment with its promise of long life. It is important to note that respecting parents is not a guarantee of long life. This statement sets forth a general principle that obedience fosters a life of self-discipline. A disciplined life-style generally helps a person live a longer, more productive life.

B. Understanding Parents
Colossians 3:21

Paul also directed his attention to the parents who have a major role in developing the parent-child relationship. Fathers are singled out in Colossians 3:21, but mothers can be included as well. Parents are not to provoke or frustrate their children. To do so will cause them to become "discouraged" (verse 21).

Ask: "In what ways can parents frustrate their children?" A common way of frustrating children is by constantly putting them down. People respond better to praise than to criticism. Praise coupled with loving discipline will go a long way in helping build good intergenerational relationships. If parents continually redo the tasks their children perform, children feel they cannot do anything right.

A constant barrage of criticism, whether verbal or unspoken, can discourage a child. Often children carry this discouragement into their adult lives. One young lady nearly ruined her life on the streets of a major city. When a counselor asked why she had gotten herself into so much trouble, she responded, "When you are continually told you are no good, you begin to believe it."

Mutual respect works both ways. Children are to honor and respect their parents. But parents are to also love, respect, and accept their children for who they are. In addition, parents are to encourage their children to become all they can be in the Lord.

NOTES

3. Care For Senior Adults

A. Do Not Forget Older Family Members
1 Timothy 5:3,4

An integral part of the intergenerational relations are senior adults. Like everyone else, their roles have changed within the last several years. One of these changes has been in longevity of life.

People are living longer today than they did a few years ago. However, senior adults are not always able to remain self-sufficient throughout their lives. Often others must care for them in their later years.

A high priority for the Early Church was caring for the widows. By the time the pastoral epistles were written, this had become an important ministry. Some, though, were abusing this ministry. Paul needed to give Timothy instructions concerning the care of widows. Paul's instructions can be applied to taking care of senior adults today.

Paul wrote that those who were "widows indeed" (1 Timothy 5:3) were to be honored. This phrase referred to widows who had no family members to take care of them. Some were allowing the local churches to take care of their obligations to their own family members (verse 4). Paul wanted families to understand their own responsibility for taking care of their widowed family members and not allow the church to be burdened with their care.

Ask: "Why is it important that families take responsibility for the care of their older family members?" Part of the intergenerational relationship structure is for families to care for each other. According to verse 4, caring for the older members of our family is religion put into practice. According to Paul, this is a way that we can repay our parents and grandparents for all the sacrifices they made for us.

NOTES

B. Provide For The Elderly
1 Timothy 5:5-8

The source of all of our help is God. Widows who were godly women understood this (1 Timothy 5:5). It is these the church was to help, not those who lived for their own pleasure (verses 6,7).

Paul concluded this passage with a stern warning. He said that anyone who fails to care for his family members is equal to an infidel, a person who has no Christian faith (verse 8). While this warning includes taking care of all family members, in this context it especially includes widows, and by extension, senior adults.

Ask: "What can Christian families provide for their older members?"

TEACHING TIP 4: Have your students share ways they have provided for the needs of older family members. Write these responses on the chalkboard or a blank transparency. Add the following if they were not mentioned by class members.

There are many things we can do to provide for the senior adults in our families. However, they need much more than just material things. They need us. Some senior adults, because they are shut-ins, lack fellowship with other Christians. Time spent with them can be very meaningful. Other senior adults may need someone to run errands for them, or to help them with tasks they are no longer able to perform.

As we minister to senior adults, we will find that our relationship with them will not be one of just giving. These wonderful people have a wealth of knowledge, experience, faith, and love to share with us. Caring for the senior adult can be one of the most rewarding experiences a family can have.

LIFE RESPONSE

There is no way to describe the value of having good intergenerational relationships. They bring peace and harmony to a home. The home becomes a place where all members are loved and respected for who they are. There is good communication and exchange of ideas.

On the other hand, bad family relationships make the home a place where no one wants to come home. The constant bickering and fighting creates tension. No one gives or receives love and respect. Screaming is the only form of communication.

What makes the difference between these two homes? First and foremost is a relationship with Jesus Christ. When Christ rules, peace rules. Secondly, parents and children respect each other as individuals. They also respect each other's opinion.

Mistakes made early in life that were not corrected can rob us of joy in later years. But mistakes can be corrected. You do not have to continue to live with bad family relationships.

As parents, you must take the lead in producing good family relationships within your home. What about your relationship with your parents? Do you need to be more concerned and helpful to them? Evaluate your relationship with your children. Do any of your actions, attitudes, or manner of discipline need changing?

God desires for you to have good relationships within your family. Ask Him to help you improve these relationships.

EVANGELISM OUTREACH

Some in your class today may be facing difficult family relationships. Their homes may be in turmoil. This turmoil may be caused by an unsaved family member. But there is a possibility that this one in your class is not saved and is part of the problem. Emphasize the importance of Christ's being the Head of the home. Explain how Christ has the power to change people's lives. He can help make the needed changes in family relationships. Give opportunity for any unsaved to accept Christ as Savior.

Dealing With Family Stress

CENTRAL TRUTH

Believers can rely on God to help them cope with stressful situations.

GOLDEN TEXT

You will keep in perfect peace him whose mind is steadfast, because he trusts in you. Isaiah 26:3, NIV

STUDY TEXT

Proverbs 23:31-35; 2 Corinthians 6:14-18; Ephesians 5:15-18; Hebrews 13:4-6

OUTLINE

1. Coping With Peer Pressures
   A. Devastating Force
   B. Antidote

2. Avoid Harmful Addictions
   A. What Is Wrong With
      A Little Wine?
   B. God's Answer

3. God Is Our Helper
   A. Safeguards Against Stress
   B. God Provides Help

OBJECTIVE

To survey the pressures society places on families and seek to deal effectively with stress.

CHECKLIST

☐ Contact four students early in the week to prepare the skit "Peer Pressure" from the teaching helps packet.

☐ Prepare sufficient copies of the work sheet "The Greatest Sources Of Family Stress Are . . ." found in the teaching helps packet. Give it to the students as they arrive. Have them fill it out and hold it until called for in the study.

☐ Duplicate the work sheet "God Our Helper" for each student.

☐ Find someone who has personally experienced problems with an addiction or with a family member who has had an addiction. Ask them to share with the class the effects of that addiction.

☐ There may be some in the class who are privately struggling with some of the things you will discuss this week. Pray that God will help you as you present this study.

DAILY BIBLE READINGS

Monday: Understand Peer Pressure.
Psalm 37:1-9

Tuesday: Overcome Peer Pressure.
Daniel 3:13-18

Wednesday: Danger Of Alcohol.
Isaiah 5:11-16

Thursday: Overcome Emotional Stress.
2 Timothy 4:9-18

Friday: Spirit-Led Life.
Romans 8:5-14

Saturday: Focus On God.
Philippians 4:6-13

Scripture Setting

King James Version

2 Corinthians 6:14. Be ye not unequally yoked together with unbelievers: for what fellowship hath righteousness with unrighteousness? and what communion hath light with darkness?

15. And what concord hath Christ with Belial? or what part hath he that believeth with an infidel?

16. And what agreement hath the temple of God with idols? for ye are the temple of the living God; as God hath said, I will dwell in them, and walk in them; and I will be their God, and they shall be my people.

17. Wherefore come out from among them, and be ye separate, saith the Lord, and touch not the unclean thing; and I will receive you,

18. And will be a Father unto you, and ye shall be my sons and daughters, saith the Lord Almighty.

Proverbs 23:31. Look not thou upon the wine when it is red, when it giveth his color in the cup, when it moveth itself aright.

32. At the last it biteth like a serpent, and stingeth like an adder.

33. Thine eyes shall behold strange women, and thine heart shall utter perverse things.

34. Yea, thou shalt be as he that lieth down in the midst of the sea, or as he that lieth upon the top of a mast.

35. They have stricken me, shalt thou say, and I was not sick; they have beaten me, and I felt it not: when shall I awake? I will seek it yet again.

Ephesians 5:15. See then that ye walk circumspectly, not as fools, but as wise,

16. Redeeming the time, because the days are evil.

17. Wherefore be ye not unwise, but understanding what the will of the Lord is.

18. And be not drunk with wine, wherein is excess; but be filled with the Spirit;

Hebrews 13:4. Marriage is honorable in all, and the bed undefiled: but whoremongers and adulterers God will judge.

5. Let your conversation be without covetousness; and be content with such things as ye have: for he hath said, I will never leave thee, nor forsake thee.

6. So that we may boldly say, The Lord is my helper, and I will not fear what man shall do unto me.

New International Version

2 Corinthians 6:14. Do not be yoked together with unbelievers. For what do righteousness and wickedness have in common? Or what fellowship can light have with darkness?

15. What harmony is there between Christ and Belial? What does a believer have in common with an unbeliever?

16. What agreement is there between the temple of God and idols? For we are the temple of the living God. As God has said: "I will live with them and walk among them, and I will be their God, and they will be my people."

17. "Therefore come out from them and be separate, says the Lord. Touch no unclean thing, and I will receive you."

18. "I will be a Father to you, and you will be my sons and daughters, says the Lord Almighty."

Proverbs 23:31. Do not gaze at wine when it is red, when it sparkles in the cup, when it goes down smoothly!

32. In the end it bites like a snake and poisons like a viper.

33. Your eyes will see strange sights and your mind imagine confusing things.

34. You will be like one sleeping on the high seas, lying on top of the rigging.

35. "They hit me," you will say, "but I'm not hurt! They beat me, but I don't feel it! When will I wake up so I can find another drink?"

Ephesians 5:15. Be very careful, then, how you live—not as unwise but as wise,

16. Making the most of every opportunity, because the days are evil.

17. Therefore do not be foolish, but understand what the Lord's will is.

18. Do not get drunk on wine, which leads to debauchery. Instead, be filled with the Spirit.

Hebrews 13:4. Marriage should be honored by all, and the marriage bed kept pure, for God will judge the adulterer and all the sexually immoral.

5. Keep your lives free from the love of money and be content with what you have, because God has said, "Never will I leave you; never will I forsake you."

6. So we say with confidence, "The Lord is my helper; I will not be afraid. What can man do to me?"

OPENING THOUGHTS

This week's study concludes the unit "Strengthening Marriage And Family Ties." In this study, we will examine a contemporary issue faced by most families—stress.

Stress can be defined as "a physical, chemical, or emotional factor that causes bodily or mental tension." Anyone raising a family knows that this definition describes what the family is facing today.

Stress can come in many ways and from many sources—both from within the family and from forces outside of the family. This week, we will look at two sources of family stress. More importantly, we will discover God's answer for stressed-out families.

You and your family do not have to live in a stressful situation. God is your Helper. Allow Him to minister to your needs this week.

BIBLE COMMENTARY

1. Coping With Peer Pressures

A. Devastating Force
2 Corinthians 6:14-18

TEACHING TIP 1: Have the students present the skit "Peer Pressure."

Peer pressure can be a major source of stress to the family. Such pressure operates on the principle of compromise. Peer pressure forces people to be what they are not, do things they would not normally do, and go where they really do not want to go.

Ask: "What is it about human nature that gives peer pressure such a grip in many lives?" Nearly all human beings have a fear of rejection or of not fitting in with those around them. This basic fear makes us susceptible to pressure by those around us. But a firm set of convictions based on God's Word will help us overcome the temptation to compromise (see Genesis 39:7-23).

One of the ways we can combat peer pressure is by understanding principles for godly living found in God's Word. In doing so, we can help each family member learn to evaluate outside influences and adhere to true and lasting godly values.

While not all peer pressure is bad, Paul recognized that the world will try to pressure us into conforming to its mold. In 2 Corinthians 6:14-18, he addressed the dangers of trying to blend in with those around us. Paul declared that believers are not to be "unequally yoked" with unbelievers. Paul drew this analogy from Deuteronomy 22:10 that prohibited the Jews from plowing with mixed breeds of animals.

While Paul's command is commonly used to prohibit marriages of believers with unbelievers, there is a broader application. As believers, we must not develop a close relationship with unbelievers that might cause us to compromise our Christian convictions or witness. When we succumb to the world's pressure, we are joining ourselves with the world. This is totally contrary to the values of true Christianity. In 2 Corinthians 6:14-16, Paul presented five rhetorical questions designed to illustrate the incompatibility of Christianity and heathenism.

TEACHING TIP 2: Have students read 2 Corinthians 6:14-16 and give the five questions listed. Write these on the chalkboard or a blank transparency. Ask the students to give suggestions as to things they face that would compare to the things Paul listed.

It is important to note that Paul was not suggesting that we do not associate with those in the world. How else can we win them if we avoid all contact with them?

The world and Christianity do not share the same values or goals. Trying to blend the two creates a struggle in which Christian values usually come in second. Because of the Holy Spirit's presence in our lives, the conviction He brings when we compromise godly standards produces stress. The only way to alleviate this stress is to ask forgiveness and begin to live by His Word.

NOTES

B. Antidote
2 Corinthians 6:17,18

TEACHING TIP 3: Take the work sheet "The Greatest Sources of Family Stress Are . . ." the students filled out at the beginning of class. Make a list of their suggestions. Be sure to include going into debt, living above one's means, paying bills with tithe money, and buying things the family cannot afford.

One antidote for peer pressure is in 2 Corinthians 6:17. God demands that His people live differently from the ways and desires of the world. If they do, God has promised that He will receive us and be our Father, and we will be His "sons and daughters" (verses 17,18).

If family members will focus their attentions on holy living and the promises of God, negative peer pressure will not have the devastating effect it could have. When we cease trying to be like the world and strive to become more like God, we find a contentment that all the things in the world can never provide.

NOTES

2. Avoid Harmful Addictions

A. What Is Wrong With A Little Wine?
Proverbs 23:31-35

Few things put more stress on a family than a member who is addicted to something. In today's society, even Christian families face this problem.

One of Satan's most deceptive lies is the belief that as long as you do something in moderation, it will not hurt you. An alcoholic may have at one time been a moderate drinker until he became addicted and lost control of his life. The compulsive gambler only wagered a few coins at first. Soon he found himself believing he was only one wager away from the "big win."

There are many forms of addiction. They include gambling, drinking, drugs, pornography, and violence. Each can create a high stress level in a home and potentially destroy the family. The addicted person can make life miserable for everyone.

God's Word provides warnings to help avoid being caught in the trap of addictive habits. The Book of Proverbs addresses the issue of alcohol. We can learn from this passage a lot about how alcoholic addiction occurs. The writer provided a vivid description of a drunkard's sorrows (23:29,30).

Verse 31 warns "Look not upon the wine . . . when it moveth itself aright." The writer pointed out how subtly addiction works. Note the words he used in verse 31 to describe its enticement. Wine "moveth itself aright" (KJV) or "goes down smoothly" (NIV). While one is drinking, it is difficult to comprehend its results. Those who began to drink probably did not intend to become alcoholics. The deception took place with the first drink.

Many alcoholics state that their actions are harmless and innocent; drinking brings them pleasure. But an addicted person is a lot like the plow animals in the early days of farming. The farmer would tie a carrot to a stick and dangle it in front of the plow animal just out of reach. The animal would trudge around the field all day trying to get a bite of that carrot. Addicts believe that one day they will find the satisfaction they desire. It is just one more experience away.

Note in verse 32 the description of the results of drinking—"it biteth like a serpent, and stingeth like an adder." Alcohol causes a person to loose control of his thinking (verse 33). Under its influence, people will do and say things that they would not do or say under normal conditions.

People who drink lose control of their equilibrium (verse 34). They become like sailors staggering around a ship in a storm. They end up in a stupor, like sailors sleeping in a ship's rigging.

Alcohol can become the master of people's lives. Even when exposed to physical pain, their only need is for one more drink (verse 35). It is impossible to measure the negative effects this and other addictions can have on a family. But be sure, these addictions take their toll.

Does this all mean that there is no help for the addict? Of course not. But addicts, whether they are addicted to alcohol, drugs, or other substance or behavior, find it very difficult to admit they have a problem, to themselves or to others. Help is available if they desire it. But they must first be willing to admit their need.

TEACHING TIP 4: Have the students you contacted earlier in the week share their experiences of living with someone who has or had an addiction.

NOTES

B. God's Answer
Ephesians 5:15-18

For the believer, part of resisting those things that cause addiction comes from an understanding of what it means to live a Christian life. In Ephesians 5:15, Paul instructed these believers to "walk circumspectly." The word can also be translated "carefully" or "accurately." Believers are to understand the importance of living a life above reproach. Such understanding will cause us to shun anything that has the potential of controlling our lives.

We are further admonished not to be foolish but to have an understanding of what the will of the Lord is (verse 17). By knowing the will of the Lord, and knowing what pleases God, then and only then, can we carry it out in our lives.

Part of God's will is not to be "drunk with wine" but "be filled with the Spirit" (verse 18). As Spirit-filled believers we are not to be controlled by anything other than the Spirit of God. Taking one drink of alcohol, popping one pill, buying one lottery ticket, or looking at one R- or X-rated film can begin the process of being brought under its control. If we never take that one step, we will never be brought under its control. Then instead of the ridiculous displays of an addicted person, we can experience the abiding presence of the Holy Spirit with its peace, joy, and love.

Adult Teacher Guide

lossians 3:5). An important principle for a happy life is: "Be content with such things as ye have" (Hebrews 13:5).

Ask: "Why is being content so important?" When a person is intent on accumulating possessions, he has switched his focus from the Lord to those possessions. Material possessions cannot provide security. And the acquiring of these possessions can cause financial stress.

Contentment is the solution to greed. But the principle of being content should never be used as an excuse to be lazy and not try to better oneself. Verse 5 is a warning not to be caught up in trying to find security in material possessions. Our security is in the Lord and His presence. He has promised that we can be content because He "will never leave thee, nor forsake thee" (verse 5). That makes Christians the most secure people in the world.

NOTES

3. God Is Our Helper

A. Safeguards Against Family Stress
Hebrews 13:4,5

Many things in our society produce stress on the family. One thing is certain, though, God wants to help families avoid as much stress as possible.

The writer of Hebrews gave us instructions that can help us reduce stress in our lives. These instructions concern developing right priorities by which we live.

Marriage relationships not grounded on biblical principles can be a source of stress. We must remember that "marriage is honorable" (Hebrews 13:4). All parts of marriage are designed by God. This includes an intimate physical relationship between a husband and wife. To violate the marriage relationship with immorality is not only sinful, but also produces stress.

The word translated "whoremongers" is the general word used to describe sexually immoral persons. Not only does adultery ruin the marriage relationship, but pornography can also put undue stress on a marriage. But when the husband and wife develop the close intimate relationship that God designed for marriage, those things that can cause stress are not allowed to take hold.

The writer of this epistle also instructed families not to be consumed with monetary greed. The word translated "conversation" in verse 5 is a word used to describe one's life-style. The life-style of a believer is not to be characterized by covetousness. In other places, covetousness is called idolatry (Co-

B. God Provides Help
Hebrews 13:6

Our families are being threatened with materialism, discontentment, frustrations, and other factors that are bent on destroying families. But we do not have to fear any of these or anything else that society may do to distract and destroy the family. If we establish our families on the Word of God, accept His way for living, and follow His directives for each person, we will not be caught up in the philosophy of this age.

We can have this confidence while living in this present world because God is our "helper" (Hebrews 13:6). We do not have to be afraid. **Ask: "How does God's being our Helper relieve stress in our lives?"**

God is on our side (Romans 8:31). We know that in any circumstance, God is working for our good (verse 28). These facts allow us to rest in Him knowing that He has everything under control. This gives us the confidence we need to live for God in an ungodly world.

NOTES

LIFE RESPONSE

The family unit is very important to God. God designed the family to be a place in which godly values are taught. A family that is not living as God intended cannot pass on the Christian character and values necessary to ensure future generations of dedicated Christians. If the family unit breaks apart because of the stresses of everyday living, many important things are left unattended. This breakdown at the family level can actually cause the Church to become weak and ineffective.

In today's world, families are facing stresses that they have never had to face before. Our families are struggling against some very powerful forces. Peer pressures are creating discontent that lead to growing debts. In addition, addictive habits are invading the family—robbing its life, joy, and influence.

Perhaps your family is going through a time of tremendous stress. Maybe the peer pressure you are facing at work or your children are facing at school seems overwhelming. You might even have a family member addicted to a life-controlling habit. If this is the case, remember: God is your Helper.

God can help you by giving you strength and wisdom. He can also help you train your children to resist being conformed to the values of the world. And He can deliver those who are controlled by habits they cannot break. God is with you and will never forsake you. Ask for His help today.

EVANGELISM OUTREACH

Family stress can have a positive effect. God sometimes uses stressful situations to show people their need for Him. When people cannot solve their own problems, they can then turn to Him for help.

There may be unsaved students in your class this week who are facing stressful situations at home. Some might have life-controlling habits. Emphasize that God will provide the help they need. At the end of class, give them opportunity to accept Christ as their Savior. 📖

I N T R O D U C T I O N

PRINCIPLES OF GODLY LEADERSHIP

Godly leaders are vital to the well-being of any society. These leaders can make the difference in society because their influence has a preserving effect. You may have students in your class that are leaders at work, in your community, or in the church. Some in your class are parents. As such, they have a place of leadership in their family. And as a Sunday School teacher, you are also a leader. This unit, which focuses on the leadership qualities of some of Israel's kings, can be a valuable study for your class.

The power of the Holy Spirit is important in the life of all leaders. Study 1 shows how Peter became a dynamic leader of the Early Church because of his baptism in the Holy Spirit. As leaders today we can have this resource of power for our lives.

Some people have trouble accepting leadership responsibilities. The same God that helped Gideon with his fear (study 2) can gently help us become fearless leaders. Effective leaders are also caring. By studying a portion of David's life (study 3), we can see how we can become a caring leader to those under us.

In addiiton, leaders are called to be faithful. A study of Asa shows how his faithfulness brought spiritual revival to Judah (study 4). In a similar way, Jehoshaphat was steadfast in the midst of a difficult situation. In study 5 you will discover how he depended upon God's wisdom and intervention when facing his enemies. Another quality of godly leadership is good stewardship. Joash (study 6) used good stewardship principles in the rebuilding of the temple.

Sometimes, though, leaders do make unwise decisions. Though the life of Hezekiah (study 7) you will learn the importance of seeking God's wisdom in every decision of life. This unit concludes with a study of King Josiah, the most godly king since David. As he found the truth of God's Word, he brought his nation back to God.

Enriching Teacher-Student Relationships

By James E. Richardson

The friendship between the teacher and his or her students is one of the greatest jobs of teaching. This relationship is not simply desirable; it is imperative. Friendship like this does not happen overnight. It requires time and careful cultivation for it to grow.

How well do you know your students? Are they merely names on a roster, or do you know what makes them cry? Did you know that Joan's 15-month-old has cystic fibrosis and will probably never live to be an adult? Had you heard that John's wife left him because he attends your church? When you know the heartaches of your class members, you can pray for them better and help them more.

Looking at your class roster, do you know what the members do for a living? What about their hobbies? This information can be a great asset in selecting illustrations for the studies. It can also help to build friendships. If you are familiar with their jobs, you can share experiences with them. If you do not know what their work involves, just by asking questions you tell them that you interested in their everyday lives.

Also, don't forget their birthdays and anniversaries. A card with a short personal greeting says, "My teacher is really interested in *me!*

Specifically, what does it take to build this type of relationship? First of all, it requries your genuine concern. You must be willing to share in the lives of your students. This means you laugh with them in their joys, but you also cry with them when they hurt. You go with them to watch their children compete in sports or perform in the school play. You also sit with them all night in the emergency waiting room at the hospital. "That's the pastor's responsiblity," you say? Not if you are genuinely concerned about your students.

Secondly, learn to be an attentive observer and listener. Experts say that as much as 85% of a person's intended message is communicated nonverbally—through gestures, tone of voice, facial expressions, or posture. Listen carefully to what the student says, but pay special attention to his behavior as he speaks. These actions often give your only clue to his burden. Show your concern immediately.

Thirdly, keep the lines of communication open in the classroom. Encourage participation and commend the students for it. Help the ones who are hesitant to participate. Don't force them to respond, but be supportive when they do. Again, this shows your concern for them personally.

The fourth element necessary to building this relationship is authentic Christian love and compassion. Our Lord had compassion on every needy person He saw. He loved each one and reached out to touch the untouchables. As teachers, we must feel and show the same compassion. In our "plastic" age, students are looking for something real and alive. Give them your genuine Christian love and concern.

Finally, a relationship like this will never reach maturity without prayer. Your students should be near the top of your daily prayer list. When particular students come to mind during the week, pray for them immediately. As this becomes part of your daily devotional life, God will begin to show you how better to pray for your class. He will show you specific burdens felt by the students. This, in turn, will increase your concern for them.

How long does it take to build this type of relationship? It varies. It may come quickly or it may take months, even years, to gain the students' confidence. The important thing is to treasure it when it does come. Confidence is the most fragile element in this realtionship. If it is ever betrayed, it may never be restored.

The successful teacher is not the one who simply imparts knowledge. He is the one who gives himself to his students as a Christian example, a concerned friend, and a trustworthy confidant.

"Teacher Growth Series" brings you information on every phase of your teaching ministry. Three articles per quarter can be read, shared with other teachers, and filed for future reference. Articles dealing with the same topics are presented at each age level from early childhood through adult. The "Teacher Growth Series" covers 36 different topics.

"Forget Not My Laws"

By Janet M. Harp

As a teacher, one of your biggest challenges is to inspire your students to delve into the treasure of God's Word. This involves not only reading the Bible, but committing portions of Scripture to memory as commanded in Proverbs 3:1. Here are some practical suggestions:

Devotions. The ideal time to begin Scripture memorization is during daily devotions. Suggest to your students that they select one verse from their daily Scripture reading to memorize and meditate on throughout the entire day. Some people find it helpful to print that verse on a 3 X 5 index card to refer to periodically as they go about their daily activities. Let each individual decide which verse and how many verses he or she wants to memorize.

Goals. Encourage your students to set realistic yet challenging goals for memorization. For one student, a verse each day is a realistic goal. For another, the goal might be two verses per week. The important principle to remember is that the goal is not to memorize a certain number of verses, but to commit the Word to memory whatever the amount may be.

Selection. Although each person should decide which verses to memorize, you can offer suggestions from these areas:

(1) Spiritual principles and guidelines: Psalm 55:22; Romans 10:9,10; Galatians 5:14,22; Ephesians 4:32; 5:18,19; 1 Timothy 6:6; 2 Timothy 2:15; James 1:22.

(2) Faith-building: Romans 10:17; 2 Corinthians 5:17; Ephesians 6:12; Philippians 4:13,19; Hebrews 13:8.

(3) Comfort and hope: Matthew 28:20; Ephesians 3:20; Philippians 4:7; Hebrews 4:16; 1 Peter 5:7.

(4) Victory: 1 Corinthians 15:54-57; Philippians 3:14; Colossians 2:10; 2 Timothy 1:7; James 4:7; 1 John 5:4.

Special Seasons. The Christmas and Easter holidays offer special opportunities to memorize Scripture central to those themes.

Family Time. The entire family can benefit from memorizing Scripture. By promoting it as a family venture, each member can encourage and assist the others.

How To. The technique for memorization is as varied as each individual. Some people memorize easily. For others the effort is much more difficult. Many people find that writing a Scripture repeatedly assists in memorization. Others find it helpful to read a Scripture aloud several times until they have it memorized, and some are able to memorize by listening to a text read by someone else.

Scripture Choruses. Your class might be encouraged to know how much Scripture they have already committed to memory. Ask how many know the chorus, "This Is The Day," and them remind them the chorus is Psalm 118:24 set to music. Here are some other well-known choruses your students can learn: "I Am Crucified With Christ" (Galatians 2:20), "I Will Enter His Gates" (Psalms 100:4), "Come Bless The Lord" (Psalm 134:1,2), "Bless His Holy Name" (Psalm 103:1), "Thou Art Worthy" (Revelation 4:10,11), "Beloved, Let Us Love One Another" (1 John 4:7,8).

These choruses are available from the Gospel Publishing House publication *Choruses And Scripture Songs*, order number 05-0444.

Testimonials. Encourage your students to testify about the benefits they have received from memorizing God's Word. The Scripture from Hebrews 13:8, "Jesus Christ the same yesterday, and today, and for ever" has been a source of strength and hope for many in time of need.

Also by committing certain Scriptures to memory, witnessing to unbelievers is easier. Instead of vague rendition, the believer can quote appropriate portions of Scripture with authority.

You First. Your students will follow your example more than any words you can speak. As you commit Scripture to memory and quote it appropriately, testify of its power, and live out its benefits in your own life, you will become a visible and forceful illustration to your class.

"Teacher Growth Series" brings you information on every phase of your teaching ministry. Three articles per quarter can be read, shared with other teachers, and filed for future reference. Articles dealing with the same topics are presented at each age level from early childhood through adult. The "Teacher Growth Series" covers 36 different topics.

TGS 11: Memorizing Scripture

TEACHER GROWTH SERIES

By John T. Maempa

Tools For Teaching

What do a mechanic, carpenter, surgeon, and electrician have in common? Their occupations differ greatly, but each depends heavily on tools and instruments to do his job. In order to be experts, they must know their tools well and how to use them.

As a Sunday School teacher, you are engaged in one of the most important ministries in the church. It is your task to help bring about spiritual understanding and changed lives as you present the truths of God's Word each week. To accomplish that weighty task effectively, you need tools that will help you communicate truth and relate it meaningfully to everyday life.

It can be said that a practitioner in any field is only as good as his tools. Professionals choose only the best. So should the Christian educator.

Radiant Life adult curriculum provides the kind of tools that make effective Christian education possible. Your task is to know what these tools are and how to use them.

God's Word

Heading the list of tools is, of course, God's Word. Your Bible ought to be the major instrument in your teaching ministry. Study it thoroughly even before concentrating on the quarterly materials.

Use the Bible in class. Give students an opportunity to read passages aloud and research important truths and concepts. God's Word must always be central in the Christian education process.

Adult Teacher Guide

At the core of every curriculum is a teacher's guide. This is the essential foundational tool designed to provide an organized and structured approach to Bible study. The *Adult Teacher Guide* features a flexible format that permits either a lecture approach or the use of a variety of methodologies that involve the students more directly in the learning process.

Perhaps not every question, teaching tip, or life application can be referred to in a given lesson. However, an effort should be made to select the kind of presentations and methodologies that will convey truth to your students most effectively.

Adult Teaching Helps Packet

Woven into the *Adult Teacher Guide* study structure is a wide variety of supplemental teaching helps found in the Adult Teaching Helps Packet. This is the primary resource for developing innovative study presentations.

The Adult Teaching Helps Packet contains overhead transparencies, work sheets, information sheets, case studies, and posters for use at various times throughout the quarter. An instruction folder describes the packet's contents and provides information on when and how each item is to be used. All packet materials are closely correlated with the *Adult Teacher Guide*.

Several work sheets and general information sheets are designed for duplication and distribution. These involve the students in inductive Bible study and research, question/answer interaction, and other involvement activities. Use these to add interest and reinforcement to each Bible study.

Overhead transparencies generally serve to highlight key facts and concepts in selected Bible studies. If an overhead projector is not available, the information may be written on a chalkboard or poster. Or, by placing a white sheet behind a transparency, you may duplicate it and hand it out as an information sheet to the students.

As you plan your studies, give careful attention to references to the Adult Teaching Helps Packet in the *Adult Teacher Guide.* Plan to incorporate these methodologies to help make Bible study come alive for you and your students.

The Bible, the *Adult Teacher Guide*, and the Adult Teaching Helps Packet are precision tools that will help you communicate life-changing truth effectively each week. Become thoroughly familiar with their design and purpose and learn to use them well.

Pentecostal Power

CENTRAL TRUTH

The Holy Spirit empowers believers for effective service.

GOLDEN TEXT

But you will receive power when the Holy Spirit comes on you. Acts 1:8 (NIV)

STUDY TEXT

Joel 2:32; Acts 1:1-8; 2:1-41

OUTLINE

1. Power Promised
   A. Command To Wait
   B. Power To Witness

2. Power Received
   A. Wind And Fire
   B. A Special Sign

3. Power Misunderstood
   A. Jews From Every Nation
   B. Perplexity Abounds

4. Power For Salvation
   A. Powerful Preaching
   B. Many Saved

OBJECTIVE

To appreciate the power of the Holy Spirit and receive His power in our lives.

CHECKLIST

☐ Read the *Adult Student Guide* noting any questions you would like to use for discussion.

☐ Using a copy of the Planning The Session sheet from the teaching helps packet, plan the most effective use of class time.

☐ Familiarize yourself with the overhead transparencies "Jews From Every Nation" and "Essentials Of The Apostle's Preaching." The first transparency shows possible locations for the spread of the gospel as these Spirit-filled Jews returned to their home cities. The second outlines Peter's sermon on the Day of Pentecost.

☐ Pray for God's help as you teach this important study. Encourage those in your class who have never received the baptism in the Holy Spirit to begin to seek for this gift from God. Offer to pray for those students who desire this empowering in their lives.

DAILY BIBLE READINGS

Monday:	Power At Creation.	Genesis 1:1-10
Tuesday:	Power For Service.	Exodus 31:1-11
Wednesday:	Power Of Wisdom.	Proverbs 9:1-10
Thursday:	Power Upon Christ.	Matthew 3:13-17
Friday:	Power For Praise.	Luke 1:67-75
Saturday:	Powerful Presence.	John 14:15-27

King James Version

Acts 1:5. John truly baptized with water; but ye shall be baptized with the Holy Ghost not many days hence.

6. When they therefore were come together, they asked of him, saying, Lord, wilt thou at this time restore again the kingdom to Israel?

7. And he said unto them, It is not for you to know the times or the seasons, which the Father hath put in his own power.

8. But ye shall receive power, after that the Holy Ghost is come upon you: and ye shall be witnesses unto me both in Jerusalem, and in all Judea, and in Samaria, and unto the uttermost part of the earth.

2:1. When the day of Pentecost was fully come, they were all with one accord in one place.

2. And suddenly there came a sound from heaven as of a rushing mighty wind, and it filled all the house where they were sitting.

3. And there appeared unto them cloven tongues like as of fire, and it sat upon each of them.

4. And they were all filled with the Holy Ghost, and began to speak with other tongues, as the Spirit gave them utterance.

13. Others mocking said, These men are full of new wine.

14. But Peter, standing up with the eleven, lifted up his voice, and said unto them, Ye men of Judea, and all ye that dwell at Jerusalem, be this known unto you, and hearken to my words:

15. For these are not drunken, as ye suppose, seeing it is but the third hour of the day.

16. But this is that which was spoken by the prophet Joel.

21. And it shall come to pass, that whosoever shall call on the name of the Lord shall be saved.

40. And with many other words did he testify and exhort, saying, save yourselves from this untoward generation.

41. Then they gladly received his word and were baptized: and the same day there were added unto them about three thousand souls.

New International Version

Acts 1:5. "John baptized with water, but in a few days you will be baptized with the Holy Spirit."

6. So when they met together, they asked him, "Lord, are you at this time going to restore the kingdom to Israel?"

7. He said to them: "It is not for you to know the times or dates the Father has set by his own authority.

8. But you will receive power when the Holy Spirit comes on you; and you will be my witnesses in Jerusalem, and in all Judea and Samaria, and to the ends of the earth."

2:1. When the day of Pentecost came, they were all together in one place.

2. Suddenly a sound like the blowing of a violent wind came from heaven and filled the whole house where they were sitting.

3. They saw what seemed to be tongues of fire that separated and came to rest on each of them.

4. All of them were filled with the Holy Spirit and began to speak in other tongues as the Spirit enabled them.

13. Some, however, made fun of them and said, "They have had too much wine."

14. Then Peter stood up with the Eleven, raised his voice and addressed the crowd: "Fellow Jews and all of you who live in Jerusalem, let me explain this to you; listen carefully to what I say.

15. These men are not drunk, as you suppose. It's only nine in the morning!

16. No, this is what was spoken by the prophet Joel.

21. " 'And everyone who calls on the name of the Lord will be saved.' "

40. With many other words he warned them; and he pleaded with them, "Save yourselves from this corrupt generation."

41. Those who accepted his message were baptized, and about three thousand were added to their number that day.

After witnessing their Lord's ascension into heaven, the disciples gathered together to await the promised empowering from on high. In just a few days they would receive the baptism in the Holy Spirit. This experience would change them and the entire world.

This same experience is available to believers in every generation. Pentecost, which brought great power and spiritual vitality to the Early Church, is intended for Christians today.

Believers will always need God's power in order to be effective witnesses. As long as the Church is in existence, God will continue to pour out His power through His Holy Spirit. As believers seek after and receive the empowering of the Spirit, they will be victorious in proclaiming the gospel to a hostile world.

BIBLE COMMENTARY

1. Power Promised

A. Command To Wait
Acts 1:1-5

The events of the Crucifixion and Resurrection had passed. The disciples, who had scattered before Christ's crucifixion, were now together again. For 40 days they had been with Jesus and understood that He was the Messiah (Acts 1:3). Then, just before He ascended into heaven, Jesus told His disciples to wait for the promise of the Father—the baptism in the Holy Spirit.

The expression "the promise of the Father" (verse 4) was referred to by Jesus in His teaching to the disciples in John 14-16. It was also referred to by John the Baptist when he proclaimed the coming Messiah (Mark 1:6-8). Jesus knew His disciples were going to need the power of the Holy Spirit. To try to minister without this power would bring failure to their efforts.

This command to wait was open-ended. There was no definite date or time set for the Holy Spirit's appearance. The disciples were to wait until the promise was fulfilled.

TEACHING TIP 1: Stress the relationship between our sense of need for the Spirit's enablement and our earnest desire for Him on the one hand and the response of God in baptizing us in the Holy Spirit on the other.

Ask: **"Why do you think desire is a prerequisite for receiving the baptism in the Holy Spirit?"** To receive the baptism in the Holy Spirit requires more than a superficial desire on our part. God is looking for more than the curious. He will fill all who seriously seek Him.

NOTES

B. Power To Witness
Acts 1:6-8

Jesus' followers still entertained the hope of seeing His kingdom's immediate physical establishment (Acts 1:6). Jesus indicated that knowing the time of His kingdom was not of supreme importance (verse 7).

Rather than receiving political power, the disciples were to be clothed with the divine power that would accompany the baptism in the Holy Spirit (verse 8).

This power was precisely what the disciples needed. It would enable them to be His witnesses. The power would make their preaching powerful. In addition, their ministries would be accompanied with signs and wonders.

The last words of Jesus recorded in Acts prior to His ascension indicate that the witness of His disciples was to go to the "uttermost part of the earth" (verse 8). This mission still continues. The gospel has yet to be proclaimed in every part of today's world. There are many people in distant lands that are still unreached. Many of our family members and next door neighbors need to hear a clear presentation of the gospel. We need the power to witness just as much today. The same power has been promised to us. We must seek God for His power with the same zeal that was evident among the first believers, that others may know salvation.

NOTES

2. Power Received

A. Wind And Fire
Acts 2:1-3

The Day of Pentecost dawned 10 days after the ascension of Christ (Acts 2:1). On this day the 120 believers were gathered together, possibly in the temple courts. God chose this occasion to pour out His Holy Spirit upon His Church.

Ask: "Why did God use the signs of wind and fire to indicate the coming of the Holy Spirit?" The arrival of the Holy

Spirit was accompanied by what sounded like a "rushing mighty wind" and what appeared to be "cloven tongues of fire" (verse 2). These symbols speak of the Spirit's power and presence.

The Old Testament contains examples of wind as a manifestation of God's power. God used a powerful wind to part the Red Sea, enabling the Children of Israel to cross over (Exodus 14:21,22). Wind, as the breath of God, blew on dry bones and they came to life (Ezekiel 37:9,10). Fire was also seen as a sign of divine presence in the account of the burning bush (Exodus 3:2) and God's appearance in fire on Mount Sinai (Exodus 19:16-20).

These believers would have recognized these signs as symbols of the Holy Spirit. There could be no doubt in their minds that the Spirit had indeed come upon them.

NOTES

B. Special Sign
Acts 2:4

The sound like the wind and what appeared to be "tongues of fire" were not the only manifestations that accompanied the Holy Spirit's coming at Pentecost. Verse 4 declares that they all began speaking with other tongues as the Spirit "gave them utterance."

While the first two signs only occurred at Pentecost, speaking in tongues is specifically mentioned in later occasions of the baptism in the Holy Spirit (see Acts 10:44-47 and Acts 19:1-7). In addition, speaking in tongues was the likely manifestation on two other occasions when people were baptized in the Spirit. In Acts 8:17,18 tongues are not specifically mentioned, but there was clearly an impressive physical sign involved. Also, when Saul was filled with the Spirit, nothing is stated about his speaking in tongues. But Paul later gave testimony that he did speak with tongues (1 Corinthians 14:18).

This special sign is evident today. Tens of millions of believers worldwide have received the baptism in the Spirit with the initial physical evidence of speaking with other tongues. Both the experiences recorded in the Book of Acts and the experiences of people today point to tongues as the initial physical evidence of the Holy Spirit's baptism.

TEACHING TIP 2: Encourage students in your class to pursue the baptism in the Holy Spirit. Stress the proper motivation in seeking the baptism—the believer's need for divine power for evangelism. Also emphasize the purpose of the initial evidence of speaking with tongues: God wants us to know assuredly that He has answered our earnest desire.

NOTES

3. Power Misunderstood

A. Jews From Every Nation
Acts 2:5-11

On the Day of Pentecost, Jerusalem would have been filled with Jews who had been dispersed to other parts of the Roman Empire. Some scholars estimate that there were over 4 million Jews dispersed throughout the ancient world. From these places great numbers of Jews would gather at Jerusalem

for the three great Jewish feasts—Passover, Pentecost, and Tabernacles. Luke stated that "Jews . . . out of every nation under heaven" (verse 5) witnessed the outpouring of the Holy Spirit upon these 120 believers. He then lists 15 different nations and provinces from which the Jews had come.

TEACHING TIP 3: Display Overhead Transparency 1 "Jews From Every Nation." Point out the distances which the dispersed Jews had to travel to come to Jerusalem for these festivals. Also point out the important part these Jews had in spreading the gospel as they responded to the gospel, were filled with the Spirit, and then returned home after this festival.

As the results of the coming of the Spirit upon these 120 believers were "noised abroad," a large crowd gathered providing an audience for the great miracle of the Holy Spirit's advent. Words cannot fully describe the amazing sight witnessed by the multitude assembled. They heard in their own language and dialects "the wonderful works of God" (verse 11).

Some have mistakenly believed that tongues were used to proclaim the gospel. While the evidence of speaking in tongues is not normally used to proclaim the gospel, God did use this sign to show His power and to get the attention of the multitude. Note that Peter later preached in a language that the whole crowd could understand (probably Aramaic).

NOTES

B. Perplexity Abounds
Acts 2:12,13

Luke records the initial reaction of those present on this occasion. Verse 12 indicates there was genuine amazement on the part of some and they asked, "What meaneth this?" They realized they were witnessing a miracle. The fact they asked this question shows that God had accomplished what He had set out to do. The stage was set for Peter to stand up and give the answer.

Others in the crowd reacted in the opposite manner. They assumed that the disciples had been drinking too much wine, and the crowd began to mock them. People today respond in essentially the same way concerning the Pentecostal experience. They ask, "What does this mean?" or "What is the purpose of speaking in other tongues?" While some mock, others genuinely want to know about the baptism in the Holy Spirit. Their interest has been aroused and they sincerely look for answers.

NOTES

4. Power For Salvation

A. Powerful Preaching
Acts 2:14-16,21

Peter's answer to the question, "What meaneth this?" was clear and emphatic. These 120 believers were not drunk. It was only 9 a.m. But what was happening was "that which was spoken by the prophet Joel" (verse 16). "The last days," which were to be characterized by the outpouring of the Holy Spirit upon God's people, had finally begun (verses 17,18). And these people were witnesses of this event.

Ask: "What was the content of the message Peter preached to this crowd?"

TEACHING TIP 4: Place Overhead Transparency 2, "Essentials Of The Apostle's Preaching" on the overhead projector, but cover it with a piece of paper. Have the students scan Acts 2:14-36. As they note specific statements, words, and phrases that made Peter's presentation of the gospel powerful, reveal the items the students point out. Stress the importance of each of these essentials if our witness is to be effective.

Peter's Spirit-empowered proclamation of the gospel was the second great miracle of Pentecost. This miracle demonstrates the true purpose of Pentecost. The same disciple who wavered before a servant girl in the courtyard of the high priest, was now powerfully proclaiming to the Jews the truth concerning Jesus and the need for them to repent. There was no hesitancy or vagueness in his words. Peter preached with power and clarity. This same power must be demonstrated in our lives if God's message is to be effectively preached in today's world.

NOTES

B. Many Saved
Acts 2:40,41

The powerful preaching of Peter had great impact on those who heard it. The same Holy Spirit who empowered Peter brought conviction to the multitude (verse 37).

Conviction of sin can only be accomplished by the Holy Spirit. Jesus said that when the Spirit came, He would convict the world of sin, righteousness, and judgment (John 16:8). People cannot be convinced of their need of God by human persuasion. The Holy Spirit is the Great Persuader.

Not all of Peter's message is recorded (Acts 2:40), but verse 41 gives the results—approximately 3,000 received Peter's message and were baptized. Unquestionably, the anointing of the Spirit cannot be measured merely by the number of people saved. But without His anointing, God's purposes cannot be effectively achieved.

The tremendous evangelistic success of Pentecost did not end on that day. The Book of Acts details the continued powerful proclamation of God's Word in Jerusalem, and the beginning of a missionary thrust that eventually took the gospel throughout the Roman Empire. Success occurred because men were filled with the power of God and were burdened to declare the message of life. This same power and burden in our lives will enable us to reach our communities, cities, nation, and world for Christ today.

NOTES

LIFE RESPONSE

The Pentecostal Movement has left an indelible imprint on the missionary accomplishments of the 20th century Church. Yet today's challenges cannot be met by yesterday's achievements. Believers must call upon God for a fresh empowering of the Holy Spirit.

The Early Church was wise enough to see its inability to adequately accomplish the task of evangelism without divine power. Thus they were obedient to Christ's command and waited for the promised Holy Spirit. Their obedience was rewarded by God. Signs and wonders followed their bold preaching of the gospel.

Today's Church must have the same realization as the Early Church. It is essential that we recognize our need for dependence on God. As the 120 waited with expectancy for power from on high, so must we.

The early pioneers of the Pentecostal Movement in this century understood this need for God's power. Their prayer meetings were characterized by passionate praying. They understood that God was a rewarder of those who diligently seek Him (Hebrews 11:6).

Until Jesus returns, God is still pouring out His Holy Spirit upon "all flesh." The baptism in the Holy Spirit is available to all who have accepted Christ as their Savior. God desires to give you this empowering for service (Luke 11:11-13). Ask Him today to fill you with His Holy Spirit. The same Holy Spirit that empowered the Early Church will empower you.

EVANGELISM OUTREACH

The baptism in the Holy Spirit is only available to those who have received Christ as Savior. But the same Spirit that empowers believers convicts unbelievers of sin. There may be some in your class who do not know Jesus as Lord and Savior. Remind them of Peter's words in Acts 2:21. All who call upon His name for forgiveness will be saved. Offer to pray with those who desire personal salvation. ⌐⌐

Accepting God's Call To Service (Gideon)

CENTRAL TRUTH

Leaders who obey God's call trust in Him for wisdom and victory.

GOLDEN TEXT

The Lord is with you, mighty warrior. Judges 6:12 (NIV)

STUDY TEXT

Judges 6:1 through 7:25

OUTLINE

1. God Calls To Service
   A. Angelic Messenger
   B. Unlikely Instrument

2. God Confirms His Call
   A. Empowered By The Spirit
   B. Seeking Reassurance

3. Obedience Brings Victory
   A. Encouraged By God
   B. God-Given Strategy

OBJECTIVE

To understand that God calls ordinary people to leadership and commit ourselves to accept His call.

CHECKLIST

☐ Fill out the Planning The Session sheet making sure to plan enough time for each segment of this week's study.

☐ Read through the study text several times. This will help in your presentation.

☐ Before beginning this unit of study, read both the student and teacher quarterlies in their entirety. This will help you keep succeeding studies in view as you teach each one.

☐ Display the poster "Have You Answered God's Call?" from the *Adult Teaching Helps Packet*. Leave it in place throughout this unit. From time to time call the students' attention to it and remind them this call includes every believer.

DAILY BIBLE READINGS

Monday:	Called To A New Land.	Genesis 12:1-9
Tuesday:	Called From Bondage.	Exodus 12:31-42
Wednesday:	Hearing God's Call.	1 Samuel 3:7-14
Thursday:	Rejecting The Call.	Mark 10:17-22
Friday:	Following Christ.	Luke 5:1-11
Saturday:	Obeying The Call.	Acts 9:10-20

Scripture Setting

King James Version

Judges 6:11. There came an angel of the Lord, and sat under an oak which was in Ophrah, that pertained unto Joash the Abiezrite: and his son Gideon threshed wheat by the winepress, to hide it from the Midianites.

14. And the Lord looked upon him, and said, Go in this thy might, and thou shalt save Israel from the hand of the Midianites: have not I sent thee?

15. And he said unto him, Oh my Lord, wherewith shall I save Israel? behold, my family is poor in Manasseh, and I am the least in my father's house.

16. And the Lord said unto him, Surely I will be with thee, and thou shalt smite the Midianites as one man.

36. And Gideon said unto God, If thou wilt save Israel by mine hand, as thou hast said,

37. Behold, I will put a fleece of wool in the floor; and if the dew be on the fleece only, and it be dry upon all the earth besides, then shall I know that thou wilt save Israel by mine hand, as thou hast said.

38. And it was so: for he rose up early on the morrow, and thrust the fleece together, and wringed the dew out of the fleece, a bowl full of water.

7:16. And he divided the three hundred men into three companies, and he put a trumpet in every man's hand, with empty pitchers, and lamps within the pitchers.

17. And he said unto them, Look on me, and do likewise: and, behold, when I come to the outside of the camp, it shall be that, as I do, so shall ye do.

18. When I blow with a trumpet, I and all that are with me, then blow ye the trumpets also on every side of all the camp, and say, The sword of the Lord, and of Gideon.

19. So Gideon, and the hundred men that were with him, came unto the outside of the camp in the beginning of the middle watch; and they had but newly set the watch: and they blew the trumpets, and brake the pitchers that were in their hands.

21. And they stood every man in his place round about the camp: and all the host ran, and cried, and fled.

22. And the three hundred blew the trumpets, and the Lord set every man's sword against his fellow, even throughout all the host: and the host fled to Beth—shittah in Zererath, and to the border of Abel—meholah, unto Tabbath.

New International Version

Judges 6:11. The angel of the Lord came and sat down under the oak in Ophrah that belonged to Joash the Abiezrite, where his son Gideon was threshing wheat in a winepress to keep it from the Midianites.

14. The Lord turned to him and said, "Go in the strength you have and save Israel out of Midian's hand. Am I not sending you?"

15. "But Lord," Gideon asked, "how can I save Israel? My clan is the weakest in Manasseh, and I am the least in my family."

16. The Lord answered, "I will be with you, and you will strike down all the Midianites together."

36. Gideon said to God, "If you will save Israel by my hand as you have promised—

37. Look, I will place a wool fleece on the threshing floor. If there is dew only on the fleece and all the ground is dry, then I will know that you will save Israel by my hand, as you said."

38. And that is what happened. Gideon rose early the next day; he squeezed the fleece and wrung out the dew—a bowlful of water.

7:16. Dividing the three hundred men into three companies, he placed trumpets and empty jars in the hands of all of them, with torches inside.

17. "Watch me," he told them. "Follow my lead. When I get to the edge of the camp, do exactly as I do.

18. When I and all who are with me blow our trumpets, then from all around the camp blow yours and shout, 'For the Lord and for Gideon.' "

19. Gideon and the hundred men with him reached the edge of the camp at the beginning of the middle watch, just after they had changed the guard. They blew their trumpets and broke the jars that were in their hands.

21. While each man held his position around the camp, all the Midianites ran, crying out as they fled.

22. When the three hundred trumpets sounded, the Lord caused the men throughout the camp to turn on each other with their swords. The army fled to Beth Shittah toward Zererah as far as the border of Abel Meholah near Tabbath.

God often used heathen nations to punish Israel when God's people sinned. This time the enemy was Midian. Militarily there was no way the Israelites could deal with the situation. Furthermore, the Midianites constantly destroyed Israel's crops. It is difficult for people to resist when they are starving and impoverished.

In the account of Gideon, we see a scenario repeated often during Israel's history. When the pressure became unbearable, the Israelites would cry to God and He would answer. This time God chose an unlikely individual named Gideon to be Israel's deliverer. There was nothing outstanding about his background, nothing to suggest the role in which God would use Him. Gideon is an encouragement to all of us "ordinary" folk who feel we are not talented enough to be of value in God's work.

BIBLE COMMENTARY

1. God Calls To Service

A. Angelic Messenger
Judges 6:11-13

The Midianites had oppressed Israel for 7 years. Each year at harvest they came in like a hoard of locusts and consumed all of Israel's crops. Thus when the angel appeared, Gideon was hiding in a winepress threshing wheat.

Ordinarily, wheat would have been threshed in the open so the wind could carry away the chaff. It would be difficult to thresh grain in a winepress. But Gideon could not afford to let the Midianites see him. They would have quickly seized his wheat.

God's people had cried to God for deliverance (Judges 6:7). In answer, God sent an angel to Gideon (verses 11,12). Many believe this angel was Jesus Christ in one of His Old Testament appearances as the Angel of the Lord (see verse 14). What is important, though, is the message he brought. God had heard and had chosen Gideon as His instrument of deliverance.

Gideon must have been startled to be addressed as a "mighty man of valor" (verse 12). He certainly did not feel like one and immediately expressed his discouragement at his people's plight (verse 13).

Ask: "Did Gideon's complaint indicate cynical unbelief?" There is a difference between honest doubt and callous skepticism. Undoubtedly Gideon was only repeating what many of his fellow Israelites were saying. They had heard of God's deliverance of His people from Egypt. Why was not God doing something about Israel's oppression by the Midianites? Have we ever asked similar questions?

NOTES

B. An Unlikely Instrument
Judges 6:14-16

It is significant that the angel did not rebuke Gideon for his question. His response was a command: "Go in this thy might" (verse 14). This expression meant that instead of lamenting he was not braver and stronger, Gideon should use the strength he did possess to answer God's commission. It is human to lament, "If only I had this or that, I could really accomplish so much." What we must do is use what we have in obedience to God and He will multiply it.

Ask: "Were Gideon's statements about himself and his family in verse 15 an attempt to evade God's commission?" His remarks do not seem to indicate false humility. He did not come from a prominent family, as he undoubtedly felt would be the qualification for a leader. Who would listen to a "nobody" like him? The expression, "least," apparently meant that even in an insignificant family he was the most unlikely to command a following. It could also have meant he was the youngest. Regardless, Gideon could not see himself as a mighty warrior and leader. Is this not an example of how God sees the potential in His people of which even they are unaware?

Often in the Bible and in church history God has chosen unlikely instruments to show what His power can accomplish even when natural attributes seem to be lacking. This should be an encouragement to all of us.

In verse 16 note the words, "I" and "thou." There are always two sides to God's call—His power and the individual's response. "I will be with thee" was all the authority Gideon needed. He was not marching under his own orders, but God's. Yet it was Gideon's hand that would smite the enemy. This is an example of God and man working together. God calls and equips His servants, and His servants yield themselves for the Lord's use. That is how God's work has always been done.

Ask: "What characteristics did Gideon possess which might account for God's choice of him as Israel's deliverer?"

TEACHING TIP 1: Lead a discussion based on the characteristics that Gideon displayed, both positive and negative. After listing these on the chalkboard or a blank transparency, have the students suggest which ones can apply to their own lives.

NOTES

2. God Confirms His Call

A. Empowered By The Spirit
Judges 6:34,35

The nature of Gideon's leadership is seen in the words, "The Spirit of the Lord came upon Gideon" (Judges 6:34). This would make the difference between success and failure. Gideon could not go in his own strength. He could not depend on his human capabilities, even though he was expected to use them to the fullest extent. Gideon was anointed and empowered by the Spirit of God. God can do great things through a person yielded to Him, even if that individual is lacking in qualities the world considers important.

Gideon began to gather men for the challenge. This hardly seems like the man hiding timidly while doing his threshing and questioning whether God was still with His people. The coming of the Spirit of God upon Gideon transformed him. There seems to be no delay between the call of God and these first steps to answer that call.

It must have encouraged Gideon to have the men from his hometown be the first to answer the summons. His own tribe, Manasseh, also rallied to him quickly, along with men from the tribes of Asher, Zebulun, and Naphtali.

Ask: "What does the quick response of these people to Gideon's call indicate?"

The response of these four northern tribes demonstrates the evidence of the Spirit's anointing on Gideon for this task. It is doubtful that Gideon could have succeeded in raising an army before the Spirit of God came upon him. His fellow Israelites sensed that God had raised him up as the deliverer they had prayed for.

NOTES

B. Seeking Reassurance
Judges 6:36-40

The timidity in Gideon's nature showed itself again. Although he was successful in gathering an army, an "if" began to fill his mind (verse 36). Even great men who seem to be fearless and full of confidence have their moments of doubt. People in the Bible really were human. And just like people today, they were subject to the same shortcomings and needed God's help. In the account of Gideon, we can see how patient the Lord is with His children when they wrestle with fears and misgivings.

Ask: "What might have been a source of hesitation on Gideon's part?" It seems strange that he would have doubts when he knew that God had promised to use him as Israel's deliverer (verse 36). Obviously Gideon did not have a great deal of confidence in himself or the call of God on his life. Even though he had heard God's promise, it is likely that he still could not quite believe that God could use him. None of us are immune to times when we are discouraged by our own frailties. God understands and can use people who are humbled by their weakness better than those who are so self-assured they do not feel they need His help. Yet it is better to wait until we

are assured of what God called us to do, rather than plunging recklessly ahead in a battle we are unprepared to fight. God did not reprove Gideon for his cautious approach.

Gideon's use of a fleece to confirm God's will is quite familiar to many people today. We have often heard of "putting out a fleece" when there is uncertainty about a course of action.

In the account, Gideon first asked that if he had understood the Lord correctly, then a fleece he put on the ground would be wet in the morning while the ground around it would be dry. God's answer was emphatic. The fleece was so wet that Gideon wrung out a bowlful of water from it.

We can admire Gideon for not being so impulsive that he rushed off to his task immediately without considering all the implications. Apparently it occurred to him that a wet fleece and dry ground was not so unusual after all. The fleece would absorb moisture more quickly than the threshing floor and would not dry nearly so fast. A real miracle would be for the fleece to be dry while the ground was wet.

Gideon decided to use the fleece method once more, although verse 39 indicates he feared he might be on the verge of incurring God's displeasure. Nevertheless, he asked for one more confirmation and God graciously answered. In the morning, the fleece was dry while the ground was wet. The writer of the Scripture wanted it clearly understood this was no mere coincidence, for he wrote that "God did so that night" (verse 40). God understands human frailty and accommodated Gideon's desire for added assurance.

When God uses human beings, He knows He is not dealing with perfection. How patient He is with our fears and questions. When the victory over Midian was won, there would be no question about Who brought it about.

TEACHING TIP 2: Discuss with the class the modern use of "fleeces" using the following questions:

Adult Teacher Guide

The gifts of the Spirit are available among God's people to confirm His working among us. We must also remember that we have God's Word and His Holy Spirit to help us know His will. To use a fleece as a delay tactic or an excuse not to obey God is wrong.

NOTES

3. Obedience Brings Victory

A. Encouraged By God
Judges 7:15

At God's instructions Gideon slipped to the outer edge of the enemy's camp at night. He overheard two soldiers talking about a strange dream one of them had. In the dream, a loaf of barley bread come rolling through the Midianite camp, knocking down every tent. The other soldier immediately realized this was a warning that the Israelites would defeat them (Judges 7:13,14). This was another way God encouraged Gideon. The dream of the barley loaf showed how God could use the seemingly weak and insignificant to overcome the mighty. When Gideon returned to his men there was no hesitation or timidity. He had heard from God and he knew victory was certain.

Ask: "What do we observe about Gideon's attitude from his statement in verse 15?" Notice Gideon's words: "The Lord hath delivered into your hand the host of Midian." There was no feeling of self-exaltation or desire to take personal credit. The victory would be God's as Gideon followed His orders carefully.

To serve the Lord expecting the applause from people or some kind of remuneration is not the proper motivation for serving Him. We may receive recognition from others, but it must not be the basis of our service. We would do well to heed Paul's admonition to servants in Colossians 3:22-24. Our service must be done with the attitude of pleasing the Lord. After all, the Lord Christ is the One we serve.

NOTES

B. God-Given Strategy
Judges 7:16-22

There can be no question that Gideon's battle strategy came from the Lord. It is a classic example of God's using weak things to confound the mighty (1 Corinthians 1:27). Gideon and his men attacked during the night (between 10 p.m. and midnight) when most of the enemy was asleep. Dividing the 300 into 3 companies made the Midianites think they were surrounded by a huge force.

Generally only leaders carried the rams horns. Thus the sound of 300 horns sounding gave the illusion of a very large army. Adding to the Midianites confusion was the sound of shattering clay jars, the many torches, and the battle cry, "The sword of the Lord, and of Gideon" (verse 18). While the Midianites were trying to collect their senses, they saw themselves surrounded by the lights from 300 torches. It is no wonder they grew so confused that they began to lash out at every figure in the darkness, killing one another by the thousands. What a victory!

NOTES

LIFE RESPONSE

Often when Christians are called on to take a place of leadership, they respond with excuses like "I do not feel worthy" or "I do not have the ability." Then they excuse themselves from any kind of Christian service.

Why did God choose a timid, self-effacing individual who seemed to have no outward qualification for such a task as delivering Israel? The Lord often uses people who do have talents and abilities. When these are yielded to Him, He can use them to accomplish great things. However, there are occasions when God wants to remind us that human skill apart from Him will never be enough. Throughout the Bible and church history, He has frequently used human instruments that others would have passed by.

If we sometimes have doubts and fears about the task to which God has called us, we should remember Gideon. He was a person who appeared to need frequent reassurance even after God had spoken clearly. The Lord is mindful of our human frailties and graciously extends added assurance to us when we struggle with our fears.

What task has the Lord called you to do? Perhaps it is to teach a Sunday School class. Maybe He has asked you to go to a neighbor to share the gospel. Whatever it is, remember that God's people have one source of strength and only one: the power of the indwelling Holy Spirit. God and one are still a majority. We need not fear taking steps of faith when we have heard from Him.

EVANGELISM OUTREACH

This week's study provides encouragement to those who do not feel they are capable of any kind of Christian service. There may even be some in your class who feel the same way about salvation. They may believe they are not capable of serving the Lord. Maybe they think they have been too ungodly. Use the example of Gideon to show that God will provide the strength for them to serve Him. Give opportunity at the end of class for any unsaved students to come to Christ.

Assuming Leadership Responsibilities (David)

CENTRAL TRUTH

Effective spiritual leaders manifest responsible leadership traits.

GOLDEN TEXT

David shepherded them with integrity of heart; with skillful hands he led them. Psalm 78:72 (NIV)

STUDY TEXT

1 Chronicles 11:1 through 13:14; Psalm 78:70-72

OUTLINE

1. Be A Caring Leader
   A. Call To Godly Character
   B. Servant's Heart

2. Nurture Fellowship
   A. Exercising Caution
   B. Responding To The Spirit

3. Recognize God's Presence
   A. Bringing Back The Ark
   B. Recognizing A Mistake

OBJECTIVE

To examine certain responsibilities of spiritual leadership and support those who lead us in the Lord.

CHECKLIST

☐ Familiarize yourself with the ark of the covenant, its construction, and its use in Israel's worship as well as the God-given directions for its care and transportation.

☐ Fill out the Planning The Session sheet. This will help ensure that you have sufficient time to cover the material as well as any teaching activities you desire to use.

☐ Make sure you relate the qualifications of a leader found in this week's study to the kind of leadership in which your students participate. This would include teaching Sunday School, serving as deacons, working with children and youth, as well as taking leadership roles in secular employment.

DAILY BIBLE READINGS

Monday:	Interceding For People.	Numbers 14:11-19
Tuesday:	Successful Leadership.	2 Chronicles 26:1-5
Wednesday:	Respecting True Worship.	2 Chronicles 30:1-5
Thursday:	A Qualified Leader.	Acts 1:21-26
Friday:	Leadership Standards.	1 Timothy 3:1-7
Saturday:	Encouragement For Leaders.	2 Timothy 1:1-7

King James Version

1 Chronicles 11:1. Then all Israel gathered themselves to David unto Hebron, saying, Behold, we are thy bone and thy flesh.

2. And moreover in time past, even when Saul was king, thou wast he that leddest out and broughtest in Israel: and the Lord thy God said unto thee, Thou shalt feed my people Israel, and thou shalt be ruler over my people Israel.

Psalm 78:70. He chose David also his servant, and took him from the sheepfolds:

71. From following the ewes great with young he brought him to feed Jacob his people, and Israel his inheritance.

72. So he fed them according to the integrity of his heart; and guided them by the skilfulness of his hands.

1 Chronicles 13:1. And David consulted with the captains of thousands and hundreds, and with every leader.

2. And David said unto all the congregation of Israel, If it seem good unto you, and that it be of the Lord our God, let us send abroad unto our brethren every where, that are left in all the land of Israel, and with them also to the priests and Levites which are in their cities and suburbs, that they may gather themselves unto us:

3. And let us bring again the ark of our God to us: for we enquired not at it in the days of Saul.

7. And they carried the ark of God in a new cart out of the house of Abinadab: and Uzza and Ahio drave the cart.

8. And David and all Israel played before God with all their might, and with singing, and with harps, and with psalteries, and with timbrels, and with cymbals, and with trumpets.

New International Version

1 Chronicles 11:1. All Israel came together to David at Hebron and said, "We are your own flesh and blood.

2. In the past, even while Saul was king, you were the one who led Israel on their military campaigns. And the Lord your God said to you, 'You will shepherd my people Israel, and you will become their ruler.' "

Psalm 78:70. He chose David his servant and took him from the sheep pens;

71. From tending the sheep he brought him to be the shepherd of his people Jacob, of Israel his inheritance.

72. And David shepherded them with integrity of heart; with skillful hands he led them.

1 Chronicles 13:1. David conferred with each of his officers, the commanders of thousands and commanders of hundreds.

2. He then said to the whole assembly of Israel, "If it seems good to you and if it is the will of the Lord our God, let us send word far and wide to the rest of our brothers throughout the territories of Israel, and also to the priests and Levites who are with them in their towns and pasturelands, to come and join us.

3. Let us bring the ark of our God back to us, for we did not inquire of it during the reign of Saul."

7. They moved the ark of God from Abinadab's house on a new cart, with Uzzah and Ahio guiding it.

8. David and all the Israelites were celebrating with all their might before God, with songs and with harps, lyres, tambourines, cymbals and trumpets.

David was the spiritual leader as well as the political leader of Israel. Israel was no ordinary nation. The Israelites were God's covenant people. For this reason it was important that their king be a spiritual man as well as one skilled in administration and military operations.

Israel's first king, Saul, failed on the spiritual side. God chose David because he was a man after His own heart. David had been a shepherd by occupation, and he carried this spirit into his rulership. Many times we see him as the shepherd of his people as well as their king.

Leaders need many qualifications, but few are as important as having a shepherd's heart. If you are in any kind of leadership position, allow David's example of leadership to encourage you to become the best leader possible.

BIBLE COMMENTARY

1. Be A Caring Leader

A. Call To Godly Character
1 Chronicles 11:1-3

A leader's task is made harder if he follows one who did not fulfill his responsibilities. David came to the throne at a time when the nation was in disarray following Saul's reign. God never intended Israel to have an earthly king. However, He accommodated their rebellious cry for a king and selected Saul as the nation's first ruler. At first Saul showed great promise, but as time went on, weaknesses in his character became apparent. But God saw the quality of David's character and chose the young shepherd boy as Saul's successor.

It has been said, "Ability may get you to the top, but only character can keep you there." The contrast between Saul and David is an example of this. Some people, when choosing a candidate for public office, have said, "Character doesn't matter as long as he or she can do the job." But many times this kind of reasoning has proved disastrous.

The people had watched David throughout the years he led Saul's military campaigns (verse 2). David had been tested by these experiences and had earned the people's confidence and trust. The same character David demonstrated must be a part of godly leaders today. Putting a novice in charge is warned against in the New Testament (1 Timothy 3:6). A young Christian must be proven through trials and testing before taking a position of leadership in a church. Godly character does not occur overnight—rather, it grows over time.

Ask: "What was the deepest longing of the Israelites in choosing another king?" Clearly they wanted one who truly cared for them. This was the glaring deficiency in Saul. Assuming leadership is a test of an individual's true nature. It soon becomes clear whether he really has a concern for those he leads or if he wants to use his position only to advance his own cause.

The people were aware that God had chosen David (1 Samuel 15:28; 16:1-13; 2 Samuel 2:4). They were ready to become part of God's plan for His people and install David in office without delay.

The covenant mentioned in verse 3 shows both sides recognized mutual responsibilities. If a ruler is to be effective he must have the total support of those he rules. In turn he is obligated to keep their interests in mind at all times.

The Hebrew word translated "integrity" means primarily uprightness. The foundational truth of Christianity is our righteousness comes from faith in Christ's work. As Christians, we walk in righteousness—uprightness—by the power of the Holy Spirit indwelling us. We demonstrate integrity through our relationship with God.

The word translated "skillfulness" means wisdom, understanding, and insight. God gives each believer gifts, but the understanding and wisdom to use these gifts comes as we seek God.

To be a caring leader, a believer can depend on God to bring about the situations that will cause him to mature. By seeking God, the believer will gain insight and wisdom to apply the things he learns from Scripture. Caring for people, like a shepherd does his sheep, will be the result.

NOTES

B. Shepherd's Heart
Psalm 78:70-72

Psalm 78 is a summary of Israel's history. **Ask: "In verses 70-72 how does the Psalmist emphasize God's sovereignty in determining his nation's course?"** The Psalmist refers to David's kingship as the result of God's choice: "He chose David." God took David from his shepherd's work; David did not seek the office.

TEACHING TIP 1: Point out that the Psalmist referred to David as God's servant (verse 70). Lead a brief discussion about what characterizes a servant's heart in a leader.

Some might think a shepherd's occupation was a poor qualification for becoming king, but in David's case it was the qualification the nation needed most. Verse 71 pictures David first as a shepherd caring tenderly for the ewes about to give birth. Then we see the same shepherd leading his nation with the same loving concern. Unlike other nations, they were God's people, His inheritance. They must have a king fit for such an awesome responsibility.

In verse 72 we see two characteristics of David that made him God's choice: integrity and skillfulness. Integrity described David's inner quality. Skillfulness focused on his abilities in the administration of the nation's affairs. There can be no question that his skillfulness was enhanced by inner integrity. Without it, the outward ability would have eventually failed.

2. Nurture Fellowship

A. Exercising Caution
1 Chronicles 12:16,17

First Chronicles 12 looks back to a time prior to Saul's death. The men listed there had supported David prior to his becoming king of Israel. David had been a fugitive constantly on the move because Saul was intent on killing him. During that period many defected to David. This was a difficult time in David's life. He knew he was God's choice as king, yet he also recognized the difficulties facing him.

God has a way of encouraging His servants just when things may seem discouraging. David knew he could not afford to take foolish risks. Nothing could have been more encouraging, however, than to have a group from the tribe of Benjamin come to him. This was Saul's own tribe. It was no light thing for these people to declare their loyalty to the one Saul considered his enemy and chief rival.

Ask: **"Was it wrong for David to question the motives of these men?"** David had been the victim of betrayal and deception before, and he could not be certain such possibilities did not still exist. David manifested the attitude Jesus said should characterize His followers—wise as a serpent and harmless as a dove. He was ready to receive anyone he was certain wanted to join his company. But he could never discount the possibility of a plot. In verse 17 David spoke of "mine enemies," showing that he recognized such people still existed.

TEACHING TIP 2: Use the following questions to lead a discussion relating David's attitude to situations today.
• How much should we trust people?
• Should we be suspicious of everyone?
• How can mistrust damage Christian fellowship?

David made it clear he would welcome this group with open arms if they had peaceful intentions. If they had been loyal to Saul in the past this would not be held against them. "Mine heart shall be knit unto you" (verse 17) is a beautiful expression of the spirit in which David would receive them. He wanted them in his group. He welcomed their fellowship and loyalty.

At some point in our lives we may have been wronged by others. Having been hurt, we might have a tendency to reject them even when they come to us desiring reconciliation. At these times we must follow David's example. When someone truly repents, we must accept him or her back into fellowship.

B. Responding To The Spirit
1 Chronicles 12:18

Ask: **"Why was Amasai's prophecy so important to David?"** As a spiritually-minded man, David would quickly recognize that the Spirit of God had inspired this utterance. The Lord understood David's cautious approach to the situation and chose to reassure him supernaturally.

Amasai's prophecy left no doubt where the group's loyalty lay: "Thine are we, David, and on thy side" (verse 18). They had come to cast their lot with David knowing there were some risks involved.

Amasai acknowledged God's choice of David and declared, "Thy God helpeth thee." He was aware that David had survived various dangerous situations because of God's help. Amasai and his men discerned the direction the Lord was leading Israel and wanted to identify with His plan and purpose.

David's response was enthusiastic. He received the men and made them captains of his army. He would not have done this if there were any lingering suspicions about their motives. God worked on both sides of the situation, showing them it was His will for them to join forces.

NOTES

3. Recognize God's Presence

A. Bringing Back The Ark
1 Chronicles 13:1-6

It was a tragic day for Israel when the ark fell into the hands of the Philistines. However, this happened because the people's spiritual life had sunk so low that their reverence for the ark had waned. They were using it as people today might employ a good luck charm. Feeling it would affect their fortunes in war, they took the ark out on the battlefield only to have the Philistines capture it (1 Samuel 4:1-11).

For the next 7 months, the Philistines felt the judgment of God because of the ark. They finally became so fearful of the ark's presence that they sent it back to Israel. For the next 80 years it remained in Kirjath-jearim at the house of a man named Abinadab. It was a red-letter day for the nation when the king and a multitude of his people started for Abinadab's house to bring back the ark. David was determined to bring the ark back to where it belonged.

Ask: "Why was it so important to David to recover the ark?" The ark was the most sacred piece of furniture in Israel's worship. Its lid was the mercy seat where the sacrificial blood was sprinkled on the Day of Atonement. It represented the presence of God.

David recognized what it meant to the covenant people not to have the ark of the covenant in their midst. During the dark days of Saul's reign there had been no attempt to bring it back. Under David, the nation was experiencing a spiritual renewal. To return the ark, David consulted first with the leaders, then with the whole nation. The response of the people was immediate and enthusiastic. They recognized the recovery of the ark as a necessity.

Today we do not need objects like the ark to help us to worship. However, spiritual lessons abound in this passage. We have an enemy far more dangerous than the Philistines. The Christian is engaged in constant spiritual warfare. The devil never stops trying to steal the truths that are the foundation of our faith. He tries to take away our prayer life, our love for the Scriptures, and our walk in the Spirit. We must be on constant guard so the enemy will not gain a foothold in our lives.

NOTES

B. Recognizing A Mistake
1 Chronicles 13:7-14

TEACHING TIP 3: At the beginning of this discussion, display overhead transparency 1 "The Right Way." Use it to emphasize the way God had commanded the ark to be transported. Then replace it with overhead transparency 2 "The Wrong Way" showing the Israelites' error in their treatment of the ark as you discuss the following.

David ignored God's commands in the Scriptures for transporting the ark. God's Word states that only the Levites were to carry the ark on their shoulders, using wooden staves thrust through rings on its sides (Exodus 25:10-15). But David put the ark on an ox-drawn cart, copying the way the Philistines had removed the ark (1 Samuel 6:1-12). All of the music, singing, and dancing by David and his people did not impress the Lord and could not cover up their disobedience. As a result, David's friend Uzza lost his life.

Ask: "Why must we guard against doing good things in the wrong way? Isn't it enough to have the right motivation?"

None of us are exempt from lapses where we seem to forget the clear teaching of God's Word and use the ways of the world as our example. Never has such temptation been greater than in these end-time days.

David was filled with fear when Uzza was struck dead. Yet David recognized he had incurred God's displeasure and did not carry his foolish error any further. For the time being the ark was not brought back to its final resting place. As the leader of his people, David had learned a serious lesson the hard way. Yet through it all he displayed his submission to the sovereign will of God.

NOTES

LIFE RESPONSE

We live in a day when it is not easy to find people who really care about others. How often have you heard someone say, "No one cares." No quality is more important in a leader than a deep concern for those he leads. He must put their interests above his own. He should never allow selfishness to cloud his responsibility to them.

A leader must know the interests, anxieties, fears, and concerns of those for whom he is responsible. Even if he is not always able to do something to help, just the knowledge that he cares is important. This caring must be sincere, because people quickly detect what is genuine in a leader's attitude.

One important ingredient in the life of a leader is a sensitivity to God's will and leadership. This must never be lacking in one who serves the Lord in leading others. A leader often needs wisdom that only God can give. He may be confronted with situations for which there seem to be no human solutions. A consistent walk in the Spirit must be cultivated and maintained. The leader must have an ear for "the still, small voice."

These same principles of leadership apply to your job. Whether you are a leader at church or at work, God can help you become a better leader. Maybe you need wisdom for a difficult situation. Perhaps you need to bring unity where there has been division. God will help you. You only need to ask Him.

EVANGELISM OUTREACH

Integrity is an important part of leadership. We cannot separate personal integrity from our job as leaders. The decisions we make reflect our moral character. There may be some in your class who are not saved. Perhaps they are in leadership positions outside of the church. Emphasize that the only way we can be a truly effective leader is to have the help of the Holy Spirit. He can provide wisdom for difficult decisions. Extend an invitation to any unsaved students to accept Christ.

Benefits Of Faithful Leadership (Asa)

Central Truth

Faithful leaders act to bring spiritual blessings to God's people.

Golden Text

Lord, there is no one like you to help the powerless against the mighty. 2 Chronicles 14:11 (NIV)

Study Text

2 Chronicles 14:1 through 16:14

Outline

1. Removing Evil Influences
   A. A King's Priority
   B. Untiring Zeal

2. Overcoming Opposition
   A. The Enemy Attacks
   B. Victory Through Prayer

3. Encouraging Spiritual Renewal
   A. God's Blessing Recognized
   B. Seeking The Lord

Objective

To discover the blessings of godly leadership and appropriate them.

Checklist

☐ Read through this week's study in the student guide. Write down any questions you would like to use for class discussion.

☐ Fill out the Planning The Session work sheet. This will help you plan each activity and how much time you will need.

☐ Familiarize yourself with the two overhead transparencies "Prayer Power" and "Spiritual Renewal" from the *Adult Teaching Helps Packet*. They will be used in Teaching Tips 2 and 3.

☐ Make sure you have an overhead projector set up prior to class.

☐ Concentrate on life application in this study. Some of your students may be caught up in materialism and need to recommit their lives to Christ. Encourage students who like Asa have taken a stand for morality and may be facing persecution and attacks from the enemy because of their stand.

☐ Pray for the anointing of the Holy Spirit upon your teaching. Use this week's study to encourage your students to pray for revival for your church and community.

Daily Bible Readings

Monday:	Rescuing Captives.	Genesis 14:13-16
Tuesday:	Delivering From Oppression.	Exodus 14:10-18
Wednesday:	Defending The Oppressed.	Isaiah 42:1-7
Thursday:	Encouraging Decisions.	Acts 15:30-35
Friday:	Fearless Leadership.	Acts 27:21-25
Saturday:	Leaders Rewarded.	Revelation 3:7-13

SCRIPTURE SETTING

King James Version

2 Chronicles 14:2. Asa did that which was good and right in the eyes of the Lord his God:

3. For he took away the altars of the strange gods, and the high places, and brake down the images, and cut down the groves:

4. And commanded Judah to seek the Lord God of their fathers, and to do the law and the commandment.

5. Also he took away out of all the cities of Judah the high places and the images: and the kingdom was quiet before him.

9. And there came out against them Zerah the Ethiopian with an host of a thousand thousand, and three hundred chariots; and came unto Mareshah.

10. Then Asa went out against him, and they set the battle in array in the valley of Zephathah at Mareshah.

11. And Asa cried unto the Lord his God, and said, Lord, it is nothing with thee to help, whether with many, or with them that have no power: help us, O Lord our God; for we rest on thee, and in thy name we go against this multitude. O Lord, thou art our God; let not man prevail against thee.

12. So the Lord smote the Ethiopians before Asa, and before Judah; and the Ethiopians fled.

13. And Asa and the people that were with him pursued them unto Gerar: and the Ethiopians were overthrown, that they could not recover themselves; for they were destroyed before the Lord, and before his host; and they carried away very much spoil.

15:9. And he gathered all Judah and Benjamin, and the strangers with them out of Ephraim and Manasseh, and out of Simeon: for they fell to him out of Israel in abundance, when they saw that the Lord his God was with him.

11. And they offered unto the Lord the same time, of the spoil which they had brought, seven hundred oxen and seven thousand sheep.

12. And they entered into a covenant to seek the Lord God of their fathers with all their heart and with all their soul;

13. That whosoever would not seek the Lord God of Israel should be put to death, whether small or great, whether man or woman.

14. And they sware unto the Lord with a loud voice, and with shouting, and with trumpets, and with cornets.

15. And all Judah rejoiced at the oath: for they had sworn with all their heart, and sought him with their whole desire; and he was found of them: and the Lord gave them rest round about.

New International Version

2 Chronicles 14:2. Asa did what was good and right in the eyes of the Lord his God.

3. He removed the foreign altars and the high places, smashed the sacred stones and cut down the Asherah poles.

4. He commanded Judah to seek the Lord, the God of their fathers, and to obey his laws and commands.

5. He removed the high places and incense altars in every town in Judah, and the kingdom was at peace under him.

9. Zerah the Cushite marched out against them with a vast army and three hundred chariots, and came as far as Mareshah.

10. Asa went out to meet him, and they took up battle positions in the Valley of Zephathah near Mareshah.

11. Then Asa called to the Lord his God and said, "Lord, there is no one like you to help the powerless against the mighty. Help us, O Lord our God, for we rely on you, and in your name we have come against this vast army. O Lord, you are our God; do not let man prevail against you."

12. The Lord struck down the Cushites before Asa and Judah. The Cushites fled,

13. And Asa and his army pursued them as far as Gerar. Such a great number of Cushites fell that they could not recover; they were crushed before the Lord and his forces. The men of Judah carried off a large amount of plunder.

15:9. Then he assembled all Judah and Benjamin and the people from Ephraim, Manasseh and Simeon who had settled among them, for large numbers had come over to him from Israel when they saw that the Lord his God was with him.

11. At that time they sacrificed to the Lord seven hundred head of cattle and seven thousand sheep and goats from the plunder they had brought back.

12. They entered into a covenant to seek the Lord, the God of their fathers, with all their heart and soul.

13. All who would not seek the Lord, the God of Israel, were to be put to death, whether small or great, man or woman.

14. They took an oath to the Lord with loud acclamation, with shouting and with trumpets and horns.

15. All Judah rejoiced about the oath because they had sworn it wholeheartedly. They sought God eagerly, and he was found by them. So the Lord gave them rest on every side.

Israel's constant backsliding allowed idolatry to be so entrenched that it was difficult to eradicate it completely. Several good kings undertook the task and had a measure of success, but under evil leaders the idols quickly reappeared.

Asa faced such a challenge when he took the throne. It is clear that he was a godly man and Israel would be greatly blessed by his leadership. One of the first things he undertook was the destruction of idols and the shrines where they were worshiped. As a result of this zeal for God's honor, Asa led successful military campaigns and saw the blessing of the Lord on His people.

Israel was indeed blessed to enjoy the leadership of such a king. Asa had the good of the nation at heart, and above all he was devoted to the Lord and determined to hold up a standard of righteousness.

BIBLE COMMENTARY

1. Removing Evil Influences

A. A King's Priority
2 Chronicles 14:2

God demands exclusive devotion to Him. The Ten Commandments forbade worship of any gods (whether persons or objects) but the one true God. No graven image was to be made lest it become an object of worship. Furthermore, God warned His people of the serious consequences of engaging in such sacrilege (Exodus 20:3-5).

Ask: "In our society, how does God's command against idolatry apply?" Without actually worshiping a piece of metal, wood, or stone, people show devotion to other things ahead of God, in effect, worshiping those things.

One of the great evils of our time is materialism. There can be no question that many people literally worship "things." They give their devotion to what will make them happier, wealthier, and more self-confident. They are willing to sacrifice a relationship with God in order to achieve these goals. They have no interest in eternity—only in the here and now. For them, all of life centers in self—the greatest idol of all.

Before King Asa dealt with any other matter, he made the elimination of idolatry his priority. Here was a king whose career was summed up in these words: "Asa did that which was good and right in the eyes of the Lord his God" (2 Chronicles 14:2). He was not seeking the favor of man. If he had, he would not have been so bold in his campaign against idolatry.

How tragic that people today are not concerned with what is good and right "in the eyes of the Lord." Many are interested only in having others regard them in a favorable light. There have been those who, like Esau, sold their spiritual birthright for momentary pleasure. Asa was not such a man. He lived with the knowledge that he was always under the eyes of the Lord and he wanted God to be pleased with what He saw.

NOTES

B. Untiring Zeal
2 Chronicles 14:3-5

Often people may speak out against some evil in order to give a favorable impression, but they are unwilling to act. Apparently they have opinions rather than convictions. But Asa did more than pay lip service to God's commandment against idolatry.

Asa saw the shrines where Israelites gathered to bow down to their heathen gods. He saw the altars of these "strange" gods (2 Chronicles 14:3) which had been imported from the wicked nations surrounding Israel. He burned with a holy zeal as he realized the covenant people were hurling insults into the face of God. He had delivered them from Egypt, given them the Promised Land, and made them a nation. Yet they were turning their backs on Him and acting as though they owed their thanks to lifeless foreign deities.

Asa removed these heathen altars, smashed the images people worshiped, and cut down the groves (poles erected to worship Asherah, a fertility goddess). As long as such objects remained, they were a source of temptation to people who were not yet caught up in idolatry. Heathen shrines were usually at the top of hills where they were constantly seen. The sight of multitudes trooping to these places might cause weaker Israelites to join the crowd.

Asa then commanded the people of Judah to "seek the Lord God of their fathers" (verse 4). **Ask: "Why is it proper to 'command' people to forsake evil and turn to the Lord?"** In our permissive society people object to restrictions of any kind. They resent having what they call the convictions of others imposed on them. However, there are principles in God's Word which must not be compromised. We need not make any apologies for insisting on moral standards for our society.

Obviously Asa's reform was an extensive campaign. There were many idol shrines. Asa did not pursue his course enthusiastically for a time and then stop. He sent his servants throughout the cities of Judah to locate the images and remove them (verse 5).

TEACHING TIP 1: Call attention to the statement at the end of verse 5, "and the kingdom was quiet before him." **Ask: "How can the removal of evil influences affect the conditions of a nation?"** List responses on a chalkboard or blank transparency. **Ask: "As believers, what can we do to see evil removed from our city?"** From student responses, list practical things that they can do to remove the evil from your city.

NOTES

2. Overcoming Opposition
A. The Enemy Attacks
2 Chronicles 14:9

Ask: "When we are living to please the Lord, why should we not be surprised if we suddenly have battles to fight?" The righteous king Asa was tested by the attack of an enemy army. Some Christians have been shocked and even discouraged when they found themselves involved in great difficulties. Have you ever wondered, "Did I commit some sin for which the Lord is punishing me?" Such thoughts should be discarded quickly. The more vigorous we are in pursuing the path of righteousness, the fiercer our struggles may be.

We can never know how strong our faith is until it is tested. The same goes for our commitment to the Lord. It is no problem to be faithful when things are going well. It is in the heat of battle that we learn the quality of our consecration.

The Ethiopian army that came against Israel was formidable. It consisted of both infantry men and chariots, which might be considered the ancient equivalent of our modern tanks. "Zerah the Ethiopian" (verse 9) was the leader of this army. Numerically speaking, Asa's army was no match for these invaders. Such circumstances, however, provide opportunity for us to learn what God can do when the human side of things looks hopeless.

NOTES

B. Victory Through Prayer
2 Chronicles 14:10-15

TEACHING TIP 2: Display Overhead Transparency 1 "Prayer Power," as you discuss 2 Chronicles 14:10-15.

Asa took up battle positions in the valley of Zephathah. Then he brought out his "secret weapon"—prayer. The Ethiopians must have been anxious to start the battle so they could proceed to annihilate the Israelites. Little did they know Who was fighting on the side of this seemingly inferior force. They would soon discover how much power their weapons had against God.

Ask: "What example did Asa set for us at this time?" We are inclined in such a situation to count figures, weighing our strength against that of the enemy. Asa did not. He did not hesitate to admit his seemingly hopeless position: "Lord, there is no one like you to help the powerless against the mighty" (verse 11, NIV). Human nature does not like to admit powerlessness. We would rather build up our egos by focusing on our own strength. However, there will be times when we try to find that strength and discover it is not there. When we finally admit we are weak is the time we are in the best position to receive help from God.

There was no panic in Asa's prayer. "We rest on thee," he said. He declared he was leading his army in the name of the Lord. This was really God's army. All the resources of heaven were on the side of the Israelites.

Note the contrast in the focus of Asa's prayer: "Thy name . . . this multitude." What could the largest multitude accomplish against people who were trusting the living God? What weapon could compare with prayer?

Asa saw the honor of God at stake for he prayed, "Let not man prevail against thee." He would not want the Ethiopian army to imagine Israel's God was no match for their military machine. Should they win the battle, they could brag about how their false gods overcame the God of Israel.

Believers today are involved in what may be the fiercest spiritual warfare of the ages. Every force seems to be arrayed against the cause of righteousness. But we are not fighting to enhance our own reputation. We are fighting for the honor of God. The standards He has set up for men to live by are being attacked today. His Name, His Word, His Church—are all targets of the powers of darkness. But we need never fear the final outcome. God can never be defeated.

Verse 12 puts the credit where it is due. It does not say the Israelites smote the Ethiopians, but that God did. He was using Asa and his army, but God was the real Leader and the real Victor.

The enemies' defeat was so complete that they could not recover. The Israelites plundered the cities of the enemies, capturing large numbers of their livestock—one of their chief sources of livelihood. It became evident to the Ethiopians that the Israelites had received help from a Source with which they had not reckoned, "for the fear of the Lord came upon them" (verse 14).

NOTES

ably to observe the Feast of Weeks (Pentecost). This was one of the annual feasts when all males were required to be in Jerusalem. These feasts served to unify the nation and keep them reminded of their dependence on God.

NOTES

3. Encouraging Spiritual Renewal

A. God's Blessing Recognized
2 Chronicles 15:9,10

Some of the people who came to Asa (1 Chronicles 15:9) were defectors from the northern kingdom. They had seen "that the Lord his God was with [Asa]." Apparently these were Israelites who anguished over the apostasy of their leaders and saw in Asa a king who would lead the nation back to God. In his military victories they recognized the Lord's hand. Asa was God's man and these people wanted to identify with him.

Ask: "In what sense can people today 'see' the Lord is with a believer?" Although witnessing is a part of being a Christian, a godly life will speak louder than words. It is much better to be told, "I can see the Lord is with you" than to make a practice of trying to impress others with our spirituality. Many people will be drawn to the Lord when they see His hand in the lives of His children.

The gathering of these Israelites to Asa was further proof that God was watching over His covenant people. Even when there was widespread apostasy among them, He preserved a faithful remnant.

Judging from the month and day this gathering took place (verse 10), it was prob-

B. Seeking The Lord
2 Chronicles 15:11-15

When repentance and revival come to a people, whether in a small community or a nation, two things must be done, one negative and the other positive. First, we must remove evil influences from our lives. Asa had vigorously pursued this course in his attacks on idolatry. However, if we are concerned only with separation from sin, there will be a vacuum in our lives. We must renew our relationship with God, by seeking Him in Bible study and prayer. Asa recognized how necessary this was and led the people in the right direction.

Ask: "What was the purpose in offering so many animals (2 Chronicles 15:11)?" The livestock was captured from the enemy during war. Instead of keeping all the animals, the Israelites showed they gave God glory for victory by dedicating in sacrifice part of the spoil of battle.

TEACHING TIP 3: Display Overhead Transparency 2 "Spiritual Renewal" as you discuss verses 12-15.

God was the originator of the covenant with His people. He did not need to renew

it, but the people did. They recognized they had wandered from the paths He wanted them to walk and were determined to change the course the nation had been taking.

The best of us have times when we sense we are not as close to the Lord as we should be. This does not mean we have backslidden. It is a case of our human frailties showing themselves and cooling off our spiritual fervor. When the Holy Spirit brings this to our attention, it is time to renew those vows of commitment and dedication. We may do it at a church altar or in the privacy of our own prayer closet. The important thing is that it be done.

These people were so earnest about seeking the Lord that they decreed the death penalty for anyone who refused (verse 13). They celebrated the time of renewal with shouting and with music. Joy was the order of the day. As a result of this renewal, God gave the nation peace (verses 14,15).

NOTES

LIFE RESPONSE

The leader who does not care about the people's relationship with God is lacking the first qualification for leadership—spiritual desire. Asa stands out in the Old Testament because those who desired to serve God in the midst of idolatry were in the minority.

We must never imagine that because our position of leadership is not a prominent one, our task is not important. There is leadership in the family, in the Sunday School, and the local church (including various groups of different ages). If we will concern ourselves with leading people in the paths of righteousness, other matters will fall into place.

It is not being fanatical or narrow minded to speak out against the evil influences of the day. Compromise ruins our relationship with God. He has commanded us not to be conformed to the present age.

It should not take us by surprise if others do not share our enthusiasm for committed Christian living. We must not be discouraged if we encounter outright opposition. Jesus warned His disciples that since He had to suffer scorn and rejection, they should not be surprised to encounter the same.

The act of commitment is not a one-time event but a daily exercise in spiritual growth. There are times when all of us need to take a fresh look at ourselves and renew our loyalty to God. Examine your commitment to the Lord. Perhaps this is a time you need to make a new commitment to serve Him.

EVANGELISM OUTREACH

This week's study provides an excellent opportunity to present the message of salvation to any unsaved in your class. There may be students in your class who worship idols of materialism or self. Emphasize the danger of idolatry and the need to remove all idols from one's life. Some may even need to lay aside friends and sinful activities. But also stress the importance of replacing those idols with a true worship of Jesus Christ. Give an invitation for these students to accept Christ as Savior. ⌷

Depending On God (Jehoshaphat)

CENTRAL TRUTH

Righteous leaders trust the Lord for guidance and help.

GOLDEN TEXT

We have no power to face this vast army that is attacking us. We do not know what to do, but our eyes are upon you.
2 Chronicles 20:12 (NIV)

STUDY TEXT

2 Chronicles 20:1-30

OUTLINE

1. Seeking The Lord
   A. Major Crisis
   B. Answer To Fear

2. Waiting On The Lord
   A. Priority Of Prayer
   B. Acknowledging Human Need

3. Prayer Brings Results
   A. Faith And Praise
   B. Enemies Defeated

OBJECTIVE

To acknowledge the importance of prayer in leadership and commit to seek the Lord.

CHECKLIST

☐ Read the entire study text to help you understand the context of this week's study.

☐ Read the corresponding study in the *Adult Student Guide*. Write down any questions you would like to use for discussion.

☐ Fill out the Planning The Session sheet. This will help you plan enough time for each activity.

☐ Duplicate enough copies of the work sheet "Prayer Analysis" from the Adult Teaching Helps Packet so each student will have one. Allow sufficient time for students to express their thoughts about Jehoshaphat's prayer, but do not allow one or two to monopolize the discussion.

☐ You may have some students in your class who are facing difficult trials and need an answer to their problems. Ask the Lord to help you as you present this study. Encourage your students to seek the Lord for the answers to their needs.

DAILY BIBLE READINGS

Monday:	Trusting The Lord. Genesis 13:8-18
Tuesday:	Results Of Obedience. Joshua 6:20-25
Wednesday:	Miraculous Deliverance. Daniel 3:19-28
Thursday:	Supreme Authority. Mark 5:1-14
Friday:	Response Of Faith. Luke 1:30-38
Saturday:	Living By Faith. 2 Corinthians 4:7-18

King James Version

2 Chronicles 20:2. Then there came some that told Jehoshaphat, saying, There cometh a great multitude against thee from beyond the sea on this side Syria; and, behold, they be in Hazazon-tamar, which is Engedi.

3. And Jehoshaphat feared, and set himself to seek the Lord, and proclaimed a fast throughout all Judah.

5. And Jehoshaphat stood in the congregation of Judah and Jerusalem, in the house of the Lord, before the new court,

6. And said, O Lord God of our fathers, art not thou God in heaven? and rulest not thou over all the kingdoms of the heathen? and in thine hand is there not power and might, so that none is able to withstand thee?

7. Art not thou our God, who didst drive out the inhabitants of this land before thy people Israel, and gavest it to the seed of Abraham thy friend for ever?

8. And they dwelt therein, and have built thee a sanctuary therein for thy name, saying,

9. If, when evil cometh upon us, as the sword, judgment, or pestilence, or famine, we stand before this house, and in thy presence, (for thy name is in this house,) and cry unto thee in our affliction, then thou wilt hear and help.

10. And now, behold, the children of Ammon and Moab and mount Seir, whom thou wouldest not let Israel invade, when they came out of the land of Egypt, but they turned from them, and destroyed them not;

11. Behold, I say, how they reward us, to come to cast us out of thy possession, which thou hast given us to inherit.

12. O our God, wilt thou not judge them? for we have no might against this great company that cometh against us; neither know we what to do: but our eyes are upon thee.

20. And they rose early in the morning, and went forth into the wilderness of Tekoa: and as they went forth, Jehoshaphat stood and said, Hear me, O Judah, and ye inhabitants of Jerusalem; Believe in the Lord your God, so shall ye be established; believe his prophets, so shall ye prosper.

22. And when they began to sing and to praise, the Lord set ambushments against the children of Ammon, Moab, and mount Seir, which were come against Judah; and they were smitten.

New International Version

2 Chronicles 20:2. Some men came and told Jehoshaphat, "A vast army is coming against you from Edom, from the other side of the Sea. It is already in Hazazon Tamar" (that is, En Gedi).

3. Alarmed, Jehoshaphat resolved to inquire of the Lord, and he proclaimed a fast for all Judah.

5. Then Jehoshaphat stood up in the assembly of Judah and Jerusalem at the temple of the Lord in the front of the new courtyard

6. And said: "O Lord, God of our fathers, are you not the God who is in heaven? You rule over all the kingdoms of the nations. Power and might are in your hand, and no one can withstand you.

7. O our God, did you not drive out the inhabitants of this land before your people Israel and give it forever to the descendants of Abraham your friend?

8. They have lived in it and have built in it a sanctuary for your Name, saying,

9. 'If calamity comes upon us, whether the sword of judgment, or plague or famine, we will stand in your presence before this temple that bears your Name and will cry out to you in our distress, and you will hear us and save us.'

10. "But now here are men from Ammon, Moab and Mount Seir, whose territory you would not allow Israel to invade when they came from Egypt; so they turned away from them and did not destroy them.

11. See how they are repaying us by coming to drive us out of the possession you gave us as an inheritance.

12. O our God, will you not judge them? For we have no power to face this vast army that is attacking us. We do not know what to do, but our eyes are upon you."

20. Early in the morning they left for the Desert of Tekoa. As they set out, Jehoshaphat stood and said, "Listen to me, Judah and people of Jerusalem! Have faith in the Lord your God and you will be upheld; have faith in his prophets and you will be successful."

22. As they began to sing and praise, the Lord set ambushes against the men of Ammon and Moab and Mount Seir who were invading Judah, and they were defeated.

There are times when we face situations we feel perfectly capable of handling. Sometimes, though, we have problems where we have to admit, "I don't have the strength." This week's study is an example of the course God's people should take when natural reasoning says defeat is inevitable.

We do not face enemy armies with their arsenal of weapons that can destroy our physical lives. Our warfare is spiritual, but the opposition is just as real. The present age is controlled by Satan and his forces. If we depend on our own strength we will not survive. Our confidence must be in God, not our own resources.

Perhaps you are struggling with a difficult situation and do not have the power or wisdom to face it. Allow Jehoshaphat's example to be an encouragment to you. God has an answer for your need.

BIBLE COMMENTARY

1. Seeking The Lord

A. Major Crisis
2 Chronicles 20:2

Even during the reign of righteous kings, the nation of Israel had little rest from wars. The enemies listed in 2 Chronicles 20:1 had a long history of hostility toward Israel. They were extremely wicked, morally degraded, and steeped in idolatry.

If we traced the route the invaders took, we would see that they were well on their way before they were detected by Jehoshaphat's men. The expression, "a great multitude," indicates the Israelite scouts were impressed by the size of the force. They realized a major crisis was developing. The movement of these troops was not something which could be dismissed lightly.

Ask: "In reference to trials and temptations, why must Christians remain spiritually alert?" Some trials we face are small; others are large and complex. Just when we think we have won a victory, something new may surface. The greatest of God's saints have had to battle "great multitudes" of adversities at some point in their lives. Often adversities come when everything has been going well and our guard is down. Such situations remind us we must always be spiritually vigilant.

Ask: "To what types of trials could the enemies Jehoshaphat faced be compared?"

TEACHING TIP 1: Lead a discussion about what types of trials the invading enemy in this week's study could represent for Christians today.

Just as soldiers must stay in constant training even during times of peace, so God's people must maintain their spiritual discipline whether things are going well or poorly. If military men are to be prepared for actual war, they cannot become lackadaisical. Their task is to live each day mentally geared for possible conflict.

Christians should not live in a state of fear, but must always be aware of the dangers they face from spiritual enemies. The present age is a hostile environment for all who live righteously. And this war will continue until the day we arrive in heaven.

One word that is often lacking in a Christian's vocabulary is "discipline." Spiritually we must stay in training. We must be as familiar with our weapons as the soldier is with his. Prayer, the Word of God, faith—these are what will not only defend us but drive the enemy back.

devote every moment to crying out to God. There is no question that earnest prayer accompanied the fasting, as it always should.

The people responded quickly, showing the godly influence of Jehoshaphat. They left their homes and made their way to Jerusalem for a great prayer meeting. Their petitions had one goal: "To ask help of the Lord" (verse 4).

NOTES

B. Answer To Fear
2 Chronicles 20:3,4

Ask: "What was the positive result of Jehoshaphat's fear?" Courage is not the absence of fear. It is the ability to act in spite of it. Fear is a wholesome quality when it alerts us to danger and helps us prepare for it. Jehoshaphat would have hardly been human if he had not felt alarmed over the danger to his people.

Yet fear did not reduce the king to a state of panic (2 Chronicles 20:3). It motivated him to do what believers should always do in a crisis. He sought help from the Source he knew would bring victory—the Lord.

Jehoshaphat's reaction showed that he had not waited for a crisis to commune with God. He was a righteous king who had already established a continuing relationship with the One he recognized as Israel's true Ruler. It is tragic when people think of prayer only when they feel the world caving in on them. It should be a daily experience to walk and talk with God.

The expression "set himself" shows a deliberate, determined effort to contact God and receive His help. Much of today's praying is halfhearted and lacking in fervor. There is not enough "setting ourselves" in prayer. Perhaps this is why we do not always receive the answers we expect.

As an example to the nation, Jehoshaphat led the way in prayer. However, he involved the people by proclaiming a time of fasting. This showed an intense desire to make contact with God. Normal pursuits and activities were laid aside in order to

2. Waiting On The Lord

A. Priority Of Prayer
2 Chronicles 20:5,6

It is a wonderful sight to see the leader of a nation leading his people in prayer during a crisis. The outcome could have been different if Israel had not been ruled by a godly king at this time.

TEACHING TIP 2: As a basis for discussion, distribute the work sheet, "Analysis Of Jehoshaphat's Prayer." Allow a few minutes for students to write their answers. Then discuss each question.

Ask: "Why is it important that prayer be the first thing we think about during trials rather than a last resort?" Unfortunately we sometimes try everything else before we consider praying. "When all else fails, try prayer" is a poor philosophy. When prayer comes first, we will be assured that our confidence will be in God.

In our day, there seems to be a determined effort to disconnect us from the past. *Tradition* is a word despised by some. Yet we have arrived where we are because of what has happened before us. We enjoy blessings today, both nationally and spiritually, because of the foundation laid by others now gone from the scene.

When Jehoshaphat addressed the Lord as "Lord God of our fathers" (verse 6), he was reminding himself and the Israelites of the relationship established with Abraham and carried on by those who followed him. Because of the "fathers" who preceded Jehoshaphat and his generation, Israel had been blessed and established in the land. There is a continuity in God's dealings with His people. Each generation builds on the work of the one before. Traditions that have played a part in our nation and in the Church should never be treated with contempt. We can learn from the defeats and victories of those who came before us.

Addressing God as "God in heaven" who rules over all human kingdoms (verse 6), Jehoshaphat recognized God's sovereignty. No man has the last word, although he often seems to think so. God does allow people the freedom to act, but in the end He will not allow man to defeat His purposes.

NOTES

B. Acknowledging Human Need
2 Chronicles 20:7-12

In 2 Chronicles 20:7, Jehoshaphat began to remind himself and the people of the past miracles of God's deliverance. Thus he was emphasizing the unchangeableness of God. The God who had driven out so many enemies from Israel was the same God to whom Jehoshaphat was praying. The expression "for ever" emphasizes the truth that God's covenant, which began with the nation's father Abraham, could not be broken.

Ask: "Why is it good to remind ourselves that difficult situations may come even to God's people?" Jehoshaphat knew evil would come against Israel (verse 9). This does not indicate sin or a lack of faith; it is simply facing reality. God does not promise us a path free of trouble. But He does assure us of His presence and help, no matter what we confront.

In verse 10, we observe a complaint that we often hear—and probably have thought about. It is distressing to treat someone well and then have evil returned for our good. Numbers 20:14-21 and Deuteronomy 2:4,5 describe the instances to which Jehoshaphat referred. God had not allowed Israel to even pass through the territory of the very people now preparing to attack them. Such injustice, of course, is simply a way of life in a fallen world. We cannot afford to let it shake our faith. But we look forward to the day when He will make all things right and vindicate His own.

As long as we live there will be times when we find our own strength totally inadequate for tests we face. We cannot come up with a strategy for dealing with the situation. Jehoshaphat's admission, "neither know we what to do" (2 Chronicles 20:12) should encourage us that we are not alone in experiencing such dilemmas.

Despite these feelings of weakness and lack of a strategic plan, Jehoshaphat concluded with an expression of confidence: "Our eyes are upon thee." This is a safe position for God's children no matter how strong the enemy is.

NOTES

3. Prayer Brings Results

A. Faith And Praise
2 Chronicles 20:20,21

In 2 Chronicles 20:20,21, we see Jehoshaphat's strong spiritual leadership as his people prepared to meet the enemy. He did not tell them how capable they were as soldiers or how many weapons they possessed. The basis of his address was, ''Believe in the Lord your God'' (verse 20). To the unconverted mind, this sounds strange, but to the believer it is not. Most Christians who have experienced spiritual battle can recall when faith was the only weapon they had.

Believing in God puts a firm foundation under our feet. Believing His Word as we read it, study it, and hear it preached and taught will give us victories that could not otherwise be won.

Verse 21 shows Jehoshaphat was not a cruel despot who imposed his will on the people. Before enacting his strategy, he consulted with them—undoubtedly the leaders. We can be certain the Lord gave them directions and that the strange battle plan was not something they had devised.

The sight of the choir leading the army against the enemy reminds us of the attack on Jericho when the ark and trumpet-blowing priests were part of the march around the city (Joshua 6:9). Jehoshaphat's singers had one theme: ''Praise the Lord; for his mercy endureth forever'' (2 Chronicles 20:21). This was a reminder to each one that their confidence was in God, not themselves.

Ask: ''Why is praise such an important part of a Christian's life?'' Praise helps us keep the focus where it should be—on God, His goodness, and His sovereignty and control. Praising Him helps us maintain thankfulness, vital to spiritual maturity.

TEACHING TIP 3: Discuss with the students the significance of the choir-led army and its application to our own spiritual warfare.

B. Enemies Defeated
2 Chronicles 20:22-30

This is not the only time in Israel's history that we see enemies destroying themselves. It happened during Gideon's victory over the Midianites (Judges 7:22).

Ask: ''How do you explain the confusion which developed in the enemy's army and caused them to turn on one another?'' The writer of this passage makes it clear in 2 Chronicles 20:22 that ''the Lord set ambushments.'' Although these ''ambushments'' are not identified, God threw confusion into the ranks of the invaders in answer to the faith of His people. In mass confusion, soldiers, who had been ready to attack the Israelites, began to slaughter each other.

What we see happening cannot be explained naturally. However, God's people had prayed. They had put their trust in Him alone. God had chosen the weak Israelites to confound the mighty, a supposedly foolish nation to confound the so-called wise (see 1 Corinthians 1:26-29).

When Jehoshaphat's army reached the scene there were no enemies to fight. All around them were the dead bodies of those who had threatened them just a short time before (2 Chronicles 20:24). Is this not a picture of some of our own experiences—not against enemy armies, but by situations just as threatening? The outcome looks hopeless. Then we pray and commit it to God. When the time for the battle arrives, the foreboding situation has vanished.

After this great victory, God brought the Israelites three specific blessings. First was the spoil of the battle. The Israelites stripped the enemies' bodies of jewels and other property. There was so much spoil it took 3 days to carry it away (verse 25).

Then the Israelites gathered in a valley they named Berachah or "blessing" to celebrate the victory (verses 26-28). Then they returned to the temple in Jerusalem for another praise service.

Finally, the fear of God came on all of the nations around Israel. Because of the Israelites' obedience, God gave them rest from war (verses 29,30). These were wonderful results of a great victory.

NOTES

LIFE RESPONSE

Just because we are Christians does not guarantee that we will not have difficulties in our lives. But when these difficult times come, what must we as Christians do? We must respond as Jehoshaphat and his people did in this study. They looked to God for His faithfulness, His mercy, and His promises. They took time to pray and ask help of the Lord.

In difficult times we must remind ourselves of God's past faithfulness and His sovereignty. He is in control no matter what outward circumstances appear to indicate. We need to admit our own lack of strength and our total dependence upon God. We, like Jehoshaphat, should not be hesitant to say, "Neither know we what to do, but our eyes are upon thee" (2 Chronicles 20:12).

To believe in the Lord is more than a mental assent to His existence. It involves complete trust and commitment. In the biblical sense, believing in the Lord is standing on His Word regardless of feelings or circumstances. It involves remembering His character, His person. This is the kind of belief that brings answers to prayer.

What "great multitude" are you facing right now? When you think about this difficult situation, do you feel afraid? This week respond to your difficulty as Jehoshaphat did to his. Begin to seek God. Rely on His might and sovereignty. Then begin to praise Him for who He is and allow His presence to bring you peace.

EVANGELISM OUTREACH

Like Jehoshaphat, believers have the power of God to help them in difficult situations when they pray. On the other hand, unbelievers will not understand God's power and will try to work out their problems in their own strength. God sometimes uses difficult situations to cause sinners to turn to Him. Emphasize God's power and His willingness to help in any difficult situation. Extend an invitation to unsaved students to accept Christ and allow Him to help them in their struggles of life.

Practicing Good Stewardship (Joash)

CENTRAL TRUTH

Wise use of resources brings glory to God.

GOLDEN TEXT

It is required that those who have been given a trust must prove faithful. 1 Corinthians 4:2 (NIV)

STUDY TEXT

2 Kings 12:1-16

OUTLINE

1. Challange To Action
   A. God's House Neglected
   B. Inexcusable Delay

2. Organize For Effectiveness
   A. An Orderly Beginning
   B. Financial Integrity
      Assured

3. Enlist Trustworthy Workers
   A. A Sacred Trust
   B. Testimony Of Faithfulness

OBJECTIVE

To recognize the importance of biblical stewardship and resolve to use our resources wisely.

CHECKLIST

☐ Read the *Adult Student Guide.* Write down any questions you might wish to use for discussion.

☐ Duplicate enough copies of the work sheets "Financial Statements" and "Financial Responsibility" from the Adult Teaching Helps Packet so each student will have one.

☐ Fill out the Planning The Session work sheet in order to help you plan for the activities you want to use in teaching this study.

☐ Emphasis the importance of supporting God's work financially. Throughout the week, look for practical, everyday examples of God's blessings on good stewardship. Stress the need to support the local church financially.

☐ With the help of a concordance, be prepared to cite various biblical passages concerning the financial responsibility of God's people. Have answers ready for students who do not understand tithing.

DAILY BIBLE READINGS

Monday:	Look For Wise Leaders.	Genesis 41:33-38
Tuesday:	Complete The Work.	Exodus 40:26-33
Wednesday:	Do Not Rob God.	Malachi 3:8-12
Thursday:	Treasures In Heaven.	Matthew 6:19-24
Friday:	Make Wise Decisions.	Matthew 7:24-27
Saturday:	Fulfill Obligations.	2 Corinthians 9:1-5

King James Version

2 Kings 12:4. Jehoash said to the priests, All the money of the dedicated things that is brought into the house of the Lord, even the money of every one that passeth the account, the money that every man is set at, and all the money that cometh into any man's heart to bring into the house of the Lord,

5. Let the priests take it to them, every man of his acquaintance: and let them repair the breaches of the house, wheresoever any breach shall be found.

6. But it was so, that in the three and twentieth year of king Jehoash the priests had not repaired the breaches of the house.

7. Then king Jehoash called for Jehoiada the priest, and the other priests, and said unto them, Why repair ye not the breaches of the house? now therefore receive no more money of your acquaintance, but deliver it for the breaches of the house.

8. And the priests consented to receive no more money of the people, neither to repair the breaches of the house.

9. But Jehoiada the priest took a chest, and bored a hole in the lid of it, and set it beside the altar, on the right side as one cometh into the house of the Lord: and the priests that kept the door put therein all the money that was brought into the house of the Lord.

10. And it was so, when they saw that there was much money in the chest, that the king's scribe and the high priest came up, and they put up in bags, and told the money that was found in the house of the Lord.

11. And they gave the money, being told, into the hands of them that did the work, that had the oversight of the house of the Lord: and they laid it out to the carpenters and builders, that wrought upon the house of the Lord,

12. And to masons, and hewers of stone, and to buy timber and hewed stone to repair the breaches of the house of the Lord, and for all that was laid out for the house to repair it.

13. Howbeit there were not made for the house of the Lord bowls of silver, snuffers, basins, trumpets, any vessels of gold, or vessels of silver, of the money that was brought into the house of the Lord:

14. But they gave that to the workmen, and repaired therewith the house of the Lord.

New International Version

2 Kings 12:4. Joash said to the priests, "Collect all the money that is brought as sacred offerings to the temple of the Lord—the money collected in the census, the money received from personal vows and the money brought voluntarily to the temple.

5. Let every priest receive the money from one of the treasurers, and let it be used to repair whatever damage is found in the temple."

6. But by the twenty-third year of King Joash the priests still had not repaired the temple.

7. Therefore King Joash summoned Jehoiada the priest and the other priests and asked them, "Why aren't you repairing the damage done to the temple? Take no more money from your treasurers, but hand it over for repairing the temple."

8. The priests agreed that they would not collect any more money from the people and that they would not repair the temple themselves.

9. Jehoiada the priest took a chest and bored a hole in its lid. He placed it beside the altar, on the right side as one enters the temple of the Lord. The priests who guarded the entrance put into the chest all the money that was brought to the temple of the Lord.

10. Whenever they saw that there was a large amount of money in the chest, the royal secretary and the high priest came, counted the money that had been brought into the temple of the Lord and put it into bags.

11. When the amount had been determined, they gave the money to the men appointed to supervise the work on the temple. With it they paid those who worked on the temple of the Lord—the carpenters and builders,

12. The masons and stonecutters. They purchased timber and dressed stone for the repair of the temple of the Lord, and met all the other expenses of restoring the temple.

13. The money brought into the temple was not spent for making silver basins, wick trimmers, sprinkling bowls, trumpets or any other articles of gold or silver for the temple of the Lord;

14. It was paid to the workmen, who used it to repair the temple.

Our attitude toward material things can indicate our spiritual perspective. When people are occupied solely with what they can gain in this present life, they forget that God is the One who has provided these resources for them to enjoy.

God wants us to enjoy those resources, but we must never forget that we are stewards, not owners. We must use these resources not just to please ourselves, but to please the One who has given them to us.

In this week's study King Joash knew he was a steward of God's resources. He could not allow the house of God to remain in a state of disrepair when the money was available for repairs. The king took vigorous corrective action to use God's resources wisely. Challenge for your students to examine how they use God's resources and begin to use them wisely and faithfully.

BIBLE COMMENTARY

1. Challenge To Action

A. God's House Neglected
2 Kings 12:4,5

TEACHING TIP 1: Distribute a copy of the agree/disagree work sheet "Financial Statements" to each student. Read each statement and have your students respond. Allow for some discussion, but do not spend too much time on this activity. This work sheet will get your students thinking about finances and to generate interest in this week's study.

The state of disrepair into which the temple had fallen reflected the attitude of a nation more interested in material things than God. Revenue for the temple came from various sources (2 Kings 12:4). Yet despite the funds that were available, the needed repair work to the temple was neglected.

Like any other building the temple deteriorated with the passing of time. In addition to this, during the reign of the wicked Queen Athaliah, idolaters had desecrated the temple by introducing Baal worship into its sacred areas (2 Chronicles 24:7). Someone was needed to mobilize the nation into action and repair the temple. God used Joash for this purpose. According to 2 Kings 12:5, Joash commanded the priests to take the money from the offerings and begin repairing the temple.

Ask: "What modern counterpart reflects the same attitude of the Israelites concerning God's house?" While the Israelites continued to bring their offerings, they did not seem to have much concern for the condition of the temple. As members of a local church, we must be concerned not only about the building (a minor concern), but about all aspects of the church. We must support the ministries of our local congregation.

Such support does involve finances. The church needs money to support a strong missions program and community outreach to the unsaved. If every Christian would tithe faithfully, there is no question that these needs would be met abundantly. But we must also recognize we are stewards of all the resources given to us by God, including our abilities. We must be concerned about the various ministries of our church and become involved in them.

It seems unusual that Joash would wait so long before he took matters into his hands. Of course he respected the priestly office and probably did not want to intrude into their duties. He had undoubtedly assumed they would carry out his orders.

Finally Joash took personal charge of the finances for the repair work, ordering the Levites not to receive any more money for this purpose (verse 7). The king was not usurping the priest's powers; he was simply taking action to correct their neglect.

Joash became a strong voice for restoring respect for the house of God. He set an example that should have come from the priests. He recognized his nation could expect God's blessings only when they walked in the path of His will. This included financial responsibility and a recognition of God's ownership of everything they had. In our age of materialism we need more people with a spirit like Joash. Biblical principles of stewardship need a new emphasis.

NOTES

B. Inexcusable Delay
2 Kings 12:6-8

The Levites were charged with collecting funds for the temple's repair. For some reason, however, they kept putting it off, and in the 23rd year of Joash's reign, no repair work had been started (2 Kings 12:6). No explanation is given for this indifference on the part of the priests, but it was inexcusable.

Obviously they did not have their priorities straight. Although they were set apart for special service to the Lord, taking care of the temple was not a burden on their hearts. They were accustomed to carrying out their daily routine and were comfortable with it. Putting forth an extra effort to do the work on the temple apparently seemed too much of an undertaking for them.

Ask: "What reasons do people give for not becoming involved in the ministry of the church today?"

TEACHING TIP 2: Write student suggestions on the chalkboard. Have them analyze them to determine which they feel are valid (there are no valid excuses; everyone can be involved in some way.) Use the following commentary to supplement the discussion.

Many claim lack of time or talent. Yet all believers have something to contribute to the ongoing ministries of their local church. Unfortunately, many do not want to take the responsibility of ministry. Yet Christ has called every believer to be a minister for Him (Matthew 28:19,20).

2. Organize For Effectiveness
A. An Orderly Beginning
2 Kings 12:9,10

Jehoiada the priest employed a unique means of raising the money. He took a chest and bored a hole in it. The king ordered that all money for the repair work be placed in this chest (2 Kings 12:9). From time to time the king's secretary and the high priest counted the money and turned it over to those who were in charge of the work of upkeep and repair (verse 10).

God is a God of order. His handiwork in creation shows organization of the highest degree. In doing His work, we must always be at our best and this requires attention to detail. When a project is begun, every person must know what his task is and what is expected of him. Authority must be delegated to capable individuals who know how to work with people and guide them in their assignments. Whether a task is large or small, organization plays a large part. Lack of it will only cause confusion and discouragement.

NOTES

B. Financial Integrity Assured
2 Kings 12:11,12

The people were assured their offerings would be used for the repair work, so they began responding faithfully. Every precaution was taken to make sure the finances were handled correctly. There was no room left for any question about the integrity of those in charge.

Ask: **"Why is it so important that God's people deal honestly in financial matters?"** Probably no area of life tests an individual's character like his attitude toward money. In recent years the spiritual decline of society has produced a looseness in regard to financial integrity. When this attitude invaded the Church, much harm resulted. God's people must do all they can to ensure that no accusing finger can be pointed at them in this area.

TEACHING TIP 3: Lead a brief discussion about areas of life besides the church where Christians must be careful to practice honesty. This might include the way income tax forms are filled out, calling a cashier's attention to the fact too much change was returned, and the proper handling of supplies at work.

Notice the various kinds of skills needed to repair the temple: carpenters, masons, and hewers of stone. Undoubtedly there were also many tasks that did not require a particular skill. Everyone was needed. Each workman contributed his part. And they were all assured of being paid on time because those in charge of finances were men of integrity.

Ask: **"How important is every individual in the ministry of the church?"** God has given each believer some ability or talent to contribute to His work. He has also placed spiritual gifts within the Church. Everyone is needed. No believer is unimportant in getting God's work done. Whether a church is large or small, there are always needs for believers to teach Sunday School, work in children or youth ministry, help with repairs around the church, and pray.

NOTES

3. Enlist Trustworthy Workers

A. A Sacred Trust
2 Kings 12:13,14

According to 2 Kings 12:13, there were many areas that required finances, but for this period of time the main attention was on repairing the temple. None of the money brought to the temple was spent on musical instruments or any of the various kinds of vessels involved in worship. All contributions went to the workmen. The people's response was tremendous and it was not long before the work began.

This decision to spend the money on repairs rather than providing additional utensils again shows accountability. When goals are defined and workers are committed to those goals, it becomes easier not to be sidetracked with other issues.

Ask: "What role does the financial accountability of an organization play in our giving to that organization?"

TEACHING TIP 4: God has called us to be wise stewards of His finances. This even includes giving to Christian organizations. Distribute the work sheet "Financial Accountability." Have the students look over the questions. While some Christian organizations are very accurate and upfront in their handling of finances, others are not. In some organizations, a majority of the money is spent on administrative expenses and very little is used for projects. Have your students take this work sheet home and use it to evaluate any ministries outside of your local church to which they give money.

The temple was the center to which the money was brought and from which it was spent to accomplish the work. Today the local church is the focal point of our mission for Christ. There are many worthy causes which constantly solicit money. Before contributing to them, each individual must make sure of the organization's financial accountability. When we bring our tithes and offerings to our local church, the supervision and accountability is in the church.

The people in Joash's day who contributed to repairing the temple saw the strictness with which everything was handled. No doubt this was an incentive for them to be free and enthusiastic with their giving.

Second Chronicles 24:14 is a parallel passage which provides an interesting sidelight. The offerings were so generous that after the workmen were paid there was enough money left to provide for the sacred vessels and musical instruments. This demonstrates that when God's people are generous in their giving, needs are supplied beyond expectations.

NOTES

B. Testimony Of Faithfulness
2 Kings 12:15,16

No matter how worthy a project is, it will succeed only in proportion to the sacrificial giving and faithfulness of those who participate. Doing God's work in any area is something never to be taken lightly. In God's eyes there are no unimportant workers or tasks. God looks for those who consider any service in His kingdom as a sacred trust which they will fulfill as the highest priority.

Second Kings 12:15 is an amazing commentary on a group of unnamed workmen. Ordinarily, receipts are required for every penny spent and a strict accounting of the time spent by every worker. This is only wise and practical. In our day it is more of a necessity than ever. However, the Scripture testifies to the corps of laborers of the temple. They were so honest that no accounting was required. The fact "they dealt faithfully" (verse 15) stands as an example for all time.

The attitude people have toward their work says a lot about their character. Even when we are engaged in secular work, we should be just as honest as these men were. This is a day when such character is rare, but it should always be seen among God's people. They should always do their work in such a way that they are not ashamed to collect their pay!

Ask: "How does this passage emphasize the dignity of work?" Tragically, our society has declined spiritually to the point that many consider "work" a bad word. However, God does not! The laborers in this passage have left their mark for all who read it as men who served the Lord by working with their hands.

When God instituted the priesthood under the law of Moses, He provided arrangements for the financial support of the priests. Joash would not deprive them of their lawful income by the arrangements for repairing the temple. Two classes of offerings called "the trespass money and sin money" (verse 16) were not brought to the temple but went directly to the priests. From that time on, gifts intended for the maintenance of the temple were kept separate from those intended for the priesthood.

NOTES

LIFE RESPONSE

We brought nothing into the world and can carry nothing out of it. However, while we are here we have been given the ability to gain resources through our earnings. These resources are gifts from God. Everything we have belongs to Him. And He has placed in our hands the responsibility of using these resources wisely.

Naturally we think first of money in regard to stewardship. To some people, acquiring money becomes an obsession, and they will sacrifice every principle to satisfy this hunger. Even God's people are under tremendous pressure to let materialism control their lives.

Being good stewards means not only paying our tithes to God, but also spending the rest of our money wisely. "Easy" credit tempts us to incur debt beyond our financial means. Unfortunately, some Christians have succumbed to this pressure until they are so financially strapped they do not give anything to God's work.

As believers we must evaluate our roles as stewards. Jesus indicated that how we handle finances determines our being able to handle "true riches" (Luke 16:11). The wise use of your resources for the kingdom of God will enhance your spiritual life and your church.

In a day when advertisements make promises that cannot possibly be fulfilled, invest in the kingdom of God. Make a commitment today to be faithful and wise in the use of the resources God provides.

EVANGELISM OUTREACH

Many who do not know the Lord live only for what they can get in the way of material possessions. Some may experience conviction concerning their selfish attitudes. This week's study emphasized that we must use our possessions to honor God. But before people can honor God with possessions, they must honor Him with their lives. Stress that God wants us to surrender our lives to Him. Offer to pray with any unsaved students who desire to surrender their lives to Christ.

Avoid Unwise Decisions (Hezekiah)

CENTRAL TRUTH

Integrity and honor can be destroyed by one foolish decision.

GOLDEN TEXT

Let the wise listen and add to their learning, and let the discerning get guidance. Proverbs 1:5 (NIV)

STUDY TEXT

2 Kings 20:1-21

OUTLINE

1. New Opportunities
   A. Unwelcome News
   B. Answered Prayer

2. Danger Of Vainglory
   A. Listening To Flattery
   B. Consorting With Evil

3. Tragedy Of Shortsightedness
   A. Warning About The Future
   B. Selfish Response

OBJECTIVE

To realize that wrong choices can mar God's purpose for our lives and avoid foolish decisions.

✓ CHECKLIST

☐ Read the *Adult Student Guide*. Write down any questions that you may wish to use for discussion.

☐ Duplicate enough copies of the work sheet "Study Review" for each student. Make sure you leave enough time at the end of class for this review and any discussion with the students concerning this week's study.

☐ Familiarize yourself with the entire record of Hezekiah's life from 2 Kings and 2 Chronicles. With the help of a concordance you can follow Hezekiah's career. Many passages in these two books are parallel. They supplement each other and often give the same information. The fact Hezekiah was a good king in so many ways makes the example of his unwise decision all the more tragic.

☐ Pray that God will help you impress upon your students the importance of seeking Him in all decisions of life.

DAILY BIBLE READINGS

Monday:	Tragic Choice.	
	Genesis 3:1-13	
Tuesday:	Wise Counsel.	
	Exodus 18:13-23	
Wednesday:	A Righteous Prayer.	
	1 Kings 3:1-10	
Thursday:	Sad Decision.	
	Matthew 26:1-4,14-16	
Friday:	Lying To God.	
	Acts 5:1-11	
Saturday:	Godly Warnings.	
	2 Timothy 2:14-21	

Scripture Setting

King James Version

2 Kings 20:1. In those days was Hezekiah sick unto death. And the prophet Isaiah the son of Amoz came to him, and said unto him, Thus saith the Lord, Set thine house in order; for thou shalt die, and not live.

2. Then he turned his face to the wall, and prayed unto the Lord, saying,

3. I beseech thee, O Lord, remember now how I have walked before thee in truth and with a perfect heart, and have done that which is good in thy sight. And Hezekiah wept sore.

4. And it came to pass, afore Isaiah was gone out into the middle court, that the word of the Lord came to him, saying,

5. Turn again, and tell Hezekiah the captain of my people, Thus saith the Lord, the God of David thy father, I have heard thy prayer, I have seen thy tears: behold, I will heal thee: on the third day thou shalt go up unto the house of the Lord.

6. And I will add unto thy days fifteen years; and I will deliver thee and this city out of the hand of the king of Assyria; and I will defend this city for mine own sake, and for my servant David's sake.

12. At that time Berodach—baladan, the son of Baladan, king of Babylon, sent letters and a present unto Hezekiah: for he had heard that Hezekiah had been sick.

13. And Hezekiah hearkened unto them, and shewed them all the house of his precious things, the silver, and the gold, and the spices, and the precious ointment, and all the house of his armor, and all that was found in his treasures: there was nothing in his house, nor in all his dominion, that Hezekiah showed them not.

16. And Isaiah said unto Hezekiah, Hear the word of the Lord.

17. Behold, the days come, that all that is in thine house, and that which thy fathers have laid up in store unto this day, shall be carried into Babylon: nothing shall be left, saith the Lord.

18. And of thy sons that shall issue from thee, which thou shalt beget, shall they take away; and they shall be eunuchs in the palace of the king of Babylon.

19. Then said Hezekiah unto Isaiah, Good is the word of the Lord which thou hast spoken. And he said, Is it not good, if peace and truth be in my days?

New International Version

2 Kings 20:1. In those days Hezekiah became ill and was at the point of death. The prophet Isaiah son of Amoz went to him and said, "This is what the Lord says: Put your house in order, because you are going to die; you will not recover."

2. Hezekiah turned his face to the wall and prayed to the Lord,

3. "Remember, O Lord, how I have walked before you faithfully and with wholehearted devotion and have done what is good in your eyes." And Hezekiah wept bitterly.

4. Before Isaiah had left the middle court, the word of the Lord came to him:

5. "Go back and tell Hezekiah, the leader of my people, 'This is what the Lord, the God of your father David, says: I have heard your prayer and seen your tears; I will heal you. On the third day from now you will go up to the temple of the Lord.

6. I will add fifteen years to your life. And I will deliver you and this city from the hand of the king of Assyria. I will defend this city for my sake and for the sake of my servant David.' "

12. At that time Merodach-Baladan son of Baladan king of Babylon sent Hezekiah letters and a gift, because he had heard of Hezekiah's illness.

13. Hezekiah received the messengers and showed them all that was in his storehouses—the silver, the gold, the spices and the fine oil—his armory and everything found among his treasures. There was nothing in his palace or in all his kingdom that Hezekiah did not show them.

16. Then Isaiah said to Hezekiah, "Hear the word of the Lord:

17. The time will surely come when everything in your palace, and all that your fathers have stored up until this day, will be carried off to Babylon. Nothing will be left, says the Lord.

18. And some of your descendants, your own flesh and blood, that will be born to you, will be taken away, and they will become eunuchs in the palace of the king of Babylon."

19. "The word of the Lord you have spoken is good," Hezekiah replied. For he thought, "Will there not be peace and security in my lifetime?"

Adult Teacher Guide

There is something depressing about watching an old building being wrecked. This sometimes happens when cities have progressed to the point that old landmarks must be removed to make room for a shopping center, or perhaps a new parking lot.

One blow from that swinging iron ball and the building will never look the same. An ugly crack appears where the blow has fallen and each succeeding swing of the ball helps bring about the total destruction of the old landmark.

Some human lives are like that. For years they may stand solid, stable, and true. Then something happens. One wrong choice can eventually bring down what was once a great character. This week's study focuses on the importance of choices. Allow Hezekiah's example to encourage you to seek God to help you make right choices.

BIBLE COMMENTARY

1. New Opportunities

A. Unwelcome News
2 Kings 20:1

No one likes to receive bad news, especially if it concerns death. Yet we know that none of us will live in this body forever. Death is an enemy that not even the righteous can escape.

Hezekiah was one of Israel's righteous kings who had exerted a strong spiritual influence on the nation. But even his service for God could not keep him from the tragedy of a fatal illness. Second Kings 20:1 begins with the record of the king's illness. Apparently Hezekiah's sickness resulted from some type of ulcer on his body. One day the Lord sent him the message through Isaiah that his earthly days were coming to an end. The sickness would result in death.

Ask: "Does Hezekiah's reaction seem unbecoming for a believer?" No one could rightfully blame the most devout believer for being shocked at the news of impending death. In Hezekiah's case, it becomes clear that his feelings involved more than concern for himself. He knew the records of some of Israel's past kings and probably wondered what would happen to the nation when he was gone. He had instituted strong reforms, but would a successor continue with them? Also, Hezekiah did not yet have a male heir to become king after his death. Hezekiah was aware of God's promise to his ancestor David that one from his lineage would always be on the throne. How would his imminent death affect that covenant?

The human side of us many times shrinks from the idea of death, even though for Christians it involves living eternally with Christ. Christians who know they are going to die will naturally have concerns about those they will be leaving. They may also realize they have unfinished business and wonder how others will carry it on.

NOTES

B. Answered Prayer
2 Kings 20:2-11

How we respond to bad news is important. While there are many reactions, such

as fear, anger, or unbelief, there is one action that is vital—seeking God. Hezekiah was a godly man who immediately sought help from the Lord (2 Kings 20:2,3). By turning his face to the wall, he indicated he wanted undisturbed communion with the Lord. His praying was also accompanied by much weeping.

Ask: "Why did Hezekiah remind the Lord of the kind of life he had lived?" This was not an expression of a self-righteous or selfish attitude. He knew one of God's promises to the righteous was a long life, and he could not understand how he could be denied this blessing.

Hezekiah's earnest praying brought quick results. Isaiah had not yet left the palace grounds when God sent him back to the king with good news of healing (verses 5-6).

TEACHING TIP 1: Lead a brief discussion of times the students had seen God reverse a situation because there was earnest, believing prayers on the part of the believer involved. Such testimonies could be personal or about others they have known.

God's message to Hezekiah was a wonderful example of God's tenderness and compassion: "I have heard thy prayer, I have seen thy tears: behold, I will heal thee" (verse 5). Our Heavenly Father is concerned about our tears. He understands every deep concern of our hearts.

God gave the king a confirming sign by telling him he would go to the temple in 3 days. This probably was a regular practice of Hezekiah. He loved God's house and set an example of worship for his people. On the third day, Hezekiah would be going to the temple to give thanks for his healing.

Few people know the length of their lives ahead of time. But God told Hezekiah that he would be given 15 more years. This would provide time to solidify the spiritual reforms he had begun. From 2 Kings 20:18,21, we know that during this time a son—Hezekiah's heir—would be born.

Verse 6 shows that God was aware of Hezekiah's concern about the danger posed by the king of Assyria. Along with the promise of healing came God's assurance that He would deliver the king and his people from this enemy.

Two reasons were given for this deliverance: "mine own sake, and for my servant David's sake." God assured Hezekiah that the covenant would be honored, for God guaranteed it by His personal word.

Whether the lump of figs (or fig poultice, verse 7, NIV) had any actual healing power is beside the point. The healing of the king was the result of God's miraculous power even if natural means were used. It seems more likely that the poultice was simply a sign or symbol of the promised healing.

Apparently God was not displeased with Hezekiah's request for a confirming sign. The Lord gave the king a choice of having the shadow on the sundial go either forward or backward. Obviously the greater miracle would be for the time to be set back. The term "degrees" probably means "steps." Sometimes sundials were constructed on stairs. The shadow would reflect the time of day by where it fell across these steps.

When Isaiah prayed, the Lord answered Hezekiah's request and brought the shadow back 10 steps. Hezekiah now had all the assurance he needed.

NOTES

2. Danger Of Vainglory

A. Listening To Flattery
2 Kings 20:12,13

Ask: "How can spiritual danger be greater during times when all is going

well than when we are in a crisis?'' When Hezekiah was sick and confronted by the possibility of death, he followed the right path carefully. Now that he had been healed and his life back to normal, it would appear he let his guard down. His spiritual sensitivity was not what it should have been. He made a foolish decision that affected his nation in days to come.

Some commentators believe the ruler of Babylon wanted Hezekiah as an ally against Assyria. Obviously Berodach-baladan was eager to impress Hezekiah with his friendship for him. When the Babylonian delegation arrived in Jerusalem with a personal letter and gift from their king, Hezekiah was immediately impressed (2 Kings 20:12). It was expected he would be courteous to the foreign dignitaries, but Hezekiah went much too far with his hospitality (verse 13).

Flattery is one of Satan's most useful tools. If the world snarls at us, we are immediately on guard. But if it shows a friendly side, we lose our sense of vigilance. There can be no question that these representatives of the Babylonian king were masters of diplomacy. Their government wanted something from Hezekiah, probably a military alliance. So they did an impressive job of selling themselves to a Jewish king who seemed incredibly naive on this occasion.

TEACHING TIP 2: Lead a discussion of how Christians today can fall prey to the overtures of the world system, the present age. Perhaps some of the students have had personal experience with the kind of temptation which confronted Hezekiah.

We are not immune to the same pitfalls Hezekiah faced. When the pressures of life force us to seek God because we have no resource but Him, temptations lose much of their power. It is in the days of prosperity and health that we must be particularly vigilant. Our enemy Satan knows ''every trick in the book,'' and he can take advantage of us at the moment we least suspect it. During such lax times, we could make bad decisions that would affect the future.

NOTES

B. Consorting With Evil
2 Kings 20:14,15

We must remember that Babylon epitomized all that was evil and against God. It was a heathen, idolatrous nation saturated with the occult. Friendship with the people from such a nation should have been the farthest thing from Hezekiah's mind.

Ask: ''Why is it possible that the very blessings God has given us so abundantly could be the means of temptation?'' God had blessed Hezekiah's nation materially as well as spiritually. His treasury was full. It would appear that Hezekiah had nothing lacking in his life financially. It is puzzling that he chose to ''show off'' all these evidences of God's blessings to these heathen.

You can be sure the Babylonian envoys would carry the news of Hezekiah's riches back home. Most definitely the rulers of Babylon would immediately have designs on them. In fact, the day would come when the Babylonian invader would carry these riches away and make captives of the Jews. Even though Hezekiah himself would die before this happened, he had set forces in motion that would show themselves later.

What an example Hezekiah is of the danger of pride. He was a good man, a righteous king, one who loved God and wanted the nation to serve Him. Yet he became so proud of what God had given him that he could not resist showing it off to enemies.

Hezekiah demonstrated a spirit of pride. He was showing off when he said, in effect, ''Look what I have!'' We must always remember that whatever we have in the way of blessings are gifts from God. Never must we allow those blessings to lift us up in pride until we lose our perspective, making ourselves to be something that we are not.

God was aware of everything that was happening and He revealed it to Isaiah. The prophet confronted Hezekiah immediately with questions: "Who were these men?" "Where did they come from?" Hezekiah's answer seems to show he felt no concern. Without hesitation he told Isaiah they were from Babylon (2 Kings 20:14).

When the prophet asked what Hezekiah had shown these envoys, he replied that they had seen everything. There was nothing in his palace that he hid from them (verse 15). Thus far the implications of his foolish decisions appear to have escaped the king.

NOTES

3. Tragedy Of Shortsightedness

A. Warning About The Future
2 Kings 20:16-18

Even though Hezekiah could not discern the wrongness of his decision, Isaiah could. God had a message for the king (2 Kings 20:16). Isaiah's prediction of the Babylonian captivity in verses 17,18 seemed unlikely. Assyria had been the greatest threat to the Jews. The Babylonians had not yet become the power they would later be.

Hezekiah's hospitality to the envoys from Babylon was apparently intended to gain favor with them. However, God sees the future. The day would come when the warning He sent through Isaiah would be fulfilled by the Babylonian invasion, leaving

Israel in shambles. Babylon would be the great oppressor of the Jews. The Babylonians would take the Jews into captivity and take all the treasures Hezekiah had shown the visiting dignitaries. Some of Hezekiah's own descendants would be captured and employed as eunuchs in the palace of Babylon. This is an example of the ongoing effects of a foolish decision. It proves we do not live in isolation and what we do will affect others.

Ask: "Does it seem strange that the actions of one man could produce such consequences?" Hezekiah was not an ordinary citizen. He was the king, the leader of his people. Those who are in positions of responsibility must be especially careful of their conduct. Their actions have effects more far-reaching than those of others.

NOTES

B. Selfish Response
2 Kings 20:19,20

Ask: "How should we interpret Hezekiah's response to Isaiah's warning?" Some commentators interpret Hezekiah's response as simply a humble submission to God's will. However, there is a hint of another, not so admirable, attitude. There was obvious relief on Hezekiah's part that the predicted judgment would not happen in his lifetime. That he was happy not to suffer for his actions even though others would was selfish and shortsighted.

God records the lives of His servants fairly. Following the account of Hezekiah's failure, the Holy Spirit inspired the writer to tell of some of the king's great achievements. He instituted projects which greatly increased Jerusalem's water supply—something very important during an enemy's siege during war. The pool, or reservoir, spoken of in verse 20, became known later as the pool of Siloam (see John 9:11).

In Hezekiah we have an example of a righteous man whose general path was a godly one. Furthermore, he led his nation in that direction. He is also a warning that we must never be unmindful of the consequences of our decisions.

TEACHING TIP 3: Distribute the work sheet "Study Review." After students have completed the work sheet, discuss their responses, making appropriate application to their lives.

NOTES

LIFE RESPONSE

Hezekiah was one of the best kings the nation of Judah had. He worked hard to bring religious reform to his nation. It was his intercession before God that brought deliverance from the Assyrian army. At a time when it seemed he would soon die, Hezekiah could look back on a life of faithful service to God. It is good to have such memories when we face our last hours on earth. We cannot be careless about our relationship with God throughout life and expect to be suddenly faithful and godly in our last days. What we are now could very well determine what we will be at the end.

Hezekiah is also an example of God's mercy. God saw his tears and sent a message of healing. But when God performs a miracle of healing for us, we have the responsibility to make sure our lives thereafter are lived in the path of His perfect will. Hezekiah apparently let down his guard when he was enjoying good health and success in his reign.

No matter how many victories we gain in the Christian life, we will be in a spiritual battle to our last day on earth. We must remember that a single act can damage, and sometimes destroy, the work of a lifetime. That act can also have repercussions in the lives of others. We are responsible to be on continual guard, being diligent to maintain spiritual sensitivity. As we seek Him, the Holy Spirit will let us know when we are making a wrong decision. And He will be faithful to direct us in the right way.

EVANGELISM OUTREACH

Although Hezekiah was a devout king, the example of his foolish decision is a lesson for the unsaved as well. Unwise decisions do affect our lives and the lives of others. By not accepting Christ, the unsaved person is making a decision to reject Him. To continually reject Him is a decision that will have eternal consequences. Allow time at the end of class to invite unsaved students to accept Christ. Some may wish to remain after class to talk to you about their spiritual need. ▭

Follow God's Leadership Manual (Josiah)

CENTRAL TRUTH

The Bible is the best source of insight for good leadership principles.

GOLDEN TEXT

I have hidden your word in my heart that I might not sin against you. Psalm 119:11 (NIV)

STUDY TEXT

2 Kings 22:1 through 23:30

OUTLINE

1. Know The Bible
   A. Read The Word
   B. Commit To Obedience

2. Obey The Bible
   A. Cleanse The Temple
   B. Stop Evil Practices

3. Celebrate Redemption
   A. Remember God's
      Deliverance
   B. Separation From Evil

OBJECTIVE

To accept the Bible as God's Word and humble ourselves under its authority.

CHECKLIST

☐ Duplicate enough copies of the work sheet "The Bible And Life" from the Adult Teaching Helps Packet so you will have one for each student. This work sheet, used in Teaching Tip 3, will help summarize the theme of the study. Be sure to allow time for group discussion.

☐ Stress the importance of Bible study. Share some personal illustrations from your own life about it's value. Give students an opportunity to share their own experiences. We do not get all the understanding of God's Word we need by attending Sunday School and church. Attention must be given to personal Bible study and meditation each day.

DAILY BIBLE READINGS

Monday:	Godly Commandments. Deuteronomy 5:17-22
Tuesday:	Covenant Renewal. Joshua 24:14-26
Wednesday:	Blessings Of The Word. Psalm 119:1-8
Thursday:	The Living Word. John 1:14-18
Friday:	Power Of The Word. 2 Timothy 4:1-5
Saturday:	Obey The Word. 2 John 1-13

SCRIPTURE SETTING

King James Version

2 Kings 23:2. The king went up into the house of the Lord, and all the men of Judah and all the inhabitants of Jerusalem with him, and the priests, and the prophets, and all the people, both small and great: and he read in their ears all the words of the book of the covenant which was found in the house of the Lord.

3. And the king stood by a pillar, and made a covenant before the Lord, to walk after the Lord, and to keep his commandments and his testimonies and his statutes with all their heart and all their soul, to perform the words of this covenant that were written in this book. And all the people stood to the covenant.

4. And the king commanded Hilkiah the high priest, and the priests of the second order, and the keepers of the door, to bring forth out of the temple of the Lord all the vessels that were made for Baal, and for the grove, and for all the host of heaven: and he burned them without Jerusalem in the fields of Kidron, and carried the ashes of them unto Beth—el.

5. And he put down the idolatrous priests, whom the kings of Judah had ordained to burn incense in the high places in the cities of Judah, and in the places round about Jerusalem; them also that burned incense unto Baal, to the sun, and to the moon, and to the planets, and to all the host of heaven.

21. And the king commanded all the people, saying, Keep the passover unto the Lord your God, as it is written in the book of this covenant.

22. Surely there was not holden such a passover from the days of the judges that judged Israel, nor in all the days of the kings of Israel, nor of the kings of Judah;

23. But in the eighteenth year of king Josiah, wherein this passover was holden to the Lord in Jerusalem.

24. Moreover the workers with familiar spirits, and the wizards, and the images, and the idols, and all the abominations that were spied in the land of Judah and in Jerusalem, did Josiah put away, that he might perform the words of the law, which were written in the book that Hilkiah the priest found in the house of the Lord.

25. And like unto him was there no king before him, that turned to the Lord with all his heart, and with all his soul, and with all his might, according to all the law of Moses; neither after him arose there any like him.

New International Version

2 Kings 23:2. He went up to the temple of the Lord with the men of Judah, the people of Jerusalem, the priests and the prophets—all the people from the least to the greatest. He read in their hearing all the words of the Book of the Covenant, which had been found in the temple of the Lord.

3. The king stood by the pillar and renewed the covenant in the presence of the Lord—to follow the Lord and keep his commands, regulations and decrees with all his heart and all his soul, thus confirming the words of the covenant written in this book. Then all the people pledged themselves to the covenant.

4. The king ordered Hilkiah the high priest, the priests next in rank and the doorkeepers to remove from the temple of the Lord all the articles made for Baal and Asherah and all the starry hosts. He burned them outside Jerusalem in the fields of the Kidron Valley and took the ashes to Bethel.

5. He did away with the pagan priests appointed by the kings of Judah to burn incense on the high places of the towns of Judah and on those around Jerusalem—those who burned incense to Baal, to the sun and moon, to the constellations and to all the starry hosts.

21. The king gave this order to all the people: "Celebrate the Passover to the Lord your God, as it is written in this Book of the Covenant."

22. Not since the days of the judges who led Israel, nor throughout the days of the kings of Israel and the kings of Judah, had any such Passover been observed.

23. But in the eighteenth year of King Josiah, this Passover was celebrated to the Lord in Jerusalem.

24. Furthermore, Josiah got rid of the mediums and spiritists, the household gods, the idols and all the other detestable things seen in Judah and Jerusalem. This he did to fulfill the requirements of the law written in the book that Hilkiah the priest had discovered in the temple of the Lord.

25. Neither before nor after Josiah was there a king like him who turned to the Lord as he did—with all his heart and with all his soul and with all his strength, in accordance with all the Law of Moses.

OPENING THOUGHTS

Imagine a nation from which the Bible has totally disappeared for many years. Think of churches being used for idolatrous worship instead of the worship of God. This was the condition of Israel when Josiah came to the throne. The effects of scriptural ignorance showed itself in the nation's life. Even the priests were not being true to their call to service.

King Josiah was unaware of the existence of the Law until the high priest discovered it in the temple. The king was horrified when he heard the words of the Law, for it showed him the nation's guilt before God. This righteous king began immediate steps to lead his people back to God.

As we look at this week's study, let us determine to make God' Word a priority in our lives. When we do, we will find God's purpose in serving Him.

BIBLE COMMENTARY

1. Know The Bible

A. Read The Word
2 Kings 23:1

Approximately 200 years prior to Josiah, king Joash had rebuilt the temple (2 Kings 12). But some of the kings that followed were not strong religious leaders. About 75 years before Josiah the godly king Hezekiah brought revival to Judah. But the 55 year reign of Manasseh and the 2 year reign of Amon that followed were low points in Judah's history. Idol worship was reintroduced into the temple. As a result, the temple came into a state of disrepair.

Josiah was 8 years old when he began to reign (2 Kings 22:1). During the eighteenth year of his reign, Josiah ordered the repair of the temple (verse 3). Evidently he had instituted the process for acquiring the money for this at an earlier date (verse 4).

In the process of repairing the temple, the book of the Law was discovered. No doubt it had been years since it had been read. When the book was brought to the king and he heard the judgments of God for idolatry, he began a campaign to rid the land of idol worship.

In 2 Kings 23:1 we discover that Josiah first called the people back to the Law. The king sent out a command for the leaders of the nation to gather in Jerusalem.

Ask: "Why was it important for Josiah to lead this reform?" We would have expected the priests to initiate national religious reform. But without the king's approval, the priest's ability to bring about this reform would probably have been hindered. Since the king was the leader, it would be more likely that the nation would follow him. When national leaders seek the righteousness of God, God blesses a nation and the people can live peaceable lives (see 1 Timothy 2:1,2).

The gathering in Jerusalem was for one purpose—the public reading of the Law. How tragic that this was the first time for the people to hear what God said about His relationship with them. He declared that as long as they obeyed Him, they could expect His blessings, but if they forsook the Law, judgment would fall on them. It is obvious that this was what made such an impression on the king when the priest read the Law to him. He knew the spiritual condition of the nation and feared what would happen if they did not get back to God.

TEACHING TIP 1: Lead a discussion concerning the importance of the Word in our lives. Ask your students to suggest ways God has helped them live holy lives through His Word. Have them share their methods for daily devotions and Bible study as well. If any in your class are not spending time daily in the Word, strongly encourage them to do so.

NOTES

B. Commit To Obedience
2 Kings 23:2,3

In order for the people to obey the Law, they had to know it. The king was going to lead his people in a commitment of obedience to the Law. After Josiah gathered the people, he began to read from the Law. The priests may have helped him and took turns reading the Law to the people. The "pillar" mentioned in verse 3 may have been one of the pillars supporting the temple, although some commentators believe Josiah stood on a raised platform. It is certain that he took a position where he could be seen and heard by everyone.

Ask: "What is the value of a public commitment such as the one described in this passage?" Sometimes our vows and pledges are a matter between us and the Lord. But there are also occasions when publicly declaring our commitment to the Lord strengthens our desire to maintain that commitment. This is why many churches have altar services for people to come and renew their vows to God.

The king would not ask the people to make a pledge that he would not make. Before all those assembled, he renewed his commitment to follow the Lord. To "walk

after the Lord" describes a daily life where we follow the Word of God. On this occasion, both the king and the people acknowledged they would begin to follow the Law.

TEACHING TIP 2: The terms "commandments . . . testimonies and . . . statutes" (verse 3) describe various aspects of God's Word. Ask the students for suggestions as to what each of the terms means. (Make sure you have looked them up in a Bible dictionary or commentary.) Then have them explain how each affects or can be applied to daily living.

The Bible has guidance for every situation we encounter in life. It has instructions for individuals and families, for the young and old, for men and women. It is important that we read the Scriptures so we will have a solid foundation on which to build our lives and our characters.

NOTES

2. Obey The Bible

A. Cleanse The Temple
2 Kings 23:4

It was not enough for Josiah and the people to pledge themselves to obey the Law. Action had to be taken to remove everything that defiled the land.

God had strictly forbidden the worship of idols. Yet such worship had been actually taking place in the temple. The fact idolatry was occurring in the temple indicates that the pagan priests were allowed in the temple. If the nation was to enjoy God's blessings again, this evil had to be removed.

Ask: "Why had the priests allowed idol worship to defile the temple?" Of all people, these men should have taken the lead to cleanse the house of God. Earlier the priests had failed to withstand the wicked king Manassah when he introduced idol worship into the temple (2 Kings 21:4,7). As a result, over a period of time the priesthood had apparently lost its sense of responsibility to God.

The same is true today. When the Church and its leaders cease to hold strong convictions and act upon them, society suffers and the forces of evil strengthen their grip. If we are going to obey the commandments set forth in the Bible, we must get rid of things in our life that are contrary to the Word.

We cannot serve the Lord effectively if we allow practices in our lives that are forbidden in the Bible. Just as the priests were called on to cleanse the temple and remove all of its defilement, God calls us to seek Him and get rid of anything that would hinder our relationship with Him or our witness of His goodness in our lives.

NOTES

B. Stop Evil Practices
2 Kings 23:5-7

Idolatry involves people. Baal worship had its priesthood. Some of the wicked kings of Israel had appointed priests to serve the people in their idolatrous practices. Josiah stopped the activities of these men. No longer would they be allowed to burn incense to these idols.

The high places were elevated locations where much of this idolatry took place. It seemed they were hard to remove. Their prominent locations kept the temptation to idol worship before the people.

Ask: "Why were there so many varieties of idol worship—Baal, Asherah, and the heavenly bodies?" When people try to replace God in their lives, they find the vacancy impossible to fill. Consequently they keep trying new activities and new kinds of religion, searching for something that will give them peace and satisfaction. Of course they never find what they are looking for, so they keep on searching.

When Josiah had the Asherah pole removed from the temple, he ordered it burned at the brook Kidron (verse 6). The ashes were then beaten into powder and sprinkled on the graves of the common people. This was to show the contempt idolatry deserved. What had once stood as an object of worship was now scattered among the locations associated with death.

Gross immorality always attended idol worship. Living quarters for the male prostitutes involved in idolatry were next to the temple. According to verse 7, Josiah ordered these houses destroyed.

In this fervent attempt to rid the land of the stench of idolatry we have an example of being not only hearers of the Word, but doers. Such a spirit is needed in our own day of spiritual declension and wickedness.

TEACHING TIP 3: To emphasize that idolatry can take many forms, ask students to mention some things today that are replacing the worship of God in the lives of people. You may want to list these on the chalkboard or a blank transparency to impress them on the minds of the students. Ask them to suggest possible actions that they can take to get rid of these things.

3. Celebrate Redemption

A. Remember God's Deliverance
2 Kings 23:21-23

The king's obedience to God's command to observe the Passover is noteworthy. Such was his desire to please the Lord that there had not been a Passover celebration like this one since the days of the judges.

Ask: "Why was it important for the Israelites to renew their observation of the Passover?" This feast reminded the people why they were God's covenant nation. The Passover emphasized that God's covenant with them was sealed by the blood of a sacrificial lamb. Had it not been for God's miraculous deliverance they would still be a nation of slaves. Also the contrast between the true worship of God and the worship of idols would be seen by the people. This would remind them of how far they had fallen from the purpose of God for their lives.

As Christians, we do not look back on literal slavery to a foreign nation. However, there is a bondage just as severe—slavery to sin. The Christian life should be a continual celebration of our deliverance from sin through the blood of Jesus.

Yet our salvation is not based on feelings. It is based on the truth revealed in the Bible. God did not allow man to devise his own plan of salvation. God set forth in the Scriptures how we can be saved from sin and become His children—by repenting of sin and accepting Christ as Savior we can be saved. Then we can enter into this wonderful celebration. We will know the deliverance from sin that Christ, the Passover Lamb, died to purchase.

B. Separation From Evil
2 Kings 23:24,25

It was not enough for the king and his people to observe the Passover. There was still work that needed to be done. There were still "workers with familiar spirits, and the wizards, and the images, and the idols, and all the abominations" (2 Kings 23:24) that needed to be taken care of.

The occult thrives in the kind of atmosphere that develops when the Bible is rejected or ignored. Man must have something to worship. When it is not the true God, other religions rush in to fill the vacuum. This is true in our own time to an astounding degree. The supernatural of the occult is attracting many followers today.

Ask: "Beside the occult, what other false religions must we beware of today?" There are many teachings which may seem more sophisticated or exciting, but which belong to a religion of works. The New Age is one example. There are other religions which have been around a long time and still claim their followers. Some are very clever in the way they word their teachings, using the same words as the true gospel, but changing the meanings. From all of these deceptions we must keep a great distance, not letting curiosity lead us to experiment with them.

False religion is not the only thing from which Christians must be separate. Ours is a permissive society which has rejected the standards of right and wrong taught in the Bible. This calls for greater attention to God's teachings in His Word. It takes self-discipline to maintain a holy walk today, but we must do it whatever the cost. When

God has paid such a price to redeem us, we can do no less than follow in the path He has shown us in the Bible.

Josiah was intent on fulfilling all the words that were written in the book of the Law. There was not a king before him "that turned to the Lord with all his heart, and with all his soul, and with all his might" (verse 25). May we have a heart like Josiah. Having read God's Word, let us determine to do all that we can to be obedient to its commands.

TEACHING TIP 4: Distribute the work sheet "The Bible And Life." Divide the class into groups of four or five students and assign each group one of the questions on this work sheet.

Have each group discuss the assigned question for about 5 minutes, then ask for a response. Discuss each response with the rest of the class.

NOTES

LIFE RESPONSE

Living without the Bible is like taking a trip across the country without a road map. The chances of arriving at the expected destination are very slim.

Life is full of twists and turns. Unexpected dangers sometimes appear. We are often faced with decisions for which we cannot find an answer. Where will we get our guidance, our direction, the values which determine the path we should take?

The prevailing philosophy in today's society is that there are no absolutes, no unchanging values. Secular humanism urges everyone to do what he feels like doing, for self is at the center of each individual's little universe. It is no wonder there is such turmoil and trouble all around us.

Just as we need a map to guide us on a trip, we need a map for our spiritual journey. The Bible, God's unerring Word, provides guidelines for living which do not change with the passing of time. In His Word we find comfort in our sorrows, the truth about God, His love, His plan of salvation, and the gift of the Holy Spirit.

To know the Bible means to meditate on it and study its teachings each day. We must not allow it to become a lost book because of our neglect. To live a victorious life, we must accept the Bible's authority as God's message to us. This means obeying its teachings in every choice, every decision. It means saying, "Not my will, Lord, but Yours." This week make sure God's Word has a primary place in your life.

EVANGELISM OUTREACH

In your outreach to unsaved students, stress the truth that the Bible alone shows us God's plan of salvation. No matter what we may think, the Word of God is the final authority. Emphasize that the plan of salvation is simple and easy to understand. God only asks that we believe on His Son as our Lord and Savior, repent of our sins, and confess Him publicly. Plan for time to extend an invitation to the unsaved at the end of the class period. Invite some of your students to pray with them.

INTRODUCTION

CHRISTIAN VALUES

Values is a word that is used quite frequently in today's society. Both liberals and conservatives proclaim that they are teaching family values. But when we examine their teachings, they seem to contradict each other. We ask, "Who is right?"

Others say that we are to teach values, but leave out religion. But one might ask, "What is the basis for the values they want to teach?" Some even proclaim that there is no such thing as absolute values. The situation of the moment determines what is right or wrong. After hearing all of the views of each group, one might wonder, *Which belief is right? Are values really that important?*

You and your students live in a world where values are questioned and teachings on values seem contradictory. This is why you must have your value system anchored in God's Word and then be able to help your students develop biblical values to live by.

The basis for all of our values must be the Bible. Study 9 emphasizes that God's Word is truth. As such, we can trust it as a basis for our values. Also true Christian values cannot be developed outside of a relationship with God (study 10). As believers, we must value that relationship above all else.

Our demonstration of Christian values is known as integrity. Study 11 examines some aspects of itegrity that need to be a part of us. Ethics, or the morality behind behavior, is another part of Christian values (study 12). Our Christian ethics will help us determine the value of life.

Lastly this unit presents a pattern for discovering true meaning in our lives (study 13). When we give God priority in our lives, we find the meaning of life that God intended us to have. As you and your students study this unit, ask God to help each of you develop a value system that is true to God's Word and brings honor to Him in daily living.

Truth: Basis For Christian Values

CENTRAL TRUTH

Christian values are derived from the Word of God.

GOLDEN TEXT

I have chosen the way of truth; I have set my heart on your laws. Psalm 119:30 (NIV)

STUDY TEXT

Psalm 19:1-4; John 1:14; 8:31,32; 14:6,7; 17:17; Romans 1:18-20; 2 Timothy 3:14-17

OUTLINE

1. Truth Revealed In Creation
   A. Universal Message
   B. Universal Response

2. The Bible Is Truth
   A. Sanctified By God's Truth
   B. Lifelong Application

3. Jesus Is The Truth
   A. The Word Made Flesh
   B. Truth Demands Obedience

OBJECTIVE

To know that Christian values are rooted in biblical truth and incorporate them into our manner of living.

CHECKLIST

☐ Read the student guide and look for ways to correlate the material from it in your teaching. Note in your presentation where you can discuss questions from the student guide.

☐ Contact a student early in the week and ask for a short report on the false concepts of Christ promoted by one or two modern cults. The report only needs to be 2-3 minutes long and offer a summary view of the cults the student chooses to study.

☐ Practice integrating the two overhead transparencies from the Adult Teaching Helps Packet, "Growing Through The Word" and "Applying God's Truth To Life," in this study.

☐ Pray that unsaved students will be convinced of Jesus Christ's ability to save them and bring them into a right relationship with God. Pray also that the students will make a new commitment to rely on Christ to help them express God's truth through the values they hold.

DAILY BIBLE READINGS

Monday: Recognizing Worldly Values.
Isaiah 59:4-9

Tuesday: Rejecting Truth.
Jeremiah 5:1-6

Wednesday: The City Of Truth.
Zechariah 8:3-17

Thursday: Truth In Worship.
John 4:20-26

Friday: Search For Truth.
Acts 17:16-23

Saturday: Prayer For Truth.
1 Timothy 2:1-6

Scripture Setting

King James Version

Psalms 19:1. The heavens declare the glory of God; and the firmament showeth his handiwork.

2. Day unto day uttereth speech, and night unto night showeth knowledge.

3. There is no speech nor language, where their voice is not heard.

4. Their line is gone out through all the earth, and their words to the end of the world. In them hath he set a tabernacle for the sun.

Romans 1:18. For the wrath of God is revealed from heaven against all ungodliness and unrighteousness of men, who hold the truth in unrighteousness;

19. Because that which may be known of God is manifest in them; for God hath showed it unto them.

20. For the invisible things of him from the creation of the world are clearly seen, being understood by the things that are made, even his eternal power and Godhead; so that they are without excuse.

John 17:17. Sanctify them through thy truth: thy word is truth.

2 Timothy 3:16. All Scripture is given by inspiration of God, and is profitable for doctrine, for reproof, for correction, for instruction in righteousness:

17. That the man of God may be perfect, thoroughly furnished unto all good works.

John 1:14. The Word was made flesh, and dwelt among us, (and we beheld his glory, the glory as of the only begotten of the Father,) full of grace and truth.

8:31. Then said Jesus to those Jews which believed on him, If ye continue in my word, then are ye my disciples indeed;

32. And ye shall know the truth, and the truth shall make you free.

14:6. Jesus saith unto him, I am the way, the truth, and the life: no man cometh unto the Father, but by me.

7. If ye had known me, ye should have known my Father also: and from henceforth ye know him, and have seen him.

New International Version

Psalm 19:1. The heavens declare the glory of God; the skies proclaim the work of his hands.

2. Day after day they pour forth speech; night after night they display knowledge.

3. There is no speech or language where their voice is not heard.

4. Their voice goes out into all the earth, their words to the ends of the world. In the heavens he has pitched a tent for the sun.

Romans 1:18. The wrath of God is being revealed from heaven against all the godlessness and wickedness of men who suppress the truth by their wickedness,

19. Since what may be known about God is plain to them, because God has made it plain to them.

20. For since the creation of the world God's invisible qualities—his eternal power and divine nature—have been clearly seen, being understood from what has been made, so that men are without excuse.

John 17:17. Sanctify them by the truth; your word is truth.

2 Timothy 3:16. All Scripture is God-breathed and is useful for teaching, rebuking, correcting and training in righteousness,

17. So that the man of God may be thoroughly equipped for every good work.

John 1:14. The Word became flesh and made his dwelling among us. We have seen his glory, the glory of the One and Only, who came from the Father, full of grace and truth.

8:31. To the Jews who had believed him, Jesus said, "If you hold to my teaching, you are really my disciples.

32. Then you will know the truth, and the truth will set you free."

14:6. Jesus answered, "I am the way and the truth and the life. No one comes to the Father except through me.

7. If you really knew me, you would know my Father as well. From now on, you do know him and have seen him."

Many values for living associated with Christianity can be found in other religions. Buddhism, for example, includes practices promoted by Christ. But the examination of Christian values must rest on a foundation that is distinct from worldly philosophy and religion.

This week's study emphasizes truth as the foundation for our values. But to say that truth is the basis for Christian values, we must define exactly what that truth is.

The Bible clearly teaches that God is the Source of truth. This week's study examines three ways in which God has proclaimed His truth to the world, culminating in Jesus Christ, the living Truth. When we accept the truth of Christ's claims, we are accepting the full revelation of God's truth. We are then in a position to apply His truth to our values.

BIBLE COMMENTARY

1. Truth Revealed In Creation

A. Universal Message
Psalm 19:1-4

"The heavens declare the glory of God; the firmament showeth his handiwork" (Psalm 19:1). Perhaps David was remembering a clear night outside of Bethlehem when he was a young shepherd caring for his father's flocks. David, like every person who looks up at the sky, was awestruck at what he saw. But David's response to God's creation was far different from that of many of his contemporaries.

Astrology had long been practiced in the ancient Near East even before David's time. But instead of worshiping the stars, David allowed the stars to remind him of the one and only God who is worthy of worship. And David realized that the real message of God's existence was apparent for all people to see.

TEACHING TIP 1: Ask a student to read Psalm 19:2-4 to the class. Have the other students note every word or phrase that describes the extent to which creation speaks of God's existence and power. List responses on the board or a blank transparency.

David's response to creation was that of a believer in the true God. David expressed his love for God by worshiping God as Creator. Christians experience the same heartfelt response to God today. But those of us who worship God in response to nature's majesty are certainly in the minority in today's world. If it were not for the grace of God that has impacted human hearts by His Holy Spirit, every single one of us would respond very differently to creation.

NOTES

when we are overcome by our trials and problems our God in a small [word] - We need to look to the heaven and see the stars, our God is bigger than the heaven - It builds our faith

B. Universal Response
Romans 1:18-20

Paul wrote of the genuinely human response to nature in his epistle to the Romans. Romans 1:18-20 gives a succinct view of the relationship between a holy God and fallen humanity. That relationship, sadly, is one characterized by "wrath" (verse 18). God's anger at human sin is justified, Paul wrote, because all people sin in spite of their knowledge of the truth.

Ask: "Where do people get this knowledge of the truth if they have never heard the gospel?" As verses 19 and 20 point out, God has shown through the visible creation ample evidence of His invisible presence and power. The creation testifies that God exists.

Ask: "What has the study of nature brought about in the world's view of who God is?" In today's world, the study of nature has led some people away from God. Many attempt to understand life through their own wisdom instead of God's. They either make nature the source of a false religion, or they twist their knowledge of nature into a claim for no religion.

Consider the first category. Just as the nations of David's day had become bound by astrology and the idolatrous worship of objects in nature, so have false religions centered around nature today. The Hindu pantheon includes almost countless gods and goddesses represented by various parts of nature. African animism associates invisible spirits with objects in nature.

In the other approach to nature, people limit their studies strictly to the material realm and deny the existence of an invisible Creator. The evolutionist explains all of nature's phenomena as the result of cause and effect over billions of years.

While not all evolutionists are antireligionists, many are quite hostile toward religion, and particularly Christianity. They perceive it as a threat to scientific inquiry. One evolutionist, when describing the creation narrative in Genesis, advocated continuing the defiance toward God that was evident in the orginal sin of Adam and Eve.

While giving powerful evidence for God's presence and creative influence, nature remains inadequate in drawing people into a relationship with God. People are reminded of God's presence by their surroundings, but human nature continues in rebellion.

NOTES

The creation in not to be worshiped — It tells of God but not of Jesus our Savior.

2. The Bible Is Truth

A. Sanctified By God's Truth
John 17:17

Certain aspects of God have been revealed to all people through His creation, history, and conscience. This is known as "general revelation." General revelation makes people aware of God, but cannot save a person from sin's eternal consequences. But God in His mercy has provided truth concerning himself beyond nature. This truth is found in His inspired Word.

In John 17:17, Jesus set forth the standard for truth—God's Word. If believers are going to develop Christian values in their lives, they must first come to the knowledge of those values. Contrary to the philosophies of this world is the truth of true Christian living found in the Bible.

In order for believers to live by Christian values, there needs to be a sanctifying work in our lives. "Sanctify them through thy truth," Christ prayed to His Father on behalf of His followers. "Thy word is truth" (verse 17).

Ask: "What is sanctification?" Sanctification is the means by which we are made holy and set apart for God's service. When we are saved, we are miraculously transformed as people separate from the lost masses of our world. While we experience sanctification at salvation, it is also a process in our lives.

NOTES

B. Lifelong Application
2 Timothy 3:14-17

"Continue thou" is a key phrase in 2 Timothy 3:14-17. It sets the tone for the statements Paul made to Timothy concerning the value of God's Word. Timothy had the privilege of being raised by a godly mother and grandmother (1:5). Their influence was responsible for the knowledge of the Scriptures Timothy received as a child (3:15). At the time Paul had written his letter to Timothy, Timothy was helping to establish the growing church in Ephesus.

Verse 15 highlights the knowledge of salvation found in the Bible. Timothy had applied this knowledge personally. He had been saved. As a growing Christian, and a minister to others, Timothy would find the wisdom in God's Word to be ever useful in developing spiritual maturity.

Ask: "What other results of studying Scripture did Paul emphasize in 2 Timothy 3:16,17?"

"Doctrine" refers to the teachings of God's truth. This is the specific information about God and His laws. "Reproof" is a rebuke, similar to conviction felt by a sinner. Those who apply God's Word to their lives will discover its rebuke when they sin. But the Bible does not simply point out sin, it gives guidance for making things right with God—restoring to a right relationship. This is "correction." In addition, further training in the godly life is possible as the believer studies the "instruction in righteousness" found in God's Word.

As Christians make Bible study a priority, they are thoroughly prepared by God for the "good works" He would have them accomplish (verse 17). Looking back to verse 14, we see the significance of Paul's injunction for Timothy to "continue" in the truth of the Word. It is a lifelong process. The written guidelines in the Bible shape the daily values by which believers live.

NOTES

3. Jesus Is The Truth

A. The Word Made Flesh
John 1:14

Ask: "Besides natural revelation and God's written Word, what is still lacking in our picture of God's truth?" God's creation speaks to the human heart of His existence and power. God's inspired written Word describes who He is and how He expects humanity to live. But even when they know the detailed guidelines of Scripture, sinful people cannot bring themselves into right relationship with God.

The culmination of God's revelation of truth is God's Son, Jesus Christ. He is the living Word of God. As John proclaimed in the opening chapter of his Gospel, it was the Incarnation—Jesus Christ in flesh—that finally allowed people to truly behold their God. The infinite God who is beyond all human comprehension has made himself accessible to humanity through Christ.

Jesus not only "was made flesh," but He "dwelt among us" (1:14). Through His life and ministry, men and women and children were presented with a flesh-and-blood portrait of their Creator. The Bible's inspired record of the Incarnation has presented the same picture to humanity in the ages since.

Jesus, "the Word," is the full expression of God to humanity. Jesus is God. Through Jesus, the unknowable is known and the invisible is revealed. It is through knowing Christ personally that our lives are changed and our sense of values conformed to God's.

NOTES

B. Truth Demands Obedience
John 8:31,32; 14:6,7

TEACHING TIP 4: Display the overhead transparency "Applying God's Truth To Life." Cover the transparency with a sheet of paper and reveal each point as it is referred to in the commentary. Ask students to suggest personal application. Write these in the spaces provided. For example, after the first point students could describe in a sentence what happened to them at the moment of salvation.

People can accept or reject God's truth revealed in creation and in His written Word. But when hearts are open to this truth, the message of creation with God's written revelation will lead to a confrontation with Jesus Christ himself. The decision then must be made as to what the sinner will do with this knowledge of the Savior. What remains is for the person confronted with Christ to accept Him as Lord.

Yet a decision for Christ involves more than momentary faith in Him. Salvation is accomplished through God's grace instantly. But a lifetime of obedience will follow as evidence of the believer's continuing submission to Christ. This is a critical point in any study of Christian values.

Jesus explained to some who were claiming to believe in Him: "If ye continue in my word, then are ye my disciples indeed" (John 8:31). The idea of "continue" can be expressed as "remain" or "hold to." Willingness to continue in obedience results in genuine knowledge of the truth and genuine freedom from sin (verse 32).

Among the crowd of Jews in this passage were those who voiced a faith in Christ, but were unwilling to allow Him to change their lives (verses 33-47). They were still focused on their own efforts to come to God. The same mistake is made today. Some people will rely on church membership to guarantee their salvation. Others will choose a pseudo-Christian cult that speaks highly of Jesus Christ but distorts or ignores His role as our atoning Sacrifice and our living Lord.

In the end, Christ alone stands as the Way to God; He alone fully expresses God's truth; He alone brings eternal life to those doomed by their sins (14:6). And only the Christ revealed in Scripture accomplishes this. There is not a false Christ today who can do what Jesus does—show us plainly our eternal Heavenly Father and allow us to "henceforth . . . know him" (14:7).

NOTES

LIFE RESPONSE

When we evaluate any claim to truth, there are several important factors to consider. Who is sharing this "truth" with us? What supporting evidence is offered? What is the significance?

In the case of God's truth, the Source is God himself. The supporting evidence is seen in creation, in His Word, and in our own transformation by Christ. The significance to our lives can only be measured in the contrast between eternal death and eternal life.

As Christians, then, we are daily reminded of the unshakeable nature of God's truth. We live in a world that has been deceived by Satan and practices deception in countless ways. We cannot afford to become entangled in that deception. But as believers, we have a responsibility to live God's truth in plain view for the benefit of the lost. This is where the ideas of "God's truth" and "Christian values" mesh.

Unbelievers who write off the glories of creation to the chance of evolution have the opportunity to rethink their worldview when confronted with the changed life of a Christian. Those who have passed off the Bible as "good literature" can gain new insight into the power of God's written Word when they see it applied in believers' lives. The individual who admires the life and teachings of Jesus Christ can watch Him actively working as the Savior of those Christians willing to live out their beliefs. This week determine to live out your Christian values.

EVANGELISM OUTREACH

For the sake of any unsaved students in your class, emphasize again that only a personal relationship with Jesus Christ can make God's truth fully effective in our lives. Without Christ, every human effort to live morally is doomed to failure. Personal faith in Christ's atonement is required in order to be forgiven of the sins that separate us from a holy God. Once in right relationship with God, we are given the power to live righteously. Invite students to accept Christ today.

A Personal Relationship With God

CENTRAL TRUTH

Every Christian has a personal relationship with God through Jesus Christ.

GOLDEN TEXT

This is eternal life: that they may know you, the only true God, and Jesus Christ, whom you have sent. John 17:3 (NIV)

STUDY TEXT

Psalm 63:1-8; Proverbs 2:1-6; Jeremiah 9:23,24; 2 Timothy 1:8-14

OUTLINE

1. Knowing God
   A. God Of Wisdom
   B. God Of Love And Justice

2. Trusting God
   A. Personal Invitation
   B. Personal Example

3. Worshiping God
   A. Search And Find
   B. Worship And Live

OBJECTIVE

To comprehend the value of a personal relationship with God and enjoy the blessings of fellowship with Him.

CHECKLIST

☐ Read the student guide when preparing to teach this study. Take time to answer the questions yourself. You may find them useful for generating class discussion.

☐ Fill in a copy of the Planning The Session sheet from the teaching helps packet to help plan the activities for this study.

☐ Make sufficient copies of the work sheet "Proclaiming Our Faith" from the Adult Teaching Helps Packet. Fill out a copy yourself in order to offer examples of possible responses to the students.

☐ Teaching Tip 3 calls for a time of class worship. Allowing one or more students to lead the class in worship might encourage the rest of the students to enter in more freely.

☐ This study is well-suited for evangelism. Portray Christ as the One who makes a personal relationship with God possible. Pray that God will open the hearts of any unsaved students to the truth of His love for them as expressed through Christ.

DAILY BIBLE READINGS

Monday:	God's Plan. Genesis 2:15-25
Tuesday:	God's Promise. Genesis 15:1-6
Wednesday:	Holy Relationship. Exodus 3:1-10
Thursday:	Meeting Christ. Mark 1:14-20
Friday:	Protected By God. Acts 16:25-35
Saturday:	Alive In Christ. Romans 6:1-11

Scripture Setting

King James Version

Proverbs 2:3. Yea, if thou criest after knowledge, and liftest up thy voice for understanding;

4. If thou seekest her as silver, and searchest for her as for hid treasures;

5. Then shalt thou understand the fear of the Lord, and find the knowledge of God.

Jeremiah 9:23. Thus saith the Lord, Let not the wise man glory in his wisdom, neither let the mighty man glory in his might, let not the rich man glory in his riches:

24. But let him that glorieth glory in this, that he understandeth and knoweth me, that I am the Lord which exercise loving-kindness, judgment, and righteousness, in the earth: for in these things I delight, saith the Lord.

2 Timothy 1:8. Be not thou therefore ashamed of the testimony of our Lord, nor of me his prisoner: but be thou partaker of the afflictions of the gospel according to the power of God;

9. Who hath saved us, and called us with an holy calling, not according to our works, but according to his own purpose and grace, which was given us in Christ Jesus before the world began;

10. But is now made manifest by the appearing of our Saviour Jesus Christ, who hath abolished death, and hath brought life and immortality to light through the gospel.

12. For the which cause I also suffer these things: nevertheless I am not ashamed; for I know whom I have believed, and am persuaded that he is able to keep that which I have committed unto him against that day.

Psalm 63:1. O God, thou art my God; early will I seek thee: my soul thirsteth for thee, my flesh longeth for thee in a dry and thirsty land, where no water is;

2. To see thy power and thy glory, so as I have seen thee in the sanctuary.

3. Because thy loving-kindness is better than life, my lips shall praise thee.

4. Thus will I bless thee while I live: I will lift up my hands in thy name.

7. Because thou hast been my help, therefore in the shadow of thy wings will I rejoice.

8. My soul followeth hard after thee: thy right hand upholdeth me.

New International Version

Proverbs 2:3. If you call out for insight and cry aloud for understanding,

4. And if you look for it as for silver and search for it as for hidden treasure,

5. Then you will understand the fear of the Lord and find the knowledge of God.

Jeremiah 9:23. This is what the Lord says: "Let not the wise man boast of his wisdom or the strong man boast of his strength or the rich man boast of his riches,

24. But let him who boasts boast about this: that he understands and knows me, that I am the Lord, who exercises kindness, justice and righteousness on earth, for in these I delight," declares the Lord.

2 Timothy 1:8. So do not be ashamed to testify about our Lord, or ashamed of me his prisoner. But join with me in suffering for the gospel, by the power of God,

9. Who has saved us and called us to a holy life—not because of anything we have done but because of his own purpose and grace. This grace was given us in Christ Jesus before the beginning of time,

10. But it has now been revealed through the appearing of our Savior, Christ Jesus, who has destroyed death and has brought life and immortality to light through the gospel.

12. That is why I am suffering as I am. Yet I am not ashamed, because I know whom I have believed, and am convinced that he is able to guard what I have entrusted to him for that day.

Psalm 63:1. O God, you are my God, earnestly I seek you; my soul thirsts for you, my body longs for you, in a dry and weary land where there is no water.

2. I have seen you in the sanctuary and beheld your power and your glory.

3. Because your love is better than life, my lips will glorify you.

4. I will praise you as long as I live, and in your name I will lift up my hands.

7. Because you are my help, I sing in the shadow of your wings.

8. My soul clings to you; your right hand upholds me.

If we listed a hierarchy of relationships we enjoy in life, we would probably establish the various levels according to such factors as how strongly we love a person, how intimately we can confide in that friend or family member, and how we seek to spend time together. But imagine being totally devoted to every person on that list. Imagine having an inexhaustible supply of love that makes the people we pass on the street just as precious to us as a relative.

The idea seems ludicrous, but that is really how God looks at humanity. His perfect love reaches out to everyone. But there is so much more involved in God's divine embrace. He desires us to draw closer to Him. But to find this closeness with God we must deepen our knowledge of God, trust Him even in life's storms, and worship Him with all our heart.

BIBLE COMMENTARY

1. Knowing God

A. God Of Wisdom
Proverbs 2:1-6

An entire range of meaning is possible when you say you "know" someone. You can simply know *who* someone is. You might study the life of a famous individual and know *about* that person. You can also *personally* know people on many different levels ranging from casual acquaintances to intimate friends and family. With such a spectrum of relationships encompassed in *knowing* different people, what does it mean to *know* God?

Looking at Proverbs 2:1-6, an important characteristic of knowing God becomes evident—those people who truly know God will rely on His wisdom and knowledge in making life's decisions. Knowing God means knowing how He feels about the situations we face and knowing which choices will be pleasing to Him.

This is made clear in verses 5 and 6. In order to get the real thrust of the passage, we can view the wisdom and knowledge called for in verses 1-4 as the same "knowledge of God" mentioned in verse 5 and "wisdom" that God is said to give in verse 6. The writer of the passage viewed this sharing of God's knowledge as being communicated directly from His mouth.

Ask: "How can we apply Proverbs 2:1-6 to Christian learning?" The Book of Proverbs illustrates repeatedly that gaining practical wisdom in life is a great blessing. Sound business policy, financial management, and relational psychology are all covered in Proverbs. Formal classroom training and practical experience are a part of gaining knowledge for job opportunities and everyday living. But we cannot ignore the practical guidance contained in God's Word. Verses 1-4, then, can serve as an encouragement to seek knowledge and wisdom of God throughout all of our life's experiences. Verses 5 and 6 serve as a reminder that all worthwhile wisdom and knowledge will connect with our relationship to God.

TEACHING TIP 1: Ask each student to share one of two kinds of testimonies with the person sitting in next seat. 1. Recall how a personal relationship with God was a source of wisdom when faced with a major decision or problem.

NOTES

B. God Of Love And Justice
Jeremiah 9:23,24

Again and again, Proverbs points to wisdom as a worthy goal that brings great reward and personal satisfaction. In today's world we find those who base their satisfaction on personal accomplishments. Physical strength or agility can gain us recognition, as can material wealth. But even though these may not be wrong in themselves, they cannot be the most important things in our life. As believers, we must put all areas of our lives in proper perspective. Our acheivements are not to be the focus of our boasting (Jeremiah 9:23).

Verse 24 goes on to put these achievements in their proper place of priority. Foundational to any satisfaction gained through human effort must be the satisfaction of knowing God personally. When our relationship with God takes first place, it enriches and gives purpose to all of life.

Ask: "How do the divine qualities listed in verse 24 shape our personal relationship with God?" Both God's love and His justice impact our lives daily. And when we know God, we experience both aspects of His nature. His love has been supremely demonstrated through Jesus Christ (John 3:16,17). His justice demands that we be accountable for our sins (Romans 3:23).

Christians can look at Jeremiah 9:24, then, and recognize that God's "loving-kindness" has saved them from His "judgment" and brought about His "righteousness" in their lives. This is the true source of personal joy. Of this we can "boast."

The knowledge of God promoted in Scripture is deeply relational. It contrasts sharply with the cognitive knowledge of God's existence we considered in last week's study. A person can believe in the Creator, admire the teachings of the Bible, and still be far away from God. On the other hand, when a personal relationship with God is established through Jesus Christ, the born-again believer knows God in a way that involves the Lord in every area of life.

NOTES

2. Trusting God

A. Personal Invitation
2 Timothy 1:8-10

"Trust me!" We have heard the expression often. But we can probably think of times when the invitation to trust has been rewarded with deception. In order for any relationship to be successful, trust must be present. This is certainly true in our relationship with God. In order to relate to God personally, we must be able to trust Him.

Our personal relationship with God is founded on the deepest kind of trust—faith. Faith requires that we trust God when He says He will forgive our sins. Faith expresses a trust that the Holy Spirit will bring about spiritual maturity in our lives. Faith involves the trust that we will one day join our Heavenly Father for all eternity.

Ask: "Does our trust in God guarantee an absence of problems in life?" A careful study of Scripture will quickly reveal that trusting God does not prevent trials or suffering. In fact, when we trust God completely, we are willing to believe He has our best interests at heart in allowing us to go through difficult experiences.

Second Timothy 1:8-10 falls within a passage that repeatedly encourages Christians to remain faithful to the cause of Christ. Timothy's trust in God was to remain firm in spite of persecution. Paul was blunt: "Join with me in suffering for the gospel" (verse 8, NIV).

An invitation to make a sacrifice on behalf of someone or some cause assumes a great degree of trust. While there are instances in which people are willing to make personal sacrifices because of their trust in an earthly cause, the cause of Christ is worthy of a far greater commitment.

Ask: "What further cause for our trusting God is found in verses 9 and 10?" Christians need only look back to the work of salvation brought about in their lives to remind them of the trust they owe God. He alone is responsible for the work of grace that transforms a sinner into a righteous member of the body of Christ. That plan of salvation has been in place since "before the world began" (verse 9). Jesus Christ has personally demonstrated God's trustworthy nature by overcoming death and bringing us eternal life (verse 10).

NOTES

B. Personal Example
2 Timothy 1:12-14

Paul's example of trust must have been a great source of encouragement to Timo-thy. The apostle's proclamation of his trust in God in verse 12 has also encouraged countless believers in the centuries since his death. How many times when in the midst of a trial can we confidently say, "I also suffer these things: nevertheless I am not ashamed; for I know whom I have believed!"

Those last seven words are powerful. When we know God intimately, we recognize that the very character of God calls for our trust. We become convinced that He will be faithful to fulfill His promises to us.

Paul was so convinced of God's trustworthy nature that he invited Timothy to follow his own example of faith (verse 13). That invitation can be voiced by many believers today to younger Christians. In fact, we have a responsibility to draw others into a deeper trust in God by testifying of God's faithfulness to us.

TEACHING TIP 2: Distribute copies of the work sheet "Proclaiming Our Faith." Ask the students to look over the categories of testimony listed. Have them write a brief statement about their own salvation experience and list the names of people with whom they can share this news. In addition, encourage the students to take time this week to write down ways in which God has proven himself trustworthy in each of the remaining categories.

Paul's charge to Timothy in verse 14 makes an important observation about the nature of our trust in God. When we trust God, we cannot depend on our own strength. On our own, we would forget God's blessings the first time adversity appeared to overwhelm us. We need the help of the Holy Spirit in order to persevere in the faith. A Pentecostal understanding of the Holy Spirit's ministry recognizes the wide variety of gifts God has promised to us. With these gifts, we will be established in the faith and can then encourage others in the body of Christ.

of God's presence that is as intense as that demonstrated in His sanctuary (verse 2). He exults in God's loving-kindness (verse 3). He anticipates the fulfillment of his desire for God with upraised hands (verse 4).

Think how our lives would be impacted if we would seek God with David's intensity. Our own society is a "thirsty land" offering temptation rather than spiritual triumph. As we commit ourselves in worship to God, He will respond with the bountiful blessings of His Spirit promised throughout the New Testament. As Pentecostal believers, we can look expectantly to the Holy Spirit to give new life to our worship and empower us for God's service.

NOTES

3. Worshiping God

A. Search And Find
Psalm 63:1-4

To know God intimately through the miracle of salvation opens to the believer the splendor of God's divine Person. Admittedly, the view in this life is limited. Only in heaven will believers be shown God's undiluted glory. But for every revelation of himself God chooses to share, the natural response is worship. Certainly the complete revelation is found in Christ. Simeon offered his worship in the temple when he saw the infant Christ. John watched the 24 elders worship the Lamb of God in heaven. One day every knee will bow and every tongue confess that Jesus Christ is Lord (Philippians 2:10,11).

Old Testament believers were not blessed with the revelation of Christ that New Testament believers had, but what God revealed of himself to them inspired the same fervor of worship. The Psalms resound with praise to God, and David's call to worship in Psalm 63 is no exception.

Reading David's heartfelt cry to God in verse 1, we sense the contrast between life in this world and the spiritual life God gives. David called out to God from "a dry and thirsty land, where no water is." Our thirst for God is made all the more intense when we recognize the emptiness of worldly pursuits. Nothing in this life can fulfill the soul like a personal relationship with God.

Verses 2-4 expand on David's desire to draw closer to God and see God at work in his life. David calls for a personal revelation

B. Worship And Live
Psalm 63:5-8

In Psalm 63:5-8, we see God's faithful response to worship. Just as David recognized his spiritual thirst (verse 1), he counted on God's satisfying his soul in verse 5. David's meditation on God in verse 6 led to renewed confidence in God's ability to be his help and uphold him (verses 7,8).

Verse 8 gives a powerful picture of both sides of our personal relationship with God. On one hand, like David, the believer's soul "followeth hard after [God]." This can also be expressed as clinging to God. All the while, however, God is upholding us.

This is the essence of the Christian's walk of faith. On the believer's side of the relationship must be the desire to hold on to God. Daily obedience to God's Word, personal communion with the Lord in prayer, a commitment to share the good news with the lost—all these are evidences of our genuine love for God. But we must recognize that God is at work in us, upholding us when we would fall and giving life to us.

As we commit ourselves to God in times of worship, this experience is intensified. In praising God, we draw closer to Him and He faithfully returns the embrace.

TEACHING TIP 3: Consider structuring your presentation of this study to allow 10-15 minutes of free time at the end of the class. Use this time to worship God with your students. You might select an appropriate chorus to begin this worship experience. This would draw the students into an atmosphere of praise that could lead naturally into a time of joyful prayer together. The material in Life Response and Evangelism Outreach could be covered before this activity.

NOTES

LIFE RESPONSE

If a spouse or a very close friend expressed a desire to make their relationship with us more enriching, what would be our response? Would we callously claim that we were satisfied with the relationship as it stood and that no changes were really necessary? Of course not! Even if the relationship were already strong, the sentiment expressed by our friend or loved one would draw from us a sympathetic response. We would look for ways to draw closer to that person.

Throughout His Word, God calls out to His people to draw ever closer to himself. How are you responding to that invitation? Are you content with the status quo of your faith? Or do you recognize that a relationship with God is one of never-ending discovery of His infinite goodness and love?

Seek to know God more intimately. Faithful study of His Word and a daily commitment to prayer are powerful tools for enriching this knowledge.

Determine to trust God's wisdom. Maintain your faith in Him even when life's outlook is bleak.

Let the language of praise be ever present in your life. Worship God for who He is and what He is helping you to become. Allow the Holy Spirit to enrich your worship with the joyful overflowing of other tongues!

As you take steps to build your personal relationship with God, you will find your other relationships will improve as well. God's love for you will transform you and help you reach out to others in love.

EVANGELISM OUTREACH

Some students in your class may only have an intellectual knowledge of God. They do not know Him personally. Use this study to portray God's love in a way that will urge unsaved students to come to Him. Pray that students who have not accepted Christ as Savior will see that they do not really know God, they are separated from the promises for which believers trust Him, and they have a barrier of sin that hinders any worship they might give. Close with an invitation to be saved.

Personal Integrity

CENTRAL TRUTH

Christian values should be reflected in a person's attitudes, decisions, and actions.

GOLDEN TEXT

Blessed are the pure in heart, for they will see God. Matthew 5:8 (NIV)

STUDY TEXT

Proverbs 11:3; 15:26; Matthew 5:8; Acts 5:1-11; Philippians 2:14,15; James 1:21-26

OUTLINE

1. Honesty
   A. Choose The Right Path
   B. Avoid Destruction
2. Purity
   A. Established Within
   B. Lighting The World
3. Discipline
   A. Lose The Baggage
   B. Be Transformed By
      God's Word

OBJECTIVE

To accept the value of personal integrity and allow the Holy Spirit to renew us in Christ.

CHECKLIST

☐ Read the student guide and answer the questions after each main point. Integrate these questions into your teaching.

☐ While the outline does not include any passages with a Pentecostal emphasis, keep in mind the study objective. Supplement the presentation of each main point with a reference to the Holy Spirit's role in bringing about that quality in the believer's life.

☐ Make sufficient copies of the work sheet "Looking In The Mirror" from the Adult Teaching Helps Packet. You can distribute this sheet at the end of the study as suggested, or you can refer to each of the three questions on the sheet at the end of each main point.

☐ During your evangelistic appeal, emphasize Christ's ability to transform our lives and help us to demonstrate true integrity. Pray that unsaved students will be receptive to this truth.

DAILY BIBLE READINGS

Monday:	Moral Purity. Genesis 39:2-12
Tuesday:	Consequences Of Sin. Joshua 7:19-26
Wednesday:	Obedient To God. Daniel 1:8-20
Thursday:	Wise Men. Matthew 2:1-12
Friday:	Righteousness Rewarded. Luke 2:25-32
Saturday:	Honest Ministry. 2 Corinthians 6:3-10

SCRIPTURE SETTING

King James Version

Acts 5:1. A certain man named Ananias, with Sapphira his wife, sold a possession,

2. And kept back part of the price, his wife also being privy to it, and brought a certain part, and laid it at the apostles' feet.

3. But Peter said, Ananias, why hath Satan filled thine heart to lie to the Holy Ghost, and to keep back part of the price of the land?

4. While it remained, was it not thine own? and after it was sold, was it not in thine own power? why hast thou conceived this thing in thine heart? thou hast not lied unto men, but unto God.

5. And Ananias hearing these words fell down, and gave up the ghost: and great fear came on all them that heard these things.

9. Then Peter said unto her, How is it that ye have agreed together to tempt the Spirit of the Lord? behold, the feet of them which have buried thy husband are at the door, and shall carry thee out.

10. Then fell she down straightway at his feet, and yielded up the ghost: and the young men came in, and found her dead, and, carrying her forth, buried her by her husband.

11. And great fear came upon all the church, and upon as many as heard these things.

Proverbs 15:26. The thoughts of the wicked are an abomination to the Lord: but the words of the pure are pleasant words.

Matthew 5:8. Blessed are the pure in heart: for they shall see God.

James 1:21. Wherefore lay apart all filthiness and superfluity of naughtiness, and receive with meekness the engrafted word, which is able to save your souls.

22. But be ye doers of the word, and not hearers only, deceiving your own selves.

23. For if any be a hearer of the word, and not a doer, he is like unto a man beholding his natural face in a glass:

24. For he beholdeth himself, and goeth his way, and straightway forgetteth what manner of man he was.

25. But whoso looketh into the perfect law of liberty, and continueth therein, he being not a forgetful hearer, but a doer of the work, this man shall be blessed in his deed.

New International Version

Acts 5:1. A man named Ananias, together with his wife Sapphira, also sold a piece of property.

2. With his wife's full knowledge he kept back part of the money for himself, but brought the rest and put it at the apostles' feet.

3. Then Peter said, "Ananias, how is it that Satan has so filled your heart that you have lied to the Holy Spirit and have kept for yourself some of the money you received for the land?

4. Didn't it belong to you before it was sold? And after it was sold, wasn't the money at your disposal? What made you think of doing such a thing? You have not lied to men but to God."

5. When Ananias heard this, he fell down and died. And great fear seized all who heard what had happened.

9. Peter said to her, "How could you agree to test the Spirit of the Lord? Look! The feet of the men who buried your husband are at the door, and they will carry you out also."

10. At that moment she fell down at his feet and died. Then the young men came in and, finding her dead, carried her out and buried her beside her husband.

11. Great fear seized the whole church and all who heard about these events.

Proverbs 15:26. The Lord detests the thoughts of the wicked, but those of the pure are pleasing to him.

Matthew 5:8. Blessed are the pure in heart, for they will see God.

James 1:21. Therefore, get rid of all moral filth and the evil that is so prevalent and humbly accept the word planted in you, which can save you.

22. Do not merely listen to the word, and so deceive yourselves. Do what it says.

23. Anyone who listens to the word but does not do what it says is like a man who looks at his face in a mirror

24. And, after looking at himself, goes away and immediately forgets what he looks like.

25. But the man who looks intently into the perfect law that gives freedom, and continues to do this, not forgetting what he has heard, but doing it—he will be blessed in what he does.

The heart is deceitful above all things, and desperately wicked: who can know it?'' (Jeremiah 17:9). This description of the human heart was made by God himself. It seems pessimistic and reveals an apparent futility of seeking to develop personal integrity. In fact, trying to do it in our own strength is futile.

This week's study examines three Christian values God wants us to display in our lives: honesty, purity, and discipline. Because Jesus was the only pure life ever lived, He is qualified to become the perfect example for us. The same disciplines He applied to His own life while living on earth are the ones we are to apply to our lives. As we commit ourselves to Jesus Christ, He will empower us to live disciplined lives and develop in us the kind of godly values He has exemplified for us.

BIBLE COMMENTARY

1. Honesty

A. Choose The Right Path
Proverbs 11:3

TEACHING TIP 1: Write the following statements on the chalkboard or blank transparency.
• ''Honesty is for the most part less profitable than dishonesty.''
• ''The surest way to remain poor is to be an honest man.''
• ''There is no well-defined boundary line between honesty and dishonesty. The frontiers of one blend with the outside limits of the other, and he who attempts to tread this dangerous ground may be sometimes in the one domain and sometimes in the other.''

Ask: ''What do these statements illustrate about the world's view of honesty.'' In order to be successful, many in the world believe one must sacrifice honesty. Others claim there is no way to establish a truth on which honesty is based. But there is a foundation for truth and honesty—God's Word.

Proverbs 11:3 is just one of numerous passages in Scripture that teach the importance of honesty. Honesty is the basis for personal integrity. What we are on the inside will affect our thoughts and actions. This proverb distinguishes the fate of those who live by honesty from that of those who practice dishonesty.

Consider the first group. Their commitment to honesty will ''guide'' them. In a world where so many cannot find purpose or direction, those committed to honest living will see a plan for their lives begin to develop. Since in the larger context of these studies we recognize God's identification with integrity, we can also recognize this guidance to be a divine blessing.

Ask: ''In light of the blessings of honesty, why do people feel they can get ahead by being dishonest?'' Some people deny the value of honesty. And when we look at the dishonest people who have become financially successful, we are tempted to sometimes agree. But there is a payday for dishonesty. The second half of verse 3 is not concerned with the momentary results of a lie. ''The perverseness of transgressors'' will bring about their personal destruction.

erty. Peter, under the anointing of the Holy Spirit, saw through their deception. The seed of dishonesty present within their hearts was not directed to men, but to God (verse 4). God sovereignly chose to immediately fulfill the principle described in Proverbs 11:3.

God's severe judgment may seem hard to understand, but this sin was committed at a crucial point in the establishment of the Church. God was divinely aware of all the damage this deception could produce if unchecked. Even in our day, we have seen the reputation of well-known Christians come to ruin because of their failure to pursue honesty at all costs. Their sin has driven others from Christ. May we recognize our responsibility to live as faithful representatives of the One who calls himself the Way, the Truth, and the Life. In doing so, we will not only avoid personal destruction, but will draw others into the body of Christ.

NOTES

B. Avoid Destruction
Acts 5:1-11

The opening chapters of Acts describe a time of great growth for the Early Church. On the Day of Pentecost alone, about 3,000 people came to Christ. Acts 2:44-47 pictures a joyous communal life in which individual needs were met by the local body.

Satan has always opposed God's purposes, and his attacks on the Church were soon in coming. In Acts 5, we see a force of evil at work that goes far beyond the self-seeking trick of a husband and wife.

TEACHING TIP 2: Have the students scan Acts 5:1-11 to find the verse that exposes the satanic influence behind Ananias and Sapphira's actions. Discuss the personal commitment to sin exhibited by these people. Verses 3 and 9 show sinful human nature in cooperation with Satan's schemes to undermine God's Church. Use the following commentary to emphasize that our human perception of dishonesty never sees the extent of its evil as God sees it.

---

2. Purity

A. Established Within
Proverbs 15:26; Matthew 5:8

A well-known collection of children's bedtime stories includes the story of a young boy who selfishly picked the largest apple from a fruit bowl. He saw how shiny and plump it looked on the outside, but was disgusted to find that it was rotten inside. The decay inside was invisible. Some people are the same way. Their appearance is attractive, but they hide inner, moral decay.

It is interesting to note that Ananias and Sapphira only kept back "part of the price" of what they sold (verse 2,3). They freely gave a portion of the money to the church. But they must have indicated that their gift was the total price received from the prop-

Ask: "Why is it foolish to try to rely on our outward appearance as the true test of character?" When we are impure, we only deceive people, not God. To try to appear falsely righteous before God is absolute foolishness. He sees the deepest recesses of the soul. And His standard for inner purity leaves no margin for error.

Consider God's evaluation of the wicked in Proverbs 15:26. He sees their very thoughts, and finds them abominable! This should be a sobering reminder even to believers. For, though we have been justified in God's sight through Christ, we still struggle with our old sin nature. Much of that struggle takes place within our minds. In light of God's divine scrutiny, we should be ever aware of how our thoughts are directed. When we realize our thoughts are displeasing to the Lord, we should immediately seek His forgiveness.

The second half of Proverbs 15:26 is encouraging to the believer. The pure in this verse can only enjoy this description thanks to God's grace; they have been redeemed by Christ. While the emphasis here is on their "pleasant words," the principle of the first half of the verse still holds. Those pleasant words must be based on an inner commitment to God. (See Matthew 12:34,35 for the true source of good and evil).

Matthew 5:8 drives home the importance of inner purity. The ones who will "see God" are pure in the deepest recesses of their being. This demand for complete purity cannot be met in human strength. Believers can enjoy being "pure in heart" only if they remain committed to following the Holy Spirit's guidance and repenting of the sins He exposes in their lives.

TEACHING TIP 3: Brainstorm with the students for attitudes and activities that can compromise the believer's purity. List their responses on the chalkboard or a blank transparency. Try to develop a practical list that includes items the students themselves often face.

B. Lighting The World
Philippians 2:14,15

Purity is not only a benefit to those who pursue it. Purity results in a testimony that can draw others to Christ. Paul emphasized this when writing to the Philippian believers.

The purity Paul emphasized was actually corporate in nature. Philippians 2:14 calls Christians to relate to one another "without murmurings and disputings." Paul was calling for this church to work together without any dissension. Of course, this requires each member of a body of believers to remain pure as well.

Verse 15 describes an important result of Christians' mutual commitment. By working together to promote the cause of Christ, believers "shine as lights in the world." Paul described the world as a "crooked and perverse nation."

Ask: "What sort of problems can disrupt the unity of a church?" Satan seeks every possible means to destroy the Church. He will use whatever weaknesses he can find in individual members to disrupt the unity and testimony of a local body. The list of potential sources for conflict is endless. Only by pursuing inner purity can each Christian ensure that he or she will be a force for spiritual growth within a church and a spiritual light within a community.

TEACHING TIP 4: Ask the students to reflect on their attitudes toward other believers. Have a time of prayer with the class. Ask God to guide individuals to seek restoration and forgiveness with any brothers or sisters in

---

Christ from whom they have drawn away in bitterness.

of God offers believers the key to overcoming temptation. As the Word is engrafted and made a part of a person's life, it becomes a powerful weapon against temptation.

3. Discipline

A. Lose The Baggage
James 1:21

Ask: "What examples of discipline are common for people in the 20th century?" Most of us have attempted at one time or another to follow a diet or exercise regimen. We disciplined our bodies. We can look back to high school or college and remember occasions when we studied for a test or researched material for a paper. We disciplined our minds. In all these cases, there are things we had to give up if we wanted to accomplish our goals.

Getting rid of hindrances to physical or mental progress illustrates the need of getting rid of hindrances to spiritual progress. James called for this kind of discipline. As believers, we need to cut off any attachment we have to the lusts of the world. The "filthiness and superfluity of naughtiness" (James 1:21, KJV) can also be understood as "moral filth and the evil that is so prevalent" (NIV) in our world.

While we might be tempted to suggest our own definitions of "filth," we need to remember that all sin fits this description in God's sight. Having been saved by His grace, and justified in His sight, believers must regard any sin at all as "filth."

Sin is "prevalent," or all around us. If we are supposed to remain untainted by evil, what can we possibly do? The solution is found in "the engrafted word." The Word

B. Be Transformed Through The Word
James 1:22-26

This idea of making God's Word an integral part of life is very crucial. Knowing *about* the Bible or having a *head knowledge* of its contents is not enough. What God has shared with humanity through His Word must be taken to heart and lived out in daily experience.

In verses 23 and 24, James illustrated this principle with a mirror. A person who reads God's Word and does not apply its truth is like someone who looks in a mirror and then forgets what he looks like. Just as a mirror reflects our outer appearance, so God's Word exposes the deepest recesses of who we are. Yet, some will read the Bible and completely ignore the state of their soul exposed within its pages.

Ask: "What are some ways people exhibit a familiarity with God's Word but show that it is not a part of their lives?" In our day the Bible has been distributed more widely than at any other time in history. Quotations from and allusions to the Bible crop up frequently in popular fiction and literature. People with even a passing interest in art will study the biblical themes painted and sculpted by history's masters. Yet countless people never allow God's Word to change them.

On the other hand, there are those who put into action the life principles of

Scripture. These people who study "the perfect law of liberty and continueth therein" are not "forgetful" (verse 25). The result: God's blessing.

If we wish to grow spiritually, we will find that a detailed study of God's Word is an indispensable practice. The Bible does not stop with showing us our need to be saved. It goes on to show us how the Holy Spirit can enrich our lives and our ministry to others. The growing believer will apply God's Word for all it is worth.

TEACHING TIP 5: Distribute copies of the work sheet "Looking In The Mirror" for the students to fill out at home. Encourage them to carefully study the passages listed and respond to the questions. They can also write in other passages that emphasize these three guidelines for living.

NOTES

LIFE RESPONSE

The world's view of honesty, purity, and discipline is far different from God's. As believers committed to living wholeheartedly for our Heavenly Father, we will recognize these differences.

Honesty is more than glibly claiming "scout's honor" for the verbal statements we make. It requires that we communicate God's truth in all that we say and do. We must recognize all forms of deception as hindrances to His truth.

Our commitment to purity must meet the same rigorous standard. We are to be perfect even as our Heavenly Father is perfect (Matthew 5:48). Having an attitude of "what you see is what you get" is not enough. What others see in us must be a reflection of God's presence.

Finally, all our disciplines in life are to focus on spiritual maturity as their goal. We must remember that we are constantly growing up into the perfect image of Christ himself (Ephesians 4:13). We can discipline ourselves in any number of areas, but if our goals are faulty, those disciplines will not earn us eternal benefits.

Personal integrity is not optional for the believer. Even when its characteristics are either ridiculed or simply imitated by those around us, integrity is still attainable. Personal integrity is possible because Christians have committed themselves to the one Person whose integrity can never be questioned. And our integrity will be strengthed as we allow God's Word to mold our lives.

EVANGELISM OUTREACH

The focus on honesty, purity, and discipline may speak to the unsaved in your class. These characteristics can only come through a relationship with Jesus Christ. Emphasize God's willingness to help all who desire to live for Him to demonstrate true honesty, purity, and discipline. God sent His Son to die on our behalf and the Holy Spirit to empower us for service. Invite unsaved students to accept Christ as their Lord and encourage all students to seek the infilling of the Holy Spirit.

Practical Christian Ethics

CENTRAL TRUTH

The truth of Scripture provides the guidelines for right living.

GOLDEN TEXT

His divine power has given us everything we need for life and godliness through our knowledge of him who called us by his own glory and goodness.
2 Peter 1:3 (NIV)

STUDY TEXT

Psalm 139:13-18; Matthew 10:29-31; 1 Peter 2:13-17; 3:8-17

OUTLINE

1. Civil Obedience
   A. Recognizing All Authority
   B. Establishing A Testimony

2. Peaceful Relationships
   A. Peace In The Church
   B. Peace In Persecution

3. Value Of Human Life
   A. God's Personal Concern
   B. Always In God's Care

OBJECTIVE

To recognize that Christian values relate to every sphere of life and resolve to apply them in daily living.

CHECKLIST

☐ Fill out the Planning The Session sheet to make sure you allow enough time for the class activities you wish to use.

☐ Read study 12 in the student guide when preparing your presentation. Answer the questions and look for ways to integrate student responses during the class.

☐ Make sufficient copies of the work sheets "Weakened Witness" and "Human Life: Affirming Its Value" from the Adult Teaching Helps Packet. They will be used in the first and third points of the study. Allow adequate time for discussion.

☐ During your evangelistic appeal, also give attention to the need for Christians to exhibit a consistent testimony before the lost that will draw them to God.

☐ Examine your own life in light of this study as you prepare to teach. Ask the Holy Spirit to show you any areas in which your life contradicts scriptural principles.

DAILY BIBLE READINGS

Monday:	Blessings Of Obedience.	Psalm 1:1-3
Tuesday:	Seek God's Wisdom.	Proverbs 2:1-11
Wednesday:	Justice Required.	Micah 6:6-8
Thursday:	Wise Living.	Romans 12:14-21
Friday:	Respect To Government.	Romans 13:1-7
Saturday:	Primacy Of Love.	1 Corinthians 13:1-13

SCRIPTURE SETTING

King James Version

1 Peter 2:13. Submit yourselves to every ordinance of man for the Lord's sake: whether it be to the king, as supreme;

14. Or unto governors, as unto them that are sent by him for the punishment of evildoers, and for the praise of them that do well.

15. For so is the will of God, that with well doing ye may put to silence the ignorance of foolish men:

16. As free, and not using your liberty for a cloak of maliciousness, but as the servants of God.

17. Honor all men. Love the brotherhood. Fear God. Honor the king.

3:8. Finally, be ye all of one mind, having compassion one of another, love as brethren, be pitiful, be courteous:

9. Not rendering evil for evil, or railing for railing: but contrariwise blessing; knowing that ye are thereunto called, that ye should inherit a blessing.

10. For he that will love life, and see good days, let him refrain his tongue from evil, and his lips that they speak no guile:

11. Let him eschew evil, and do good; let him seek peace, and ensue it.

12. For the eyes of the Lord are over the righteous, and his ears are open unto their prayers: but the face of the Lord is against them that do evil.

Psalm 139:14. I will praise thee; for I am fearfully and wonderfully made: marvelous are thy works; and that my soul knoweth right well.

15. My substance was not hid from thee, when I was made in secret, and curiously wrought in the lowest parts of the earth.

16. Thine eyes did see my substance, yet being unperfect; and in thy book all my members were written, which in continuance were fashioned, when as yet there was none of them.

17. How precious also are thy thoughts unto me, O God! How great is the sum of them!

18. If I should count them, they are more in number than the sand: when I awake, I am still with thee.

Matthew 10:29. Are not two sparrows sold for a farthing? and one of them shall not fall on the ground without your Father.

31. Fear ye not therefore, ye are of more value than many sparrows.

New International Version

1 Peter 2:13. Submit yourselves for the Lord's sake to every authority instituted among men: whether to the king, as the supreme authority,

14. Or to governors, who are sent by him to punish those who do wrong and to commend those who do right.

15. For it is God's will that by doing good you should silence the ignorant talk of foolish men.

16. Live as free men, but do not use your freedom as a cover-up for evil; live as servants of God.

17. Show proper respect to everyone: Love the brotherhood of believers, fear God, honor the king.

3:8. Finally, all of you, live in harmony with one another; be sympathetic, love as brothers, be compassionate and humble.

9. Do not repay evil with evil or insult with insult, but with blessing, because to this you were called so that you may inherit a blessing.

10. For, "Whoever would love life and see good days must keep his tongue from evil and his lips from deceitful speech.

11. He must turn from evil and do good; he must seek peace and pursue it.

12. For the eyes of the Lord are on the righteous and his ears are attentive to their prayer, but the face of the Lord is against those who do evil."

Psalm 139:14. I praise you because I am fearfully and wonderfully made; your works are wonderful, I know that full well.

15. My frame was not hidden from you when I was made in the secret place. When I was woven together in the depths of the earth,

16. Your eyes saw my unformed body. All the days ordained for me were written in your book before one of them came to be.

17. How precious to me are your thoughts, O God! How vast is the sum of them!

18. Were I to count them, they would outnumber the grains of sand. When I awake, I am still with you.

Matthew 10:29. Are not two sparrows sold for a penny? Yet not one of them will fall to the ground apart from the will of your Father.

31. So don't be afraid; you are worth more than many sparrows.

James posed a crucial question to all Christians: "What doth it profit, my brethren, though a man say he hath faith, and have not works? can faith save him?" (James 2:14). Paul explained, "For by grace are ye saved through faith; and that not of yourselves: it is the gift of God: not of works, lest any man should boast" (Ephesians 2:8,9). An apparent contradiction is resolved when we recognize faith as the necessary element for salvation and understand James' reference to works as meaning visible evidence of saving faith. In other words, the Christian who accepts the truths of the gospel practices them.

Christian ethics is more than mere theory. In order for ethics to be valuable, they must be evident in everyday practical living. This week's study focuses on how three aspects of Christian ethics impact our lives.

BIBLE COMMENTARY

1. Civil Obedience

A. Recognizing All Authority
1 Peter 2:13,14

> TEACHING TIP 1: Read 1 Peter 2:13,14 to the class. Point out Peter's emphasis on levels of human authority. Brainstorm with the class and develop a list of governmental positions starting at the national level and working down to local officials. Make a chart of this list on the board or a blank overhead transparency.

How often do we observe people in authority making mistakes in judgment or even immoral choices that we feel are beneath our own "margin for error"? We are sometimes tempted to think that such faults disqualify these men and women from receiving our continued respect and obedience.

Peter very likely heard such opinions expressed by Christians in his day. Nero was in power as emperor when this epistle was written (approximately A.D. 62-64). Under him were pagan governors, many of which oppressed those in their assigned provinces. Under these govenors were garrisons of Roman soldiers who could be cruel and demanding when enforcing the Empire's laws, and lazy and licentious in their spare time.

What would Peter have said to any Christian who tried to ignore the civil authorities of his day? Verses 13,14 gives us an answer: believers are to obey the laws of the land. Peter never suggested that Christians' opinions of their leaders could affect this principle.

Ask: "What can a Christian do if civil laws violate scriptural principles?" The phrase "for the Lord's sake" is an important part of verse 13. It sets the overall qualification for obedience to human laws. God would never expect a Christian, or anyone else for that matter, to sin for His sake. Even Peter, when commanded with the other apostles to stop preaching about Jesus in Jerusalem, made it clear that God's command to continue preaching would have to be obeyed (Acts 5:27-29).

As long as civil laws do not call for any compromise of our Christian testimony, Christians are obligated to obey them. Christians are also obligated to show respect to the leaders who enforce those laws, even when those leaders' personal lives are not Christlike.

reading the case study, have them answer the questions at the bottom. After a few minutes, have each group summarize their decisions and give opportunity for discussion.

Ask: "How can the guidelines found in verse 17 be applied to the immoral society in which we live?" Christians are to "honor" or esteem everyone. They are to respect others' rights and personal concerns. Love is to be another important characteristic of their lives. Foundational to believers' treatment of other people is their commitment to honor God in all that they do. Finally, Christians will "honor the king," or live faithfully according to society's laws whenever they do not conflict with the other principles listed in the verse.

NOTES

B. Establishing A Testimony
1 Peter 2:15-17

In regard to any unique society or group of people, rumor has a way of growing rapidly within a surrounding community. The Early Church was no stranger to the suspicions of the world. Rumors abounded concerning certain practices of Christianity. Christians were accused of moral attrocities committed in secret meetings and these were hidden from public view.

Peter, though, did not want anything to hinder the believers' testimony. Establishing a godly testimony is the central thrust of Peter's call for civil obedience. As verses 15 and 16 emphasize, Christians need to put to rest false accusations by publicly showing themselves to be citizens of solid standing.

TEACHING TIP 2: With the students' help, make two lists on the chalkboard or a blank transparency. The left list should include laws or public ordinances commonly faced each day. These can include traffic regulations, signs in buildings, and even recognized unspoken guidelines for public behavior. The right list should describe the opinions that people might develop toward Christians who ignore these regulations.

Distribute the case study sheet "Weakened Witness." Divide the class into three groups and assign each group one of the case studies. After

2. Peaceful Relationships

A. Peace In The Church
1 Peter 3:8-12

Christianity is not just an individual experience. The Bible repeatedly describes the Christian as a member of the body of Christ and strongly associated with the other members of that Body. How believers get along with one another is a powerful indicator of the extent to which they have allowed Christian values to define their lives. And the way Christians treat one another will strongly influence how the world accepts their testimony of faith in Christ.

As Peter continued his epistle, he stressed the importance of their commitment to brothers and sisters in Christ. These believers needed one another, and 1 Peter 3:8,9 gives attention to their need for unity, love, compassion, and forgiveness.

Verses 10 and 11 give more attention to the individual. The person that desires God's blessings will control personal speech and actions and seek a peaceful life. Verse 12 then contrasts God's attitude toward those who live righteously with those who "do evil."

Ask: "How do these guidelines for individuals impact the corporate life of the Church?" As each Christian in a local body of believers guards against evil speech and actions, relationships with other Christians will grow and the Church will move forward with God's blessing.

NOTES

B. Peace In Persecution
1 Peter 3:13-17

Sometimes we think that when we live an honest life-style in this world, everyone will treat us kindly. But this is not always the case. While Peter stressed that people often respond positively to good behavior, he did not rule out the attacks of the wicked on those who faithfully live for God (1 Peter 3:13,14).

Ask: "What is the key to maintaining spiritual victory in times of persecution?" Peter called on believers to "sanctify the Lord" in their hearts (verse 15). In other words, "set apart Christ as Lord" (NIV) or "concentrate on being completely devoted to Christ" (Phillips). Such complete devotion to Christ's lordship will make us receptive to the steps God would lead us to take in the midst of persecution.

Ask: "What is your natural reaction to people you know to be hostile to the gospel?" When we find ourselves in an environment where our faith is ridiculed, our natural tendency is to keep quiet about what we believe. We sometimes use the idea of "life-style" evangelism as an excuse to quietly live according to biblical standards without sharing the gospel with others. But we are called to be ready with a defense of what we believe, regardless of the situation. In verse 15, Peter encouraged these believers to be ready at all times to defend the truth of the gospel. This is not self-righteous or obnoxious preaching, but humbly sharing the truth.

When Christ is reigning in our hearts, His peace is available to us when troubles would overwhelm our own strength. The Holy Spirit will empower us to proclaim the gospel when our own wisdom can never hope to answer the world's criticism.

We may not overcome our enemies immediately or even in this life. But the truth of the gospel will eventually triumph. There will come a day when all who have mocked our stand for Christ will "be ashamed" at their false accusations (verse 16).

When we recognize Christ as the Lord He truly is, we can trust all of life's circumstances to His care. As verse 17 points out, there may be times when God allows us to "suffer for well doing." Our responsibility is to ensure that no suffering we face is punishment because we have done evil. When we are committed to demonstrating

Christian values, we will please God and enjoy His favor, even if we receive the brunt of the world's hatred for Christ.

NOTES

3. Value Of Human Life

A. God's Personal Concern
Psalm 139:13-18

TEACHING TIP 4: Distribute copies of the work sheet "Human Life: Affirming Its Value" Give the class some time to think of examples and biblical solutions for each of the categories listed. Discuss their responses.

One woman, who unapologetically shared her pro-abortion views in a national newsmagazine, said: "People make bad decisions for which they should not have to pay with their whole lives. I was pregnant with two unborn children and I chose, for completely selfish reasons, to deny them life so that I could better my own."

Ask: "What is the correct way for Christians to respond to such an attitude?" Perhaps no other issue has focused Christians' attention on the value of human life more than abortion. But society expresses a disregard for human life in many other ways besides abortion. Thus we need to proclaim the sanctity of life in all areas of life as well.

In the argument for life, the world focuses on what they call the "quality" of life. Their argument goes like this: When something interferes with my life (an unwanted pregnancy, elderly parents), then my life quality suffers. Thus, I must do something to enhance the quality of my life. But as believers, we must make our decisions based in God's Word and His values.

David was awed when he considered God's personal awareness of all that he was. Psalm 139:13-18 describes God's knowledge as being so complete that He knows a person even before that person exists. God even knew about him in his mother's womb.

At no point does God lose sight of a person either. He does not forget about the person He creates. Verses 17 and 18 focus on the number of God's thoughts concerning the Psalmist specifically. Applying this passage to ourselves, we recognize God's equal concern with all that we are and all that we do.

Human life has value. Every individual is precious in God's sight. Any disregard for life is sin. Murder in any form and a lack of concern for those deprived of the necessities of life point to a disregard for our Creator. A faithful proclamation of the gospel is the necessary foundation for any measures taken to adequately address these societal tragedies.

NOTES

B. Always In God's Care
Matthew 10:29-31

A well-known song made a personal application of Matthew 10:29-31. Since God watches the sparrow, we can be reassured to know that God is watching over each of us. When we know that God is watching over us, we also realize that He is aware of all that happens to us.

Ask: "Why would Jesus refer to sparrows and the hairs on our head when

describing His Heavenly Father's concern for us?'' To think about sparrows dying, or God counting the hairs on our head may seem trivial, but Jesus used these images to emphasize the great value God places on each of us. The word translated ''sparrows'' had come to mean any common, small bird that was available as cheap food for the poor. By extension, sparrows can represent anything of very little value. If God directs His attention even to those things valued slightly or not at all by humans, imagine His care for those lives He has created in His own image!

TEACHING TIP 5: Have your students read Matthew 10:29-31. Ask them to consider the great value God

places on them. Then have them silently name the difficult situation they may be in. Assure them that their Heavenly Father sees their need.

NOTES

LIFE RESPONSE

This week's Golden Text must be kept in focus when applying the points we have studied. The first half of 2 Peter 1:3 is crucial: ''[God's] divine power has given us everything we need for life and godliness'' (NIV).

On the basis of our personal righteousness, we can never hope to be consistently obedient. In the strength of our own emotions, we cannot hold on to peace. And even the most loving individual is incapable of valuing human life sufficiently. It is when we are relying on human strength that we compromise our testimony and misrepresent the gospel.

But the Christian life is not a display of human achievement. It is evidence of God's power at work within fallible human beings. God has given us everything we need to live for Him. He has saved us through the sacrifice of His own Son. He has poured out His Holy Spirit so that we can be equipped with spiritual gifts, enjoying victory over sin, and actively ministering to others. He offers His love and guidance daily in order that we might resist the world's

temptations and keep our sights on eternity's goal.

''Practical Christian Ethics,'' then, is much more than our deciding to put spiritual principles into practice. It is allowing God to move in our lives and bring out those attitudes and actions that please Him and draw others to Him. Christian ethics must be a part of our everyday lives.

EVANGELISM OUTREACH

Use the central ideas behind the second and third points of this study to draw unsaved students to Christ. Help them recognize Him as the Source of genuine peace in a troubled life. Point out that even when other people fail to acknowledge their personal worth, Jesus Christ sees their true value. He has already given His life on their behalf. He knows everything about them. Invite any who wish to turn their lives over to Christ to either pray with you in class or meet with you afterward.

Living A Meaningful Life

CENTRAL TRUTH

A fulfilling life is found in loving devotion to God.

GOLDEN TEXT

Fear God and keep his commandments, for this is the whole duty of man. Ecclesiastes 12:13 (NIV)

STUDY TEXT

Genesis 1:27-30; Ecclesiastes 12:1,7,13,14; Matthew 6:25-33

OUTLINE

1. Acknowledge God's Purpose
   A. Created In God's Image
   B. Servants Of God

2. Give Priority To God
   A. Freed From Worry
   B. Free To Serve

3. Honor God
   A. Throughout Life
   B. With All Of Life

OBJECTIVE

To comprehend that God gives meaning to our lives and submit to Him.

CHECKLIST

☐ Read study 13 in the student guide when preparing your presentation. Answer the questions and look for ways to integrate these questions into your presentation.

☐ The Adult Teaching Helps Packet contains two overhead transparencies, "Giving My Worries To God" and "Dedicating My Life To God." Become familiar with them and how they are to be used. Make sure you have an overhead projector set up prior to class.

☐ This study is an important conclusion to the study of Christian values. Without a total dedication to God, your students will not develop Christian values in their lives. Pray for the anointing of the Holy Spirit as you present this study.

☐ Some of your students may be trying to find fulfillment in material things. During your evangelistic appeal, be sure to emphasize that only through Christ can life have its full meaning.

DAILY BIBLE READINGS

Monday: Honorable Life.
Deuteronomy 34:1-12

Tuesday: Act Of Faith.
Joshua 2:15-21

Wednesday: Praise The Lord.
Psalm 146:1-10

Thursday: Exemplary Life.
Matthew 11:2-15

Friday: Knowing Christ.
Philippians 3:7-14

Saturday: Growing In Faith.
Jude 17-25

Scripture Setting

King James Version

Genesis 1:27. So God created man in his own image, in the image of God created he him; male and female created he them.

28. And God blessed them, and God said unto them, Be fruitful, and multiply, and replenish the earth, and subdue it: and have dominion over the fish of the sea, and over the fowl of the air, and over every living thing that moveth upon the earth.

29. And God said, Behold, I have given you every herb bearing seed, which is upon the face of all the earth, and every tree, in the which is the fruit of a tree yielding seed; to you it shall be for meat.

30. And to every beast of the earth, and to every fowl of the air, and to every thing that creepeth upon the earth, wherein there is life, I have given every green herb for meat: and it was so.

Matthew 6:25. Therefore I say unto you, Take no thought for your life, what ye shall eat, or what ye shall drink; nor yet for your body, what ye shall put on. Is not the life more than meat, and the body than raiment?

31. Therefore take no thought, saying, What shall we eat? or, What shall we drink? or, Wherewithal shall we be clothed?

32. (For after all these things do the Gentiles seek:) for your heavenly Father knoweth that ye have need of all these things.

33. But seek ye first the kingdom of God, and his righteousness; and all these things shall be added unto you.

Ecclesiastes 12:1. Remember now thy Creator in the days of thy youth, while the evil days come not, nor the years draw nigh, when thou shalt say, I have no pleasure in them.

7. Then shall the dust return to the earth as it was: and the spirit shall return unto God who gave it.

13. Let us hear the conclusion of the whole matter: Fear God, and keep his commandments: for this is the whole duty of man.

14. For God shall bring every work into judgment, with every secret thing, whether it be good, or whether it be evil.

New International Version

Genesis 1:27. So God created man in his own image, in the image of God he created him; male and female he created them.

28. God blessed them and said to them, "Be fruitful and increase in number; fill the earth and subdue it. Rule over the fish of the sea and the birds of the air and over every living creature that moves on the ground."

29. Then God said, "I give you every seed-bearing plant on the face of the whole earth and every tree that has fruit with seed in it. They will be yours for food.

30. And to all the beasts of the earth and all the birds of the air and all the creatures that move on the ground—everything that has the breath of life in it—I give every green plant for food." And it was so.

Matthew 6:25. "Therefore I tell you, do not worry about your life, what you will eat or drink; or about your body, what you will wear. Is not life more important than food, and the body more important than clothes?

31. So do not worry, saying, 'What shall we eat?' or 'What shall we drink?' or 'What shall we wear?'

32. For the pagans run after all these things, and your heavenly Father knows that you need them.

33. But seek first his kingdom and his righteousness, and all these things will be given to you as well.

Ecclesiastes 12:1. Remember your Creator in the days of your youth, before the days of trouble come and the years approach when you will say, "I find no pleasure in them."

7. And the dust returns to the ground it came from, and the spirit returns to God who gave it.

13. Now all has been heard; here is the conclusion of the matter: Fear God and keep his commandments, for this is the whole duty of man.

14. For God will bring every deed into judgment, including every hidden thing, whether it is good or evil.

If someone were to ask you what you would do if you were given unlimited resources to "live life to the fullest," what would be your response? You might daydream of the ultimate vacation, a dream home, or unlimited opportunities to improve your education or practical skills.

But what if someone told you that you already had the capacity to live life to the fullest? Jesus said, "I am come that they may have life, and that they might have it more abundantly" (John 10:10). While serving Jesus does not guarantee material prosperity, it does guarantee fulfillment.

During this study, keep in mind that Jesus Christ is the key to fulfillment in your life. You truly acknowledge God's purpose for you when you give priority to Him; you honor Him with your life as you submit yourself to the lordship of His Son.

BIBLE COMMENTARY

1. Acknowledge God's Purpose

A. Created In God's Image
Genesis 1:27

William Paley, an 18th-century English theologian and philosopher, wrote Natural Theology, a systematic defense for the existence of God based on the "argument from design." This argument is founded on an analogy between complex man-made objects and complex objects in nature. Paley's most famous illustration concerned a watch found on the ground. Just as no one would suggest that such an intricate timepiece came into existence without a designer, so no one should suppose that nature's design is simply by chance. Believing in God's existence as Creator, Paley proposed, was just as reasonable as believing in the existence of the unknown watchmaker.

"When we come to inspect the watch," Paley wrote, "we perceive . . . that its several parts are framed and put together for a purpose." Purpose—this is a key point in Paley's argument. And purpose is a very important point when considering our own identity as members of the human race— God's highest creation.

As Christians, we must recognize that God has a purpose for our very existence. This is brought to light very early in the Genesis creation account. The first aspect of this truth is seen in Genesis 1:27. We are created "in the image of God." This is stated twice in the verse for clear emphasis.

Ask: "How are we created in the image of God? Does God have a body like ours?" Rather than supposing that God has a body and that He created us to look like Him, it is better to focus on attributes God created in us. These attributes—our mental and moral being—show we belong to God. Because we have been created in God's image, we should pattern ourselves after Jesus, the complete revelation of the image of God.

We would do well to remind ourselves of this connection with our Creator whenever we are tempted to live in a way inconsistent with His holy standards. We bear His imprint, and we were intended to live as testimonies of His goodness. While the Fall tragically marred the full manifestation of God's image in us, those who accept Jesus Christ as their Savior are restored to right relationship with God. Believers are being transformed into the image of Christ (see Romans 8:29). Christ is the perfect expression of God's image in humanity. And this image can be restored in us through Him (Ephesians 4:20-24).

toward goals He has established for us. Just as we studied last week in connection with Psalm 139:13-18, God is intimately involved with our lives from conception, and directs His thoughts toward us continually.

NOTES

B. Servants Of God
Genesis 1:28-30

Just as there is purpose *in* God's creation, there is purpose *for* God's creation. The creation narrative includes a brief outline of responsibilities given to Adam and Eve.

TEACHING TIP 1: Ask two or three students to read Genesis 1:28-30 from different Bible versions. List on the chalkboard or a blank overhead transparency each of the points God made in connection with Adam and Eve's life on earth.

Clearly, God established humanity at the top of His created order and gave people the responsibility to both populate and care for the world in which He placed them. In our society, we increasingly see two extremes in thought and practice concerning humanity's environmental responsibility. On the one hand, there are cases of gross failure to use good stewardship in the handling of our natural resources. On the other hand, we see a philosophy that places human life on the same scale as all other life and views the earth a god or goddess.

Ask: "What can God's mandate to Adam and Eve really indicate to us today?" When we keep a balanced perspective on Genesis 1:27-30 and apply it individually, we recognize that God has a task for each person to carry out. As God's servants, we can find meaning in each day of our lives. Each day God is leading us further

2. Give Priority To God

A. Freed Of Worry
Matthew 6:25-32

TEACHING TIP 2: Display the overhead transparency "Giving My Worries To God" as you discuss this material. Cover the transparency with a sheet of paper and reveal each point as its associated verse is presented.

Even as we acknowledge that God has a purpose for our lives, we can be overwhelmed by the demands of life. Life is full of challenges, and we can become discouraged by them. But believers need not be bound by pessimism. Looking at Matthew 6:25-32, we find a powerful antidote to life's worries—faith.

"Take no thought" in verse 25 simply means "Don't worry." Jesus was not telling us to quit planning or using good sense in organizing our lives. He was telling us to get rid of the worry that can so easily paralyze us. Jesus' teaching on God's provision is a soothing mental balm for all the worries we allow to pile up in our lives.

Jesus' illustrations in verses 26 and 28 point to the supply available to us from our

Creator. The same God who feeds the birds and "clothes" the flowers will feed and clothe us as well (verses 26,30).

The call to "take no thought" appears again in verse 31. This time, Christ's comparison of such thinking with the Gentiles in verse 32 gives an indication of what He is really warning against. The Gentiles represent those people who have no faith in God. They are completely self-absorbed. Material needs and desires take up all of their attention. This is not to be the case with the Christian.

TEACHING TIP 3: In order to keep Jesus' statements in perspective, ask the students to brainstorm for biblical statements calling for or illustrating planning and diligent work. The following passages could be included if responses are slow in coming: Proverbs 6:6-11; 10:4,5; 12:11; 14:23; 31:10-27; Matthew 25:14-30; 2 Thessalonians 3:10,11; 1 Timothy 5:8.

The Christian is to be a diligent worker, but work in itself is never to become the believer's preoccupation. Jesus' statements regarding the necessities of life are intended to establish a godly set of priorities for living, as verse Matthew 6:32 makes clear.

NOTES

on God instead of circumstances. Christians who direct their attention toward God will find their commitment rewarded. As they discern what God wants them to do with their lives and respond in obedience, He promises to supply those things that they need (Matthew 6:33).

Ask: "What conditions did Jesus include in this promise?" Two points are critical here. Believers are to seek both God's "kingdom" and His "righteousness." References to the Kingdom point to the fulfillment of God's will. "Righteousness" emphasizes the state of the heart, an inner commitment to holiness that should affect every thought and motive.

Our lives are wonderfully transformed when we apply these guidelines. Seeking God's kingdom and His righteousness draws our attention away from the endless worry Jesus warned against. We are freed to serve God and others as we trust the Lord to supply our needs. Christians in every walk of life have found God to be faithful to meet their needs as they have dedicated their lives to carrying out His will and conforming to His righteous standards.

TEACHING TIP 4: Conclude this part of the study with a time of testimonies emphasizing God's divine care and provision in response to obedience to His will. You might bring to class a written example from the life of a well-known Christian to start.

NOTES

B. Free To Serve
Matthew 6:33

Jesus' call to replace worry with faith necessarily focuses the believer's attention

3. Honor God

A. Throughout Life
Ecclesiastes 12:1,7

TEACHING TIP 5: Display the overhead transparency "Dedicating My Life To God" as you discuss this material. Cover the transparency with a sheet of paper and reveal each point as its associated verse is presented.

If there is a single book of the Bible specifically structured around the search for meaning in life, it is the Book of Ecclesiastes. With a surface reading, however, Ecclesiastes appears to present very little meaning at all. In fact, "Meaningless! Meaningless!" is the heart's cry of the narrator as he surveys the different pursuits people follow.

But while the bulk of Ecclesiastes gives examples of meaningless living, the book's conclusions offer the true path to personal fulfillment. Simply put, all meaning in life is found in God.

Ecclesiastes 12:1-7 describes one part of this truth. All of life should be lived to please God. But the journey into old age truly lacks meaning if a life has not been committed to God. Looking at verses 1 and 7 in particular, we see that a life committed to God early on will be ready to meet the Creator when death inevitably arrives.

For many, the temptation is to say, "I'll serve God . . . tomorrow." God, in His mercy, does continue to speak to human hearts even after years of rejection. And there are those Christians who are wonderfully saved in their later years and are grateful to see decades of worldly living put under the atoning blood of Christ.

But Ecclesiastes directs us toward a much better path. The full life is one that is lived for God from youth to old age. When the strength of one's youth is committed to God, God's blessing carries the believer through the difficult path to death. This person can anticipate life's end and a welcome into God's presence.

NOTES

B. With All Of Life
Ecclesiastes 12:13,14

Faithfully living for God refers to more than simply time. Our faithfulness must involve every part of life. Ecclesiastes 12:13,14 closes the book with an all-inclusive look at life. "Now all has been heard," the narrator says. "Here is the conclusion of the matter" (NIV).

The conclusion is found in the second half of verse 13. To fear God and obey Him is "the whole duty of man." All of life, from the years of play as a child through life's quest for achievement to the quiet reflection of old age, is to be characterized by reverence for our Creator and obedience to His holy standards of living.

This evaluation of life's purpose is important. Since the great spectrum of life's pursuits has the potential of drawing us closer to God, what should we do when we discover personal practices that seem to have no connection with our Lord whatsoever? The obvious answer is to get rid of them. Overcoming our own attachment to those things that do not please God is a challenge, but as we reject them in the power of His Spirit we will find true meaning in life.

Ask: "As you examine your life, what things do you see that are getting in the way of your honoring God completely?"

TEACHING TIP 6: Give the students some time for personal reflection.

> Without asking for a show of hands or any other form of personal identification, ask all the students to keep those questionable areas of their lives in focus and seek the Holy Spirit's help in either making necessary adjustments to those practices or eliminating them completely.

As Ecclesiastes 12:14 makes clear, God overlooks nothing about our lives. Heaven's record of all we do is absolutely complete. But as we come to God through Christ, we enjoy the inestimable privilege of receiving Christ's atonement for our sin. Rather than facing God's judgment for our sins, we can look forward to His approval and eternal blessing. By trusting Christ as our Savior, we can then honor God throughout our lives.

NOTES

LIFE RESPONSE

Solomon was very likely the author of Ecclesiastes. Certainly, the biographical details concerning his life and reign are a powerful illustration of many of the book's principles.

Solomon had everything that people naturally believe give meaning to life. He had vast wealth, enormous personal talent, unquestioned authority, and time on his hands to use them as he saw fit. But Solomon did not commit all of his life to God, and those personal resources in themselves could not prevent him from making a mess of his life.

It does not matter how much money or talent or influence you have—without God you will find life to be an empty shell of an existence. On the flip side of this truth is a very encouraging principle. It does not matter how little money or talent or influence you have—if you commit your life to God, He will make sure your days are touched with His presence and sense of purpose for your life. God takes care of the birds and flowers, so He will take care of you.

What can you do to find meaning in life? Submit yourself to God. Give Him all your worries, all your mistakes, and everything else about you that seems to get in the way of your own happiness and sense of fulfillment. As you do, He will transform you. He desires to make you like His Son, the One who showed us how to find total meaning in this life through total obedience to His Father.

EVANGELISM OUTREACH

Each point of this study has emphasized a personal relationship with God as the key to a meaningful life. Emphasize again that no attempt to find meaning in life will be successful without establishing a personal relationship with God by accepting Jesus Christ as Savior. Invite unsaved students to commit their lives to Christ today. Pray for the Holy Spirit's guidance in presenting this invitation. A call to salvation should always be a time of encouragement rather than intimidation. ◻

Adult Teacher Guide